THE ROUGH GUIDE TO

San Francisco

Rough Guide Credits

Text Editor:	Don Bapst
Managing Editor	Andrew Rosenberg
Series Editor:	Mark Ellingham
Editorial:	Martin Dunford, Jonathan Buckley, Jo Mead, Kate Berens, Amanda Tomlin, Ann-Marie Shaw, Paul Gray, Helena Smith, Judith Bamber, Orla Duane, Olivia Eccleshall, Ruth Blackmore, Geoff Howard, Claire Saunders, Gavin Thomas, Alexander Mark Rogers, Polly Thomas, Joe Staines, Lisa Nellis, Andrew Tomičić, Richard Lim, Duncan Clark, Peter Buckley, Sam Thorne, Lucy Ratcliffe (UK); Mary Beth Maioli, Stephen Timblin (US)
Online:	Kelly Cross, Anja Mutić-Blessing, Jennifer Gold (US)
Production:	Susanne Hillen, Andy Hilliard, Link Hall, Helen Ostick, Julia Bovis, Michelle Draycott, Katie Pringle, Robert Evers, Mike Hancock, Robert McKinlay, Zoë Nobes
Cartography:	Melissa Baker, Maxine Repath, Ed Wright
Picture Research:	Louise Boulton, Sharon Martins
Finance:	John Fisher, Gary Singh, Edward Downey, Mark Hall, Tim Bill
Marketing & Publicity:	Richard Trillo, Niki Smith, David Wearn, Jemima Broadbridge, Chloë Roberts, Birgit Hartmann (UK); Simon Carloss, David Wechsler (US)
Administration:	Tania Hummel, Demelza Dallow, Julie Sanderson

Acknowledgements

The **editor** would like to thank Peter Gerhäuser, Lee Anne and Tony Willis, Anibal Martinez, Kelly Cross, Emma Chynoweth, Silke Kerwick, Mike Hancock, Julia Bovis, Michelle Draycott, Melissa Baker, Maxine Repath, Russell Walton, Mary Beth Maioli, Stephen Timblin, Martin Dunford, and Andrew Rosenberg.

Mike Meyer would like to thank Feng Dan, the K, the San Francisco History Museum, the San Francisco Public Library, the University of California Berkeley, the Sonoma Chamber of Commerce, Silver Oak, the rangers at Bay Area state parks and National Park Service.

Ken Miller would like to thank Jenny Gotwals, Noah Leff, the staff of *Get Lost* Books, and his friends and family.

Thanks also to the many readers who have sent us suggestions for updates via mail and through our Web site – too many to list here. Your contributions are greatly appreciated.

This fifth edition published October 2000 by Rough Guides Ltd, 62–70 Shorts Gardens, London WC2H 9AH.

Distributed by the Penguin Group:
Penguin Books Ltd, 27 Wrights Lane, London W8 5TZ.
Penguin Putnam, Inc. 375 Hudson Street, New York, NY 10014, USA.
Penguin Books Australia Ltd, 487 Maroondah Highway, PO Box 257, Ringwood, Victoria 3134, Australia.
Penguin Books Canada Ltd, 10 Alcorn Avenue, Toronto, Ontario M4V 1E4, Canada.
Penguin Books (NZ) Ltd, 182–190 Wairau Road, Auckland 10, New Zealand.
Printed in England by Clays Ltd, St Ives PLC
Typography and original design by Jonathan Dear and The Crowd Roars.
Illustrations throughout by Edward Briant.

384pp. Includes index

A catalogue record for this book is available from the British Library.

ISBN 1-85828-526-7

THE ROUGH GUIDE TO

San Francisco

Written by Deborah Bosley

With additional contributions by
Mike Meyer and Ken Miller

Help us update

We've gone to a lot of trouble to ensure that this fifth edition of *The Rough Guide to San Francisco* is accurate and up-to-date. However, things inevitably change, and if you feel we've got it wrong or left something out, we'd like to know: any suggestions, comments or corrections would be much appreciated. We'll credit all contributions and send a copy of the next edition – or any other *Rough Guide* if you prefer – for the best correspondence.

Please mark letters "Rough Guide to San Francisco" and send to:
Rough Guides, 62–70 Shorts Gardens, London WC2H 9AH or
Rough Guides, 4th Floor, 345 Hudson St, New York, NY 10014.

Email should be sent to:
mail@roughguides.co.uk

Online updates about Rough Guide titles can be found on our Web site at *www.roughguides.com*

Rough Guides

Travel Guides • Phrasebooks • Music and Reference Guides

We set out to do something different when the first Rough Guide was published in 1982. Mark Ellingham, just out of University, was traveling in Greece. He brought along the popular guides of the day, but found they were all lacking in some way. They were either strong on ruins and museums but went on for pages without mentioning a beach or taverna. Or they were so conscious of the need to save money that they lost sight of Greece's cultural and historical significance. Also, none of the books told him anything about Greece's contemporary life – its politics, its culture, its people, and how they lived.

So with no job in prospect, Mark decided to write his own guidebook, one which aimed to provide practical information that was second to none, detailing the best beaches and the hottest clubs and restaurants, while also giving hard-hitting accounts of every sight, both famous and obscure, and providing up-to-the-minute information on contemporary culture. It was a guide that encouraged independent travelers to find the best of Greece, and was a great success, getting shortlisted for the Thomas Cook travel guide award, and encouraging Mark, along with three friends, to expand the series.

The Rough Guide list grew rapidly and the letters flooded in, indicating a much broader readership than had been anticipated, but one which uniformly appreciated the Rough Guides' mix of practical detail and humor, irreverence and enthusiasm. Things haven't changed. The same four friends who began the series are still the caretakers of the Rough Guide mission today: to provide the most reliable, up-to-date and entertaining information to independent-minded travelers of all ages, on all budgets.

We now publish 150 titles and have offices in London and New York. The travel guides are written and researched by a dedicated team of more than 100 authors, based in Britain, Europe, the USA, and Australia. We have also created a unique series of phrasebooks to accompany the travel series, along with the acclaimed series of music guides, and a best-selling pocket guide to the Internet and World Wide Web. We also publish comprehensive travel information on our Web site: *www.roughguides.com*

Contents

List of maps

MAP SYMBOLS

Interstate
US Highway
Highway
Tunnel
Pedestrianized road
Ferry route
Chapter division boundary
River
Airport
Accommodation
Church (regional maps)
Historic house
Stadium
Lighthouse
Mountain range
Mountain peak
General point of interest
Information center
Post office
Public transit stop
Parking
Building
Church
Cemetery
National Park
Park

Introduction

One day, if I do go to heaven, I'm going to do what every San Franciscan does who goes to heaven. I'll look around and say, "It ain't bad, but it ain't San Francisco."

Herb Caen, legendary San Francisco journalist

One of America's most beautiful cities, and one whose locals are not afraid to harp on such a claim, especially when designing tourist brochures, **SAN FRANCISCO** sits poised on the 47-square-mile fingertip of a peninsula at the western edge of America – the perfect location for a place that considers itself the last stronghold of civilization in California's lunatic fringe. Indeed, the city has much to gloat about, not least the breathtaking natural beauty that surrounds it – from rugged coastline and tranquil bay waters to rambling, fog-capped hills and dense, unspoiled woods. Along the steep streets of the city itself, sit a cluster of distinct neighborhoods – by turn quaint or hip, lined by rows of preserved Victorian houses or dotted with chic clubs in converted warehouses. Residents like to think of their home as the cultured northern counterpart to sunny Los Angeles, mass entertainment capital of southern California, and to an extent they're right – this was the place that birthed the United Nations and became forever associated in the public consciousness with the literary Beat and gay rights movements. Still, San Francisco is undeniably Californian; after all, this is also the city where blue jeans, mountain biking and topless waitressing first took off.

From its earliest days as a stop on the Spanish chain of Missions, through its explosive expansion during the Gold Rush and right up into the present-day Internet boom, San Francisco's turbulent history is relatively short. Named for **Saint Francis of Assisi**, the kindly monk who harbored society's outcasts, the city sprang up almost overnight in the late 1840s from a sleepy fishing village named Yerba Buena. The hilly terrain did not daunt the rough-and-ready prospectors who built on it according to a grid pattern that ignored even the steepest inclines; with its whimsical architecture, its vast irrigated park on the site of a former sand dune, and its cliff-hugging resort buildings, the late nineteenth-century city defied the elements and served as much as a playground as an economic center, luring writers, architects, immigrants, and thousands of transient sailors eager to "make it" in the newest, westernmost, metropolis. Though earthquakes, fires, droughts, landslides, and other natural disasters have put the city's very existence to the test, residents have never taken long to rebuild and resettle, refusing to give in to nature's tantrums. Politically, San Franciscans are known for the same unbreakable character, infusing their city with an activist spirit most evident in the high visibility of once disenfranchised groups, especially Asian-Americans, gays, and people with AIDS.

Many visitors to the city today are drawn as much by its nonconformist spirit as by the sights; for some, it's a veritable pilgrimage site. But the most common lure of San Francisco is its easy charm – with inescapably quaint pastel street scenes and blossoming parks offset by a sophisticated selection of international cuisine and world-class clubs, making it the ideal American city in which to linger without the encumbrance of a serious agenda. Indeed, despite all its activity, San Francisco remains a small town, where having a car is a liability due to traffic-jammed streets and a dearth of parking spaces. Provided you don't mind hills, every major sight in town is a short walk, bike or bus ride away.

Though San Francisco is undoubtedly the focus of the Bay Area, there's much in the surrounding parts to take in too. The **East Bay** is centered around the up-and-coming port city of **Oakland** and the University of California's flagship campus in hipster **Berkeley**. To the south, the **Peninsula** contains fast-growing Silicon Valley, with **San Jose** as its hub, home to many computer giants. North of San Francisco, across the Golden Gate Bridge, **Marin County** boasts enormous wealth in spots like the postcard-perfect towns of **Sausalito** and **Tiburon**, plus prime biking and hiking trails in the **Marin Headlands**. Further north, the lush beauty continues in California's famed **Wine Country**.

Climate and When To Go

The city of San Francisco emphatically does not belong to the California of monotonous blue skies and slothful warmth. Flanked on three sides by water, it is regularly invigorated by the fresh winds that sweep across the peninsula. The **climate** is among the most stable in the world, with a daytime temperature that rarely ventures more than 5°F either side of a median 60°F but can drop much lower at night. Summer does offer some sunny days, of course, but it also sees heavy **fog** roll in through the Golden Gate to smother the city in gloom. This thick mist does much to add romance to the city, but it can also dash hopes of tanning at the beach or having a timely departure from one of the local airports. The western half of the city sees the worst of the fog on summer mornings; later in the year, cooler inland temperatures prevent the fog from taking root. Winters bring most of the city's rainfall, sometimes in quite torrential storms. Almost everywhere else in the Bay Area is warmer than San Francisco, especially in the summer when the East Bay basks in sunshine, and the Wine Country and other inland valleys are baking hot.

As for **when to go**, if you want to avoid the crowds, it makes sense not to come in the summer, although even then most of the tourist congestion is confined to a few of the most popular parts of the city, and is rarely too off-putting. The nicest times to visit are late May and June, when the hills are greenest and covered with wildflowers, or in October and November, when you can be fairly sure of good weather and reduced crowds at tourist attractions.

Average temperatures (°F) and Rainfall

	Jan	Feb	March	April	May	June	July	Aug	Sept	Oct	Nov	Dec
Max °F	55	59	61	62	63	66	65	65	69	68	63	57
Min °F	45	47	48	49	51	52	53	53	55	54	51	47
Rainfall	4.7	3.8	3.1	1.5	0.7	0.1	0	0	0.3	1.0	2.5	4.4

Part 1

The Basics

Getting there from Britain and Europe

Although flying to San Francisco from Europe is pretty straightforward, choosing the best route can be more complicated than you might think, with prices fluctuating wildly according to how and when you go. Some airlines have nonstop services from Britain, but the majority of options are so-called "direct" flights, which can land several times, waiting an hour or so at each stop – a flight is called direct as long as it keeps the same flight number throughout its journey. The first place the plane lands is your point of entry into the US, which means you'll have to collect your bags and go through customs and immigration formalities there, even if you're continuing on to San Francisco on the same plane. This can be a real pain after a ten-hour journey, so it's worth finding out before you book a ticket.

All international flights use the main San Francisco International Airport (SFO); for transportation details from there into the city, as well as from the two other Bay Area airports, see p.28.

> One word of **warning**: it's not a good idea to buy a **one-way** ticket to the States. Not only are they rarely good value compared to a round-trip ticket, but US immigration officials usually take them as a sign that you aren't planning to go home, and may refuse you entry.

Fares, routes, and agents

Although you can fly to the US from any of the regional airports, the few **nonstop flights** from Britain to San Francisco are from London (see box, p.4). The nonstop flight time is around eleven hours from London to San Francisco; add an hour at least for each intervening stop on **direct flights**, twice that if you have to change planes. Following winds ensure that return flights are usually an hour or so shorter than outward journeys. Because of the time difference between Britain and the West Coast (eight hours almost all year), flights usually leave Britain mid-morning, while flights back from the US tend to arrive in Britain early in the morning.

Generally, the most expensive time to travel is **high season**, roughly between June and August and around Christmas. April, May, September and October are slightly less pricey, and the rest of the year is considered **low season**. Keep an eye out for slack-season bargains – November to mid-December is often the cheapest time to go. Additionally, make sure to check the exact dates of the seasons with your operator or airline; you might be able to make major savings by shifting your departure date by a week – or even a day. **Weekend rates** for all return flights tend to be around £20 more expensive than those in the week.

Britain remains one of the best places in Europe to obtain flight bargains, though fares vary widely according to season, availability and the current level of inter-airline competition. The comments that follow can only act as a general guide, so be sure to shop around carefully for the best offers by checking the travel ads in the weekend papers, on the holiday pages of ITV's *Teletext* and, in London, scouring *Time Out* and the *Evening Standard*. Free magazines aimed at young travelers, like *TNT*, are also useful resources.

Standby deals (open-dated tickets which you pay for and then decide later when you want to fly – if there's room on the plane) are few and far between, and don't give great savings: in general you're better off with an **APEX ticket**. The con-

Flights from Britain

The following carriers operate daily **nonstop** or **one-stop flights** between Britain and San Francisco.

American Airlines via Chicago from Heathrow; via Dallas from Gatwick.

British Airways nonstop from Heathrow and around three one-stop flights from Gatwick.

Continental via Houston or Newark from Gatwick.

Delta via Cleveland, Cincinnati or Atlanta from Gatwick.

TWA via St Louis from Gatwick.

United several nonstop from Heathrow and one-stop via Dallas from Heathrow.

Virgin Atlantic nonstop from Heathrow and Gatwick.

The following carriers operate **direct flights** from regional airports to North America:

American Airlines, from Manchester and Birmingham to Chicago; May to October also from Glasgow to Chicago.

British Airways, from Manchester to New York.

Continental, from Glasgow, Birmingham and Manchester to Newark.

Delta, from Manchester to Atlanta.

Northwest, from Glasgow to Boston.

Virgin Atlantic, from Manchester to Orlando.

Alternative routes to San Francisco include:

Air Canada from Glasgow to Toronto, with direct flights on to San Francisco.

Air France via Paris (CDG).

KLM via Amsterdam.

Lufthansa via Frankfurt.

Airlines

Air Canada ☎ 0870/524 7226; *www.aircanada.ca*

Air France ☎ 0845/084 5111; *www.airfrance.com*

American Airlines ☎ 08457/789789; *www.aa.com*

British Airways ☎ 0845/773 3377; *www.britishairways.com*

Continental ☎ 01293/776464; *www.flycontinental.com*

Delta ☎ 0800/414767; *www.delta-air.com*

KLM ☎ 0870/507 4074; *www.klm.com*

Lufthansa ☎ 0845/773 7747; *www.lufthansa.com*

Northwest ☎ 01424/224400; *www.nwa.com*

TWA ☎ 08457/333333; *www.twa.com*

United ☎ 0845/844 4777; *www.ual.com*

Virgin Atlantic ☎ 01293/747747; *www.fly.virgin.com*

Toll-free phone numbers for airlines in the United States are listed on p.11.

ditions on these are pretty standard whomever you fly with – seats must be purchased seven days or more in advance, and you must stay for at least one Saturday night; tickets are normally valid for up to six months. Some airlines also do less expensive Super-APEX tickets, which fall into two categories: the first are approximately £150 cheaper than an ordinary APEX but must be bought 21 days in advance and require a minimum stay of seven days and a maximum stay of one month; the second are around £100 less than an APEX, must be purchased fourteen days in advance and entail a minimum stay of a week and a maximum stay of two months – such tickets are usually nonrefundable or changeable. **Open-jaw tickets** can be a good idea, allowing you to fly into San Francisco (for example), and back from LA for little or no extra charge; fares are calculated by halving the return fares to each destination and adding the two figures together.

Sample Airfares from Britain

The prices given below (in £ sterling) are a general indication of the minimum transatlantic airfares currently obtainable from specialist companies; youth discount fares are cheaper, especially for one-way tickets. Remember to add £55 airport tax to these figures. Each airline decides the exact dates of its seasons. Prices are for departures from London.

Low Nov–March (except Christmas)		Shoulder Apr, May, Sep, Oct		High June–Aug, Christmas	
one-way	return	one-way	return	one-way	return
182	276	249	260	346	429

This makes a convenient option for those who want a fly-drive holiday (see p.7).

For an overview of the various offers, and unofficially discounted tickets, go straight to an **agent** specializing in low-cost flights (we've listed some below). Especially if you're under 26 or a student, they may be able to knock up to thirty percent off the regular APEX fares when there are no special airline deals.

Finally, if you've got a bit more time, or want to see some more of the USA, it's often possible to stopover in **another city** – New York especially – and fly on from there for little more than the cost of a direct flight to California. Also, with increased competition on the **London–Los Angeles** route, thanks to Virgin Atlantic among others and price wars between US carriers, the cost of a connecting flight from LA to San Francisco has been brought down to as low as £40. You could also opt for cut-price seats on a **charter flight** from the UK to San Francisco or Los Angeles; these are particularly good value if you're traveling from a British city other than London although they tend to be limited to the summer season, and have fixed departure and return dates. Brochures are available in most high-street travel agents, or contact the Charter Flight Centre in London (☎020/7565 6799).

Courier flights

It's still possible, if not as common as it used to be, for those on a very tight budget to travel as **couriers** (for example £200 return to the West Coast). Two airlines have dedicated courier flight departments: British Airways (☎0870/606 1133) and Virgin (☎020/8897 5246 or 8897 5247). Virgin offers opportunities to travel at discounted rates (as low as £250 return to San Francisco) in return for allowing a package to be delivered. You call to say when you'd like to travel (ie you must come up with the date first), then they can tell you if a courier flight is available; there are no waiting lists. Discounts are about 30 percent on standard economy return. There are no customs requirements if you're going to San Francisco (these only apply on

Low-cost agents in Britain

Bridge The World 47 Chalk Farm Rd, London NW1 8AN (☎020/7916 0990; *www.b-t-w.co.uk*).

Destination Group 14 Greville St, London EC1N 8SB (☎020/7400 7000; *www.destination-group.com*).

Flightbookers 177 Tottenham Court Rd, London W1P 0LX (☎020/7757 2320; *sales@flightbookers.co.uk*).

STA Travel 86 Old Brompton Rd, London SW7 3LQ (☎0870/160 6070; *www.statravel.com*); branches nationwide.

Trailfinders 42–50 Earls Court Rd, London W8 6EJ (☎020/7937 5400; *www.trailfinders.com*); branches nationwide.

Travel Bug 597 Cheetham Hill Rd, Manchester M8 5EJ (☎0161/721 4000); 125 Gloucester Road, London SW7 4TE (☎020/7835 2000; *www.flynow.com*).

Travel Cuts 295a Regent St, London W1B 2HN (☎020/7255 2082; *www.travelcuts.com*).

USIT Campus, 52 Grosvenor Gardens, London SW1 0AU (national call centre ☎0870/240 1010; *www.usitcampus.co.uk*)

USIT Council, 28a Poland St, London W1V 3DB (☎020/7287 3337).

Specialist holiday operators

Airtours Wavell House, Helmshore, Rossendale, Lancs BB4 4NB (☎01706/240033; *www.airtours.co.uk*). Multi-centre holidays including combinations of Los Angeles, San Francisco, and Las Vegas.

American Adventures 64 Mount Pleasant Ave, Tunbridge Wells, Kent TN1 1QY (☎01892/512700; *www.americanadventures.com*). Small-group touring and adventure holidays on the West Coast; also hosteling with Road Runner International (see below).

American Airlines Holidays PO Box 5, 12 Coningsby Rd, Peterborough PE3 8XP (☎0870/605 0506). Flight-plus-accommodation and fly-drive deals.

Bon Voyage 18 Bellevue Rd, Southampton, Hants SO15 2AY (☎023/8024 8248). Flight-plus-accommodation deals in San Francisco, Los Angeles, and Palm Springs.

British Airways Holidays Astral Towers, Bettsway, London Rd, Crawley, West Sussex RH10 2XA (☎01293/723121). City breaks in Los Angeles, San Diego, and San Francisco, and fly-drive deals (including motorhomes).

Connections 10 York Way, Lancaster Rd, High Wycombe, Bucks HP12 3PY (☎01494/473173; *www.connectionsworldwide.net*). Tailor-mades, including short breaks in Los Angeles and San Francisco.

Contiki Travel Wells House, 15 Elmfield Rd, Bromley, Kent BR1 1LS (☎020/8290 6777). West Coast coach tours.

Destination Group 14 Greville St, London EC1N 8SB (☎020/7400 7000; *www.destination-group.com*). Tailor-mades; can arrange accommodation and fly-drive deals.

Explore Worldwide 1 Frederick St, Aldershot, Hants GU11 1LQ (☎01252/760000; *www.explore.co.uk*). Small-group walking tours, camping or staying in hotels.

Flydrive USA PO Box 45, Bexhill-on-Sea, East Sussex TN40 1PY (☎01424/224400). Flight-plus-accommodation and fly-drive combinations.

Funway Holidays 1 Elmfield Park, Bromley, Kent BR1 1LU (☎020/8466 0222). Tailor-mades in Los Angeles, San Diego, San Francisco, and Palm Springs.

Kuoni Kuoni House, Dorking, Surrey RH5 4AZ (☎01306/742888; *www.kuoni.co.uk*). Multi-center flight-plus-accommodation-plus-car deals featuring Los Angeles, San Francisco, and San Diego.

North America Travel Service 7 Albion St, Leeds LS1 5ER (☎0113/246 1466); 241 Kensington High St, London W8 6EL (☎020/7938 3737). Also branches in Nottingham, Manchester, and Barnsley. Tailor-mades: flights, accommodation, car hire, and so on.

Premier Holidays Westbrook, Milton Rd, Cambridge CB4 1YQ (☎01223/516516; *www.premierholidays.co.uk*). Flight-plus-accommodation deals throughout California.

Road Runner International 64 Mount Pleasant Ave, Tunbridge Wells, Kent TN1 1QY (☎01892/512700). Hosteling version of American Adventures touring and adventure packages (see above).

Top Deck Travel 131 Earls Court Rd, London SW5 9RH (☎020/7370 4555; *www.topdecktravel.co.uk*). Agents for numerous adventure-touring specialists.

Travelpack Clarendon House, Clarendon Rd, Eccles, Manchester M30 9TR (☎08705/747101). Escorted tours and tailor-made holidays throughout California.

TrekAmerica Malvern House, 4 Waterperry Court, Middleton Rd, Banbury OX16 4QB (☎01295 256777; *www.trekamerica.com*). Touring-adventure holidays.

United Vacations PO Box 377, Bromley, Kent BR1 1LY (☎020/8313 0999). City breaks, tailor-mades and fly-drives.

Virgin Holidays The Galleria, Station Rd, Crawley, West Sussex RH10 1WW (☎01293/456789; *www.virginholidays.co.uk*). Packages to a wide range of California destinations.

courier flights to New York and Tokyo) and you can take the usual 23kg of luggage, and stay in San Francisco for up to six weeks.

Courier firms offer opportunities to travel at discounted rates in return for delivering a package or escorting a cargo. There'll be someone to check you in and to meet you at your destination, which minimizes any red-tape hassle. You may have to travel light (but not necessarily, if you're escorting a cargo of several tons), and accept tight restrictions on travel dates. For phone numbers, check the *Yellow Pages*, as these businesses come and go.

Flights from Ireland

Aer Lingus flies to California **direct from Ireland** and Delta flies to Atlanta and New York from Dublin. The cheapest flights – if you're under 26 or a student – are available from USIT. Student-only return fares to San Francisco range from IR£359 to IR£525 (also add IR£31 airport tax to any fares). Ordinary APEX fares are only marginally higher.

USIT can be contacted at Aston Quay, O'Connell Bridge, Dublin 2 (☎01/677 8117). Aer Lingus is at 40 O'Connell St, Dublin 1 and Dublin Airport (☎01/886 8888; *www.aerlingus.ie*), and Delta Air Lines is at 24 Merrion Square, Dublin 2 (☎01/676 8080 or 1800/768080).

Flights from Europe

It is generally far cheaper to fly nonstop to San Francisco from London than any other European city. However, for the best deals to New York from Brussels and Paris, contact **Nouvelles Frontières**, 87 boulevard de Grenelle, 75015 Paris (☎41.41.58.58) and 2 boulevard M. Lemonnier, 1000 Brussels (☎02/547 4444).

Other options are the cut-price charter flights occasionally offered from major European cities; ask at your nearest travel agent for details. In Germany, look for discount **youth-fare deals** which United offers (to those under 26 booking 72 hours or less in advance) from Frankfurt, its continental hub (☎069/605020).

Packages

Packages – fly-drive, flight/accommodation deals and guided tours (or a combination of all three) – can work out cheaper than arranging the same trip yourself, especially for a short-term stay. The obvious drawbacks are the loss of flexibility and the fact that most schemes use hotels in the mid-range bracket, but there is a wide variety of options available. High-street travel agents have plenty of brochures and information about the various combinations.

Fly-drive deals, which give cut-rate (sometimes free) car rental when buying a transatlantic ticket, always work out cheaper than renting on the spot, and give especially great value if you intend to do a lot of driving. However, if you're planning to stay pretty much within San Francisco itself, having a car is a bonus but not strictly necessary. You'll probably have to pay more for the flight than if you booked it through a discount agent, but competition between airlines (especially Northwest and TWA) and tour operators means it's well worth phoning to check on current promotions.

Northwest Flydrive offers excellent deals for not much more than an ordinary APEX fare; for example, a return flight to San Francisco and a week's car rental costs around £300 per person in low season. Several of the other companies listed (see box opposite) offer similar, and sometimes cheaper, packages. Watch out for hidden extras, such as local taxes and drop-off charges, which can be as much as a week's rental, and insurance (see p.15); the combined extras can bump up a week's hire from the most basic £35 to £145. Remember, too, that while you can drive in the States with a British license, there can be problems renting vehicles if you're under 25. For complete car-rental details, see "Getting around the City," p.28.

There's really no end of combined **flight-and-accommodation deals** to San Francisco and, although you can often do things cheaper independently, you won't be able to do the same things cheaper – in fact, the equivalent room booked separately will normally be a lot more expensive – and you can leave the organizational hassles to someone else. Drawbacks include the loss of flexibility and the fact that you'll probably have to stay in hotels in the mid-range to expensive bracket, even though less expensive accommodation is almost always available.

A handful of tour operators offer quite deluxe packages, of which Virgin Holidays are among the least expensive: for example, seven nights in San Francisco plus return flight costs around £559 in low season, £849 per person in high season. Discount agents can set up more basic packages for around £500 each. Pre-booked accommodation schemes, under which you buy vouchers for use in a specific group of hotels, are not normally good value.

If you want to combine your stay in San Francisco with trips out into the rest of California, particularly the state's extensive wilderness areas, the best tour agents to contact in Britain are the long-established TrekAmerica and Explore Worldwide. TrekAmerica's specialist **touring and adventure packages** include transportation, camping accommodation (equipment, except a sleeping bag, is provided), food and a guide;

small groups (limited to 13) are transported around by minibus. A typical ten-day trek, including San Francisco, will cost around £425; flights to the US are not included and extras include hotels in large towns en route and a food kitty of US$35 per week, with many meals cooked and eaten communally. Based in California, the more unconventional **Green Tortoise** (see p.15), has a similar set-up although there's plenty of time to leave the group and do your own thing. If you're interested in **backcountry hiking** to balance out a week in the city, the San Francisco-based Sierra Club (730 Polk St, SF, CA 94110 ☎415/776-2211) offers a range of tours that take you into parts of the state that most people never see; other options may be available through travel agents.

Entry requirements

Citizens of **Britain**, **Ireland** and most **European countries** do not require **visas** for stays in the United States of less than ninety days. Instead you are simply asked to fill out the **visa waiver** form handed out on incoming planes. You must, of course, also be in possession of a valid **passport**. Immigration control takes place at your initial point of arrival on American soil. Visitors on the visa waiver scheme are also allowed to cross into Mexico and Canada. For more information, contact the American embassies in Britain (5 Upper Grosvenor St, London W1A 1AE; ☎020/7499 9000), Scotland (3 Regent Terrace, Edinburgh EH7 5B; ☎0131/556 8315), or Ireland (Queens House, 14 Queen St, Belfast BT1 6EQ; ☎028/9032 8239).

Getting there from Australia and New Zealand

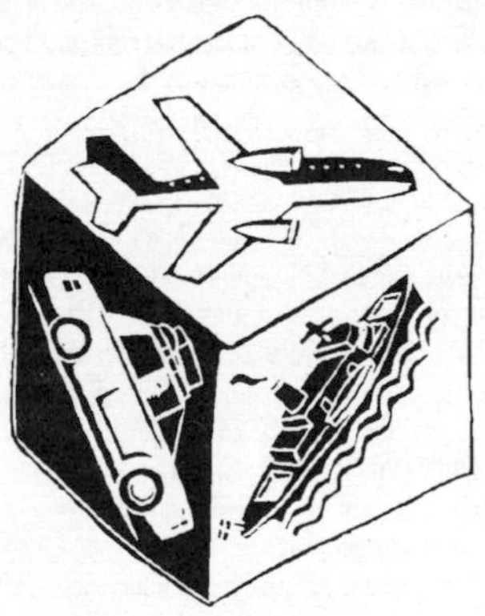

From Australia and New Zealand, Los Angeles and San Francisco are the main points of entry to the US, with Los Angeles being a bit better served. With any of the American carriers, you can continue on to New York for around US$180 on top of the fare to the West Coast. Some flights stop off in Honolulu, Hawaii; you can usually stay over for as long as you like at no extra charge. A less direct, but cheaper option is to go via Asia with a carrier like JAL (Japan Airlines) or Korean Air. These often include a one-night stopover in a hub city such as Osaka or Seoul.

Fares and tickets

Tickets purchased direct from the airlines tend to be expensive, and you'll get much better deals on fares from your local **travel agent**, as well as the latest information on limited specials, fly-drive, accommodation packages, stopovers en route and round-the-world fares. The best discounts are through Flight Centres and STA, who can also advise on visa regulations.

Airfares are seasonally adjusted, with **low season** typically from mid-January to end-February, and October to November; **high season** is end May to August and December to mid–January; **shoulder season** is the rest of the year.

From Australia, there are daily direct flights to San Francisco with United Airlines from Sydney (around A$1765 low season, A$2350 high sea-

Airlines

Air New Zealand Australia ☎13 2476; New Zealand ☎09/357 3000; *www.airnz.com*

America West Airlines Australia ☎02/9290 2232; *www.americawest.com*

American Airlines Australia ☎1300/650 747; New Zealand ☎09/309 0735 or 0800/887 997; *www.aa.com*

Delta Air Lines Australia ☎02/9251 3211 or 1800/500 992; New Zealand ☎09/379 3370; *www.delta-air.com*

JAL (Japan Airlines) Australia ☎02/9272 1111; New Zealand ☎09/379 9906; *www.japanair.com*

Korean Air Australia ☎02/9262 6000; New Zealand ☎09/307 3687; *www.koreanair.com*

Qantas Australia ☎13 1313; New Zealand ☎09/357 8900 or 0800/808 767; *www.qantas.com*

United Airlines Australia ☎13 1777; New Zealand ☎09/379 3800; *www.ual.com*

son); and Air New Zealand from Sydney and Melbourne (A$1775/2400). Qantas flies from Cairns, Brisbane, Sydney and Melbourne via LA starting at A$1800 in low season, while the lowest fares are with JAL, which flies out of Sydney, Brisbane and Cairns for A$1265/2000, with a transfer in Tokyo. Korean Air from Sydney via Seoul comes in as next cheapest, costing A$1530/2100. If you're flying out from any of the other eastern capitals, the fares should be about the same, whereas fares from some western cities, like Perth and Darwin, cost around A$400 more.

Discount travel agents

Anywhere Travel Sydney ☎02/9663 0411; *anywhere@ozemail.com.au*

Budget Travel Auckland ☎09/366 0061 or 0800/808 040

Destinations Unlimited Auckland ☎09/373 4033

Flight Centres Sydney ☎13 1600; Auckland ☎09/358 4310. *www.flightcentre.com.au*

Northern Gateway Darwin ☎08/8941 1394; *oztravel@norgate.com.au*

STA Travel Sydney; nearest branch ☎13 1776, fastfare telesales ☎1300/360 960; Auckland ☎09/309 0458; fastfare telesales ☎09/366 6673; *traveller@statravel.com.au*; *www.statravel.com.au*

Student Uni Travel, Sydney ☎02/9232 8444; *sydney@backpackers.net*

Thomas Cook Sydney ☎13 1771, direct telesales ☎1800/201 002; Auckland ☎09/379 3920. *www.thomascook.com.au*

Trailfinders Sydney ☎02/9247 7666

Travel.com.au Sydney ☎02/9249 5444 or 1800/000 447. *travel.com.au*

USIT Beyond Auckland ☎09/379 4224 or 0800/788 336. *usitbeyond.co.nz*

YHA Travel Sydney ☎02/9261 1111. *yha@yhansw.org.au*; *www.yha.com.au*

Specialist agents and tour operators

Adventure World North Sydney ☎02/9956 7766 or 1300/363 055; Auckland ☎09/524 5118. Agents for a vast array of international adventure-travel companies that operate trips out of San Francisco and LA.

American Town and Country Holidays Melbourne ☎03/9877 3322. Specially tailored packages to San Francisco.

Creative Holidays Sydney ☎02/9386 2111. Fly-drive holidays and flight-accommodation package deals to San Francisco. Bookings through travel agents.

Journeys Worldwide Brisbane ☎07/3221 4788. Individually prepared San Francisco itineraries.

Sydney International Travel Centre Sydney ☎02/9299 8000. US specialists with an extensive range of accommodation, air passes, car rental and tours in and around San Francisco.

Coupon deals valid in the continental US are available with your main ticket, allowing you to fly onward to destinations across the States. You can expect to pay around A$400 for the first three, and between A$70 and $100 for subsequent tickets (a maximum of ten total).

From New Zealand, the best deals to San Francisco are out of Auckland on JAL, via Tokyo (NZ$1799 low season), and on United Airlines direct (NZ$1850/2700). Korean Air costs from NZ$1899, while Air New Zealand and Qantas both fly via LA for around NZ$1999/2799. Fares from Christchurch are usually the same as from Auckland, but you should add on about NZ$100 for flights out of Wellington.

If you intend to take in San Francisco as part of a much longer trip, then your best bet may be a **round-the-world ticket**, which offers good value, working out to be just a little more than an all-in ticket. Qantas and British Airways are part of the One World airline consortium, which offers six stopovers worldwide from A$2400/NZ$2999. Another option is the "Star Alliance" fare on offer from Air New Zealand and United Airlines, costing from A$2699/NZ$3199, depending on mileage.

Entry requirements

Australian and New Zealand citizens who have full **passports** do not require a **visa** for trips to the United States of less than ninety days, providing they arrive on a commercial flight with an onward or return ticket. You'll simply fill in the **visa waiver form** on your incoming flight. Visitors on the visa waiver scheme are also entitled to cross into Mexico and Canada and return to the US. For further details, such as those involving longer stays, contact the **American embassies** in Australia (Moonah Place, Canberra, ACT ☎02/6214 5600; premium-rated visa information service: ☎1902/941 641) or New Zealand (29 Fitzherbert Terrace, Thorndon, Wellington ☎04/472 2068).

Getting there from North America

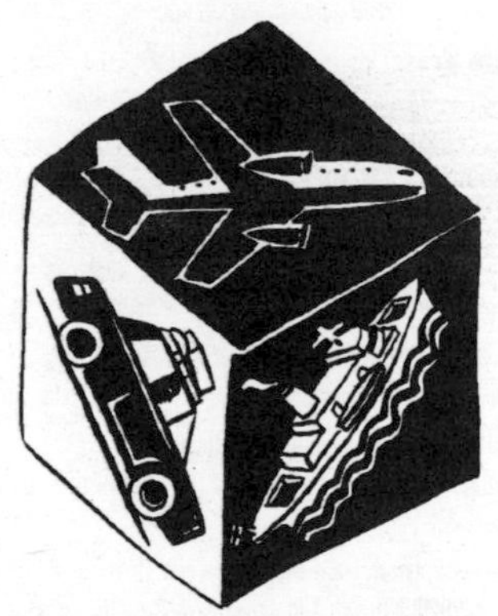

Getting to San Francisco from elsewhere in North America is never a problem; the Bay Area is well serviced by air, rail, and road networks.

All the main airlines operate daily scheduled flights into San Francisco from points across the continent. Flying remains the best if most expensive way to travel. Otherwise, driving is the American – indeed the Californian – way as cars offer the greatest freedom and convenience. Trains can be painfully slow and not a particularly good value. Buses are least expensive, but they are even slower and less comfortable.

By air

Besides the main **San Francisco International Airport** (SFO), two other airports, both in the Bay Area, may be useful – particularly **Oakland International** (OAK), across the bay but easily accessible. The third Bay Area airport, **San Jose Municipal** (SJO), forty miles south, is a bit out of the way but has good connections with the western US, Los Angeles especially.

Airlines in the US and Canada

Aer Lingus ☎ 1-800/474-7424; *www.aerlingus.ie*

Aero California ☎ 1-800/237-6225

Aeromexico ☎ 1-800/237-6639; *www.aeromexico.com*

Air Canada in Canada ☎ 1-800/263-0882; in US 1-800/776-3000; *www.aircanada.ca*

Air France in US ☎ 1-800/237-2747; in Canada ☎ 1-800/667-2747; *www.airfrance.fr*

Alaska Airlines ☎ 1-800/426-0333; *www.alaska-air.com*

Aloha Airlines ☎ 1-800/367-5250; *www.alohaair.com*

America West Airlines ☎ 1-800/235-9292; *www.americawest.com*

American Airlines ☎ 1-800/433-7300; *www.aa.com*

American Trans Air ☎ 1-800/435-9282; *www.ata.com*

British Airways ☎ 1-800/247-9297; *www.british-airways.com*

British Midland ☎ 1-800/788-0555; *www.iflybritishmidland.com*

Canadian Airlines in Canada ☎ 1-800/665-1177; in US ☎ 1-800/426-7000; *www.cdnair.ca*

Continental Airlines domestic, ☎ 1-800/525-0280; international ☎ 1-800/231-0856; *www.flycontinental.com*

Delta Air Lines in US ☎ 1-800/241-4141; in Canada ☎ 1-800-221-1212; *www.delta-air.com*

Frontier Airlines ☎ 1-800/432-1359; *www.frontierairlines.com*

Hawaiian Airlines ☎ 1-800/367-5320; *www.hawaiianair.com*

Lufthansa in US ☎ 1-800/645-3880; in Canada ☎ 1-800/563-5954; *www.lufthansa.com*

Northwest/KLM Airlines domestic ☎ 1-800/225-2525; international ☎ 1-800/447-4747; *www.nwa.com*

Reno Air ☎ 1-800/433-7300; *www.aa.com*

Southwest Airlines ☎ 1-800/435-9792; *www.southwest.com*

TWA domestic ☎ 1-800/221-2000; international ☎ 1-800/892-4141; *www.twa.com*

United Airlines ☎ 1-800/241-6522; *www.ual.com*

US Airways domestic, ☎ 1-800/428-4322; international, ☎ 1-800/622-1015; *www.usairways.com*

Virgin Atlantic Airways ☎ 1-800/862-8621; *www.virgin-atlantic.com*

Note that not all the above airlines fly domestic routes within the US. The **toll-free directory inquiries** number is ☎ 1-800/555-1212.

As airlines tend to match each other's prices, there's generally little difference in the quoted fares. Barring a **fare war**, round-trip prices start at around $318 from New York, and $238 from Chicago. What makes more difference than your choice of carrier are the conditions governing the ticket – whether it is fully refundable or not, the time and day and, most importantly, the **time of year** you travel. Least expensive of all is a non-summer-season midweek flight that stays over a Saturday night, booked and paid for at least three weeks in advance. While it's good to call the airlines directly to get a sense of their official fares, it's also worth checking with a reputable **travel agent** (such as the ones listed overleaf) to find out about any **special deals** or student/youth fares that may be available. Agents can also alert you to restrictions that aren't immediately apparent when finding deals on your own **online**.

In addition to the big-name scheduled airlines, a few lesser-known carriers run no-frills flights, which can prove to be very good value. Southwest flies budget flights from a host of American cities; American Trans Air has some of the best fares from Chicago, with round trips starting around $235. Flights to New York are frequent, so competition between carriers is fierce, with round-trip flights starting at $225. Boston and DC tend to be slightly higher. For flights to Hawaii, fares start around $325, and round trips to the Mexican resorts of Puerto Vallarta, Cancun, and Cabo start around $219.

Travelers intending to fly from **Canada** are likely to find that, with less competition on these routes (Canadian only flies nonstop to SF from

Discount travel companies in the US and Canada

Council Travel offices in the US: Head office 205 E 42nd St, New York, NY 10017 ☎212/822-2700; *www.counciltravel.com*. Other main offices at **530 Bush St, San Francisco, CA 94108 ☎415/421-3473**; 221 West Portal Ave, San Francisco, CA 94127 ☎415/566-6222; 2486 Channing Way, Berkeley, CA 94712 ☎510/848-8604; 3300 M St NW, 2nd Floor, Washington, DC 20007 ☎202/337-6464; 1153 N Dearborn St, Chicago, IL 60610 ☎312/951-0585; 273 Newberry St, Boston, MA 02116 ☎617/266-1926; 2000 Guadalupe St, Suite 6, Austin, TX 78705 ☎512/472-4931; 1314 NE 43rd St, Suite 210, Seattle, WA 98105 ☎206/632-2448.

STA Travel offices in the US: Nationwide information ☎1-800/777-0112; *www.sta-travel.com*. Other main offices at **51 Grant Ave, San Francisco, CA 94108 ☎415/391-8407**; 10 Downing St, New York, NY 10014 ☎212/627-3111; 7202 Melrose Ave, Los Angeles, CA 90046 ☎213/934-8722; 297 Newbury St, Boston, MA 02115 ☎617/266-6014; 429 S Dearborn St, Chicago, IL 60605 ☎312/786-9050; 4341 University Way NE, Seattle, WA 98105 ☎206/633-5000; 3730 Walnut St, Philadelphia, PA 19104 ☎215/382-2928.

Travel CUTS offices in Canada: Head office, 187 College St, Toronto, ON M5T 1P7 ☎416/979-2406; *www.travelcuts.com*. Other main offices at MacEwan Hall Student Centre, University of Calgary, Calgary, AB T2N 1N4 ☎403/282-7687; Student Union Building, University of Alberta, Edmonton, AB T5N 3K5 ☎403/492-2592; 2085 Union St, Montréal, PQ H2X 3K3 ☎514/284-1368; 1 Stewart St, Ottawa, ON K1N 6H7 ☎613/238-8222; 2383 Ch Ste Foy, Suite 103, Ste Foy, Quebec, PQ G1V 1T1 ☎418/654-0224; Place Riel Campus Centre, University of Saskatchewan, Saskatoon, SA S7N 0W0 ☎306/975-3722; 567 Seymour St, Vancouver, BC V6B 1P2 ☎604/681-9136; University Centre, University of Manitoba, Winnipeg, MA R3T 2N2 ☎204/269-9530.

For travel agents **in San Francisco**, see p.328.

Vancouver; other routes are monopolized by Air Canada), fares are somewhat higher than they are for flights wholly within the US. You may find that it's worth the effort to get to a US city first, and fly on to San Francisco from there.

By train

If you have the time and inclination to enjoy the view of the rest of the US on your way to San Francisco or if you need the creature comforts of a private cabin and dining car (and can afford them), then an **Amtrak train** may be just the ticket for you. There's only one long-distance train per day from the north or east, and only a few from the south, but all three routes are among the most scenic on the entire Amtrak system.

The most spectacular train journey to San Francisco, the **California Zephyr**, runs all the way from Chicago passing through the Rockies west of Denver. After climbing alongside raging rivers through gorgeous mountain **scenery**, the route drops down the west flank of the Rockies and races across the Utah and Nevada deserts by night, stopping at Salt Lake City and Reno. The next day the train climbs up and over the mighty Sierra Nevada, following the route of the first transcontinental railroad on its way into Oakland, where you change to a bus for the ride into San Francisco.

Note that Amtrak trains arrive in Emeryville and Oakland across the Bay; they do not enter San Francisco itself. A free shuttle service is provided to the Ferry Building on the Embarcadero and to Market Street in front of the San Francisco Shopping Center in San Francisco. See p.61 and p.300.

A shorter but equally memorable route is the **Coast Starlight**, winding along the coast north from Los Angeles. The most incredible section is between Santa Barbara and San Luis Obispo, a 100-mile coastline ride during which it's not unusual to see seals, dolphins, or even whales in the waters offshore. (The other LA–SF Amtrak routes head inland by bus to Bakersfield then by rail north through the dull San Joaquin Valley. Avoid these if at all possible.)

The final route to San Francisco, also called the Coast Starlight, is the southbound leg of the

AMTRAK RAIL PASSES

Foreign travelers have a choice of four **rail passes** that include the Bay Area; the **Coastal Pass** permits unlimited train travel on the West coast.

	15-day (June–Aug)	15-day (Sept–May)	30-day (June–Aug)	30-day (Sept–May)
Far Western	$245	$190	$320	$250
Western	$325	$200	$405	$270
Coastal	—	—	$285	$235
National	$440	$295	$550	$385

For all information on **Amtrak fares and schedules**, and to make reservations, use the toll-free number ☎ **1-800/USA-RAIL** or check *www.amtrak.com*. (The site often offers to send you a brochure instead of giving information online, if so, check *www.aptms.com.au* for complete Amtrak listings and fares.) Do not call individual stations. For information on Canadian rail, check with VIA at ☎ 1-888/842-7245 or *www.viarail.ca*.

above journey. Starting out in Seattle, it runs south along the Puget Sound and across the Columbia River to Portland, past the mountains and forests of the Pacific Northwest. Unfortunately, it passes through the prettiest stretch, around Mt Shasta, by night, though, as its name suggests, it's still a lovely ride in the dark.

One-way cross-country coach fares are around $300, though Americans traveling round-trip can take advantage of "**All-Aboard America**" fares, which are zone-based and allow three stopovers in between your origin and eventual return. This enables you to visit one or more additional cities without paying any extra. Travel within the West (from Denver to the Pacific) costs $208 between September and May or $238 June to August; within the West and Midwest (west of Chicago), it costs $268/328; and for the entire USA it's $328/388). Amtrak also runs a promotion from October through November in which a companion travels free with the purchase of a full-fare ticket. **Foreign travelers** can take advantage of the rail passes detailed in the box above. While Amtrak's basic fares are quite a good value, if you want to travel in a bit more comfort the cost rises quickly. **Sleeping compartments**, which include small toilets and showers, start at around $100 per night for one or two people, but can climb as high as $400 depending on class of compartment, number of nights, season, etc; all include three meals a day.

On production of a passport issued outside the US or Canada, the passes can be bought at Amtrak stations in the US. In the **UK**, buy them from Destination Marketing, 2 Cinnamon Row, York Place, London SW11 3TW (☎ 020/253 9009); in **Ireland**, contact USIT (☎ 01/602 1600); in **Australia**, Rail Plus (☎ 1300/555 003); and in New Zealand, Rail Plus (☎ 09/303 2484).

You can also get a North America Rail Pass, a joint promotion between Amtrak and VIA that allows 15 or 30 days of unlimited travel on the US and Canadian rail system. Thirty-day passes in the peak season (June 1–Oct 15) cost $645, and $450 at all other times. The 15-day pass requires travel to originate in the northeast of the continent. Peak

CANADIAN VISITORS

Canadian citizens do not need a special visa to enter the States (unless planning to stay more than ninety days), but it is a good idea to bring your **passport** on a visit as far as San Francisco. If you cross the border by car, know that your trunk is subject to search, though it's rarely a hassle getting across.

If you need more information, contact the **Canadian Embassy**, 100 Wellington St, Ottawa, ON K1P 5T1 (☎ 613/238-5335).

Trains to and from San Francisco

A daily **Amtrak** shuttle bus departs from San Francisco from the San Francisco Shopping Center, 835 Market St (8am and 8.25pm); Pier 39 at Fisherman's Wharf (8.15am and 8.35pm); and the Ferry Building (8.40am and 8.55pm) to the Emeryville depot, from where the Coast Starlight train runs mornings northeast to Sacramento, Portland, and Seattle and evenings south to Los Angeles and San Diego. Amtrak's Capitol Corridor route links Oakland with San Jose (four daily, 1hr). San Francisco–San Jose commuters rely on **Caltrain** (☎1-800/660-4287). Thirty-three trains make the trip each way daily, with express ones clocking in at 45min, and regulars taking 1hr 30min ($4–5.25 each way). The San Francisco station is at Fourth and King Streets.

fare is $400, and off-peak $300. There's a 10 percent discount for students bearing a Student Advantage Card in the US or an ISIC card in Canada.

By bus

Bus travel is the most tedious and time-consuming way to get to San Francisco, and, for all the discomfort, won't really save you much, if any, money. You will undoubtedly meet some decidedly unique characters among your fellow passengers, so if it's truly seedy Americana you're after, this is the way to go. **Greyhound** (☎1-800/231-2222) is the sole long-distance operator; its fares average around 10¢ a mile if you buy your ticket the day of travel – which adds up to around $300 coast-to-coast. You can do it more cheaply by purchasing tickets two or three weeks in advance, sometimes cutting the price down by more than half.

Greyhound's **Ameripass**es are good for unlimited travel within a certain time and cost $199 for 7 days, $299 for 15 days, $409 for 30 days and $599 for 60 days. Because they're valid from the day of purchase, it doesn't make sense to buy them in advance. **Foreign visitors** can buy Ameripasses before leaving home, in which case they will be validated once travel starts. In the UK, they cost £105–130 (7-day), £218–268 (30-day) or £299–355 (60-day) depending on the season. Greyhound's general sales agent for the UK is Greyhound International UK, Kings Place, Wood St, Kingston-upon-Thames KT1 1JY (☎0870/888 0223; *www.greyhound.com*). In Australia the passes are available from Canada & America Travel Specialists, 343 Pacific Highway, Crows Nest, Sydney (☎02/9922 4600), and in New Zealand from Walshes World, 6/18 Shortland St, Auckland (☎09/379 3708).

By car

Driving your own car gives the greatest freedom and flexibility, but if you don't have one (or don't trust the one you do have), one option worth considering is a **driveaway**. Companies operate in most major cities, and are paid to find drivers to take a customer's car from one place to another. The company will normally pay for your insurance and your first tank of gas; after that, you'll be expected to drive along the most direct route and to average 400 miles a day. Companies are keen to use foreign travelers (German tourists are ideal, it seems), but if you are at least 21 and can convince them you're a safe bet, they'll take something like a $350 deposit, which you get back after delivering the car in good condition. Availability varies greatly, but usually there are as many cars leaving San Francisco as there are arriving. Auto Driveaway, 350 Townsend St (☎415/777-3740), is the main San Francisco company using drivers; look under "Automobile Transporters and Driveaways" in the *Yellow Pages* for your local branch office.

Though it's not really necessary if you're planning to stay in San Francisco itself, **renting a car** for travel to the outlying areas involves the usual story of phoning your local branch of one of the majors (Avis, Hertz, Budget, Thrifty, etc – listed on p.32) of which Thrifty tends to be the cheapest. Most companies have offices at destination airports, and

Buses to and from San Francisco

Greyhound unless specified otherwise.

San Francisco to: Los Angeles (19 daily; 8–12hr; or 1 Green Tortoise weekly; 12hr); Redding (5 daily; 6hr); Reno (7 daily; 6hr); Sacramento (17 daily; 2hr 20min); San Diego (8 daily; 12hr); San Jose (13 daily; 1hr 30min); San Rafael (2 daily; 1hr).

Green Tortoise

One alternative to Long-Distance Bus Hell is the slightly more cheerful **Green Tortoise**, whose buses, furnished with foam cushions, bunks, coolers and sound systems, ply the major cities of the West Coast, running between Los Angeles, San Francisco, and Seattle (departing at 8pm; 24hrs; $59). In summer, they also cross the country to New York and Boston in ten or fourteen days ($349/389), allowing plenty of stops for hiking, river-rafting, and hot springs. Other Green Tortoise trips include excursions to the major national parks (in 16 days for $499), and north to Alaska, as well as winter trips to Central America and Mexico. Green Tortoise has year-round excursions to Yosemite.

Main office: 494 Broadway, San Francisco, CA 94133 ☎1-800/867-8647 or ☎415/834-1000

addresses and phone numbers are comprehensively documented in the *Yellow Pages*.

Also worth considering are **fly-drive deals**, which give cut-rate (and sometimes free) car rental when buying an air ticket. They usually work out cheaper than renting on the spot and are especially good value if you intend to do a lot of driving.

Packages

Many operators run all-inclusive **packages** which combine plane tickets and hotel accommodation with (for example) sightseeing, wining and dining, or excursions to tourist sites. Even if the "package" aspect doesn't thrill you to pieces, these deals can still be more convenient and sometimes even work out to be more economical than arranging the same thing yourself, providing you don't mind losing a little flexibility. With such a vast range of packages available, it's impossible to give an overview – major travel agents will have brochures detailing what's on offer.

Health and insurance

Most travel agents and tour operators will offer you an insurance policy when you book your flight or holiday, and some will insist you take it. These policies may not be as competitive as others available on the market, so do your homework before buying, and check that you're not already covered on any plans or credit cards you already hold.

Canadians should find that their **provincial health plans** cover most of their health insurance needs. Bank and credit cards (particularly American Express) often provide certain levels of medical or other insurance, and travel insurance may also be included if you use a major credit or

For advice on personal safety, and how to cope with emergency situations – including phone numbers to report lost checks or credit cards, see p.26.

Rough Guides Travel Insurance

Rough Guides now offer their own **travel insurance**, customized for our readers by a leading UK broker and backed by a Lloyds underwriter. It's available for anyone, of any nationality, traveling anywhere in the world, and we are convinced that this is the best-value scheme you'll find.

There are two main Rough Guide insurance plans: **Essential**, for effective, no-frills cover, starting at £11.75 for 2 weeks; and **Premier** – more expensive but with more generous and extensive benefits. Each offer European or Worldwide cover, and can be supplemented with a "Hazardous Activities Premium" if you plan to indulge in sports considered dangerous, such as skiing, scuba-diving, or trekking. Unlike many policies, the Rough Guides schemes are calculated by the day, so if you're traveling for 27 days rather than a month, that's all you pay for. You can alternatively take out annual **multi-trip insurance**, which covers you for all your travel throughout the year (with a maximum of 60 days for any one trip).

For a policy quote, call the Rough Guides Insurance Line on UK freefone ☎0800/015 0906, or, if you're calling from outside Britain on ☎44 1243 621 046. Alternatively, get an online quote at *www.roughguides.com/insurance*.

charge card to pay for your trip. **Homeowners' or renters'** insurance may also cover theft and loss of valuables while you're on vacation.

Travelers from **outside North America** should be sure their coverage includes a sensible amount for medical expenses, a necessity when you're traveling to the US – this should be at least £1,000,000, which will cover the cost of an air ambulance to fly you home in the event of serious injury or hospitalization.

Most **North American travel insurance** policies apply only to items lost, stolen, or damaged while in the custody of an identifiable, responsible third party – hotel porter, airline, luggage consignment, etc. Even in these cases you will have to contact the local police within a certain time limit.

If you have a serious **accident** while in San Francisco, don't worry about being left to die on the sidewalk; emergency medical services will

Hospital emergency rooms open at all times

California Pacific (formerly Davies) **Medical Center** Castro and Duboce sts ☎415/600-6000 has 24hr emergency care and a doctors' referral service.

Highland Hospital 1411 E 31st St, Oakland ☎510/533-3712

Kaiser Permanente 2425 Geary Blvd ☎415/202-2000

Lyon Martin Women's Health Services 1748 Market St, Suite 201 ☎415/565-7667

Pacific Medical Center 2333 Buchanan St at Washington St ☎415/923-3333

San Francisco General Hospital 1001 Potrero Ave near 22nd St ☎415/206-8000 or ☎206-8111 emergency; also has a 24hr emergency walk-in service and rape treatment center ☎415/821-3222.

University of California Medical Center Parnassas Ave at Third ☎415/476-1037

Also, if you're short of funds, check in with the **Castro-Mission Health Center**, 3850 17th St (☎415/487-7500). It offers a drop-in medical service with charges on a sliding scale depending on income, and free contraception and pregnancy testing. **The Haight-Ashbury Free Clinic**, 558 Clayton St (Mon–Thurs 9am–9pm, Fri 9am–5pm; ☎415/487-5632), provides a general health-care service with special services for women and detoxification, by appointment only. **New Leaf**, 1853 Market St at Guerrero (☎415/626-7000), offers outpatient mental health services on a sliding fee scale.

get to you quickly and charge you later. For emergencies or ambulances, dial ☎**911**, the nationwide emergency number.

Should you need to see a **doctor**, lists can be found in the *Yellow Pages* under "Clinics" or "Physicians and Surgeons." A basic consultation fee is $50–75, payable in advance, but if you have medical insurance, give them your policy card and you won't have to pay anything when checking in. Medications aren't cheap either – keep all your receipts for later claims on your insurance policy. For **dental care**, contact the Dental Society Referral Service (☎415/421-1435).

Many **minor ailments** can be remedied using the fabulous array of potions and lotions available in **drugstores**. Foreign visitors should bear in mind that many pills available over the counter at home need a prescription in the US – most codeine-based painkillers, for example – and that local brand names can be confusing. Conversely, many over-the-counter cold and flu medications sold in the US pack double or triple the wallop of their European counterparts. Ask for advice at the **pharmacy** in any drugstore or supermarket.

Travelers from Europe do not require **inoculations** to enter the US.

Information and maps

Advance information can be obtained by post from the California Office of Tourism, 801 K St, Sacramento, CA 95814 (☎916/322-2881 or 1-800/862-2543), though the best source of specific information on San Francisco is the San Francisco Convention and Visitors Bureau, Suite 900, 201 Third St, San Francisco, CA 94103 (Mon–Fri 8.30am–5pm; ☎415/974-6900). The bureau publishes the *San Francisco Visitor Planning Guide* which includes detailed, if somewhat selective, information about accommodation, entertainment, exhibitions, and stores, as well as a handy map; they'll send it to you for free if you leave your address on their answering machine.

Tourist offices

The **San Francisco Visitor Information Center**, on the lower level of Hallidie Plaza at the end of the cable-car line at 900 Market St (Mon–Fri 8.30am–5pm; ☎415/391-2000; *www.sfvisitor.org*), has free maps of the city and the Bay Area, oodles of pamphlets on hotels and restaurants, and can help with lodging and travel plans. Its staff speaks several languages, as well. Besides giving out the free *San Francisco Visitor Guide*, the center also sells **CityPass** (*www.citypass.net*, $33.25, children $24.25), a booklet of tickets to six popular attractions – the Exploratorium, Palace of the Legion of Honor, Steinhart Aquarium and Academy of Sciences, M.H. de Young Museum, the Museum of Modern Art, and the Blue and Gold Fleet's San Francisco Bay cruise – that can work out to half off total admission, as long as you visit all six sights within nine days. The pass now includes a 7-day Muni/Cable Car passport for unlimited public transportation within the city.

All the various **Bay Area regions** also have at least one main source of information and usually some kind of visitors' bureau; almost every town will have at least one office operated by the local **Chamber of Commerce**. Where useful we've listed them under the appropriate sections of the Bay Area chapters.

MAP AND TRAVEL BOOK SUPPLIERS

Australia

The Map Shop, 6 Peel St, Adelaide, ☎08/8231 2033.

Mapland, 372 Little Bourke St, Melbourne, ☎03/9670 4383.

Perth Map Centre, 1/884 Hay St, Perth, ☎08/9322 5733.

Travel Bookshop, Shop 2, 175 Liverpool St, Sydney, ☎02/9261 8200.

Worldwide Maps and Guides 187 George St, Brisbane, ☎07/3221 4330.

New Zealand

Mapworld, 173 Gloucester St, Christchurch ☎03/374 5399.

Specialty Maps, 46 Albert St, Auckland ☎09/307 2217.

UK

Aberdeen Map Shop, 74 Skene St, Aberdeen ☎01224/637999.

Blackwell's Map and Travel Shop, 53 Broad St, Oxford ☎01865/792792.

Daunt Books, 83 Marylebone High St, London ☎020/7224 2295.

Heffers Map Shop, 3rd Floor, Heffers Stationery Department, 19 Sidney St, Cambridge ☎01223/568467.

James Thin Melven's Bookshop, 29 Union St, Inverness ☎01463/233500.

John Smith and Sons, 57–61 St Vincent St, Glasgow ☎0141/221 7472.

National Map Centre, 22–24 Caxton St, London ☎020/7222 4945 or 7222 2466.

Stanfords, 12–14 Long Acre, London ☎020/7836 1321; 52 Grosvenor Gardens, London; 156 Regent St, London; 29 Corn St, Bristol ☎0117/929 9966.

The Travel Bookshop, 13–15 Blenheim Crescent, London ☎020/7229 5260.

Maps by **mail or phone order** are available from Stanfords ☎020/7836 1321.

Ireland

Easons Bookshop, 40 O'Connell St, Dublin ☎01/873 3811.

Fred Hanna's Bookshop, 27–29 Nassau St, Dublin ☎01/677 1255.

Maps

Most of the tourist offices we've mentioned can supply you with good **maps**, either for free or for a small charge; supplemented with our own, these should be enough for general sightseeing and touring. The best of the commercially available alternatives are the easy-to-read city plans published by Rand McNally and Gousha Publications, both of which have especially detailed sections on downtown. They also do maps of Oakland and the East Bay, San Jose and the Peninsula, and Marin County. For the habitually lost, Flashmaps does a handbook on the city. The **American Automobile Association** – "Triple A" – based at 1000 AAA Drive, Heathrow, FL 32746 (☎1-800/222-4357), provides free maps and assistance to its members, and to British members of the **AA** and **RAC**; they also have an office in San Francisco, 150 Van Ness Ave (Mon–Fri 8.30am–5.30pm; ☎415/565-2012), near the Civic Center, and other locations all over the Bay Area. Give them a day's notice, your membership number and your desired route, and they'll put together a **TripTik** for you – a detailed map of the best routes to take.

Hodges Figgis Bookshop, 56–58 Dawson St, Dublin ☎01/677 4754.

Waterstone's, Queens Building, 8 Royal Ave, Belfast ☎028/9024 7355.

Canada

Open Air Books and Maps, 25 Toronto St, Toronto, ☎416/363-0719.

Ulysses Travel Bookshop, 4176 St-Denis, Montréal ☎514/289-0993.

World Wide Books and Maps, 714 Granville St, Vancouver, ☎604/687-3320.

United States

Adventurous Traveler Bookstore, PO Box 1468, Williston, VT ☎1-800/282-3963; *www.AdventurousTraveler.com.*

Book Passage, 51 Tamal Vista Blvd, Corte Madera, CA ☎415/927-0960.

The Complete Traveler Bookstore, 199 Madison Ave, New York, NY ☎212/685-9007; 3207 Fillmore St, San Francisco, CA ☎415/923-1511.

Distant Lands, 56 S Raymond Ave, Pasadena, CA ☎626/449-3220; *www.distantlands.com.*

Forsyth Travel Library, 9154 W 57th St, Shawnee Mission, KS ☎1-800/367-7984.

Get Lost, 1825 Market St, San Francisco, CA ☎415/437-0529. Travel books, travel books, travel books. Plus maps and gear.

Map Link Inc, 25 E Mason St, Santa Barbara, CA ☎805/692-6777.

Phileas Fogg's Books & Maps, #87 Stanford Shopping Center, Palo Alto, CA ☎1-800/533-FOGG.

Rand McNally,* 444 N Michigan Ave, Chicago, IL ☎312/321-1751; 150 E 52nd St, New York, NY ☎212/758-7488; 595 Market St, San Francisco, CA ☎415/777-3131; 1201 Connecticut Ave NW, Washington, DC ☎202/223-6751.

The Savvy Traveler, 310 S Michigan Ave, Chicago, IL ☎312/913-9800.

Sierra Club Bookstore, 85 Second St, San Francisco, CA ☎415/977-5600.

Travel Books and Language Centre, 4931 Cordell Ave, Bethesda, MD ☎1-800/220-2665.

***Note**: Rand McNally now has 24 stores across the US, though their San Francisco store is cramped and not particularly well-stocked; call ☎1-800/333-0136 (ext 2111) for the location of your nearest store, or for **direct mail** maps. For a good map store in the city, head for Get Lost, listed above.

For something more detailed, such as **hiking** or **cycling** routes, it's best to wait till you're in San Francisco to map out a trail. Ranger stations in parks and wilderness areas all sell good-quality local maps for $1–2, and camping stores generally have a good selection as well. Most bookstores will have a range of local trail guides, the best of which we've listed under "Books" in Contexts.

The Internet

Due to San Francisco's major role in the computer industry and the city's status as pretty much *the* US new-media capital, there are many quirky **Web sites** that serve San Francisco with maps, bookstores, flight options, or other useful information. We've listed both practical and fun sources here, other sites are sprinkled throughout the guide. Also, don't forget our own site (*www.roughguides.com*), which will lead you to plenty more on San Francisco and other locations around the world. If that doesn't satiate, go to a search engine such as *www.hotbot.com* and plug in the words "San Francisco" – you should net thousands of options.

San Francisco on the Internet

California's Edge *www.californiasedge.com* Travel and culture site for the entire California coast.

Emperor Norton's homepage *www.notfrisco.com* Features the colorful historical character's complete biography (see box, p.55) along with the complete text of his many proclamations; the site also contains the San Francisco Almanac, links to San Francisco oral history, and a selection of virtual vintage postcards.

The List *www.foopee.com/punk/the-list/* The only concert calendar ska, punk and indie fans will need in the Bay Area.

Literary Kicks *www.charm.net/~brooklyn/Places/SanFrancisco.html* For the word on the Beats and the iconoclastic legacy they left on San Francisco.

The Museum of the City of San Francisco, *www.sfmuseum.org* The actual museum, which used to be in the Cannery, has closed, but the Web site gives a peek at its collection (now in storage) of Gold Rush and 1906 earthquake knickknacks, along with a chronology of the local rock scene in the 1960s.

Napa Valley *www.napavalley.com* Useful information for visiting this renowned wine-producing valley, plus links to some vineyards' Web sites.

San Francisco Arts Monthy *www.sfarts.org* Comprehensive review of what's on around town in music, theater, dance, and festivals.

San Francisco Bay Traveler *www.sfbaytraveler.com* Travel specific site with a good archive of Bay Area travel features, links to maps, hotels, and airlines.

San Francisco Jazz Organization *www.sfjazz.org* A comprehensive listing of jazz performances in the city.

San Francisco Magazine *www.sffocus.com* Good for restaurant listings and features on upscale treats like spas, hair salons, and designer boutiques.

San Francisco Reservations *www.hotelres.com* Check hotel room availability and make reservations online.

SF Rave Calendar *www.hyperreal.org* Those wearing day-glo gear can tune into the local rave community here.

SF Station *www.sfstation.com* Serves up alternative events listings and reviews, and points you to the trendsetting shops.

Sunshine Daydream *www.sunshinedaydream.com* Your one-stop site for mountain biking, rock climbing and other outdoor activities.

Webcastro *www.webcastro.com* A comprehensive guide to the Castro, a gay neighborhood with a history of activism and pride.

Telephones, mail, and email

Telephones

The vast majority of San Francisco telephones are the push-button kind, emitting a different audio tone for each button pressed. Some numbers, particularly those of consumer services, employ letters as part of their "number," for example ☎992-*BART*, for information on the Bay Area Rapid Transit system. The letters are printed on the buttons. For help, call the operator (☎0).

The San Francisco **area code** – a three-figure number that must precede the seven-figure number if you're calling from another region – is ☎415. All San Francisco phone numbers are within this area code but we've included the ☎415 prefix as a reminder, as the Bay Area has no less than five area codes. The others are: East Bay (☎510), the Wine Country (☎707), Palo Alto (☎650), San Jose (☎408) and Santa Cruz (☎831). To phone one area code from another you have to dial a 1 before the code and number – for example ☎1-707/963-9611 for Robert Mondavi Winery in the Napa Valley.

Public telephones sometimes actually work and can be found almost everywhere. Local calls are 35¢. Most phones don't take incoming calls, so be sure and have plenty of change if you plan to talk for any length of time. **Toll-free calls** (☎1-800 or ☎1-888 numbers) are, indeed, free, and many government agencies, car rental firms, hotels, and so on use them. Phone numbers with the prefix ☎1-900 are pay-per-call lines, generally quite expensive and almost always involving either sports or phone sex.

Nonlocal calls ("zone calls") – to numbers misleadingly located within the same area code yet out of the most immediate calling zone – are more expensive than local ones. Pricier still are **long-distance calls** (to a different area code and always prefixed by a 1), for which you'll need pockets of change or a calling card (see below). Nonlocal calls and long-distance calls are far cheaper if made between 6pm and 8am, and calls from **private phones** are always much cheaper than those from public phones. Detailed rates are listed at the front of the **telephone directory**.

If you're broke, you can call **collect** and charge the person whom you call. Dial "0" then the area code and phone number. An operator will answer, ask your name, call the intended recipient and ask if they will accept the charges. Cheaper still would be to use a private agency like ☎1-800/COLLECT.

Making a telephone call from a hotel room is usually more expensive than from a pay phone, though some budget hotels offer free local calls from rooms – ask when you check in. Some phones accept **credit cards**, but a better bet, if you make a lot of calls from the road, is to get a **calling card** linked to your long distance account.

Useful numbers

Emergencies ☎911 Ask to be connected with the appropriate emergency service: fire, police or ambulance.

Local directory information ☎411

Operator ☎0

Long-distance directory information ☎1-(area code)/555-1212

Directory inquiries for toll-free numbers ☎1-800/555-1212

International telephone calls

To call **San Francisco** from the rest of the world (excluding Canada), the US country code is always ☎1. Thus from the UK you dial ☎00-1-415, followed by the seven-digit number. When placing an **international call** from San Francisco, it's best to do so between 6pm and 7am, when the rates are lowest. It's also wise to get a **calling card** before you leave home if you're going to be making a lot of these calls. The charges will then be billed to your regular account, so you don't have to pay as you go. In Britain contact BT (☎0800/345600 or 345144), Cable & Wireless (☎0500/700101), or Swiftcall (☎020/7488 2001 or 0800/769 0800); in Ireland, Swiftcall (☎01/205 7834); in Australia, Telstra (☎1800/038 000) or Optus (☎1300/300 937); and in New Zealand, Telecom (☎04/801 9000). You can get assistance from the **international operator (☎00)**, who may also interrupt every three minutes asking for more money, and call you back for any money still owed immediately after you hang up. To call **direct**, dial 011 followed by the country code (a complete listing of codes can be found in the front section of the *Yellow Pages*):

Australia 61

Ireland 353

New Zealand 64

United Kingdom 44

Phone cards are a popular way of calling from any phone, and can be purchased at post offices, newsstands, convenience stores and some hotels in denominations of $5, $10, and $20. They work out to be a lot cheaper than feeding coins into a pay phone, especially when calling abroad.

Mail services

Post offices are usually open Monday to Friday from 9am until 5pm, and Saturday from 9am to 1pm; there are blue **mail boxes** on many street corners. Ordinary **mail within the US** costs 33¢ for a letter weighing up to an ounce; the sender's address should be written on the envelope. **Air mail** between the West Coast and Europe generally takes about a week. Postcards, aerograms and letters weighing up to half an ounce (a single thin sheet) cost 60¢.

The last line of the address is made up of an abbreviation denoting the state (California is "CA") and a five-figure number – the **zip code** – denoting the local post office. (The additional four digits you will sometimes see appended to zip codes are helpful but not essential.) Letters that don't carry any zip code are generally returned to the sender or lost. To find a zip code for an address without one, phone the United States postal service toll free (see box).

Letters can be sent c/o **General Delivery** (what's known elsewhere as **poste restante**) to:

Your Name
General Delivery
San Francisco CA 94142
USA

You can collect general delivery mail (bring your ID) from the main post office, 101 Hyde St, in the Civic Center (Mon–Fri 8.30am–5.30pm, Sat 10am–2pm; ☎1-800/275-8777), but letters will only be held for thirty days before being returned to sender, so make sure there's a return address on the envelope. If you're receiving mail at some-

Main Bay Area post offices*

Rincon Finance Station, 180 Steuart St (Mon–Fri 7am–6pm, Sat 9am–2pm)

Sutter Street Station, 150 Sutter St (Mon–Fri 8.30am–5pm)

SoMa, 266 Harrison St

Chinatown 867 Stockton St

North Beach 1640 Stockton St

Marina 2055 Lombard St

Oakland Main 1675 Seventh St, Oakland

Berkeley Main 2000 Allston Way, Berkeley

*In San Francisco unless indicated; to call any of the post offices, dial ☎1-800/275-8777.

one else's address, it should include "c/o" and the regular occupant's name; otherwise it too is likely to be returned.

Rules on sending **parcels** are very rigid: packages must be sealed according to the instructions given at the start of the *Yellow Pages*. To send anything out of the country, you'll need a green **customs declaration form**, available from a post office. **Postal rates** for sending a parcel weighing up to one pound are $9.75 to Europe, $11.20 to Australasia. Packages can be guaranteed for **overnight delivery** in the US by private companies. The most popular and omnipresent is Federal Express at 1150 Harrison St near the Civic Center (☎415/877-9000). For other FedEx locations (there are several dozen around town) call ☎1-800/463-3339.

Faxes and email

Public **fax** machines, which may require your credit card to be "swiped" through an attached device, are found at photocopy centers (such as the omnipresent Kinko's chain), libraries, and, occasionally, bookstores.

Email is, of course, a great way of communicating with folks while you're off on your travels. In San Francisco, you can get **free Internet access** at the Main Library (Civic Center, between Seventh and Eighth sts ☎415/557-4400), but you'll have to get a membership, which requires a local address, and you're limited to 30 minutes at a time. Downtown's locations, such as the Microsoft Store in the Sony Metreon mall at Fourth Street, or Computown at 710 Market or CompUSA nearby all have free Internet terminals, as does the Green Tortoise hostel, for guests. Otherwise, if you want to sip some coffee while you're corresponding via computer, check out the cybercafés *Internet Alfredo* (1 McCoppin ☎415/437-3140, $7.50 per hour), *Coffee Net* (774 Harrison ☎415/495-7447, $5 per hour), and *Chat Café* (18th St at Sanchez ☎415/626-4700, free with purchase of meal).

Costs, money, and banks

This book contains detailed price information for lodging and eating in San Francisco. Make sure to study prices in those sections (p.217 & p. 233) when planning your trip.

Your biggest single expense is likely to be **accommodation**. Few hotel or motel rooms cost under $50 – it's more usual to pay no less than $75 for anything halfway decent. Although dorm beds in hostels costing around $15 do exist, they're far from luxurious, though some, granted, are located in prime spots of town.

As for **food**, $20 a day is enough to get you an adequate life-support diet, but if you can manage $50 per day and upward you should spend it and get the most out of this cuisine-conscious city. Beyond this, everything hinges on how much sightseeing, taxi-taking, drinking, and socializing you do – in San Francisco it's easy to get through a bank roll in a couple of days.

Rates for traveling around using the Muni (☎415/673-6864) system are very reasonable. If you're going to be in the city for at least a week or two, consider a one-month **Fast Pass** ($35) sold at all underground Muni stations – the pass permits unlimited BART and Muni use throughout San Francisco. See "Getting around the city," p.28.

Money: a note for foreign travelers

Even when the exchange rate is at its least advantageous, most European visitors find virtually everything to be better value in the US than it is at home, though San Francisco's prices have more in common with New York than those of any other American metropolis, so you shouldn't expect to scrape by on a minuscule budget.

Generally speaking, one **pound sterling** will buy $1.50–1.70; one **Canadian dollar** is worth between 70¢ and 90¢; one **Australian dollar** is between 60¢ and 80¢; and one **New Zealand dollar** is worth 50¢ to 70¢.

Bills and coins

US currency comes in **bills** worth $1, $5, $10, $20, $50, and $100, plus various larger (and rarer) denominations. Confusingly, all are the same size and same green color, making it necessary to check each bill carefully. The dollar is made up of 100 cents in **coins** of 1¢ (known as a **penny**), 5¢ (a **nickel**), 10¢ (a **dime**) and 25¢ (a **quarter**). Very occasionally you might come across **JFK half-dollars** (50¢), **Susan B. Anthony dollar coins**, or a **two-dollar bill**. Exact change (quarters and $1 bills are the most useful) is needed for buses, vending machines, and telephones, so always carry plenty.

To make the most of the surrounding regions, especially if there are two or more of you, renting a **car** can be a very good investment.

Sales tax of 8.5 percent is added to virtually everything you buy in stores, save food, but it isn't part of the marked price.

Carrying, changing and accessing money

If you don't already have a **credit card**, you should definitely get one before you set off. For many services, it's simply taken for granted in many places that you'll be paying with plastic. Credit cards serve as a form of ID here; when renting a car (or even a bike) or checking into a hotel you'll almost certainly be asked to show a credit card to establish your creditworthiness – even if you intend to settle the bill in cash. **Visa**, **MasterCard**, **Diners Club**, **Discover**, and **American Express** are the most widely accepted.

You'll also need to carry a certain amount of **cash**. With MasterCard or Visa it is also possible to withdraw cash at any bank displaying relevant stickers, or from appropriate automatic teller machines (**ATMs**). ATM cards held by visitors from other states, and overseas cash-dispensing cards linked to international networks such as **Cirrus** and **Plus**, should work in most Californian machines, though you should check with your bank before you leave home. This may be the best way of accessing money, not only because this method of financing is safer, but with highly favorable exchange rates and at only a dollar or two per transaction, it's economical as well. Check what penalties your bank assesses for using a competitor's cash machine; voters in San Francisco in 1999 approved a measure that would make it illegal for local banks to "double dip" – or charge an ATM access fee on top of the one already charged by the primary establishment – though the banking industry is challenging that verdict in court.

Diners Club cards can be used to cash personal checks at Citibank branches. American Express cards can only get cash, or buy traveler's checks at American Express offices (check the *Yellow Pages*) or from the traveler's check dispensers at most major airports. Most **Canadian** credit cards issued by hometown banks will be honored in the US.

US dollar traveler's checks are a safe way of carrying money for both American and foreign travelers; they offer the great security of knowing that lost or stolen checks will be replaced. You should have no problem using the better-known checks, such as American Express and Visa, in shops, restaurants, and gas stations (don't be put off by "no checks" signs, which only refer to personal checks). Be sure to have plenty of the $10 and $20 denominations for everyday transactions.

Banks in San Francisco are generally open from 9am until 5pm or 5.30pm Monday to Thursday, and 9am to 6pm on Friday. Most major banks will change dollar traveler's checks for their face value – though there's little point in doing this as the checks are as good as cash – and

Exchange offices

American Express, 560 California St between Kearny and Montgomery (Mon–Fri 9am–5pm; ☎415/536-2600). Park at the garage at 635 Sacramento, as they validate.

Thomas Cook, 75 Geary St (Mon–Fri 9am–5pm; Sat 10am–4pm; ☎415/362-3452).

Wire services

Australia

American Express Moneygram ☎1-800/230-100; **Western Union** ☎1-800/649-565.

New Zealand

American Express Moneygram ☎09/379 8243 or 0800/262 263; **Western Union** ☎09/270 0050.

Britain

American Express Moneygram ☎0800/894887; **Western Union** ☎0800/833833.

US and Canada

American Express Moneygram ☎1-800/543-4080; **Western Union** ☎1-800/325-6000

change foreign traveler's checks and currency. Exchange bureaus, always found at airports, tend to charge slightly less commission: Thomas Cook and American Express are the biggest names. Rarely, if ever, do hotels change foreign currency. **Emergency phone numbers** to call if your checks and/or credit cards are stolen are on p.27. To find the nearest bank that sells a particular brand of traveler's check, or to buy checks by phone, call the following numbers: American Express (☎1-800/673-3782), Citicorp (☎1-800/645-6556), MasterCard International/Thomas Cook (☎1-800/223-7373), Visa (☎1-800/227-6811).

Each of the two main ATM networks operates a **toll-free** line to let customers know the location of their nearest machine; **Plus System** is ☎1-800/THE-PLUS and **Cirrus** is ☎1-800/4CIRRUS.

Emergencies

Assuming you know someone who is prepared to send you money in a crisis, the quickest way is to have them wire the money instantaneously from the Western Union office nearest them to the one nearest you, subject to the deduction of 10 percent commission. Western Union operates terminals at many small convenience stores and check-cashing stores throughout the city (call ☎1-800/325-6000 for the nearest location). American Express Moneygram offers a similar service.

It's also possible to have money wired directly from a bank in your home country to a bank in the US, although this is somewhat less reliable because it involves two separate institutions. If you go this route, the person wiring the funds to you will need the telex number of the bank the funds are being wired to. Having money wired from home is never convenient or cheap, and should be considered a last resort.

If you have a few days' leeway, sending a postal **money order**, exchangeable at any post office, is cheaper still. The equivalent for foreign travelers is the **international money order**, for which you need to allow up to seven days in the international air mail before arrival. An ordinary check sent from overseas takes 2–3 weeks to clear.

British travelers in difficulties have the final option of throwing themselves on the mercy of the **British Consulate**, 1 Sansome St (☎415/981-3030), who won't be at all pleased to see you but may deign to offer assistance. In worst cases only they may repatriate you, but they will never, under any circumstances, lend you money. Likewise stranded Australian travelers can call upon the **Australian Consulate**, seventh floor, 1 Bush St (☎415/362-6160) and New Zealanders the **New Zealand Consulate**, Suite 700, One Maritime Plaza (☎415/399-1255).

Crime and personal safety

Though no one could pretend that San Francisco is trouble-free, by and large the worst areas for crime are also the most unusual places for tourists to visit, so you're unlikely to have to deal with any of the threatening environments of some other US cities. Violent crime is down sharply, and most of what does occur is drug-related and generally concentrated in deprived areas such as Hunter's Point, on San Francisco's southeast waterfront, or West Oakland. In downtown San Francisco, only the Tenderloin and quieter spots of SoMa need a bit of extra vigilance. By being careful (walking with a purpose; taking care to avoid darkened streets and doorways), you're unlikely to have problems even in these places, though you may well feel distinctly uncomfortable.

Mugging and theft

The biggest problem for most travelers is the threat of **mugging**. It's impossible to give hard and fast rules about what to do if you're confronted by a mugger. Whether to run, scream, or fight depends on the situation – but most locals would just hand over their money and do whatever the mugger says.

Of course, the best strategy is simply to **avoid being mugged**. Following a few basic rules helps minimize the danger: *don't* flash money around; *don't* peer at your map (or this book) at every corner, thereby announcing you're a lost stranger; even if you're terrified or drunk (or both), *don't* appear so; *avoid* dark streets, especially ones you can't see the end of; in the early hours stick to the roadside edge of the pavement so it's easier to run into the road to attract attention; and cross the road or turn around immediately if you see that danger lies ahead on the same block.

If **the worst happens** and your assailant is toting a gun or a knife, try to stay calm: remember that he (for mugging is generally a male pursuit) is probably scared, too. Keep still, don't make any sudden movements – and hand over your money. When he's gone you'll be shocked, but try to find a cab to take you to the nearest police station, or **phone ☎911** and the police will send an officer to the scene, who'll take you to the nearest station. Here, report the theft and

Main SF and Bay Area police stations

San Francisco Police Dept 850 Bryant St, SoMa ☎415/553-1373

Central Station 766 Vallejo St, North Beach ☎415/553-1532

Mission Station 630 Valencia St, Mission District ☎415/558-5400

Northern Station 1125 Fillmore, Western Addition ☎415/553-1563

Golden Gate Park Station Stanyan and Waller sts ☎415/753-7280

Potrero Station 2300 Third St, Hunter's Point ☎415/553-1021

Richmond Station 461 Sixth Ave ☎415/553-1385

Oakland Police Dept 455 Seventh St ☎510/238-3744

Berkeley Police Dept 2171 McKinley Ave ☎510/644-6743

Stolen traveler's checks and credit cards

Keep a record of the numbers of your traveler's checks separately from the actual checks; if you lose them, ring the issuing company on the toll-free number below. If you had American Express-issued monies, go to the branch office at 560 California St between Kearny and Montgomery (Mon–Fri 9am–5pm; ☎415/536-2600). Park at the garage at 635 Sacramento, as they validate. You can also try the Travel Service Office, 455 Market St at First Street (Mon–Fri 8.30am–5.30pm, Sat 9am–2pm) or at 333 Jefferson at Jones in Fisherman's Wharf (Mon–Thurs 10am–6pm, Fri–Sat 10am–9pm, Sun 11am–6pm). They'll ask you for the check numbers, the place you bought them, when and how you lost them and whether it's been reported to the police. All being well, you should get the missing checks reissued within a couple of days – and perhaps an emergency advance to tide you over.

Emergency numbers

American Express	
(checks)	☎1-800/221-7282
(credit cards)	☎1-800/992-3404
Diners Club	☎1-800/234-6377
MasterCard	☎1-800/307-7309
Thomas Cook	☎1-800/287-7362
Visa	
(checks)	☎1-800/227-6811
(credit cards)	☎1-800/336-8472

get a reference number on the report to claim insurance and traveler's check refunds. For specific advice to women in case of mugging or attack, phone the Rape Crisis Line (☎415/647-7273).

Another potential source of trouble is having your **hotel room burgled**. Always store valuables in the hotel safe when you go out; when inside, keep your door locked and don't open it to anyone you are suspicious of. If they claim to be hotel staff and you don't believe them, call reception on the room phone to check.

Stolen passports

Needless to say, having bags containing travel documents snatched is a big headache, none more so for foreign travelers than **losing your passport**. If the worst happens, go to the nearest consulate (see listings in Directory, p.326) with any remaining ID – plane tickets, driving license, etc – and they will issue you with an emergency **temporary passport**, basically a sheet of paper saying you've reported the loss, which will get you out of America and back home.

Car crime

Crimes committed against tourists driving **rental cars** in the US have garnered headlines around the world in recent years. In major urbanized areas, any car you rent should have nothing on it – such as a particular license plate – that makes it easy to spot as a rental car. When driving, under no circumstances stop in any unlit or seemingly deserted urban area – and especially not if someone is waving you down and suggesting that something is wrong with your car. Similarly, if you are "accidentally" rammed by the driver behind, do not stop immediately but drive on to the nearest well-lit, busy area and **phone ☎911 for assistance**. Keep your doors locked and windows never more than slightly open. Do not open your door or window if someone approaches your car on the pretext of asking directions. Hide any valuables out of sight, preferably locked in the trunk but not in the glove compartment. In fact, locals often leave their glove compartments open (check to see that a light doesn't go on and drain your battery) to show potential thieves there's nothing worth breaking a window for. Store any valuables you don't need for your journey in your hotel safe.

Getting around the city

Getting around San Francisco is best done on foot as the city center is compact. Walking the dense metropolis reveals numerous surprises, often in the form of stunning homes and bustling marketplaces. The hills can be brutal on your legs and feet, so wear comfortable shoes and consider the occasional flat – if less direct – detour. Watch traffic when crossing the street, and don't start off until the light has been green for a few seconds. You may see outlines of bodies painted on street corners; they represent real people killed on city streets, stenciled by activist Ken Kelton (*www.pedsafe.com*) over the past two years to raise awareness of pedestrian safety.

San Francisco's **public transportation** system, **Muni**, though much maligned by locals for its unpredictable schedule, covers every neighborhood via its system of cable cars, buses, and trolleys. **Cycling** is another good option, as marked bike routes lead to all major points of interest. If you're considering journeying further north to Marin County and the Wine Country or south to San Jose and Santa Cruz, consider renting a **car** as public transport, while extant, is infrequent and complicated.

Points of arrival

By air

All international and most domestic flights arrive at **San Francisco International Airport** (SFO), inconveniently located about fifteen miles south of the city. San Mateo County Transit (SamTrans) **buses** leave every half-hour from the upper level of the airport; the #KX express ($3) takes around 25 minutes to reach the Transbay Terminal downtown, while the slower #292 ($1.10) stops everywhere and takes nearly an hour. On the #KX, you're allowed only one carry-on bag; on the #292, you can bring as much as you want provided you can carry it onto the bus yourself. Another alternative from the airport is the excruciatingly slow #193 bus to the Daly City BART station ($1.10), where a train downtown will run you an additional $2.10. The SFO Airporter bus ($10) picks up outside each baggage claim area every fifteen minutes and travels to Union Square and the Financial District in about thirty minutes. The blue **Supershuttle, American Airporter Shuttle** and the **Yellow Airport Shuttle** minibuses depart every five minutes from the upper level of the circular road and take passengers to any city-center destination for around $12 a head. Be ruthless – competition for these and the several other companies running shuttle service is fierce and queues nonexistent. **Taxis** from the airport cost $25–30 (plus tip) to any downtown location, more for East Bay and Marin County – definitely worth it if there is more than one of you. If you're planning to drive, the usual **car rental** agencies operate free shuttle buses to their depots, leaving every 15 minutes from the upper level. Driving from SFO, head north on gritty US-101 or northwest on prettier I-280 for the 20–30-minute drive downtown.

Several domestic airlines (including America West, Southwest and United) fly into **Oakland International Airport** (OAK; see p.138 for details), across the bay. This is actually no further from downtown San Francisco than SFO, and is efficiently connected with the city by the $2 AirBART shuttle bus, which drops you at the Coliseum BART station, from where San Francisco's downtown stops are fifteen minutes away ($2.75).

The third regional choice, the **San Jose International Airport** (SJO), should really only be considered if you're staying in Silicon Valley on high-tech business. Fares in and out of SJO tend to be higher than to the other airports and public transportation to the city is inconvenient

SAN FRANCISCO PUBLIC TRANSPORTATION

Useful bus routes

#5 From the Transbay Terminal, west alongside Haight-Ashbury and Golden Gate Park to the ocean.

#7 From the Ferry Terminal (Market St) to the end of Haight St and to Golden Gate Park.

#15 From Third St (SoMa) to Pier 39, Fisherman's Wharf, via the Financial District and North Beach.

#20 (Golden Gate Transit) From Civic Center to the Golden Gate Bridge.

#22 From the Marina up Pacific Heights and north on Fillmore.

#28 and **#29** From the Marina through the Presidio, north through Golden Gate Park, the Richmond and the Sunset.

#30 From the CalTrain depot on Third St, north to Ghirardelli Square, via Chinatown and North Beach, and out to Chestnut St in the Marina district.

#38 From Geary St via Civic Center, west to the ocean along Geary Blvd through Japantown and the Richmond, ending at Cliff House.

Muni Train Lines

Muni F-Market Line Restored vintage trolleys from around the world run downtown from the Transbay Terminal up Market St and into the heart of Castro.

Muni J-Church Line From downtown to Mission and the edge of the Castro.

Muni K-Ingleside Line From downtown through the Castro to Balboa Park.

Muni L-Taraval Line From downtown west through the Sunset to the zoo and Ocean Beach.

Muni M-Ocean View From downtown west by the Stonestown Galleria shopping center and San Francisco State University.

Muni N-Judah Line From the Caltrain station, past the new baseball stadium, along South Beach to downtown west through the Inner Sunset to Ocean Beach.

From the Muni N-Judah line (at Ninth Ave) or from buses #5 (at Seventh Ave) and #38 (at Sixth Ave), you can connect to **bus #44** which goes by the De Young Museum, Asian Art Museum, Japanese Tea Garden, California Academy of Sciences, and Steinhart Aquarium in Golden Gate Park. A Muni transfer will get you **discounts** (usually $2 off admission) at these places.

Cable-Car Routes

Powell & Hyde From Powell St/Market along Hyde through Russian Hill to Fisherman's Wharf.

Powell & Mason From Powell St/Market along Mason via Chinatown and North Beach to Fisherman's Wharf.

California Street From the foot of California St at Robert Frost Plaza in the Financial District through Nob Hill to Polk St.

By bus and train

All San Francisco's **Greyhound** services use the **Transbay Terminal** at 425 Mission St, south of Market Street, near the Embarcadero BART station in the South of Market (SoMa) district; the terminal might eventually become a stop for trains and BART as well. **Green Tortoise** buses stop behind the Transbay Terminal on First and Natoma. **Amtrak** trains stop across the bay in **Oakland**, where free shuttle buses run passengers across the Bay Bridge to the Transbay Terminal. Though technically closer to San Francisco than Oakland don't get off at **Emeryville**, where consistent public transportation to the city is non-existant.

By car

From the east, the main route **by car** into San Francisco is I-80, which runs all the way from

Chicago, through Reno and Sacramento. I-5, fifty miles east of San Francisco, serves as the main north–south route, connecting Los Angeles with Seattle. From I-5, I-580 takes you west to the Bay Area. US-101 also runs the length of California from north to south, but if you have time and can tolerate a dramatically winding road, take Hwy-1, The Pacific Coast Highway, which traces the edge of California with snaking, cliff-side pavement.

Muni

The city's public transportation is run by the **San Francisco Municipal Railway**, or Muni (☎415/673-6864; *www.transitinfo.org*). A comprehensive network of **buses**, **trolleys**, and **cable cars** run up and over the city's hills, while the underground **trains** become **streetcars** when they emerge from the downtown metro system to split off and serve the suburbs. On buses and trains the flat **fare** (correct change only) is $1; with each ticket you buy, ask for a **free transfer** – good for another two rides on a train or bus in any direction. Local groceries have begun, largely unsuccessfully, to vend **single-ride tokens** (80¢). Cable cars cost $2 one-way, and do not accept transfers, though showing the conductor a valid one should take $1 off the fare, a rule often ignored by both conductors and booths selling tickets.

If you plan on riding the cable car more than once or simply wish to explore the town, pick up a one-day Muni **Passport** ($6), from the Visitor Center. The Passport is valid for unlimited travel on the Muni system, including cable cars, and BART stations (see below) within the city limits. The Passport is also available in three-day and seven-day denominations ($10, $15).

A **Fast Pass** costs only $9 for a week but excludes cable cars, though the $35 pass is valid for a full calendar month and includes unlimited transportation on the historic vehicles. Passes are available from the Visitor Center and from select grocery stores such as those in the Safeway chain. Muni trains stop running around midnight or 1am depending on the line and are replaced with lumbering night-owl shuttle bus services. Some buses run all night, in theory, though service is greatly reduced after midnight. For more information, pick up the handy Muni map ($2.95) from the Visitor Information Center or kiosks around town. **Bikes** are allowed on Muni buses equipped with bicycle racks (on the front of the bus).

BART and other public transportation services

Along Market Street downtown, Muni shares the station concourses with **Bay Area Rapid Transit (BART)** (☎510/464-7161 or 415/989-2278; *www.bart.org*), which is the fastest way to get to the East Bay and suburbs east and south of San Francisco. Tickets aren't cheap ($2.65 one way across the bay), but trains follow a fixed schedule; free schedules are available at all stations. Tickets can be purchased on the station concourse, and can store as much cash as you want to put on them. Save your ticket, as you use it for both entering and exiting the train. The **CalTrain** commuter railway (depot at Fourth and Townsend, SoMa) links San Francisco along the peninsula south to San Jose. **Golden Gate Ferry** boats (☎415/923-2000) leave from the Ferry Building at the Embarcadero, crossing the bay past Alcatraz to Sausalito and Larkspur in Marin County. **Blue & Gold Fleet** (☎415/773-1188) sails to Sausalito and Tiburon (Marin County) from Pier 41 at Fisherman's Wharf. The **Alameda–Oakland ferry** (☎510/522-3300) sails between Oakland's Jack London Square, the Ferry Building, and Fisherman's Wharf ($4.50 one-way), and, in summer, to Angel Island (daily May–Oct; $13 round-trip). **Bikes** are allowed on BART except during peak commute hours. When entering BART with a bike, go through the blue gate for wheelchairs next to the ticket window, then carry your bike downstairs to the BART platform. Board at the rear of the car and stand with the bicycle in the open area around the doors.

Driving – taxis and cars

Taxis ply the streets (especially downtown), but finding an available one can be a pain. Try Veterans (☎415/552-1300) or Yellow Cab (☎415/626-2345). Fares (within the city) are roughly $1.70 to start the meter, $1.80 for the first mile and $1.50 per mile thereafter.

The only reason to **rent a car** in San Francisco is if you want to explore the Bay Area beyond the city, and getting north or south along the coast or into Wine Country are compelling enough reasons to do so. **Driving** in town, pay attention to San Francisco's attempts to control downtown traffic: The posted speed limit is rarely over 30mph, and is well-enforced. In addition, it's almost impossible to make a left

Road conditions

The California Department of Transportation (aka CalTrans) operates a **toll-free 24-hour information line** (☎ 1-800/427-ROAD) giving up-to-the-minute details of road conditions throughout the state. On a touch-tone phone simply input the number of the road ("5" for I-5, "29" for Hwy-29, etc) and a recorded voice will tell you about any relevant weather conditions, delays, detours, and snow closures, etc. From out of state, or without a touch-tone phone, similar information is available on ☎ 916/445-1534.

turn anywhere in town, meaning you'll have to get used to making a "California left" – looping the next block in three right turns in order to make your turn. Cheap, available **parking** is even rarer than a left-turn signal, but it's worth it to play by the rules: police issue multiple tickets for illegally parked vehicles and won't hesitate to tow your car if it's violating any posted laws. Downtown, plenty of garages exist, most advertising rates beginning at $2.50 – note that price is for 15 minutes, not an hour. New public garages under Union Square downtown, Portsmouth Square in Chinatown, or Ghirardelli Square near Fisherman's Wharf are cheaper than the private garages. Metered spots on the street usually fill up fast, but a good bet is to prowl the residential areas for a spot, where you can leave your car for up to two hours. Take care to observe the San Francisco law of curbing wheels – turn wheels in to the curb if the car points downhill and away from the curb if it points up. Violators are subject to a $20 ticket. Bear in mind that **driving while intoxicated (DWI)** is a very serious offense. If a police officer smells alcohol on your breath, he/she is entitled to administer a breath, saliva, or urine test. If you fail, you may be liable for up to six months in the slammer and a fine of anywhere from $390 to $1000. You may lose your license for six months and/or your car for thirty days. You may even have to enroll in an unimaginably tedious DWI education program. If you refuse to take the test to begin with, you automatically lose your license for one year.

Bridge tolls are collected only upon entering San Francisco by car. Entering by way of the Golden Gate Bridge costs $3, while approaching from Oakland via the Bay Bridge runs $2.

Driving for foreign visitors

UK nationals can **drive** in the US on a full UK driving license (International Driving Permits are not always regarded as sufficient). Drivers from Australia or New Zealand should contact their local National Roads and Motoring Association (NRMA) or Automobiles Association (AA) before departure, to obtain an International Driving Permit.

Fly-drive deals are good value if you want to **rent** a car (see box, overleaf), though you can save up to sixty percent simply by booking in advance with a major firm. If you choose not to pay until you arrive, be sure you take a written confirmation of the price with you. Remember that it's safer not to rent a car straight after a long transatlantic flight, and that standard rental cars have **automatic transmissions**.

As for **rules of the road**, you must drive on the right and front-seat passengers must always wear seat belts. There are several **types of road** – the wide, straight, and fast **Interstate Highways** (prefixed "I"); **State Highways** (ie Hwy-1); and **US Highways** (ie US-101) – though in San Francisco and the more built-up parts of the Bay Area most roads are better known by their local name. Hwy-1, for instance, is known as 19th Avenue, or PCH for Pacific Coast Highway. The speed limit in the city and other built-up areas is 30–35mph; otherwise, it's a maximum of 55–70mph, depending on the highway or interstate. Keep an eye on signposted limits – there are no **spot fines**, but if given a **speeding** ticket, reckon on a fine of at least $75.

Accidents involving more than $500 in damages or any injury or death must be reported to the Department of Motor Vehicles within ten days or participants risk losing their licenses.

Hitching

The usual advice given to **hitchhikers** is that they should use their common sense; in fact, of course, common sense should tell anyone that hitchhiking in the US is a bad idea. We do not recommend it under any circumstances.

Cycling, scooting, and motorcycling

In general, **cycling** is a cheap and healthy method of getting around San Francisco and the Bay Area, some parts of which have cycle lanes, though they are designed to avoid traffic rather than to trace the shortest point-to-point distances. Also keep in mind that city drivers can be a mean bunch, and wearing a helmet is essential. If you get tired out, local buses are often equipped to carry bikes strapped to the outside. In **country areas**, there's much scenic, and sometimes even level, land, especially in parts of the Wine Country. Bikes can be **rented** for $25 a day, $100–140 a week, from outlets usually found close to beaches, university campuses or simply in areas that are good for cycling; see the appropriate sections of the *Guide*, or contact local visitor centers. Good-value city rental shops include **Park Cyclery** (1749 Waller St ☎415/751-7368), which provides mountain bikes for $12 per hour, $25 a day, and offers weekly rates from $120.

American Rentals rents **scooters** and **motorcycles**, with liability insurance and helmets included in the price. A scooter for one starts at $50/day, while a two-seater begins at $65/day. Motorcycles begin at $150/day.

Organized tours

One way to orient yourself is an **organized tour**. Gray Line Tours (☎415/558-9400), for example, take you around the city by bus in three-and-a-half fairly tedious hours for around $28 a head. Likewise, Tower Tours (☎415/434-TOUR) can zip you around to all the major must-sees for $30, with deals that combine city stops with Muir Woods, Alcatraz, or even Monterey, Wine Country

Car rental

Toll-free numbers for the big international **car-rental firms** are listed below; most have outlets at both the airport and downtown, and all compete with bargain rates and special offers. Prices vary depending on the time of year and the size of the car you choose, though you should always ask about any special discounts available. Compacts start between $140 and $230 per week, with Dollar and Reliable at the cheaper end of the spectrum. Inquire carefully about rates, especially since they can vary between downtown and airport locations. If you are tied into any **AirMiles** scheme, check the special offers on car rental; good discounts and special deals are offered by most airlines in conjunction with the major car-rental firms. **Unlimited mileage** is fairly standard, so you can plan long trips without fear. Bear in mind that any insurance included in the rental is probably only basic third-party coverage (a legal requirement for all drivers), to cover damage to other vehicles. Read the small print carefully for details on **Collision Damage Waiver (CDW)**, also known as Liability Damage Waiver (LDW), that specifically covers the car you are driving. It is usually extra, about $9–13 a day, but it's well worth considering – without it you're liable for every scratch to the car, even those not your fault. Some credit-card companies offer automatic CDW coverage to anyone using their card; check with the credit company and read all the fine print beforehand in any case.

You should also check your **third-party liability**. The standard policy often only covers you for the first $15,000 of the third party's claim against you, a paltry sum in litigation-conscious America. Companies strongly advise taking out third-party insurance, which costs a further $10–12 a day but indemnifies the driver for up to $2 million. California law requires all drivers to carry a minimum amount of liability insurance: $15,000 for single death or injury and $5000 property damage.

Companies are becoming more particular about checking up on the driving records of would-be renters and refusing to rent to high-risk drivers. As a result, it has become increasingly difficult to rent a car unless you are over 25 – rates for people younger than this can go through the roof. If you're **under 25** and have a valid driver's license, rent from **City-Rent-a-Car**, 1748 Folsom St (☎415/861-1312), a family-owned local operator that rents everything from Porsches to minivans.

If you **break down** in a rented car, use the emergency number pinned to the dashboard.

San Francisco offices

Alamo, 687 Folsom St ☎415/882-9440

Avis, 675 Post St ☎415/885-5011

City-Rent-a-Car, 1748 Folsom St ☎415/861-1312

Dollar, 364 O'Farrell St ☎415/771-5300

Critical Mass

Getting around downtown San Francisco gets even more problematic the last Friday of each month, when at evening rush hour the so-called **Critical Mass** takes shape. Loosely organized by cyclists to promote bicycle awareness, this ride-cum-demonstration – as many as five thousand bikers taking off from Justin Herman Plaza through downtown's busiest streets – has been going on since 1992.

It was a largely tension-free event – even sanctioned by the police, who allowed the cyclists to proceed unimpeded through traffic lights and stop signs – until one ride in summer 1997, when a route over the Golden Gate Bridge caused longer delays than usual. This led Mayor Willie Brown to try to impose stricter regulations on Critical Mass claiming, "If it were a group of Hell's Angels on motorcycles doing the same thing, I'd be run out of town if I didn't try to bust every one of them."

He didn't, though there were large-scale arrests when a number of bikers, who had agreed to ride down less-traveled streets in a late-summer compromise, broke off from their planned route and disrupted a speech Brown was trying to give at the time. It has been more low-key since then; if you want to watch, or even participate, just show up around 5pm at Justin Herman Plaza on the appointed Friday.

Enterprise, 1133 Van Ness Ave ☎ 415/441-3369

Hertz, 433 Mason St ☎ 415/771-2200

Reliable, 349 Mason St ☎ 415/928-4414

Thrifty, 520 Mason St ☎ 415/788-8111

In North America

Alamo ☎ 1-800/354-2322; *www.goalamo.com*

Avis ☎ 1-800/331-1212; *www.avis.com*

Budget ☎ 1-800/527-0700; *www.budget.com*

Dollar ☎ 1-800/421-6868; *www.dollar.com*

Enterprise ☎ 1-800/325-8007; *www.pickenterprise.com*

Hertz ☎ 1-800/654-3131; *www.hertz.com* in Canada ☎ 1-800/263-0600

National ☎ 1-800/227-7368; *www.nationalcar*.com

Payless ☎ 1-800/729-5377

Rent-a-Wreck ☎ 1-800/535-1391; *www.rent-a-wreck.com*

Snappy ☎ 1-800/669-4800

Thrifty ☎ 1-800/367-2277; *www.thrifty.com*

In the UK

Alamo ☎ 0800/272200

Avis ☎ 0990/900500

Budget ☎ 0800/181181

Dollar (Eurodollar) ☎ 01895/233300

Hertz ☎ 0990/996699

Holiday Autos ☎ 0990/300400

National (Europcar/InterRent) ☎ 08457/222525

Thrifty ☎ 0990/168238

In Australia

Avis ☎ 1800/225 533

Budget ☎ 1300/362 848

Hertz ☎ 1800/367 227

In New Zealand

Avis ☎ 09/526 2800

Budget ☎ 09/375 2270

Hertz ☎ 09/309 0989

Walking tours

A great way to get to know the quieter, historical side of San Francisco and her neighborhoods is to take a **walking tour**. The better ones keep group size small and are run by natives who truly love their subject matter and jobs. Some, like those sponsored by the library, are free, though reservations are recommended for all tours, regardless of the season.

All About Chinatown (☎415/982-8839). Led by Chinatown native and director of the Chinese Historical Society of America, Linda Lee, who takes you through the heart and history of the neighborhood; $25 two-hour walk, $35 three-hour walk, including dim sum lunch.

Barbary Coast Trail (☎415/775-1111). Free guided tours run by the San Francisco Historical Society, highlighting dozens of official Gold Rush, Comstock Lode, and 1906 earthquake-era sites downtown.

City Guides, San Francisco Public Library (☎415/557-4266; *www.wenet.net/users/jhum/*). Free daily themed walks through every nook and cranny of San Francisco, covering sights related to topics ranging from the Gold Rush to the Beat generation.

Cruisin' the Castro (☎415/550-8110; *www.webcastro.com/castrotour/*). Ms Trevor Hailey leads you through her beloved neighborhood, the Castro, and explains how and why San Francisco became the Gay Capital of the world. Tour includes the story of the rise and murder of Harvey Milk, the city's first openly gay politician, as well as a visit to the "Names Project" center of the AIDS Memorial Quilt; $40, includes brunch.

Footnotes Literary Walk (☎415/381-0713; *www.tactileheart.com*). San Francisco has harbored dozens of famous writers including Mark Twain, Dashiell Hammett and Jack Kerouac. Guide Shelley Campbell leads a three-and-a-half-hour walk around North Beach detailing their exploits; $20, or $35 including a lunch at *Tavolino Ristorante*.

Haight-Ashbury Flower Power Walking Tour (☎415/863-1621; *sixties.astrid.net*). Learn about the Human Be-in, Grateful Dead, Summer of Love, and also the Haight's distant past as a Victorian resort destination; $15.

Precita Eyes Mission Mural Walk (☎415/285-2287). Two-hour presentation by mural artists leads around the Mission District's outdoor paintings. Includes a slide presentation on the history and process of mural art. Saturdays, 1.30 pm; $7.

Victorian Home Walk (☎415/252-9485). Leisurely two-hour tour through Pacific Heights and Cow Hollow past the Painted Ladies. Learn to tell the difference between a Queen Anne and a San Francisco Stick; $20.

or Yosemite in a day. Considerably more exciting is the El Volado Mexican Bus Tour (☎415/546-3747) through the Mission District, a nighttime ride on a colorfully decorated vehicle to a number of local Mexican restaurants and salsa clubs for drinking and dancing.

For awesome views of the bay, take a chilly 75-minute **bay cruise** operated by the Red & White (☎415/447-0597) and Blue & Gold (☎415/705-5555) fleets and from pier 41 and pier 43 1/2 – though be warned that everything may be shrouded in fog, giving little justification for the $17 ticket. If you want to take a loop out by boat out under the Golden Gate Bridge and back, several independent operators trawl for your business along Fisherman's Wharf ($10/person). Excruciatingly expensive **aerial tours** of the city and Bay Area in light aircraft are available from several operators, such as San Francisco Helicopter Tours (☎1-800/400-2404), which offers a variety of spectacular flights over the Bay Area beginning at $79 per passenger for a 20-minute flight.

For tours of the Wine Country and other parts of the Bay Area, see the relevant Bay Area chapters.

Traveling with children

San Francisco is very much a place for adults – more so than, say, LA, where Disneyland and Universal Studios are major attractions. Still, kids can take solace in the fine beaches, neighborhood parks and tech-loaded malls like Sony's Metreon on Fourth Street in SoMa. Other kid-stops in town tend to lean toward the educational – science museums, zoos, and the like – though huge amusement parks are across the bay in Vallejo and down the coast in Santa Cruz, where the classic 1940s-style boardwalk with its famous wooden rollercoaster drives every child into giddy throes of joy.

Activities

Of San Francisco's few specifically **child-oriented attractions** – all of which are listed in the relevant chapters of this book – the **Exploratorium** in the Marina District is particularly excellent, as is the **Steinhart Aquarium** in **Golden Gate Park**. **Zeum** (Wed–Fri noon–6pm, Sat & Sun, 11am–5pm ☎415/777-2800), on the rooftop of Yerba Buena Gardens in SoMa, is a children's play paradise: an entire city-block-sized area devoted to films, bowling, ice skating (☎415/777-3727), and hands-on technology exhibits and art tables. For something a little wilder, the **San Francisco Zoo** offers children the chance to pet tarantulas and feed the big cats, while **Pier 39** at Fisherman's Wharf has plenty of underwater creatures to admire in its Underwater World.

If you want to take your children on a **boat ride**, the best value is the Golden Gate Ferry to Larkspur or Sausalito, which departs from the Ferry Building at the foot of Market Street; children can ride for around $3.

For full-day family excursions from San Francisco, try the **Great America** amusement park in San Jose, or the animal-themed **Marine World/Africa USA** in Vallejo, accessible by Transbay ferry.

Getting around

On most domestic routes, children less than two years old are classified as "lap children," and provided they stay on your lap, they can fly for free. On most international flights, however, you'll have to pay about ten percent of the ticket price for the same service. Discounts of up to fifty percent apply to children below the age of twelve, but over that the full standard fare is applicable.

For traveling around the city, the **Muni** system is by and large clean, efficient, and safe, and children travel for just 35¢. If you want to travel beyond the city limits it is usually easier to bundle children into a **car**.

Gay and lesbian San Francisco

San Francisco's reputation as a city of gay celebration is not new – in fact it may be a bit outdated. Though still considered by many to be the gay capital of the world, the gay community here has made a definite move to the mainstream, a measure of its political success. The exuberant energy that went into the posturing and parading of the 1970s has taken on a much more sober, down-to-business attitude, and these days you'll find more political activists organizing conferences than drag queens throwing parties. Being an openly gay politician or businessperson here is not as much of an issue to locals as it might be elsewhere in the United States, making it easy to forget things were not always this way.

As recently as the 1970s, gay public school teacher **Tom Ammiano**'s coming out as a way to raise awareness of discrimination against gays in the San Francisco school system made front-page headlines. Ammiano has since gone on to become a wildly popular local politician who vied with current mayor Willie Brown for the job in 1999 in a write-in campaign that led to an unprecedented run-off.

Ever since its early gold-rush-era days, when men came unaccompanied to town to seek their fortunes, San Francisco has been a gayer city than most, long before the term was even coined. At saloons and dancehalls catering to the rough-and-ready prospectors and merchants who came to Barbary Coast to seek their fortunes, a bandana worn around a man's arm meant he wanted to be led in a dance. This **hanky code** actually evolved into a complex symbolic language, recognized predominantly in today's leather scene most visible in the SoMa district.

The **first bar** openly catering to a predominantly homosexual crowd was in full operation at Pacific and Kearney by 1908. Later, during World War II, the military purged suspected homosexuals at their point of embarkation. For those expecting to serve in the Pacific war zone, this meant they got off in San Francisco; unable to face the stigma of a return home, many remained, and the city became something of a refuge for gays. Still, patrons of the many gay clubs and bars that began popping up around town grew accustomed to random round-ups and surprise busts by local police.

It wasn't until the "Bohemian" *Black Cat Café* at 710 Montgomery began welcoming gays and lesbians that the city's official attitude toward homosexuality changed. This was the result of a landmark **1950 court case** won by the *Black Cat* which decided, for the first time, that businesses cannot be discriminated against for catering to homosexuals.

Gay ranks were once again swelled by those who lost their government jobs during the McCarthy era purge. In the same influx came the **Beats**, among them Allen Ginsberg, whose *Howl* was tried for obscenity largely due to its descriptions of homosexuality. His victory further raised awareness, as did the *laissez-faire* attitudes of the 1960s.

The **Seventies** were notorious for the bar-and-bathhouse culture and the busy and often anonymous promiscuity which went with it. But the party began dying down in 1978, with the tragic City Hall murder of openly gay supervisor Harvey Milk and mayor George Moscone by disgruntled former councilman Dan White. The killer's lenient sentencing resulted in the "White Night" riots of 1979 against San Francisco police (see p.109).

Around the same time, came the recognition of **AIDS** followed by the closure of the city's bathhouses, which some gay rights advocates saw as progress, others as an infringement on civil liberties. For better or worse, the gay community took a more sober and political tone in the Eighties, lobbying to raise AIDS awareness in the mainstream.

Lesbians, though less directly affected by the epidemic than gay men, were particularly active in the AIDS movement. The lesbian scene flowered in the 1980s, but today, though women's club nights do exist, lesbian culture is less in evidence in San Francisco than it once was and is centered more around cafés and bookstores than bars and clubs.

Politically, San Francisco's gay and lesbian scene is stronger today than ever. The annual

Contacts and resources

Bisexual Resources Line (☎415/703-7977). Contacts and voicemail boxes of various bisexual groups.

Dignity, 1329 Seventh Ave (☎415/681-2491). Catholic worship and services.

Gay Health Care 45 Castro (☎415/861-2400). Health services for a fee.

Gay/Lesbian Lawyers, 235 Montgomery (☎415/956-5764). Inquiries regarding legal problems and legal representation.

Gay Therapy Center, 3393 Market St (☎415/558-8828). Counseling and help with coming out.

Lesbian/Gay Switchboard, Pacific Center, 2712 Telegraph Ave, Berkeley, CA 94705 (☎510/841-6224). 24hr counseling and advice. Contacts and activities referral service.

Lyric (☎415/863-3636). For gays and lesbians 23 and younger, discussion groups, movie nights, camping and sporting events, women's issues.

Travel Alternatives Group (☎1-800/464-2987). A consortium of gay and gay-friendly travel agents. Call from anywhere in the US and your call is routed to the one nearest to the place you're calling from.

Publications

New clubs and groups spring up all the time, and you should keep an ear to the ground as well as referring to the many free **local gay publications**: the *Bay Area Reporter*, *Bay Times*, *Creampuff*, *Frontiers*, and *Odyssey* all give listings of events, services, clubs, and bars in the city and Bay Area. Women should also keep an eye out in bookstores for *On Our Backs*, the sporadic *Female F.Y.I.* and *Bad Attitude*, three magazines that often have pointers to lesbian organizations in town. Alternatively, a must-have for every visiting gay man with a sense of humor is *Betty & Pansy's Severe Queer Review*, listing everything from the best place to eat upscale food to the best cruising alleys – in unashamedly explicit detail. The free *Columbia Fun Maps* (*www.funmaps.com*) highlights gay-friendly establishments in San Francisco.

San Francisco Lesbian/Gay/Bisexual/Transgender Pride Celebration Parade is the single biggest event in the city (see festivals, p.41).

Despite the tolerant attitude of the city, it is, nevertheless, part of more conservative California. Though San Francisco allows **domestic partnerships** registration, which offers same-sex couples a few of the rights and benefits enjoyed by married heterosexual couples, the state's notorious **Knight Initiative** (or Proposition 22) passed with a solid majority in March 2000 insuring that "only marriage between a man and a woman is valid or recognized in California," ensuring that the rights of same-sex couples are limited to the few token benefits afforded by the domestic partnership legislation not recognized beyond the city limits.

Many gay tourists coming to San Francisco for the first time are disappointed to find no major gay and lesbian **community center**. Things are likely to take an important upturn in summer 2001, with the opening of one at Market and Octavia streets (☎415/437-2257). Besides providing the established community with a wide variety of resources, the center will be a place to provide guidance and support to the staggering number of gay and lesbian youth who arrive in San Francisco daily from less tolerant parts of the country, many of them ending up, sadly, on the city's streets.

Specifically **gay accommodation** is listed on p.227; the best of San Francisco's **gay and lesbian bars and clubs** are detailed on p.277.

Neighborhoods

Traditionally, *the* area for gay men has been the **Castro** – though gay life these days is much less ghettoized and there are bars and clubs all over town, with those in the **SoMa** area particularly popular. Rent boys and pushers prowl **Polk Street**, not the safest area at 2am, but neither is it a danger zone if you use common sense. Lesbian interests are more concentrated in the East Bay than the city, although women's activities thrive in the **Mission**.

Women's San Francisco

In the West Coast's most politically progressive city, women are treated with respect and courtesy almost everywhere and commonly hold positions of power and authority. The gains of the last twenty years are considerable and visible. San Francisco is safer than most American metropolises (see p.26), though common sense still applies: look as if you know where you are going, take taxis at night and never hitch. Women traveling alone are not at all unusual but the successful ones learn to deal with any harassment firmly and loudly. While there is more chance of being mugged in San Francisco than raped – the city has one of the lowest incidences of rape of any metropolitan area in the US – you may feel safer if you carry whistles, gas, and sprays; useless in the event of real trouble but a confidence booster that can ward off creeps. The SoMa area of the city's clubs is underlighted at night, so exercise caution when walking back from living it up.

The flip side of San Francisco's gay revolution has in some women's circles led to a separatist culture, and women's resources and services are sometimes lumped together under the lesbian category. While this may be no bad thing, it can

Contacts and resources for women

Bay Area Women and Children's Resource Center, 318 Leavenworth St (☎415/474-2400). Services, information, and clothing.

Lyon Martin Women's Health Services, 1748 Market, Suite 201 (☎415/565-7667). Targets lesbian-bisexual-transgender community, but encourages all women to come for anonymous AIDS testing, gynecological care, pregnancy tests, counseling, and legal help. Nonprofit, and operating since 1979.

Planned Parenthood, 815 Eddy St, Suite 200 (☎415/441-5454), and in Glide Memorial Church at 330 Ellis St, Room 504 (☎415/922-6957). They offer counseling, post-coital contraception, HIV testing, contraception, pregnancy testing, and abortions.

Radical Women/Freedom Socialist Party, New Valencia Hall, 1908 Mission St (☎415/864-1278). Socialist feminist organization dedicated to building women's leadership and achieving full equality. Meetings, discussion groups, and poetry readings held on various issues; call for details.

Rape Crisis Center and Hotline, 1841 Market St (☎415/647-7273). 24hr switchboard.

Rape Treatment Center San Francisco General Hospital, 1001 Potrero (☎415/821-3222).

Shelley's Body Therapy, 1041 Guerrero St (☎415/282-1779). Specializes in massages for pregnant women and infants, but popular with all women for her healing touch after a hard day of walking.

Women's Building, 3543 18th St (☎415/431-1180). Central stop in the Mission for women's art and political events. A very good place to get information also – the women who staff the building are happy to deal with the most obscure of inquiries.

Women's Needs Center, 1825 Haight St (☎415/487-5632). Low-cost health care and referral service.

Specific **accommodation** options for women are listed on p.220.

be hard to tell which organizations exist irrespective of sexuality. Don't let this stop you from checking out anything that sounds interesting; nobody is going to refuse you either entry or help if you're not a lesbian – support is given to anybody who needs it. Similarly women's health care is very well provided for in San Francisco and there are numerous clinics you can go to for routine gynecological and contraceptive services: payment is on a sliding scale according to income, but even if you're flat broke, you won't be refused treatment.

Travelers with disabilities

Travelers with mobility problems or other physical disabilities are likely to find San Francisco to be much more in tune with their needs than most places, thanks partly to the passage and rigorous local enforcement of the Americans with Disabilities Act (ADA) that requires equal access for those with physical limitations. Steep hills aside, the Bay Area is generally considered to be one of the most barrier-free cities around, catering well to physically challenged travelers. All public buildings must be wheelchair-accessible and have suitable toilets, most city street corners have dropped curbs, and most city buses are able to kneel to make access easier and are built with space and hand grips for wheelchair users. Elevators at BART and Muni stations allow access to these trains. Most hotels and restaurants (certainly any built in the last ten years or so) have excellent wheelchair access.

Getting to and around San Francisco

Most **airlines**, transatlantic and within the US, do whatever they can to ease your journey and will usually let attendants of people with more serious disabilities accompany them at no extra charge. The Air Carriers' Access Act of 1986 obliged all domestic air carriers to make the majority of their services accessible to travelers with disabilities within five to nine years.

National organizations

Mobility International USA, PO Box 10767, Eugene, OR 97440 (voice and TDD ☎541/343-1284). Answers transportation queries and operates an exchange program for people with disabilities.

Society for the Advancement of Travelers with Handicaps (SATH), 347 Fifth Ave, #610, New York, NY 10016 (☎212/447-7284; *www.sath.org*). A nonprofit travel-industry grouping which includes travel agents, tour operators, hotel and airline management, and people with disabilities. It will pass on any inquiry to the appropriate member; allow plenty of time for a response.

Travel Information Service, Moss Rehabilitation Hospital, 1200 W Tabor Rd, Philadelphia, PA 19141 (☎215/456-9600).

Twin Peaks Press, Box 129, Vancouver, WA 98666 (☎360/694-2462 or 1-800/637-2256). Publisher of the *Directory of Travel Agencies for the Disabled* ($19.95), listing more than 370 agencies worldwide; *Travel for the Disabled* ($14.95); the *Directory of Accessible Van Rentals* and *Wheelchair Vagabond* ($9.95), loaded with personal tips.

Almost every **Amtrak train** includes one or more coaches with accommodation for passengers with disabilities. Guide dogs travel free, and Amtrak will provide wheelchair assistance at its train stations, adapted seating on board and a fifteen-percent discount on the regular fare, all provided at least 24 hours' notice is given (though 48 hours is preferable). Passengers with hearing impairment can get information on ☎1-800/523-6590.

When traveling by **Greyhound** and **Amtrak Thruway buses**, the "Helping Hand" scheme offers two-for-the-price-of-one tickets to passengers unable to travel alone (carry a doctor's certificate). Buses are now required to be accessible. Call 48 hours in advance for reservations and check schedules for accessible cars. Similarly, many **tour companies**, such as Grayline, have wheelchair-accessible buses available with 48 hours' notice.

The major **car-rental** firms can, given sufficient notice, provide vehicles with hand controls (though these are usually only available on the more expensive models, and you'll need to reserve well in advance). The American Automobile Association (see p.18) produces the *Handicapped Driver's Mobility Guide* for **drivers with disabilities** (available from Quantum-Precision Inc, 225 Broadway, Suite 3404, New York, NY 10007). There are no longer differences in state **parking regulations for motorists with disabilities**; the Department of Transportation has decreed that all state licenses issued to persons with disabilities must carry a three-inch-square international access symbol, and each state must provide placards bearing this symbol, to be hung from the rear-view mirror – the placards are blue for permanent disabilities, red for temporary (maximum of six months). More information can be obtained from your state motor-vehicle office.

As in other parts of the world, the rise of the **self-service gas station** is unwelcome for many drivers with disabilities. The state of California has addressed this by changing its laws so that most service stations are required to provide full service to drivers with disabilities at self-service prices.

Information

The California Office of Tourism's free 200-page *California Travel Planning Guide* lists "handicap facilities" at accommodations and attractions (though perhaps a bold capital **H** would have been easier to pick out than mentions in the text – and some attractions which do have facilities for visitors with disabilities are not listed as accessible). The *San Francisco Lodging Guide* (free from the San Francisco CVB, PO Box 6977, San Francisco, CA 94101 ☎415/391-2000) lists many "wheelchair-accessible" properties – hotels, motels, apartments, B&Bs, hostels, RV parks – in the city and surrounding counties; as always, travelers should call to confirm details.

San Francisco's **Mayor's Council on Disabilities**, PO Box 1595, San Francisco, CA (☎415/252-3112), puts out an annual guide for visitors with disabilities. They also have information on services for deaf and blind visitors and can arrange wheelchair rentals. The **Center for Independent Living**, 2539 Telegraph Ave in Berkeley (☎415/543-6222 or 510/841-4776), has long been one of the most effective organizations in the world for people with disabilities; it has a variety of counseling services and is generally a useful resource.

Accommodation

The big motel and hotel chains are often the safest bet for accessible **accommodation**, though any lodging that is retrofitted or upgraded must meet the current ADA rules.

Choice Travel (☎1-818/367-4693 or 1-800/494-3999, fax 1-818/833-0840) is one of a handful of agencies that specializes in providing travel services to people with disabilities and other special needs. They are particularly helpful in booking accommodation.

Festivals and holidays

Someone is always celebrating something in San Francisco, and, while many of these are uniquely local affairs, most have their roots in the ethnic or national holidays of other countries, highlighting the region's diverse background. Street fairs and block parties take place all over the city throughout the summer months and, at the bigger events, like the Chinese New Year parade in February or Gay Freedom Day in June, it seems as if the entire city is joining in.

Festivals

The first big event in San Francisco's festival season is the **Chinese New Year** celebration, at the end of January or early February, depending on the lunar calendar. A week of low-key activities in and around Chinatown culminates in the Golden Dragon Parade, in which hundreds of people march through downtown leading a 75-foot-long dragon. To find out more, contact the **Chinatown Chamber of Commerce** (730 Sacramento St; ☎415/982-3000).

On March 17, the whole city dresses up in emerald hues to celebrate **St Patrick's Day**, which is marked by excessive consumption of green-tinted beer and by a lengthy parade through downtown. The *Shannon Arms* (915 Taraval; ☎415/665-1223) is a relatively unknown dive packed shoulder-to-shoulder with many of SF's Irish.

Other celebrations continue the international flavor, starting with late April's low-key **Cherry Blossom Festival** in Japantown and picking up steam around the **Cinco de Mayo**, celebrating the Mexican victory at the battle of Puebla with a 48-hour party in the Mission over the weekend nearest to May 5. San Jose also hosts one of the largest Cinco de Mayo parties in the country (☎408/977-0900). Late in May or early in June, the Mission explodes in another burst of color, when the lively **Carnaval** happenings take over the district's streets.

June is the biggest party month, with the boisterous, music- and fun-filled **Festival on the Lake** on Oakland's Lake Merritt, followed by numerous San Francisco **street fairs** – the **North Beach Fair**, the **Haight Street Fair**, and the **Union Street Spring Festival** to name three of the biggest. The month's main event is the **San Francisco Lesbian/Gay/Bisexual/Transgender Pride Celebration Parade**, with crowds of up to a half a million packing Market Street for the city's biggest parade and party. Afterward, City Hall is the scene for a giant block party, with outdoor discos, live bands and numerous craft and food stands.

In July, consider a trip thirty miles south of San Jose to tiny Gilroy, garlic capital of the world, for the annual **Garlic Festival** (☎408/842-6436). Apart from the **4th of July** fireworks at Crissy Field in the Presidio, the city is comparatively quiet for the rest of the month. But late in August, the **X Games** heat things up again, when 350 of the world's best alternative sports athletes compete for prize money in categories such as freestyle motocross, wakeboarding and skysurfing.

In late September/early October, The Marina and Embarcadero play host to the visiting US Navy during **Fleet Week**, a time when servicemen get to drink for free in the city's bars and citizens get to tour the military hardware, as well as enjoy the aerial acrobatics of the Blue Angels precision flying team as they roar their fighter jets over the bay in stunning maneuvers. Usually held over the fourth weekend of September at Fort Mason is the **San Francisco Blues Festival** featuring local and national acts. Around the same time, San Francisco's wildest party turns the

SoMa district black, when the **Folsom Street Fair** draws hundreds of thousands of people, many of them in the latest leather and latex styles, some in search of a good public flogging.

The **Castro Street Fair**, in early October, is far tamer in comparison, but it gets the district in the mood for one last burst of pre-winter activity on **Halloween** (October 31), when locals and tourists from around the world dress up and strut their stuff, promenading from bar to bar as area kids beg door-to-door for sweets. Halloween also provides the basis for one of the Bay Area's most unexpected events, the **Pumpkin Festival** in Half Moon Bay, when local farmers open their fields to jack-o'-lantern hunters and host a range of pumpkin-based cooking and eating competitions.

Finally, before the city gears up for the Christmas celebrations, **Mexico's Day of the Dead** is celebrated on the first Thursday of November in the Mission, where people costumed to look like skeletons parade the streets. Christmas and the holiday season kicks off at Thanksgiving with the lighting of the tree and menorah in Union Square, also the site of a raucous New Year's celebration on December 31.

Public holidays

Banks and offices, and many but not all stores, will be closed for the full day on the following **public holidays**:

January 1 **New Year's Day**
January 15 **Martin Luther King Jr's Birthday**
Third Monday in February **Presidents' Day**
Late March/early April **Easter Monday**
Last Monday in May **Memorial Day**
July 4 **Independence Day**
First Monday in September **Labor Day**
Second Monday in October **Columbus Day**
November 11 **Veterans' Day**
Fourth Thursday in November **Thanksgiving Day**
December 25 **Christmas Day**

The media

San Francisco is a bit of a media backwater compared to Los Angeles or New York City, but what it lacks in high-power status it makes up with in-depth coverage of local news and features. Two daily papers are part of large media conglomerates, meaning you can expect a lot of wire stories from agency journalists and little verve on the editorial page. Several free weekly alternative press publications fill the vacuum, concentrating on local politics, art, and personals. San Francisco's television is much the same as anywhere else in America, but the city's radio stations are excellent, offering an amazing range of music, the best of which is commercial-free, 24 hours a day.

Newspapers

The city's two major daily **newspapers** have competed for decades, though economic necessity saw the morning *Chronicle* (25¢) and afternoon *Examiner* (25¢) reach a joint-operating agreement in 1965 to produce the Sunday edition ($1.50) in tandem. In 1999, an announcement that the Hearst corporation would purchase the *Chronicle* and sell the *Examiner* came as a shock to employees and readers alike. The *Examiner* was finally purchased by Ted Fang, publisher of the thrice-weekly freebie, the *Independent*, early in 2000, and it remains to be seen how diverse a voice the papers will remain under the new ownerships. For the moment, both papers are heavy on local news, with extensive arts and food reporting; Sunday edition's "Datebook" (also known as the "Pink Pages") contains previews and reviews for the coming week.

The city's alternative press picks up the slack the more conservative dailies leave behind, resulting in two fine free weekly papers, *The Bay Guardian* (*www.sfbg.com*) and *SF Weekly*

San Francisco TV	
2 KTVU FOX	9 KQED PBS
4 KRON NBC	20 KBWB WB
5 KPIX CBS	26 KTSF Chinese
7 KGO ABC	44 KBHK UPN

(*www.sfweekly.com*), available Wednesdays from racks around town. Both offer more in-depth features on local life and better music and club listings than the dailies. They also have some funky personals ads should you be looking for a mate.

More detailed information on the East Bay can be found in its daily, the *Oakland Tribune*, and its alternative free weekly, the *East Bay Express* (replete with more personals). Down south, look to the *San Jose Mercury News*, the thick daily that focuses on the Peninsula.

Television

San Francisco **TV** is pretty much the standard network barrage, frequently interrupted by loud commercials. Game shows and talk shows fill up most of the morning schedule until lunchtime, when you can take your pick of any of a dozen daily soaps. Most hotels provide access to **cable networks** such as CNN, the round-the-clock news channel, and the mainstream pop of MTV and sports of ESPN. See updated listings in the daily papers.

Radio

Bay Area **radio**, in contrast, is probably the best in the US, with some eighty stations catering to just about every conceivable taste. **AM** stations tend to be either all news, chat and phone-in shows, or shit-kicking country-and-western tunes. A better option is the **FM** band, which is

SAN FRANCISCO RADIO

AM

560 KSFO Talk radio.

680 KNBR Sports and sports commentary.

740 KCBS News, talk shows, and excellent commentaries.

810 KGO News, and the most intense talk shows.

1050 KTCT "The Ticket" covers live major sports.

FM

88.5 KQED Classical music, talk, community affairs.*

89.5 KPOO Community-based radio – blues, reggae, soul.

90.3 KUSF Excellent college station with alternative rock, news, and offbeat issues. Only accessible on the western side of town.

90.7 KALX Voted best US college station most years for its blend of anything-but-mainstream rock and reggae, though the UC Berkeley-based signal rarely makes it across the bay.

91.1 KCSM Diverse but consistently high-quality programming, especially good for late-night jazz.

91.7 KALW Jazz, classical, bluegrass and the like, plus news programming, including BBC.*

94.1 KPFA Long-running, listener-supported Berkeley station known for its in-depth investigative reporting as well as arts programs.

94.9 KYLD Urban Top 40; hip hop, soul and the like.

95.7 KZQZ Top 40 bubblegum pop.

97.3 KLLC Vaguely alternative rock.

98.9 KSOL Spanish hits.

100.7 KJOI Adult standards.

102.9 KBLX "The Quiet Storm": soul, jazz, and lots of house.

104.1 (Free radio Berkeley) Pirate radio featuring political talk shows and independent, non-programmed music.

104.5 KFOG Best of the adult rock stations with lots of oldies and the best of newies.

105.3 KITS "Live 105": popular modern/alternative rock station with those who like it loud and fast.

106.1 KMEL Soul, house. Very funky; the best hip-hop station in the area.

* *Indicates National Public Radio programming.*

broadcast in stereo. The bulk of these stations are commercial, but by far the best are the dozen noncommercial stations, located at the far left end of the radio dial (88–92 FM). Most of these are affiliated with a college or university, and in the main their programming is anarchically varied, from in-depth current affairs discussions to mind-boggling industrial thrash. Local fave KPFA received much media attention during the summer of 1999 when listeners took to the streets to protest the new owners' plans to replace local programming with national, piped-in material.

Staying on

San Francisco may be a great place to live, but anyone planning an extended legal stay should apply for a special working visa at any US embassy at least six months *before* setting off for the States. There are a whole range of visas, depending on your skills and length of stay, but unless you've got relatives (parents or children over 21), or a prospective employer to sponsor you, your chances at best are slim. For details on finding long-term accommodation, see Chapter 20, "City Directory."

Work and study

Illegal work hasn't been easy to come by ever since the government introduced fines of up to $10,000 for businesses caught employing a foreigner without a **social security number** (which effectively proves you're part of the legal workforce). Understandably, most are now reluctant to employ travelers. If you do secure an address in town, you can get a social security card without becoming a resident of the US; essentially the card becomes your taxpayer ID number, meaning you'll have the same taxes deducted from your pay (about 25 percent) as a US resident, but you'll reap none of the benefits come retirement or unemployment.

Any work you do find will be of the casual washing-up/babysitting and farmhand variety – traditionally low-paid cash work. Even restaurants can be reluctant to employ foreign waiters because of the visibility of the work. Making up a fictitious social security number, or borrowing one from somebody else, is of course completely illegal, as are **marriages of convenience**; usually inconvenient for all concerned and with a lower success rate than is claimed.

One option is to throw your hat into the **information technology** whirlpool; if you know HTML and can design a Web page or service workstations, check *www.craigslist.org* for the latest Multimedia Gulch and Silicon Valley postings. There are dozens of new job offers every day for those with sought-after tech skills, regardless their nationalities.

Foreign students have a slightly better chance of a prolonged stay in San Francisco than other low-techies, especially for those who can arrange some sort of "year abroad" through their university at home. In the UK, study and work programs for students and recent graduates in the US are offered by CIEE **(Council on International**

Educational Exchange), 52 Poland St, London W1V 4JQ (☎020/7478 2000; work programs ☎020/7478 2007; study programs ☎020/7478 2004; *www.ciee.org*). CIEE Australia is at Level 8, University Centre, 210 Clarence St, Sydney (☎02/9373 2730; *www.councilexchanges .org.au*).

Otherwise you can apply directly to a Bay Area university: if they'll have you (and you can afford the painfully expensive fees charged to overseas students), it can be a great way to get to know the city, and maybe even learn something useful. The US grants more or less unlimited visas to those enrolled in full-time further education. San Francisco State University is a magnet for foreign students from Europe and Asia, despite the fact that tuition alone for them runs upwards of $9000/year (versus $2000 for residents).

Another possibility for students is to get onto an Exchange Visitor Program, for which participants are given a J-category visa that entitles them to accept paid summer employment and apply for a social security number. However, most of these visas are issued for jobs in American **summer camps**, which aren't everybody's idea of a good time. They fly you over (a charge of £195 covers a return flight to New York, visa, insurance, and travel to the camp), food and board is provided and some pocket money, and after a summer's work (usually nine weeks from the beginning of June) you end up with around US$500 and 10 weeks to blow it in. If you live in Britain and are interested, contact BUNAC (British Universities' North America Club; 16 Bowling Green Lane, London EC1R 0BD; ☎020/7251 3472; *www.bunac.org.uk*; registration fee from £70; also training placements with companies); Camp America (37 Queens' Gate, London SW7 5HR; ☎020/7581 7373); or Camp Counsellors USA, 6 Richmond Hill, Richmond-on-Thames TW10 6QX (☎020/8332 2952). If you live in Australia or New Zealand, contact your local branch of STA Travel.

For young women – in most cases – working as an **au pair** is a viable option, and in 1996 10,000 people applied for **au pair visas** to the **United States**, introduced in 1986. However, in wake of the 1997 case of Louise Woodward, young British woman who was charged with murdering the nine-month-old baby she was employed to care for, applicants for au pair visas to the US will have to prove that they have at least 200 hours' experience with infants, 24 hours' training in child development and 8 hours' child safety training, including certification in CPR. Applicants will also have to undergo testing to provide a personality profile. The London-based organization Au Pair in America (same address as Camp America; ☎020/7581 7322) can arrange visas and placements. Their Au Pair scheme is open to both men and women aged 18–26, though women are mostly preferred. There is a placement fee of £35, a £67 contribution toward insurance and a good faith deposit of £268; the combined amount includes the interviewing and selection process, visa and flight to the US. On-the-job payment while in the US is about $139 per week; if you last the whole year you get your good faith deposit back in American dollars, which you can then use to fund further US travels.

If you manage to land a day job and have some extra time, you might spend some time moonlighting as a **volunteer**. For information, check with Bay Area Volunteer Information Center (*www.meer.net/users/taylor*); San Francisco Volunteer Center, 425 Jackson (☎415/982-8999, www.vcsf.org); or Volunteer Centers of the Bay Area (☎1-800/227-3123; *www.volunteerbayarea.com*). Friends of the Urban Forest (☎415/543-5000), a locally organized tree planting group devoted to greening San Francisco's neighborhoods, could always use a hand digging, planting, and maintaining trees. Or check in at Glide Memorial Church, 330 Ellis (☎415/771-4014) for helping out in the soup kitchen, as well as Project Open Hand (☎415/447-2404) to volunteer to deliver meals to home-bound HIV and AIDS sufferers. In the East Bay, try the Berkeley Emergency Food and Housing Project (☎510/649-4145) or the St. Vincent de Paul Society (☎510/451-7676).

Part 2

The City

Chapter 1

Introducing the City

Surrounded by the shimmering waters of the San Francisco Bay to its east and the crashing waves of the Pacific Ocean to its west, San Francisco sits on a hilly peninsula at the United States' final frontier. The city's nearly four dozen hills serve as handy markers between its shifting moods and characters; as a general rule, geographical elevation is synonymous with wealth: the higher up you are, the better the views – barring fog, of course – and the higher the rents. Commercial square-footage is surprisingly limited for a city of nearly a million people and is mostly confined to the downtown area; elsewhere, neighborhoods are primarily residential, giving the place an undeniable smalltown feel despite its status as the second densest city in the country.

See chapters 14 to 20 for comprehensive details of accommodation, restaurants, and other facilities in San Francisco.

One of the flattest stretches of land, created by landfill and bulldozing, is located at the top right-hand corner of the peninsula and comprises **downtown**. Almost entirely contained within the pie wedge formed by the diagonal artery of Market Street to the south, Van Ness Avenue (a continuation of Hwy-101) to the west, and the bay to the east, the compact district is the obvious focus for initial explorations. Lined with the city's stores and tallest office buildings, Market Street begins at the water's edge of the **Embarcadero**, and runs alongside the boxy corporate high-rises of the **Financial District**, past the shopping quarter of **Union Square**, also home to a number of upscale hotels. Just north of Union Square is **Chinatown**, a tight cluster of apartments, restaurants, temples, and stores built around historic Portsmouth Square. Nearby, the towering **Transamerica Pyramid** makes a useful landmark to orient yourself by, shadowing historic Jackson Square's restored redbrick buildings, most of them converted into prime office space.

Diagonal Columbus Avenue separates Portsmouth from Jackson Square, heading northwest and forming the backbone of **North Beach**, the old Italian enclave once haunted by Beat writers, and still popular among pasta eaters and espresso drinkers. To either side of Columbus stand the peaks of three of San Francisco's steep hills: **Telegraph Hill** to the east, perch of the unmistakeable Coit Tower,

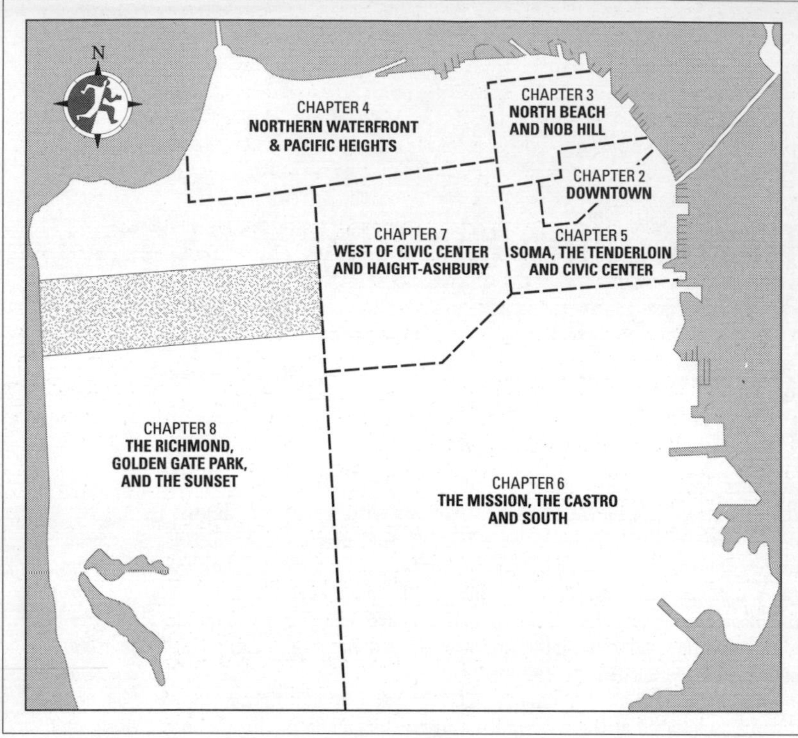

Russian Hill to the west, reached by curvy Lombard Street, and **Nob Hill** to the southwest, capped by stately Grace Cathedral along with some of the city's poshest hotels – though the area was once the province of robber barons.

Along the northern edge of the peninsula, **Fisherman's Wharf** is thoroughly loathed by locals, but draws plenty of visitors to its tacky waterfront piers; it's also the departure point for ferries to one-time island prison **Alcatraz**. Trails along the water's edge lead west past the clutch of museums in **Fort Mason** and the ritzy **Marina** district, home of the Palace of Fine Arts and some of the city's best shopping. High above, on the hills just to the south, the ornate mansions and Victorians of **Pacific Heights** make for splendid viewing; from this perch you'll spot too the **Presidio**, a vast expanse of green stretching west to the Golden Gate Bridge.

For a complete listing of outdoor activities in San Francisco, see p.318.

Back near downtown, west of Union Square, the gritty **Tenderloin**, a run-down section of cheap hotels and sleazy porn shops, will snap you back to reality. It sits uneasily next to the **Civic Center**, where the painstakingly restored City Hall is the imposing focus of a concentrated few blocks of public buildings and cultural venues. Cross Market Street and you'll hit **South of Market** (or **SoMa**), once the city's major industrial enclave, but now more of a new media center, with the offices of many Internet start-ups. It has gained some cultural cachet, too, with the development of the Yerba Buena Gardens and the San Francisco Museum of Modern Art. SoMa's waterfront, long-neglected South Beach, has recently been rezoned for housing and businesses, anchored by the Giants' brand new PacBell Ballpark.

Inland, the **Mission** district was built around Mission Dolores, the oldest building in San Francisco. The neighborhood's diverse population, which includes a large Hispanic community, is privy to a dense concentration of cafés, restaurants, and entertainment that runs along Valencia Street. Just west is an equally energetic neighborhood, the **Castro**, the nominal center for San Francisco's gay population, and home to most of the best gay bars and clubs.

For an overview of the history of San Francisco's gay community, see p.36.

North of the Castro, the **Haight-Ashbury** district was once San Francisco's Victorian resort quarter before hippies and flower children took over. Today it's a rag-tag collection of used-clothing stores and laid-back cafés, though prices here have kept pace with more chic parts of town. Nearby are a few areas of only marginal interest to visitors: tiny **Japantown**, the slightly tatty **Western Addition**, and unexciting – save for some decent nightlife – **Lower Haight**.

Surrounding the central parts of the city, the western and southern sides of San Francisco are where most locals actually live, in districts like the **Richmond**, whose two main drags, Clement and Geary streets, are liberally sprinkled with a number of the city's best ethnic restaurants. The Richmond is hugged by the Golden Gate National Recreation Area to the north, along the coast of which you can pick up the four-mile Pacific Coast Trail; expansive, man-made **Golden Gate Park**, meanwhile, borders the south of the district, and holds a number of fine museums, gardens and the like in its confines. South of the park, the **Sunset** district's homogenous single-story townhomes stretch on relentlessly; relief can be found throughout on the western coast, home to the city's best **beaches**.

The 49-Mile Drive

If you have your own vehicle, you can orient yourself by way of the breathtaking **49-Mile Drive**, a route that takes in the most important scenic and historic points in the city in around a half a day. Marked by blue-and-white seagull signs, it circuits the Civic Center, Japantown, Union Square, Chinatown, Nob Hill, North Beach, and Telegraph Hill, before skirting Fisherman's Wharf, the Marina, and the Palace of Fine Arts – after which it passes the southern approach of the Golden Gate Bridge and winds through the Presidio. From here it sweeps along the ocean, past the zoo and doubles back through Golden Gate Park, vaulting over Twin Peaks and dipping down to Mission Dolores then back to the waterfront for a drive past the Bay Bridge, the Ferry Building and the Financial District. Maps of the entire route are available for $1 from the Visitor Information Center on Market Street at the Powell street cable-car terminus.

Chapter 2

Downtown San Francisco

San Francisco spreads fairly evenly over most of its 49 square miles, but the main concentration of activity is in its oldest and easternmost plot, jammed between the waterfront and the steeply rising hills. It's difficult to draw clear borders, as the parameters shift according to continuous development and whomever you ask, but most of what the locals call downtown is clustered within a square mile around the northern side of Market Street – San Francisco's main commercial and traffic drag, which bisects the northeastern corner of the peninsula. The area ends abruptly at the edge of the bay, where the vistas have been greatly improved by the recent tearing down of the Embarcadero Freeway.

In keeping with its quirky history and unique personality, downtown San Francisco is a real mixed bag, conforming to no overall image. One block is thronged with multinational banks, the next is home to Chinese markets and sidewalk evangelists, and throughout are plenty of upscale department stores, private clubs, smart restaurants, and the other hallmarks of an affluent city.

At the heart of it all sits **Union Square**, San Francisco's liveliest urban space, equally populated by shoppers, street musicians, and beggars. As the city's main hotel and shopping district, at the junction of its major transportation lines (including cable cars), it makes a logical starting point for downtown wanderings. Rimming the **Financial District** – San Francisco's only real high-rise quarter – at the eastern edge of the peninsula, the revitalized waterfront **Embarcadero** rests atop landfill, much of it made up of the remains of ships abandoned by eager 49ers during the Gold Rush. Inland, **Jackson Square** and the **Barbary Coast** were once situated along the natural waterfront and are the city's oldest historic districts, hiding in the shadows of the modern city and home to both antique galleries and prestigious architectural firms. Still further inland, you'll find **Portsmouth Square**, site of where the city was founded. Hugging the square on three sides, bustling **Chinatown** is home to the second-largest Chinese community outside Asia, and inevitably many of the best Asian restaurants in the city.

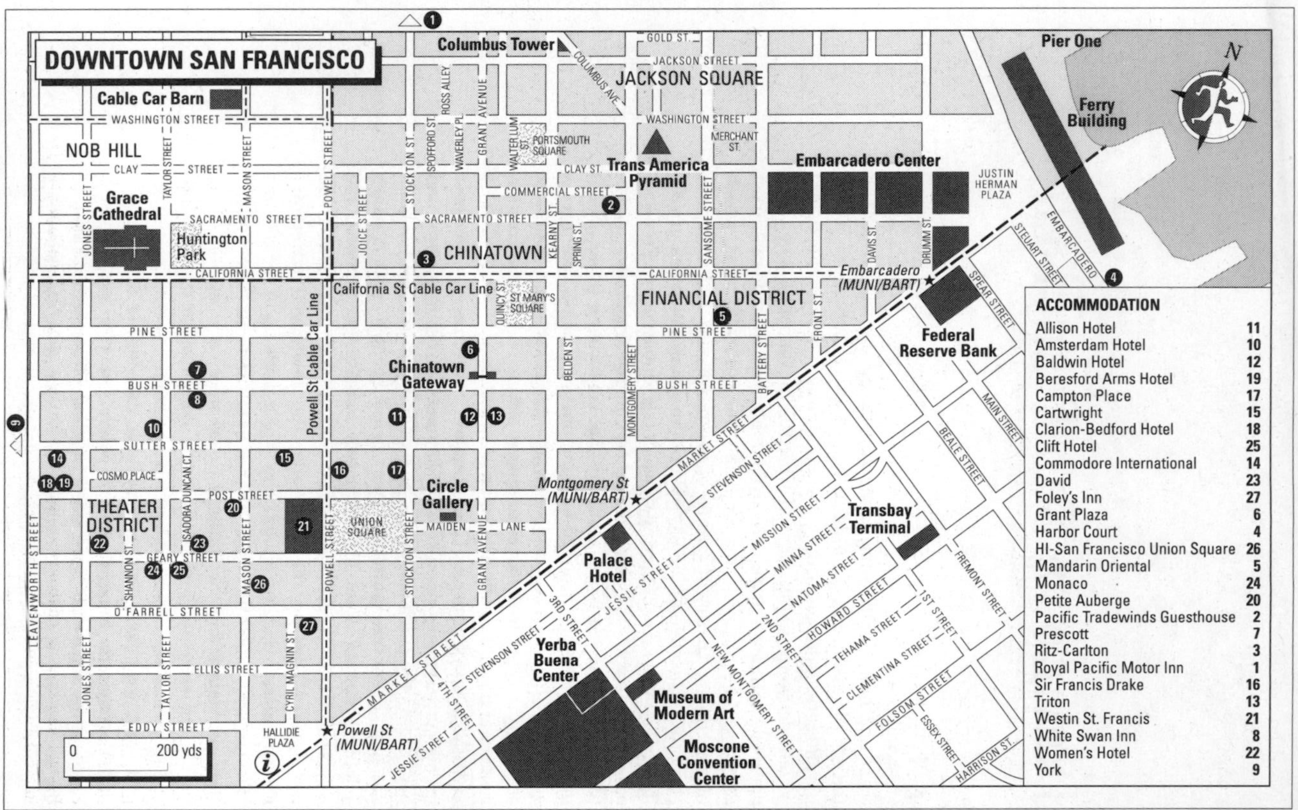

DOWNTOWN SAN FRANCISCO
Cable Car Barn
NOB HILL
Grace Cathedral
Huntington Park
Columbus Tower
CHINATOWN
Chinatown Gateway
JACKSON SQUARE
Trans America Pyramid
FINANCIAL DISTRICT
Embarcadero Center
Embarcadero (MUNI/BART)
Montgomery St (MUNI/BART)
Powell St (MUNI/BART)
Pier One
Ferry Building
JUSTIN HERMAN PLAZA
Federal Reserve Bank
Transbay Terminal
Palace Hotel
Yerba Buena Center
Museum of Modern Art
Moscone Convention Center
Circle Gallery
UNION SQUARE
THEATER DISTRICT
PORTSMOUTH SQUARE
ST MARY'S SQUARE
HALLIDIE PLAZA
California St Cable Car Line
Powell St Cable Car Line
WASHINGTON STREET
CLAY STREET
SACRAMENTO STREET
CALIFORNIA STREET
PINE STREET
BUSH STREET
SUTTER STREET
POST STREET
GEARY STREET
O'FARRELL STREET
ELLIS STREET
EDDY STREET
JONES STREET
TAYLOR STREET
MASON STREET
POWELL STREET
STOCKTON ST.
GRANT AVENUE
KEARNY ST.
MONTGOMERY STREET
SANSOME STREET
BATTERY STREET
FRONT ST.
DAVIS ST.
DRUMM ST.
MARKET STREET
MISSION STREET
HOWARD STREET
FOLSOM STREET
EMBARCADERO
STEUART STREET
SPEAR STREET
MAIN STREET
BEALE STREET
FREMONT STREET
1ST STREET
2ND STREET
3RD STREET
4TH STREET
LEAVENWORTH STREET
200 yds
ACCOMMODATION
Allison Hotel 11
Amsterdam Hotel 10
Baldwin Hotel 12
Beresford Arms Hotel 19
Campton Place 17
Cartwright 15
Clarion-Bedford Hotel 18
Clift Hotel 25
Commodore International 14
David 23
Foley's Inn 27
Grant Plaza 6
Harbor Court 4
HI-San Francisco Union Square 26
Mandarin Oriental 5
Monaco 24
Petite Auberge 20
Pacific Tradewinds Guesthouse 2
Prescott 7
Ritz-Carlton 3
Royal Pacific Motor Inn 1
Sir Francis Drake 16
Triton 13
Westin St. Francis 21
White Swan Inn 8
Women's Hotel 22
York 9

As with most of central San Francisco, **walking** is the best way of sightseeing, though from Union Square – or even better, from California Street – you can hop on a cable car up the steep incline towards Nob Hill, where you can hop off at Grant Avenue to enter Chinatown. It's possible, if exhausting, to cover the entire downtown area in a day, but unless you're on the tightest of schedules, you'll get much more out of downtown (and indeed all of San Francisco) just ambling around.

Union Square and around

Union Square and around

The best place to start a visit to San Francisco is under the palm trees of its commercial center, **UNION SQUARE**. North of Market Street and bordered by Powell and Stockton streets, the area always bustles with activity: cable cars clank past crowds of consumers and tourists who gravitate to the many upscale department stores, boutiques, hotels and theaters situated nearby. The 97-foot-tall Corinthian column in the center of the square commemorates Admiral Dewey's success in the Spanish–American War, though the site takes its name from its role as gathering place for Unionist speechmakers on the eve of the Civil War. The voluptuous female figure atop the monument was modeled on **Alma de Bretteville**, who married into the wealthy Spreckels family and later founded the Palace of the Legion of Honor art museum at Land's End (see p.124).

A four-story parking garage was recently added under the plaza, and given the dearth of spots downtown, it may be the best place to leave your car.

The square was built where a massive sand dune known as O'Farrell's Mountain once stood under the direction of Mayor Geary, who bequeathed the land to the city for use as a public plaza in 1850. Aside from being a pleasant place to sit and people-watch, it's the

The Emperor Norton

Joshua Norton was a 49er from London who'd amassed a considerable fortune in San Francisco speculating on real estate and commodities during the heady years of the Gold Rush. His attempt to corner the rice market in 1854 resulted in bankruptcy, however, and he disappeared for a few years, seemingly another casualty of greed. But one day in 1859 he reappeared, marched into the offices of the *San Francisco Bulletin* dressed in lavish military dress, including a plumed hat, sabre, and epaulettes, and proclaimed himself Emperor of the United States, a statement the editor printed on the front page; a month later, Norton added for himself the title Protector of Mexico. Businesses accepted the currency he printed and advertised that the emperor patronized their shops and restaurants. Among the countless edicts he issued were a proposal to President Lincoln, suggesting he wed Queen Victoria to cement relations between the US and UK, and a call for the building of a bridge to Oakland, positing a route that was realized 75 years later with the completion of the Bay Bridge. He was also said to be the inspiration for the character of the King in Mark Twain's *Adventures of Huckleberry Finn*.

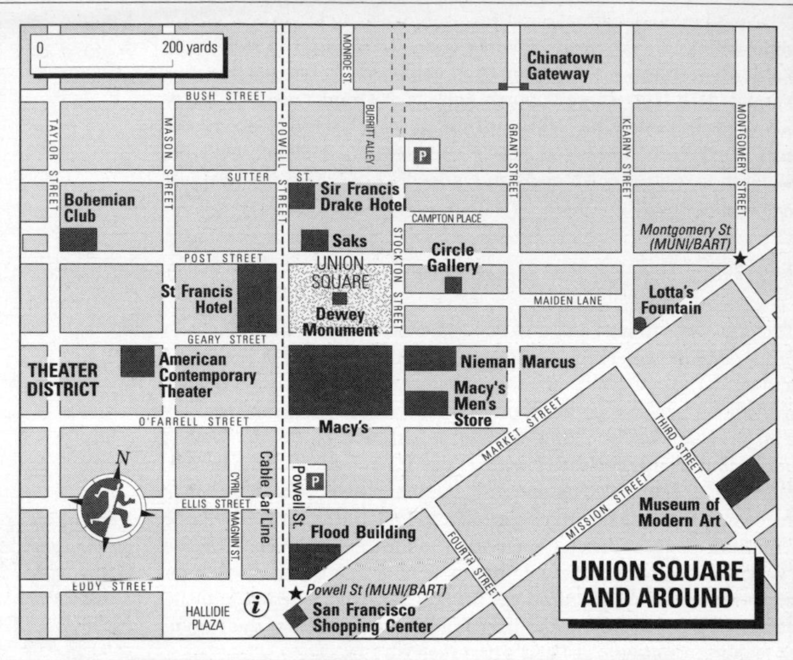

center of one of the most profitable shopping areas in the country, as well as the site of the city's Christmas tree lighting each holiday season, a tradition started back in the mid-1800s by local kook Joshua Norton (see box p.55).

The opulent **Westin St Francis Hotel**, across the cable-car tracks on Powell Street, is steeped in San Francisco lore: Al Jolson died here while playing poker, and just outside, in 1975, President Gerald Ford was nearly assassinated by ex-FBI agent Sara Jane Moore. Perhaps even more legendary, parts of **Dashiell Hammett's** detective stories, such as *The Maltese Falcon*, were set in the hotel; the writer worked as a Pinkerton detective here during the Twenties, investigating the rape and murder case against silent film star Fatty Arbuckle. Though its status is not what it used to be, visiting dignitaries still frequent it – their nations' flags hoisted out front during their stays – and just inside the entrance you can check out paintings of famous folks who have slept here. Step further inside to see the 10-foot-tall Rococo Viennese clock in the lobby and to catch a ride in the glass elevator at the back of the building for a great vista of downtown. Hammett fans should check out *John's Grill*, 63 Ellis St, for Sam Spade's favorite eating spot, and **Burritt Alley** – two blocks north of the square on Bush, near Stockton Street – where a plaque marks the spot that Spade's partner, Miles Archer, was shot and killed.

Union Square and around

Along Post and Sutter Streets, just north of the *St Francis*, are some of downtown's least visible landmarks: some fourteen **private clubs** hidden behind discreet facades. Money isn't the only criteria for membership to these highly esteemed institutions, though being *somebody* usually is. Most notorious is the **Bohemian Club** at Post and Taylor; better known for its Bohemian Grove retreat at the Russian River, where ex-presidents and corporate giants assemble for Masonic rituals and schoolboy larks; the San Francisco chapter is housed in a Lewis Hobart Moderne-style building. Organized in the late 1872 as a breakfast club for newspapermen, it evolved into a businessmen's club with an arty slant, numbering Ambrose Bierce, Jack London, Bret Harte, and Frank Norris among its members. A plaque on the Taylor Street corner bears the group's logo, an owl, along with the motto, "Weaving Spiders Come Not Here," and a bronze bas-relief of Bret Harte characters marks the Post Street corner.

Also west of Union Square, on Geary Street, is San Francisco's smallish **THEATER DISTRICT**, a collection of rep houses anchored by the American Conservatory Theater's **Geary Theater**, at no. 415. The company usually performs major plays – and the obligatory holiday-season run of *A Christmas Carol* – five nights a week, with rush tickets available ninety minutes before the show; not long ago Tom Stoppard chose to debut his *Invention of Love* here instead of London or New York.

Music, theater, and dance options are detailed from p.291 onwards.

A huge, newly renovated **Macy's** department store flanks the south end of Union Square, and heralds the prominence of shopping in the area, some of the best of which can be found down **Maiden Lane**, a chic little urban walkway that was once called Morton Street and was one of San Francisco's lowest-class red-light districts before the 1906 earthquake and fire. Nowadays, aside from some prohibitively expensive boutiques, the lane's main sight is the only **Frank Lloyd Wright-designed building** in San Francisco, at no. 140, an intriguing circular space that was something of a trial run for the Guggenheim in New York; it's now occupied by the Xanadu ethnic art gallery (see p.316).

A few blocks away, where Kearney Street intersects with Geary and Market, **Lotta's Fountain**, an overlooked landmark, sits modestly amidst the tall downtown buildings. Named in honor of actress Lotta Crabtree, one of the first children brought to San Francisco by pioneering families, the fountain served as a message center following the 1906 earthquake, where people passed about news to family and community members lost in the chaos. A few years later, it enjoyed more attention when world-renowned opera diva Luisa Tetrazinni sang a free Christmas Eve performance atop it in 1910, an event that drew tens of thousands of people.

If you're moving on from Union Square, **cable cars** run north along Powell Street; the long lines to catch one begin at the terminus of **Hallidie Plaza**, where Powell and Market Streets meet. While you

The Cable Cars

It was the invention of the **cable car** that made high-society life on San Francisco's hills possible and practical. Since 1873, the trolleys have been an integral part of life in the city, thanks to Scots-born designer Andrew Hallidie. "My attention was called to the great cruelty and hardship to the horses engaged in that work," he wrote. "I devoted all of my available time to the careful consideration of the subject." Hallidie designed a pulley system around the thick wire rope patented by his father in England and widely used in the gold and silver mines in eastern California. "Hallidie's folly," as disbelieving locals dubbed his enterprise, succeeded wildly, launching a transportation and real-estate revolution. High sections of San Francisco like Nob Hill suddenly became accessible, and businesses and homes were constructed along cable-car routes, spreading the urban landscape westward. At their peak, just before the 1906 earthquake, more than six hundred cable cars traveled 110 miles of track throughout the city. But the massive quake tore up the tracks, and over the years usage dwindled further in favor of the automobile. The three lines that remain are a result of a civic campaign undertaken in 1964 when nostalgic citizens voted to preserve the last seventeen miles (now down to ten) as a moving historic landmark. There are 44 cars in use – each unique – and around 23 miles of moving cable underground. Since the mid-1980s Muni has been rebuilding the cars by hand, a process that is taking longer than the originally estimated ten years to complete and as much as 3000 hours and $275,000 per car.

The Powell & Mason and the Powell & Hyde lines run from Hallidie Plaza off Union Square at Powell and Market streets to Fisherman's Wharf. The Powell & Hyde line is the steepest, reaching a hair-raising 21-degree grade between Lombard and Chestnut streets – the number may not sound so frightening, but wait till you're hanging off the side of the cable car for dear life as you take the white-knuckle plunge back downhill in the other direction. The oldest cable car route, the California line, climbs Nob Hill along California Street from the Embarcadero, rattling past the fanciest hotels in the city. During their ascent, cars fasten onto a moving two-inch cable which runs continuously beneath the streets, then release the cable at the top of each hill to glide down the other side. The cars' conductors are typically a cheerful lot, and are receptive to passengers' questions; each boasts a signature bell-ringing style most prominently displayed during the Cable Car Bell Ringing Contest, held every July in Union Square. For more history and background, visit the **Cable Car Museum and Powerhouse** (p.77).

wait to "ride the rope," admire the grand **Flood Building**, at 870 Market St, overlooking the plaza. This flat-iron building, constructed in 1904 by the silver-mining Flood family, is one of the few structures that remained standing after the 1906 earthquake and fire. If the line to catch a car at the plaza is too long, you may wish to try to get on a block north; drivers usually leave a bit of extra room on board at the start of the journey. The San Francisco Visitor Center hides downstairs from the cable-car terminus near the entrance to the Powell Street BART/Muni station located there.

The Financial District and around

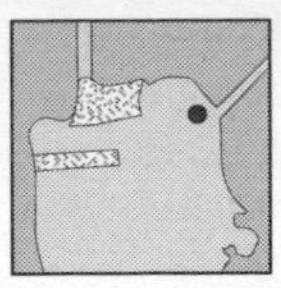

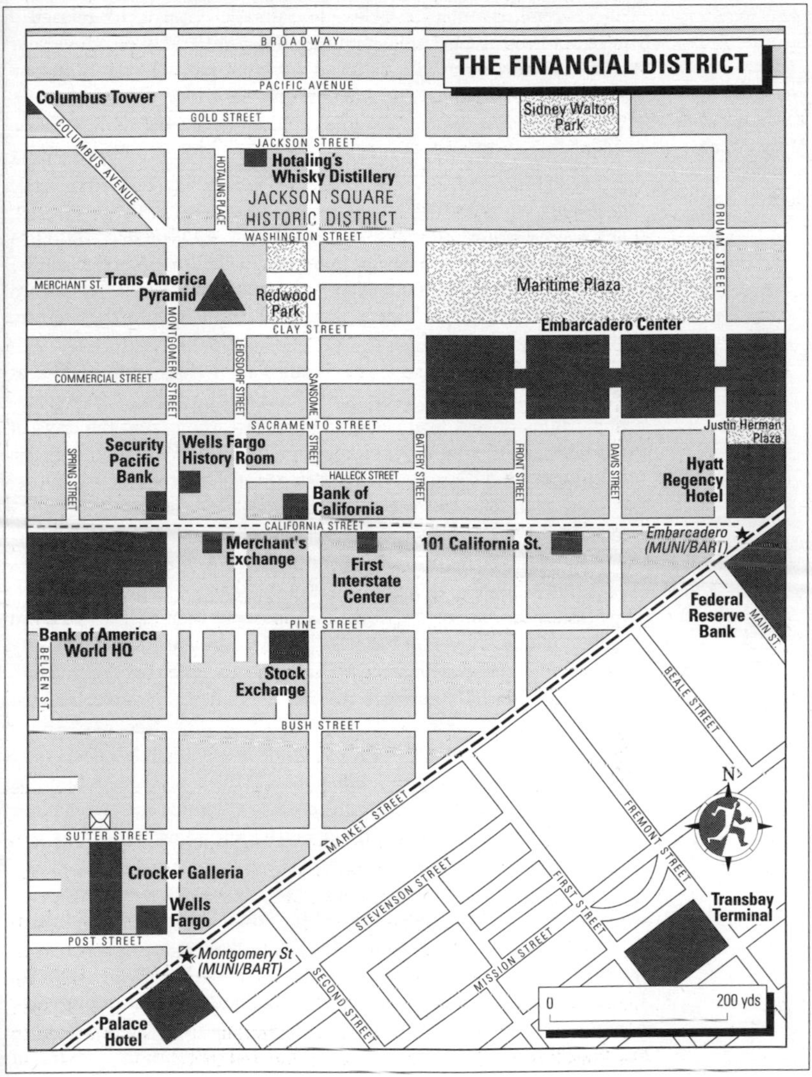

From Hallidie Plaza to the waterfront, Market Street traces the southern edge of the **FINANCIAL DISTRICT**, San Francisco's patch of banks and other trade-related businesses, which hold court in buildings that consitute a veritable hodgepodge of architectural styles and periods, from Palladian piles to postmodern redoubts. Scattered between the investment companies are the copy centers and computer boutiques that serve the offices above, with an occasional restaurant of note, usually set up in alleyways, like those tucked off the corner of Kearney and Pine streets. San Francisco's movers and shakers distinguish themselves from the rest of the American financial community on the last business day of the year, when local custom dictates that office workers throw their desk calendar pages out of the window. Standing on the street and looking skywards, the scene is reminiscent of a ticker-tape parade – not to be missed if you're in town for Christmas and New Year. On Friday evenings year round, the bars buzz with relieved workers, but after 7pm and on weekends, the Financial District is nearly deserted.

The bars and restaurants of downtown San Francisco are detailed on the map on p.240.

Predictably, the district's sights are themed around money. For a hands-on grasp of modern finance, the **World of Economics Gallery** in the **Federal Reserve Bank**, 101 Market St (Mon–Fri 9am–6pm), is unbeatable: computer games allow you to engineer your own inflationary disasters, while exhibits detail recent scandals and triumphs. Outside the bank is the starting point of the **California Street cable-car line**, which leads you out of the Financial District, past Chinatown and up to Nob Hill, though it is a more thrilling ride back down, swooping from quiet mansions into a sea of bustling high-rises.

Just off California Street, the **Wells Fargo History Museum**, at 420 Montgomery St (Mon–Fri 9am–5pm; free), traces the less glamorous origins of San Francisco's big money, right from the days of the Gold Rush, through exhibits of mining equipment, gold nuggets, photographs, and a genuine retired stagecoach. Across Montgomery, the Ionic columns and robust stone details of the 1922 **Security Pacific Bank**, at Montgomery and California, are thoroughly overpowered by the ominous hulk of the **Bank of America** headquarters (California's biggest financial institution) across California Street. Though not the tallest, this broad-shouldered monolith of dark-red granite dominates the San Francisco skyline and has divided the city into fans and those who would like to see it razed to the ground. Finished in 1971, it challenged the city not only with its size, but also with the startling contrast of its hue – San Francisco used to be known as "a city of white" – but with time it has assimilated well and even become the subject of admiration. At the top of the building is the handsome *Carnelian Room* (see p.274), which is a great place to go for drinks and sweeping vistas, though be warned – this is a jacket-and-tie affair.

Surprisingly, some fine **art** is tucked away in hidden corners of the district. Several blocks north, the **Merchants' Exchange Building** at 465 California St was designed by Willis Polk and has a series of nineteenth-century marine paintings by Irish painter William Coulter. At the entrance of its **Grain Exchange Hall** are four huge columns, beyond which the six vast oil canvases depict the history of San Francisco as a seaport. This room was the original center of commercial life in the city, monitoring the comings and goings of every Pacific Coast ship. It was also the place where shippers, warehousemen and traders would gather to do their bidding.

Just south of here,the imposing **Pacific Stock Exchange** sits at the corner of Pine and Sansome streets, though you'll have to make do with viewing its grand pillared entrance, since it closed its doors to traders in 2000, opting to begin an electronic exchange system; the exchange holds the lease on the landmark building until mid-2001, and the air is ripe with speculation on who will take over.

Two other interesting museums hide amidst the caverns of commerce: the **Pacific Heritage Museum**, at 608 Commercial St (Tues–Sat 10am–4pm; free), exhibits Asian art in the former US Subtreasury Building, now beautifully sky-lit and fronting a bench-lined inland avenue that used to be San Francisco's longest pier.

Another retreat from the charging midday throngs is the **Crocker Galleria** rooftop garden at 50 Post St near Market Street. Skip the three floors of expensive boutiques and opt for a sack lunch amidst the office workers who enjoy theirs here.

The Embarcadero

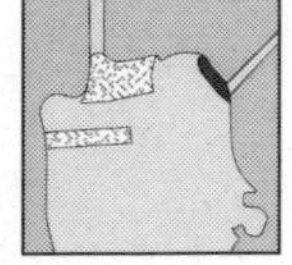

At the northeastern edge of the Financial District, the thin, long waterfront district known as **THE EMBARCADERO** has become a magnet for restaurateurs and hoteliers of repute, taking advantage of the wonderful vistas from its bayfront windows. During the 1930s, before the building of the bridges that connect the city to Oakland and Marin County, this was the main point of arrival for 50,000 cross-bay commuters a day. It's still a transportation hub, but the main focus of the area is now the self-contained complex of offices, hotels and stores housed in four huge modern blocks known as **Embarcadero Center**, recently freed from the shadow of the contentious double-decker freeway that shared its name. Building One is the only one you might be compelled to enter, crowned by the Sky Deck (daily 9.30am–9pm; $7), from which you can observe the cityscape from the 41st floor.

Cut off from the rest of San Francisco by the freeway until it was torn down in 1992, the **Ferry Building**, at the foot of Market Street, was modeled in 1898 on the cathedral tower in Seville, Spain. Most of it collapsed during the 1906 temblor and was rebuilt that same year. A few ferries still dock here (see p.183), but the characterless office units inside do little to suggest its former importance. You can walk inside and loll in the shadow of the Ghandi statue on the many park benches overlooking the water. The area in front of the Ferry Building is the site of the much-loved **Ferry Plaza Farmers' Market** (year-round Sat 8.30am–1.30pm, also April–Nov Tues 10.30am–2.30pm), a good place for local produce; live local bands electrify the atmosphere.

The **Vaillancourt Fountain** in **Justin Herman Plaza** at the foot of market usually triggers a strong emotional reaction; people either love or hate its tangled mass of concrete tubing. During an impromptu free U2 concert here in 1988, Bono left his mark on the structure by spray-painting, "Rock and Roll Stops the Traffic." When someone hung a banner from a window reading, "SF loves U2," he stopped the concert, thinking "SF" stood for Sinn Fein. Today, skateboarders and trick-bike riders share the open concrete square with seagulls and pigeons, and on the last Friday of every month, cyclists gather here to promote the bike as an environmentally sound alternative to driving, an event known as **Critical Mass**.

For the background and details on Critical Mass, see box on page 33.

The five-mile **waterfront** which stretches north and south from the foot of Market Street was teeming during the first half of the twentieth century with ships loading and unloading their cargo. The area experienced something of a slump after World War II, but recent development, including the building of a new Muni station and the extension of the cable-car lines, has brought San Franciscans back here to jog, bike and skate. The addition of several wooden public piers to the north provides scenic rest-stops on the way to Fisherman's Wharf (see p.78), while to the south lie the marina and the San Francisco Giant's new baseball stadium PacBell Ballpark (see p.97).

The waterfront was also the site of one of the more notorious episodes of twentieth-century San Francisco, when, on the eve of America's involvement in World War I, on July 22, 1916, ten members of a massive pro-war demonstration were killed by a bomb. Though there was no tangible evidence of any link, the city's union leaders were held responsible for the attack as they opposed US intervention in the war; they were charged, and found guilty (on perjured testimony) of murder. Tom Mooney, a prominent longshoremen's activist, was sentenced to death, and it took twenty years of lobbying and protest before he was freed and his name cleared. His alleged co-conspirator, Warren Billings, spent most of his life behind bars before being pardoned in 1961. The site of the bombing is now filled by the brick fortress headquarters of the **Southern Pacific Railroad Corporation** at the tail end of Market Street.

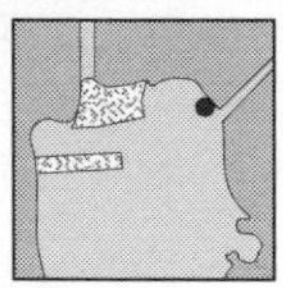

Jackson Square

A century or so ago, the eastern flank of the Financial District formed part of the **Barbary Coast**, where hundreds of ships abandoned by prospectors rushing to the Gold Rush became hotels, bars, stores and, eventually, the landfill on which the neighborhood of **JACKSON SQUARE** stands today. From the 1860s to 1900s, San Francisco grew to be the busiest port on the West Coast, and once on dry land, sailors clambered for entertainment. This then-rough-and-tumble waterfront district gave the city an unsavory reputation and earned the nickname "Baghdad by the Bay," packed as it was with saloons and brothels around evocatively named places like Murderer's Corner and Deadman's Alley, where hapless young males were given Mickey Finns and shanghaied into involuntary servitude on merchant ships. William Randolph Hearst's *Examiner* lobbied frantically to shut down the quarter, resulting in a 1917 California law prohibiting prostitution. Remains of San Francisco's earliest days can be seen today in the restored redbrick buildings of Jackson Square's **historic district,** bordered by Washington, Columbus, Sansome, and Pacific streets.

Begin your explorations at the **Transamerica Pyramid,** at the foot of diagonal Columbus Avenue and Washington, downtown San Francisco's most unmistakeable (though some would say unfortunate) landmark – so tall and thin, it looks more like a squared-off rocket than a pyramid. Designed by LA-based architect William Pereira, the building does have four triangular sides, rising from a square city block to a lofty point high above. A brass plaque in the lobby is the sole reminder that this was once the site of San Francisco's prime literary and artistic crossroads, the **Montgomery Block**. From 1853, when it was built, until 1959, when it was torn down and made into a parking lot, the four-story building was the city's most important meeting place. Though built as an office block for lawyers, doctors, and businesspeople, it was soon taken over by writers and journalists and evolved into a live-in community of bohemian poets, artists, and political radicals. Rudyard Kipling, Robert Louis Stevenson, Mark Twain, and William Randolph Hearst all rented office space here. Twain met a fireman named **Tom Sawyer** – who later opened a popular San Francisco saloon – in the basement steam baths. Ambrose Bierce, Bret Harte, and Joaquin Miller were frequent visitors to its *Bank Exchange* bar and restaurant. Later habitues included George Sterling, Maynard Dixon, and **Sun Yat-sen**, who ran a local newspaper, *Young China*, from his second-floor office. Rumor has it that he wrote the first Chinese constitution here and even orchestrated the successful overthrow of the Manchu (Qing) Dynasty in 1911. A shimmering statue of Dr Sun stands three blocks away in Chinatown (see p.66).

For a suggested reading list of books on the history of San Francisco, see p.348.

Next door to the Transamerica Pyramid is a pleasant **redwood-tree park** with fountains, perfect for an outdoor lunch. Across the street, the winding brickwork, hitching posts, and antique lamps of **Hotaling Place** recall the neighborhood's past, though there's little to focus on. Nearby Jackson Street does hold, at nos. 451–455, the **Hotaling Building**, once a wholesale whiskey operation and miraculously spared in the 1906 fire to the great relief of a city badly in need of its alcohol. A piece of doggerel from the time reads, "If as they say God spanked the town for being over frisky, why did he burn the churches down and spare Hotaling's whiskey?" **Pacific Avenue**, originally Pacific Street, the old heart of the Barbary Coast, is now perhaps the most anodyne stretch of the Jackson Square district.

Montgomery Street, at the square's western edge, holds a number of handsome facades, many with further literary and libertine associations. Just down from Jackson Street, 732 Montgomery St was the home of San Francisco's first literary magazine, the *Golden Era*, founded in the 1850s, which helped launch the careers of Bret Harte and Mark Twain. Writers John Steinbeck and William Saroyan later spent many a night drinking in the vanished *Black Cat Café* down the street. In the middle of the block, **722–728 Montgomery Street** (The Belli and Genella buildings) have had their original stucco stripped and have been done up in overwrought Victorian mode. The building has served as a theater – Lotta Crabtree of Lotta's Fountain fame began singing here on her way to becoming America's highest-paid entertainer – a Turkish bath, a tobacco warehouse, and finally an auction room, before becoming the headquarters of America's first famous lawyer, the late swashbuckling San Francisco barrister Melvin Belli, who would fire off the rooftop cannon after winning a case. Belli's widow announced plans a year after her husband's 1996 death to turn the site into a museum, and the mayor even came to the groundbreaking, but work stopped when a drawn-out ownership battle froze all progress. Today, the building has fallen into disuse, hidden from view by shuttered windows, encroaching ivy, and gnarled tree branches, giving the place a ruined feel.

Heading west on Jackson or Pacific Street leads you back to Columbus and the distinctive green-copper siding of the **Columbus Tower**, 906 Kearney St, the border between the Financial District, Chinatown, and North Beach. Director and San Francisco native Francis Ford Coppola owns the building, and his *Neibaum-Coppola Café* on the ground floor serves sandwiches, pasta, and his wine. Coppola's office hovers above, in the rounded tower that gives the building its name.

Portsmouth Square

One block south of Columbus Tower on Kearny and Washington streets, **Portsmouth Square** was San Francisco's original city center and the first port of entry. It was here that Englishman William Richardson received permission in 1835 from Mexican rulers to begin a trading post on the coast of the bay, known as Yerba Buena. John Montgomery came ashore in 1846 to claim the hamlet for the United States, raising a flag whose original location is marked by the one flying in the square today. In 1848, Sam Brannan's cry of "Gold!" here sent property prices and development skyrocketing as hungry prospectors poured in.

The sunny square holds four monuments besides the American flag: a statue of the galleon *Hispaniola* from *Treasure Island* is a monument to writer **Robert Louis Stevenson**, who loved to lounge here watching people during his brief residence in San Francisco in 1879; a nearby plaque honors California's first public school, built here in 1848; another pays tribute to Andrew Hallidie, whose first cable-car line ran on Clay Street, down the steps from the stairs; on a more modern note, Thomas Marsh's bronze *Goddess of Democracy* was erected in memory of the 1989 Tian'anmen Square protests. All around the square, dozens of elderly Chinese practice t'ai chi, play Chinese chess, and watch grandchildren climb the new playground equipment, and every Saturday evening from spring through autumn (6–11pm), a **nightmarket** animates the square with performances of classical opera and traditional music surrounded by stalls selling everything from fresh honey to leather jackets. All are reminders of the proximity of one of San Francisco's best-loved neighborhoods.

Chinatown

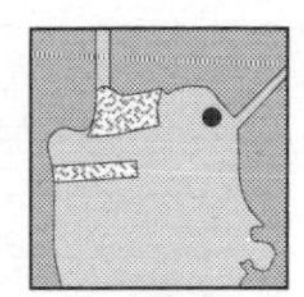

At the foot of Nob Hill, and just blocks from Union Square, **CHINATOWN**'s densely populated 24 square blocks smack in the middle of San Francisco make up the second-largest Chinese community outside Asia, after New York City. A busy area, populated by big numbers of Taiwanese, Vietnamese, Korean, Thai, and Laotian as well, the neighborhood has its roots in the Chinese laborers who migrated to the area after the completion of the transcontinental railroad, and the arrival of Chinese sailors keen to benefit from the Gold Rush. The city didn't extend much of an initial welcome to Chinese immigrants, however; they were met by a tide of vicious racial attacks, and further stymied by the 1882 Chinese Exclusion Act, a law that prevented new immigration and barred thousands of single Chinese men from both dating local women and bringing wives from China. A rip-roaring prostitution and gambling quarter developed – filling the void created by the racist laws – controlled by gangs known as *tongs*.

Chinatown's restaurants are listed on p.240.

After World War II, conditions got progressively better, what with the loosening of immigration laws, and the population began to swell again. Much of the seediness began to recede, though the energy remained. Indeed today the area bristles with activity by day; at night it's a blaze of neon, thanks mainly to the abundance of Chinese restaurants, which draw crowds from all over. Overcrowding is compounded by a brisk tourist trade, most of which is centered along **Grant Avenue**, the neighborhood's main east–west artery, lined with

Chinese New Year

If you're visiting at the end of January or in February, make an effort to catch the citywide celebration of **Lunar New Year**, known as **Chinese New Year**, when downtown streets from Market to Columbus nearly self-combust with energy and noise. Floats and papier-mâché dragons trundle up Kearney Street alongside a cavalcade of local politicians, movie stars and writers. Carnival booths are set up on Portsmouth Square, and the sound of firecrackers fills the air.

gold-ornamented portals, brightly painted balconies and some of the tackiest stores and facades in the city, though pockets of authenticity do remain elsewhere.

You can approach Chinatown from pretty much any direction, but the most dramatic entrance to the neighborhood is via the **Chinatown Gate**, on Grant Avenue at Bush Street, a large dragon-clad archway with a four-character inscription that reads, "*Xia tian wei gong*," or "The reason to exist is to serve the public good." It's hard to see how that idea is carried out on the blocks ahead; Grant's sidewalks are paved with plastic Buddhas, cloisonné "health balls," noisemakers, and chirping mechanical crickets that assault the ear and eye from every doorway. Before its commercial days, Grant was named Dupont Street, a wicked ensemble of opium dens, bordellos, and gambling huts policed, if not terrorized, by *tong* hatchet men – though little of this legacy remains.

One leftover from the neighborhood's early days is the redbrick and granite **Old St Mary's Church**, on the corner of Grant and California, one of the few San Francisco buildings to survive the 1906 fire; a good photo display of the damage to the city and the church resides in its entranceway. Across California Street in St Mary's Square, a Benjamin Bufano statue of **Dr Sun Yat-Sen**, founder of China's first democratic revolution, glistens in the sun.

Parallel to Grant Avenue, on **Waverly Place**, three opulent but skillfully hidden **temples** (nos. 109, 125 and 146), their interiors a riot of black, gold and vermilion, are still in use and open to visitors. The temples do not charge admission, but ask for a donation and the absence of cameras and camcorders. At the intersection of Waverly and Sacramento, the **Clarion Music Center** is an educational resource center for world music, a vendor of ethnic musical instruments from around the planet, and a concert hall for international music events (see p.286). A bit to the north, running between Jackson and Washington streets, **Ross Alley** has a few kitschy places of interest, the first of which is the **Golden Gate Fortune Cookie Company**, no. 56, specializing in racy fortunes. Fortune cookies were invented in San Francisco by Golden Gate Park's Japanese Tea Garden proprietor Makota Hagiwara, whose recipe was borrowed and promoted by restaurants in Chinatown. Next door is **Jun Yu's Barbershop**, where for $8 you can get a cut to resemble the Hollywood star of your choice. Moving west, **Stockton Street** is crammed with exotic fish and produce markets, bakeries, and herbalists. Inside the **Ellison Herb Shop**, at no. 805, Chinatown's best-stocked herbal pharmacy, you'll find clerks filling orders the ancient Chinese way – with hand-held scales and abacuses – from drug cases filled with dried bark, roots, sharks' fins, cicadas, ginseng, and other staples.

Back on Grant Avenue, near Washington, the best of Chinatown's very few **bars** is *Li Po's* at no. 916, unique for its caverned entranceway and dimly lit interior. Some of the hundred-plus **restaurants** in this part of Chinatown are historical landmarks in themselves, notably ***Sam Woh***, at 813 Washington St, a cheap and churlish ex-haunt of the Beats where Gary Snyder taught Jack Kerouac to eat with chopsticks and had them both thrown out with his loud and passionate interpretation of Zen poetry.

Going back a bit further in time, Chinatown's history is well documented in the **Chinese Historical Society of America** at 650 Commercial St (Tues–Fri 10am–4pm; donations), which traces the beginnings of the Chinese community in the US and has a small but worthy collection of photographs, paintings and artifacts from the pioneering days of the nineteenth century. Visitors interested in Buddhism should head to **Buddha's Universal Church** at 720 Washington St, where America's largest Zen sect gives free tours on the second and fourth Sunday of each month, the only time it's open to the public. This five-story building was painstakingly built by the sect's members from an exotic collection of polished woods, adorned everywhere by the mosaic images of Buddha. The **Chinese Cultural Center**, inside the *Holiday Inn* at 750 Kearny St (Tues–Sun 10am–4pm), hosts a sporadic program of art shows, mostly contemporary.

Chinatown has some of the cheapest good food in town, especially during lunch when a plate of fried noodles and dumplings can be procured at any grotty cafeteria for as little as $3.

Chapter 3

North Beach and Nob Hill

Inland North Beach was named in the days when the area sat along the original waterfront, before the peninsula grew outward on landfill. Today, the sunny neighborhood sits in a valley sheltered by several hills, and is best-known as a home to the city's Italian community – and former stomping ground of various Beat poets. Though somewhat eroded by gentrification, it retains an appealing, worn-in feeling, its gently sloping streets lined with plenty of cafés and bars that invite lingering.

Within walking distance, flanking either side of North Beach, **Telegraph** and **Russian hills** are more residential in flavor, with beautiful homes and hidden gardens along steep streets that lead to pedestrian steps. Good for strolling and taking in the views of the waterfront, these neighborhoods are well removed from the consumer-driven madness below. Flanking Russian Hill just to the north, **Nob Hill** is even more sedate and tranquil, a high mount of cathedrals, opulent hotels, and mansions developed by the barons of the Gold Rush and silver's Comstock Lode. Formerly too high for the hoisting building materials, it, like Russian Hill, blossomed with the invention of the **cable car**; riding on one up the steep inclines is still an exhilarating experience that no visitor should miss.

North Beach

Bordering Chinatown at the junction of Grant and Broadway avenues and Fisherman's Wharf to the south, **NORTH BEACH** has always been a gateway for immigrants. Though storied today as "Little Italy," the district has played host to Chinese, Chileans, and Irish before taking on its present mien in the 1900s, when Italians turned the area into a soulful quarter of espresso shops, delis, wine bars, and salami grocers. Drawn to its freewheeling European flavor and sleazy Broadway nightclubs, writers like Lawrence Ferlinghetti, Allen Ginsberg, and Jack Kerouac made North Beach the nexus of the **Beat generation** in the 1950s and a beacon for similarly-oriented beatniks from all over the

world (see box overleaf). The ensuing immigration of hippies and flower children helped transform San Francisco into a testing ground for the experiments of free love and expression of the Summer of Love.

Though developing artists and poets can no longer afford to live here, the stretch of the neighborhood that runs along diagonal **Columbus Avenue** remains one of San Francisco's livelier districts. Walking north from Columbus Tower (see p.64), you'll pass the area which hosted some of the biggest names of the 1950s San Francisco scene. Politically conscious comedians like Mort Sahl, Dick Gregory, and the legendary Lenny Bruce performed at the *Purple Onion* nightclub and the *Hungry I* (now a sex joint on Broadway), as did San Francisco author Maya Angelou, in her earlier guise of singer and dancer. These landmarks have now changed beyond recognition, but the district still trades on a reputation earned decades ago.

The bars and restaurants of North Beach are detailed on the map on p.245.

City Lights Bookstore at 261 Columbus Ave (Sun–Thurs 10am–11.30pm, Fri–Sat 10am–12.30am) may be your most appropriate introduction to North Beach. Much more than a place to get a

The Beats in North Beach

North Beach has always been something of a literary hangout: it served as temporary home to both Mark Twain and Jack London among other boomtown writers. But it was the **Beat generation** that really put the place on the map as the literary capital of California when Lawrence Ferlinghetti opened America's first bookstore selling only paperbacks – City Lights – in 1953. The first Beat writings had emerged a decade earlier in New York's Lower East Side where Jack Kerouac, Allen Ginsberg, and William Burroughs bemoaned the conservative political climate. Frustrated, they moved out West, most of them settling in North Beach where they were surrounded by an esoteric cluster of artists and hangers-on. In 1957, a storm of controversy rose up when police moved in on City Lights to prevent the sale of Ginsberg's poem *Howl* under charges of obscenity – an episode the press latched onto immediately, inadvertently hyping the Beats to national notoriety, as much for their hedonistic antics as for the literary merits of their work. The Supreme Court heard the case and acquitted Ginsberg, ruling that so long as a work has "redeeming social value," it cannot be considered pornographic. Within six months, Jack Kerouac's *On the Road*, inspired by his friend Neal Cassady's benzedrine monologues and several cross-country trips, shot to the top of the bestseller lists.

Besides developing a new, more personal style of fiction and poetry, the Beats eschewed most social conventions of the time, and North Beach soon became synonymous across the nation with a wild and subversive lifestyle. The Beats became as much an industry as a literary movement when tourists, promised sidewalks clogged with black-bereted, goateed trend-setters banging bongos, began pouring into North Beach on "Beatnik Tours." The legend has yet to die, aided by City Hall's granting of Ferlinghetti's wish to rename city streets after the literary figures made famous by his press (as well as a host of other local writers not directly linked with the Beat movement); the alley next to the bookstore, for example, is now known as Jack Kerouac Street.

Howl T-shirt, it's actually one of San Francisco's best bookstores and is still owned by Ferlingetti who's now in his eighties. The upstairs poetry section is expansive, including everything from $1 mini-books and poster-size poems from beatnik legends to various collections and anthologies; the basement contains, among other surprises, an excellent selection of hard to find works-in-translation. Next to the bookstore, across Jack Kerouac Street, **Vesuvio's**, an old North Beach bar where the likes of Dylan Thomas and Kerouac got sauced, remains a haven for the lesser-knowns (and hordes of backpackers in search of them) to pontificate on the state of the arts.

For more on City Lights, see p.310.

From *Vesuvio's*, a short walk south on the other side of Columbus leads to William Saroyan Place and *Spec's Adler Museum Café*, a small wooden bar packed with mementos left by the thousands of sailors who've drunk underneath its exposed-brick walls. Heading north, at the crossroads of **Columbus and Broadway**, poetry meets porn in a raucous assembly of coffeehouses and strip joints. Most famous was the **Condor Club**, where Carol Doda's revealing of her silicone-implanted breasts started the topless waitress phenomenon. Now reincarnated as the (fully-clothed) *Condor Sports Bar*, the landmark site still preserves the notorious set of neon nipples that once glowed above the door in its museum, along with photos and clippings from the *Condor Club*'s heyday, which no doubt reached its apex in a sexual escapade involving a bouncer and waitress, who climbed atop the club's rising piano and accidentally hit the lever, sending the man up to the ceiling where he was crushed to death. The seediness continues nearby at **The Lusty Lady**, at 1033 Kearney, if not the only female owned-and-operated strip club in the world then likely the only unionized one. Beat tourists will want to continue a few blocks down to **1010 Montgomery St**, at the corner of Broadway, where Ginsberg lived when he wrote *Howl*, though there's nothing really to see save the outside of the house.

The late, great drag club Finochhio's, *once located on Columbus Avenue, was closed in 1999 after 63 years in business when owners could no longer pay the rent.*

At the intersection of Columbus, Grant, and Broadway, a large history **mural** on the left side of the intersection depicts the area's Chinese, Italian and maritime past. Lyle Tuttle's **Tattoo Museum**, 841 Columbus Ave (Sun–Thurs noon–9pm, Fri & Sat noon–10pm), exhibits art of a different sort, with extensive displays of body drawings and the various tools used to paint them into flesh over the years. The museum is also a working tattoo parlor, should you want a permanent souvenir.

Continuing north on Columbus Avenue, you enter the heart of the old Italian neighborhood, an enclave of narrow streets and leafy enclosures dotted with minor landmarks like *Cafe Trieste*, 609 Vallejo (☎415/982-2605), where the jukebox blasts out opera classics to a heavy-duty art crowd, toying with cappuccinos and browsing slim volumes of poetry. On Saturday afternoons, the café hosts free opera performances. Photos of its star patrons line the walls, and legend has it that Francis Ford Coppola wrote the screenplay for *The Godfather* at the table under his picture. Walk north along quiet **Grant Avenue**, the neighborhood's best shopping street, lined with a variety of cool clothing and knickknack stores. The city's oldest bar, *The Saloon*, is at no. 1232; a rare North Beach survivor of the 1906 fire, it's little more now than a hole in the wall.

Nearby, North Beach's plaza, grassy **Washington Square Park**, usually hums with Chinese practicing t'ai chi and young people tossing frisbees. Local legend Lillie Coit's not-subtle fascination with firefighters can be seen on the Columbus side in the form of a bronze **statue of volunteer firemen** holding hoses. The statue of **Benjamin Franklin** in the center of the park, meanwhile, was donated by dentist and prohibitionist H.D. Cogswell, who installed taps at the base of the monument in the vain hope that people would drink water from them rather than try to get their hands on bootleg liquor.

On the north side of the park, the white lacy spires of the **Church of St Peter and Paul** look like a pair of fairy-tale castles rising beneath the shadow of Telegraph Hill's Coit Tower (see p.73). Step inside to see the wonderful *La Madre del Lume*, a painting of a Madonna, child on hip, reaching into the inferno to pull out a sinner. In 1954, local baseball phenom Joe DiMaggio and Marilyn Monroe had their wedding pictures taken here (though the actual marriage took place earlier at City Hall). DiMaggio's legacy lives on a few blocks to the north at the recently renamed **Joe DiMaggio North Beach Playground**, on Greenwich Street, where he practiced baseball as a kid.

The blocks south of Columbus are largely residential, though **Fugazi Hall** at 678 Green St, between Columbus and Powell, is one of the neighborhood's symbols of Italian pride. Donated to the community in 1912 by local figure John Fugazi, a banker who founded the Transamerica Corporation, this elaborate terra-cotta ornamented building is now host to San Francisco's longest-running show, *Beach Blanket Babylon*. An upper-floor room holds photographs depicting the history of the local Italian community. Other memorabilia can be found at the intimate **North Beach Museum** (Mon–Thurs 9am–4pm, Fri 9am–6pm; free), on the mezzanine level of the Eureka Bank, 1435 Stockton St, near Columbus. Filled with old photographs and heirlooms, it is the best peep into the area's unique history of the Italian- and Chinese-Americans.

For more on Beach Blanket Babylon, *see p.293.*

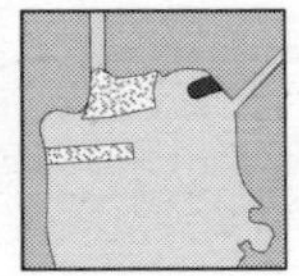

Telegraph Hill and Russian Hill

The hills that flank North Beach are host to some of the best views and most expensive homes in San Francisco. To the east of Columbus, the narrow wooden alleys and steep steps of **Telegraph Hill** – named for an old communications station that once stood here – are capped by Coit Tower. West of Columbus, **Russian Hill** is highlighted by the curves of Lombard Street, though it has also gained repute as the fictitious home of the cast of Armistad Maupin's *Tales of the City*. Both are fantastic places to spend an afternoon wandering around, provided you have strong legs, a light load, and plenty of water – the neighborhoods are primarily residential, with cafés and grocers few and far between.

Telegraph Hill

Dominated by **Coit Tower**, **TELEGRAPH HILL** is a quiet cluster of hill-hugging homes with breathtaking views. The most direct path up the hill is Filbert Street, a very steep climb past clapboard houses and flowery gardens up to Telegraph Hill Boulevard. One alternative is to drive, but there's only a handful of parking spots atop the hill, and the wait for a place can verge on the eternal. You could catch the infallibly infrequent Muni bus #39 to the top, but the ten-minute walk up is faster – if tiring – and allows you to drink in the panorama of North Beach and the bay below. Once atop the hill, it's easy to see

Lillie Hitchcock Coit

Lillie Hitchcock Coit (1844–1929) came to San Francisco at the age of seven only to lose some of her new friends in a series of city fires. Moved by her experiences, she helped the short-handed Knickerbocker Engine Company (No. 5 of the Volunteer Fire Department) tow its engine up Telegraph Hill one day. The grateful firefighters of the first engine to ever make it up the hill made Coit their mascot; she so relished the role that she embroidered the number five on her clothing and began signing her name with a five after it. Despite marrying wealthy Easterner Howard Coit in 1868, Lillie continued attending firemen's balls and playing poker with "her" men of Company No. 5. Local stories abound of her exploits, including scenes of dashing away from society balls and chasing after clanging fire engines. What's certain of her legacy, however, stands atop Telegraph Hill in the shape of the tower that was constructed after her 1929 death with the $125,000 she'd left "to be expended in an appropriate manner for the purpose of adding to the beauty of the city which I have always loved." The result was a concrete tower, designed by Arthur Brown, architect of City Hall, that bears an unmistakeable resemblance to a firehose nozzle.

why it was used as a signal tower for ships entering the Golden Gate. A watchman atop the hill would identify the boat's origin and name via the flags flying on the mast, and relay the information via telegraph to the docks along Fisherman's Wharf. A plaque in front of a statue honoring Christopher Columbus in **Pioneer Park**, which lies at the foot of the tower, marks the watchman's spot.

Within Pioneer Park, and the best viewpoint in all of Telegraph Hill, is **Coit Tower** (daily 10am–6pm; $3.75), a 212-ft pillar bequeathed to the city by Lillie Coit. While waiting to ascend to the top, take some time to admire the murals at the interior's base, site of a WPA project that employed artists to decorate public and government buildings. Students of famed Mexican muralist **Diego Rivera** – known for his links with Russian Communists – were selected to adorn the tower's entranceway with frescoes. Though the paintings are thematically linked, the styles vary greatly. One section depicts muscle-bound Californians working on the land; another shows a man reading Marx in front of a wall of books written by left-leaning authors like Upton Sinclair and Jack London; still others contemplate apocalyptic newspaper headlines. The murals were completed in 1934, during a longshoreman's dispute that escalated into a general strike after police killed two demonstrators. When rumors about the "subversive" frescoes reached the authorities, the Art Commission ordered that a hammer and sickle be removed from one and even tried to close the tower until tempers cooled. A picket of the tower was mounted by local unions, keeping it in the headlines until authorities caved in and allowed the exhibit to open several months later. You can take a free tour of the murals Tuesdays and Thursdays at 10.15am and Saturday at 11am.

Descending Telegraph Hill on the eastern side, the beautifully landscaped **Greenwich Steps**, which cling to the hill at a 45-degree angle,

Blue Jeans

The Gold Rush resulted in fortunes for those without panhandles, too; merchants, hoteliers, financiers, and inventors supporting the miners all profited as well, giving San Francisco an entrepreneurial legacy still alive today. One of the first self-made millionaires in town was a merchant named **Levi Strauss**, who arrived in 1853 from New York with bolts of tan canvas he intended to sell for tent material. He soon learned that miners needed sturdier pants, so Strauss cut some of his cloth into trousers. News of the rugged product spread via word of mouth among the miners, and by 1860, Strauss ran out of canvas. He began using blue cloth from Nimes, France, or fabric "de Nimes," soon Americanized into "denim." Legend has it that the blue trousers resembled uniform worn by Italian sailors from Genoa, or "Genes" in French, which was Americanized into "jeans." The rest, as they say, is history. Levi's is still headquartered in San Francisco; the company's flagship store off Union Square, at 300 Post St, features a Shrink-to-Fit tub where you and your jeans take a dip into hot water before standing in a body drier.

and the equally lovely **Filbert Steps**, which drop down even more steeply, pass glitzy homes and gardens looking out over the Bay Bridge before plateauing at Montgomery Street. Filbert Street gives access to narrow footpaths like **Darell Place** and **Napier Lane** that cut off to either side; Napier Lane is one of the last boardwalk streets in the city, lined with bucolic cottages and overflowing greenery.

Backtrack to Montgomery Street to check out the fine Art Moderne apartment building at no. 1360 in which Lauren Bacall lived in the classic Bogart and Bacall film *Dark Passage*. Off Montgomery, at 60-62 Alta Street, you'll find the former home of **Armistead Maupin**, who penned much of the *Tales of the City* here; begun as a column in the *San Francisco Chronicle*, the book did much to preserve San Francisco's reputation as a capital of free expression.

Back at the foot of Greenwich Street, head east to **Levi Strauss Plaza**, headquarters of blue-jean inventors Levi Strauss & Co, (hence the "SF" on the pocket rivets); an exhibit on blue-jean history and the company's less successful products can be found inside the main building in the complex, but the allure of the plaza lies more in its lovely pond and park.

Russian Hill

West of North Beach, elegant **RUSSIAN HILL**, named for six unknown Russian sailors who died on an undocumented expedition here in the early 1800s and were buried on its southeastern tip, has the odd point of interest, but most people come here for the white-knuckle drive down Lombard Street – a narrow, tightly curving one-way block with a 5mph speed limit and some very rich, if annoyed, homeowners along its sides. Residents have proposed numerous times that the road be closed, to no avail. Surrounded by palatial dwellings and herbaceous borders, Lombard is featured as often as the Golden Gate Bridge in San Francisco publicity shots, and at night when the tourists leave and the city lights twinkle below, it makes for a thrilling drive. At the top of the street is the tiny but immaculate **Alice Marble Park**, good for taking a breather or stretching out in the sun.

It's easy to get your bearings in the neighborhood, as the cable-car tracks along **Hyde Street** neatly divide the district in two. Not far away, the **San Francisco Art Institute**, at 800 Chestnut St (Tues–Sat 10am–5pm; free), the oldest art school in the West, has long been central in the development of the arts in the Bay Area – Jerry Garcia and Lawrence Ferlinghetti are former students, and Ansel Adams started the photography department – and has four excellent galleries, three dedicated to painting and one to surrealist photography. The highlight of the institute is unquestionably the **Diego Rivera Gallery**, with an outstanding mural executed by the painter in 1931 at the height of his fame. A small **cafeteria** at the back of the building's annex – where Janis Joplin flipped burgers before making a name for herself – offers cheap refreshments and a fantastic vista of North Beach, Telegraph Hill, and the bay.

Walking south from the institute for four blocks on Jones Street, you'll find vine-covered, wooden-planked **Macondray Lane**, a pedestrian-only "street" thought to be one of the inspirations for Barbary Lane in Maupin's *Tales of the City*. Continue on Jones two more

San Francisco's Steepest Streets

Though no street can match Lombard for its fabled curves, the wait to go down them may force you to consider another itinerary if pressed for time or seeking release from tourist throngs. The city's second-twistiest street lays coiled in the Potrero Hill neighborhood, on Vermont Street between McKinley and 22nd Street. It has five full and two half-turns, compared to Lombard's eight. Another San Francisco thrill that'll test the brakes of your rental car is to take a ride down any of the city's steepest streets. Don't worry about traffic on these routes; most people prefer not to brave them, even if that forces them to make an elaborate detour. We've included the hill's neighborhood to help find it on a map.

	degree
1) Filbert between Leavenworth and Hyde Russian Hill	31.5
2) 22nd Street between Church and Vicksburg Castro/Noe Valley	31.5
3) Jones between Union and Filbert Russian Hill	29.0
4) Duboce between Buena Vista and Alpine Lower Haight	27.9
5) Jones between Green and Union Russian Hill	26.0
6) Webster between Vallejo and Broadway Pacific Heights	26.0
7) Duboce between Alpine and Divisadero Lower Haight	25.0
8) Jones between Pine and California Nob Hill	24.8
9) Fillmore between Vallejo and Broadway Pacific Heights	24.0

blocks and head up the steps on the steep, small hill at Vallejo Street for a hidden swath of unnamed green with an inspiring view of the Bay Bridge. The home at 40–42 Vallejo St was designed c.1900 by San Francisco architect Willis Polk, an early example of the wood-shingle-covered style seen scattered about the city. Continue east On Vallejo and cross Taylor Street to **Ina Coolbrith Park**, a small, peaceful outpost of green that clings to the hillside, named after California's first poet laureate.

For complete reviews of San Francisco's galleries, see p.314.

A few blocks west of the the park, at 1067 Green St, stands one of the city's few remaining octagonal houses. The **Freusier Octagon House**, built in the 1870s, is closed to the public, but the outside still merits a look for its shape as much as its age. Back down off Hyde Street, the small alley known as Russell Street offers, at no. 29, the little cottage where Jack Kerouac lived in 1952, though only for six months, during which time he began an affair with Carolyn Cassady at her husband Neal's urging. Kerouac also had time to produce some of his best work in the building, inspired by the tape-recorded sessions with Neal for *Visions of Cody*. He revised *On the Road* in the house as well as writing *Doctor Sax*. Carolyn Cassady's own rich memoir, *Heartbeat*, chronicles this period, with some vivid descriptions of the city itself.

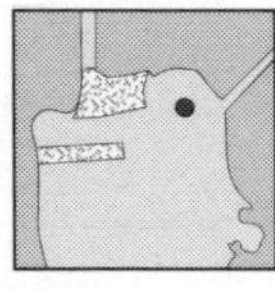

Nob Hill

From Nob Hill, looking down upon the business wards of the city, we can decry a building with a little belfry, and that is the stock exchange, the heart of San Francisco; a great pump we might call it, continually pumping up the savings of the lower quarter to the pockets of the millionaires on the hill.

Robert Louis Stevenson

The posh hotels and Masonic institutions of **NOB HILL**, south of Russian Hill and west of Chinatown, exemplify San Francisco's old wealth; it is, as Joan Didion wrote, "the symbolic nexus of all old California money and power." Once you've made the stiff climb up (or taken the California cable car), there are very few real sights as such, apart from the astounding views over the city and beyond, but this is a pleasant enough place to stroll between the ornate facades of opulent dwellings.

Originally called California Street Hill, the 376-foot-high hill used to be scrubland occupied by sheep. The invention of the cable car made it accessible to Gold Rush millionaires, and the area became known as Nob Hill (from "nabob," a Moghul prince or "snob" or "knob," as in rounded hill) after **The Big Four** – Leland Stanford, Collis P. Huntington, Mark Hopkins, and Charles Crocker – came to the area to construct the Central Pacific Railroad, and built their mansions here. Ostentatious designs from redwood culled from the Marin Headlands were the fashion, though one man, James C. Flood,

For reviews of Nob Hill's hotels, see p.320.

bucked the trend by building his home in brownstone; quite fortuitous, as after the 1906 earthquake and fire only his house, and the uncompleted *Fairmont Hotel*, were left standing here.

Nob Hill

Flood's mansion, constructed in 1886 at the cost of a cool $1 million, remains at the corner of California and Mason streets. Note the hand-wrought brass fence, worth nearly a million itself today, for which Flood employed a full-time polisher. The building is now the private **Pacific Union Club**, a retreat for the rich, closed to the public. Across the street, at 950 Mason St, the other survivor of the 1906 fire has been restored to its former opulence. The **Fairmont Hotel**, setting for the 1980s television series *Hotel*, has a great rooftop garden behind the lobby from which you can watch the cable cars clank up Powell Street directly below; downstairs is perhaps the the city's most unique locale for a cocktail, the *Tonga Room* (see p.276). Ride the glass elevator at the back of the hotel's modern wing for an inspiring view of San Francisco. Across California Street, you'll find another jaw-dropping view and even more startling prices at San Francisco's most famous vista-bar, *The Top of the Mark* in the *Mark Hopkins Hotel*, where Tony Bennett supposedly found his inspiration for *I Left My Heart in San Francisco*.

One block west on California stands one of the biggest hunks of sham-Gothic architecture in the US, the Episcopal **Grace Cathedral** (Sun–Fri 7am–6pm, Sat 8am–6pm; free tours Mon–Fri 1–3pm, Sat 11.30am–1.30pm, Sun 12.30–2pm.) The block the cathedral stands on was originally occupied by the homes of the Crocker family, who donated the site to the Episcopal Church after losing their dwellings in the 1906 fire. Construction on the building, which was modeled on Notre Dame, began soon after, though most of it was finished with reinforced concrete in the early 1960s. Detractors point to its rushed inception, compared to the centuries-long construction of usual cathedrals, as proof that the rich think they can buy salvation. The entrance, adorned with faithful replicas of the fifteenth-century Ghiberti doors of the Florence Baptistry are worth a look, as is the allegorical stained glass around the cathedral walls. The labyrinth floor tapestry near the entrance duplicates the sacred design at Chartres Cathedral. Another cloister maze is outside, intended as a place for quiet contemplation. Just to the right of the main entrance is the AIDS Interfaith Chapel, with an altarpiece by the late artist Keith Haring. The best time to visit is on Sunday at 11am, when the choral service fills the chapel with sound powerful enough to move the unGodly.

Across from Grace Cathedral, the prim grounds of **Huntington Park** seem more suitable for a wine picnic than any other activity. At the nearby intersection of Mason and Washington streets, the **Cable Car Museum and Powerhouse**, at 1201 Mason St (daily 10am–5pm; free), gives testament to the development of this largely outdated mode of transportation. The system's entire history and inner workings are uniquely displayed here.

For more on the cable cars, see box, p.58.

Chapter 4

The northern waterfront and Pacific Heights

San Francisco's northern waterfront gathers on its banks everything from the tacky to the refined, often changing without warning. Standing sentry at the city's northeastern shore are the masts and bunting that identify San Francisco's number-one crowd-puller, Fisherman's Wharf. Each year, millions of visitors plow through its overpriced commercial gimmickry for a glimpse of what remains of a nearly obsolete fishing industry. As you move west from the wharf, things improve dramatically. Aquatic Park is a small beach that draws a few hardy bathers, though it's better known as the home of the fine Maritime Museum. A great, paved path leads from here along the coastal cliffs to Fort Mason – an old military installation that was rescued from the clutches of development and now has an impressive grouping of small museums, workshops, theaters, and an excellent youth hostel. Continuing west, the waterfront becomes a focus for the fancy yacht clubs that make up the northern tip of the Marina district; at the neighborhood's westernmost point rises the distinctive Palace of Fine Arts. To the Marina's south are the city's finest collection of designer fashion shops, boutiques and Victorian neighborhoods in the boroughs of Pacific Heights and Cow Hollow.

If you're a keen walker, you may want to stroll the extra mile from the Marina along the waterfront's parkland of Marina Green and Crissy Field, the restored edges of the **Presidio**. A former army base turned over to public use, it is a good example of San Francisco's ability to combine beauty with utility – its 1500 acres of hand-planted trees harbor walking trails, cycling routes, and picnic spots with panoramic views. Better still, the many eucalyptus groves provide an inspiring approach to the orange spires of the city's most famous landmark, the **Golden Gate Bridge**.

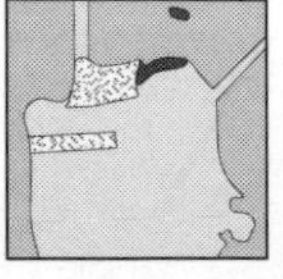

Fisherman's Wharf, Alcatraz, and the northern waterfront

San Francisco's neighborhoods don't often go out of their way to court tourists, but **FISHERMAN'S WHARF**, along with the adjoining waterfront district, is a major exception. An inventive use of statistics allows the area to proclaim itself the most visited attraction in the entire country; in fact, this overcrowded ensemble of waterfront kitsch and fast-food stands make for a rather misleading introduction to the city. Unless you have squirming kids in need of a cotton-candy fix, the best thing you can do with Fisherman's Wharf is skip it all together, and head for the parkland around Fort Mason and the Marina, a far more agreeable segment of waterfront.

Fisherman's Wharf, Alcatraz, and the northern waterfront

Hard as it might be to believe now, Fisherman's Wharf was once a serious fishing port. The few fishermen that can afford the exorbitant mooring charges these days are usually finished by early morning and get out before the tourists arrive. You can still find some decent **seafood** here at some of the better restaurants, but worthwhile sights or remnants of the fishing trade are few and far between.

Restaurants in the Fisherman's Wharf area are reviewed from p.247 onward.

The most endearing sight at the wharf is a large colony of boisterous sea lions (no feeding allowed) that have taken over a number of floating platforms between piers 39 and 41. Though no one seems able to explain why, these wild animals have made the wharf their home for over eight years and, protected by the Marine Mammal Act, are free to come and go as they please. To see more aquatic life, check out **Underwater World**, at Pier 39 (daily 9am–9pm; $12.95 adults, $6.50 kids; ☎415/623-5300), which puts you on a moving walkway and scoots you through a giant aquarium in a 400ft acrylic viewing tunnel. The experience is surprisingly informative, thanks largely to the audio tour included in admission price which manages, mysteriously, to stay pretty well in synch with the fishes' movements.

Dotting the wharf are plenty of **street performers** eager to take in some of your dough as well, the most unique of which is **Bush Man**, who lurks camouflaged behind a lightpole near Pier 43, from which he leaps out to startle passersby; enough seem to find this amusing to drop a steady stream of change into his bucket.

The wharf thrives on souvenir sales, and one of the more tasteful malls in which to purchase them is **The Cannery** on Jefferson Street at Leavenworth, an old fruit-packing factory that was part of a c.1900 industrial wharf. It's since been converted into three floors of shops and restaurants centered around a shady courtyard. Nearby **Ghirardelli Square**, at 900 N Point St, marks the western edge of the Wharf, a boutiquey mall that is a far cry from its days as a chocolate factory, though its handsome redbrick facade and red-neon sign remain a landmark. Slightly more upmarket than the Cannery, its careful refurbishment took six years, though its gift and clothing shops are certainly nothing special – even if the **Ghirardelli Chocolate Manufactory** on the ground floor of the clock tower building still packs people in. The boats and storage sheds around Pier 45's **Fish Alley** (officially Tonquin St), across from the foot of Leavenworth, give a glimpse backstage at a world few people care to

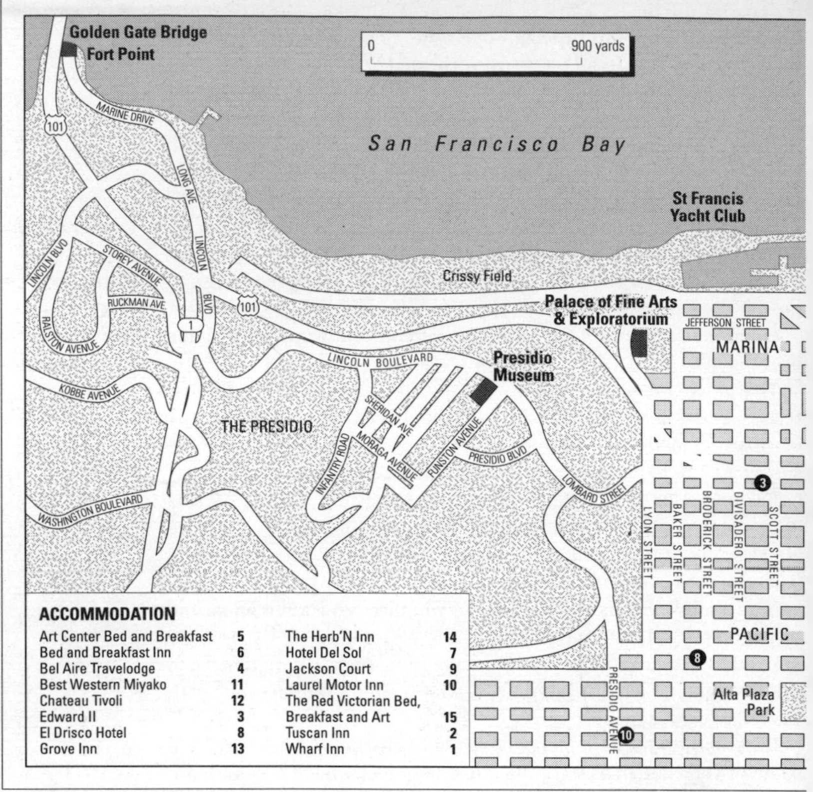

get more than a quick whiff of. On the pier's east side is the **USS Pampanito** (daily 9am–8pm; $5), a submarine that sank five Japanese ships during World War II. Though hardly a must, sub and ship lovers will find it worth a quick tour.

Details of bay cruises can be found on p.183.

Bay cruises depart from piers 39, 41, and 431/2 several times a day. Provided the fogs aren't too heavy, they give good city views, and passing under the Golden Gate Bridge from the water is an awesome experience. Keep in mind that the bay can be very cold and very choppy, so dress accordingly and expect to get splashed.

Alcatraz

Visible from the waterfront, the rocky little islet of **Alcatraz** – commonly referred to as "The Rock" – rising out of San Francisco Bay was once home only to a few pelicans and odd gannet (*alcatraz* in Spanish). In the late nineteenth century, the island became a military fortress, and in 1934 it was converted into America's most dreaded

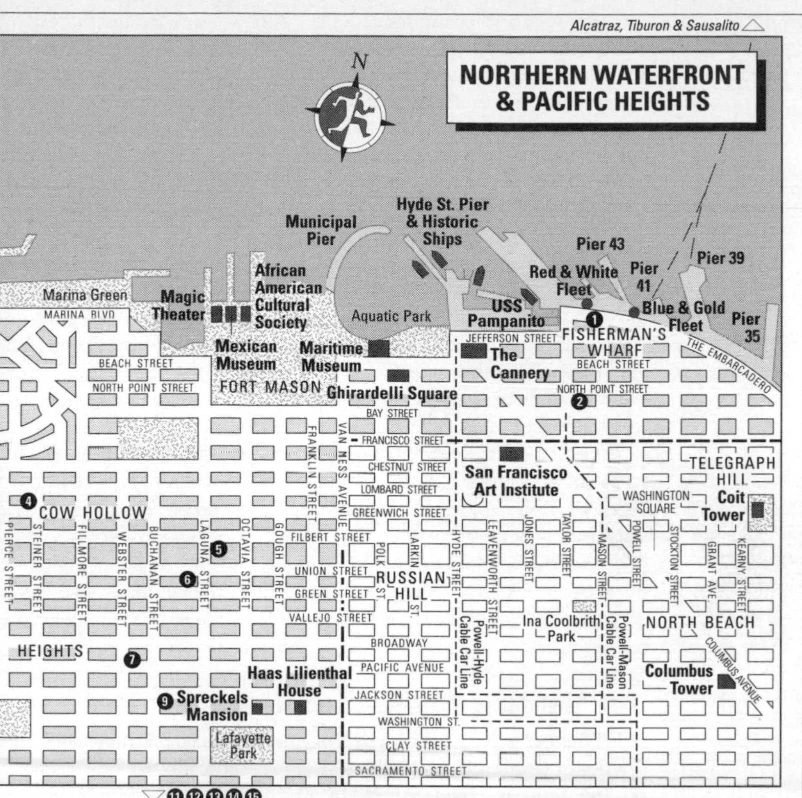

high-security prison. Surrounded by freezing, impassable water, it was an ideal place for a jail, and safely kept some of America's most wanted criminals behind bars – Al Capone and Machine Gun Kelly were just two of the villains imprisoned here. If upon visiting the conditions don't seem quite as inhuman as presented in Hollywood films, the tiny, lonely cells with their heavy, clanging doors still must have taken their toll on prisoners, especially considering the jail's proximity to the vibrant city just across the waters. But escape from the island really was impossible due to the violent currents churning constantly in the icy bay. In all, nine men managed to get off "The Rock," but there is no evidence that they made it to the mainland.

For all its usefulness as a jail, the island turned out to be a fiscal disaster. After years of generating massive running costs, not to mention whipping up a storm of public protest for its role as a prison for petty criminals, it closed in 1963. The remaining prisoners were distributed among decidedly less horrific detention centers, and the island remained abandoned until 1969, when a group of Native Americans staged an occupation as part of a peaceful attempt to claim the island for their people – citing treaties which designated all federal land not in use as automatically reverting to their ownership. The occupation soon fell victim to infighting and intrusion from other countercultural demonstrators. Using all the bureaucratic trickery it could muster, the government finally ousted the floundering movement in 1971, claiming the operative lighthouse qualified it as active.

These days the island's only function is as a tourist attraction, and at least 750,000 visitors each year take the excellent hour-long, self-guided audio **tours** ($4) of the abandoned prison, which include some sharp anecdotal commentary, campy reenactments of prison life (featuring improvised voices of characters like Capone and Kelly) and even the chance to spend a minute (which feels like forever) in a darkened cell.

Check in at the National Park Service's Web site for updated hours and restrictions for visiting the rock, at www.nps.gov/alcatraz/.

Blue and Gold fleet (frequent departures from 9.30am, last boat back at 4.30pm; $12.25 including audio tour, $8.75 without; ☎415/705-5555; *www.blueandgoldfleet.com*) runs **boats** to Alcatraz, leaving from Pier 41. Advance reservations are strongly recommended, especially in peak tourist season; you should book at least two weeks in advance. In summertime, the company also has a day-tour that combines a visit to Alcatraz with a stop at Angel Island ($33.25).

The Maritime Museum and Hyde Street Pier

A bit further west of the wharf, beyond Ghirardelli Square, lies the border of **Golden Gate National Recreation Area** (see box, below). At the foot of Hyde Street, in **Aquatic Park**, is the **Maritime Museum**, (daily 10am–5pm; free), housed in a great Moderne building on Beach Street at the foot of Polk, which is known as the Aquatic Park Casino. This bold, Art Deco, streamlined imitation of a luxury liner, with three curving levels, steel railings, and porthole windows features permanent WPA exhibits inside, tracing the saga of the people and merchant ships that shaped the development of the city back in the Barbary Coast days. Hundreds of artifacts, photographs and documents chart San Francisco's seafaring history, but the most

The Golden Gate National Recreation Area

Established in 1972 to protect much-needed park space for the city, the **Golden Gate National Recreation Area** encompasses almost seventy square miles of waterfront property, including Ocean Beach (see p.130), Lincoln Park (p.124), parts of the Presidio (see p.88), Aquatic Park (see above), and even portions of Marin County (see p.181), across the Golden Gate Bridge. With some twenty million visitors each year, it's one of the most visited national parks in the US.

interesting items are the panoramic photos of the city taken from an identical spot on Nob Hill nearly a century apart, and Hilaire Hiler's 1939 **mural** in the main room, symbolizing the lost continent of Atlantis in 37 individual hallucinogenic panels.

Actual seafaring vessels are on display at the **Hyde Street Pier** (daily 9.30am–5.30pm; $5, free first Tues each month), part of the Maritime Museum's collection. Originally the pier was used to serve the Sausalito ferries before the opening of the Golden Gate Bridge; today several of the ships docked here are open to the public. The *Balclutha* is the most interesting, a tireless vessel of the late 1800s that journeyed round Cape Horn, returning with wine and spirits from London, coal from Wales, and hardware from Antwerp. The boat was put into retirement in the 1930s, to be dragged out and done up for bit parts in such films as *Mutiny on the Bounty* before its current job as a showboat. The *Eureka*, once the largest passenger ferry in the world, is the only surviving large ferryboat in the US with a wooden hull. The rest are a bit more mundane: the *Alma* is a flat-bottomed workhorse that used to carry hay and lumber around the bay; the *C.A. Thayer* is one of two remaining schooners from a fleet of nine hundred that carried lumber from the Pacific Northwest; the *Hercules* tug was used for taking log rafts down the West Coast and towing sailing vessels to sea.

Fort Mason and the Palace of Fine Arts

FORT MASON is half a mile further west along the waterfront, best reached by walking along the start of the Golden Gate Promenade, a scenic stretch of pavement popular with joggers and rollerbladers that continues right past Fort Mason along the northern edges of the Marina and the Presidio.

Originally a Civil War defense installation dating from the late 1700s, it was used by Spanish soldiers from the Presidio in 1797, and came under the auspices of the US Army in 1850, but failure to occupy the land immediately led squatters to build homes here. The squatters took thirteen years to evict, in a gradual program of building, but the Fort sheltered the homeless once again as a refugee center after the 1906 earthquake and fire. It saw its greatest action during World War II, when 1.6 million soldiers passed through on their way to the Pacific War Zone, and again in the early 1950s during the Korean War, when it was a logistical support center. Eventually Fort Mason was turned over to public use in the 1970s through the efforts of congressman and environmentalist Philip Burton, who blocked plans to turn over the land to private speculation.

Its old shed-like buildings, collectively known as **Fort Mason Center**, are occupied by around fifty nonprofit groups, several theaters, two galleries, four museums, a youth hostel, and *Greens*, an elegant vegetarian restaurant with the best views from any table in the city – giant windows look over the masts of the marina to the Golden Gate Bridge (see review p.248). The centerpiece of the complex's museums is the **Museum of Craft and Folk Art** (Tues–Fri & Sun 11am–5pm, Sat 10am–5pm; $3), with its expansive array of exhibits from around the world. Displays at the **Museo Italo-Americano** (Wed–Sun noon–5pm; $3) relate to the culture and history of the Italian community in the US; the rather better **Mexican Museum** (Wed–Fri noon–5pm, Sat & Sun 11am–5pm; $4), while awaiting construction of a new building South of Market, still exhibits its large collection of funky folk art and representational works. The **San Francisco African-American Historical and Cultural Society** (Wed–Sun noon–5pm; $2), meanwhile, commemorates local black leaders and historical figures.

Fort Mason's museums are all free on the first Wed of the month when they are open till 7pm.

San Francisco's most theatrical piece of architecture lies a few hundred yards further west at Marina Boulevard and Baker Street. **The Palace of Fine Arts** is not the museum its name suggests, but a huge, freely interpreted classical ruin by Bernard Maybeck, originally built of wood and plaster for the Panama Pacific International Exhibition in 1915 – held to celebrate the rebirth of the city after the 1906 catastrophe. The weeping figures on the colonnade, by sculptor Ulric Ellerhusen, are said to represent the melancholy of life without art. These lachrymose ladies – conceived along with the rest of the ornate building out of great optimism for post-earthquake San Francisco – were saved from immediate demolition after the exhibition by sentimental San Franciscans. The structure crumbled with dignity until the late 1950s when a wealthy resident put up the money for its restoration. It's the sole survivor of many such triumphal structures built for the Exhibition, which stretched from here all along the waterfront to Fort Mason. Surrounded by Monterey cypresses, a swan-filled lagoon and other picturesque touches of urban civility, it makes for the best picnic spot in the neighborhood.

For information on whale-watching trips from Fort Mason to Point Reyes, see p.196.

Next door, the best kids' museum in San Francisco, the **Exploratorium** (summer daily 10am–6pm, Wed until 9pm; rest of year Tues–Sun 10am–5pm, Wed until 9pm; $9 adults, free first Wed of the month; ☎415/561-0362 for Tactile Dome reservations), has over 650 hands-on exhibits demonstrating scientific principles of electricity, sound waves, lasers, and more. Its traveling flea circuses, showcases of frogs, and giant, completely dark labyrinth called the "Tactile Dome," explored on hands and knees (reservations required) should keep children of all ages enthralled for hours.

The Marina

The area situated between Fort Mason and the Palace of Fine Arts, the **MARINA** district, is one of the city's greenest districts, enjoying a prime waterfront location and lots of open space; its swanky yacht clubs, jogger-laden paths, and parks sprinkled with kite-flyers testify to the presence of the young, image-conscious professionals who call it home. Ironically, though it was built specifically to celebrate the rebirth of the city after the massive earthquake of 1906, the Marina was the worst casualty of the earthquake in 1989 – tremors tore through fragile landfill and a good number of homes collapsed into a smoldering heap. Then-Mayor Alioto ordered that residents could re-enter their homes for only fifteen minutes to grab their belongings before they were razed forever; he lost the district, and his mayorship, in the following election. Rebuilding was immediate, however, and the only reminder of the destruction is how new many of the current structures are.

Before the 1915 Panama-Pacific International Exhibition, the Marina didn't exist at all. On the bay north of Pacific Heights, a sea wall was erected parallel to the shoreline, and the marshland in between was filled with sand pumped up from the bottom of the ocean. Dredging left enough deep water for the creation of the **St Francis** and **Golden Gate Yacht Clubs**, which occupy prestigious spots at the foot of Baker Street. Slightly to the east is **Marina Green**, a large stretch of turf frequented for the most part by fitness fanatics. For less strenuous exercise, walk the **Golden Gate Promenade** that runs parallel to Marina Boulevard, continuing a couple of miles further before reaching the eponymous bridge. A massive landscaping project is now underway to reseed **Crissy Field**, the long swath of land and tidal marsh that reaches from Marina Green to the bridge.

The neighborhood's commercial center runs along **Chestnut Street** near Fillmore. The street has a reputation as a haven for swinging singles, and the local watering holes are known as "high intensity breeder bars." Even the local Safeway has been dubbed "The Body Shop" because of the inordinate amount of cruising that goes on in the aisles.

For bars situated in the Marina District, see p.277.

Cow Hollow

Originally a small valley of pastures and dairies in the post-Gold Rush years, **COW HOLLOW** takes its name from the days when cows rather than shoppers grazed the land between Russian Hill and the Presidio, and women would bring their loads to one of the only sources of freshwater in town which came to be known as Washerwoman's Lagoon. Problems with open sewage, and complaints from neighbors up on prestigious Pacific Heights about the smell of the cows saw the area transformed in the 1950s, when enterprising merchants decided its old clapboard dwellings along **Union Street** had possibilities. The area's gorgeous old Victorian houses have since been refitted, especially around Filbert and Green streets, and the stretch of Union between Van Ness and Divisadero now holds one of the city's densest concentrations of boutiques and cafés. Shopping is, indeed, what the neighborhood is best for, and numerous upscale types converge here to look for the perfect dress, lingerie or cabinet handle.

For complete listings of Cow Hollow's shops, see Chapter 18, "Shops and galleries."

Though there's little here in the way of actual sights, the historic **Octagon House Museum** on the corner of Union and Gough streets (☎415/441-7512; donation) is worth a peek if you happen to be there during its very limited hours of operation; tours of the home's Colonial- and Federal-period furniture, porcelain, and portraits are given on the second Sunday and second and fourth Thursdays of the month, from noon to 3pm (closed January). Built in 1861, at a time when it was believed that increased exposure to sunlight benefited one's health, the house remains in excellent condition. Look for the display of signatures from 54 of the 56 men who signed the Declaration of Independence. Next door, leafy **Allyne Park** feels more like someone's backyard than a public space, but its redwood trees and comfy benches are an idyllic place to rest. The last of the district's original thirty farmhouses and barns stands at **2040 Union**; today it houses a collection of rather pricey clothing and houseware shops. The western border of the neighborhood is **Fillmore Street**, where Allen Ginsberg first read *Howl* at **no. 3119** when the address was a gallery.

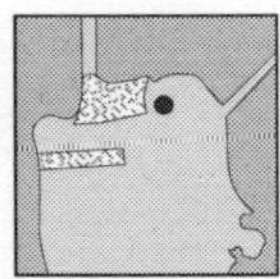

Pacific Heights

Looming above Cow Hollow on one side and Japantown on the other, wealthy **PACIFIC HEIGHTS** is home to some of the city's most monumental Victorian piles and stone mansions – a millionaires' ghetto, beautifully poised around two windswept parks. A local joke has it that when the bright young things of the Marina grow up and have kids, they climb the hill to Pacific Heights and look down on all the fun they used to have. Even when these hills were bare back in the 1860s, their panoramic views of the ocean earmarked them as fashionable territory as soon as the gradient-conquering cable cars linked them with downtown. The lavishly proportioned mansions that teeter precipitously atop these hills today are the chosen domains of stockbrokers, business magnates, and the odd best-selling novelist, like Erle Stanley Gardner, the creator of Perry Mason, who set up his one-man fiction factory here, producing 82 novels that sold some three hundred million copies.

The neighborhood is neatly divided by Fillmore Street: to the west are the large dwellings that earned the neighborhood its reputation; to the east, swanky Art Deco apartment buildings that do little to damage it. Known as the **Upper Fillmore**, the stretch of Fillmore Street above California Street is where locals go to shop, dine, and otherwise spend their cash.

West of Fillmore Street, lower Pacific Heights is centered on restful **Alta Plaza Park**, at Clay and Steiner Streets, where local dog-walkers earn their keep by exercising pampered pooches. You can enjoy good views of St Mary's Cathedral and Civic Center from its crest or play a game of tennis on the upper courts. Barbra Streisand fans will recognize the park as the site of the famous scene in *What's Up Doc?*, in which she drives the car down the steps on the south side. Look closely and you'll see the cracks left in the steps after the scene was shot here. North of the park, the territory becomes solidly residential, home to well-tended gardens and immaculate houses. West, at the intersection of Broadway and Lyon, a set of steps leads down a steep incline, passing several grandiose homes and offering a magnificent view of the Palace of Fine Arts and the Bay.

South of Alta Plaza park, at the furthest reaches of Pacific Heights, lies San Francisco's most beautiful and overlooked church, **St Dominic's**, at the nondescript intersection of Bush and Steiner streets. Though established in the mid-nineteenth century, the current structure – a glorious mixture of styles firmly grounded in English Gothic with a striking four-spire tower and flying buttresses running along either side – wasn't begun until 1923 and was only completed in 1974. Badly damaged during the 1989 earthquake, the structure was renovated and retrofitted to prevent further damage. Inside resides a treasure trove of original European sacred art: the

Victorians

Constructed from redwood culled from the Marin Headlands across the Golden Gate, San Francisco's Victorian houses enjoyed their greatest popularity in the late 1800s, when they were preferred by homeowners who could afford to use "signature details," such as turrets, towers, gables, and anything else that could be tacked onto a home to differentiate it from those of the neighbors. But the earthquake and fire of 1906 burned most of the grandest exmaples (especially a heavy concentration on Nob Hill) to the ground, and the axe-stripped hillsides of Marin County didn't have enough building material left to replace them. Besides, a post-1906 trend made such ornamentation and embellishment unfashionable, ushering in an era of muted stone and stucco.

More recently, the nostalgia of wealthy young homebuyers has resurrected the Victorians' popularity. A preservation effort undertaken in 1976 by the National Endowment for the Arts found 13,487 Victorians in the city, and restoration work to save crumbling edifices in the Haight-Ashbury, Western Addition, Bernal Heights, Noe Valley, and other southern neighborhoods ensued. Today, Victorian restoration is a lucrative profession – a "saved" home rarely sells less for $500,000, no matter how seedy the neighborhood it lies in.

There are three main styles of Victorians to look out for. The **Italianate**, a tall, narrow rowhouse popular in the 1870s, is distinguished by a slanted bay window jutting from the front; examples can be seen at 2115–2125 Bush St. The **San Francisco Stick**, popular in the 1880s, is like the Italianate but has a false front capped by a gable or "French cap" and is often crowded with elaborate millwork; there's a fine cluster at 1801 Laguna St. Perhaps the best-known style of Victorian is the **Queen Anne**, characterized by its steep gables, plaster garlands, arches, and art-glass windows; it was the favorite style of the 1890s. A fine example at 1701 Franklin St dates from 1895.

white-oak confessionals, shrines, and secondary altars were hand carved in Oberammergau, Germany, while the high altar was carved of botticino marble at Pietrasanta, Italy, and shipped to San Francisco in 76 crates. Carved in Liège, Belgium, the statuary, such as the angels under the rood beam and the statue of the Virgin in the Lady Chapel, is incredibly intricate, as are the stained-glass windows from Paris which line the nave.

East of Fillmore, the windswept, cypress-dotted peak of **Lafayette Park** is a popular local hangout. Facing it to the north are several mansions worth admiring if you're wandering round the neighborhood, among them the squat brownstone at 2150 Washington St, the **Phelan Mansion**, built by former mayor James Phelan, an anti-Asian protectionist who later, as senator, pushed to bring a poet laureateship to California. Not far away, at 2080 Washington St, is the **Spreckels Mansion**, a gaudily decadent white-stone palace and home now to romance pulpist Danielle Steele, who pumped a not-so-small fortune into the structure's restoration and upkeep. Unfortunately, neither of these are open to the public, nor are the set of old Queen Anne Victorians a block away at 2000–2010 Gough St. For that, head another block east to the ornate **Haas-Lilienthal House** at 2007 Franklin St (Wed & Sun noon–3pm; $5), a grand symbol of old wealth, with intricate wooden towers outside, and Tiffany art-glass and stenciled leather paneling inside. A bit south, the stretch of California Street from Franklin west to Fillmore holds more Victorians, notably the Egyptian-flavored one at no. 2026, distinguished by its blue-and-gold trim and bust of King Tut over the entrance.

To the south, the city's newest and most conspicuous Catholic church is **St Mary's Cathedral** (☎415/567-2020) at Gough and Geary. Built in 1971, the cathedral has been the butt of local humor ever since, due to a modernist design that many have likened to a washing machine agitator (hence its nickname, "Our Lady of the Maytag"). Take a look inside at its open, 190-foot vaulted space which rounds delicately inward; the massive organ within is a spectacle in itself, especially when it's played during the wildly popular Christmas Midnight Mass, though bad acoustics don't do it justice.

West of Pacific Heights, Sacramento Street leads into **Laurel Heights**, a smart collection of antique shops and used designer-clothing stores. There's not really much to deter you on your way to the Presidio, but it's a nice enough strip to make for good idle window shopping.

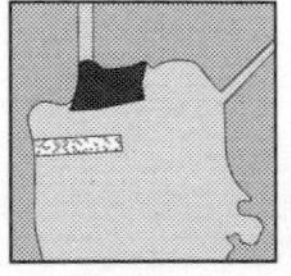

The Presidio

Occupying most of the northwest tip of the San Francisco peninsula, the **PRESIDIO** covers some 1500 acres and is home to 75 miles of forested roads. After a hundred years of sporadic US military use, it became a national park in October 1994, though many of the park's buildings have been leased out to various private interests, and wrangling continues over how to develop the new national park. The Presidio Trust Board favors tearing down much of the abandoned military housing to create open space. Mayor Willie Brown pushed to convert the uninhabited buildings into low-income housing – dwellings he later announced would be put on the market at full value. *Star Wars* creator George Lucas, meanwhile, won tentative approval to build a huge film studio on part of the land, bringing conservationists to court with concerns about the impact such a project would have on the environment. For the moment, the Presidio offers little more than a scenic ride through its eucalyptus-scented highways or a leisurely hike through its numerous trails. Strolling or cycling along part of the **Pacific Coast Trail**, part of the Golden Gate National Recreation Area, is not-to-be-missed for the stunning views across the bay and back to the skyline. Tracing the northern limit of town from the western side of the Golden Gate Bridge through Lincoln Park and all the way to Land's End past Ocean Beach (see p.121), there are plenty of side trails winding down to the waterfront to explore. Plan three or four hours for a leisurely one-way hike.

For the best places in the city to rent bicycles and skates for use in the Presidio and the city's other outdoor spaces, see p.320.

In the 1770s, the Presidio was founded as a frontier station for the Spanish Empire, which garrisoned the distant peninsula to forestall British and Russian claims on the San Francisco Bay. In 1822, it became the northernmost outpost of the new Mexican republic, who abandoned it in 1835 to move north to Sonoma. By 1846, it was occupied by the American armed forces, who billeted their soldiers here for the Modoc War in 1870 and their campaigns against the Apaches in the southwest. The US Army started to develop the inherited adobe structures, but the Presidio didn't take on its present appearance until the 1880s, when an environmentally minded major initiated a program of forestation that changed it from a windswept, sandy piece of coastline into a dense thicket. Afterward it served mainly as a medical and administrative army base; the only time its harbor defenses were activated was for a brief period during World War II. Today, almost thirty acres of the Presidio is given over to the **San Francisco National Military Cemetery** – a sobering sight and, surprisingly, the only graveyard in San Francisco.

The main entrance to the Presidio is by way of Lombard Street, west of Pacific Heights and the Marina, where a huge gate bearing the figures of Liberty and Victory leads to the main quadrangle of buildings that once functioned as a military headquarters. There's a small chapel and adobe officers' mess, but the only thing you can actually visit is the **Presidio Museum**, on Lincoln Boulevard and Funston Avenue (Wed–Sun noon–4pm; free), in the original hospital building. In addition to bits on military history, detailed models and maps trace how San Francisco's appearance has changed over the centuries, showing which parts of the city were wiped out by the

1906 earthquake. Further along, the **Presidio Visitor Center**, in Building 102 on the west side of Montgomery Street (daily 9am–5pm; ☎415/561-4314), is a good source of information if you wish to explore the area further; pick up the free *ParkNews* here for details on the numerous walks, tours and activities offered in the Golden Gate National Recreation Area year-round.

The Presidio is at its most dramatic at the **Fort Point National Historic Site** at the head of Marine Drive (Wed–Sun 10am–5pm; free), a brick fortress seawall built in the 1850s to guard the bay. You may recognize it as the site of Kim Novak's suicide attempt in Alfred Hitchcock's *Vertigo*. From here, where the surf crashes and the Pacific stretches interminably, you get a good sense of the Presidio as the westernmost frontier of the nation. It was originally to have been demolished to make way for the Golden Gate Bridge, but the redesign of the southern approach left it intact, and the bridge high above adds to the theatricality. Supposedly, the water here makes for one of the best local surfing spots, provided you don't mind risking your life in the violent currents and undertow.

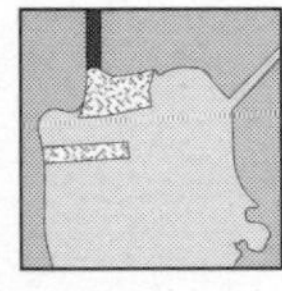

The Golden Gate Bridge

The orange towers of the **Golden Gate Bridge** – arguably the most beautiful, certainly the most photographed bridge in the world – are visible from almost every point of elevation in San Francisco. The only cleft in northern California's 600-mile continental wall, for years this mile-wide strait was considered unbridgeable. As much an architectural as an engineering feat, the Golden Gate took only 52 months to design and build, and was opened in 1937. Designed by Joseph Strauss, it was the first really massive suspension bridge, with a span of 4200ft, and until 1959 ranked as the world's longest. If the towers don't seem to be the same distance from the center of the bridge, that's because they're not. In order to save Fort Point, Strauss designed the southern anchoring tower to be planted far from shore. The bridge connects the city at its northwesterly point on the peninsula to Marin County and Northern California, rendering the hitherto essential ferry crossing redundant, and was designed to withstand winds of up to a hundred miles an hour and to swing as much as 27ft. Handsome on a clear day, the bridge takes on an eerie quality when the thick white fogs pour in and hide it almost completely.

Cyclists heading south across the bridge are always routed along the east side, while cyclists heading north must take the west side from Mon–Fri, and the east side on weekends.

You can either drive, bike, or walk across. To bike is the most thrilling of the options as you teeter along under the bridge's towers, but the half-hour walk across it really gives you time to take in its enormous size and absorb the views of the city behind you and the headlands of Northern California straight ahead. Pause at the midway point and consider the seven or so suicides a month who choose this spot, 260ft up, as their jumping-off spot. Monitors of such events speculate that victims always face the city before they leap, which may be due to the fact that the western walkway is closed to pedestrians. In 1995, when the suicide toll from the bridge had reached almost 1000, police kept the figures quiet to avoid a rush of would-be suicides going for the dubious distinction of being the thousandth person to leap.

Chapter 5

SoMa, the Tenderloin, and Civic Center

While much of San Francisco is depicted as a quaint residential utopia at the edge of the sea, the SoMa, Tenderloin, and Civic Center areas to the west and south of downtown are about as urban as neighborhoods come, with a conspicuous lack of greenery and plenty of well-worn pavement.

After languishing for decades as a blighted urban wasteland, SoMa has taken a once unimaginable upswing in recent years, thanks in part to Internet startup companies attracted to the district's low rents. Groundbreaking art and music communities were the first to take advantage of the deal, but, now, the increased prosperity of the tech industry threatens to drive them out. For the moment, the majority of the neighborhood still retains its gritty appearance, and much of the district booms every night with the muffled reverberations of underground dance clubs, but nearer to the downtown, just south of Market Street, a new **museum and entertainment complex** draws daytime visitors, as does the new **baseball stadium** along the waterfront to the east.

The adjoining districts of the Tenderloin and Civic Center reveal harsher realities, with heavy drug traffic and prostitution in evidence along with a shocking number of homeless people wandering about; their almost constant presence in front of City Hall is an ironic reminder of governmental failure to resolve the city's major shortage of affordable housing. Thus far, sporadic attempts to improve the situation have ranged from well-meaning misses to bound-to-fail cosmetic gestures. While the refurbished City Hall and the adjoining **Opera** and **Symphony** buildings are popular attractions, most visitors will only venture near them when searching for cheap accommodation or hurrying to a performance.

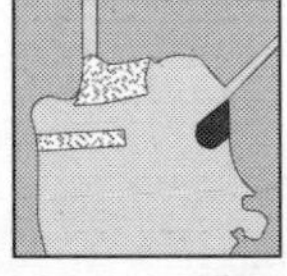

SoMa (South of Market)

SoMa, the distinctly urban district South of Market Street, stretches diagonally from the Mission in the southwest to the waterfront in the

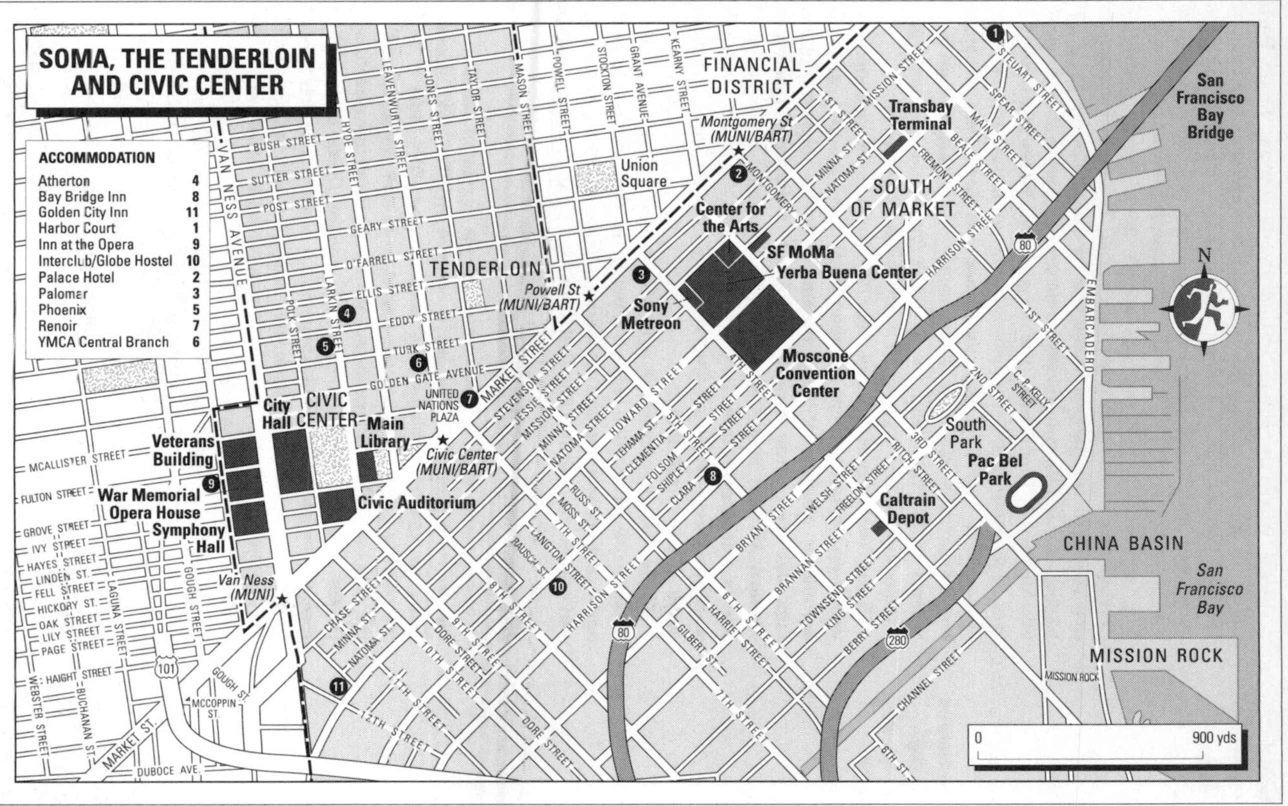

SOMA, THE TENDERLOIN AND CIVIC CENTER
ACCOMMODATION
Atherton 4
Bay Bridge Inn 8
Golden City Inn 11
Harbor Court 1
Inn at the Opera 9
Interclub/Globe Hostel 10
Palace Hotel 2
Palomar 3
Phoenix 5
Renoir 7
YMCA Central Branch 6
San Francisco Bay Bridge
San Francisco Bay
CHINA BASIN
MISSION ROCK
EMBARCADERO
FINANCIAL DISTRICT
SOUTH OF MARKET
TENDERLOIN
CIVIC CENTER
Transbay Terminal
Union Square
Center for the Arts
SF MoMa
Yerba Buena Center
Moscone Convention Center
Sony Metreon
South Park
Pac Bel Park
Caltrain Depot
Main Library
Civic Auditorium
City Hall
Veterans Building
War Memorial Opera House
Symphony Hall
Montgomery St (MUNI/BART)
Powell St (MUNI/BART)
Civic Center (MUNI/BART)
Van Ness (MUNI)
UNITED NATIONS PLAZA
N
0
900 yds

northeast, where the streets around **Rincon Hill** and **South Park** were once home to wealthy business leaders working in the Financial District. Further inland was concentrated the large working-class community into which **Jack London** (author of *Call of the Wild*) was born. The advent of the cable car changed the neighborhood's face, and by 1900, it was increasingly given over to industrial development, creating an enduring imprint. The poorer community that remained was largely driven out by fires following the 1906 earthquake, and Rincon Hill was eventually cleared in 1930 to make way for the new **Bay Bridge**. The decades after World War II saw the area converted almost exclusively to an industrial and shipping district, and oversized gray warehouse complexes still dominate most of the landscape today. Nevertheless, odd pockets remain from SoMa's glory days, and the latest wave of development and regeneration makes it a popular, activity-filled destination.

For more on the Bay Bridge, see p.136.

Today, SoMa's northern end, near downtown, is the location of an impressive entertainment complex that has sprouted suddenly around the refurbished **Yerba Buena Gardens** – anchored by the high and low culture appeals of the **San Francisco Museum of Modern Art** and Sony's **Metreon** mall. By night, the office-lined streets near Market Street are virtually deserted – unlike the district's southern streets, which are filled with bars and clubs that don't really come alive until nightfall.

To the east, the waterfront is looking brighter these days, thanks in part to the destruction of the freeway in the 1989 earthquake, with spiffy new upscale housing complexes blooming at the water's edge and a brand new bayside **Pac Bell Park** for the San Francisco Giants.

Rincon Center and around

A block inland from the waterfront, at the corner of Mission and Steuart, is the **Rincon Center**, at 101 Spear St, an office and residential court highlighted by its impressive landmark post office. Built in 1939, the building's interior boasts the largest work ever commissioned by the WPA – a series of 27 murals on California's history by expat Russian painter Anton Refreiger, inspired by populist Diego Rivera. More recently, the interior of the building became home to a vaguely upscale food court popular at lunchtime with those who work in the surrounding buildings. Nearby, the little-known **Jewish Museum of San Francisco** (Mon–Wed & Sun noon–5pm, Thurs noon–8pm; $5, free first Mon of month; ☎415/543-8880), is tucked discreetly into a nondescript building at 121 Steuart St and has an impressive collection of contemporary work by Jewish artists along with exhibits on Jewish-American heritage. Around the corner, dwarfed by the much larger buildings that surround it, the **California Historical Society**, at 678 Mission St near Second Avenue (Tues–Sat 11am–5pm; $2), offers a collection of ephemera from the state's history, including maps, newspapers, and an excellent collection of photographs.

Walking west from the Rincon Center along Mission, you'll pass the unsightly **Transbay Terminal**, focus of much commuter activity as the departure and arrival point for Greyhound and AC Transit buses. At Mission's intersection with New Montgomery Street, the **Pacific Telephone Building**, a product of architecture's golden age in the 1920s, stands like a gently tapered, subtly shadowed mountain detailed in terra-cotta.

SoMa (South of Market)

For information on transportation from the Transbay Terminal, see p.29.

At the corner of Market and New Montgomery in the heart of downtown, the **Palace Hotel** (now owned by Sheraton) was built in 1875 by the banker William Ralston during the height of the city's ascension as the west coast's financial center. The Rococo structure served as a landmark for the city's new guilded gentry. Unfortunately the building was severely burned in 1906 and after numerous remodelings, much of its former splendor has been diminished, the main exception being the ornate Garden Court dining room, where you can have high tea under the original 1875 Austrian Crystal chandeliers suspended from the glass ceiling, which is a remnant of the post-earthquake remodeling of the hotel in 1909. In a subsequent remodeling in 1989, the 72,000 panes of glass were dismantled, cleaned, and retouched to the tune of $7 million.

San Francisco Museum of Modern Art and around

The brightest recent arrival to SoMa, and one that has brought much respectability to an otherwise rather provincial local art scene, has been the **SF Museum of Modern Art** at 151 Third St (Fri–Tues 11am–6pm, Thurs 11am–9pm, closed Wed; $9, $4.50 Thurs 6–9pm, free the first Tues of the month; ☎415/357-4000). Designed by Swiss architect Mario Botta, the structure cost a reported $62 million, and now competes with the Getty and MoCA in Los Angeles to be the West Coast's premier exhibition space, playing host to touring shows from New York and Europe while struggling to assemble a collection worthy of its housing. In the meantime, the building itself steals the show: a huge central skylight floods the space with light, while the upper galleries are connected by a vertigo-inducing metal catwalk that challenges the definition of "adventurous" art.

The museum's top floor permanent collection focuses on painters in the **California school**, such as Richard Diebenkorn, and the works of Mexican painters Frida Kahlo and Diego Rivera, both of whom were major presences in the city. There is also a notable collection of **abstract expressionist** works by Mark Rothko, Jackson Pollock, Robert Rauschenberg, Clyfford Still and Philip Guston, along with an extensive collection of works by German artists Sigmar Polke and Anselm Keifer. There is also a smattering of Impressionism, cubism and surrealism by big names like Matisse, Picasso, and Dali, though with most significant canvases by these artists housed in other museums, the SF MoMA has wisely turned its spotlight on its other holdings. The photography department is particularly strong, with numerous prints by early innovators such as Cartier-Bresson, Alfred Steiglitz, and Man Ray in the permanent collection, along with touring shows by the likes of Roy deCarava and Germaine Krull. But what has really distinguished the SF MoMA from its contemporaries is a strong interest in architecture, design, and **new media** works; it's in these areas that you'll generally find the museum's most interesting temporary exhibitions, often drawing attention to lesser-known names such as Archigram and Bill Viola.

Across the street from the SF MoMA is the **Yerba Buena Center for Art**, 701 Mission St at Third (Tues–Sun from 11am to 6pm; $5, free the first Thurs of the month; ☎415/978-2787), a smaller, funkier companion to the main museum. Spread out along the periphery of the Yerba Buena Gardens, the Center for Art is a loosely connected complex of low-lying buildings, including a gallery space and large theater. Like the museum, the gallery frequently hosts touring exhibitions from other cities, but its smaller confines are also home to more intimate exhibitions of local artists' work, particularly during the sporadically scheduled Bay Area Now exhibition. The small second floor screening room shows works by local experimental filmmakers, as well as themed programs of cult and underground films.

The neighboring **Yerba Buena Gardens** are a postage stamp-sized patch of green, covered each midday with lunching office workers. The gardens routinely offer free musical entertainment that can include everything from traditional Chinese music to jazz: a welcome repose after exploring the cavernous downtown streets. Stretching along the park's eastern face is a fifty-foot granite waterfall **memorial** to Martin Luther King, Jr. On the Mission Street of the gardens, **St. Patrick's Church** serves a primarily Filipino congregation and holds a regular series of free classical music concerts at midday on Wednesdays.

If it's your brain you're looking to rest, wander to **the Metreon**, Sony's new urban mall, at the corner of Fourth and Mission. Aesthetically, the place is baffling – something protrudes from virtually every surface to grab your attention. The space is also chock-a-block with big-name retail outlets, such as the first-ever **Microsoft** store. For the kids there is a Where the Wild Things Are play area and a massive **IMAX** theater in the multiplex.

For information on films at the Metreon, see p.296.

Steps away is the new home of the **Ansel Adams Center for Photography** at 655 Mission St (daily 11am–5pm, except holidays, $5); the expanded space showcases a solid collection of the famed local landscape photographer's work in addition to regular exhibitions by a wide range of contemporary photographers. Nearby, carefully hidden on the second floor of 814 Mission St, the **Cartoon Art Museum** (Wed–Fri 11am–5pm, Sat 10am–5pm, Sun 1–5pm; $5) encompasses a tiny space that houses touring exhibitions by such twentieth-century masters as Charles Schulz (*Peanuts*) and French illustrator Moebius; there's also a worthwhile cartoon bookshop in its confines.

A block further south on Folsom Street is the rather sterile **Moscone Convention Center**, named after the assassinated mayor, only worth visiting if you have a trade-show to attend inside. Further south and in towards the bay, **South Park**, between Bryant and Brannan streets, is a leafy sanctuary of a picturesque European-style commons around which trendy shops and cafés occupy the first floors of the last remaining nineteenth-century houses in the neighborhood. The square has, in recent years, become a haven for young multimedia professionals (*Wired*, the industry's main rag, has offices just around the corner at Bryant and Third streets), many of whom take their lunches here. Poke your head down **Jack London Alley** for a glance at the small plaque at the semi-industrial corner of Third Street and Brannan which marks London's **birthplace**.

For information on the devlopment of the tech industry in the Bay Area, see box p.170.

Pac Bell Park, China Basin, and Mission Rock

Pac Bell Park, the San Francisco Giants' new home, is undoubtedly a major improvement over the team's much-maligned old home at Candlestick Park, which is prone to gusts of brutally cold wind. The new stadium, in one of the sunniest parts of town, with an outfield that opens onto the Bay and an extremely short right-field fence – rumored to have been specifically designed to allow team star Barry Bonds to hit home runs more easily – made its debut on opening day of the 2000 season; tickets are a hot commodity, as is parking. In an effort to get fans to leave their cars at home, the city built an extension to Muni along the Embarcadero specifically for the stadium, though with only 5000 on-site parking spaces for 50,000 fans, even mass transit can be overwhelmed for big games. If you want to see the stadium but not the team, twice hourly tours leave Lefty O'Doul Plaza between 10am and 2pm on off days. Tickets cost $10 – more than the price of a cheap seat – and sadly you don't get to see the giant Coke bottle in the outfield salute Giant home runs.

Often obscured by the new development, the spirit of blue-collar, industrial San Francisco still exists around the abandoned docks and old shipyards known as **China Basin** and **Mission Rock** along the eastern edge of SoMa. Not much goes on here now, but the area has an isolated quality suited to desolate walks. The easiest way to reach the area is to follow Third Street south from Market as it curves round to meet the docks at the **switchyards** where the drawbridge crosses China Basin Channel. In the 1930s the docks were the site of deadly clashes between striking longshoremen and the city police, one of the country's largest labor uprisings of the twentieth century; to this day the union maintains a reputation for radicalism. Later, it was here that **Jack Kerouac** worked as a brakeman in the Fifties, at the same time writing the material that was later to appear in *Lonesome Traveler*, detailing scenes of SoMa's skid-row hotels,

SoMa (South of Market)

drunks, and whores. This was also the location of the former port where freight ships used to dock from Asia. Today, the odd ship will sail by, but it's more likely to be the military ships from the Oakland Naval Base cruising the bay than the freighters that used to jam the waterways. A few small boat clubs remain along the waterfront, but most people come on weekends to visit *The Ramp*, a creaky wooden structure on Pier 50 that offers beer and burgers. The site of several distressingly large homeless encampments, the area is generally best avoided after dark.

For more on Jack Kerouac's San Francisco connection, see box on p.70.

Folsom Street

On the western side of SoMa, and not much to look at by day, the strip of **Folsom Street** between Eighth and Eleventh streets comes alive at night – its clubs and restaurants catering to every subculture under the stars. Longtime home to the city's leather community (French postmodern critic Michel Foucault claimed to have a near-spiritual relationship with the place), the leather scene actually maintains a relatively low profile for most of the year, except in September during the **Folsom Street Fair**, an orgy of chaps and public whippings, reputed, remarkably, to be the largest street fair in the state.

For a complete listing of SoMa bars and clubs, see p.277.

The surrounding blocks hide a variety of art spaces and galleries, though your chances of simply stumbling across them are rather slim. If you happen to be here during daytime hours, wander back east to Sixth and Mission streets to look at **Defenestration**, a Quixotic piece of public art involving furniture that has been bolted to the outside of an abandoned building. Just don't linger too long – it's one of the nastier corners in town.

For a list of SoMa galleries, see p.315.

The Tenderloin and Polk Gulch

The **TENDERLOIN**, a small, uninviting area on the north side of Market Street between the Civic Center and Union Square, has long been one of the shabbiest sections of town, overrun with flophouses and homeless vagrants; in fact, one explanation for the district's name is that nineteenth-century police were rewarded with choice cuts of steak for serving a particularly perilous tour of duty here. You should still exercise caution here today, especially at night in the vicinity of Taylor Street around Turk and Eddy, though you probably won't find yourself here unless staying in one of the many budget lodgings. In any case, you should be safe as long as you keep your wits about you and don't mind vagrants asking you for money. On a more positive note, waves of Pakistani and South Asian immigrants have begun transforming the neighborhood while establishing numerous spots for a cheap, flavorful meal.

Glide Memorial Church at 330 Ellis St and Taylor provides a wide range of social services for the neighborhood's downtrodden, includ-

San Francisco's sex industry

San Francisco established itself as a center of sin long before the Mitchell brothers opened shop. During the **Gold Rush era**, thousands of unaccompanied men passed through the city before heading off to the hills in pursuit of sudden wealth; when they returned to town with a bit of gold in their pocket, they often lost it at one of over one hundred houses of ill repute that had taken root in the city. This booming **prostitution** business, often in league with organized gambling halls, actually offered poor women a form of advancement in society; successful madams were able to move with the city's elite. Gaming parlor owner **Belle Cora**, mythologized as the most beautiful woman in the city, was involved with a prominent judge, while the reputed madam **Sarah Althea Hill** sued her longstanding customer, Senator William Sharon. Still, for most it was a miserable existence, and it was in this lawless environment that the women's suffrage movement began to gain force, led in large part by religious activists campaigning against pauperism and vice. By the beginning of the twentieth century the brothels were rapidly shutting their doors, while rebellious women such as Gertrude Stein led a charge into salon society.

Still, San Francisco's reputation as the **sex capital** of America remained ingrained in the popular mythology, and after World War II the city's massage parlors and strip joints thrived again with the sudden presence of numerous GIs who stayed on after being discharged from their service here. Later, after AIDS hit the 1980s, many sex establishments shut down – especially the city's notorious gay bathhouses – only to resurface a decade later in different forms. Today, the city retains a laissez-faire attitude about sex, though a somewhat bizarre zoning law dictates that sex clubs, while legal, may not have private rooms on-site, delighting the city's exhibitionists and voyeurs while frustrating shyer patrons.

San Francisco's matter-of-fact attitude towards sex is most evident at places like the **Lusty Lady** at 1033 Kearny St near Broadway (☎415/391-3991), a strip club that gets political correctness points for being owned and operated by women. Perhaps the best example of how the sex industry has evolved into the 21st century can be found at the **Power Exchange**, at 86 Otis near Mission (☎415/487-9944); touting itself as the largest sex club in the world, this former power station unblinkingly advertises three floors of "playrooms" including an "Electrified Forest," Egyptian and Medieval theme rooms, and plenty of equipment for whippings, floggings, fetish, and more vanilla activities. Less extravagant but equally indicative of San Francisco's sex-positive culture is **Eros** at 2051 Market near Fourteenth Street (☎415/864-3767). This squeaky-clean safe-sex club caters to a gay male clientele, but students of all genders can often participate in the sex workshops and classes held here – some for college credit. Only in San Francisco.

ing a shelter and soup kitchen for the local homeless. Thanks to the forceful personality of Pastor Cecil Williams, a major political figure in the city, the church also conducts a remarkable Sunday service, backed by his rollicking choir. From local resident Sharon Stone to drag queens dressed like her, you never know who will be in the next seat. If you're not stopping by on a Sunday, it's worth stepping inside anyway to see the AIDS Memorial Chapel – the alterpiece triptych was the last work artist Keith Haring completed before his death from the disease.

At the western limits of the Tenderloin, on Polk Street, between O'Farrell and California, lies **POLK GULCH**, a congregating point for the city's transgender community, and a hub for the flesh trade. Several historically famous gay bars line the street, as do young hustlers and prostitutes. The intersection of O'Farrell and Polk is home to a neighborhood landmark of sorts, the **Mitchell Brother's O'Farrell Theater** (11.30am–2am; ☎415/776-6866). The Mitchell boys achieved considerable notoriety in the 1970s when they persuaded a young Ivory Soap model named Marilyn Chambers to star in their porno film *Behind the Green Door*, which they debuted at the Cannes film festival. While the pair slowly slipped back into obscurity over the ensuing decades, they made a tragic return to tabloid fame when Jim Mitchell shot and killed his brother Artie.

For bars situated in the Polk Gulch area, see p.278.

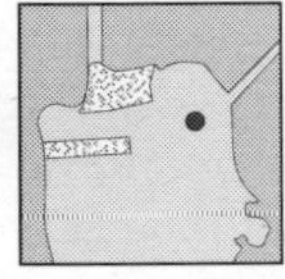

Civic Center

Born out of a grand, celebratory architectural scheme, the **CIVIC CENTER**, a little ways southwest of the Tenderloin, is an impressive layout of majestic federal and municipal Beaux Arts buildings focusing on the grand dome of City Hall, designed by Arthur Brown and completed in 1915, just in time for the Panama Pacific International Exhibition. The complex surrounding City Hall is a watered-down version of planner Daniel Burnham's ambitious schemes for the city, which would have seen grand avenues fanning out across San Francisco, including one extending to the Panhandle of Golden Gate Park. Drawn up with the help of architect Willis Polk, the plans won the wholehearted approval of city leaders, only to be delayed by the massive earthquake and fire of 1906. Political difficulties after the quake delayed the project further, and although Burnham doggedly pursued his vision of a "City Beautiful," the project was only finished after his death. He no doubt would be saddened by the complex today: it's still a fine collection of buildings, but the elegant layout has become the focus of San Francisco's most glaring social problem – the homeless. Periodically, police evict the hundreds of street people who inhabit the nearby plazas, but with housing in perpetually short supply, no long-term solution is in sight. Being San Francisco's center for the performing arts – by night, beautifully lit and swarming with dinner-suited San Franciscans heading in and out of the opera, ballet, and symphony – the problem was not one that could be easily hidden, and although the authorities have since established a number of shelters, the Civic Center, along with the adjacent Tenderloin, remains the most intensely down-and-out area of town.

Using the Civic Center Muni and BART station as your starting point, you'll emerge from underground facing the **United Nations**

Plaza just south of the main quadrangle. Built to commemorate the founding of the UN here in 1945, it is an attractive design with fountain and flags that is generally home to a refugee camp of squatters and skateboarders. From dawn until dusk Wednesdays and Sundays are the exceptions, when the site serves as a **Farmer's Market**, the city's largest and most inexpensive fruit and vegetable market.

Originally housed on the north side of the plaza, the **Main Library** moved into its current location at Grove and Larkin in 1996, amidst both fanfare and controversy. The building's sleek new design, which included a large, light-filled central atrium, didn't include much room for books, and portions of the library's holdings have repeatedly been sold off in order to squeeze everything into the new stacks. At the top floor of the striking structure is the San Francisco History Center, used primarily for research, but with an interesting collection of old prints, maps and photographs. A trip up the stairway will reward you with an elongated sculpture listing the names of prominent local authors. Just one level below, the James C. Hormel Gay and Lesbian Center is the first of its kind in the nation, topped by a dome with a mural depicting leading figures in gay rights and literary movements.

Next door, centered around the collection of former Olympic Committee head Avery Brundage, the **Asian Art Museum** will soon show one of the largest collections of Asian Art in the Western world. After spending the past decade attempting to escape from an earthquake-damaged building in Golden Gate Park, the museum is finally moving into the library's former home at Larkin and McAllister, and is due to open in 2002. Because of space limitations in its previous location, the museum was only able to display a fraction of its holdings at any given time, but the new digs will allow more of its thorough collection of ten thousand paintings, sculptures, ceramics, and textiles from all over Asia to come out of mothballs, including the oldest known Chinese Buddha image, from 338 AD. In the meantime, some temporary exhibits are still on display at the museum's temporary location in Golden Gate Park.

For more information on the Asian Art Museum's temporary home in Golden Gate Park, see p.128.

Dominating the quadrangle at its far end on Polk Street, **City Hall** is arguably the best-looking building in town. Modeled on St Peter's basilica in Rome, this Baroque structure of granite and marble with a grandiose green-copper dome forms the nucleus of the Civic Center. The interior is as grand as its facade, with a large Baroque marble staircase dominating the center, leading up to opulent arches and balustrades, all beneath a gold-inlaid dome. For years the elegant building was buried in scaffolding, but, thankfully, after extensive work to repair the effects of time and weather, not to mention a seemingly never-ending seismic retrofit to make sure it would withstand another earthquake, City Hall's refurbished dome was recently reopened for public viewing. It was here in 1978 that conservative ex-supervisor Dan White got past security guards to assassinate Mayor George Moscone and supervisor Harvey Milk; later, when White was found guilty of manslaughter (not murder), it was the scene of violent demonstrations as gay protesters set fire to police vehicles and stormed the doors of the building – an event that became known as the "White Night Riot."

For more on the assassination of Harvey Milk, see box p.109.

Directly behind City Hall on Van Ness Avenue are San Francisco's cultural mainstays, most elegant of which is the **War Memorial Opera House**. The United Nations Charter was signed here in 1945; today it's home to the San Francisco Opera and Ballet. Reopened in 1997 after extensive earthquake-proofing engineering work, it's a suitably refined structure, its understated grandeur a sharp contrast to the giant modernist fishbowl of the **Louise M Davies Symphony Hall** one block down. Built in 1980, at a cost of almost $35 million, the symphony hall has some fans in the progressive architecture camp, though the general consensus is that it's an aberration of the otherwise tastefully harmonious scheme of the Civic Center. Both buildings enjoy a healthy patronage, and come nightfall the formally dressed arrive by the busload. Sadly, few performances are subsidized, so prices remain generally high.

See p.291 for details of ballet and opera performances.

If your budget doesn't stretch to a night at the opera, you can at least get a sense of its history and success at the **San Francisco Performing Arts Library and Museum**, 399 Grove St (Wed 1–7pm, Thurs–Fri 10am–4pm, Sat noon–4pm; free), between the opera house and symphony hall. Primarily a research center, with the largest collection of performing arts material outside of New York, the museum has more than two million painstakingly collected programs, photographs, posters, books, videos, and press clippings concentrating on music, dance, theater, and opera. Performing-arts fans could spend hours raking through the memorabilia, the highlight of which is the Isadora Duncan collection, focusing on the influential dancer who was born in the city in 1877.

For other galleries and accompanying reviews, see p.315.

Next to the War Memorial Opera House, the **Veteran's Building** houses the gallery of the **San Francisco Arts Commission** (Wed–Sat noon–5.30pm) in its lobby, a terrific place to discover up-and-coming Bay Area artists. The commission also puts on the provocative window installations a couple blocks away at 155 Grove St and administers **Exploration: City Site**, an open-air lot used for environmental installations, next door at no. 165. Back near the Performing Arts Library, the Vorpal Gallery (Tues–Sat 11am–6pm; ☎415/397-9200) at 393 Grove St, has earned a reputation for consistently high-class contemporary paintings and has a room dedicated to surrealist sketch artist M.C. Escher. Less prestigious, but worth a look, is the San Francisco **Women Artists Gallery** at 370 Hayes St, concentrating mostly on photographs, paintings, and crafts.

Chapter 6

The Mission, the Castro, and south

Largely sheltered from the coastal fog by the looming hills of **Twin Peaks**, the central neighborhoods of the **Mission** and the **Castro** may lack a concentration of notable sights, but the shortage is more than made up for by the great street life, as well as the density of restaurants, clubs and shops in each, making these districts the most popular neighborhoods in town for going out on the town.

Long a focus of San Francisco's largely working-class **Hispanic community**, the Mission District has in the past decade experienced an influx of affluent yuppies, driving rents to once unthinkable heights. Still, the district retains its unmistakeable color, visible in painted **murals** and authentic Hispanic restaurants. The Mission is also home to the **oldest building** in San Francisco, the Mission Dolores, from which it takes its name, and a trendy strip of alternative and upscale venues along **Valencia Street**.

Slightly to the west, at the foot of Twin Peaks (San Francisco's highest and most central point), the Castro was claimed by the city's **gay community** during the 1970s and quickly became the gayest neighborhood in the world, a title still unchallenged to this day. Besides, the landmark **Castro Theater** there's little here to see but rows of quaint houses and trendy shops, but the neighborhood's outgoing population makes it one of the best places for a people-watching stroll on a sunny day.

Further south, **Noe Valley**, **Bernal Heights**, and **Potrero Hill** are pleasant if sleepy neighborhoods, and not crucial on any must-see itinerary; though near the southern border of the city, **Candlestick Park**, a storied sports arena turned over to the San Francisco 49ers when the Giants moved to Pac Bell Park, might make a decent pilgrimage for sports fans.

The Mission

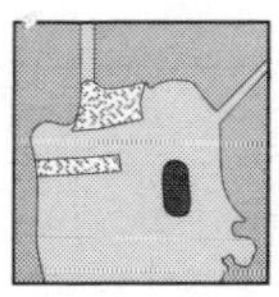

Contained in a flat hollow between the Castro and Potrero Hill, the **Mission** district stretches south from SoMa to Bernal Heights, with

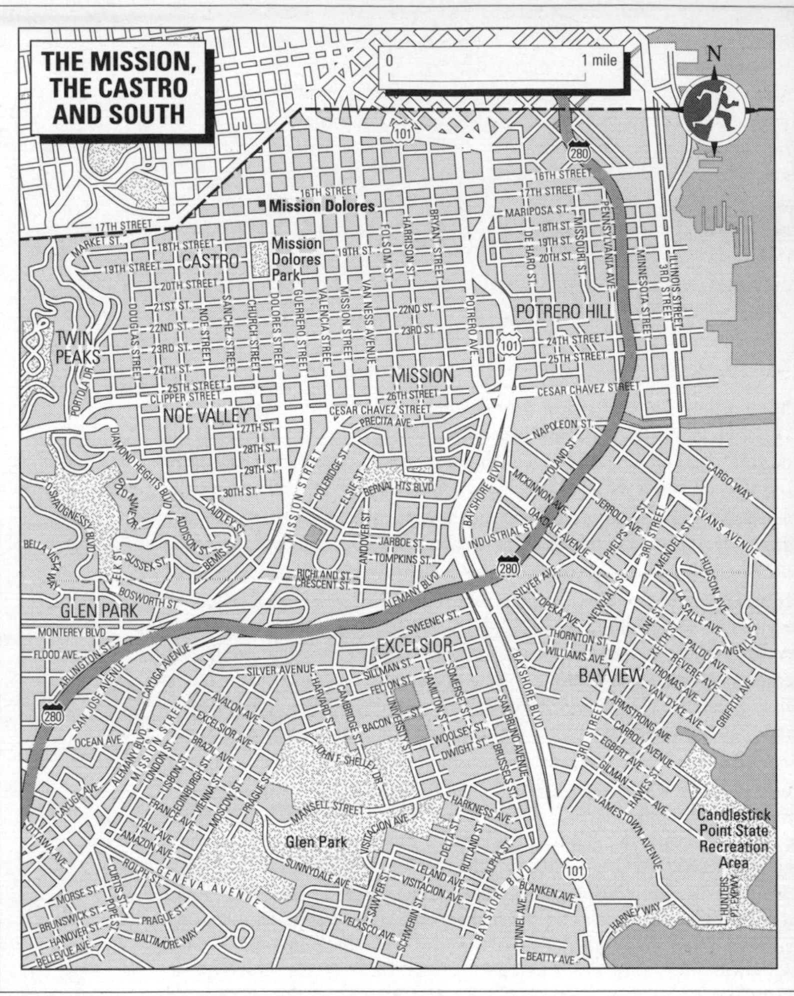

most activity contained between the 16th and 24th Street BART stations. It's a colorful if noisy melange of junk shops and taquerias with a concentration of trendy new restaurants, shops, theaters, and nightclubs along Valencia Street that has earned it a reputation as one of the hippest neighborhoods in the US. The one consistency to the district is its gloriously sunny skies – shielded by hills, the district is protected from the cold fog that plagues most of the rest of the city.

Mission Dolores was first built by Spanish missionaries in 1776, the sixth mission in the El Camino Reál chain. The first Mass celebrated at Mission Dolores on June 29 of that year marked the official founding of the city, though the community was then known as **Yerba Buena**. With California's annexation following the Mexican–American war, the mission's vicinity became home to succeeding waves of immigrants, first Scandinavians, followed during the Gold Rush by a significant Irish influx, who, since the 1950s, have migrated to the more suburban Sunset and Richmond districts, but whose presence is still reflected in the names on numerous store and bar awnings. The currently predominant Latin American community traces its roots back to a massive population influx during a period of intense political turmoil in Central and South America in the late-1960s and 1970s.

For more information on the history of the California Missions, see p.332.

Mission Dolores

Mission San Francisco de Asis, more commonly known as **Mission Dolores**, at Sixteenth Street and Dolores, (daily 9am–4pm; $1) is concrete evidence of the city's Hispanic origins. The adobe building – the second to stand on the site and dating from 1791, having survived both the 1906 and 1989 earthquakes – is squat and relatively spare, while the more prominent basilica next door, built in 1913, is a riot of ornate designs, though it holds nothing of historic interest. In the older structure, a few simple pews face a wooden altar, hand-carved in Mexico around the beginning of the eighteenth-century; redwood beams line the ceiling, painted with designs mimicking decorative styles from the local Ohlone population, while plaques on the floor mark the burial sights of prominent locals, including William Leidesdorff, an African-American businessman who funded the construction of the first city hall. Outside, the rose-lined backyard cemetery – made famous in Hitchcock's *Vertigo* – holds the graves of many early settlers, including the first mayor of San Francisco and California's first governor, not to mention the remains of over 5000 Native Americans.

Dolores Park and around

A short walk down the stately, palm-tree-lined Dolores Street, arguably the most attractive stretch of asphalt in the city, will bring you to the slope of **Dolores Park**, a magnet for sunbathers. The park's southwestern corner provides a spectacular view of the downtown skyline – particularly striking late afternoons when the fog rolls in – and is also much more easily accessible than vistas of Twin Peaks. Though much of the park is little more than an unusually scenic place to walk dogs, the elevated southwest corner transforms on weekends into the so-called **Dolores Beach**, a haven for members of the Castro gay community to bronze their gym-toned muscles.

Continuing south, the hillsides between 19th and 24th streets contain a warren of quiet side streets hosting Victorian mansions

THE MISSION & THE CASTRO
N
Twin Peaks
Levi Strauss Building
Mission Dolores
Castro Theater
Women's Building
Dolores Park
Bernal Heights Park
THE CASTRO
THE MISSION
NOE VALLEY
101
WEBSTER ST.
BUCHANAN ST.
LAGUNA ST.
HERMANN ST.
DUBOCE AVENUE
HOWARD ST.
12TH ST.
FOLSOM STREET
11TH ST.
10TH ST.
HARRISON ST.
VALTER ST.
SANCHEZ ST.
BELCHER ST.
14TH STREET
CASTRO STREET
MARKET STREET
15TH ST.
15TH STREET
LANDERS PLACE
GUERRERO STREET
VALENCIA STREET
JULIAN AVENUE
MISSION STREET
VAN NESS AVENUE
SHOTWELL STREET
FLORIDA STREET
SHARON ST.
BEAVER ST.
16TH STREET
DOLORES STREET
ALBION STREET
HOFF ST.
CAPP ST.
TREAT AVENUE
HARRISON STREET
ALABAMA STREET
POND ST.
17TH STREET
DORLAND STREET
18TH STREET
CHURCH STREET
HANCOCK STREET
19TH STREET
COLLINGWOOD STREET
CUMBERLAND STREET
20TH STREET
LIBERTY STREET
21ST STREET
HILL STREET
HILL ST.
22ND STREET
CHATTANOOGA STREET
CAPP STREET
ALVARADO STREET
SANCHEZ STREET
VICKSBURG STREET
FAIR OAKS STREET
SAN JOSE AVENUE
23RD STREET
DIAMOND STREET
NOE STREET
ELIZABETH STREET
24TH STREET
BALMY ST.
JERSEY STREET
25TH STREET
CLIPPER STREET
26TH STREET
CESAR CHAVEZ STREET
PRECITA AVENUE
PRECITA AVE.
BESSIE ST.
SHOTWELL ST.
MANCHESTER ST.
FOLSOM ST.
TREAT ST.
HARRISON ST.
COSO AVE.
TIFFANY AVE.
28TH STREET
VALLEY STREET
29TH STREET
DAY STREET
30TH STREET
COLERIDGE STREET
PROSPECT AVENUE
WINFIELD STREET
ELSIE STREET
RIPLEY ST.
VIRGINIA AVE.
EUGENIA AVE.
BERNAL HEIGHTS BLVD
POWHATTAN AVENUE
WHITNEY ST.
CHURCH ST.
CHENERY ST.
CORTLAND AVE.
SANTA MARINA ST.
BOCANA ST.
WOOL ST.
GATES ST.
BANKS ST.
PRENTISS ST.
ACCOMMODATION
24 Henry 3
Andora Inn 9
Beck's Motor Lodge 1
Beck's Motor Lodge 5
Black Stallion Inn 8
Dolores Park Inn 7
Inn on Castro 6
San Francisco International Guest House 10
Twin Peaks Hotel 4
The Willows 2
0 600 yds

largely untouched by earthquakes and fires. Most are relatively quaint and modest, but a crow's-nested and cupola-encrusted few are quite spectacular, particularly along the secluded stretch of **Liberty Street** between 20th and 21st streets.

A few blocks away, a landmark of more recent origin can be found at the **Women's Building**, 3543 Eighteenth St and Guerrero (daily 10am–2pm). Founded in 1971, the building hosts and sponsors a variety of community groups, workshops and events. In an amusing updating of the early teetotaling history of the feminist movement, the building had to wage an extended public battle to evict an unwanted tenant – a den of iniquity and drink known as the *Dovre Club* – from a prime street-level location; a café now occupies the newly liberated space. Walk around the corner to see the Women's Building's most spectacular face: a brightly colored mural depicting a Native American woman that towers benevolently over the neighborhood.

For more information on Victorians, see box, p.87.

Valencia Street

Between Sixteenth and 24th streets, trendy **Valencia Street** is packed with boutiques, theaters, used furniture stores, thrift stores, bookstores, restaurants, and cafés. Though gentrification has taken root in places, this stretch of shops includes some of the best thrift shops in town.

The only actual sight in the area, the original **Levi's factory building**, is a few blocks removed from the main action at 250 Valencia St, near Fourteenth St (tours Tues & Wed 9am, 11am & 1.30pm; ☎415/565-9155). The denim jeans began their existence during the heady days of the Gold Rush, when leftover tent material was transformed into the distinctly unfashionable apparel of **miners** looking for something sturdy to wear while slogging through mountain rivers. Though the pants Levi's makes today bear only a remote resemblance to the original item, the popularity of the company's jeans has endured, outlasting countless trends.

For more information on these and other Valencia Street shops and galleries, see p.298.

Mission Street

Just one block east of Valencia, yet worlds away culturally, **Mission Street** is the commercial hub of the city's **Latino community**, lined with five-and-dime shops selling a virtually identical stock of kitschy religious items, along with numerous locally famous **taquerias**. Attracted by relatively low real-estate prices, a crop of trendy new bars has sprung up along the street, their snazzy signs often glowing incongruously beside struggling grocery and clothing stores. Though quickly becoming one of the city's hottest nightlife districts, you should still exercise significant caution here at night as the area is rife with gang activity, especially between Fourteenth and Nineteenth streets. On Mission Street's southern end, the **Mission**

For information on festivals in the Mission, see p.41.

Cultural Center at no. 2868 holds the Galeria Museo, devoted exclusively to Hispanic art.

East of Mission Street the pace is noticeably slower, especially in the heart of the district along 24th Street, where the strong sense of community pride and Hispanic heritage is evidenced by some 200 **murals**. The greatest concentration of work can be found on **Balmy Alley**, an unassuming back way between Treat and Harrison, where the walls are covered from block to block. Started during a small community organizing event in 1973, this tiny street has been the spiritual center of a burgeoning Latino arts movement that has grown out of both the US civil rights struggle and pro-democracy movements in South America. For a tour of the artwork, call the **Precita Eyes Mural Arts Center** 2981 24th St at Harrison (Mon–Fri 10am–5pm, Sat & Sun 11am–4pm, $5–10; ☎415/285-2287), which has sponsored most of the paintings since its founding in 1971.

For information on shops and galleries on Mission Street, see p.298.

Bernal Heights and Potrero Hill

South of the Mission, residential districts stretch down the peninsula past the city limits. For a lovely, little-seen view of the city, consider a steep walk up Folsom Street to lofty **Bernal Heights Park**. Downhill to the south is **Liberty Street**, Bernal Heights' remote main drag – a quiet strip of shops and restaurants that can be pleasantly undercrowded compared with those in more central neighborhoods.

Further south, a hike up quiet **POTRERO HILL** affords more attractive views of the city. Like so much of San Francisco, the neighborhood has become rather gentrified in recent years and Eighteenth Street, its central artery, now boasts a small strip of cafés and gourmet sandwich shops. Still, it remains unpretentious and solidly residential, a pace and atmosphere more evocative of a country village than a major city – it even has its own weekly newspaper. There's precious little to do, but its leafy streets are perfect for a morning stroll, taking in the panoramic views of downtown and the docks and pausing for a coffee.

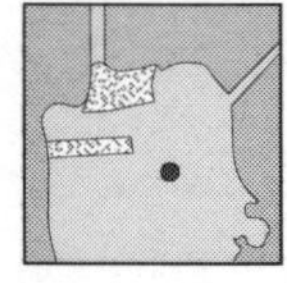

The Castro

Oddly enough, for a neighborhood bursting with energy, there's not an awful lot to *do* in the **CASTRO**, though the district consistently manages to lure gay and lesbian tourists from the four corners of the earth. Sprawling up and down several hillsides between the Lower Haight, Mission, and Noe Valley, in the eastern shadows of Twin Peaks, it's a large area, though the main concentration of street life takes place along Castro Street, between Market and 19th Street. The most logical place to begin exploring the neighborhood is at **Harvey Milk Plaza**, on the corner of Castro and Market, where a massive twenty by thirty foot **rainbow flag** flaps in the breeze above the underground Muni stop. The flag was recently updated by its designer, Gilbert Baker, to include the eight colors he'd originally intended it to carry; back in 1978, tight funds prevented him from including turquoise and fuchsia fabrics along with the more standard shades of red, orange, yellow, green, blue, and purple that have become familiar as the symbol for gay freedom.

For a list of bars in the Castro, see p.279.

Walking in any direction along either street, you will encounter heavy foot traffic, which is fine, since the best way to while away an afternoon or evening here is to simply wander around **people-watching**. If you're lucky, you might even pass one of the outrageous **Sisters of Perpetual Indulgence**, volunteers who dress as white-faced nuns to promote safe-sex and HIV awareness in a camp parody of Catholic pageantry. The neighborhood's various side streets are slightly less frequented and are lined with neat rows of brightly painted Victorians, though none necessarily worth seeking out in itself.

The district's one major sight is the **Castro Theater**, a true Art Deco movie palace at 429 Castro St (☎415/621-6120), with a neon sign that rises high above the crowds, visible from the heights of Twin Peaks and beyond. Designed in Spanish Baroque by Timothy Plueger, who is also responsible for the landmark Paramount

For an insider's view of the Castro Trevor Hailey's "Cruisin' The Castro" walking tour is just about unbeatable; see Walking Tours, p.34.

The Assassination of Harvey Milk

In 1977, eight years after New York's Stonewall riots brought gay political activism into the spotlight, Castro camera shop-owner Harvey Milk won his campaign to be elected to the board of city supervisors – the city's first openly gay elected official, an honor that earned him the nickname "Mayor of Castro Street." It came as a horrifying shock when, in 1978, Milk's former fellow supervisor, Dan White – an ex-cop who had resigned from the board, supposedly in response to low wages, and was later denied an attempt to resume office – walked into City Hall and shot both Milk and Mayor George Moscone dead. White was angered that the liberal policies of Moscone and Milk didn't accord with his conservative views: a staunch Catholic, White was a spokesman for San Francisco's many blue-collar Irish families and, as an ex-policeman, saw himself at the vanguard of the family values he believed gay rights were damaging. At his trial, during which the prosecution never once mentioned the word "assassination" or recognized a political motive for the killings, White claimed that harmful additives in his fast-food-laden diet had driven him temporarily insane – a plea which came to be known as the "Twinkie defense," after the brand name for the airy cream cakes he liked consuming by the boxful – and was sentenced to five years' imprisonment for manslaughter. The gay community exploded when the news of White's light sentence was delivered by the media, and the "White Night" riots that followed were among the most violent San Francisco has ever witnessed, as protesters stormed City Hall, turning over and burning police cars as they went. White was released from prison in 1985 and, unable to find a job, committed suicide shortly afterwards. The anniversary of Milk and Moscone's murders is marked by a candlelight procession from the Castro to City Hall each November 27th.

Halloween in the Castro

Radio shock-jock Howard Stern once described Halloween as "the Gay Christmas," and if you're in the Castro on the night of October 31, you'll be hard pressed to counter his argument. Originally an informal Castro district event, the local celebration of the holiday provided local drag queens with an opportunity to strut their stuff without fear of a harassment by typically intolerant local policemen. By the 1980s, the party began attracting significant numbers of straight locals, some eager for an excuse to cut loose, others gawking at the outrageous outfits and still others looking for a fight. The festivities eventually became too rowdy: shop owners reported destruction to their property, and many neighborhood residents complained about the noise and mess. City Hall responded by creating an "official" party, luring much of the rowdy element away from the residential Castro district into the heavily policed public square of Civic Center. Once again, the drag queens, along with their more respectful admirers, rule the night during the witching hour back in the Castro, where the crowd is thicker with costumed revelers than drunken tourists. The sheer number and variety of costumes alone make it one of the city's most colorful annual events.

Theater in Oakland (see p.143), the building's ornate balconies, wall-mounted busts of heroic figures and massive ceiling ornamentation provide ample visual stimulation, even without a film showing on the gigantic screen, though you'll have to come for a show to see inside; arrive early for pre-screening performances on the "mighty" Wurlitzer organ. The musical medley always draws to a close with Judy Garland's hit *San Francisco*, with the crowd merrily clapping along.

For history on the gay and lesbian movement in San Francisco, see, p.36.

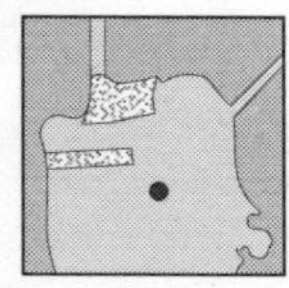

Twin Peaks

A quiet neighborhood perched above the city, **Twin Peaks** has one sight on display: San Francisco. Boasting 360° **panoramic views** of the Bay and the Pacific Ocean, it's certainly worth the quick ride up the hill on the curving streets that wind alongside some of the city's priciest, yet remarkably unstriking, homes. Thanks to television, the Peaks now boast the city's most prominent landmark: a massive, oddly stylish **antenna tower** that can be seen from throughout the city and from airplanes on thick San Francisco days, when it pokes up through the highest peaks of downy white fog.

For information on the well-curated schedule of avant garde and revival cinema at the Castro Theater, see p.295.

According to Native American mythology, the Peaks were created when a married couple argued so violently that the Great Spirit separated them with a clap of thunder. Spanish explorers had a more corporeal inspiration for naming them "Breasts of an Indian Girl," but Americans eventually settled on the current literal name. From these lofty heights in 1905, architect Daniel Burnham worked on his plans for the city, which he intended to sculpt into broad thoroughfares. Despite the opportunity offered by the earthquake and fire of the following year, commercially minded civic authorities lacked the vision to carry it out, and the ideas were largely forgotten, except for his plans for the Civic Center.

Twin Peaks

To get to the peaks by car, continue uphill on Market Street from the Castro till it turns into Portola, then turn right on **Twin Peaks Boulevard**. If you're on foot, you can take the #37 bus part way, though you're still left with a significant climb. Be warned: the peaks are a major tour-bus destination and it's not unusual to encounter throngs of photographers lining the pinnacle. A good option for avoiding the rabble lies just downhill, where the small promontory of **Tank Hill**, at the end of Belgrave Avenue just off Seventeenth Street, offers equally impressive views, though on foggy days you should avoid the area entirely, unless you enjoy playing hide-and-seek in cold, damp fog.

Noe Valley and south

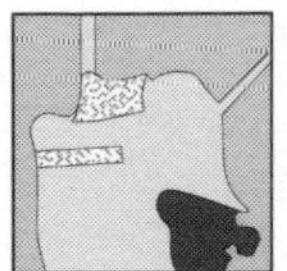

Just a couple of blocks from the Castro and Mission, the quiet bedroom community of **NOE VALLEY** feels worlds apart, thanks to some very steep hills that help keep the area isolated. The neighborhood's heart is **24th Street**, full of restaurants and cafés, and along which baby strollers often seem to outnumber cars. The Muni ride along Church Street (crucial, unless you want to tackle the killer hill) from the Castro is pleasant enough, passing scenic Dolores Park (see p.105), but once you get here, odds are you'll be hard pressed to find anything to do besides sip coffee, shop for cardigans, or brunch at one of the overpacked eating places on a weekend morning.

South of the Mission and Castro there isn't much more to do. The industrial and shipping industries that were once vital here have fallen by the wayside while waves of gentrification have pushed poor residents toward the geographic margins. Sitting atop a hill, above the housing projects and tract homes, is **City College** at 50 Phelan Ave near Ocean Avenue; the institution's theater is its most notable spot, decorated with a mural by the Mexican socialist painter **Diego Rivera**, whose work is seen throughout the Mission, though unless you stop in for a performance, actually getting in to see the painting can be tricky.

The only major attraction in the city's southern half is the chilly promontory of Candlestick Point, home of the former **Candlestick Park**, now known by the distinctly awkward official name "3Com Park at Candlestick Point." Locals still call it by the old name – or "the Stick," for short – and regard the stadium with equal amounts of nostalgia and disdain. Once the home of baseball's **San Francisco Giants**, the ballpark is notorious for its brutal and capricious winds and the otherworldly fog bank that sometimes settles on the field. An even more surreal scene was broadcast live to the nation in October

1989, when a championship game between the Giants and the Oakland A's was rudely interrupted by the Loma Prieta earthquake. With the Giants gone, the stadium's remaining tenant is the **San Francisco 49ers** football team. A stadium renovation and the construction of a mall nearby was recently approved by voters – though some who voted "yes" to the proposal were apparently quite deceased at the time, which has lead to ongoing legal wrangling. Muni 47X buses bound for the stadium leave Van Ness and Market on game days, or take the 9X from outside the Montgomery Street BART station.

Chapter 7

West of Civic Center and Haight-Ashbury

Wedged into the geographical center of the city, the districts west of the Civic Center, once too crime-infested to lure tourists, have come into their own, forming a diverse cluster of largely residential communities. Compact **Hayes Valley** – born out of the rubble of the unsightly elevated freeway that stood here until the 1989 earthquake knocked it down – is an increasingly popular shopping and dining spot, thanks largely to its proximity to the San Francisco Opera and Symphony. Just west of there, **Alamo Square** is the setting for some of San Francisco's best-known and most photographed Victorians, while the **Lower Haight** district which borders the square to the south has become the hub of an emerging local DJ scene.

To the north of Hayes Valley, the **Western Addition** was once home to the city's worst housing projects and incidents of violent crime; it, too, has been experiencing something of a revival, especially in the **Fillmore** at its northern end, which is digging up its jazz roots to attract visitors. Still further north, **Japantown** is really not much more than a Tokyo-style mall of sushi bars, tempura houses, and Japanese book and paper stores, though it is, by far, the best place in town to enjoy an authentic Japanese meal.

West of these districts, stretching out to Golden Gate Park, the **Haight-Ashbury** was once an upper class enclave at the city's outskirts; the district burned itself into the nation's consciousness during a few short summers in the late 1960s, when the small neighborhood was the center of the nationwide hippie movement. While the ornate Victorian architecture of many residences in the Haight (as the district is commonly known) provides evidence of the area's genteel prehistory, the chance to catch a few remaining wafts of anti-establishment rebellion is what draws most visitors.

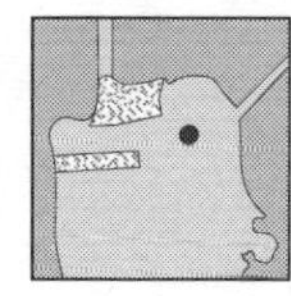

Hayes Valley and around

While the massive 1989 Loma Prieta earthquake razed large parts of the Marina district, it also helped create a new neighborhood smack

in the center of town. Previously overshadowed by the hulking mass of the central freeway, fashionable **HAYES VALLEY** bloomed into existence when structural damage to the highway forced the city to knock it down. The welcome rays of sunshine encouraged an intimate, tight-knit community to sprout just a few blocks from the oversized architecture of the city's Civic Center. Though there's little in the way of sights in the neighborhood, which occupies just a few blocks on **Hayes Street** between Franklin and Octavia, there's plenty here to spend money on – an article of clothing at one of the district's chic **boutiques** will probably set you back at least a couple of hundred bucks. At night the streets are full of black-tie wearing music lovers out for a fancy meal before heading over to the War Memorial Opera House or Symphony Hall in neighboring Civic Center.

For a complete description of Civic Center, see p.100.

Up the steep incline of Hayes Street, the spectacular **Alamo Square** park sits at the intersection with Steiner Street. A staple of every tour-bus company in town, the park's southeast slope attracts small flocks of amateur photographers eager to snap a picture of the "**Painted Ladies.**" These six colorful Victorian houses, originally built in 1894 and lovingly restored during the nostalgia craze of the 1970s have become one of the most clichéd images of the city. The **view** beyond the houses is more brilliant still – on a clear day you can see over the city and across the bay all the way to the hills of North Berkeley.

For more information on Victorians, see box p.87.

A few blocks south, the portion of Haight Street between Divisadero and Fillmore known as **Lower Haight** features a smattering of bars, restaurants, and shops – mostly record stores catering to local DJs at the forefront of the Bay Area club scene. As in the surrounding districts, there are few daytime sights, though proto-beatnik **Kenneth Rexroth**, best known among literary scholars as an important translator of Chinese poetry, lived at 250 Scott St; Kerouac and some of his compadres crashed at his pad upon first arriving in San Francisco, gaining a quick initiation into the local creative community.

For listings of clubs in the Lower Haight, see p.288.

South of Haight Street and east along Duboce Avenue lies **Duboce Park**, a pleasant patch of green, hugely popular with dog lovers who come here to let their best friends run about leash-free. Just past the park to the east is the rather incongruous mass of the new **US Mint** (the old Mint is in SoMa, though neither can be toured), one of four currency-producing factories in the country, rising somewhat menacingly on a granite escarpment at Duboce Avenue and Webster Street near the mega-supermarket, Safeway, one of the most cruisey grocery stores in the country for members of all sexes and orientations.

The Western Addition and Japantown

A short trip north of Hayes Valley on Fillmore Street leads you to the **WESTERN ADDITION**, once the most relentlessly poor and dangerous neighborhood in the city, but somewhat changed thanks to the trickling in of affluent, bargain-hungry renters and investors. Still, on every block between Fulton Street and Geary, boarded-up shops, vacant lots, and abandoned housing projects remain firmly in place. As with most of this central area, there's little to see here, though the corner of Fillmore and Geary offers the district's one significant attraction – the **Fillmore Auditorium**, where in the 1960s promoter Bill Graham put on carnivalesque psychedelic rock shows for thousands of hallucinating hippies. Recently, in an effort to speed up improvements to the district, Mayor Brown has declared the Fillmore Street strip south of Geary a **jazz redevelopment district**, with plans calling for the street's reconfiguration into an open-air mall centered around a new live-music venue belonging to the stellar **Blue Note** record label, legendary for 1950s bop recordings by the likes of Miles Davis.

Before the devastation of the 1906 earthquake, the Western Addition (then known as the Fillmore) served as San Francisco's main shopping district, but Fillmore Street's economic fortunes declined as the city was rebuilt. Wealthier residents moved uphill, and the intersection of Geary and Fillmore became home to a large **Japanese community**. Japanese immigrants first came to the area via Hawaii, where they had worked on sugar plantations at the start of century, and grew in number to occupy some forty blocks, but when anti-Japanese hysteria swept California following the bombing of Pearl Harbor, the federal government began incarcerating much of the Japanese community in camps in the Southwest US. The immigrants were forced to quickly sell off property at below-market prices, mainly to **African-Americans** eager to own houses in the city's center, and soon jazz clubs and black-owned businesses lined the streets. In the early 1960s, civic planner **Justin Herman** was appointed to "renew" the district; instead, he demolished block after block of nineteenth-century Victorian housing, displaced the residents with little compensation and replaced their old homes with acres of drab modernist housing projects. When all was said and done, the Fillmore no longer existed – renamed the Western Addition – and Herman had a public park along the Embarcadero named in his honor.

For reviews of Japantown restaurants, see p.260.

One positive, if unintentional, outcome of Herman's scheme was that it allowed a small, but hearty community of Japanese to reclaim the blocks along the Western Addition's northern perimeter. That area, **JAPANTOWN**, is centered around a glorified mall officially known as the **Japanese Cultural and Trade Center** (or *Nihonmachi*). The enclosed space stretches for several blocks between Fillmore and Laguna, just south of Pacific Heights, and is surrounded by a densely concentrated Japanese community. Topped by the five-tiered, 100-foot **Peace Pagoda**, the mall is a strangely logical combination of Japanese aesthetics and American influences. An important shopping and meeting place for the local community, the Center doesn't offer much – if anything – in the way of sights, though it's packed with excellent Japanese restaurants. The other main highlight is the **Kabuki Hot Springs** at 1750 Geary Blvd at Fillmore (Mon–Fri 10am–10pm; Sat & Sun 9am–10pm; ☎415/922-6000), where San Franciscans of all ethnic and national origins love to steam their cares away in gender-segregated saunas and pools before getting a shiatsu massage. In the basement of the Center is the multiplex **AMC Kabuki 8** theater, 1881 Post St at Fillmore, taken over every May by the **San Francisco International Film Festival**, which screens foreign films hailing from places as remote as Kazakhstan and Burkina Faso.

Japantown's ethnicity is most evident in spring when the **Cherry Blossom** festival brings Japanese culture into the streets with taiko drum performances and numerous food kiosks. Another small window into the neighborhood's soul is offered by the **Buddhist Church of San Francisco** at Pine Street near Octavia Street, which offers services in both Japanese (Sun 1.30pm) and English (Sun 9.30am). The building's plain exterior hides a sumptuous interior filled with relics of the Buddha, donated by the King of Siam in 1935.

Haight-Ashbury

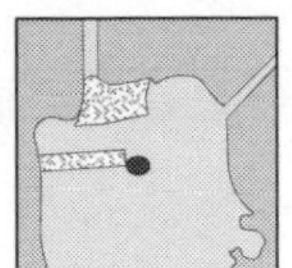

Two miles west of downtown San Francisco, the **HAIGHT-ASHBURY** neighborhood lent its name to an era, giving it a fame that far outstrips its size. Small and dense, "The Haight" spans no more than eight blocks of attractive Edwardian and Victorian buildings, centered around the junction of Haight and Ashbury streets. Since it emerged in the 1960s as the focus of the countercultural scene, it has gone slightly upmarket but still remains one of San Francisco's most racially and culturally mixed neighborhoods, with radical bookstores, laid-back cafés, record stores, and secondhand clothing boutiques recalling its days of international celebrity.

Until 1865, the Haight was no more than a pile of sand dunes, claimed in part by squatters, when a forward-thinking supervisor called Frank McCoppin spearheaded the development of the dunes into the area now known as Golden Gate Park. The landscaping of the Panhandle that leads into the park, the creation of a cable-car line along Haight Street, and the opening of an amusement park along the oceanfront, all drew people out to what was then the western edge of town. Development continued, and by the 1890s the Haight was a thriving middle-class neighborhood. After the 1906 earthquake, new building gathered pace and the neighborhood's desirability grew. That rapid growth was checked by the 1930s Depression, which turned many of the respectable Victorian homes into low-rent rooming houses. During the 1950s, students from San Francisco State College (which, at the time, was nearby) began to move into the neighborhood, creating a local youth culture that took lasting root (see box, overleaf).

Today, nostalgia for a long dormant counterculture draws most visitors here – transforming the neighborhood into something of an alternative culture shopping mall, complete with numerous places to get pierced or buy a bong. Consequently, the district has one of the highest concentrations of oddball characters per square foot of any neighborhood in the country. On a darker note, the street's long association with drugs has kept the number of people seeking, selling, and using them here alarmingly high; the hippie mystique continues to draw numerous youths, many of them ending up hooked and homeless. You'll also have to contend with persistent, if harmless panhandlers.

For clothing and record store reviews, see p.298.

Counterculture in the Haight

The **first hippies** were an offshoot of the **Beats**, many of whom had moved out of their increasingly expensive North Beach homes to take advantage of the low rents and large spaces in the run-down Victorian houses of the Haight. The post-Beat bohemia that began to develop here was a small affair at first, involving the use of drugs and the embrace of Eastern religion and philosophy, together with a marked anti-American political stance. Where the Beats had been a small, cliquish group who emphasized self-indulgence as an escape from social oppression, the hippies, on the face of it at least, attempted to be more embracing by emphasizing such concepts as "universal truth" and "cosmic awareness." The use of **drugs** was crucial and seen as an integral, and positive, part of the movement – LSD especially, the effects of which were just being discovered, despite an esoteric following in psychoanalytical circles for decades before.

Naturally, it took a few big names to get the ball rolling, the pivotal occasion coming in January 1966, when early LSD guinea pig and Stanford drop-out **Ken Kesey** and his **Merry Pranksters** hosted a "Trips Festival" in the Longshoremen's Hall at Fisherman's Wharf. The Pranksters handed out flyers asking "Can you pass the acid test?" and the festival was attended by thousands, most on acid. Along with a "Be-In" at Golden Gate Park later the same year, the festival set a precedent for wild living, challenging authority and dropping out of the social and political establishment. At the time, LSD was not illegal and was being hyped as an avant-garde art form, consciousness-raising in its effects. Pumped out in private laboratories and promoted by the likes of Harvard professor **Timothy Leary** with the prescription "Turn on, tune in, drop out," LSD galvanized a generation into believing that it could be used to raise the creativity of one and all. The Haight Street scene quickly began to attract

The best way to see the neighborhood is to simply walk west up Haight Street, beginning on the east end at **Buena Vista Park** – a thickly wooded hillside patch of nature surrounded by rows of extravagantly turreted mansions – heading towards Golden Gate Park. While the park's grassy lower stretch is sometimes home to sunbathers (on those rare days when there's sun in the often-foggy Haight), its dark, overgrown upper reaches can be pretty spooky and are also a popular gay cruising spot. Don't be fooled by the name: the trees block any chance of a view of the city.

Just across Haight from the park at 112 Lyon St is an impressive Victorian, once the home of the larger-than-life rock diva **Janis Joplin**, who got evicted for, of all things, owning a dog. A bit further west at 710 Ashbury St, the **Grateful Dead** house draws numerous pilgrims, many of whom still tape notes to the front porch long after Jerry Garcia's death. The location was made famous by photos of the band taken here around the time of the band's notorious 1967 drug bust.

Another worthy 1960s hangover is the **Haight-Ashbury Free Clinic** at 558 Clayton St. By American standards, it's quite a phe-

national attention, as local bands the **Grateful Dead**, **Jefferson Airplane**, and **Big Brother and the Holding Company** began to make names for themselves, and, backed by the business weight of **Bill Graham**, the psychedelic music scene became a genuine force nationwide. It wasn't long before large numbers of kids from all over America started turning up in the Haight for the free food, free drugs . . . and free love. Money became a dirty word, the hip became "heads," the others "straights," and by 1966's **Summer of Love**, this busy little intersection had attracted no fewer than 75,000 transitory residents in its short life as the focus of alternative culture.

But along with all the nice middle-class kids who simply wanted to get stoned came the outcasts, the crazies, and the villains. **Charles Manson** recruited much of his "family" in the Haight, and as heroin and speed increasingly replaced LSD as the drugs of choice, the enormous flow of drugs through the neighborhood made it inviting prey for organized crime.

By the end of the Sixties, it had become clear that the peace and love era was coming to an end. With the police riots at the **Chicago Democratic Convention**, the assassination of the Reverend Martin Luther King, and the killing of Bobby Kennedy, bad vibes set in. In 1969, the Rolling Stones organized a concert in **Altamont**, California, (see p.165) hoping to recapture the spirit of Woodstock and to counter allegations that the Stones had ripped off their fans during a long US tour. The acid on supply was bad, and the concert was a tragic failure; members of the Hells Angels biker gang, hired as security, took it upon themselves to beat members of the audience. The terrifying image of the brutal stabbing of one fan in the midst of the oblivious, drugged-out crowd was captured in the documentary filmed during the event. *Gimme Shelter* immortalized the moment that marked the end of a cultural movement, and the Haight-Ashbury district descended in a hazy, hungover blur into a grim era of crime and decay.

nomenon, providing free health care since the 1960s when drug-related illnesses became a big problem in the Haight. It survives – barely – on contributions and continues to treat drug casualties and the poor, both disproportionately large groups in this part of the city. A block further west, at 636 Cole St, is the former home of **Charles Manson**; it was while staying at this nondescript blue building that Manson recruited most of the members of his murderous cult. Near Cole, at 1775 Haight St, is the home that once belonged to the **Diggers**, a short-lived anarchist art group with an anonymous leadership that took a break from writing Dadaist manifestos to give free food and shelter to the increasing numbers of homeless filling the neighborhood. To this day, the sidewalk in front of the building is a popular gathering spot for local wanderers.

North of Haight Street, you hit the **Panhandle**, the finger-slim strip of greenery that eventually leads to Golden Gate Park but is generally considered to be part of the Haight. The Panhandle was landscaped before the rest of the park back in the 1870s, and for a while was the focus of high-society carriage rides, where the well-dressed would go to show off. In post-quake 1906, it became a refuge for fleeing families, with some thirty thousand living in tents. During the 1960s, it was the scene for outdoor rock concerts by the likes of Jimi Hendrix that caused considerable wear and tear on the delicate landscape. Today it's rather seedy: home to vagrants and the few guitar-strumming hippies that remain, though its bike paths and playgrounds also ensure steady use by neighborhood residents.

For an excerpt from Hunter S. Thompson's writings on San Francisco, see p.343.

Back in the opposite direction, a few blocks south of Haight Street, at 130 Delmar near Frederick, is the site of the **Jefferson Airplane** house. Though there's not a lot to see at this modest abode, Grace Slick's legendary rock band rose to such psychedelic superstardom here in the late 1960s with the alternative lifestyle anthems *White Rabbit* and *Somebody to Love*, that many fans still make the pilgrimage. Still further south, just below the southeast corner of Golden Gate Park, lies **Hunter S. Thompson**'s former house at 318 Parnassus St near Willard. Again, there's not much to see, but while at work on his book *Hell's Angels*, the legendary "gonzo journalist" routinely held wild parties here, some of them not ending until somebody shot out the lights.

Chapter 8

The Richmond, Golden Gate Park, and the Sunset

As late as the 1940s, much of what today comprises San Francisco's **Sunset** and **Richmond** districts was little more than a giant row of sand dunes, stretching out to the ocean; snootier residents of more central districts might tell you that not much has changed in the decades since. But despite their long patches of relentlessly suburban architecture, both neighborhoods offer a few rewarding pockets to entice explorers, including numerous good, cheap restaurants and the odd cultural outpost. More than the tourist-saturated downtown neighborhoods, these somewhat somnambulant districts are windows into residential San Francisco in all its domesticated diversity.

To a remarkable degree, the landscape of the city's western half is defined by its greenery, most notably the sculpted expanse of **Golden Gate Park**. Though the park is home to museums, ball fields, and bandstands, none can compare to the park itself, a wildly diverse organic environment shaped by humans. At the park's western edge, the city's **coastline** has a hauntingly desolate beauty – a reminder of this small peninsula's tenuous fingerhold at the very edge of the Western Hemisphere. The beaches begin just west of Golden Gate Bridge with the popular crescents of **Baker** and **China beaches**. Rapidly rising cliffs mark the city's northwest corner, beginning at Lincoln Park, home to the unjustly overlooked **Palace of the Legion of Honor**, which houses a fine art collection. Hiking below the park to the rugged promontory of **Lands End** affords striking views of Marin across the mouth of the Bay. Turning south, things become more civilized again at the **Cliff House** and the former **Sutro Baths**, the lone remnants of what was once an amusement park, retaining a few endearingly shopworn diversions today.

Beginning at the base of the cliffs is the aptly named **Ocean Beach**, a thin strip of sand that extends down to the city's southern border where it widens at the blustery heights of **Fort Funston** at the southwestern reaches of the Sunset district. Nearby, verdant **Stern Grove** is soothing and lush, while the **San Francisco Zoo** is distinctly haggard, though the only one in town. Though much of the rest of the district is

THE RICHMOND, GOLDEN GATE PARK & THE SUNSET

0 — 1 mile

ACCOMMODATION	
Ocean Park Motel	3
Oceanview Motel	1
Sunset Motel	2

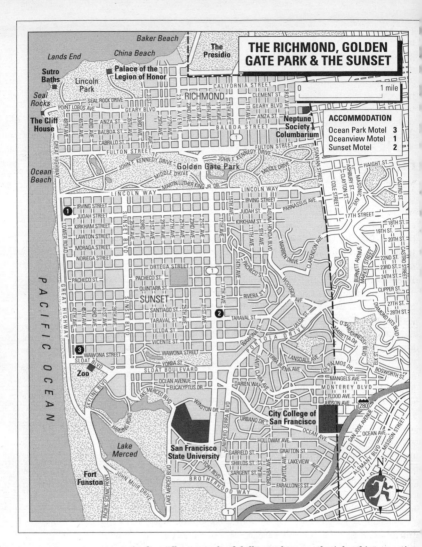

a seemingly endless march of dull tract homes, the inland intersection of Ninth Avenue and Irving (not far from the Haight-Ashbury) has sprouted a miniature **restaurant row**.

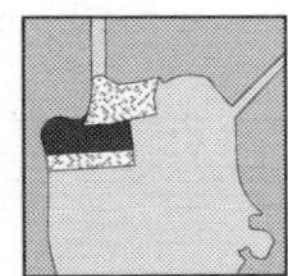

The Richmond and the beaches

Often referred to as "new Chinatown," the **RICHMOND** is actually a melting pot of numerous ethnicities, due perhaps in part to its massive size, which has allowed the neighborhood to comfortably accommodate successive waves of Jewish, Irish, Asian, and Russian immigrants. Because of these distinct settlements, successive blocks in the district have entirely different characters – from the comfortably chic **Sea Cliff** section (home to local celeb Robin Williams) to the dim sum houses and frantic commerce of **Clement Street** and the foggy solitude at the end of **Geary Boulevard**. The entire district is wrapped with sandy **beaches** to the north and south as well as the jagged coastal beauty of **Lincoln Park**.

Clement Street and Geary Boulevard

Nowhere is the Richmond's intimate mix of ethnicities more evident than on the commercial strip of **Clement Street** between Arguello – where the airy **Temple Emmanu-El** is a rare public bastion of the city's Jewish population – and Park Presidio Boulevard. A short stroll brings you past Irish bars, Chinese dim sum bakeries, French bistros, Russian delis, and South Asian noodle houses, not to mention the dense warrens of the city's best used bookstore, **Green Apple Books**.

For a review of Green Apple Books and other city bookstores, see p.310.

Just south, the district's main driving thoroughfare, **Geary Boulevard**, offers a similar mix of cultures, but the street's massive width makes it less than pleasant for strolling. Hidden just off of Geary, behind the Coronet movie theater, which has the biggest screen in town, the **Neptune Society Columbarium**, at 1 Lorraine Court near Anza (erratic hours; ☎415/771-0717), is a miniature-scale monument to the city's heady Gold Rush-era high society – or at least to those society members who were cremated and placed in the thousands of urns held here. Built in 1898 at the entrance to an exclusive cemetery and highlighted by Tiffany stained-glass windows, the names on the bronze and copper plaques lining the walls mirror the city's social register: the remains of the Kaiser, Magnin, Brannan, and Folgers families all reside in this odd combination between a chapel and a Roman temple, memorialized with such unusual tributes as a martini shaker and a baseball.

The beaches and around

Rimming the western edge of the Presidio, just north of the Richmond, **Baker** and **China beaches** are popular outdoor destinations for locals unwilling to brave the weekend gridlock on Golden Gate Bridge in search of sunnier recreation. Anyone expecting a prototypically Californian spectacle similar to the Venice Beach boardwalk in Los Angeles is going to be sorely disappointed. Even on the sunniest days (which can be unnervingly unpredictable given the foggy climate, especially in summer) the water here is bone-chillingly cold, and since both beaches sit at the mouth of the bay, currents are perilously strong, making swimming inadvisable year

For information on the Presidio, see p.88.

round. That said, either of these beaches is an enjoyable place to while away an afternoon, as the odd mix of nude sunbathers and families on outings makes for some enjoyable people watching. The approaches from both the east (the Presidio) and the west (Lincoln Park) along Lincoln Boulevard offer some spectacular views of the surrounding landscape along with the bridge. To get there by Muni take bus #29, which offers a pleasant tour through the Presidio.

Both beaches suffered turbulent early histories that speak to the city's at-times tense relationship to its cross-Pacific rivals. In 1905 the army placed an enormous 95,000lb cannon in an underground bunker on the hill above Baker Beach, at the base of cliffs protecting the Presidio's western flank. Despite heightened militarization of both sides of the bay during World War II, the cannon was subsequently declared obsolete and melted down for scrap, unfired in its forty-year career. A replacement cannon was set up in 1977 for exhibition purposes only, and if you stop by between 10am to 2pm on the first weekend of each month, you might catch the rangers giving a demonstration of how the cumbersome object would have been aimed and fired.

Treacherous trails descending from the ruins of more coastal defense structures just north of Baker Beach and south of the bridge, lead to isolated, picturesque **Golden Gate Beach**, popular with local nudists who like basking in the sun on the sheltered stretch of sand, which also affords a stunning view of the bridge and across the bay.

To the south, **China Beach** – barely separated from Baker Beach by an outcropping of rock that's easily navigated at low tide – got its name in 1870 when it was home to an encampment of Chinese fishermen. When the government acted on rampant anti-Chinese bigotry and imposed tight restrictions on immigration, the beach was supposedly a landing place for illegal aliens. These days, it's the best of the slim pickings when it comes to swimming in town, thanks to comparatively calm currents, as well as changing rooms and showers. Worlds apart from hardscrabble immigrant lean-tos, the **Sea Cliff** neighborhood surrounding the beach is one of the city's wealthiest, with ostentatious arches guarding the entrance to each street. Unfortunately for residents, the neighborhood's quiet comfort is literally not well founded – during a period of near-biblical rainfall in 1997, massive sinkholes developed in the area, swallowing entire mansions.

The Palace of the Legion of Honor and Lands End

The stately **Palace of the Legion of Honor** (Tues–Sun 9.30am–5pm; $8, free with a ticket from the de Young Museum; ☎415/863-3330) is dramatically situated in **Lincoln Park**, which offers the most striking coastal beauty in the city. Approaching the Palace from any direction involves a steep climb through the park's golf course – miss a chip shot here, and your ball will end up in the ocean several hundred feet below. The museum itself is no less staggering: built in 1920, its parade of white columns is a copy of Paris' Légion d'Honneur. Adding to the monumentality is a cast of Rodin's *The Thinker*, set dramatically on a pedestal in the center of the museum's front courtyard.

In keeping with its European exterior, the museum houses a fine collection of Renaissance paintings by Titian and El Greco, and sculpture by Giambologna. The seventeenth-century collection focuses on works by the Dutch and Flemish masters, including canvases by Rembrandt, Rubens, and Haals. The museums' Impressionist and post-Impressionist galleries are particularly strong, with representative paintings by Manet, Monet, Renoir, Courbet, Degas, and Cézanne. A separate room is devoted to more Rodin sculptures, one of the best collections of its kind in the world, including bronze, porcelain, and stone pieces such as *The Athlete*, *Fugit Amor*, *The Severed Head of John the Baptist*, *Fallen Angel*, and a small cast of *The Kiss*; the small, decorous space seems barely able to contain Rodin's kinetic style. An eclectic array of touring shows gets exhibited in the basement space – a skylight opening into the central courtyard lets you sneak a peak before entering. On the path from the museum down to the Lands End trails is a somber final work, George Segal's sculpture *The Holocaust*, a blunt remembrance of the horrors inflicted in Nazi concentration camps.

For more Rodin in the Bay Area, see Stanford University, p.171.

Curving along the cliffs beneath the Legion of Honor are the trails rounding the point of **Lands End**, one of the few true wilderness areas left in the city. Littering the base of the jagged cliffs are the broken hulls of ships that have failed to navigate the Golden Gate's violent currents; with luck, at low tide you can see chunks of the wooden wreckage. The main trail is a popular though slightly treacherous jogging path, but the land recedes inland into shady cypress groves that are a popular gay cruising spot. Arrive just before dusk for spectacular views of Marin. Both Lands End and the Palace of the Legion of Honor can be reached by taking the #38 bus on Geary Boulevard and transferring to the #18 at the Lincoln Park Golf Course.

Cliff House, Seal Rock, and the Sutro Baths

The last remnants of a once-impressive amusement park complex, the **Cliff House** at 1090 Point Lobos Rd (Mon–Thurs 9am–1.30am, Fri–Sun 8.30am–1.30am) remains a favorite stopping point, even if it no longer has any rides. In any case, no mechanical gimmick could possibly compare with the House's natural setting, poised midway between the point of Lands End, to the north, and Ocean Beach, stretching to the south. The cliff-hugging building, with its souvenir shops and constant stream of visitors, has the sleepy aura of a resort out of season.

For information on dining at Cliff House, see p.261.

A few traces of the house's carnival past remain, though they've been all but hidden away down an outdoor flight of stairs just to the right of the entrance to the Cliff House's main dining room, where a large concrete landing offers views of **Seal Rock**, which is also a popular nesting spot for birds. To the right is a park service station offering maps and information on the Golden Gate National Recreation Area (which covers much of the city's western seaboard), along with an arresting photographic display of the numerous ships that have run aground on the rocks below. To the left, tucked directly under the Cliff House's restaurant, is the **Musée Méchanique** (Mon–Fri 11am–7pm, Sat & Sun 10am–8pm; ☎415/386-1170), an odd collection of historic arcade games. With the mere drop of a coin you can be greeted by a giant chortling puppet, study the goings-on at a c.1900 opium den, watch a can-can dancer kick up her legs, or be titillated by a rather tame century-old nudie show. Toward the back of the cramped space, several newer video games are tucked away, including some from the early 1980s such as Pac Man and the like. Across the landing from the museum is a **Camera Obscura** (11am–sunset, weather permitting; $1), one of the last of its kind in the country. Using a rotating mirror – and a trick of light – the camera allows entrants to see a panoramic view of the surrounding area.

Back toward Lands End and down a path from the Cliff House are the ruins of the **Sutro Baths**, generally filled with brackish sea water, though photos back at the Cliff House ranger station reveal what a splendid spa this used to be. Built by the Prussian immigrant Adolph Sutro (who also built the Cliff House), the baths were a seaside jewel – 100,000 feet of stained glass covering more than three acres of sculpted pools filled with fresh and salt water. Sutro packed his "Tropical Winter Gardens" with fountains, gardens, sculptures, and historical bric-a-brac from around the world. The lone dramatic rem-

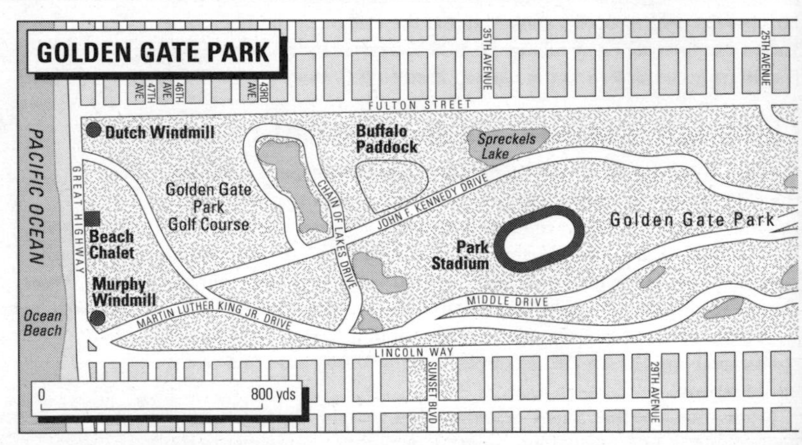

nant of Sutro's grandiose palace is a tunnel through the rocks, on the far end of the pools from the Cliff House, which fills with the crashing of waves during high tide. Back at the top of the hill, across Point Lobos Avenue from the Cliff House in Sutro Heights Park, only a massive parapet survives from Sutro's once lavish house.

Golden Gate Park

Developed in the late nineteenth century, many years before the neighborhoods that surround it, **GOLDEN GATE PARK** manages to be both a pastoral retreat for San Franciscans and a bastion of local culture, with more than a thousand acres of gardens and forest, complemented by some of the city's best museums. Spreading three miles or so west from the Haight, it was designed in 1871 by park commissioner **William Hall**, mimicking the style of Frederick Law Olmsted (who also created Central Park in New York). Hall used a dyke to protect the park's western side from the sea, and **John McLaren**, the Scottish park superintendent for 56 years, sculpted numerous miniature environments from what was then an area of wild sand dunes by planting several thousand trees here. The resulting living masterpiece is a rugged landscape which undergoes a natural transition as it approaches the ocean, subject on the park's western half to strong winds and chilly temperatures. It's perhaps fitting then that most of the cultural institutions are situated on the eastern half of the park, with the more open western side better for outdoor activities.

If you're entering by car or bike, follow Fell Street west until it becomes **John F. Kennedy Drive**, along which most of the major

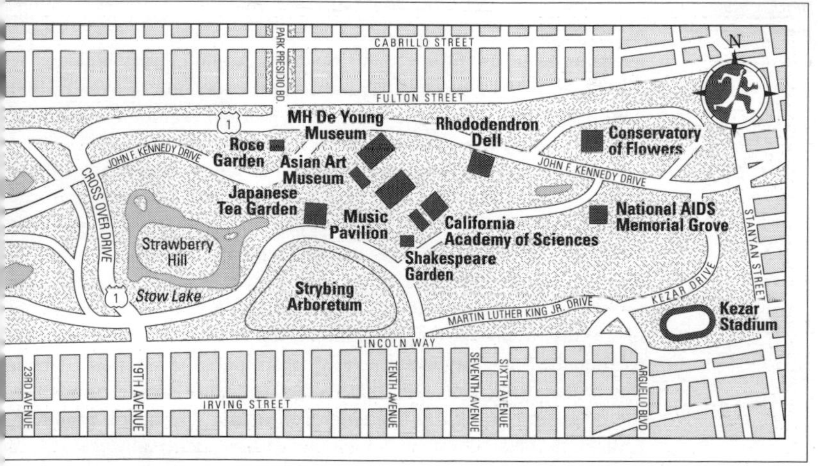

draws are located. The **Conservatory of Flowers** sits just inside this northeastern entrance, a Victorian horticultural museum modeled on the Palm House at London's Kew Gardens. Though the interior has been closed since 1995 when the mostly glass building suffered severe damage in a winter storm, the rolling greens in front of the building are still a popular gathering spot, with numerous rollerbladers and cyclists zipping past. The Conservatory is expected to open the doors to its greenhouses in the next couple of years, though no one seems willing to commit to an exact date just yet. Just south of here is a **children's play area**, complete with a jungle gym, sand pit and classic merry-go-round (25¢ per child), as is the **National AIDS Memorial Grove**, on Middle East Drive, one of the park's most recent additions. Nearby, on a small set of **lawn bowling greens**, elderly locals play in suitably restrained fashion.

Of the park's numerous museums, the **M.H. de Young Museum**, off JFK Drive (Wed–Sun 9.30am–5pm; $7, $2 off with Muni transfer and free first Wed of each month; ☎415/863-3330), is the largest, if not the most exciting; its rather cramped collection covers everything from ancient Greek and Roman artifacts to more than a hundred early American works bequeathed by John D. Rockefeller III. The British galleries feature Neoclassical and Rococo works from the reign of George III, most notably the contributions of Thomas Gainsborough, John Constable, Henry Raeburn, and Sir Joshua Reynolds. Rubens, Rembrandt, and other seventeenth-century European painters are also well represented. The museum had its origin in the California Midwinter International Exposition of 1894, a venture that was so successful that the Fine Arts Building (around which the current museum was built) was turned over to newspaper publisher M.H. de Young with the purpose of establishing a permanent museum.

A $12.50 Golden Gate Park Explorer Pass gets you into all the park's museums and other attractions, representing a 25 percent reduction of total admission costs.

For over a decade now, the **Asian Art Museum** has shared a building with the de Young, but as it will be entirely relocated into roomier galleries in the former San Francisco Public Library building by 2002 (see p.101), most of the permanent collection of over 10,000 paintings and decorative objects is in storage. Temporary exhibits occupy what space remains.

Opposite, the **California Academy of Sciences** (daily 10am–5pm; summer daily 9am–6pm; $8.50, $1 off with Muni transfer and free first Wed of each month) is a perfect place to amuse restless children. There's a natural-history museum with a thirty-foot skeleton of a 140 million-year-old dinosaur, depictions of the solar system, life-size replicas of elephant seals and other California wildlife, and a colony of twenty black-footed penguins. The Academy's "educational" earthquake ride – simulating a range of tremors – is a popular exhibit for thrill-seeking kids and adults alike. The show-stealer, though, is the collection of 14,500 specimens of aquatic life in the **Steinhart Aquarium** (daily 10am–5pm; included with Academy admission). The feeding of the penguins at 11.30am and 4pm is always a popular scene, as is the Fish Roundabout; where the viewing area at the center of this donut-shaped fish tank creates the sensation of being underwater. Alligators and other reptiles lurk in a thankfully less intimate exhibit known as the Swamp. The **Morrison Planetarium** (schedule varies; $2.50, $1.25 for children, $7 laser rock shows; ☎415/750-7141) offer the typical array of sky shows by day and rock music-oriented laser shows – which draw smoked-out teens (and those who still act like them) – by night.

In 1907 Makota Hagiwara invented the fortune cookie to deliver thank you notes, popularizing them during the1915 Panama exposition.

Slightly west of the museums, the popular **Japanese Tea Garden** (daily 9am–5.30pm; $2.50) was built in 1894 for the California Midwinter Exposition and beautifully landscaped by the Japanese Hagiwara family, who looked after the garden until World War II, when along with other Japanese-Americans they were sent to internment camps. A massive bronze Buddha dominates the garden, whose gently curved bridges, winding footpaths, still pools filled with shiny carp, and leafy bonsai and cherry trees lend the place a peaceful feel despite the busloads of tourists pouring in every day. The best way to enjoy the garden is to get there around 9am when it first opens for a tea and Japanese cookie breakfast in the teahouse for $2.50.

For a less crowded outdoor alternative, wander south to the **Strybing Arboretum** (Mon–Fri 8am–4.30pm, Sat & Sun 10am–5pm), with entrances across from the Tea Garden or at Ninth Avenue and Lincoln Way. The 75-acre botanic garden is home to more than 7000 varieties of plants, with miniature gardens focusing on plants from different regions of the world – desert to tropical. For a tour, stop by the Ninth Avenue entrance at 1.30pm any day of the week, or 10.30am Saturdays or Sundays. Just outside the Arboretum's north entrance is the **Shakespeare Garden**, showing off every flower and plant mentioned in the writer's plays.

To enjoy the somewhat quieter corners of the park head west through the many flower gardens and eucalyptus groves towards the ocean. Though you can wander quite aimlessly about, a number of activities may catch your fancy as well. **Boat rental** is available on the vast and marshy **Stow Lake** (near Nineteenth Ave) for $10–14 per hour, a pleasantly serene option at midweek when it's relatively uncrowded. Sitting at the water's center is Strawberry Hill, a large fake hill that can be reached by a footbridge. Meanwhile, the Golden Gate Park Stables at John F. Kennedy Drive and 36th Avenue offer **horse-riding** for around $25 per hour. On weekend afternoons the large soccer field nearby is the scene of some very heated games between South and Central American intramural squads.

Perhaps the most unusual thing about Golden Gate Park is its small herd of bison, roaming around the **Buffalo Paddock** off JFK Drive near 38th Avenue; you can get closest to these noble giants in their feeding area at the far west end. Continuing west along JFK, you'll pass the **Queen Wilhelmina Tulip Garden** before coming to the 1902 **Dutch Windmill** at the northwest corner of the park; restored to working order, the windmill once pumped water to the park's Strawberry Hill reservoir. At the southwest corner of the park, the companion **Murphy Windmill** stands in a somewhat sorrier state, never having been restored for lack of funds. Between the two structures, facing the highway, is the **Beach Chalet**, a two-story, white-pillared building designed by Willis Polk; housing a series of 1930s frescoes depicting the growth of San Francisco as a city and the creation of Golden Gate Park, it also holds a small visitors' center that provides information about the park's numerous guided walking tours. Upstairs there's a lively brewery-restaurant, great for late weekend brunches.

For places to rent skates and bicycles in and around Golden Gate Park, see p.320.

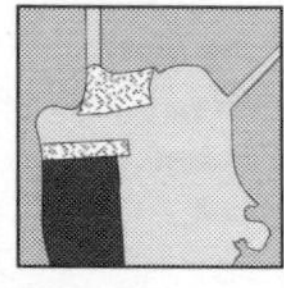

The Sunset and the western coast

Built following World War II to provide cheap housing for returning soldiers, much of the **SUNSET** district suffers from intense suburban malaise. The visual tedium of around forty blocks of nearly identical stucco housing in pastel colors – originally sold for only $5000 a unit – is barely interrupted by as much as a corner store or laundromat. It's hardly worth the trip out, except on your way to the beach and other coastal sights, though you may find a few spots of interest around the intersection of Ninth Avenue and Irving Street, where a heavy concentration of restaurants and stores has formed. This oddly situated dining district serves refugees from the nearby Haight-Ashbury, as well as students at the **University of California, San Francisco (UCSF)**.

For reviews of restaurants in the Sunset, see p.261.

About forty blocks west of the university, buffeted by sea breezes and fog, the thin barrier of **Ocean Beach** seems to constantly be on the brink of either being washed out to shore or blown into locals' backyards. Aside from a small community of particularly hearty surfers, the windy beach is the almost exclusive territory of joggers and dog walkers. During the evenings, bonfires are permitted on the southern portions of the beach near Sloat Boulevard, their flickering light adding a haunted touch.

Just south, where Sloat Boulevard meets the coast, the **San Francisco Zoo** (10am–5pm daily; $9; ☎415/753-7061) makes for a disappointing visit, as it's largely outmoded, despite improvements over the years. Some sections are considerably more appealing than others, notably the **Primate Discovery Center**, which includes a family of gorillas. Also notable is an unusual emphasis on mammals and marsupials from Australia, displayed in the open-pen **WalkAbout**. A similar approach is taken in the **Rainbow Landing**, which surrounds visitors with brightly colored lorikeets resembling miniature parrots. Otherwise, the animals look pretty tired of the place themselves; with zoo funding mired in a never-ending series of political disputes, big changes are unlikely for some time.

A worthwhile summer detour along the Ocean Beach's southern run is the small **Stern Grove** park, a leafy ravine of eucalyptus, redwood and fir trees sheltering a natural amphitheater where a popular free Sunday concert series is held each summer – make sure to stop in early for good seats on the lawn. The symphony and opera make annual appearances at the festival, along with a good roster of jazz and world music performers. The park is tucked at the base of **WEST PORTAL**, a pleasant row of shops and restaurants near the point where the K, L, and M Muni lines emerge from the subway tunnel. Further south, a seemingly endless string of malls runs along Route 1, briefly interrupted by the unappealing campus of **San Francisco State University** – long known for its populism and political activism, though it resembles nothing so much as a 1960s housing complex gone to seed.

A freshwater pond tucked between the university's campus and the shoreline, undervisited **Lake Merced** provides a quiet getaway, though most of the surrounding greenspace is given over to golf courses. Boats can be rented from the **boathouse** at 1 Harding Rd off Skyline Boulevard (Mon–Thurs 11am–midnight, Fri 11am–2am, Sat & Sun 10am–2am; $9 per hour; ☎415/681-2727), which has a pleasant restaurant and bar. It's hard to believe that this was the site of one of the most notorious events in California history; back in 1859 David Broderick, the state's most prominent politician and a US Senator, was challenged to a duel here by David Terry, the Chief Justice of the state's Supreme Court. Terry, a southern sympathizer who dreamed of bringing California into the confederacy, shot and killed Broderick, and quickly fled the state.

It is worth continuing on to the city's southernmost corner, where a steep bluff holds the scenic heights of **Fort Funston**. Aside from a few concrete bunkers, there isn't even much evidence of a fort here, but the cliff-hugging dunes that drop off to the beach below have attracted a crowd of hang-gliding enthusiasts – on a gusty day watching the daredevils swoop and twirl along the cliff face is a true pleasure. For a more traditional method of descending, wooden stairs lead down the cliffs to little-used Burton Beach, though swimming is not an option and high tides can make sunbathing spots scarce.

Part 3

The Bay Area

Chapter 9

Introducing the Bay Area

Of the six million people who make their home in the San Francisco **Bay Area**, only one in eight lives in the city of San Francisco. Everyone else is spread around the many smaller cities and suburbs that ring the bay, either south on the peninsula or across the Golden Gate and Bay bridges that span the chilly waters of the natural harbor. Though there's no denying the subordinate role these places play in relation to San Francisco, each is a distinct environment meriting individual exploration.

Across the gray-steel **Bay Bridge**, eight miles from downtown San Francisco, the East Bay (covered in chapter 10) is perhaps the most culturally interesting of the surrounding areas. As it contains the lively, left-leaning cities of **Oakland** and **Berkeley** – home to Berkeley University – the region boasts some of the best bookstores, restaurants, and live music venues in the greater Bay Area. The weather's generally much sunnier and warmer over here, and it's easily reached by the BART trains that race under the bay. The remainder of the East Bay is filled out by Contra Costa County, which includes the short-lived early state capital of California, **Benicia**, and the **Mount Diablo State Park** which towers 4000 feet over the dry surroundings.

South of the city, the **Peninsula**, covered in chapter 11, holds some of San Francisco's oldest and most upscale suburbs, spreading down through the computer-rich **Silicon Valley** and into **San Jose** – California's fastest-growing city, and larger actually than San Francisco – though apart from a few excellent museums there's not a lot to see. Along the peninsula's western frontier, the **beaches** are sandy, clean and uncrowded, and there are a couple of youth hostels dramatically situated in old lighthouses perched on cliffs along the Pacific.

For some of the most beautiful land- and seascapes in California, cross the Golden Gate Bridge or ride a ferry boat north across the bay to **Marin County**, described in chapter 12; this mountainous peninsula is one-half wealthy suburbia and one-half unspoiled hiking country, with dense **redwood forests** rising up directly alongside the thundering Pacific Ocean. A range of 2500-foot peaks divides the county down the middle, separating the yacht clubs and plush bay-view houses of **Sausalito** and **Tiburon** from the nearly untouched

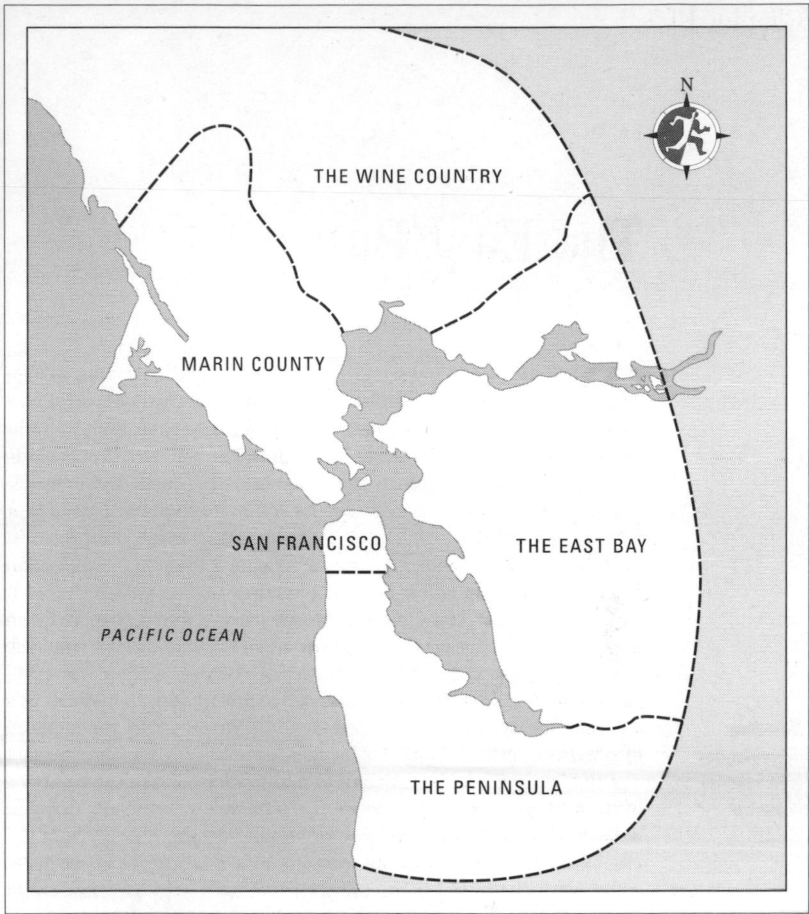

wilderness that runs along the Pacific coast through **Muir Woods** and the **Point Reyes National Seashore**.

Finally, no visit to San Francisco is complete without seeing the **Wine Country**, detailed in chapter 13. Just north of Marin, the sunny cradle of the Sonoma and Napa valleys makes an excellent day- or weekend-trip for its wineries, spas, and countless recreational activities, while to their northwest, another scenic valley lies along the **Russian River** – lesser known but just as worthwhile.

Public **transportation** throughout these regions is quite good by US standards, although it is primarily aimed at commuters, not visitors. Unless you have more time than money, it is probably wiser to rent a car – many of the best places outside San Francisco are simply inaccessible without one.

Full listings of accommodations, restaurants, and other facilities in the Bay Area are provided in chapters 14 to 19.

Chapter 10

The East Bay

The largest and most-traveled bridge in the US, the **Bay Bridge** heads east from downtown San Francisco, part graceful suspension bridge and part heavy-duty steel truss. Built in 1933 as an economic booster during the Depression, the structure is made from enough steel cable to wrap around the earth three times. Completed just seven months before the more famous (and better-loved) Golden Gate, it works a lot harder for a lot less respect: local scribe Herb Caen dubbed it "the car-strangled spanner," a reflection of its often-clogged lanes. Indeed, a hundred million vehicles cross it each year, though you'd have to search hard to find a postcard with an image of its silvery mass; its only claim to fame – apart from the much-broadcast videotape of its partial collapse during the 1989 earthquake – is that **Treasure Island** (see box, p.140), where the two halves of the bridge meet, hosted the 1939 World's Fair, the memory of which still evokes pride for locals.

East Bay accommodation reviews begin on p.222.

Though commuters returning to San Francisco take the top level of the bridge – passing between the structure's statuesque towers, with the skyline dramatically before them – heading away from the city in the opposite direction, traffic is routed along the lower deck, where dark shadows obstruct any view of hard-working, blue-collar **Oakland**. The city traditionally earned its livelihood from shipping and transportation services, as evidenced by the enormous cranes in the massive Port of Oakland, but is in the beginning stages of a renaissance as it lobbies to attract businesses and workers from the information technology industry. Oakland spreads north along wooded foothills to **Berkeley**, an image-conscious university town that looks out across to the Golden Gate and collects a mixed bag of international students, heavily pierced dropouts, aging 1960s radicals, and Nobel prize-winning nuclear physicists in its cafés and bookstores.

Reviews of East Bay restaurants begin on p.263; bars and clubs listings start on p.281.

Parts of Oakland and Berkeley blend together so much as to make them indistinguishable, and the hills above them are topped by a twenty-mile string of **regional parks**, providing much needed fresh air and quick relief from the concrete grids below. The rest of the

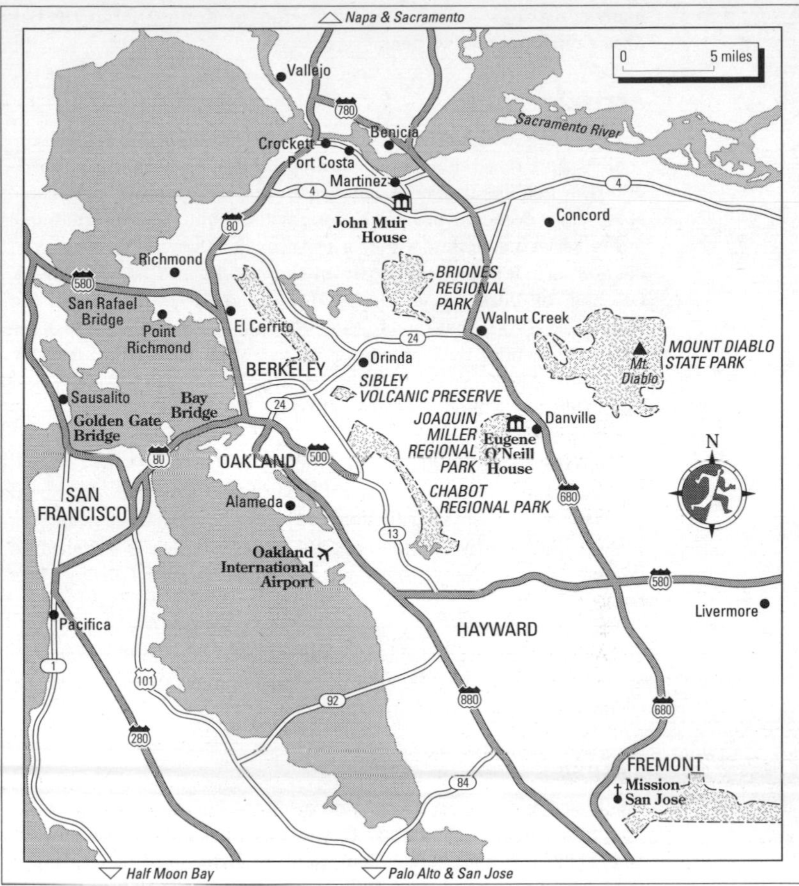

East Bay is filled out by **Contra Costa County**, a huge area that contains some intriguing, historically important waterfront towns – well worth a detour if you're on your way to the Wine Country – as well as some of the Bay Area's most inward-looking suburban sprawl.

The Wine Country is detailed in Chapter 13.

Curving around the **North Bay** from the oil-refinery landscape of Richmond, and facing each other across the narrow **Carquinez Strait**, both **Benicia** and **Port Costa** were vitally important during California's first twenty years of existence after the 1849 Gold Rush; they're now strikingly sited but little-visited ghost towns. In contrast, standing out from the soulless dormitory communities that fill up the often baking hot **inland valleys**, are the preserved homes of an unlikely pair of influential writers: the naturalist John Muir, who, when not out hiking around Yosemite and the High Sierra, lived most of his life near **Martinez**, and playwright Eugene O'Neill, who wrote many of his angst-ridden works at the foot of **Mount Diablo**, the Bay Area's most impressive peak.

Arrival

Most visitors to San Francisco arrive at SFO, though it is just as convenient and reasonable to fly into **Oakland Airport** (☎510/577-4000), which lies the same distance from downtown San Francisco. Most major domestic airlines – along with a number of international ones – serve the facility, which is less crowded than its San Francisco counterpart. It's an easy trip from the airport into San Francisco, Oakland, or Berkeley via the AirBART Shuttle (every 15min; $2; ☎510/562-7700) that runs to the Coliseum BART station. There are also several door-to-door shuttle buses, such as Bayporter ($15; ☎510/467-1800), that run from the airport to locations in the East Bay. They also make the run into San Francisco; expect to pay around $30.

The **Greyhound** station is in a dodgy part of northern Oakland alongside the I-980 freeway at 2103 San Pablo Ave near 21st Street (☎510/834-3213). **Amtrak** terminates at Second Street near Jack London Square in West Oakland, but a better option is to get off at Richmond and change onto the ultramodern BART trains (see below).

The most enjoyable way to arrive in the East Bay is aboard a Blue and Gold Fleet **ferry** ($4.50 each way; ☎510/522-3300), which sails every hour from San Francisco's Ferry Building and Pier 39 to Oakland's Jack London Square.

Transportation connections to Oakland are detailed on p.30.

Transport

The East Bay is linked to San Francisco via the underground BART transbay **subway** (Mon–Sat 6am–midnight, Sun 9am–midnight; ☎415/989-BART from San Francisco or ☎510/465-BART from the East Bay; *www.bart.org*). Three lines run from Daly City through San Francisco and on to downtown Oakland, before diverging to service East Oakland out to Fremont, Berkeley, north to Richmond, and east into Contra Costa County as far as Concord. Bikes are allowed on most trains, and one-way fares range from $1.10–4.45. If you're relying on BART to get around a lot, buy a **high-value ticket** ($5, $10, or $20) to avoid having to stand in line for a new ticket from machines on the station concourse. The cost of each ride is deducted from the total value of the ticket.

For a map of BART, see the color section at the back of the book.

From East Bay BART stations, pick up a **coupon** saving you 35¢ on the $1.35 fares of the revamped **AC Transit** (☎510/839-2882), which provides a good **bus service** around the entire East Bay area, especially Oakland and Berkeley. AC Transit also runs buses on a number of routes to Oakland and Berkeley from the Transbay Terminal in San Francisco. These operate all night, and are the only way of getting across the bay by public transit once BART has shut down. You can pick up excellent free maps of both BART and the bus system from any station. A smaller-scale bus company that can also prove useful, the **Contra Costa County Connection** (☎925/676-7500), runs buses to most of the inland areas, including the John Muir and Eugene O'Neill historic houses.

One of the best ways to get around is by **bike**; a fine **cycle route** follows Skyline and Grizzly Peak boulevards along the wooded crest of the hills between Berkeley and Lake Chabot. You can rent touring bikes or mountain bikes from Around the World, 2416 Telegraph Ave in Oakland (☎510/835-8763; $25), and from Cal Adventures, 2301 Bancroft Way on the UC Berkeley campus (☎510/642-4000; $25). For those interested in **walking tours**, the city of Oakland sponsors free "discovery tours" (☎510/238-3050) of various neighborhoods. A popular excursion is the free Oakland Historical Landmark Tour (Sun 1–3.30pm; ☎510/835-1306), beginning in front of the Oakland Museum at 10th and Fallon, taking in Chinatown, Lake Merritt, Preservation Park, and Jack London Square.

Car rental companies are listed on p.32.

If you're **driving** from San Francisco, allow yourself plenty of time to get there: the East Bay has some of California's worst traffic, with the Bay Bridge and I-80 in particular jam-packed sixteen hours a day. If entering San Francisco via the Bay Bridge on a weekend night, allow at least an hour for the crossing.

Information

The **Oakland Visitor Information Booth**, on Broadway between Water and Embarcadero Streets in Jack London Square (daily 11am–5pm; ☎1-800/262-5526), offers free maps and information, as does its counterpart at 550 Tenth St near the 12th Street BART station in downtown Oakland (Mon–Fri 8.30am–5pm; ☎510/839-9000). In Berkeley, check in at the **Berkeley CVB**, 2015 Center St (Mon–Fri 9am–5pm; ☎510/549-7040) for free maps of the town and a list of what's on. The **Berkeley TRiP Commute Store** (Mon–Wed & Fri 8.30am–5.30pm, Thurs 9am–6pm; ☎510/644-7665), right beside the visitor center at 2033 Center St, sells passes to all local public transportation and gives free information on how to reach local points of interest on the system.

For listings of all major points of interest and the bus routes that'll lead you there, pick up a copy of the free pamphlet, *UC Berkeley Student Guide to East Bay Hot Spots* from the CVB. For an excellent brochure on hiking, cycling, and riding in the many parks and trails that top the Oakland and Berkeley hills, contact the **East Bay Regional Parks District**, 11500 Skyline Blvd (☎510/562-7275). The widely available (and free) *East Bay Express* has the most comprehensive listings of what's on in the vibrant East Bay music and arts scene. The troubled daily *Oakland Tribune* (50¢) is also worth a look for its coverage of local politics and sporting events.

For more on Bay Area publications, see p.42. For specific guides, see p.350.

Treasure Island

Offering great views of San Francisco and its bay, **Treasure Island** was constructed off the eastern edge of the peninsula with dirt dredged from the floor of the bay during construction of the Bay Bridge in 1936. Intended eventually to become an international airport and hub to Pan Am's great China Clippers, Treasure Island captured the imagination of the world in 1939 when it hosted the World's Fair (better known as the Golden Gate Exposition) in the cavernous Art Deco airport buildings.

With the outbreak of World War II in 1941, the Navy comandeered Treasure Island for a base, giving the city some land further south to build the SFO airport. The Navy finally surrendered its lease to the island in September of 1997, and the future of the property – one of San Francisco's most valuable pieces of real estate – is up in the air, though many of the Navy's former housing units have already been converted into residences – both subsidized and privately owned. Still, development efforts are somewhat tangled in red tape, and for the moment, Treasure Island remains an undervisited place from which to take in unspoiled views of the San Francisco skyline.

To get there, take the offramp from either direction on the Bay Bridge, and follow its curves to the Coast Guard gate, beyond which there's a small **museum** in the large auditorium at 410 Palm Ave (daily 10am–3pm; free; ☎415/395-5067), which shows a film on the fair and contains an extensive collection of memorabilia from the China Clippers and the historic exposition. The building itself served as the set of Berlin's Nazi-era airport in *Raiders of the Lost Ark*, not so ironic considering the grand, sharp lines in the building's design, reflective of the conservative politics of World Fair organizers. Outside, there's a telescope (25¢) for snagging close-ups of sea lions, passing ships, or points on the San Francisco skyline. On Sundays, from 6am to 4pm, the island hosts the city's largest **flea market**, at Avenue C and 4th Street (parking $5; ☎415/255-1923), featuring antiques, farmer's produce, flowers, and snacks.

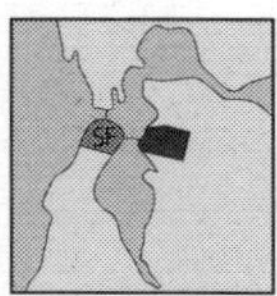

Oakland

As solidly working class as San Francisco is upwardly mobile, **Oakland** is one of the busiest ports on the West Coast and the western terminal of the rail network. Though there are few major sights to lure tourists to "Oaktown," as snootier San Franciscans sometimes refer to the city, a quick hop over from San Francisco on BART or the Bay Bridge is more than justified by the climate – rated the best in the US, it keeps the East Bay sunny and mild when San Francisco is cold and dreary – making for great hiking around the redwood and eucalyptus-covered hills above the downtown.

Still, Oakland has more historical and literary associations than important sights. It's the spawning ground of some of America's most unabashedly revolutionary **political movements** such as the militant **Black Panthers** (see box, p.147), who drew national attention to African-American issues, and the **Symbionese Liberation Army**, who demanded a ransom for kidnapped heiress Patty Hearst

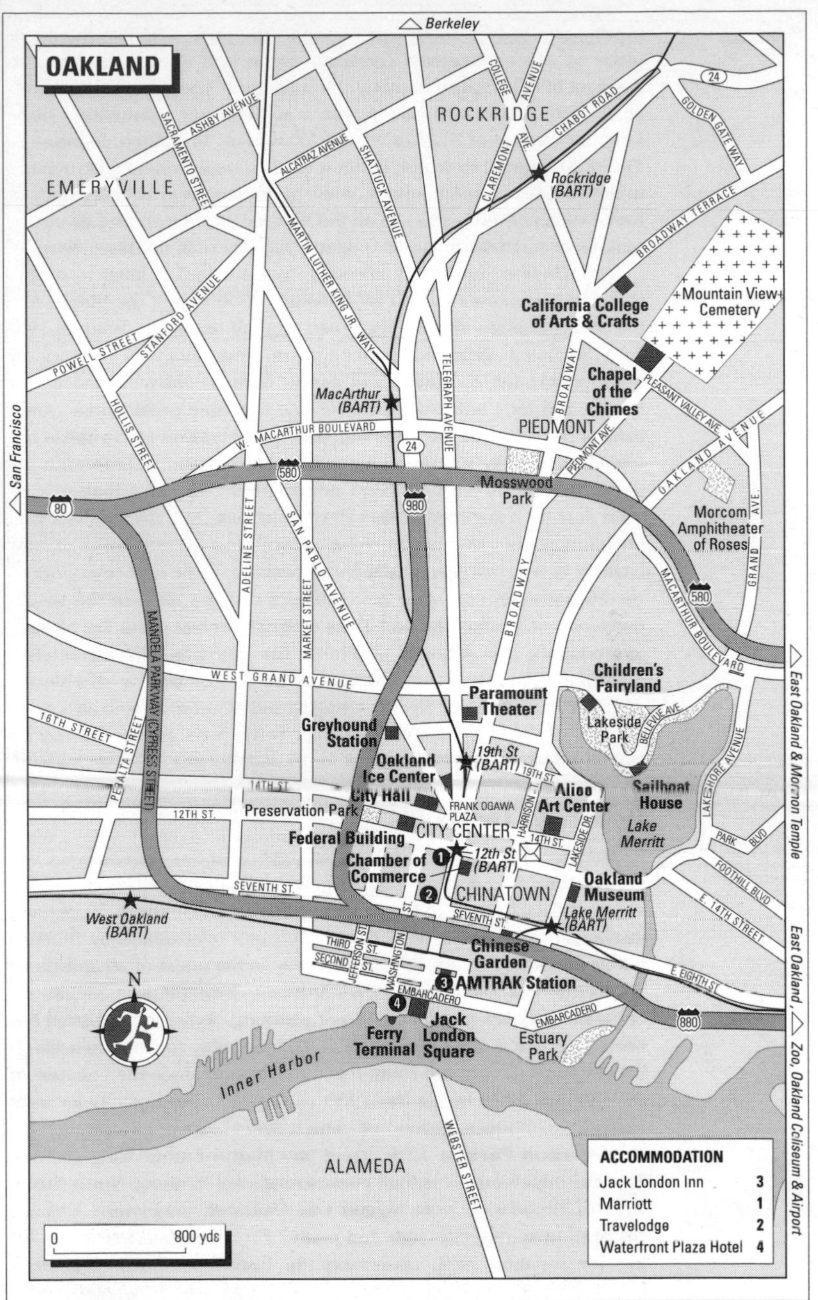
OAKLAND
Berkeley
San Francisco
East Oakland & Mormon Temple
East Oakland, Zoo, Oakland Coliseum & Airport
ROCKRIDGE
EMERYVILLE
PIEDMONT
CITY CENTER
CHINATOWN
ALAMEDA
Rockridge (BART)
MacArthur (BART)
19th St (BART)
12th St (BART)
Lake Merritt (BART)
West Oakland (BART)
California College of Arts & Crafts
Mountain View Cemetery
Chapel of the Chimes
Mosswood Park
Morcom Amphitheater of Roses
Children's Fairyland
Lakeside Park
Paramount Theater
Greyhound Station
Oakland Ice Center
City Hall
Preservation Park
Frank Ogawa Plaza
Alice Art Center
Sailboat House
Lake Merritt
Federal Building
Chamber of Commerce
Oakland Museum
Chinese Garden
AMTRAK Station
Ferry Terminal
Jack London Square
Estuary Park
Inner Harbor
N
0 800 yds
ACCOMMODATION
Jack London Inn 3
Marriott 1
Travelodge 2
Waterfront Plaza Hotel 4

in the form of free food distribution to the poor. It's also the birthplace of literary legends **Gertrude Stein** and **Jack London**, who grew up here at approximately the same time, though in entirely different circumstances – Stein was a stockbroker's daughter, while London, author of *Call of the Wild*, was an orphaned delinquent. The waterfront area where London used to steal oysters and lobsters in now named in his memory, while Stein, who was actually born in East Oakland (see p.147), is all but ignored, not surprising given her famous proclamation about Oakland that "there is no there there."

Nevertheless, until very recently, locals found it hard to argue: Oakland businesses have a long history of deserting the place once the going gets good; the city's own football team, the Raiders, defected to Los Angeles for thirteen years. Residents who've stuck by the city through its duller and darker days recently elected a new mayor, former California governor and one-time presidential candidate **Jerry** "Moonbeam" **Brown**, who has promised to revitalize the town and slash its infamous crime rate without cramping its distinctive style. With his term not up until 2003, it remains to be seen how he'll succeed at this Herculean task, but already he's well on his way to meet his promise of bringing 10,000 affluent new citizens downtown, especially those basking in the new "e-conomy." Increasingly popular with dot-commers and the like are the neighborhoods of **Rockridge** and **Lake Merritt**, whose rents are already approaching San Francisco prices. The city has also attracted a significant number of lesbians, who've formed a distinctive community near Lake Merritt along Grand Avenue, as well as a great number of artists, pushed from their SoMa lofts across the bay by sky-high rents and resettled now in the warehouses of West Oakland.

Downtown Oakland

Coming by BART from San Francisco, get off at the 12th Street–Civic Center station and you're at the new, open-air shopping and office space of **City Center** in the heart of **downtown Oakland**, a compact district of spruced-up Victorian storefronts overlooked by modern hotels and office buildings that has been in the midst of an ambitious redevelopment program for over a decade. Fraught with allegations of illegal dealings and incompetent planning, so far the program has been less than a complete success. To make way for the moat-like I-980 freeway – the main route through Oakland since the collapse of the Cypress Freeway in the 1989 earthquake – entire blocks were cleared of houses, some of which were saved and moved to **Preservation Park** at 12th Street and Martin Luther King Jr Way. The late nineteenth-century commercial center along Ninth Street west of Broadway, now tagged **Old Oakland**, underwent a major restoration some years ago, but many of the buildings are still waiting for tenants. Still, observing the historic facades, especially between Clay and Washington, provides a glimpse of what Oakland once was. By way of contrast stroll a block east of Broadway, between Seventh and Ninth streets, to Oakland's **Chinatown**, whose bakeries and restaurants are as lively and bustling – if not as picturesque – as those of its more famous cousin across the Bay. Every year on the last weekend in August the vibrant **Chinatown Street Fest** brings out traditional performing artists, food vendors, and cooking and arts demonstrations, drawing a good 100,000 people.

Oakland's restaurants are detailed beginning on p.263.

While much of downtown Oakland may have the look of a permanent building site, it's actually home to a wide array of architectural styles. The city experienced its greatest period of growth in the early twentieth century, and many of the grand buildings of this era survive a few blocks north along Broadway, centered around the gigantic grass knoll of **Frank Ogawa Plaza** and the awkwardly imposing 1914 **City Hall** on 14th Street. The first government building designed as a skyscraper, it was restored after the 1989 earthquake, and the foundation now rests on 113 giant, but concealed, rubber shock absorbers so that it will sway rather than crumble in the Big One. Two blocks away at 13th and Franklin stands Oakland's most unmistakeable landmark, the chateauesque lantern of the **Tribune Tower**, the 1920s-era former home of the *Oakland Tribune* newspaper.

Further north, around the 19th Street BART station, are some of the Bay Area's finest early twentieth-century buildings, highlighted by the outstanding Art Deco interior of the 1931 **Paramount Theater** at 2025 Broadway (tours 10am first and third Sat of the month; $1; ☎510/465-6400), which shows Hollywood classics and hosts occasional concerts by big-name stars as well as performances by the Oakland Ballet and Oakland Symphony. The theater was designed by Timothy L. Pflueger, the San Francisco architect behind the Pacific Coast Stock Exchange, the Castro Theater, and many of the buildings on Treasure Island. Pflueger enlisted the help of a group of artists to contribute to the Paramount's design, as evidenced by the building's eclectic mix of accoutrements, from the illuminated "fountain of light" stained-glass ceiling in the entrance, to the mosaics and reliefs which adorn every inch of the interior. Pflueger became the Bay Area leader of the Moderne, or Art Deco style, counting among his friends the artist Diego Rivera.

For more information on Diego Rivera, see p.73.

Nearby buildings are equally flamboyant, ranging from the wafer-thin Gothic "flatiron" office tower of the **Cathedral Building** at Broadway and Telegraph, to the Hindu temple-like facade of the magnificent 3500-seat **Fox Oakland** (now closed) on Telegraph at 19th – the largest movie house west of Chicago at the time it was built in 1928 – and, across the street, the 1931 **Floral Depot**, a group of small, modern storefronts faced in black-and-blue terracotta tiles with shiny silver highlights.

West of Broadway, the area around the Greyhound bus station on San Pablo Avenue is fairly seedy. Once the main route in and out of

Oakland before the freeways were built, many of the avenue's roadside businesses are now derelict, especially around the isolated industrial districts of Emeryville. Still, an effort by local architects to transform the place into a glitzy architectural centerpiece is underway, the most intriguing evidence of which is the new **Civic Center**, at Park Avenue and Hollis Street, in which the original 1902 town hall has been wrapped in a sheer glass box that provides 15,000 additional square feet of stylized office space. Despite the push to gentrify the area, prostitutes and drug-dealers still hang out under the neon signs of the dingy neighboring bars and gambling halls such as the *Oaks Card Club*, where Oaktown rapper M.C. Hammer used to work.

Lake Merritt and the Oakland Museum

Five blocks east of Broadway, the eastern third of downtown Oakland comprises **Lake Merritt**, a three-mile-circumference tidal lagoon that was bridged and dammed in the 1860s to become the centerpiece of Oakland's most desirable neighborhood. All that remains of the many fine houses that once circled the lake is the elegant **Camron-Stanford House**, on the southwest shore at 1418 Lakeside Drive, a graceful Italianate mansion whose sumptuous interior is open for visits (Wed 11am–4pm, Sun 1–5pm; $4). The lake is also the nation's oldest wildlife refuge, and migrating flocks of ducks, geese, and herons break their journeys here. Its north shore is lined by **Lakeside Park**, where you can rent canoes and rowboats ($4 per hour), and a range of sailing boats and catamarans ($4–10 per hour) from the **Sailboat House** (summer daily 10am–5pm; rest of year Fri–Sun 10am–4.30pm; ☎510/238-2196), provided you can convince the staff you know how to sail. A miniature Mississippi riverboat makes thirty-minute lake **cruises** ($1) on weekend afternoons, and kids will like the puppet shows and pony rides at the **Children's Fairyland** (summer daily 10am–5.30pm; rest of year Fri–Sun 10am–5.30pm; $3.25), along Grand Avenue on the northwest edge of the park. Every night, the lake is lit up by its Necklace of Lights, a source of local pride, and on the first weekend in June, the park comes to life during the **Festival at the Lake**, when all of Oakland gets together to enjoy nonstop music and performances from local bands and entertainers.

For other children's activities in the Bay Area, see p.35.

Two blocks south of the lake, or a block up Oak Street from the Lake Merritt BART station, the **Oakland Museum** (Wed–Sat 10am–5pm, Sun noon–5pm; $6, free Sun after 4pm) is perhaps Oakland's most worthwhile stop, not only for the exhibits but also for the superb modern building in which it's housed, topped by a terraced rooftop sculpture garden that gives great views out over the water and the city. The museum covers three topics on as many floors, the first of which treats California's **ecology** in exhibits simulating a walk from the seaside through various natural habitats and climate zones right up to the 14,000-foot summits of the Sierra Nevada mountains. The second floor deals with California's **history**, from Native American habitats to the Spanish colonial and Gold Rush eras to the present day. Artifacts on display include the guitar that Berkeley-born Country Joe MacDonald played at the Woodstock festival in 1969. On the third floor resides a broad survey of works by Californian artists and craftspeople, some highlights of which are pieces of c.1900 Arts and Crafts furniture. You'll also see excellent **photography** by Edward Muybridge, Dorothea Lange, Imogen Cunningham, and many others. A collector's gallery housed in the museum rents and sells works by California artists.

West of the museum, the newly opened **Alice Arts Center**, 1428 Alice St at 14th Street (☎510/652-0752), is home to the Oakland Ensemble Theater and host to weekly concerts and performances by East Bay artists.

The waterfront

Half a mile down from Downtown Oakland on AC Transit bus #51, at the foot of Broadway on the **waterfront**, **Jack London Square** is Oakland's main concession to the tourist trade. Accessible by direct ferry from San Francisco, this somewhat anesthetic complex of harborfront boutiques and restaurants, anchored by a huge Barnes and Noble bookstore, was named after the self-taught writer who grew up pirating shellfish around here, though it's about as distant from the wandering spirit of the man as could be. London's best story, *The Call of the Wild*, was written about his adventures in the Alaskan Yukon, where he carved his initials in a small cabin that has been reconstructed here. Another relic, **Heinold's First and Last Chance Saloon**, is a tiny slanting bar built nearby in 1883 from the hull of a whaling ship where Jack London actually drank, as the collection of yellowed portraits of him on the wall attest.

No Jack London enthusiast should fail to visit his Sonoma Valley ranch, see p.211.

In recent years, the square has seen the addition of a nine-screen multiplex cinema and **Yoshi's World Class Jazz House**, on the Embarcadero between Clay and Washington, the Bay Area's, if not West Coast's, premier jazz club, transplanted from further inland. There is also a massive $200 million plan to revamp the square into a top-notch entertainment venue by 2005, including the ambitious introduction of a lighted, moving sidewalk to make the center – isolated from the downtown by I-580 where it passes over Broadway – more accessible.

For information on Yoshi's, *see p.288.*

Within the square, **The Ebony Museum of Arts**, at 30 Alice St on the second floor of the shopping complex (Tues–Sun noon–6pm; donation), is worth a visit for its African art and pop-American counterculture collectibles. Docked at the pier at the foot of Clay Street is the USS *Potomac*, FDR's presidential yacht, restored to its former glory and open for both historical cruises and dockside tours. Otherwise, a few short blocks inland lies a warehouse district with a

Ferry services from San Francisco are detailed on p.30.

Two hour USS Potomac *cruises depart at 10am & 1.30pm, mid-May–mid-Nov, the first and third Thurs, and the second and fourth Sat of each month, for $30; dock-side tours are given Wed 10am–4pm and Sun noon–4pm, for $3; call ☎510/839-8256 for more information.*

couple of good places to eat and drink lurking among the train tracks (see on p.263) and most lively early in the morning, from about 5am when a daily **Produce Market**, along Third and Fourth streets, gives you the opportunity to buy fruits and vegetables direct from the growers.

Alameda

AC Transit bus #51 continues from Broadway under the inner harbor to **Alameda**, a quiet and conservative island of middle America dominated by a large, empty naval air station, closed by President Clinton in 1995 – although massive nuclear-powered aircraft carriers still dock here occasionally. The fine houses along the original shoreline on Clinton Street were part of the summer resort colony that flocked here to the *contra costa* or "opposite shore" from San Francisco, near the now demolished Neptune Beach amusement park. The island has since been much enlarged by dredging and landfill, and 1960s apartment buildings now line the long, narrow shore of **Robert Crown Memorial Beach** along the bay – a quiet, attractive spot, though development has begun to encroach on the last pocket of affordable real estate in the form of chain stores.

West Oakland

West Oakland – an industrial district of warehouses, rail tracks, 1960s housing projects, and decaying Victorian houses – may be the nearest East Bay BART stop to San Francisco, but it is light years away from that city's prosperity, and apart from a marvelous stock of c.1900 houses there's little here to tempt tourists today.

Historically, the district couldn't have been more colorful. The heart of the Bay Area's entertainment scene was situated near the West Oakland BART station along **Seventh Street** from the end of Prohibition in 1933 right up through the early 1970s, when the buildings were torn down in the name of urban renewal. Today, Seventh Street runs west between the docks and storage yards of the Oakland Army Base and the Naval Supply Depot, ending up at **Port View Park**, a good place to watch the huge container ships that pass by. The small park stands on the site of the old transbay ferry terminal, used by as many as 40 million passengers annually before the Bay Bridge was completed in 1936. Despite the obvious poverty, it's more safe and settled than it may appear, though the only time anyone pays any attention to it is when something dramatic happens. The Black Panthers once held court in West Oakland (see box opposite), and in 1989, Black Panther Huey Newton was gunned down here in a drug-related revenge attack; later the same year, the double-decker I-880 freeway that divided the neighborhood from the rest of the city collapsed in on itself during the earthquake, killing dozens of commuters. Local African-

Black Panthers

Formed amidst the poverty of West Oakland in 1966 by black-rights activists Huey Newton and Bobby Seale, the leather jacket and beret-sporting members of the **Black Panther Party for Self-Defense** captured the media spotlight with their militant rhetoric and occasional gun battles with police.

The party was actually started as a civil-rights organization influenced by Malcolm X's call to black Americans to rely on themselves for defense and dignity. Mixing socialism with black pride, the Panthers aimed to eradicate poverty and drug use in America's inner cities, arguing that if the government wouldn't do it, they would. One of the first acts of the party was to establish patrols in local communities to monitor police brutality.

The Panthers' membership grew as the group captured the national spotlight over the trial of Newton for the murder of an Oakland police officer in 1969. Released from prison a year later when his conviction was overturned, Newton sought to revamp the Panthers' image – tainted by increasingly negative and sensational press coverage – by developing "survival programs" in black communities, including the establishment of free medical clinics, breakfasts for children, shelter for the homeless, and jobs for the unemployed. But infighting over leadership within the party took a heavy toll, and when Netwon fled to Cuba in 1974 to avoid prosecution for drug use, a series of resignations ensued. By the end of the 1970s, stripped of its original leadership and attacked by newspaper accounts of illicit internal activities, the group disbanded.

In 1999, former party Chief of Staff David Hilliard began giving school groups tours of West Oakland, stressing the positive contributions of the Panthers to the neighborhood, such as stoplights at dangerous intersections, health care centers, and food programs. Hilliard is now in a court battle with Newton's widow over ownership of the Black Panther name, though he still conducts **Black Panther Legacy Tours** ($20–25; ☎510/986-0660) through the Huey P. Newton Foundation on the last Saturday of each month. Tours depart at noon across from the main library on W 18 St.

American leaders successfully resisted government plans to rebuild that concrete eyesore; the broad, street-level **Nelson Mandela Parkway** has replaced it, thereby removing the physical justification for the "other side of the freeway" stigma once linked to the place. Given its cheap rents and open spaces situated so closely to San Francisco, West Oakland's future is sure to include some major new developments.

East Oakland

The bulk of Oakland spreads along foothills and flatlands to the east of downtown, in neighborhoods obviously stratified along the main thoroughfares of Foothill and MacArthur boulevards. Gertrude Stein grew up here, though when she returned years later in search of her childhood home it had been torn down and replaced by a dozen Craftsman-style bungalows – the simple 1920s wooden houses that cover most of **East Oakland**, each fronted by a patch of lawn and divided from its neighbor by a narrow concrete driveway.

For books by and about Bay Area literary figures, see p.348.

A quick way out from the gridded streets and sidewalks of the city is to take AC Transit bus #64 from downtown east up into the hills to **Joaquin Miller Park**, the most easily accessible of Oakland's hilltop parks. It stands on the former grounds of "The Hights," the misspelled home of the "Poet of the Sierras," Joaquin Miller, who made his name playing the eccentric frontier American in the literary salons of 1870s London. His poems weren't exactly acclaimed – even if he did manage to rhyme "teeth" with "Goethe" – but his prose account, *Life Amongst the Modocs*, documenting time spent with the Modoc people near Mount Shasta, does stand the test of time. It was more for his outrageous behavior that he became famous, wearing bizarre clothes and biting debutantes on their ankles. For years, Japanese poet and sculptor Yone Noguchi, father of Isamu Noguchi, lived here; according to one story, he worked the sprinkler while Miller impressed lady visitors with a Native American rain dance.

Perched in the hills at the foot of the park, the pointed towers of the **Mormon Temple**, 4770 Lincoln Ave, look like missile-launchers designed by the Wizard of Oz – unmissable by day or floodlit night. In December, speakers hidden in the landscaping make it seem as if the plants are singing Christmas carols. Though you can't go inside the temple itself (unless you're a confirmed Mormon), there are great views out over the entire Bay Area from the grounds, and a small adjoining museum explains the tenets of the faith (daily 9am–9pm; free; ☎510/531-1475). If asked, the docent will give a 25-minute tour of the structure, after which you can watch any or all of the 12-part video about the temple. There's also a branch of the Mormon's **genealogical research library** (daily 7am–8pm; ☎510/531-3200) where you can try tracing your family's ancestry, regardless of your faith, as long as you don't mind that your own name may be baptized into the Mormon faith without your consent.

Two miles east along Hwy-13 sits the attractive campus of **Mills College**. Founded in 1852 as a women-only seminary, it's still decidedly female after a much-publicized 1990 struggle against turning co-ed, although the graduate class is now open to both sexes. Mills is renowned for its music school, considered one of the best and most innovative in the US, and is worth a visit for its **art gallery** (Sept–June Tues–Sat 11am–4pm, Sun noon–4pm; free), which has a fine collection of Chinese, Japanese, and pre-Columbian ceramics. A broad stream meanders through the lushly landscaped grounds, and many of the buildings, notably the central campanile, were designed in solid California Mission style by Julia Morgan, architect of Hearst Castle as well as nearly five hundred Bay Area structures. Further east, reachable by AC Transit bus #56, is **Oakland Zoo** in Knowland Park, once one of the worst zoos in the country, though many of its once-cramped quarters have been replaced with large naturalistic

The Oakland Zoo is open daily 10am–4pm; entrance is $6.50.

habitats. The most noteworthy is the **Malayan Sun bear** exhibit, the largest of its kind in the States.

Some twenty miles of tract house suburbs stretch along the bay south to San Jose, and the only vaguely interesting area is around the end of the BART line in **FREMONT**, where the short-lived Essanay movie studios were based. Essanay, the first studios on the West Coast, made more than 700 films in three years, including Charlie Chaplin's *The Tramp* in 1914. Not much remains from those pre-Hollywood days, however, and the only real sight is the **Mission San Jose de Guadalupe** on Mission Boulevard south of the I-680 freeway (daily 10am–5pm; donation). Built in 1797 as the fourteenth mission in the chain of 21 that run along the El Camino Reál (see p.332), the structure was completely rebuilt in 1985 to look as it did in the early 1800s. One of the least-visited missions in the chain, it's probably the most striking of the five in the Bay Area, with crystal chandeliers suspended from its rustic wooden nave and trompe l'oeil balconies painted on its walls. The reconstruction of the church was so faithful to the original that even the gigantic original bells hung in the belfry are suspended from rawhide straps, just as they were more than two hundred years before.

North Oakland and Rockridge

The horrific 1991 **Oakland fire**, which destroyed 3000 homes and killed 26 people, did most of its damage in the high-priced hills of **North Oakland**. It took the better part of two years, but most of the million-dollar houses have been rebuilt, and though the lush vegetation that made the area so attractive will never be allowed by nervous residents to grow back, things are pretty much back to normal. Which is to say that segregation is still in place, these bayview homes, some of the Bay Area's most valuable real estate, look out across some of its poorest – the neglected flatlands below that were the proving grounds of Black Panthers Bobby Seale and Huey Newton in the 1960s.

Broadway is the dividing line between the two halves of North Oakland, and also gives access (via the handy AC Transit #51 bus) to most of what there is to see and do. The **Morcom Amphitheater of Roses**, on Oakland Avenue three blocks east of Broadway (April–Oct daily dawn–dusk; free; ☎510/238-3187), has eight acres of pools, trees, and roses – best seen from May to September when they're in full bloom. Nearby **Piedmont Avenue** is lined by a number of small bookstores and cafés; a mile north along the avenue, the **Mountain View Cemetery** was laid out in 1863 by Frederick Law Olmsted (designer of New York's Central Park and Golden Gate Park) and holds the elaborate dynastic tombs of San Francisco's most powerful families – the Crockers, the Bechtels, and the Ghirardellis. You can jog or ride a bike around the well-tended grounds, or just wonder at the enormous turtles in the pond. Next door, the columbarium, known as **Chapel of the Chimes**, at 4499 Piedmont Ave (daily 9am–5pm; free; ☎510/654-0123), was enhanced by Julia Morgan of Hearst Castle fame during her decade-long involvement with the structure beginning in 1921. The edifice is remarkable for its seemingly endless series of urn-filled rooms, grouped together around sky-lit courtyards, bubbling fountains, and intimate chapels – all connected by ornate staircases of every conceivable length and furnished with comfortable chairs. Morgan wanted the space to sing of life, not death, and she's succeeded. Visit the strangely peaceful place during one of the regular concerts held here (call ahead for schedule) for a completely unique – and distinctly Californian – experience.

For those keenly interested, there's a free monthly tour of the Mountain View Cemetery on the second Saturday of every month, leaving from the gates at 10am.

Back on Broadway, just past College Avenue, Broadway Terrace climbs up along the edge of the fire area to **Lake Temescal** – where you can swim in summer – and continues to the forested ridge at the **Robert Sibley Regional Preserve**, which includes the 1761-foot volcanic cone of Round Top Peak, offering panoramas of the entire Bay Area. The peak has been dubbed the **Volcanic Witch Project** by local media for five strange mazes carved into the dirt in canyons around the crater and lined with stones. No one is sure who began the project, but navigating any of the designs leads to its center, where visitors add to the pile of eclectic offerings ranging from trinkets to cigarettes to poetry. Skyline Boulevard runs through the park and is popular with cyclists, who ride the twelve miles south to Lake Chabot or follow Grizzly Peak Boulevard five miles north to Tilden Park through the Berkeley Hills.

Most of the Broadway traffic, and the AC Transit #51 bus, cuts off onto College Avenue through Oakland's most appealing shopping district, **Rockridge**. Spreading for half a mile on either side of the Rockridge BART station, the quirky stores and restaurants here, despite their undeniable yuppie overtones, are some of the best around. Both in geography and atmosphere, it's as near as Oakland gets to the café society of neighboring Berkeley.

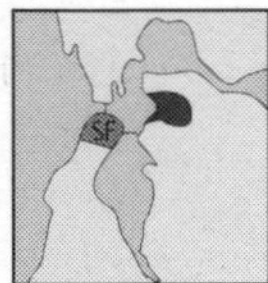

Berkeley

This Berkeley was like no somnolent Siwash out of her own past at all, but more akin to those Far Eastern or Latin American universities you read about, those autonomous culture media where the most beloved of folklores may be brought into doubt, cataclysmic of dissents voiced, suicidal of commitments chosen – the sort that bring governments down.

Thomas Pynchon *The Crying of Lot 49*

More than any other American city, **BERKELEY** conjures up an image of 1960s student dissent. When college campuses across the

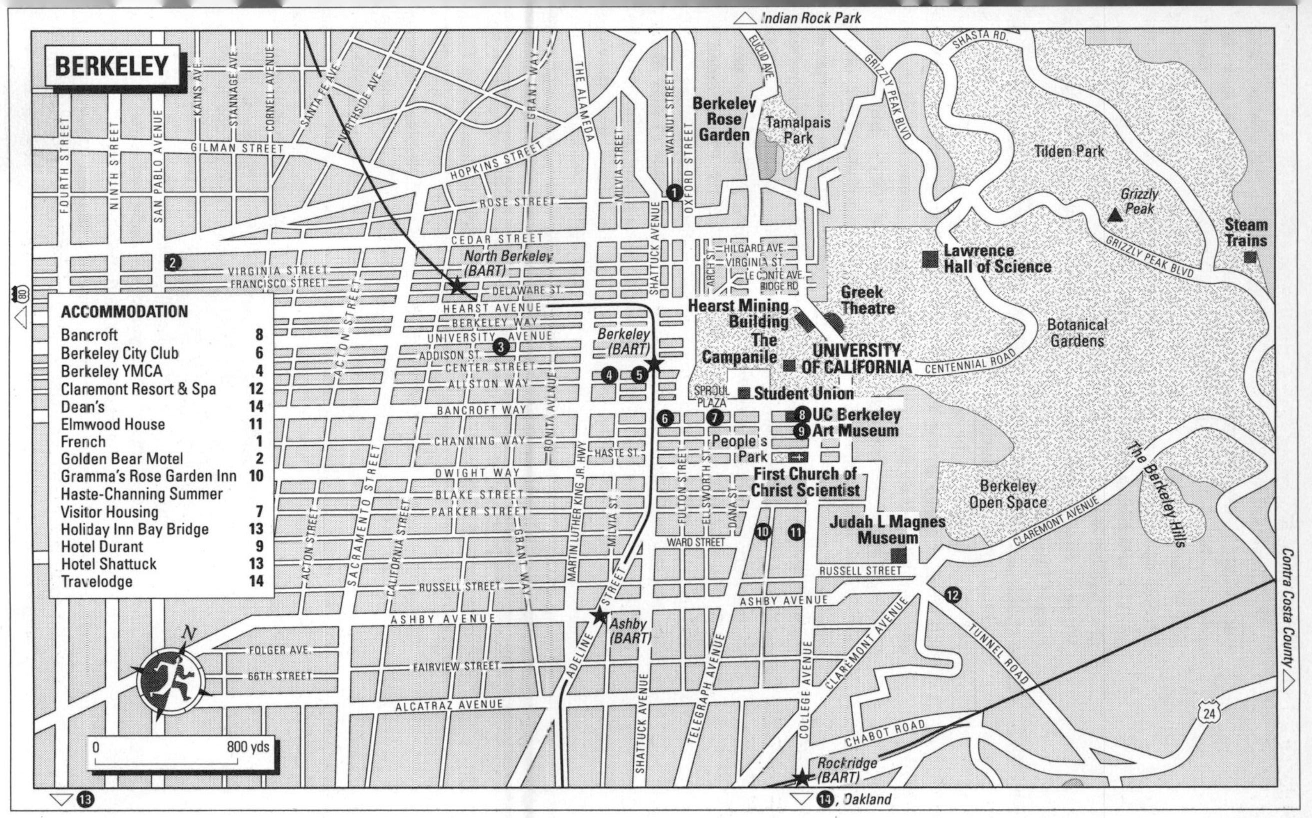
BERKELEY
ACCOMMODATION
Bancroft 8
Berkeley City Club 6
Berkeley YMCA 4
Claremont Resort & Spa 12
Dean's 14
Elmwood House 11
French 1
Golden Bear Motel 2
Gramma's Rose Garden Inn 10
Haste-Channing Summer Visitor Housing 7
Holiday Inn Bay Bridge 13
Hotel Durant 9
Hotel Shattuck 13
Travelodge 14
Indian Rock Park
Contra Costa County
Oakland
Steam Trains
Lawrence Hall of Science
Tilden Park
Grizzly Peak
Botanical Gardens
The Berkeley Hills
Berkeley Open Space
Greek Theatre
UNIVERSITY OF CALIFORNIA
Hearst Mining Building
The Campanile
Student Union
SPROUL PLAZA
UC Berkeley Art Museum
People's Park
First Church of Christ Scientist
Judah L Magnes Museum
Berkeley Rose Garden
Tamalpais Park
North Berkeley (BART)
Berkeley (BART)
Ashby (BART)
Rockridge (BART)
SHASTA RD.
EUCLID AVE.
GRIZZLY PEAK BLVD
CENTENNIAL ROAD
CLAREMONT AVENUE
TUNNEL ROAD
CHABOT ROAD
COLLEGE AVENUE
TELEGRAPH AVENUE
SHATTUCK AVENUE
ADELINE STREET
MARTIN LUTHER KING JR. HWY
THE ALAMEDA
OXFORD STREET
WALNUT STREET
MILVIA STREET
MILVIA ST.
GRANT WAY
HOPKINS STREET
GILMAN STREET
ROSE STREET
CEDAR STREET
VIRGINIA STREET
FRANCISCO STREET
DELAWARE ST.
HEARST AVENUE
BERKELEY WAY
UNIVERSITY AVENUE
ADDISON ST.
CENTER STREET
ALLSTON WAY
BANCROFT WAY
CHANNING WAY
HASTE ST.
DWIGHT WAY
BLAKE STREET
PARKER STREET
RUSSELL STREET
ASHBY AVENUE
FOLGER AVE.
66TH STREET
FAIRVIEW STREET
ALCATRAZ AVENUE
BONITA AVENUE
CALIFORNIA STREET
SACRAMENTO STREET
ACTON STREET
SANTA FE AVE.
NORTHSIDE AVE.
KAINS AVE.
STANNAGE AVE.
CORNELL AVENUE
SAN PABLO AVENUE
NINTH STREET
FOURTH STREET
HILGARD AVE.
VIRGINIA ST.
LE CONTE AVE.
RIDGE RD
ARCH ST.
FULTON STREET
ELLSWORTH ST.
DANA ST.
WARD STREET
0
800 yds

nation were protesting against the Vietnam War, it was the students of the University of California, Berkeley, who led the charge – gaining a name as the vanguard of what was increasingly seen as a challenge to the authority of the state. Full-scale battles were fought almost daily here at one point, on the campus and on its surrounding streets, and there were times when Berkeley looked almost on the brink of revolution itself: students (and others) throwing stones and gas bombs were met with tear-gas volleys and truncheons by National Guard troops under the nominal command of Governor Ronald Reagan.

Such action was inspired by the mood of the time and, in an increasingly conservative America, Berkeley politics are nowadays far more middle-of-the-road. But despite an influx of conformist students, a surge in the number of exclusive restaurants, and the dismantling of the city's rent control program, something of the progressive legacy manages to linger in the city's independent bookstores and at sporadic political demonstrations, if not on the agenda of the city council. In recent years, the most entertaining cause célèbre on campus was Naked Man, an undergrad who refused to wear clothing while attending class. More seriously, in 1999, the entire Berkeley community was outraged when Pacifica, the parent company of local leftist radio station KPFA 94.1 FM, decided to change the station's programs to less subversive themes in an attempt to draw funding. When staff members wouldn't play along, Pacifica sent in armed security guards to remove them from the premises, and the ensuing standoff was broadcast live, drawing thousands of militant supporters. For now, KPFA remains on the air, as unrepentant as ever, though relationships with management are unsurprisingly strained.

The **University of California**, right in the center of town, completely dominates Berkeley and makes a logical starting point for a visit. Its many grand buildings and 30,000 students give off a definite energy that spills down the raucous stretch of **Telegraph Avenue** which runs south from the campus and holds most of the studenty hangouts, including a dozen or so lively cafés, as well as a number of fine bookstores. Older students, and a good percentage of the faculty, congregate in **North Berkeley**, popularly known as Northside, popping down from their woodsy hillside homes to partake of goodies from the "Gourmet Ghetto," a stretch of Shattuck Avenue crammed with restaurants, delis, and bakeries. Of quite distinct character are the flatlands that spread through **West Berkeley** down to the bay, a poorer but increasingly gentrified district that mixes old Victorian houses with builder's yards and light industrial premises sandwiched around the restaurants and houseware shops of **Fourth Street**. Along the bay itself is the **Berkeley Marina**, where you can rent sailboards and sailboats or just watch the sun set behind the Golden Gate.

The University of California

Caught up in the frantic crush of students who pack the **University of California** campus during the semesters, it's nearly impossible to imagine the bucolic learning environment envisaged by its high-minded founders. When the Reverend Henry Durant and other East Coast academics decided to set up shop here in the 1860s, these rolling foothills were still largely given over to dairy herds and wheat fields, the last remnants of the Peralta family's Spanish land-grant *rancho* which once stretched over most of the East Bay. One day in 1866, while surveying the land, an inspired trustee recited "Westward the course of the empire takes its way," from an eighteenth-century poem by George Berkeley. Moved by the moment, all assembled agreed to name their school after the Irish bishop and philosopher who penned the phrase. Construction work on the two campus buildings – imaginatively named North Hall and South Hall – was still going on when the first 200 students, including 22 women, moved here from Oakland in 1873.

Since then an increasing number of buildings have been squeezed into the half-mile-square main campus, and the state-funded

Berkeley's bookstores

Berkeley's **bookstores** are as exhaustive as they are exhausting – not surprising for a university town. Perfect for browsing and taking your time, you won't be made to feel guilty or obliged to buy a book you've been poring over for ages. Listings for more bookstores can be found beginning on p.310.

Black Oak Books, 1491 Shattuck Ave (☎510/486-0698). Huge selection of secondhand and new books for every interest; also holds regular evening readings by internationally acclaimed authors.

Cody's Books, 2454 Telegraph Ave (☎510/845-7852). The flagship of Berkeley booksellers, with an excellent selection of fiction, poetry, and literary criticism.

Comics and Comix, 2502 Telegraph Ave (☎510/845-4091). Great selection of comic books, both current and classic.

Easy Going, 1385 Shattuck Ave (☎510/843-3533). The essential bookstore for every traveler. Packed with printed travel paraphernalia, it offers a wide selection of guidebooks and maps for local, countrywide, and worldwide exploration.

Moe's Books, 2476 Telegraph Ave (☎510/849-2087). An enormous selection of new and used books on four floors with esoteric surprises in every field of study; for academics, book-collectors, and browsers. There's also an excellent art section on the top floor.

Serendipity Books, 1201 University Ave (☎510/841-7455). With an incredible selection of first edition and out-of-print books. A must for collectors of first editions and obscure fiction and poetry.

Shakespeare and Company, 2499 Telegraph Ave (☎510/841-8916). Crammed with quality secondhand books at reasonable prices. The best place to linger and scour the shelves for finds.

Shambala Booksellers, 2482 Telegraph Ave (☎510/848-8443). Have a transcendental out-of-body experience where Eastern and Western religious traditions meet in this cozy store near campus.

university (known to students as merely "Cal" or "UC," but rarely "Berkeley") has become one of America's most prestigious, with so many Nobel laureates on the faculty it's rumored you have to win one just to get a parking permit. UC Berkeley physicists built the first cyclotron, and plutonium was discovered here in 1941 along with the elements californium and berkelium; as such, it was the setting for sketches for the first atomic bomb. Nuclear weaponry and over-crowding aside, the beautifully landscaped campus, stepping down from the eucalyptus-covered Berkeley Hills toward the Golden Gate, is eminently strollable. With maps posted everywhere, you'd have to try hard to get lost – though enthusiastic students will show you around on a free ninety-minute **tour** (Mon–Sat 10am, Sun 1pm; ☎510/642-5215) which depart from the **University of California's Visitor Services** office, 101 University Hall, at the corner of Oxford and University.

A number of footpaths climb the hill from the Berkeley BART station on Shattuck Avenue, but the best way to get a feel for the place is to follow Strawberry Creek from the top of Center Street across the southeast corner of the campus, emerging from the groves of redwood and eucalyptus trees at **Sproul Plaza**. It's the largest public space on campus, enlivened by street musicians playing for quarters on the steps of the **Student Union** building and conga drummers pounding away in the echoing courtyard below. The Plaza is also lined with tables staffed by student groups advocating one thing or another – from free love to sexual abstinence.

Sather Gate, which bridges Strawberry Creek at the north end of Sproul Plaza, marks the entrance to the older part of the campus. Up the hill, past the imposing facade of Wheeler Hall, the 1914 landmark **Campanile** (Mon–Fri 10am–4pm, Sat & Sun 10am–5pm; $1) is modeled after the one in the Piazza San Marco in Venice; take an elevator to the top for a great view of the campus and the entire Bay Area. At the foot of the tower stands redbrick **South Hall**, the sole survivor of the original pair of buildings.

Inside the plain white building next door, the **Bancroft Library** (Mon–Fri 9am–5pm, Sat 1–5pm) displays odds and ends from its exhaustive accumulation of artifacts and documents tracing the history of California, including a faked brass plaque supposedly left by Sir Francis Drake when he claimed all of the West Coast for Queen Elizabeth I. It also contains a collection of manuscripts and rare books, from Mark Twain to James Joyce – though to see any of these you'll have to show some academic credentials. Around the corner and down the hill, just inside the arched main entrance to Doe Library, you'll find the **Morrison Reading Room**, a great place to sit for a while and read foreign magazines and newspapers, listen to a CD, or just ease down into one of the many comfy overstuffed chairs and unwind.

Also worth a look if you've got time to kill is the **Museum of Paleontology** (Mon–Thurs 8am–10pm, Fri 8am–5pm, Sat 10am–5pm,

Sun 1–10pm; free) in the nearby Valley Life Sciences Building, which explores evolutionary concepts with hundreds of fossils, skeletons, and geological maps through the displays lining the corridors on the lower floors. From here it's a quick walk to the collection of cafés and restaurants lining Euclid and Hearst avenues, and the beginning of North Berkeley (see p.157).

The Hearst family name appears with disturbing regularity around the Berkeley campus, though in most instances this is due not to the notorious newspaper baron William Randolph but to his altruistic mother, Phoebe Apperson Hearst. Besides inviting the entire senior class to her home every spring for a giant picnic, she sponsored the architectural competition that came up with the original campus plan, and donated a good number of the campus buildings, including many that have since been destroyed. One of the finest survivors, the 1907 **Hearst Mining Building** on the northeast edge of the campus, conceals a delicate metalwork lobby topped by three glass domes, above aging exhibits on geology and mining – which is how the Hearst family fortune was originally made, long before scion W.R. took up publishing. Currently undergoing extensive seismic retro-fitting and renovation, the building is closed until further notice. Another Hearst legacy is the **Greek Theatre**, modeled after the amphitheater at Epidarus, Greece, which hosts a summer season of rock concerts.

Higher up in the hills, above the 80,000-seat Memorial Stadium, the lushly landscaped **Botanical Garden** (daily 9am–5pm; free) defeats on-campus claustrophobia with thirty acres of plants and cacti. Near the crest, with great views out over the bay, a full-size fiberglass sculpture of a whale stretches out in front of the space-age **Lawrence Hall of Science** (daily 10am–5pm; $6), an excellent museum and learning center that features earthquake simulations, model dinosaurs, and a planetarium, plus hands-on exhibits for kids in the Wizard's Lab. Both the gardens and the Lawrence Hall of Science are accessible on weekdays via the free UC Berkeley Shuttle bus from the campus or the Berkeley BART station.

In the southeast corner of the campus, the **Hearst Museum of Anthropology** in Kroeber Hall (Wed–Sun 10am–4.30pm, Thurs until 9pm; $3, free Thurs) holds a variety of changing exhibits as well as an intriguing display of artifacts made by Ishi, the last surviving Yahi Indian who was found near Mount Lassen in Northern California in 1911. Anthropologist Alfred Kroeber – father of sci-fi writer Ursula Le Guin – brought Ishi to the museum (then located on the UC San Francisco campus), where he lived under the scrutiny of scientists and journalists – in effect, in a state of captivity – until his death from tuberculosis a few years later.

For more information on arts in Berkeley, see p.291.

The brutally modern, angular concrete of the **University Art Museum** across Bancroft Way (Wed–Sun 11am–5pm, Thurs until 9pm; $6, free Thurs 11am–noon and 5–9pm) is in stark contrast to the campus' older buildings. Its skylit, open-plan galleries hold works by Picasso, Cézanne, Rubens, and other notables, but the star of the show is the collection of Fifties American painter Hans Hofmann's energetic and colorful abstract paintings on the top floor. The museum is renowned for its cutting-edge, changing exhibitions: the main space hosts a range of major shows – such as Robert Mapplethorpe's controversial photographs – while the Matrix Gallery focuses on lesser known, generally local artists.

Telegraph Avenue and South Berkeley

Downtown Berkeley lies west of the university campus around the Berkeley BART station on Shattuck Avenue, though most activity is centered on **Telegraph Avenue**, which runs south of the university from Sproul Plaza. This thoroughfare saw some of the worst of the Sixties riots and is still a frenetic bustle, especially the four short blocks closest to the university, which are packed to the gills with cafés and secondhand bookstores. Sidewalk vendors hawk handmade jewelry and brilliantly colored T-shirts, while down-and-outs hustle for spare change and spout psychotic poetry.

People's Park, now a seedy and overgrown plot of land half a block up from Telegraph between Haste Street and Dwight Way, was another battleground in the late Sixties, when organized and spirited resistance to the university's plans to develop the site into dormitories brought out the troops, who shot dead an onlooker by mistake. To many, the fact that the park is still a community-controlled open space (and outdoor flophouse for Berkeley's legions of pushers and homeless) symbolizes a small victory in the battle against the Establishment, though it's not a pleasant or even very safe place to hang about, especially after dark. A mural along Haste Street bears the words of student leader Mario Savio: "There's a time when the operation of the machine becomes so odious... that you can't take part." Though the words may serve as inspiration to some of the parks current residents, the university actually owns the land, and has long threatened to develop it, with or without their approval. Recent efforts to invade the space with volleyball and basketball courts were met with short-lived but violent protests in 1991, when rioters trashed Telegraph Avenue storefronts, and a nineteen-year-old woman enraged at the university's plans for the park was shot dead by police while trying to assassinate the Chancellor. In early 2000, community leaders rallied in the park to show resistance to the university's proposal to develop much-needed student dormitories on the land, but in light of the current housing shortage, Berkeley's students generally support the idea, showing just how much things have changed since the Sixties.

Directly across Bowditch Street from People's Park stands one of the finest buildings in the Bay Area, Bernard Maybeck's **First Church of Christ, Scientist**. Built in 1910, it's an eclectic but thoroughly modern structure, laid out in a simple Greek Cross floor plan and spanned by a massive redwood truss with carved Gothic tracery and Byzantine painted decoration. The interior is only open on Sundays for worship and for tours at 11am, but the outside is worth lingering over, its cascade of many gently pitched roofs and porticoes carrying the eye from one handcrafted detail to another. It's a clever building in many ways: while the overall image is one of tradition and craftsmanship, Maybeck also succeeded in inconspicuously incorporating such materials as industrial metal windows, concrete walls and asbestos tiles into the structure – thereby cutting costs.

Free tours of the First Church are offered the first Sunday of the month at 12.15pm.

Many of the largely residential neighborhoods elsewhere in **South Berkeley** – especially the Elmwood District around College Avenue – are worth a wander, with a couple of specific sights to search out. One of these is the **Judah L. Magnes Museum**, a few blocks south of the campus at 2911 Russell St (Sun–Thurs 10am–4pm; free). Located in a rambling old mansion, it has California's largest repository of Judaica, and exhibits detail the history of Jewish life from ancient times to the present day, along with sacred and ceremonial art. The other South Berkeley attraction is much harder to miss, towering as it does over the Berkeley–Oakland border. The half-timbered castle imagery of the **Claremont Hotel** gives a fairly clear hint as to what's inside – it's now one of the Bay Area's plushest resort hotels, with the Tower Suite going for upwards of $600 per night. Built in 1914, just in time for San Francisco's Panama-Pacific Exposition, the *Claremont* was designed to encourage day-trippers out across the bay in the hope that they'd be so taken with the area they'd want to live here. The ploy worked, and the hotel's owners (who incidentally also owned the streetcar system that brought people here, and all the surrounding land) made a fortune.

North Berkeley

North Berkeley, also called "Northside," is a subdued neighborhood of professors and postgraduate students, its steep, twisting streets climbing up the lushly overgrown hills north of the campus. At the foot of the hills, some of the Bay Area's finest restaurants and delis – most famously *Chez Panisse*, started and run by Alice Waters, the acclaimed inventor of California cuisine – have sprung up along Shattuck Avenue to form the so-called "Gourmet Ghetto," a great place to pick up the makings of a tasty alfresco lunch.

The restaurants of the "Gourmet Ghetto" are detailed beginning on p.263.

Euclid Avenue, off Hearst and next to the north gate of the university, is a sort of antidote to Telegraph Avenue, a quiet grove of coffee joints and pizza parlors frequented by grad students. Above Euclid – if you want to avoid the fairly steep walk, take bus #65 (daily) or the #8 (weekdays only) from Shattuck Avenue – there are few more pleasant places for a picnic than the **Berkeley Rose Garden** (daily dawn–dusk; free), a terraced amphitheater filled with some three thousand varietal roses and looking out across the bay to San Francisco. Built as part of a WPA job-creation scheme during the Depression, a wooden pergola rings the top, stepping down to a small spring.

Along the crest of the Berkeley hills, a number of enticing parks give great views over the bay. The largest and highest of them, **Tilden Park** (daily 8am–10pm; free; ☎510/562-7275), encompasses some 2065 acres of near wilderness. Kids can enjoy a ride on the carved wooden horses of the carousel (weekends 11am-6pm; $1) or take the mini-steam train through the grove of redwood trees (weekends 11am–6pm; $1.50). In the warm months, don't miss a swim in clean Lake Anza (lifeguard on duty May–Oct daily 11am–6pm; $2.50), rare among Bay Area lakes in that swimming is permitted. To reach Tilden, head north from campus on either Claremont Avenue (passing the *Claremont Hotel*) or Grizzly Peak Boulevard (follow the signs from Euclid Ave). Both routes snake 1600 feet to the crest of the Berkeley hills, providing stunning views and myriad hiking trails.

You can get to Tilden Park from downtown Berkeley via AC Transit bus #67 (weekends only).

The homes built on Northside's steep hills in an eclectic range of styles, are some of the finest and most impressively sited in the Bay Area, designed to meld seamlessly into the wooded landscape. Many were constructed by members of the Hillside Club c.1900 a slightly bohemian group of Berkeleyans who also laid out many of the pedestrian paths that climb the hills. Perhaps the single most striking of these hillside homes, the **Rowell House** – a half-timbered chalet built in 1914 by architect John Hudson Thomas – stands alone at the top of the path up from **Codornices Park**, where it crosses Tamalpais Road. Many of the other houses nearby were designed and built by Bernard Maybeck, architect of the Palace of Fine Arts, First Church of Christ, Scientist, and other notable Bay Area buildings; the homes he built for himself and his family still stand around the junction of Buena Vista Way and La Loma Avenue, a hundred yards south.

Nearer to town at the north end of Shattuck Avenue and close by the shops and cafés along Solano Avenue, the gray basalt knob of **Indian Rock** stands out from the foot of the hills, challenging rock-climbers who hone their skills on its forty-foot vertical faces. (Those who just want to appreciate the extraordinary view can take the steps around its back.) Carved into similarly hard volcanic stone across the street are the mortar holes used by the Ohlone to grind acorns into flour. In between, and in stark contrast, stands the rusting hulk of a Cold War-era air-raid siren.

You can take the #7, #15, or #43 bus from downtown Berkeley to the top of Solano.

West Berkeley and the waterfront

From downtown Berkeley and the UC campus, **University Avenue** runs downhill toward the bay, lined by increasingly shabby frontages of motels and massage parlors. The liveliest part of this **West Berkeley** area is around the intersection of University and San Pablo avenues – the pre-freeway main highway north – where a community of recent immigrants from India and Pakistan have set up stores and restaurants that serve some of the best of the Bay Area's rare curries.

The area between San Pablo Avenue and the bay is the oldest part of Berkeley, and a handful of hundred-year-old houses and churches – such as the two white-spired Gothic Revival structures on Hearst Avenue – survive from the time when this district was a separate city, known as Ocean View. The neighborhood also holds remnants of Berkeley's industrial past, and many of the old warehouses and factory premises have been converted into living and working spaces for artists, craftspeople, and computer-software companies. The newly polished and yuppified stretch of **Fourth Street** between Gilman and University features upscale furniture outlets and quaint gourmet delis, as well as some outstanding restaurants. An odd toss-in to this area is **Berkeley Steamworks**, 2107 Fourth St (☎510/845-8992), the only Bay Area bathhouse that remained open during the AIDS crisis and still has private rooms, unlike San Francisco's sex clubs.

For the story of San Francisco's sex industry, see box on p.99.

One place you should visit here is the **Takara Sake Tasting Room**, just off Fourth Street south of University Avenue at 708 Addison St (daily noon–6pm; free). Owned and operated by one of Japan's largest producers, this plant is responsible for more than a third of all sake drunk in the US. You can sample any of the five varieties of California-strain sake (brewed from Californian rice), best drunk warm and swallowed sharply. Though no tours are offered, they will show you a slide presentation of the art of sake brewing.

The I-80 freeway, and the still-used rail tracks that run alongside it, pretty well manage to cut Berkeley off from its waterfront. The best way to get there is to take AC Transit bus #51, which runs regularly down University Avenue. Once a major hub for the transbay ferry services – to shorten journey times a three-mile-long pier was constructed, much of which still sticks out into the bay – the **Berkeley Marina** is now one of the prime spots on the bay for leisure activities, especially windsurfing and kayaking. There's a very long pier you can walk out on, where you can chat with the local fishermen and suck in the fresh salty air while getting a great view of San Francisco and its two bridges.

The North Bay and inland valleys

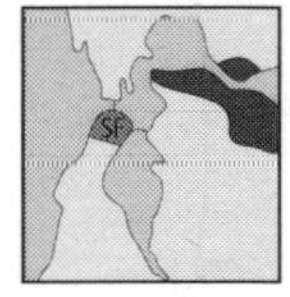

Compared to the urbanized bayfront cities of Oakland and Berkeley, the rest of the East Bay is sparsely populated, and places of interest are few and far between. The **North Bay** is home to some of the Bay Area's heaviest industry – oil refineries and chemical plants dominate the landscape – but also holds a few remarkably unchanged waterfront towns that merit a side trip if you're passing by. Away from the bay, the **inland valleys** are a whole other world of dry rolling hills, dominated by the towering peak of **Mount Diablo**. Dozens of tract-house developments have made commuter suburbs out of what were once cattle ranches and farms, but so far the region has been able to absorb the numbers and still feels rural, despite having doubled in population in the past twenty years.

The North Bay

North of Berkeley there's not a whole lot to see or do. Off the Eastshore Freeway in **ALBANY**, Golden Gate Fields has **horse-racing** from October through June, while **EL CERRITO**'s main contribution to world culture was the band Creedence Clearwater Revival, who staged most of their *Born on the Bayou* publicity photographs in the wilds of Tilden Park in the hills above; El Cerrito is still home to one of the best record stores in California, Down Home Music, at 10341 San Pablo Ave (see p.314).

For details on horse racing in Albany, see p.323.

RICHMOND, at the top of the bay, was once a boomtown, building ships during World War II at the Kaiser Shipyards, which employed 100,000 workers between 1940 and its closure in 1945. Now it's the proud home of the gigantic Standard Oil refinery, the center of which you drive through before crossing the **Richmond–San Rafael Bridge** ($2) to Marin County. About the only reason to stop in Richmond is that it marks the north end of the BART line, and the adjacent Amtrak station is a better terminal for journeys to and from San Francisco than the end of the line in West Oakland. If you find yourself with time to fill, check out the **Richmond Museum of History** at 400 Nevin Ave (Wed–Sun 1–4pm; free), which exhibits artifacts, photos, and antique items illustrating the history of Richmond during the first half of the twentieth century. Also worth a visit, **The National Institute of Art and Disabilities** at 551 23rd St (Mon–Fri 8.30am–4pm; free) exhibits art created by artists with developmental and physical disabilities, for view in an open studio and gallery space where the artists are often at work.

Amtrak services to the San Francisco area are detailed on p.12.

If you're heading from the East Bay to Marin County, **Point Richmond**, a cozy little town tucked away at the foot of the bridge between the refinery and the bay is worth a glance for its shoreline and its many Victorians – rapidly becoming occupied by upwardly mobile professionals from San Francisco. Brickyard Landing is a redeveloped docklands with modern bayview condos, tennis courts and a private yacht harbor built around disused brick kilns. The Red and White Ferry terminal ($5 one-way; ☎510/464-1030 for recorded schedules) operates from the end of Harbor Way South to and from Pier 43 1/2 at Fisherman's Wharf. The rest of the waterfront is taken up by the broad and usually deserted strand of **Keller Beach**, which stretches for half a mile along the sometimes windy shoreline.

Heading toward Point Molate on Hwy-580, take the last exit before the Richmond–San Rafael Bridge and follow Western Drive out to the deserted **Winehaven**, built in 1908 as the largest winery in the world. A colossal, empty brick castle remains on the water's edge, surrounded by a small, planned mini-community of prefabricated early 1900s homes. Later used as a military barracks, these houses and the great distillery sit lonely in the countryside.

Nowadays, there's no shortage of excellent wineries in the Bay Area; see Chapter 13, "The Wine Country," for details.

The Carquinez Strait

At the top of the bay some 25 miles north of Oakland, the land along the **Carquinez Strait** is a bit off the beaten track, but it's an area of some natural beauty and much historic interest. The still-small towns along the waterfront seem worlds away from the bustle of the rest of the Bay Area, but how long they'll be able to resist the pressure of the expanding commuter belt is anybody's guess. AC Transit #74 runs every hour from Richmond BART north to **CROCKETT** at the west end of the narrow straits – a tiny town cut into the steep hillsides above the water that seems entirely dependent upon the massive C&H Sugar factory at its foot, whose giant neon sign lights up the town and the adjacent Carquinez Bridge.

From Crockett the narrow **Carquinez Strait Scenic Drive**, an excellent cycling route, heads east along the Sacramento river. A turn two miles along drops you down to **PORT COSTA**, a small town that lived off ferry traffic across the straits to Benicia until it lost its livelihood when the bridge was built at Crockett. It's still a nice enough place to watch the huge ships pass by on their way to and from the inland ports of Sacramento and Stockton. If you don't have a bike (or a car) you can enjoy the view from the window of an Amtrak train which runs alongside the water from Oakland and Richmond, not stopping until Martinez at the eastern end of the straits, two miles north of the John Muir house (see p.163).

Benicia

On the north side of the Straits, and hard to get to without a car, **BENICIA** is the most substantial of the historic waterfront towns, but one that has definitely seen better days. Founded in 1847, it initially rivaled San Francisco as the major Bay Area port and was even the state capital for a time; but despite Benicia's better weather and fine deep-water harbor, San Francisco eventually became the main transportation point for the fortunes of the Gold Rush, and the town very nearly faded away altogether. Examples of Benicia's efforts to become a major city stand poignantly around the very compact downtown area, most conspicuously the 1852 Greek Revival structure that was used as the **first State Capitol** for just thirteen months. The building has been restored as a museum (daily 10am–5pm; $2), furnished in the legislative style of the time, complete with top hats on the tables and shining spittoons every few feet.

Pick up a walking-tour map of Benicia's many intact Victorian houses and churches from the **tourist office**, on 601 First St (Mon–Fri 8am–5pm, Sat & Sun 11am–3pm; ☎707/745-2120), and follow it to the steeply pitched roofs and gingerbread eaves of the **Frisbie-Walsh house** at 235 East L St – a prefabricated Gothic Revival building that was shipped here in pieces from Boston in 1849 (an identical house was put up by General Vallejo as his residence in

Sonoma; see p.210). Across the City Hall park, the arched ceiling beams of **St Paul's Episcopal Church** look like an upturned ship's hull; it was built by shipwrights from the Pacific Mail Steamship Company, one of Benicia's many successful nineteenth-century shipyards. Half a dozen former brothels and saloons stand in various stages of decay and restoration along First Street down near the waterfront, from where the world's largest train ferries used to ply the waters between Benicia and Port Costa until 1930.

In recent years Benicia has attracted a number of artists and craftspeople; you can watch glass-blowers and furniture-makers at work in the **Yuba Complex** at 675 and 701 East H St (Mon–Fri 10am–5pm, Sat 10am–4pm). Ceramic artist Judy Chicago and sculptor Robert Arneson are among those who have worked in the converted studios and modern light industrial parks around the sprawling fortifications of the old **Benicia Arsenal** east of the downtown area, whose thickly walled sandstone buildings formed the main Army storage facility for weapons and ammunition from 1851 up to and including the Korean War. One of the oddest parts of the complex is the Camel Barn, part of the **Benicia Historical Museum** (Wed–Sun 1–4pm; free). The structure used to house camels that the Army imported in 1856 to transport supplies across the deserts of the Southwestern US. The experiment failed, and the camels were kept here until they were sold off in 1864.

Vallejo and Six Flags Marine World

Across the Carquinez Bridge from Crockett, the biggest and dullest of the North Bay towns – **VALLEJO** – was, like Benicia, an early capital of California, though it now lacks any sign of its historical significance. In contrast to most of the other Gold Rush-era towns that line the Straits, Vallejo remained economically vital, largely because of the massive military presence here at the **Mare Island Naval Shipyard**, a sprawling, relentlessly gray complex in the center of town, right on Hwy-29, and covering an area twice the size of Golden Gate Park. Closed in late 1997, its less than glamorous history – the yard built and maintained supply ships and submarines, not carriers or battleships – is recounted in a small **museum** in the old city hall building at 734 Marin St (Tues–Sat 10am–4.30pm; $1.50), where the highlight is a working periscope that looks out across the bay.

The best reason to come to Vallejo, however, is the newly renovated **Six Flags Marine World** (daily 10am–10pm; $34; ☎707/643-ORCA), five miles north of Vallejo off I-80 at the Marine World Parkway (Hwy-37) exit. Billing itself as the nation's only oceanarium, wildlife, and theme park, it offers a well-above-average range of performing sea lions, dolphins, and killer whales in approximations of their natural habitats, as well as water-ski stunt shows and several newly constructed roller coasters, including the flying, floorless *Medusa*, on which your legs dangle as you zoom through loops at 65mph. It can be a fun day out, especially for children.

The most enjoyable way to get here from San Francisco is on the Blue and Gold Fleet **ferry** from Fisherman's Wharf, which takes an hour each way and costs $15 round trip (☎415/773-1188 for details). You can also take BART, getting off at the El Cerrito Del Norte stop where you catch the Vallejo BARTLink bus (☎707/648-4666) to the park.

The inland valleys

Most of the inland East Bay area is made up of rolling hills covered by grasslands, slowly yielding to suburban housing developments and office complexes as more and more businesses abandon the pricey real estate of San Francisco. The great peak of **Mount Diablo** is twice as high as any other Bay Area summit, and surrounded by acres of campgrounds and hiking trails; other attractions include two historic homes that serve as memorials to their literate and influential ex-residents, John Muir and Eugene O'Neill.

BART tunnels from Oakland through the Berkeley Hills to the leafy-green stockbroker settlement of **ORINDA**, continuing east through the increasingly hot and dry landscape to the end of the line at **CONCORD**, site of a controversial nuclear weapons depot. A few years ago, a peaceful, civilly disobedient blockade here ended in protester Brian Wilson losing his legs under the wheels of a slow-moving munitions train. The event raised public awareness – before it happened few people knew of the depot's existence, and it earned Wilson a place in a Lawrence Ferlinghetti poem – but otherwise it's still business as usual.

Martinez and John Muir's house

From the Pleasant Hill BART station, one stop before the end of the line, Contra Costa County Connection buses leave every thirty minutes for **MARTINEZ**, the seat of county government, passing the preserved home of naturalist **John Muir** (Wed–Sun 10am–4.30pm; $2), just off Hwy-4 two miles south of Martinez. Muir, an articulate, persuasive Scot whose writings and political activism were of vital importance in the preservation of America's wilderness, spent much of his life exploring and writing about the majestic Sierra Nevada mountains, particularly Yosemite. He was also one of the founders of the **Sierra Club** – a wilderness lobby and education organization still active today (see p.8 for more). Anyone familiar with the image of this thin, bearded man wandering the mountains with his knapsack and notebook might be surprised to see his very conventional, upper-class Victorian home, now restored to its appearance when Muir died in 1914. Built by Muir's father-in-law, only those parts of the house Muir added himself reflect much of the personality of the man, not least the massive, rustic fireplace he had built in the East Parlor so he could have a "real mountain campfire." The bulk of Muir's personal belongings and artifacts are displayed in his study on the upper floor, and in the adjacent room an exhibition documents the history of the Sierra Club and Muir's battles to protect America's wilderness.

The small cemetery holding **Muir's grave**, a pilgrimage site for conservationists, was acquired in 2000, by the National Park Service, which discourages visitors since the site is bordered by private property. Nonetheless, Muir's plot, tucked back in the pear orchard and not marked with a trail, draws hundreds each year, many led by a rule-bending park ranger. If you want to leave an offering or pay homage to the father of America's national park system, inquire at Muir's home.

Behind the bell-towered main house is a large, still productive orchard where Muir cultivated grapes, pears, and cherries to earn the money to finance his explorations (you can sample the fruits free of charge, pre-picked by staff gardeners). Beyond the orchard is the 1849 **Martinez Adobe**, homestead of the original Spanish land-grant settlers and now a small **museum** of Mexican colonial culture. The contrast between Mexican and American cultures in early California is fascinating and, as a bonus, the building's two-foot-thick walls keep it refreshingly cool on a typically hot summer day.

Eugene O'Neill and Mount Diablo

At the foot of Mount Diablo, fifteen miles south, playwright **Eugene O'Neill** used the money he got for winning the Nobel Prize for Literature in 1936 to build a home and sanctuary for himself, which he named **Tao House**. It was here, before 1944 when he was struck down with Parkinson Disease, that he wrote many of his best-known plays: *The Iceman Cometh*, *A Moon for the Misbegotten* and *Long Day's Journey into Night*. Readings and performances of his works are sometimes given in the house, which is open to visitors, though you must reserve a place on one of the free guided **tours** (Wed–Sun 10am & 12.30pm; ☎925/838-0249). Inside, O'Neill's study is slowly being restored to its original condition; the effort involves a nationwide search for the Chinese furniture he purchased from Gump's during the home's construction. There's no parking on site, so the tours pick you up in the tiny town of **Danville**, off I-680 south of Walnut Creek and north of Dublin and San Ramon, home of the **Blackhawk Automotive Museum,** 3700 Blackhawk Plaza Circle (Wed–Sun 10am–5pm; $8), an impressive collection of classic and antique cars from Britain, Germany, Italy, and the US from 1920 to 1960, and artwork inspired by them. The nearby shops of Blackhawk Plaza are frequented by the richest of the East Bay's rich.

As for **Mount Diablo** itself, it rises up from the rolling ranchlands at its foot to a height of nearly four thousand feet, its summit and flanks preserved within **Mount Diablo State Park** (daily 8am–sunset; parking $5). North Gate Road the main route through the park, reaches to within three hundred feet of the top, its terminus a popular place to enjoy the marvelous view: on a clear day you can see over two hundred miles in every direction. Three developed campgrounds with running water and restrooms are open here year-round (June–Sept Sun–Thurs, $15 & Fri–Sat, $16; Oct–May daily, $12; ☎1-800/444-PARK). To reach the park, you'll need a car or the ability to cycle a long way uphill, though the Sierra Club sometimes organizes day-trips: check with the park's interpretive center at the summit (March–Oct Wed–Sun 11am–5pm; Nov–Feb Thurs–Sun 11am–4pm; ☎925-837-2525; *www.mdia.org*) for details.

The North Bay and inland valleys

Two main entrances lead into the park, both well marked off I-680. The one from the southwest by way of Danville passes by the **ranger station**, where you can pick up a trail map ($1) which lists the best **day-hikes**. The other runs from the northwest by way of Walnut Creek, and the routes join together five miles from the summit. March and April, when the wildflowers are out, are the best times to come, and since mornings are ideal for getting the clearest view, you should drive to the top first and then head back down to a trailhead for a hike, or to one of the many picnic spots for a leisurely lunch. In summer it can get desperately hot and dry, and parts of the park are closed because of fire danger.

Livermore and Altamont

Fifteen miles southeast of Mount Diablo on the main road out of the Bay Area (I-580) or via WHEELS #12X from the Dublin/Pleasanton BART, the rolling hills around sleepy **LIVERMORE** are covered with thousands of shining, spinning, high-tech **windmills**, placed here by a private power company to take advantage of the nearly constant winds. The largest wind farm in the world, you'll probably have seen it used in a number of TV ads as a space-age backdrop to hype flashy new cars or sexy perfumes. Though the federal government provides no funding for this non-polluting, renewable source of energy, it spends billions of dollars every year designing and building nuclear weapons and other less sinister applications of modern technology at the nearby **Lawrence Livermore Laboratories**, where much of the research and development of the nuclear arsenal takes place, though reassuringly, none of the weapons themselves are actually stored here. A small **visitor center** (Mon–Thurs 1–5pm, Fri 10am–5pm; free; ☎925/423-3272) two miles south of I-580 on Greenville Road, holds hands-on exhibits showing off various scientific phenomena and devices. Their most popular tour, a two-hour look at Nova, the world's largest laser, is limited to US citizens for purposes of national security. Call a few days ahead to reserve your place, and bring your passport.

Up and over the hills to the east, where I-580 joins I-5 for the four-hundred-mile route south through the Central Valley to Los Angeles, stand the remains of **Altamont Speedway**, site of the nightmarish Rolling Stones concert in December 1969 (see p.119). Wisely, the band didn't respond to a local promoter's request to hold an anniversary concert at the site in 1999.

For the Bay Area's best motorcycle route, beginning in Livermore, see p.321.

Chapter 11

The Peninsula

The city of San Francisco sits at the tip of a five-mile-wide **Peninsula**. Home of old money and new technology, it stretches south from San Francisco along the bay for fifty miles of relentless suburbia, past the wealthy enclaves of Hillsborough and Atherton, winding up in the futuristic roadside landscape of the **Silicon Valley**. **San Jose**, now California's third largest city, having driven San Francisco into fourth place, is the hub of the technological boom that is redefining international communications, spurred by Stanford University in nearby **Palo Alto**.

There was a time when the region was largely agricultural, but the tech industry has replaced orange groves and fig trees with office complexes and parking lots. The resultant inflated economy has doubled and tripled rents from the valley in most directions out; new homes simply can't be built as fast as six-figure consultants are brought in. Surprisingly, however, most of the land along the **coast** – separated from the bayfront sprawl by a ridge of redwood-covered peaks – remains rural and undeveloped; it also contains some excellent **beaches** and a couple of affably down-to-earth communities, all well served by public transportation.

Transport and information

Peninsula accommodation options begin on p.223, restaurants on p.268, and bars on p.282.

BART only travels down the Peninsula as far as Daly City, from where you can catch **SamTrans** (☎ 1-800/660-4287) buses south to Palo Alto or along the coast to Half Moon Bay. For longer distances, **Caltrain**, run by the same company, offers an hourly rail service from its terminal at Fourth and Townsend streets in downtown San Francisco, stopping at most bayside towns between the city and San Jose ($1–5); Greyhound (☎ 1-800/231-2222) runs regular **buses** along US-101 to and from their San Jose terminal at 70 S Almaden, on the corner of Santa Clara Street. The Santa Clara Valley Transit Authority (VTA) (☎ 408/321-2300) runs buses and modern trolleys around metropolitan San Jose. If you're going to be spending most of your time there, it's possible to fly direct into

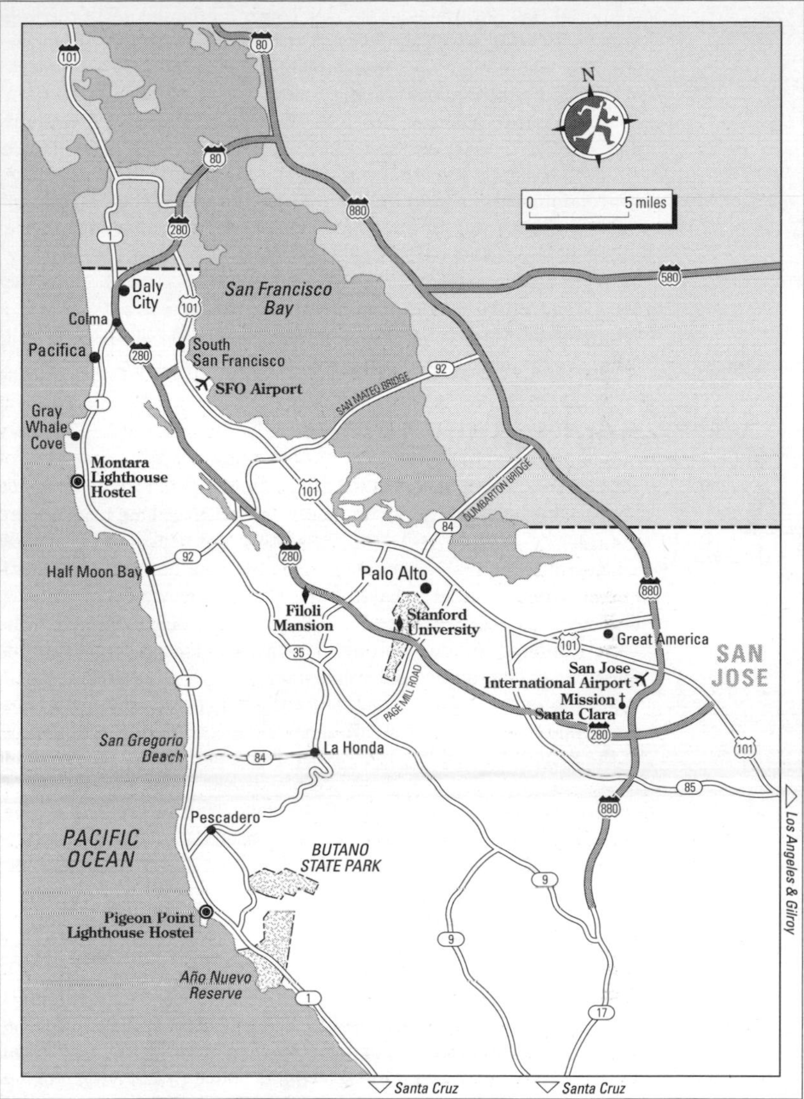

San Jose International Airport (SJO), close to downtown San Jose (see p.28).

The **Palo Alto Chamber of Commerce**, 325 Forest Ave (Mon–Fri 9am–noon & 1–5pm; ☎650/324-3121; *www.paloaltoonline.com*), has lists of local restaurants and cycle routes; for information on Stanford University, call its visitor center (☎650/723-2560) in the

Memorial Hall library under Hoover Tower, or get a copy of the free *Stanford Daily*, published weekdays. To find out what's on in the area and where, pick up a free copy of the *Palo Alto Weekly*, available at most local shops. At the southern end of the bay, the **San Jose's Visitor Center**, at 333 W San Carlos St (Mon–Fri 8am–5.30pm, Sat & Sun 11am–5pm; ☎408/295-9600 or 1-800/SAN-JOSE; *www.sanjose.org*), with another branch in the convention center across the street (same hours), is the best bet for tourist information; for local news and events pick up a copy of the excellent *San Jose Mercury* newspaper (*www.mercurycenter.com*) or the free weekly *Metro* (*www.metroactive.com*). Along the coast, the **Half Moon Bay Chamber of Commerce**, at 520 Kelly Ave (Mon–Fri 9am–4pm, Sat 10am–3pm; ☎650/726-5202), gives out walking-tour maps and information on accommodation.

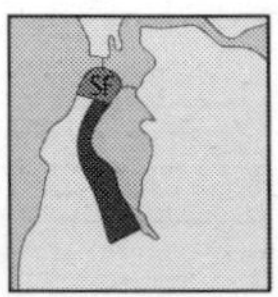

South along the bay

US-101 runs **south** from San Francisco along the bay, lined by light-industrial estates and shopping malls, to San Jose. One place along the freeway worth a visit is the **Coyote Point Museum** (Tues–Sat 10am–5pm, Sun noon–5pm; $3), four miles south of the airport off Poplar Avenue in a large bayfront park, where examples of the natural life of the San Francisco Bay – from tidal insects to birds of prey – are exhibited in engaging and informative displays, enhanced by interactive computers and documentary films.

More scenic **I-280** runs parallel to US-101, avoiding the worst of the bayside mess by cutting through wooded valleys down the center of the Peninsula. Just beyond the San Francisco city limits, the road passes through **COLMA**, a unique place once made up entirely of cemeteries, which, other than the military burial grounds in the Presidio, are prohibited within San Francisco. Besides the expected roll call of deceased San Francisco luminaries like Levi Strauss and William Hearst, are a few surprises, such as Wild West gunman Wyatt Earp. If you're interested, contact the Colma Historical Association (☎650/757-1676) for graveyard tour information, as venturing here on your own can be downright confusing.

Beyond Colma, the scenery improves quickly as I-280 continues past the **Crystal Springs Reservoir**, an artificial lake which holds the water supply for San Francisco – pumped here all the way from Yosemite. Surrounded by twenty square miles of parkland, hiking trails lead up to the ridge from which San Francisco Bay was first spotted by eighteenth-century Spanish explorers; it now overlooks the airport to the east, but there are good views out over the Pacific coast, two miles distant.

At the south end of the reservoir, just off I-280 on Canada Road in the well-heeled town of **WOODSIDE**, luscious gardens surround the palatial **Filoli Estate** (tours Tues–Thurs 9.30am, 11.30am &

1.30pm; $10; advance reservations required ☎650/364-2880). The 45-room mansion, designed in 1915 in Georgian style by San Francisco architect Willis Polk, may look familiar – it was used in the TV series *Dynasty* as the Denver home of the Carrington clan. It's the only one of the many huge houses around here that you can visit, although the sixteen-acre grounds featuring formal gardens with reflecting pools are what make it worth coming, especially in the spring when everything's in bloom.

Palo Alto and Stanford University

PALO ALTO, just south and three miles east of Woodside between I-280 and US-101, is a small, leafy community, and despite its proximity to Stanford, retains little of the college-town vigor of its northern rival, Berkeley. In recent years, Palo Alto has become somewhat of a social center for Silicon Valley's nouveau riche, as evidenced by the trendy cafés and chic new restaurants that have popped up along its main drag, **University Avenue**. The booming computer-industry job market has made more than a few people wealthy, and this is where many of them come to spend their cash; small houses in the quaint neighborhoods surrounding the downtown area can cost close to a million dollars.

The town doesn't have a lot to offer in terms of sights other than its older Spanish colonial homes along **Ramona Street** between Hamilton and University Avenues, but it's a great place for a lazy stroll and a gourmet meal. The 1925-style home at 520–526 Ramona, built right around a live oak tree, is impressive for its carved wooden doors, wrought-iron balconies, tiled roof, and interior fountains. If you get tired of nostalgic walks and browsing in overpriced designer furniture stores – one of the town's main preoccupations – try cycling around the town's many well-marked bike routes; a range of bikes is available for $12–25 a day from Action Sports Limited at 401 High St (☎650/328-3180), near the Caltrain station a block west of University Avenue. Be aware, however, that **East Palo Alto**, on the bay side of US-101, has a well-deserved reputation for gang- and drug-related violence, with one of the highest per capita murder rates of any US city. It wasn't always this way: founded in the 1920s as the utopian Runnymeade colony – an agricultural, poultry-raising cooperative – there are a few surviving sights, which the local historical society (☎650/329-0294) can point out for you. Otherwise, the area's renown ends as the place Grateful Dead guitarist Jerry Garcia grew up and is about as far as you can get off the San Francisco tourist trail.

Across the Caltrain tracks from town and spreading out from the west end of University Avenue, **Stanford University**, is by contrast one of the tamest places you could hope for. The university is among the top – and most expensive – in the United States, though when it opened in 1891, founded by railroad magnate Leland Stanford in

The Origins of Silicon Valley

The Sub-35-year-old Billionaire is really a new life-form, an economic mutation that emerged from this little pond of vigorous capitalist Darwinism. It's as if dinosaurs had suddenly hatched again in the Alviso mudflats off San Jose.

– Po Bronson *The Nudist on the Late Shift*

Though the name "**Silicon Valley**" is of relatively recent origin, Santa Clara county's history of electronic innovation reaches back to 1909, when **Lee de Forrest** completed work on the **vacuum tube** – a remarkably simple device that made possible numerous technological achievements from television to radar – at Stanford University.

Stanford's entrepreneurial spirit was best embodied by **Frederick Terman**, a professor of radio engineering who encouraged his students to found their own local companies rather than bury themselves within massive corporations. When the school decided to raise some cash for post-World War II expansions, Terman helped convince the university to lease land to two students' fledgling local company, **Hewlett Packard**, and helped found the Stanford Industrial Park, earning himself the nickname "Father of Silicon Valley." The unique public–private partnership between the school and its alumni made the Valley central to development of both radar, television, and microwave products, attracting a freethinking engineering community that thrived in the former agricultural region's hothouse intellectual environment.

It was from these roots that the modern Silicon Valley bloomed in the late 1970s, when the local folks at **Intel** invented first the **silicon semiconductor** and then the **microprocessor**, both radically smaller and more efficient than vacuum tube technology, and initiated the computer revolution. In 1976, the "two Steves," **Wozniak and Jobs**, former high school friends from Los Altos, founded Apple Computers in a garage, creating the first hardware for their systems using scavenged parts from calculators and money raised by selling a VW bus; the new computers sold for $666.66 a piece. Capitalizing on the new market, a young Stanford student named **Steve Yang** founded **Yahoo**, a portal that allowed casual computer users to explore the **Internet**, which had previously been used as a computer network for government officials and academics. Since then the Bay Area and the world has never been the same.

memory of his dead son, it offered free tuition. Ridiculed by East Coast academics, who felt that there was little need for a second West Coast university (after UC-Berkeley), Stanford was defiantly built anyway, a defiant hybrid of Mission and Romanesque buildings on a huge arid campus that covers an area larger than the whole of downtown San Francisco.

Stanford, whose reputation as an arch-conservative think-tank was enhanced by Ronald Reagan's offer to donate his video library to the school (Stanford politely declined), hasn't always been an entirely boring place, though you wouldn't know it to walk among the preppy future-lawyers-of-America that seem to comprise the majority of the student body. Ken Kesey came here from Oregon in 1958 on a writing fellowship, working nights as an orderly on the psychiatric ward of one local hospital, and getting paid $75 a day to test experimental drugs (LSD among them) in another. Drawing on both experiences, Kesey wrote *One Flew over the Cuckoo's Nest* in 1960 and quickly became a counterculture hero.

Approaching from the Palo Alto Caltrain and SamTrans bus station, which acts as a buffer between the town and the university, you enter the campus via a half-mile-long, palm-tree-lined boulevard which deposits you at its heart, the **Quadrangle**, bordered by the phallic **Hoover Tower** and the colorful gold-leaf mosaics of the **Memorial Church**. Like the rest of the campus, the church was constructed in memory of Leland Stanford, Jr., and its elaborate, mosaic entrance has an fittingly elegiac feel.

From here, the campus's covered sidewalks and symmetrical red-roofed brownstone buildings designed by Frederick Law Olmsted (of Central and Golden Gate parks fame) branch out around a central fountain. Free hour-long **walking tours** (☎650/723-2560), conducted by students depart from the Memorial Auditorium just east of Hoover Tower (daily 11am & 3.15pm).

The highlight of any trip to campus is the **Iris and B. Gerald Cantor Center for Visual Arts** (Wed–Sun 11am–5pm, Thurs till 8pm; free; ☎650/723-4177), one of the finest museums in the Bay Area, comprising 27 galleries, spread over 120,000 square feet, and containing treasures from six continents, some dating back to 500 BC. Housed in the old Stanford Museum of Art at the intersection of Lomita Drive and Museum Way (to the north of Palm Drive as you approach Stanford's "Quad"), the Cantor Center is the result of a decade-long, $37 million refurbishing effort undertaken to repair the museum's damage from 1989's Loma Prieta earthquake. Inside, amidst a collection of photography, painting, sculpture, craft, ceramics, and artifacts from around the world, is the stunning *Plum Garden, Kameido*, by Japanese artist Hiroshige, along with a wealth of artwork collected by Leland Stanford, Jr., on his fateful trip to Asia, where he caught typhoid fever and died at age 15. The museum contains a wealth of some two hundred **Rodin sculptures**, including a *Gates of Hell* flanked by a shamed *Adam and Eve*, displayed in an attractive outdoor setting on the museum's south side.

For information on the Palace of the Legion of Honor's Rodin collection, see p.124.

If you keep up on the latest trends in subatomic behavior, you won't want to miss the **Stanford Linear Accelerator** (Mon–Sat by appointment only; ☎650/926-3300), a mile west of the central campus on Sand Hill Road, where infinitesimally small particles are crashed into one another at very high speeds to see what happens. For a bird's-eye view of the campus (and the rest of the Bay Area) head up one of the **hiking trails** that leads from the gate along Junipero Serra Boulevard at Stanford Avenue to Stanford's giant communications dish atop the foothills to the west of the campus.

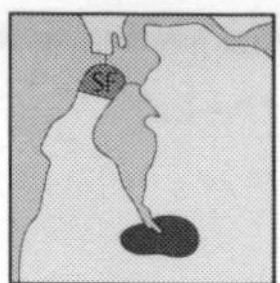

San Jose

Burt Bacharach could easily find his way to **SAN JOSE** today – heading south from San Francisco, it's about an hour's drive (on those rare occasions when traffic is actually fluid) into the heart of the heat and smog that collects below the bay. The fastest growing city in California is not strong on sights – though in area and population it's already close to twice the size of San Francisco and growing fast. San Jose's highest priority is the development of a culture outside the engineering lab, a project it's undertaking with the same sort of zeal as it brings to computing, with new museums, shopping centers, restaurants, clubs, and performing arts companies mushrooming throughout the compact downtown area. Granted, San Jose's nightlife and culture is no match for San Francisco's, and residents head north for weekends on the town; still, there are enough pleasant nooks in San Jose to fill the downtime of a business trip, including a few cultural gems that draw tourists from the surrounding area in increasing numbers.

Sitting at the southern end of the peninsula, San Jose has emerged as the civic heart of Silicon Valley, spurred by the growth of local behemoths Apple, Intel, and Hewlett Packard and surrounded by miles of faceless high-tech industrial parks where the next generations of computers are designed and crafted. Though it's seen now by some as the city of the future, San Jose's 1777 founding makes it one of the oldest settlements – and the oldest city – in California, and for centuries was little more than a sleepy agricultural community of prune farms.

Perhaps the best thing about San Jose today is that the coast is just 45 minutes away, west on Hwy-17, over the mountains residents call "The Hill." It's a wild drive, and worth it, if only to escape the heat of the valley, where summer temperatures hang around 100°F, but are a cool 70°F along the coast.

Downtown San Jose

Downtown, the only sign of San Jose's history is the 1797 **Peralta Adobe**, at 184 W St John St (Tues–Sun noon–5pm; $6), notable more for its having survived the encroaching suburbia than anything on display in its sparse, whitewashed interior. Admission includes a tour of the Victorian **Fallon House** across the street, a mansion built in 1855 by the city's seventh mayor, a frontiersman in the Fremont expedition. Guided tours through the fifteen period-furnished rooms include a comprehensive video presentation on the home and the adobe.

The two blocks of San Pedro Street which run south of the adobe form a restaurant row known as **San Pedro Square**, clearly marked by an iron gate at the intersection with W Santa Clara Street. There's no central plaza as such, just a collection of some of San Jose's best eateries and a considerable amount of activity on weekend nights.

For San Jose restaurant reviews, see p.268.

San Jose's most popular downtown attractions are best reached on foot, with the main places of interest centered around the palm-dotted **Plaza de Cesar Chavez**, just two blocks south of San Pedro Square, an oval island of green in the midst of Market Street, clustered around a modern fountain. To the north of the plaza, the **Cathedral Basilica of St Joseph** stands on the site of the first Catholic parish in California, which was built in 1803. The present building was dedicated in 1997, and is worth entering for a glimpse of its painted cupola, stained-glass windows and stations of the cross; Masses are held daily, often in Spanish.

Next door to the church at 110 S Market St is the **San Jose Museum of Art** (Tues–Wed & Fri–Sun 10am–5pm, Thurs 10am–8pm; $7, free the first Thursday of the month; ☎408/294-2787; *www.sjmusart.org*), set in an 1892 post office building with a contemporary new wing added in 1991, the museum contains more than a thousand twentieth-century works, with the spotlight on post-1980 Bay Area artists. The sweeping, open galleries are flooded with light, as is the attached café, including an outdoor patio facing the Plaza. Through a special partnership, the museum regularly features work from the permanent collection of the Whitney Museum of American Art in New York.

Facing the southwest corner of the plaza, downtown's biggest draw is the **Tech Museum of Innovation**, at 201 S Market St (summer daily 10am–6pm, Thurs till 8pm; rest of year Tues–Sun 10am–5pm; $8; ☎408/294-TECH; *www.thetech.org*), with its hands-on displays of high-tech engineering spread over three floors plus an inevitable IMAX theater. Highlights include a chance to design your own virtual roller coaster, regular demonstrations of high-tech surgical instruments and the chance to communicate with interactive robots. Unfortunately, the queues to access many of the best exhibits can seem endless, and, unless you're a computer nerd yourself, you may still leave the museum feeling like you've just read a particularly impervious software manual.

Just west of the Tech, the **Children's Discovery Museum,** 180 Woz Way (Tues–Sat 10am–5pm, Sun noon–5pm; $6 adults, $4 children under 18; ☎408/298-5437; *www.cdm.org*), draws raves from kids and parents alike for its hands-on displays, such as a real fire truck that can be climbed on, a Model A Ford, a Wells Fargo stagecoach, a bubble room, and a play table, where kids can fingerpaint and draw – though it's all aimed at the pre-adolescent set.

For reviews of San Jose's bars, see p.282.

A few blocks east of the museum and just south of Plaza de Cesar Chavez lies San Jose's entertainment district, **SoFA** (short for South First Street), with half-a-dozen clubs and a popular wine bar. By day, the **Institute of Contemporary Art** at 451 First St (Tues–Sat noon–5pm; free; ☎408/283-8155), is a bright space exhibiting contemporary work by mainly local artists.

North along First Avenue, the **Pavilion** shopping center recently underwent a major city-led renovation in an effort to revitalize the surrounding district which lay stagnant for decades, though it remains to be seen how well the rather sterile space will catch on. One block over on Second Street, the blue building resembling a giant Lego is the home of the **San Jose Repertory Theatre** (☎408/367-7255; *www.sjrep.com*); the resident company has formed a relationship with Dublin's Abbey, which exports its players and programs during specific engagements.

For information on purchasing tickets to a San Jose Sharks game at the San Jose Arena across Hwy-87 from the downtown, see p.320.

Outer San Jose

Continue west on Alameda and you enter the **Alameda Business District**, where, away from under the shadow of downtown's sparkling office buildings, you get something of a feel for the old farm town San Jose once was. Within a cluster of cafés, restaurants, and shops is the city's only revival cinema, The Towne at 1433

Alameda (☎408/287-1433). Next door, on the corner of Hester and Alameda, is *Uncommon Grounds*, a café housed in the historic 1926 Bank of Italy building, worth a peek for the ornate interior alone.

Further north on Alameda, some of San Jose's more intriguing sights languish in the suburbs. The **Rosicrucian Museum**, 1342 Naglee Ave (daily 10am–5pm; $7), is situated in an elaborate complex of buildings designed in ancient-Egyptian style, a full replica of Akhenaten's Temple in Luxor among them. The museum itself holds an astounding collection of Assyrian and Babylonian artifacts, including ancient amulets, jewelry, decorative art, and both animal and human mummies – one of them acquired, as guides will proudly tell you, through an early Neiman Marcus catalog. Though the museum is rather dark and musty, there's an unmissable flashlit tour through a subterranean replica of a real Egyptian tomb – actually a composite of three tombs – re-created in painstaking detail here. When earnest members of the Rosicrucian's mysterious order lead you through the depths of the gloomy space, they seem convinced that the figures illuminated on its walls are alive and well.

Two blocks west of the museum is the San Jose **rose garden** (daily dawn–dusk; free), a beautiful expanse of green lined with rose bushes and centered on a fountain that's a popular wading pool for local kids. There are nice views of the Santa Cruz mountains to the west too.

The nearby **San Jose Historical Museum**, at 1650 Senter Rd in Kelley Park (Tues–Sun noon–5pm; $6; ☎408/287-2290; *www.serve.com/sjhistory*), is a 25-acre historic town that tries to replicate nineteenth-century San Jose and Santa Clara Valley, through a series of restored buildings – among them a vintage ice-cream parlor – and an historic trolley system. Just down the road, peek into the **Japanese Friendship Gardens** (free), at 1300 Senter Rd, modeled after the Korakuen Garden in San Jose's Japanese sister city, Okayama, with ornate footbridges spanning koi-stocked ponds.

A special all-inclusive pass to the San Jose Historical Museum, the Peralta Adobe and the Fallon House is available at any of the three museums ($10).

Further west, out in San Jose's suburbs, the **Winchester Mystery House**, 525 S Winchester Blvd, just off I-280 near Hwy-17 (daily 9.30am–4.30pm; $12.95) belonged to Sarah Winchester, heiress to the Winchester rifle fortune, who was convinced upon her husband's death that he had been taken by the spirits of the men killed with his weapons. The ghosts told her that unless a room was built for each of them, the same fate would befall her. Work on the mansion took place 24 hours a day for the next thirty years, though the house was never finished and is a hodgepodge of extensions and styles: extravagant staircases lead nowhere and windows open onto solid brick walls. Ever since construction on the house stopped, the place ran rampantly commercial; today, visitors are channeled through a gauntlet of ghastly gift stores and soda stands to get in and out.

East of downtown, off US-101, are an assortment of attractions. San Jose's **Flea Market**, at 1590 Berryessa Rd (Wed–Sun dawn–dusk;

☎408/453-1110; *www.sjfm.com*), features more than 2000 vendors plying their wares. For the more culturally inclined, the **Mexican Heritage Plaza** at 1700 Alum Rock Ave near King, (Tues–Fri noon–6pm; Sat & Sun 10am–4pm; ☎408/928-5500; free; *www.mhc-viva.org*), has two gallery spaces featuring temporary exhibits of work by Mexican and Mexican-American artists; there are also frequent film, theater, cultural, and community events, highlighting this community that makes up nearly a quarter of San Jose's population.

North of San Jose, the small community of **Santa Clara** holds a few sights of its own. The late eighteenth-century **Mission Santa Clara de Asis**, just south of the Alameda (Route 82), is one of the least impressive structures in the chain of missions that runs along the California Coast on the traces of the El Camino Reál. But while there's little left to see of the original mission-era buildings that formed the original complex, which burned in a 1926 fire, it's interesting to note how what remains has been integrated into the campus of the Jesuit-run University of Santa Clara. The bell in the church's belfry is original, a gift from King Carlos IV of Spain in 1798, and the **de Saisset Museum** (Tues–Sun 11am–4pm; $1 donation suggested) on the grounds traces the history of the mission through a permanent display of objects recovered from its ruins, along with changing shows of contemporary art. At the north end of the grounds, a towering Benjamin Bufano sculpture stands near the entrance to the **Triton Museum**, 1505 Warburton Ave (Tues 10am–9pm, Wed–Sun 10am–5pm; ☎408/247-3754; *www.triton-museum.org*; $2 donation suggested), which features mainly Californian artists' work.

For information on the history of California's missions, see Contexts, p.332.

Santa Clara's other notable stop is the **Intel Museum**, at 2200 Mission College Blvd (Mon–Fri 8am–5pm; free; ☎408/765-0503), which showcases the process of making computer chips – actually, more interesting than it sounds.

North of the city, **Paramount's Great America** (daily Sat & Sun 10am–10pm; summer daily 10am–10pm; $34) is a huge, hundred-acre amusement park on the edge of San Francisco Bay, just off US-101. Hardly in the same league as Disneyland, the range of high-speed thrills and chills – from the new loop-the-loop *Stealth*, where your legs dangle freely as you zoom 65mph through inversions, to *Drop Zone*, where you freefall for over two hundred feet – is nevertheless impressive if you like this kind of thing or have kids who do.

A few miles north on US-101 and east on Hwy-237 takes you to the tiny town of **Alviso**, a predominantly Latino community with excellent tacquerias. Follow the railroad tracks two miles north to the ghost town of **Drawbridge**, little more than a few weathered wooden buildings, though nearly a hundred salt-box homes stood here in the 1930s. The town met with a swift demise when a sewage plant was built nearby in the 1960s, and by the 1980s, Drawbridge was added to the San Francisco Bay National Wildlife Refuge (☎510/792-0222), which has sadly discontinued guided tours until further notice.

The Coast

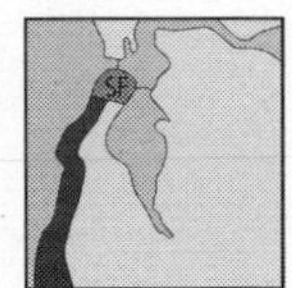

The **coastline** of the peninsula south from San Francisco is worlds away from the valley of the inland: mostly undeveloped, a few small towns, and countless beaches trace the 75 miles south to the mellow summer fun of Santa Cruz and Capitola. Along the way, bluffs protect the many nudist beaches from prying eyes and make a popular launching pad for hang-glider pilots. **Skyline Boulevard** follows the coast south from San Francisco, beginning where the earthquake-causing San Andreas Fault enters the sea at Fort Funston and passing the repetitious tracts of proverbial ticky-tacky houses that make up Daly City, before heading inland toward Woodside at its intersection with Hwy-1, which continues south along the coast – a relaxing drive affording jaw-dropping views of the ocean, though on summer and weekend afternoons you'll find the route clogged with campers creeping along at 30mph and few opportunities to pass. Try hitting the road early in the morning; provided the fog isn't obscuring everything, expect a magic ride.

San Pedro Point and Pacifica

San Pedro Point, a popular surfing beach fifteen miles south of the city proper, along with the town of **PACIFICA**, marks the southern extent of San Francisco's suburban sprawl. Stop in at the ultra-friendly **Chamber of Commerce**, 225 Rockaway Beach Ave (Mon–Fri 9am–noon & 1–5pm; Sat & Sun 10am–4.30pm; ☎650/355-4122), for free maps of the area, including trail guides for **Sweeney Ridge**, from where Spanish explorer Gaspar de Portola discovered the San Francisco Bay in 1769. Worth a quick spin, the **Sanchez Adobe**, 1000 Linda Mar Ave, Pacifica (Tues–Thurs 10am–4pm, weekends 1–5pm), is an 1846 hotel and speakeasy, now a museum with various Native American artifacts on display.

Pacifica's old **Ocean Shore Railroad Depot**, now a private residence, is one of the few surviving remnants of an ill-advised train line between San Francisco and Santa Cruz. Wiped out during the 1906 earthquake, the line was in any case never more than a third complete. Its few patrons had to transfer back and forth by ferry to connect the stretches of track that were built, the traces of which you can still see scarring the face of the bluffs. Over 100 photos of the attempt can be seen at *Ash's Vallemar Station Restaurant* at 2125 Hwy-1 at Reina Del Mar (☎650/359-7411). The continually eroding cliffs make construction along the coast treacherous at best, as evidenced a mile south by the **Devil's Slide**, where the highway is washed away with some regularity in winter storms. The slide area was also a popular dumping spot for corpses of those who fell foul of rum-runners during Prohibition, and is featured under various names in many of Dashiell Hammett's detective stories. You may notice signs along the route saying "Tunnel Yes," the product of local landowners desiring the state to construct a tunnel through the region, rather than continually patching up the road from rockslides and erosion. While theoretically possible, the enormous price tag has thus far prevented its realization.

Gray Whale Cove and Montara Lighthouse

Just south of the Devil's Slide, the sands of **Gray Whale Cove State Beach** (daily dawn–dusk; $5 parking) are clothing-optional. Despite the name it's not an especially great place to look for migrating gray whales, but the stairway at the bus stop does lead down to a fine strand of sand. Two miles south, the red-roofed buildings of the 1875 **Montara Lighthouse**, set among the windswept Monterey pine trees at the top of a steep cliff, have been converted into a youth hostel (see p.230), where guests can take a dip in a jacuzzi perched out on the coastal rocks where violent waves come crashing in at high tide.

Just south of the hostel, on California Street, the **James V. Fitzgerald Marine Reserve** (☎650/728-3584; free) has three miles of diverse oceanic habitat, peaceful trails, and, at low tide, the best tidal pools of the Bay Area. The ranger often gives guided interpretive walks through the reserve at low tide, the best time to explore. Call for low-tide times. At the south end of the reserve, **Pillar Point** juts out into the Pacific; just to the east, along Hwy-1, fishing boats dock at **Pillar Point Harbor**. **Mavericks Beach**, just south off Pillar Point beyond an enormous communications dish, has what are said to be the largest waves in North America, attracting some of the world's best (and craziest) surfers when conditions are right; just watching them can be an exhilarating way to spend an hour or so. The beach hosts the annual **Mavericks Surf Contest**, an event so secretive and dependent on the right wave-creating conditions that invitations are emailed to participants just two days in advance, with those who can make it (sometimes flying in from as far away as Australia) competing for a $10,000 prize supplied by surfboard companies. There's a long breakwater to walk out on, too, but remember to never turn your back on the ocean; rogue waves have crashed in and swept unsuspecting tourists to their deaths. Slightly further to the south lie **Dunes Beach** and **Venice Beach**, two more beautiful expanses of sand and ocean. You can ride a horse along these beaches from the **Sea Horse Ranch**, at Hwy-1 one mile north of Hwy-92 (☎650/726-2362; $20 per hour). The surrounding villages of **PRINCETON-BY-THE-SEA** and **EL GRENADA** have good roadside lunch stops like the *Highway One Diner*, in El Grenada, off Hwy-1, serving freshly caught fish and hamburgers. Further along, the best of the local surfing is just offshore at **Miramar Beach**; after dark, head for the beachfront *Douglass Beach House* (☎650/726-4143), an informal jazz club and beer bar facing the sands.

Half Moon Bay

HALF MOON BAY, twenty miles south of the city, takes its name from the crescent-shaped bay formed by Pillar Point. Lined by miles of sandy beaches, the town is surprisingly rural considering its proximity to San Francisco and Silicon Valley, and sports a number of ornate Victorians around its center. The oldest of these, built in 1849, is at the north end of Main Street, just across a little stone bridge over Pillarcitos Creek. The **Chamber of Commerce** (see p.177 for details) on Hwy-1 has free walking tour maps of the town and information on the annual **Pumpkin Festival** for which the place is well known, celebrating the harvest of the area's many pumpkin farms, just in time for Halloween when the fields around town are full of families searching for the perfect jack-o'-lantern to greet the hordes of trick-or-treaters. Free, basic campgrounds line the coast in **Half Moon Bay State Park**, half a mile west of the town.

Buy delicious fresh strawberries from roadside farm stands, or pick your own at the Anderatti family farm on Kelly Avenue, west of Hwy-1.

San Gregorio State Beach, ten miles south of Half Moon Bay, is at its best in the spring, after the winter storms, when flotsam architects construct a range of driftwood shelters along the wide beach south of the parking area. On hot summer days, the beach is packed with well-oiled bodies, but the sands around the bluffs to the north are quieter. You can bathe nude at **San Gregorio Private Beach** ($5); follow Hwy-1 one mile north of San Gregorio Road and watch for the small white gate on the left that subtly marks the entrance to the parking area. The beach attracts a predominantly gay crowd, which arrives early in the day in search of "condos" – the makeshift driftwood houses that line the beach.

The Butano Redwoods and the Año Nuevo State Reserve

If you've got a car and it's not a great day for the beach, head up into the hills above, where the thousands of acres of the **Butano redwood forest** feel at their most ancient and primeval in the grayest, gloomiest weather. About half the land between San Jose and the coast is protected from development in a variety of state and county parks, all of which is virtually deserted. Any one of a dozen roads heads through endless stands of untouched forest, and even the briefest of walks will take you seemingly miles from any sign of civilization. Hwy-84 climbs up from San Gregorio through the Sam McDonald County Park to the hamlet of **LA HONDA**, from where you can continue on to Palo Alto, or, better, loop back to the coast via Pescadero

For information on mountain bike and hiking trails around San Mateo and Santa Cruz counties, see p.323

Road. A mile before you reach the quaint town of **PESCADERO**. Cloverdale Road heads south to **Butano State Park**, where you can hike and camp overlooking the Pacific.

Back on Hwy-1, five miles south of Pescadero you can stay the night in the old lighthouse-keeper's quarters and soak your bones in another marvelous hot tub at the **HI-Pigeon Point Lighthouse Hostel**. The calmest, most pleasant beach in which to wade is at **Bean Hollow State Beach**, a mile north of the hostel. If you're here during December through March, continue south another five miles to the **Año Nuevo State Reserve** for a chance to see one of nature's most bizarre spectacles – the mating rituals of the northern elephant seal. These massive, ungainly creatures, fifteen feet long and weighing up to three tons, were once found all along the coast, though they were nearly hunted to extinction by whalers in the nineteenth century. During the mating season the beach is literally a seething mass of blubbery bodies, with the trunk-nosed males fighting it out for the right to sire as many as fifty pups in a season. At any time of the year you're likely to see a half dozen or so dozing in the sands. The reserve is also good for bird watching, and in March you might even catch sight of migrating gray whales.

For more information on the Pigeon Point Lighthouse hostel, see p.230.

The slowly resurgent Año Nuevo seal population is still carefully protected, and during the breeding season the obligatory guided tours – designed to protect spectators as much as to give the seals some privacy – begin booking in September (hourly 8am–4pm; ☎650/879-0227). Otherwise tickets are usually made available to people staying at the *Pigeon Point Hostel*, and SamTrans (☎1-800/660-4287) sometimes runs charter-bus tours from the town of **San Mateo** on the bay side of the Peninsula. South of Año Nuevo, its clear sailing down Hwy-1 to Santa Cruz, Monterey and Southern California.

Chapter 12

Marin County

Across the Golden Gate from San Francisco, **Marin County** (pronounced "Ma-RINN") is an unabashed introduction to Californian self-indulgence: an elitist pleasure zone of conspicuous luxury and abundant natural beauty, with sunshine, sandy beach-

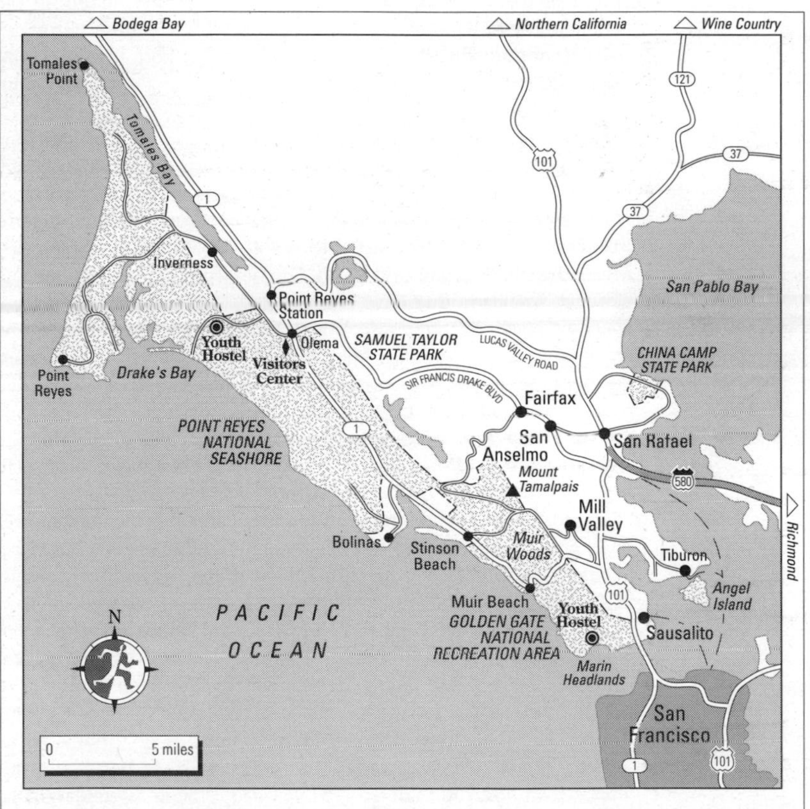

es, high mountains, and thick redwood forests. Reportedly the second-wealthiest county in the US, Marin has attracted a sizeable contingent of Northern California's wealthiest young professionals, though the place still retains much of its New Age feel and reputation that it gained back in the 1970s. Even if many of the cocaine-and-hot-tub devotees who populated the swanky waterside towns back then have traded in their drug habits for mountain bikes – which were invented on the fire roads of Mount Tamalpais – life in Marin still centers around personal pleasure. The throngs you see hiking and cycling at weekends, not to mention the hundreds of esoteric self-help practitioners – rolfing (deep-tissue massage), rebirthing, and soul-travel therapists fill up the classified ads of the local papers – prove that Marinites work hard to maintain their easy air of physical and mental well-being.

Flashy modern ferry boats, appointed with fully stocked bars, sail across the bay from San Francisco and give a good initial view of the county. As you head past desolate Alcatraz Island, curvaceous **Mount Tamalpais** looms larger until you land at its foot in one of the chic bayside settlements of **Sausalito** or **Tiburon**. **Angel Island**, in the middle of the bay but accessible most easily from Tiburon, provides relief from the excessive style-consciousness of both towns, retaining a wild untouched feeling among the eerie ruins of derelict military fortifications.

Sausalito and Tiburon (and the lifestyles that go with them) are only a small part of Marin. The bulk of the county rests on the slopes of the ridge of peaks that divides the peninsula down the middle, separating the sophisticated harborside towns in the east from the untrammeled wilderness of the Pacific coast to the west. The **Marin Headlands**, just across the Golden Gate Bridge, hold time-warped old battlements and gun emplacements that once protected San Francisco's harbor from would-be invaders, and now overlook hikers and cyclists enjoying the acres of open space and wildlife. Along the coastline that stretches north, the broad shore of **Stinson Beach** is the Bay Area's finest and widest stretch of sand, beyond which Hwy-1 clings to the coast past the rural village of **Bolinas** to the phenomenal valleys, forests, and seascapes around **Point Reyes**. Whale and seal watchers congregate here year-round for glimpses of migrations and matings.

Inland, the heights of Mount Tamalpais, and specifically its sister park to the east, **Muir Woods**, are a magnet to sightseers and nature-lovers, who come to wander through one of the few surviving stands of the native coastal redwood trees. Such trees covered most of Marin before they were chopped down to build and rebuild the dainty wooden houses of San Francisco. The long-vanished lumber mills of the rustic town of **Mill Valley**, overlooking the bay from the slopes of Mount Tam, as it's locally known, bear the guilt for much of this destruction; the oldest town in Marin County is now home to an eclectic bunch of art galleries and cafés. Further north, Marin's largest town, **San Rafael**, is best bypassed, though the undervisited

SAN FRANCISCO–MARIN COUNTY FERRIES

Because ferry schedules change slightly four times a year, you should check recent changes to the following **timetable** of arrival and departure times before sailing. Current schedules are always available from the terminals.

GOLDEN GATE TRANSIT FERRIES (☎415/923-3000)

San Francisco–Larkspur: Mon–Fri depart 6.35am, 7.20am, 7.50am, 8.20am, 8.55am, 10.45am, 11.25am, 12.45pm, 1.35pm, 3.05pm, 3.25pm, 3.45pm, 4.30pm, 4.50pm, 5.20pm, 6.15pm, 6.30pm, 7.35pm & 8.45pm; Sat, Sun & holidays 10.45am, 12.45pm, 2.45pm, 4.45pm & 6.45pm.

Larkspur–San Francisco: Mon–Fri depart 5.50am, 6.50am, 7.05am, 7.35am, 8.15am, 8.45am, 9.45am, 10.35am, 11.45am, 12.35pm, 2.20pm, 2.35pm, 3.45pm, 4.15pm, 4.50pm, 5.10pm, 5.40pm, 6.50pm & 7.50pm; Sat, Sun & holidays 9.45am, 11.45am, 1.45pm, 3.45pm & 5.45pm.

San Francisco–Sausalito: Mon–Fri depart 7.40am, 9.15am, 10.25am, 11.45am, 1.10pm, 2.35pm, 4.10pm, 5.30pm, 6.40pm & 8pm; Sat, Sun & holidays 11.30am, 1pm, 2.30pm, 4pm, 5.30pm & 6.55pm; also May–Sept 8.05pm.

Sausalito–San Francisco: Mon–Fri depart 7.05am, 8.15am, 11.05am, 12.25pm, 1.55pm, 3.20pm, 4.45pm, 6.05pm & 7.20pm; Sat, Sun & holidays 10.50am, 12.15pm, 1.45pm, 3.15pm, 4.45pm & 6.10pm; also May–Sept 7.30pm.

BLUE AND GOLD FLEET FERRIES (☎415/773-1188)

San Francisco–Sausalito: Mon–Fri depart 11am, 12.15pm, 1.50pm, 3pm & 4.50pm; Sat, Sun & holidays 10.40am, 12.25pm, 1.50pm, 3.15pm, 4.45pm & 6.30pm; also May–Sept Fri & Sat 8.25pm.

Sausalito–San Francisco: Mon–Fri depart 11.50am, 1.05pm, 2.25pm, 3.35pm, 5.45pm & 8pm; also May–Sept Fri 8.50pm; Sat, Sun & holidays 11.20am, 1.05pm, 2.30pm, 3.55pm, 5.25pm & 7.10pm; also May–Sept Sat 9pm.

San Francisco–Tiburon: Mon–Fri depart 11am, 12.15pm, 1.35pm, 2.45pm, 4.05pm & 4.50pm; Sat, Sun & holidays 9.30am, 11.30am, 2pm, 4pm, 4.45pm & 6.30pm; also May–Sept Fri & Sat 8.25pm.

Tiburon–San Francisco: Mon–Fri depart 11.25am, 12.40pm, 1.55pm, 3.10pm, 5.25pm & 7.45pm; also May–Sept Fri 9.10pm; Sat, Sun & holidays 10.35am, 12.25pm, 2.35pm, 5.05pm, 5.50pm & 7.30pm; also May–Sept Sat 9.20pm.

preserved remnants of an old Chinese fishing village in nearby **China Camp State Park** are worth a stroll. The northern reaches of Marin County border the bountiful wine-growing regions of the Sonoma and Napa valleys, detailed in Chapter 13.

Arrival and transport

Just getting to Marin County can be a great start to a day out from San Francisco. Golden Gate Transit **ferries** (see box, above) leave from the Ferry Building on the Embarcadero, crossing the bay past Alcatraz Island to **Sausalito** and **Larkspur**; they run approximately every thirty minutes during the rush hour, less often the rest of the day, and every two hours on weekends and holidays. Tickets cost $4.80 one-way to Sausalito, $2.85 to Larkspur Monday to Friday ($4.80 weekends); refreshments are served on board. The more expensive ($12 round trip) Blue and Gold Fleet (see box, overleaf) sails from Pier 41 at Fisherman's Wharf to **Sausalito** and **Tiburon** – from where the *Angel Island Ferry* ($6 round trip, plus $1 per bicycle; ☎415/435-2131) nips back and forth to **Angel Island State Park** daily in summer, weekends only in the winter. Blue and Gold Fleet provides additional service to Angel Island ($10) and Tiburon from the Ferry Building downtown during commute hours ($6 one way).

Marin County accommodation listings begin on p.224; restaurants are covered on p.270 and bars on p.282.

Golden Gate Transit also runs a comprehensive **bus service** around Marin County and across the Golden Gate Bridge from the Transbay Terminal in San Francisco (in Marin County, call ☎415/455-2000; in San Francisco ☎415/923-2000), and publishes a helpful and free system map and timetable, including all ferry services. Bus fares range from $1.25 to $4.50, depending on the distance traveled. Basic GGT bus routes run every thirty minutes throughout the day, and once an hour late at night. GGT commuter services, which run only during the morning and evening rush hours, can be the only way to get to some places. Also, San Francisco's Muni bus #76 runs hourly from San Francisco direct to the Marin Headlands on Sundays only. Golden Gate Transit bus route #40, the only service available between Marin County and the East Bay, runs from the San Rafael Transit Center to the Del Norte BART station in El Cerrito ($2 each way).

If you'd rather avoid the hassle of bus connections, Gray Line ($30; ☎415/558-9400) offers four-hour **guided bus tours** from the Transbay Terminal in San Francisco, taking in Sausalito and Muir Woods (daily 9am, 10am, 11am, 1.30pm & 2.30pm); the Blue and Gold Fleet ferry also operates a boat-and-bus trip to Muir Woods, via Tiburon, for $32 round trip.

One of the best ways to get around Marin is by **bike**, particularly using a mountain bike to cruise the many trails that crisscross the county, especially in the Marin Headlands. If you want to ride on the road, **Sir Francis Drake Highway** – from Larkspur to Point Reyes – makes a good route, though it's best to avoid weekends, when the roads can get clogged up with cars. All ferry services (except Alcatraz) allow bicycles.

Information

Three main on-the-spot sources can provide further **information** on Marin County: the **Marin County Visitors Bureau**, 1013 Larkspur Landing Circle, Larkspur (Mon–Fri 9am–5pm; ☎415/499-5000; *www.visitmarin.org*), the **Sausalito Chamber of Commerce**, Fourth Floor, 777 Bridgeway (Tues–Sun 11.30am–4pm; ☎415/332-0505), and the **Mill Valley Chamber of Commerce**, 85 Throckmorton

(Mon, Tues, Thurs & Fri 11am–4pm ☎415/388-9700), in the center of the town.

For information on **hiking** and **camping** in the wilderness and beach areas, depending on where you're heading, contact the **Golden Gate National Recreation Area**, Building 201, Fort Mason Center, San Francisco (Mon–Fri 9.30am–4.30pm; ☎415/556-0560) or in Sausalito at Fort Cronkhite (☎415/331-1540); Mount Tamalpais State Park, 801 Panoramic Highway, Mill Valley (daily 8.30am–10.30pm; ☎415/388-2070); or the Point Reyes National Seashore, Bear Valley Visitors Center, Point Reyes (Mon–Fri 9am–5pm, Sat & Sun 8am–5pm; ☎415/663-1092). Information on **what's on** in Marin can be found in the widely available local freesheets, such as the down-to-earth *Coastal Post* or the New-Agey *Pacific Sun*.

Across the Golden Gate: Marin Headlands and Sausalito

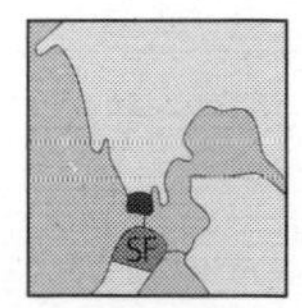

The largely undeveloped **Marin Headlands** of the Golden Gate National Recreation Area across the Golden Gate Bridge from San Francisco, afford some of the most impressive views of the bridge and the city behind. Heading north from the city, take the first turn as you exit the bridge (Alexander Ave) and follow the sign that leads, confusingly, back to San Francisco – the circular trip back to the bridge heads first to the west along Conzelman Road and up a steep hill. You'll pass through a largely undeveloped land, dotted by the concrete remains of old forts and gun emplacements standing guard over the entrance to the bay, dating from as far back as the Civil War and as recent as World War II. The coastline here is much more rugged than it is on the San Francisco side, making it a great place for an aimless clifftop hike or a stroll along one of the beaches dramatically situated near the crashing waves at the bottom of treacherous footpaths.

For information on renting bikes in the Bay Area, see p.320.

The first installation you'll see as you climb the steep hill up the Headlands is **Battery Spencer**, the largest and most impressive of artillery sites, cut through a hillside above the southwestern tip of the

Biking the Coastal Trail

San Franciscans love the Headlands for their many excellent, groomed mountain-bike trails, the best of which is the **Coastal Trail**. Beginning at the northern end of the Golden Gate Bridge, it climbs up the mountain facing back to the city before plummeting down into Rodeo Valley to the west. At Rodeo Beach, where you can also pick up the trail on foot, it continues along the quiet coast, past gun embankments, to Tennessee Valley beach, from where cyclists can loop back to Bunker Road via the marked Miwok Trail. Contact the **Marin Headlands Information Center** (daily 9.30am–4.30pm; ☎415/331-1540), to obtain a detailed map on this and other trails in the area.

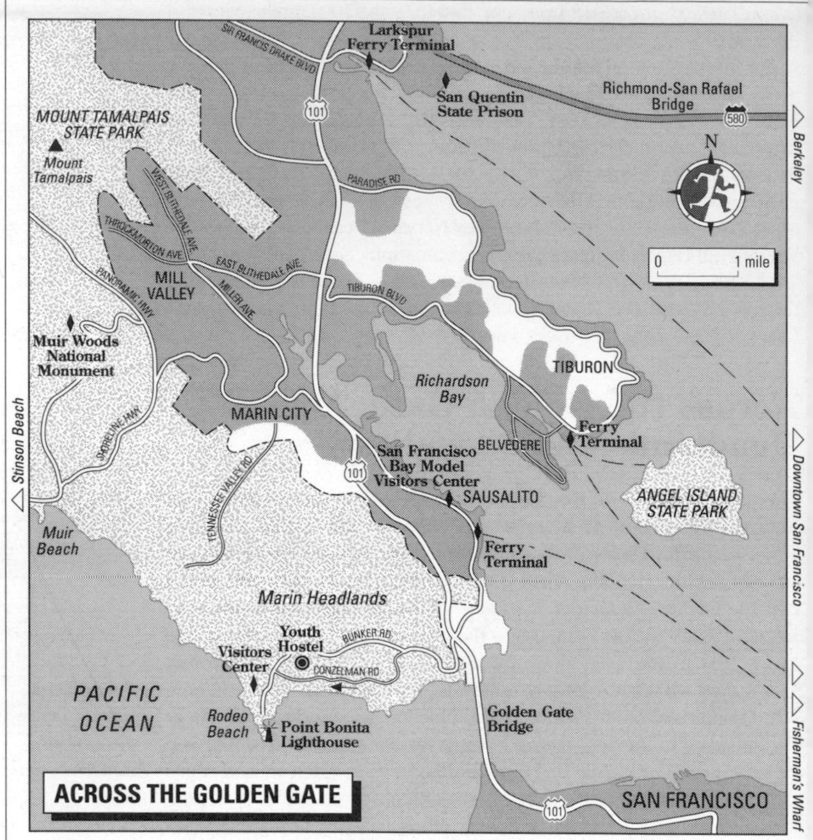

peninsula. Continue along Conzelman until it turns into a one-way road for incredible views of the city from any of the many turnouts; at the road's end, walkways lead from a parking area to bird-watching trails and vistas of **Rodeo Beach** and the lighthouse far below.

A single-lane road at the edge of the parking area descends steeply to the **Point Bonita Lighthouse** (tours Sat–Mon, 12.30–3.30pm free), standing sentry at the very end of the Headlands. You have to walk the last half-mile from an even smaller parking area down to the beckoning structure, a beautiful stroll that takes you through a tunnel cut into the cliff, and across a precarious suspension bridge. The lighthouse casts its beam over 25 miles out to sea.

Heading back on Conzelman, fork off to the left, heading northeast onto Bunker Road. To the left lies the **Nike Missile Site**, an abandoned 1950s ballistic missile launchpad, complete with disarmed nuclear missiles (Wed–Fri 10am–5pm; free guided tours first Sunday of every month 12.30–3.30pm; ☎415/331-1453). A bit further on, the **Marin Headlands Information Center**, alongside Rodeo Lagoon (daily 9.30am–4.30pm; ☎415/331-1540), has free maps of popular hiking trails in the area and information on the **historical walk** (Sat) which loops 5.5 miles into Gerbode Valley, telling the story and of the ruins of **Marincello**, a town begun and abandoned in the late 1960s in the headlands near Tennessee Valley. A bit further along Bunker Road, the largest of **Fort Barry**'s old buildings has been converted into the spacious but homey *HI-Marin Headlands Hostel*, an excellent base for more extended explorations of the inland ridges and valleys.

To the west, Bunker Road snakes down to wide, sandy **Rodeo Beach**, which separates the chilly ocean from the marshy warm water of **Rodeo Lagoon**, where swimming is prohibited to protect nesting seabirds. North of the lagoon, the **Marine Mammal Center** rescues and rehabilitates injured and orphaned sea creatures, which you can visit while they recover; there's also a series of displays on the marine ecosystem and a bookstore. Follow Bunker Road due east and you'll pass through a long, one-way tunnel, before emerging at Alexander Avenue. Turning left takes you to Sausalito, turning right reaches US-101.

Across the Golden Gate: Marin Headlands and Sausalito

Full details of the Marin Headlands Hostel *can be found on p.230.*

To get to Rodeo Beach using public transportation, take the #76 Muni bus from San Francisco – Sun and holidays only.

Sausalito

SAUSALITO, along the bay below US-101, is a pretty, smug little town of exclusive restaurants and pricey boutiques along a picturesque waterfront promenade. Expensive, quirkily designed houses climb the overgrown cliffs above **Bridgeway Avenue**, the main road and bus route through town. Sausalito used to be a fairly gritty community of fishermen and sea-traders, full of bars and bordellos, and fifty years ago served as one of the settings for Orson Welles' murder mystery, *The Lady From Shanghai*. Despite its upscale modern pretensions, the town still makes a fun day out from San Francisco by ferry, with boats arriving next to the Sausalito Yacht Club in the center of town. Hang out in one of the waterfront bars and watch the crowds strolling along the esplanade, or climb the stairways above Bridgeway and amble around the leafy hills.

If you have sailing experience, split the $130 daily rental fee of a four- to six-person sailboat at Cass's Marine, 1702 Bridgeway (☎415/332-6789). Another way of experiencing the water is to rent a sea kayak; try Sea Trek (☎415/332-4465) where rentals start at $20 for two hours' worth of paddling the bay.

One of Sausalito's biggest family draws is actually back by the bridge at Fort Baker, the **Bay Area Discovery Museum**, 557 McReynolds Rd (June 15–Sept 15 Tues–Sun 10am–5pm; Sept 16–June 14 Tues–Thurs 9am–4pm, Fri–Sun 10am–5pm; $7 adults, $6 kids; ☎415/487-4398), a hands-on children's museum aimed at explaining the area's aquatic ecosystem via an underwater sea tunnel, aquariums, and fishing from the pier.

For ideas of Bay Area places to take children, see p.35.

The old working wharves and warehouses that made Sausalito a haven for smugglers and Prohibition-era rum-runners are long gone; most have been taken over by dull steakhouses such as the *Charthouse*. However, some stretches of it have, for the moment at least, survived the tourist onslaught. Half a mile north of the town center along Bridgeway Avenue, an ad hoc community of exotic barges and houseboats, some of which have been moored here since the 1950s, is perennially threatened with eviction to make room for yet another luxury marina and bayview office development. In the meantime, many of the boats – one looks like a South Pacific island, another like the Taj Mahal – can be viewed from the marina behind the large brown shed at 2100 Bridgeway that houses the **Bay Model Visitor Center**, 2100 Bridgeway (Tues–Sat 9am–4pm; donation; ☎415/332-3871). Elevated walkways lead you around a massive working scale model of the bay, along with its surrounding deltas and aquatic inhabitants, simulating changing tides and powerful currents and offering insight on the enormity and diversity of this confluence of waters.

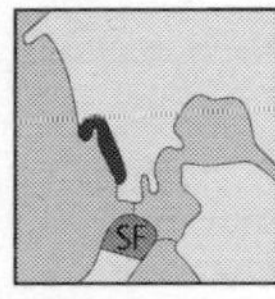

The Marin County coast to Bolinas

The **Shoreline Highway**, Hwy-1, cuts off west from US-101 just north of Sausalito, following the old main highway towards Mill Valley (see p.191). The first turn on the left, Tennessee Valley Road, leads up to the less-visited northern expanses of the Golden Gate National Recreation Area. You can take a beautiful three-mile hike from the parking lot at the end of the road, heading down along the secluded and lushly green **Tennessee Valley** to a small beach along a rocky cove, or you can take a guided tour on horseback from Miwok Livery at 701 Tennessee Valley Rd ($40 per hr; ☎415/383-8048). The stables also offer English lessons, day camps, and extended camps for children.

Hwy-1 twists up the canyon to a crest, where **Panoramic Highway** spears off to the right, following the ridge north to Muir Woods and Mount Tamalpais (see p.190). Be warned, however, that the hillsides are usually choked with fog until 11am, making a drive both dangerous and visually uninteresting.

Golden Gate Transit bus #63 to Stinson Beach follows the Panoramic Highway every hour on weekends and holidays only.

Two miles down from the crest, a small unpaved road cuts off to the left, dropping down to the bottom of the broad canyon to the **Green Gulch Farm and Zen Center** (☎415/383-3134), an organic farm and Buddhist retreat, with an authentic Japanese tea house and a simple but refined prayer hall. On Sunday mornings the center is opened for a public meditation period and an informal discussion of Zen Buddhism, after which you can stroll down to Muir Beach. If you already have some experience of Zen, inquire about the center's

Guest Student Program, which enables initiates to stay from three days to several weeks at a time (it costs about $10 a night). If you just want a weekend's retreat, you can also stay overnight in the attached *Lindisfarne Guest House* (see p.228) and take part as you choose in the communal life. Residents rise well before dawn for meditation and prayer, then work much of the day in the gardens, tending the vegetables that are eventually served in many of the Bay Area's finest restaurants (notably *Green's* in San Francisco – see p.248).

Beyond the Zen Center, the road down from Muir Woods rejoins Hwy-1 at **Muir Beach**, usually uncrowded and beautifully secluded in a semicircular cove. Three miles north, **Steep Ravine** drops sharply down the cliffs to a small beach, past very rustic $30-a-night cabins and a $10-a-night campground, bookable through Mount Tamalpais State Park (see overleaf). A mile on is the small and lovely **Red Rocks** nudist beach, down a steep trail from a parking area along the highway. **Stinson Beach**, which is bigger, and more popular despite the rather cold water (it's packed on weekends in summer, when the traffic can be nightmarish), is a mile further. You can rent boogie boards for $8 and wetsuits for $10 a day from the Livewater Surf Shop, 3448 Shoreline Hwy (☎415/868-0333), or kayaks for $35–60 per day a bit further down the road at the Stinson Beach Health Club, 3605 Shoreline Hwy (☎415/868-2739).

Bolinas and southern Point Reyes

At the tip of the headland, due west from Stinson Beach, is the village of **BOLINAS**, though you may have a hard time finding it – road signs marking the turnoff from Hwy-1 are removed as soon as they're put up, by locals hoping to keep the place to themselves. The campaign may have backfired, though, since press coverage of the "sign war" has done more to publicize the town than any road sign ever did; to get there, take the first left beyond the estuary and follow the road to the end. Bolinas is surrounded by federal property: the Golden Gate National Recreation Area and Point Reyes National Seashore. Even the lagoon was recently declared a National Bird Sanctuary. Known for its leftist hippie culture, the village itself is a small colony of artists, bearded handymen, stray dogs, and writers, and there's not a lot to see – though you can get a feel for the place (and pick up tasty sandwiches and bags of fresh fruit and vegetables) at the Bolinas People's Store in the block-long village center.

The late trout-fishing author Richard Brautigan and basketball diarist Jim Carroll both lived in Bolinas.

Beyond Bolinas, the rocky beach at the end of Wharf Road west of the village is great for calm surf waves. **Duxbury Reef Nature Reserve**, half a mile west at the end of Elm Road, is well worth a look for its tidal pools, full of starfish, crabs and sea anemones. Otherwise, Mesa Road heads north from Bolinas past the **Point Reyes Bird Observatory** (☎415/868-0655) – open for informal tours all day, though best visited in the morning. The first bird observatory in the US, this is still an important research and study center. If you time it right you may be able to watch, or even help, the staff as they put colored bands on the birds to keep track of them. Beyond here, the unpaved road leads onto the **Palomarin Trailhead**, the southern access into the Point Reyes National Seashore (see p.195). The best of the many beautiful hikes around the area leads past a number of small lakes and meadows for three miles to **Alamere Falls**, which throughout the winter and spring cascade down the cliffs onto **Wildcat Beach**. **Bass Lake**, the first of several lakes along the trail, is a great spot for a swim, best entered by swinging out and dropping from one of the ropes that hang from the trees above its shore.

Back at the turnoff from Hwy-1, the Bolinas–Fairfax road leads due east through redwoods and grassy hillside – a superb drive as long as the road has not been closed for one of the frequent landslides or washouts that occur here. When you reach the T in the road, turn left to get to Fairfax, or right to scale Mount Tamalpais.

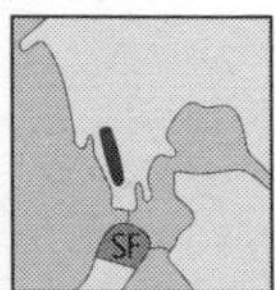

Mount Tamalpais and Muir Woods

Mount Tamalpais dominates the skyline of the Marin peninsula, hulking over the cool canyons of the rest of the county in a crisp yet voluptuous silhouette and dividing the county into two distinct parts: the wild western slopes above the Pacific coast and the increasingly suburban communities along the calmer bay frontage. Panoramic Highway branches off from Hwy-1 along the crest through the center of **Mount Tamalpais State Park** (☎415/338-2070, *www.mtia.net*), which has some thirty miles of hiking trails and many campgrounds, though most of the redwood trees which once covered its slopes have long since been chopped down to form the posts and beams of San Francisco's Victorian houses (see p.87). One 560-acre grove of these towering trees does remain, however, protected as the **Muir Woods National Monument** (daily 8am–sunset; $2), a mile down Muir Woods Road from Panoramic Highway. It's a tranquil and majestic spot, with sunlight filtering through the 300ft trees down to the laurel and fern-covered canyon below. The canyon's steep sides are what saved it from Mill Valley's lumbermen, and today it's one of the few old-growth redwood groves between San Francisco and the fantastic forests of Redwood National Park, up the coast near the Oregon border.

For detailed guides to the intricate trail network in Muir Woods and other Bay Area parks and reserves, see p.350.

Its proximity to San Francisco makes Muir Woods a popular target, and the paved trails nearest the parking lot are often packed with bus-tour hordes. However, if you visit during the week, or outside midsummer, it's easy enough to leave the crowds behind, especially if you're willing to head off up the steep trails that climb the canyon sides. Winter is a particularly good time to come, as the streams are gurgling – the main creek flows down to Muir Beach, and salmon have been known to spawn in it – and the forest creatures, including the colonies of ladybugs that spend their winter huddling in the rich undergrowth, are more likely to be seen going about their business.

Keep an eye out for the various species of salamanders and newts that thrive in this damp environment; be warned, though, that some are poisonous and will bite if harassed.

One way to avoid the crowds, and the only way to get here on public transportation, is to enter the woods from the top by way of a two-mile hike from the **Pan Toll Ranger Station** on Panoramic Highway – which is a stop on the Golden Gate Transit #63 bus route. As the state park headquarters, the station has maps and information on hiking and camping, and rangers can suggest hikes to suit your mood and interests. From here the **Pan Toll Road** turns off to the right along the ridge to within a hundred yards of the 2571-foot summit of Mount Tamalpais, where there are breathtaking views of the distant Sierra Nevada, and red-necked turkey vultures listlessly circle. Hike the 0.3-mile wood-planked trail up to Gardner Lookout from the parking lot for an even better view.

Mill Valley

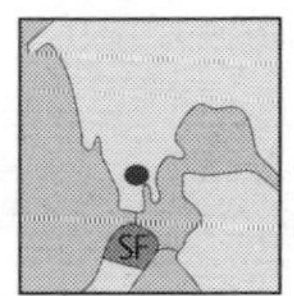

From the East Peak of Mount Tamalpais, a quick two-mile hike downhill follows the **Temelpa Trail** through velvety shrubs of chaparral to **MILL VALLEY**, the oldest and most enticing of Marin County's inland towns – also accessible every thirty minutes by Golden Gate Transit bus #10 from San Francisco and Sausalito. Originally a logging center, it was from here that the destruction of the surrounding redwoods was organized, though for many years the town has made a healthy living out of tourism. The **Mill Valley and Mount Tamalpais Scenic Railroad** – according to the blurb, "the crookedest railroad in the world" – was cut into the slopes above the town in 1896, twisting up through nearly three hundred tight curves in under eight miles. The trip proved so popular with tourists that the line was extended down into Muir Woods in 1907, though road-building and fire combined to put an end to the railroad by 1930. You can, however, follow its old route from the end of Summit Avenue in Mill Valley, a popular trip with daredevils on all-terrain bikes, which were, incidentally, invented here. The route is also used each June for the **Dipsea**, a tooth-and-nail seven-mile cross-country footrace across the mountains to Stinson Beach.

For a complete listing of film festivals in the Bay Area, see p.296.

Upscale Mill Valley now makes a healthy living out of tourism, especially during the **Mill Valley Film Festival** (☎415/383-5346, *www.finc.org*) in early October, which draws Bay Area stars like Robin Williams, Sharon Stone, and a host of up-an-coming directors. The restored town is centered around the redwood-shaded square of the **Depot Bookstore and Café** (Mon–Sat 7am–10pm, Sun 8am–10pm; ☎415/383-2665), a popular hangout at 87 Throckmorton Ave; there's a small **visitor center** doubling as the chamber of commerce next door (Mon–Tues & Thurs–Sat 10am–4pm; ☎415/388-9700), offering free maps of Mount Tam and hiking trails.

Across the street, at no. 74, the *Pleasure Principle* (☎415/388-8588) is a reminder of the Northern California eclecticism that lurks beneath Mill Valley's posh facade – this self-declared UFO headquarters also advertises a collection of vintage porn.

Tiburon and Angel Island

TIBURON, at the tip of a narrow peninsula three miles east of US-101, is, like Sausalito, a ritzy harborside village to which hundreds of people come each weekend, many of them via direct Blue and Gold Fleet **ferries** from Pier 41 in San Francisco's Fisherman's Wharf. It's a relaxed place, a bit less touristy than Sausalito, and if you're in the mood to take it easy and watch the boats sail across the bay, sitting out on the sunny deck of one of the many cafés and bars can be idyllic. There are few specific sights to look out for, but it's pleasant enough to simply wander around, browsing the galleries and antique shops. The best of these are grouped together in **Ark Row**, at the west end of Main Street, where the quirky buildings are actually old houseboats that were beached here early in the twentieth century. On a hill above the town stands **Old St Hilary's Church** (April–Oct Wed–Sun 1–4pm), a Gothic beauty that is best seen in the spring, when the surrounding fields are covered with multicolored buckwheat, flax, and paintbrush.

Tiburon is known for a couple of good bike rides – though you'll have to bring a bike over via the ferry or from Sausalito, as there are no rental shops here. Begin by cruising around the many plush houses of **Belvedere Island**, just across the Beach Road Bridge from the west end of Main Street, enjoying the fine views of the bay and Golden Gate Bridge. More ambitious bikers can continue along the waterfront bike path, which winds from the bijou shops and galleries three miles west along undeveloped Richardson Bay frontage to a bird sanctuary at **Greenwood Cove**, where a pristine Victorian house is now the western headquarters of the National Audubon Society and open for tours on Sundays (10am–4pm). A small interpretive center has displays on local and migratory birds and wildlife.

Another fine ride heads east from Tiburon along winding Paradise Road, around the mostly undeveloped headland three and a half miles to **Paradise Beach**, a county park with a fishing pier and close-up views of passing oil tankers heading for the refinery across the bay in Richmond. If you want to make a full circuit, Trestle Glen Boulevard cuts up and over the peninsula from near Greenwood Cove, linking with Paradise Road two miles northwest of Paradise Beach.

Angel Island

The pleasures of Tiburon are soon exhausted, and you'd be well advised to take the hourly Angel Island Ferry (10am–4pm; $7 round trip, plus $1 per bicycle; ☎415/435-2131) a mile offshore to the largest island in the San Francisco Bay, ten times the size of Alcatraz. **Angel Island** is now officially a state park, but over the years it's served a variety of purposes, everything from a home for Miwok Native Americans to a World War II prisoner-of-war camp. It's full of ghostly ruins of old military installations, and with oak and eucalyptus trees and sagebrush covering the hills above rocky coves and sandy beaches, feels quite apart from the mainland. The island offers some pleasant biking opportunities: a five-mile road rings the island, and an unpaved track (plus a number of hiking trails) leads up to the 800ft hump of **Mount Livermore**, with panoramic views of the Bay Area.

The ferry arrives at **Ayala Cove**, where a small snack bar selling hot dogs and cold drinks provides the only sustenance available on the island – better to bring a picnic if you plan to spend the day here. The nearby **visitor center** (daily 9am–4pm; ☎415/435-1915), in an old building that was built as a quarantine facility for soldiers returning from the Philippines after the Spanish–American War, has displays on the island's history. Around the point on the northwest corner of the island the **North Garrison**, built in 1905, was the site of a prisoner-of-war camp during World War II, while the larger **East Garrison**, on the bay a half mile beyond, was the major transfer point for soldiers bound for the South Pacific.

Quarry Beach around the point is the best on the island, a clean sandy shore that's protected from the winds blowing in through the Golden Gate; it's also a popular landing spot for kayakers and canoeists who paddle across the bay from Berkeley. **Camping** on Angel Island (☎1-800/444-7275) costs $10 per night ($11 Fri & Sat), well worth it for the view of San Francisco and the East Bay at night. The campground's nine sites fill up fast, so reserve well in advance. For **tours** of Angel Island, contact Angel Island TramTours (☎415/897-0715; *www.angelisland.com)*, which rents mountain bikes ($25 per day), gives daily tram tours (Mon–Fri 11.15am, 12.30pm, 2pm & 3.15pm; Sat & Sun 3.15pm; $10) and leads all-day kayak trips around the island (May–Oct weekends; $100).

For information on getting to Angel Island from Fisherman's Wharf, see p.82.

Sir Francis Drake Boulevard and central Marin County

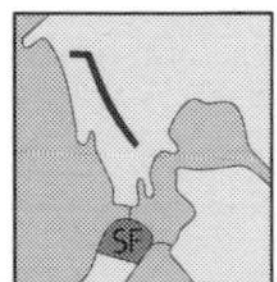

The quickest route to the wilds of the Point Reyes National Seashore, and the only way to get there on public transportation, is by way of **Sir Francis Drake Boulevard**, which cuts across central Marin County through the inland towns of **San Anselmo** and **Fairfax**, reaching the coast thirty miles west at a crescent-shaped bay where, in 1579, Drake supposedly landed and claimed all of what he called

Sir Francis Drake Boulevard and central Marin County

Nova Albion for England. The route makes an excellent day-long cycling tour, with the reward of good beaches, a youth hostel, and some tasty restaurants at the end of the road.

The Larkspur Golden Gate Transit **ferry**, which leaves from the Ferry Building in San Francisco, is the longest and, surprisingly, least expensive of the bay crossings. Primarily a commuter route, it docks at the modern space-frame terminal at Larkspur Landing. The monolithic, red-tile-roofed complex you see on the bayfront a mile east is the maximum-security **San Quentin State Prison**, which houses the state's most violent and notorious criminals, and of which Johnny Cash sang, "I hate every stone of you." If you arrive by car over the Richmond-San Rafael Bridge, you can follow road signs off Hwy-101 to the **San Quentin Prison Museum**, Building 106, Dolores Way (Mon–Fri 10am–4pm & Sat 11.45am–3.15pm; $2; ☎415/454-8808), for a glimpse at the institution's history. The tour takes about an hour, during which you'll see a prison cell, a replica of the gas chamber, the original gallows, and the solitary confinement pen known as "The Dungeon." At the end of the tour, you can buy prisoner-made artwork and even a collection of the inmates' favorite recipes, collected in the book, *Cooking with Conviction*.

For more on San Francisco's ferry building, see p.61.

San Anselmo, Fairfax, and Point Reyes Station

SAN ANSELMO, set in a broad valley two miles north of Mount Tam, calls itself "the antiques capital of Northern California" and sports a tiny center of specialty shops, furniture stores, and cafés that draws out many San Francisco shoppers on weekends. The ivy-covered **San Francisco Theological Seminary** off Bolinas Avenue, which dominates the town from the hill above, is worth a quick visit for the view and architecture. At serene **Robson-Harrington Park** on Crescent Avenue you can picnic among well-tended gardens, and the very green and leafy **Creek Park** follows the creek that winds through the town center, but otherwise there's not a lot to do but eat and drink – or browse through fine bookstores, such as Oliver's Books, at 645 San Anselmo Ave.

Center Boulevard follows the tree-lined creek west for a mile to **FAIRFAX**, a much less ostentatiously hedonistic community than the harborside towns, though in many ways it still typifies Marin lifestyles, with an array of wholefood stores and bookstores geared to a thoughtfully mellow crowd. From Fairfax, the narrow Bolinas Road twists up and over the mountains to the coast at Stinson Beach, while Sir Francis Drake Boulevard winds through a pastoral landscape of ranch houses hidden away up oak-covered valleys.

Ten miles west of Fairfax along Sir Francis Drake Boulevard, **Samuel Taylor State Park** has excellent camping (see p.231 for details); five miles more brings you to the coastal Hwy-1 and

OLEMA, a hamlet at the entrance to the park with a decent food and lodging choice in the guise of the *Olema Inn* (see p.228).

Sir Francis Drake Boulevard and central Marin County

A mile north sits the tourist town of **POINT REYES STATION**, a good place to stop off for a bite to eat or to pick up picnic supplies before heading off to enjoy the wide open spaces of the Point Reyes National Seashore just beyond. Trailhead Rentals, a half-mile from the Point Reyes Visitor Center, at 88 Bear Valley Rd (☎415/663-1958), rents mountain bikes for $24 per day – a great way to get around.

The Point Reyes National Seashore

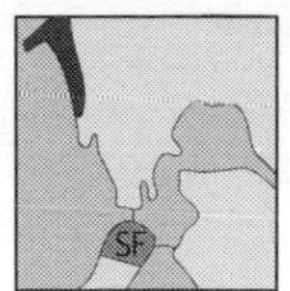

From Point Reyes Station, Sir Francis Drake Boulevard heads out to the westernmost tip of Marin County at Point Reyes through the **Point Reyes National Seashore**, a near-island of wilderness surrounded on three sides by more than fifty miles of isolated coastline – pine forests and sunny meadows bordered by rocky cliffs and sandy, windswept beaches. This wing-shaped landmass, something of an aberration along the generally straight coastline north of San Francisco, is in fact a rogue piece of the earth's crust that has been drifting slowly and steadily northward along the San Andreas Fault, having started some six million years ago as a suburb of Los Angeles. When the great earthquake of 1906 shattered San Francisco, the land here – the epicenter – shifted over sixteen feet in an instant, though damage was confined to a few skewed cattle fences.

The park's **visitor center** (Mon–Fri 9am–5pm, Sat, Sun & holidays 8am–5pm; ☎415/663-1092), two miles southwest of Point Reyes Station near Olema, just off Hwy-1 on Bear Valley Road, holds engaging displays on the geology and natural history of the region. Rangers dish out excellent hiking and cycling itineraries, and have up-to-date information on the weather, which can change quickly and be cold and windy along the coast even when it's hot and sunny here, three miles inland. Keep in mind that the point-to-point distances within Point Reyes are relatively vast and speed limits are slow, doubling most laymen's estimates of travel time. The rangers can help you realistically plan your itinerary and arrange for any hiking permits you'll need; they can also help with reservations at the various hike-in **campgrounds** within the park. Nearby, a replica of a native Miwok village has an authentic religious **roundhouse**, and a popular hike follows the Bear Valley Trail along Coast Creek four miles to **Arch Rock**, a large tunnel in the seaside cliffs that you can walk through at low tide.

For details of the Point Reyes Hostel, *see p.230.*

North of the visitor center, Limantour Road heads west six miles to the **HI-Point Reyes Hostel**, continuing on another two miles to

Gray Whales

The most commonly spotted whale along California's coast, the **gray whale** migrates annually from its summer feeding grounds near Alaska to its winter breeding grounds off Baja California and back again. Some 23,000 whales make the 13,000-mile round trip, swimming just a half-mile from the shoreline in small groups, with pregnant females leading the way on the southbound journey. Protected by an international treaty from hunters since 1938, the gray-whale population has been increasing steadily each year and its migration brings out thousands of humans hoping to catch a glimpse of their fellow mammals. Point Reyes is a favorite watching spot, as are the beaches along Hwy-1 south to Santa Cruz. For information on whale-watching expeditions or the latest information on the migration, contact Oceanic Society Expeditions, Bldg E, Fort Mason, San Francisco, CA 94123 (☎415/441-1106), or see p.323 for more details.

the coast at **Limantour Beach**, one of the best swimming beaches and a good place to watch the seabirds in the adjacent estuary. Bear Valley Road rejoins Sir Francis Drake Boulevard just past Limantour Road, leading north along Tomales Bay through the village of **INVERNESS**, so-named because the landscape reminded an early settler of his home in the Scottish Highlands. Eight miles west of Inverness, a turn leads down past **Johnson's Oyster Farm** (Tues–Sun 8am–4pm; ☎415/669-1149) – which sells bivalves for around $9 a dozen, less than half the price you'd pay in town – to **Drake's Beach**, one likely landing spot of Sir Francis in 1579 (whose journal makes the exact location unclear). Appropriately, the coastline here resembles the southern coast of England, often cold, wet and windy, with chalk-white cliffs rising above the wide sandy beach. The road continues southwest another four miles to the very tip of Point Reyes. A precariously sited **lighthouse** (Thurs–Sun 10am–5pm; tours first and third Sat of each month; free) stands firm against the crashing surf. The bluffs here are an excellent place to spot sea lions and, from mid-March to April and late December to early February, migrating gray whales.

The northern tip of the Point Reyes seashore, **Tomales Point**, is accessible via Pierce Point Road, which turns off Sir Francis Drake Boulevard two miles north of Inverness. Jutting out into Tomales Bay, it's the least-visited section of the park and a refuge for hefty **tule elk**; it's also a great place to admire the lupines, poppies, and other wildflowers that appear in the spring. The best swimming (at least the warmest water) is at **Heart's Desire Beach**, just before the end of the road. Down the bluffs from where the road comes to a dead end, there are excellent tidal pools at rocky **McClure's Beach**. North of Point Reyes Station, Hwy-1 continues along the coast past the famed oyster beds of Tomales Bay and through Bodega Bay, where Alfred Hitchcock's *The Birds* was shot, up to Mendocino and the Northern California coast.

San Rafael and northern Marin County

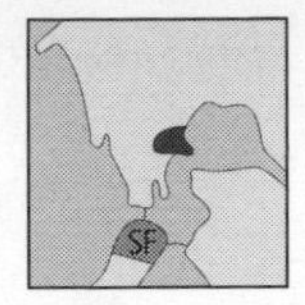

You may pass through **SAN RAFAEL** on your way north from San Francisco, but there's little worth stopping for. The county seat and the only big city in Marin County, it has none of the woodsy qualities that make the other towns special, though you'll come across a couple of good restaurants and bars along Fourth Street, the main drag. Its one attraction is the old **Mission San Rafael Arcangel** on Fifth Avenue at A Street (daily 11am–4pm; free), in fact a scaled-down 1949 replica built near the site of the 1817 original, and thus the least interesting of the chain to visit.

For information on the history of the California missions, see p.332.

Better to head out of town to the **Marin County Civic Center** (Mon–Fri 9am–5pm; tours Wed 10.30am; free; ☎415/499-6646), which spans the hills just east of US-101 a mile north of central San Rafael. A strange, otherworldly complex of administrative offices, it has an excellent performance space that resembles a giant viaduct capped by a bright-blue-tiled roof. These buildings were architect **Frank Lloyd Wright**'s one and only government project, and although the huge circus tents and amusement park at the core of the designer's conception were never built, it does have some interesting touches, such as the atrium lobbies that open directly to the outdoors.

From the Civic Center, North San Pedro Road loops around the headlands through **China Camp State Park** (☎415/456-0766), an expansive area of pastures and open spaces that's hard to reach without your own transportation. It takes its name from the intact but long-abandoned Chinese shrimp-fishing village at the far eastern tip of the park, the sole survivor of the many small Chinese communities that once dotted the California coast. The ramshackle buildings, small wooden pier, and old boats lying on the sand are pure John Steinbeck, though today there's a chain-link fence to protect the site from vandals. On the weekend you can get beer and sandwiches from the old shack at the foot of the pier, but the atmosphere is best during the week at sunset, when there's often no one around at all. There's a hike-in **campground** with thirty primitive sites ($16) at the northern end of the park, about two miles from the end of the Golden Gate Transit bus #23 route.

Six miles north of San Rafael, the **Lucas Valley Road** turns off west, twisting across Marin to Point Reyes. Although George lives and works here, it was not named after the *Star Wars* filmmaker Lucas, whose sprawling **Skywalker Ranch** studios are well hidden off the road. Hwy-37 cuts off east, eight miles north of San Rafael, heading around the top of the bay into the Wine Country of the Sonoma and Napa valleys (see Chapter 13).

Chapter 13

The Wine Country

Coming from San Francisco, a trip to the golden, arid Napa and Sonoma valleys, known jointly as the **Wine Country**, can feel like entering another country. With its cool, oak-tree-shaded ravines climbing up along creeks and mineral springs to chaparral-covered ridges, it would be a lovely place to visit even without the vineyards, but as it is, the "Wine Country" tag dominates almost everything here, including many often overlooked points of historical and literary interest.

The area doesn't actually produce all that much wine – only five percent or so of the California total – but what it does produce is far and away the best in the country, not surprising considering that the region has been producing wine since the days of the Spanish missions. Most of the vines actually withered during Prohibition, and, more recently, phylloxera – an insidious plant lice – all but decimated what remained, necessitating the transplant of root stock from Europe into the Californian soil. Growers are still struggling against mother nature and increased land costs – inflated by the sudden trend among retired millionaires living out their dream of owning a little winery – but many viticulturists nevertheless manage to turn out premium vintages that satisfy wine snobs around the world.

Predictably, the region is also among America's wealthiest and most provincial, a fact that draws – and repels – a steady stream of tourists. For every grape on the vine there seems to exist a quaint bed-and-breakfast or spa; in fact, tourism is gaining on wine production as the Wine Country's leading industry, so expect clogged highways and full hotels during peak season (March–Oct).

Around **Napa**, nothing is cheap, and the town itself can be quickly done, though you can board the over-hyped **wine train** here. Highway 29, takes you north through the valley, along a string of somewhat monotonous villages until reaching a few places of greater interest further up. **St Helena** has retained much of its c.1900-homestead character, and **Calistoga**, at the top of the valley, is famous for its hot springs, massages, and spas.

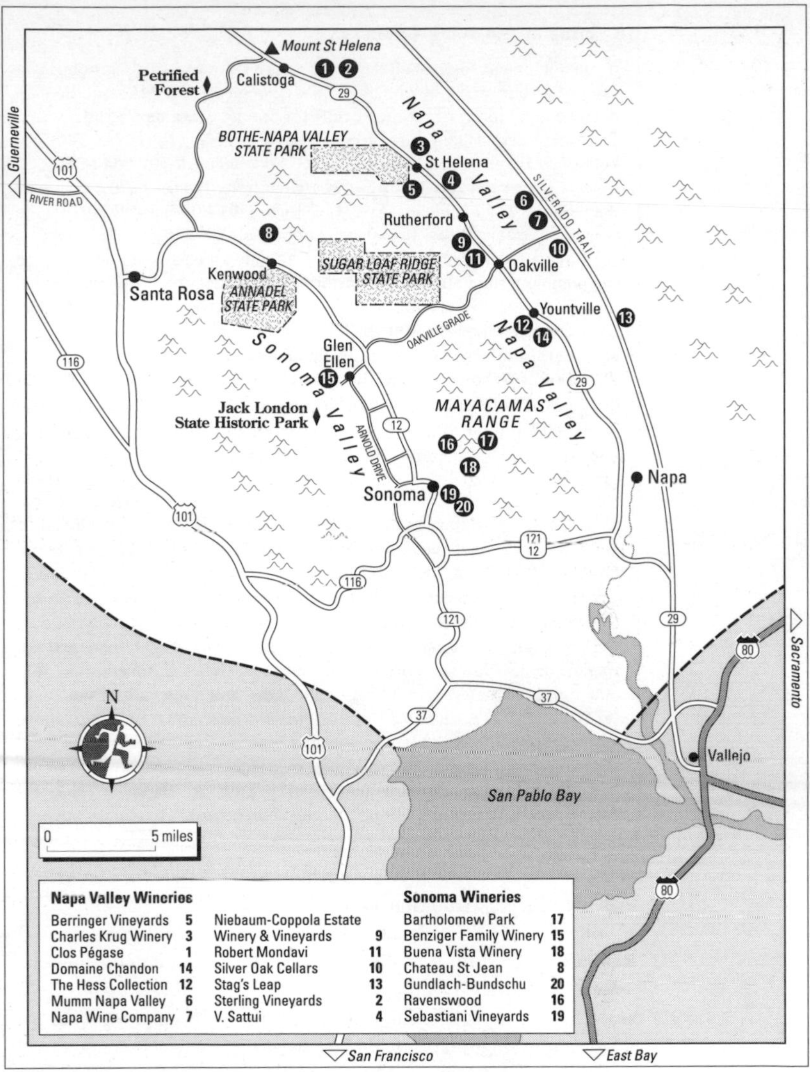

On the western side of the **Mayacamas Mountains**, which separate the two valleys, the smaller back-road wineries of the **Sonoma Valley** reflect the more down-to-earth nature of the place, which is both more beautiful and less crowded than its neighbor to the east. The town of **Sonoma** itself is by far the most attractive of the Wine Country communities, retaining a number of fine Mission-era structures around its gracious central plaza. **Santa Rosa**, at the north end

Cycling in the Wine Country

If you don't want to drive all day, **cycling** is a great way to get around. You can bring your own bike on Greyhound (though it costs $10, and the bike must be in a box), or rent one locally for around $25 a day, $120 a week. Try Napa Valley Bike Tours, 4080 Byway East, Napa (☎707/255-3377); Yountville Bike Rentals, Vintage 1870, Yountville (☎707/944-9080); St Helena Cyclery, 1156 Main St, St Helena (☎707/963-7736); Getaway Bike Shop, 1117 Lincoln Ave, Calistoga (☎1-800/859-BIKE); or the Sonoma Cyclery, 20093 Broadway, Sonoma (☎707/935-3377).

Both main valleys are generally flat, although the peaks in between are steep enough to challenge the hardiest of hill-climbers. If the main roads through the valleys are full of cars, as they are most summer weekends, try the smaller parallel routes: the **Silverado Trail** in Napa Valley and pretty **Arnold Drive** in Sonoma Valley. For the more athletically inclined, the **Oakville Grade** between Oakville in the Napa Valley and Glen Ellen in the Sonoma Valley has challenged the world's finest riders: Coors Classic tours were routed over the grade several years ago. The **King Ridge-Meyers Grade** – a 55-mile loop with a tough 4500-foot climb – begins at the north end of the bridge over the Russian River in Monte Rio and heads along the Cazadero Highway up into the hills, taking in the river, the redwoods, and the solitary mountains before finally descending to the coast and Hwy-1. Contact the Santa Rosa Cycling Club, PO Box 11761, Santa Rosa, CA 95406 (☎707/544-4803) for a complete itinerary for this or any area rides. Alternatively, plot your own route with the *Bicycle Rider Directory* (see Contexts, p.350).

Most local firms organize **tours**, providing bikes, helmets, food, and sag wagons in case you get worn out. In Calistoga, Getaway Adventures (☎1-800/499-2453) offers trips of varying lengths, and Napa Valley Bike Tours (☎707/255-3377; *www.napavalleybiketours.com*) sets up more leisurely tours – highlighted by gourmet lunches – all over the Napa area. More ambitious (and quite expensive) overnight tours are run most weekends by Backroads Bicycle Tours, 1516 Fifth St, Berkeley (Mon–Fri 8am–5pm; ☎510/527-1555; *www.backroads.com*).

of the valley, is the region's sole urban center, handy for budget lodgings but otherwise unremarkable.

Still further northwest, around two hours from San Francisco, the **Russian River Valley** is a sleepy backwater community hidden in among the redwoods lining the Russian River before it spills into the sea. This is one of the most intimate places to discover California wines, along single-lane roads that twist through peaceful vineyards. The valley's seat, **Guerneville**, has the most nightlife and lodging, and is a summertime resort, especially popular with San Francisco's gay community.

Many people are content to visit the Wine Country as a day-trip from San Francisco, visiting a few of the wineries and maybe having a picnic or a meal before heading back to the city. But if you really want to absorb properly what the region has to offer, plan to spend at least one night here, pampering yourself in one of the many (generally pricey) **hotels** and **bed and breakfast inns** that provide the bulk of the area's accommodation options. At peak times rooms of all descriptions get snapped up, so if you have a hard time finding a place, make use of one of the many **accommodation services** here: Bed and Breakfast Inns of Napa Valley (☎707/944-4444); Bed and Breakfast Association of Sonoma Valley (☎707/938-9513); Reservations Unlimited (☎707/252-1985); or the Napa Valley Visitors Bureau (☎707/226-7459). From November to February, lodging prices drop considerably, often up to fifty percent less than rates during peak season.

For specific Wine Country accommodation recommendations, see Chapter 14; restaurants are covered on p.271, and bars on p.283.

Arrival and transport

The Wine Country region spreads north from the top of the San Francisco Bay in two parallel, thirty-mile-long valleys, **Napa** and **Sonoma**, divided by the Mayacamas Mountains. As long as you avoid the rush-hour traffic, the area is a little over an hour's drive from San Francisco along either of two main routes: through Marin County via the Golden Gate Bridge (head north on US-101 then east on US-37 and north on US-121), or through the East Bay via the Bay Bridge (head east on I-80 then north on US-29). Good highways ring the region, and a loop through the hearts of the two valleys is conceivable in one-day's time – provided you leave San Francisco at the crack of dawn. If you wish to take in the adjoining **Russian River Valley** to the northwest, you should plan on staying overnight, unless you wish to bypass Napa and Sonoma entirely by taking US-101 straight there – a two-hour drive barring traffic – exiting at River Road, about five miles north of Santa Rosa, and heading west another fifteen miles to Guerneville.

As the Wine Country's attractions are spread over a fairly broad area, a **car** is pretty much essential. There are other options however: Golden Gate Transit (☎415/923-2000) runs commuter buses every hour for the two-hour, $5.45 ride between the city, Sonoma and Santa Rosa, while Greyhound (☎1-800/231-2222) has only one bus daily to Napa and Sonoma, which leaves San Francisco's Transbay Terminal at an inconvenient 3pm for Napa ($24 round trip) or 3.30pm for Sonoma ($21 round trip). From Santa Rosa, Sonoma County Transit (☎707/576-RIDE) buses serve the entire Valley on a comprehensive, if less than frequent, schedule, and the Mendocino Transit Authority (☎1-800/696-4MTA) runs one bus daily up the Russian River Valley as far north as Fort Bragg and Mendocino ($26.50 round trip). Another option for the carless is to sign up for a Gray Line **guided bus tour** (☎415/558-9400) from San Francisco. These cost $46, and leave from the Transbay Terminal at 9am. The tour covers both valleys, and visits three wineries, including Sebastiani in downtown Sonoma and Sutter Home in St Helena, with a stop for lunch in Calistoga. The tour returns to San Francisco around 6.30pm. You can also take the Sonoma Airporter bus (6 daily;

For the location of the Transbay Terminal in San Francisco, see p.95.

For more on the Ferry Building in San Francisco, see p.61.

1hr 30min; $20; ☎707/938-4246 or 1-800/611-4246) from SFO to Sonoma City Hall – reservations required. It also stops at the corner of Geary Boulevard and Park Presidio in San Francisco's Richmond District, and makes six return trips to the city daily.

Twelve daily Blue and Gold Fleet **ferries** travel from the Ferry Building in San Francisco to Vallejo ($10 round trip; ☎415/773-1188), and are met by hourly Napa Valley Transit buses (Mon–Sat; ☎1-800/696-6443) which continue on to the city of Napa and beyond. Blue and Gold also runs a Wine Country tour leaving daily from Pier 41 (weekdays 11am, weekends 9.30am; $52).

The **Wine Train** (1 daily; 3hrs; full meal and ticket $27.50–99; ☎1-800/427-4124 or 707/253-2111) runs from Napa's station at 1275 McKinstry St (located off of First St east from downtown), but is more a wining and dining experience than a means of transportation. On all itineraries, which range from simple rides on deli snack cars to interactive dinner theater, the 10-car train of restored 1950s Pullman cars chugs up the valley to St Helena, with a stop at Grgich Hills Cellars winery. The scenery en route is pleasant, but nothing that you couldn't experience by car.

Information

Not surprisingly, the Wine Country has a well-developed network of **tourist information** outlets, though the rivalry between the two valleys makes it next to impossible to find out anything about Sonoma when you're in Napa, and vice versa. Both the **Napa Valley Visitors Bureau**, 1310 Napa Town Center off First Street in downtown Napa (daily 9am–5pm; ☎707/226-7459), and the **Sonoma Valley Visitors**

Ballooning in the Wine Country

The most exciting way to see the Wine Country is on one of the widely touted **hot-air balloon rides** over its valleys. These usually lift off at dawn (hot air rises more strongly in the cold morning air) and last sixty to ninety magical minutes, winding up with a champagne brunch. The first, and still the best, of the operators is Napa Valley Balloons (☎707/253-2224), who fly out of Yountville. Others include Balloons Above the Valley, Napa (☎707/253-2222) and Air Flambuoyant, Sonoma (☎1-800/456-4711). It's around $175 a head, but really worth every cent – floating at 4000 feet with a bubbling glass of champagne in your hand as the fog lifts slowly off the valleys below is an unforgettable experience. Make reservations a week in advance, especially in summer, though with the increasing amount of balloon companies, same-day drop-bys are a possibility.

If balloons are too light for your taste, consider the nostalgic thrill of taking to the air in a solid World War II-era propeller biplane. Vintage Aircraft Company, 23982 Arnold Drive, Sonoma (☎707/938-2444), has 1- or 2-person flights that take in the Sonoma Valley between loops and rolls. Choose from four flight patterns: Scenic, Aerobatic, Kamikaze, and – gulp – Dawn Patrol, which takes you out on the longest, most daring route. Flights are 15 to 40 minutes and cost $89–199.

Bureau, 453 First St E, at the center of the plaza in Sonoma (daily 9am–5pm; ☎707/996-1090), should be able to tell you all you need to know about their respective areas. From San Francisco into Sonoma, there's a friendly branch office of the Sonoma Valley Visitors Bureau in the Vianza Winery, 25200 Hwy-121. A handy Napa Valley guide includes detailed listings and map, but doesn't come cheap at ($5.95); Sonoma Valley's guide (free) is smaller but equally effective in helping you organize your tasting and tourism agenda in the area.

The Napa Valley

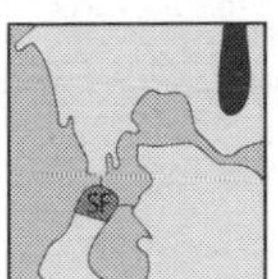

A thirty-mile strip of gently landscaped corridors and lush hillsides, the **Napa Valley** looks more like southern France than the rest of Northern California. In spring the valley floor is covered with brilliant wildflowers which mellow into autumnal shades by grape-harvest time. Local Native Americans named the fish-rich river which flows through the valley "Napa," meaning "plenty"; the name was adopted by Spanish missionaries in the early 1800s, but the natives themselves were soon wiped out. The few ranches the Spanish and Mexicans managed to establish were in turn taken over by Yankee traders, and by the 1850s the town of Napa had become a thriving river port, sending agricultural goods such as prunes to San Francisco and serving as a supply point for farmers and ranchers. The 1852 opening in town of White Sulphur Springs, California's first mineral springs resort, made Napa the vacation choice for San Francisco's elite. Sun-loving settlers such as Jacob Beringer came too; in 1870, Beringer realized that the valley's rocky, well-drained soil resembled that of his homeland, Mainz, a major wine region in Germany, and by 1875 he and his brother had established what has become America's oldest continually operating winery today.

Before long Napa was bypassed by the railroads and unable to compete with other, deep-water Bay Area ports, but the area's fine climate saved it from oblivion, with plenty of visitors pouring in to enjoy the scenery, hot springs, and growing number of wineries. Today, especially in summer, the area is overrun with visitors from all over the world, making the off-season months the time to come, though there are enough smaller wineries in the valley's lesser traveled byways to make a day-trip in even the busiest months of summer worthwhile.

If you're looking for an alternative route from Calistoga to Napa, the Silverado Trail offers some breathtaking views of the Wine Country without the commercialism of Hwy-29.

Napa, Yountville, and Oakville

Ironically, the rather congested town of **NAPA** lacks both excitement and charm and is best avoided in favor of the wineries and smaller towns north along Highway 29, though it does at least have a decent number of good restaurants (see p.271). A collection of chain stores and an ugly, broken clock anchor the downtown, situated on a curve

Napa Valley wineries

Almost all of the Napa Valley's wineries offer tastings, though comparatively few have tours. There are over three hundred wineries in all, producing wines of a very high standard, so your taste should ultimately determine the ones you visit. The following selections, listed alphabetically, includes some longstanding favorites, plus a few lesser-known hopefuls. Keep in mind that the intention is for you to get a sense of a winery's product, and perhaps buy some, rather than get drunk on the stuff, so don't expect more than a sip or two of any one sort – though some wineries do sell wines by the glass. Unlike in Europe where buying directly from the wine maker brings down the price, you can usually get wines cheaper in California supermarkets than at the wineries themselves, but if you find something you like from a smaller producer, buy it on the spot, as it may not be available elsewhere.

Berringer Vineyards, 2000 Main St, St Helena ☎707/963-4812. Napa Valley's most famous piece of architecture, the Gothic "Rhine House," modeled on the ancestral Rhine Valley home of Jacob Beringer, graces the cover of many a wine magazine. Expansive lawns and a grand tasting room, heavy on dark wood, make for a regal experience. Forty-five-minute tours and tastings daily 9.30am–5pm.

Charles Krug Winery, 2800 St Helena Hwy, St Helena ☎707/967-2200. Founded in 1861 by a Prussian immigrant, this winery was purchased by Cesare Mondavi in 1943 and is now owned by son Peter and family. Peter's brother, Robert, left in 1966 after a family dispute to start his own winery, renowned today for its huge roster of varietals, including the usual whites and reds, and an especially highly rated sangiovese reserve. Tours by appointment and tastings daily 10.30am–5.30pm; $3–6.

Clos Pégase, 1060 Dunaweal Lane, Calistoga ☎707/942-4981. A flamboyant upstart at the north end of the valley, this high-profile winery emphasizes the links between fine wine and fine art, with a sculpture garden around buildings designed by postmodern architect Michael Graves. Tours daily at 11am and 2pm; tastings daily 10.30am–5pm, $2.50.

Domaine Careneros, 1240 Duhig Rd, Napa ☎707/257-0101. Newly created Austro-Hungarian-style castle surrounded by rolling hills of vineyards in all directions. A breathtaking setting for tasting wine and picnicking in the sun. Tastings and tours daily 10.30am–6pm.

Domaine Chandon, 1 California Drive, Yountville ☎707/944-2280. Sparkling wines from this progeny of France's Moët & Chandon are known to challenge the authentic champagne of France. Enormous and modern, this winery and gallery is a standard stop on most itineraries. Highly regarded, if expensive, restaurant. Tastings daily 10am–8pm; tours daily 11am–5pm.

The Hess Collection, 4411 Redwood Rd, Napa ☎707/255-1144. A bit off the

of the Napa River. The **Napa County Historical Society**, across from the visitors bureau at 1219 First St (Tues & Thurs noon–4pm; ☎707/224-1739), has free, informative materials and photographic displays on the region's pre-wine era. It's housed in the town's proud old courthouse, which looks like a relic from another era compared to the modern, characterless buildings that comprise downtown.

beaten track, this secluded winery features, in addition to its superior wines, a surprisingly good collection of modern art and nice view of the valley. Self-guided tour. Tastings daily 10am–4pm; $2.50.

Mumm Napa Valley, 8445 Silverado Trail, Rutherford ☎707/942-3434. Opened in 1986 by Joseph E. Seagram & Sons and G.H. Mumm, France's renowned champagne house, the sparkling wines here are good, but the sweeping views of the surrounding valleys steal the show. The winery's tours are particularly engaging and witty, and the informative guides never lose sight of the primary purpose: fun. Tastings daily 10.30am–6pm, $3.50–6; hourly tours 11am–4pm.

Niebaum-Coppola Estate Winery & Vineyards, 1991 St Helena Hwy, Rutherford ☎707/968-1100. Francis Ford Coppola purchased this Inglenook estate in 1975, originally established by Gustav Niebaum in 1879. Memorabilia from the director's career is on display in the entryway to the massive new tasting room, which features a signature Rubicon wine. Tours and tastings daily 10am–5pm; $7.50, includes glass.

Robert Mondavi, 7801 St Helena Hwy, Oakville ☎707/963-9611. Long the standard-bearer for Napa Valley wines ("Bob Red" and "Bob White" are house wines at many California restaurants), they have the most informative and least hard-sell tours. Tours and tastings daily 10am–4.30pm, with reservation. Tastings free with tour, $2–5 without.

Silver Oak Cellars, 915 Oakville Cross Rd, east off Hwy-29, Oakville ☎1-800/273-8809. Lovers of cabernet sauvignon shouldn't miss Silver Oak, where tastings in the fire-warmed stone-and-wood room are a bargain at $5. Plus, you get to keep the beautiful glass. Bottle sales are limited to one per person ($50). Tastings daily 10am–4.30pm; tours by appointment.

Stag's Leap, 5766 Silverado Trail, east of Yountville ☎707/944-2020. The winery that put Napa Valley on the international map by beating Chateau Lafitte-Rothschild at a Paris tasting in 1976, and still quite highly rated. From Hwy-29, turn right on Yountville, then right on Silverado Trail. Tastings daily 10am–4.30pm; tours by appointment.

Sterling Vineyards, 1111 Dunweal Lane, Calistoga ☎707/942-3359. Famous for the aerial tram ride from the parking lot which brings visitors to the wine tasting and tour, though the extravagant white mansion, modeled after a monastery on the Greek island of Mykonos, makes the visit worthwhile. Tastings of their wide selection of reds and whites are on the View Terrace, overlooking the spectacular scenery below; 10.30am–4.30pm, self-guided tour.

V. Sattui, 1111 White Lane, St Helena ☎707/963-7774. Small family-owned winery right off Hwy-29, with award-winning wines – the riesling and gamay rouge are particularly good. Sattui wines are only sold at the winery or through the mail. The adjoining gourmet deli has a large selection of cheeses and breads that can be enjoyed within the popular tree-shaded picnic grove. Tastings daily 9am–6pm.

Nine miles north on Hwy-29, **YOUNTVILLE** was named in honor of George C. Yount, the valley's first settler of European descent in 1831. There's not much to grab your attention, just some antique shops, restaurants, and the stores at **Vintage 1870**, at 6525 Washington St (daily 10.30am–5.30pm), a shopping and wine complex in a former winery that also rents bikes with helmets for $20 a day. You may as well push three more miles on Hwy-29 to smaller **OAKVILLE** which holds no less than a dozen wineries of interest to serious aficionados including the massive Robert Mondavi Winery. More down to earth is the **Oakville Grocery**, at 7856 St Helena Hwy, a delightfully crowded deli, spilling over with the finest local and imported foods. Nearby, at no. 7830–40, the **Napa Wine Company** (☎707/944-1710) serves as a cooperative for more than fifty small boutique wineries, with an excellent tasting room featuring varietals that have made it into the *Wine Spectator's* top ten.

St Helena

For information on hotels in St. Helena, see p.224. For reviews of restaurants in town, see p.271.

Some eighteen miles north from Napa, **ST HELENA** is the first in a series of restored villages dotted with antique shops, though this one does boast the greatest concentration of wineries and a nice complement of places to stay and eat. Hwy-29 becomes the town's Main Street here, and is lined by some of the Wine Country's finest nineteenth-century brick buildings, most of which stand in prime condition, holding inns, bakeries, and shops. The historic bakery at no. 1357 is the best place to meet local wine growers, who assemble to chat or check the community bulletin board on the wall.

The **Silverado Museum** (Tues–Sun noon–4pm; free), housed in St Helena's former Public Library building just off Main Street in the center of town, has a collection of some eight thousand articles relating to Robert Louis Stevenson, who spent just under a year in the area, honeymooning and recovering from an illness. It's claimed to be the second most extensive collection of Stevenson artifacts in the US, though the only thing of interest to any but the most obsessed fan is a scribbled-on manuscript of *Dr Jekyll and Mr Hyde*. The other half of the building is taken up by the **Napa Valley Wine Library** (same hours), a briefly entertaining barrage of photos and clippings relating to the development of local viticulture. On the north side of town, at 1515 Main St, the **Ambrose Bierce House** (☎707/963-3003; $169–195) has been converted into a bed-and-breakfast containing memorabilia related to the misanthropic ghost-story writer who lived here for some fifteen years before mysteriously vanishing when he headed off to fight for Pancho Villa in the Mexican Revolution.

Calistoga

Beyond St Helena, towards the far northern end of the valley, the wineries become prettier and the traffic a little thinner, though it swells again at the very tip of the valley at **CALISTOGA**, a town that takes pride in being the source of the sparkling water that adorns every Californian supermarket shelf. Sam Brannan, the young Mormon entrepreneur who made a mint out of the Gold Rush, established a resort community here in 1860. In his groundbreaking speech, as legend has it, he attempted to assert his desire to create the "Saratoga of California," but got tongue-tied, thus coining the town's name.

Though Calistoga now boasts nearly twenty wineries and some of the valley's fanciest bistros, its main attraction still has nothing to do with wine, rather another pleasurable activity: soaking in the soothingly hot water that bubbles up here from deep inside the earth. It's a homey, health-conscious kind of place, which draws jaded city dwellers each weekend, demanding reservations for accommodation a solid two weeks in advance in summer months. The extravagant might enjoy *Dr. Wilkinson's Hot Springs*, 1507 Lincoln Ave (☎707/942-4102; treatments from $50, rooms $89–149 per night), a legendary health spa and hotel whose heated mineral water and volcanic ash tension-relieving treatments have been featured on TV's *Lifestyles of the Rich & Famous*. Down the street, **The Mount View Spa**, 1457 Lincoln Ave (☎1-800/772-8838), can wax your chin for $25 and detoxify, exfoliate, and nourish your body with an enzymatic sea-mud wrap for $75. At $180, the Urban Escape Package soaks, massages, and wraps your body for over two hours. If swaddled luxury is not what you're after, a number of more down-to-earth establishments can be found just off Lincoln Avenue, the mile-long main drag. **Golden Haven Hot Springs**, 1713 Lake St (☎707/942-6793), offers a one-hour mud bath, hot mineral jacuzzi and blanket wrap for $49. If that's still too expensive, ask a local resident to spray you down with the garden hose – given Calistoga water's restorative reputation and the town's resourcefulness at cashing in on it, even that might set you back a few bucks.

Calistoga accommodation options are listed on p.224.

Heading out of town on steep, winding Hwy-128, you'll find more picturesque scenery and evidence of Calistoga's lively underground activity at the **Old Faithful Geyser of California** (daily 9am–6pm; $6), two miles north on Tubbs Lane; spurting boiling water sixty feet into the air at forty-minute intervals, it's still nowhere near as high as the venerable spouter of Yellowstone National Park from which it borrows the name. The water source was discovered during oil-drilling here in the 1920s, when search equipment struck a force estimated to be up to a thousand pounds per square foot; the equipment was blown away and, despite heroic efforts to control it, the geyser has continued to go off like clockwork ever since. Landowners finally realized that they'd never tame it and turned it into a high-yield tourist attraction.

The **Petrified Forest**, five miles west of Calistoga on the steep road over the hills to Santa Rosa (daily 10am–5pm; $4), made the roster of California Historical Landmarks, though Robert Louis Stevenson dubbed it "a pure little isle of touristry among the solitary hills." Indeed, unless you're a geologist or really into hardened wood, you may not fully appreciate the importance of these fossils, some of the largest in the world, up to 150 feet long. The forest here was petrified by the action of the silica-laden volcanic ash which gradually seeped into the decomposing fibers of trees uprooted during an eruption of Mount St Helena some three million years ago.

Mount St Helena

The clearest sign of the local volcanic unrest is the massive conical mountain that marks the north end of the Napa Valley, **Mount St Helena**, about eight miles north of Calistoga. The 4343-foot summit is worth a climb for its great views – on a very clear day you can see Point Reyes and the Pacific coast to the west, San Francisco to the south, the towering Sierra Nevada to the east, and impressive Mount Shasta to the north. It is, however, a long steep climb (ten miles round-trip) and you need to set off early in the morning to enjoy it – take plenty of water.

For a list of suggested readings by and about Bay Area writers, see p.348.

The mountain and most of the surrounding land is protected and preserved as the **Robert Louis Stevenson Park** (daily 8am–sunset; free), though the connection is fairly weak: Stevenson spent his honeymoon here in 1880 in a bunkhouse with Fanny Osborne, recuperating from tuberculosis and exploring the valley. In Stevenson's novel, *Silverado Squatters*, he describes the highlight of the honey-

Sonoma wineries

Thirty-nine fine **wineries** are scattered all over the Sonoma Valley, but there's a good concentration in a well-signposted group a mile east of Sonoma Plaza, down East Napa Street. Some are within walking distance, but often along quirky back roads, so take a winery map from the tourist office and follow the signs closely. Even more convenient, the handy Wine Exchange of Sonoma, at 452 First St E (☎707/938-1794), is a commercial tasting room where for a small fee, you can sample the best wines from all over California. Local winemakers congregate here after 5pm for the bar's selection of 300 beers.

Bartholomew Park, 1000 Vineyard Lane, Sonoma ☎707/935-9511. A lavish Spanish Colonial building, with some great topiary in the gardens and extensive vineyards. The winery is set 100 yards from a replica of an 1862 structure which burned down; the furnishings and fixtures inside the newer structure give a sense of what being a wine-maker in Napa once entailed. Villa: Wed, Sat & Sun 10am–4pm ☎707/938-2444; winery tours and tastings daily 10am–4.30pm.

Benziger Family Winery, 1883 London Ranch Rd, Glen Ellen ☎707/935-4046. Beautiful vineyard perched on the side of an extinct volcano next to Jack London State Park. Free tram tours through the fields six times daily, self-guided tour and free tastings. Their selection of whites are among the best in the Wine Country, and their reserve reds are exceptional. Daily 10am–5pm.

Buena Vista Winery, 18000 Old Winery Rd, Sonoma ☎707/252-7117. Oldest and grandest of the wineries, established in 1857, although the wine itself has a reputation for being pretty mediocre. The tasting room, a restored state historical landmark, features a small art gallery. Tastings daily 10.30am–5pm; tours daily at 11am and 2pm.

moon as the day he managed to taste eighteen of local wine baron Jacob Schram's champagnes in one sitting. A plaque marks the spot where his bunkhouse once stood, but little else about the park's winding roads and dense shrub growth evokes its former notoriety.

The Sonoma Valley

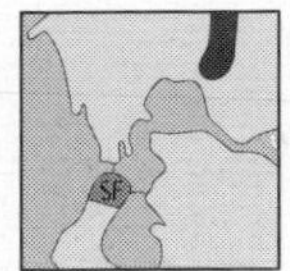

On looks alone the crescent-shaped Sonoma Valley beats Napa Valley hands down. This smaller, altogether more rustic valley curves between oak-covered mountain ranges from **SONOMA** a few miles north along Hwy-12 to the hamlet of **Glen Ellen** and **Jack London State Park**, and ends at the booming bedroom community of **Santa Rosa**. The area is known as the "Valley of the Moon," a label that's mined by tour operators for its connection to longtime resident Jack London, whose book of the same name retold a Native American legend about how, as you move through the valley, the moon seems to rise several times from behind the various peaks. Long a favorite among visitors, Sonoma has been claimed, at different moments of its relatively brief history, by Spain, England, Russia, and Mexico.

Chateau St Jean, 8555 Sonoma Hwy, Kenwood ☎ 707/833-4134. The quality of the Chateau's premium wines is suited to the landmark, 1920s-era buildings set against the slopes of Sugarloaf Ridge. There's a curious tower to climb for the view. Self-guided tours. Tastings daily 10am–4.30pm, $5.

Glen Ellen Winery, 14301 Arnold Drive, Glen Ellen ☎ 707/939-6277. Glen Ellen is the Bay Area's best-tasting inexpensive wine; you can often find a bottle in the supermarket for around $5. They also make a wide array of more upscale reds and whites of superior quality. Their tasting room, in a barn-like structure in Jack London Village on the banks of Sonoma Creek, is as fine a place as any to stock up and sample. A museum displays antiques and photos from the winery and town's 120-year history. Tastings daily 10am–5pm.

Gundlach-Bundschu, 2000 Denmark St, Sonoma ☎ 707/938-5277. Set back about a mile away from the main cluster of wineries, GunBun, as it's known to locals, is highly regarded, having stealthily crept up from the lower ranks. The plain, functional building is deceptive – this is premium stuff and definitely not to be overlooked. The winery also hosts the Sonoma Valley Shakespeare Festival, actually a summer-long celebration of the Bard. Three plays are staged annually, running July–September, Friday through Sunday. Tickets are $20 each, but $48 gets you a season-long pass to all performances. Daily 11am–4.30pm; tours Sat & Sun only.

Ravenswood, 18701 Gehricke Rd, Sonoma ☎ 707/938-1960. Noted for their "gutsy, unapologetic" zinfandel, the staff at this unpretentious winery is particularly friendly and easygoing, and the tasting room is well-known to locals for its summer barbecues. Tastings daily 10am–4.30pm; tours by appointment.

Sebastiani Vineyards, 389 Fourth St E, Sonoma ☎ 1-800/888-5532 or 707/938-5532. One of California's oldest family wineries, only four blocks from central Sonoma. Free tastings and tours via tram every half-hour. Daily 10am–5pm.

The Sonoma Valley

The US took over in 1846 during the Bear Flag Revolt against Mexico, which took place in Sonoma's central plaza when locals raised the flag of an independent California Republic.

Sonoma Valley's **wineries** are generally more intimate and casual than their Napa counterparts, even though the Sonoma Valley fathered the wine industry from which Napa derives its fame. Colonel Agostin Haraszthy first started planting grapes here in the 1850s, and his Buena Vista winery in Sonoma still operates today.

Sonoma

Retaining a good deal of its Spanish and Mexican architecture, **SONOMA** emanates from the grassy central **plaza**, where wild chickens – escapees from an attempt to turn the bordering Sonoma State Historic Park into a living nineteenth-century exhibit – patrol the grounds. It's a sleepy setting for relaxing in one of the great coffee shops and restaurants that ring the plaza, which was also the site of the Bear Flag Revolt, the 1846 action that propelled California into independence from Mexico, and then statehood. In this much-romanticized episode, American settlers in the region, who had long lived in uneasy peace under the Spanish and, later, Mexican rulers, were threatened with expulsion from California along with all other non-Mexican immigrants. In response, a band of thirty armed settlers – including the infamous John Freemont and Kit Carson – descended upon the disused and unguarded *presidio* at Sonoma, taking the retired and much-respected commander, Colonel Mariano Guadalupe Vallejo, as their prisoner. Ironically, Vallejo had long advocated the American annexation of California and supported the aims of his rebel captors, but he was nonetheless bundled off to Sutter's Fort in Sacramento and held there while the militant settlers declared California an independent republic. The Bear Flag, which served as the model for the current state flag, was fashioned from a "feminine undergarment and muslin petticoat" and painted with a grizzly bear and single star. Raised on Sonoma Plaza, where a small plaque marks the spot today, the Bear Flag flew over the Republic of California for three weeks, at which point the US declared war on Mexico and, without firing a shot, took possession of the entire Pacific coast. The subsequent arrival in 1856 of General Joe Hooker – who traveled with groups of ladies employed to cheer up the troops known at first as "Hooker's girls" then as "hookers" – gave the English language one of its most familiar slang expressions.

Preserved in the sprawling **Sonoma State Historic Park** (daily 10am–5pm; $3 combined entry to all sites) are a number of historic buildings and relics, including the restored **Mission San Francisco Solano de Sonoma**. This last and northernmost of the California missions was the only one established in Northern California by nervous Mexican rulers fearful of expansionist Russian fur traders. While the church is small and unremarkable – not an exact copy of the original mission chapel – the original priests' quarters have at least been preserved. To the west of the mission stands the **General Vallejo Home**, the leader's ornate former residence, dominated by decorated filigree eaves and slender Gothic-revival arched windows. The chalet-style storehouse next door has been turned into a **museum** of artifacts from the general's reign.

For a more detailed history of California's missions, see p.332.

Glen Ellen and Jack London State Park

Continuing north on Hwy-12, you'll come upon the cozy hamlet of **GLEN ELLEN**, whose main street (Hwy-12, or Arnold Drive as it's also known) is a three-block-long collection of boutique shops and restaurants along the banks of Sonoma Creek. More interestingly, Glen Ellen is the home of **Jack London State Park** (daily 9.30am–6pm; $6 per car), which begins a half-mile up London Ranch Road past the Benziger Family winery, and covers 140 acres of ranchland the famed author of *The Call of the Wild* owned with his wife. From a small parking lot near the entrance, a one-mile walk on a groomed trail through the woods leads to the ruins of **Wolf House**, which was to be the London ancestral home. "My house will be standing, act of God permitting, for a thousand years," wrote London. In 1913, a month before they were to move in, the house burned to the ground, sparing only the boulder frame. Mounted blueprints point out the splendor it was to contain: plans included a manuscript room, stag party room, sleeping tower, gun room, and indoor reflecting pool. Nearby is the final resting place of London – a red boulder from the house's ruins under which his wife Charmian sprinkled his ashes. Just off the parking lot, The **House of Happy Walls** (daily 10am–5pm; free) houses an interesting collection of souvenirs he and Charmian picked up traveling the globe: manuscripts, rejection letters (more than 600), the couple's letter of resignation from the Socialist Party, and plenty of photographs.

Opposite the parking lot from the house, the **Sonoma Cattle Co** (☎707/996-8566) offers daily horseback rides, weather permitting, starting at $25. A nearby trail leads past a picnic ground to the cottage (daily 10am–4pm; free) where London died; a video display gives background to his life, his wife, and the era. The trail continues west toward the mountains and into the woods, ending at the lake London had built so he and Charmian could fish and swim, a great place to relax with a bottle of wine.

Santa Rosa and the north

Sixty miles due north of San Francisco on US-101, and about twenty miles from Sonoma on Hwy-12, **SANTA ROSA**, with 130,000 people, is by far the largest town in Sonoma County, though it's largely given over to shopping centers, roadside malls, and inexpensive lodging establishments. The downtown area is centered around **Courthouse**

Square, bordered by B, D, 4th, and 3rd streets and filled with bookstores, cafés, and restaurants. One side of the square is lined by an indoor shopping mall, across from which, via an underpass, is **Historic Railroad Square**, a redeveloped strip of redbrick-facade boutiques. Across the street, you'll find the **Santa Rosa Visitors Center**, at 9 Fourth St (Mon–Fri 8.30am–5pm, Sat & Sun 10am–3pm; ☎707/577-8674), which has a rather curt staff and a wall crowded with pamphlets that don't do much to recommend the town.

The place's biggest claim to fame is its list of former residents who went on to fame and fortune. The late *Peanuts* creator **Charles Schulz** (originally from St Paul, MN) lived here, and built the **Redwood Empire Ice Arena**, 1667 West Steele Lane (☎707/546-7147), as a gift to the community, though he also enjoyed skating here himself. An adjoining building holds **Snoopy's Gallery**, a museum and gift shop of all things *Peanuts*-related (daily 10am–6pm; free).

The **Luther Burbank Home and Gardens**, at the junction of Santa Rosa and Sonoma avenues (Tues–Sun 10am–3.30pm; free), remembers California's best-known horticulturist, who created these splendid gardens, which include some of his most unusual hybrids, around his sunny, if unremarkable home.

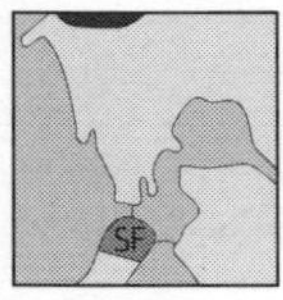

The Russian River Valley

Just northwest of Santa Rosa, the remote **Russian River Valley** contains some of the most secluded vineyards and bucolic landscapes in the state. Back in the Twenties and Thirties it was a recreational resort for well-to-do city folk, who abandoned the area when newly constructed roads took them elsewhere. Drawn by lower-than-city rents, hippies started arriving to fill the void in the late Sixties, and the Russian River took on a non-conformist flavor. Today, an injection of affluent Bay Area property seekers, many of them gay, has sustained the region's economy, especially at **GUERNEVILLE**, where a collection of bars and resorts catering to the gay tourist trade – along with a funky mix of loggers, sheep farmers, and wealthy weekenders – keep the place jumping every summer.

Despite this combination and two exclusive **Women's Weekends** (☎707/869-2971) – in early May and late September – the town can still seem a bit backward. Though tolerance is the rule, not all the longtime locals follow it, and there have been more than a few stories of same-sex couples getting turned away from vacant rooms in "family inns" just steps from the predominantly gay resorts. Still, during high season, Guerneville packs enough gay and lesbian nightlife into its few narrow blocks along River Road to keep gay tourists coming back every year.

Weekend visitors of all orientations flock here for the canoeing, swimming, and sunbathing that comprise the bulk of local activities:

Russian River Valley Wineries

The Guerneville Chamber of Commerce (see overleaf) issues an excellent *Russian River Wine Road* map, which lists all the **wineries** that spread along the entire course of the Russian River. Unlike their counterparts in Napa and Sonoma, the wineries here neither organize guided tours nor charge for wine-tasting. Some of the varietals produced here are of remarkably good quality, if not as well known as their Wine Country rivals.

Hop Kiln, 6050 Westside Rd, Healdsburg ☎707/433-6491. This recently established winery built around a registered historic landmark – the hop kiln – produces award-winning varietals such as cabernet sauvignon and zinfandel. Have a bottle with a picnic lunch near the pond, which is teeming with wildfowl. Tastings daily 10am–5pm.

Korbel Champagne Cellars, 13250 River Rd, two miles east of Guerneville ☎707/887-2294. Even if you're not doing the wineries, you shouldn't miss this place. The bubbly itself – America's best-selling premium champagne – isn't anything you couldn't find in any supermarket, but the wine and brandy are sold only from the cellars, and are of excellent quality. The estate is lovely, too, surrounded by hillside gardens covered in blossoming violets, coral bells and hundreds of varieties of roses – perfect for quiet picnics. A microbrewery and upscale deli are also on the premises. Daily May–Sept: tours 10am–3.45pm, tastings 9am–5pm; Oct–April: tours 10am–3.45pm, tastings 9am–4.30pm.

Martini & Prati, 2191 Laguna Rd, Santa Rosa ☎707/823-2404 This family-owned winery since 1902 has a number of varietals; you can fill your own jug of table wine from a tank then organize picnic fixings in the adjoining Italian grocery. Tastings daily June–Oct 10am–5pm; Nov–May 11am–4pm.

Topolos at Russian River Vineyards, 5700 Gravenstein Hwy, Forestville, five miles from Guerneville along Hwy-116 ☎707/887-1575. One of the Russian River Valley's most accessible wineries, specializing in zinfandels. Popular restaurant serves California dishes influenced by Greece – dine on the patio and feast your eyes on the wildflower gardens. Winery tours by appointment. Tastings daily 11am–5.30pm.

Villa Pompei, 5700 River Rd, Santa Rosa ☎707/545-5899. Small family operation specializing in pinot noir, sangiovese, and zinfandel, situated on a hill with a dramatic view of the Russian River Valley. Tastings daily 10am–5pm.

Johnson's Beach, on a placid reach of the river in the center of town, is the most frequented spot, with canoes ($12 a day), pedal boats ($5 an hour) and tubes ($3 a day). But Guerneville's biggest natural asset is the magnificent **Armstrong Redwoods State Reserve** (daily, 8am to one hour after sunset; $6 parking; ☎707/869-2015), two miles north at the top of Armstrong Woods Road – 700 acres of massive redwood trees, hiking and riding trails, and primitive camping sites. Take food and water and don't stray off the trails: the densely forested central grove is quite forbidding and very easy to get lost in. One of the best ways to see it is on **horseback**; the Armstrong Woods Pack Station (☎707/887-2939) offers guided horseback tours that range from a half-day trail ride ($40) to a three-day pack trip ($450). A natural amphitheater provides the setting for the **Redwood Forest Theatre**, which stages dramatic and musical productions during the summer. More musical happenings occur at the **Russian River Jazz Fest** (☎707/869-3940; $40), the first weekend after Labor Day, and a popular time to come here – events take place right on Johnson's Beach. The mid-June **Russian River Blues Festival**, also on the beach (☎707/869-3940; *www.russianriverbluesfest.com*; $35–75), is quite happening too.

The **Chamber of Commerce**, at 16200 First St (Mon–Fri 9am–5pm; 24hr info line ☎707/869-3533), has good free **maps** of the area and **accommodation** listings, while the friendly **Russian River Region Visitors Bureau**, across the street at 14034 Armstrong Woods Rd (☎1-800/253-8800 or 707/869-9212), can also recommend places to stay. To get the most out of the wilderness, though, you're best off camping, and the whole region is dotted with campgrounds every few miles. There are a couple of free primitive sites in the woods, and $7 walk-in backcountry sites in the state reserve. All the state campgrounds, however, are first-come, first-served, so be there before they open at 8am to claim one, especially if you are visiting during a holiday or festival.

For camping options in the Russian River, see p.232.

Part 4

Listings

Chapter 14

Accommodation

Visitors are San Francisco's number-one business, and the city is full of motel, hotel, bed and breakfast, and hostel rooms of a consistently high standard. Such standards, however, have their price, and with room rates averaging over $100 per night, accommodation will almost certainly be the major expense of your stay. Though annual visitors far outnumber San Francisco's 750,000 people, there are, surprisingly, only thirty thousand or so beds available in town, and strict building codes limit the number of new hotels that can be built; gone, consequently, are the days when you could show up in San Francisco without reservations, hoping to stumble upon a great deal in a prime location.

Prices start at about $50 a night for the most basic **hotel** room, with the most luxurious properties more than ten times as expensive. If availability – or your budget – is low and you've got a car, **motels** are legion along the highways and bigger roads throughout the Bay Area, at an average rate of around $50 a night. In all cases, bear in mind that all quoted room rates are subject to a **fourteen percent room tax**.

For **B&Bs**, the city's fastest-growing source of accommodation, consult the list on p.226, or contact a specialist agency such as Bed and Breakfast California (12711 McCartysville, Saratoga, CA 95070; ☎1-800/872-4500 or 408/867-9662; *www.bbintl.com*) or Bed and Breakfast San Francisco (PO Box 420009, San Francisco, CA 94142; ☎415/931-3083).

The Visitor Information Center (☎1-888/782-9673; *www.sfvisitor.org*) can provide the latest accommodation options; and San Francisco Reservations (22 Second St, Fourth Floor, San Francisco, CA 94105; ☎1-800/677-1500 or 415/227-1500; *www.hotelres.com*) will find you a room from around $85 a double. British visitors can reserve rooms

Accommodation price codes

All the prices of hotels, motels, and bed and breakfasts in this chapter have been graded with the symbols below, according to the cost of the least expensive double room throughout most of the year. Bear in mind that for hotels, motels, and bed and breakfasts you will have to pay room tax – currently 14 percent of the total bill – on top of these rates.

① up to $30	⑤ $100–150
② $30–50	⑥ $150–200
③ $50–75	⑦ $200–300
④ $75–100	⑧ $300+

Accommodation

When you arrive at your hotel or motel, ask if there are discounts available for American Automobile Association members (that is, if you're a member) or if the hotel has any discount deals with the airline on which you flew.

through **Colby International** (☎0151/220 5848)

If you just can't find a room, or if you're just plain broke, **transient hotels** with shared bath and toilet in the developing South of Market and the seedy Tenderloin now start at around $30 per night or $120 a week.

Hostels are plentiful, cheap, and a good place to meet fellow travelers. Some are located on the scenic edge of the bay or along the western coast. Reservations are strongly recommended, particularly for the network of International Youth Hostels situated in prime waterfront locations like Fort Mason, Marin Headlands, and lighthouses, though some of the private hostels may have a last-minute bed available.

Camping isn't an option in San Francisco itself, and though throwing down a bag in Golden Gate Park or the Presidio may seem tempting, it's illegal within the city, and can be dangerous, as well. However, outside town are some splendid sites in the East Bay, Marin County, the Wine Country, and along the peninsula.

Hotels and B&Bs are listed below by neighborhood, with hostels listed separately. In case you're arriving on a late flight, or leaving on an early one, we've also listed a few places to stay near the **airport**. Hostels and campgrounds are listed by location around the Bay Area.

Hotels and motels

San Francisco **hotels** and **motels** have a reputation of high quality, cleanliness, and fine service. Especially at the lower price ranges, it can be hard to tell the difference between the two, the main distinction being that hotels are usually more centrally located than motels and provide more "extras" like room service, laundry, and a health club. Motels are situated outside downtown and generally offer a "no-frills" stay, thinner walls, and possible traffic noise.

One thing to consider in searching for a room is **parking**; motel rooms come with a place to park the car, something not guaranteed with a hotel. While the higher-end downtown hotels should have a parking garage available free-of-charge for guests, most of the under-$100 hotels do not, meaning you'll have to park overnight in a garage, which can run upwards of $15.

Standard rooms usually come with color TV (sometimes with cable), a phone (local calls free; non-415 area codes, including Oakland, for a fee), a bathtub with shower, and heating/air conditioning. Increasingly, hotels are rewiring to provide a phone jack for Internet access in each room.

Rooms around Union Square, North Beach, Nob Hill, Chinatown, and the Marina average about $100/night for a double room, but many have suites available for three or more people for a tad more, or will provide cots for additional guests for a small fee.

Staying in the heart of the Tenderloin, Civic Center, or SoMa neighborhoods may seem like a bargain ($30 a night – $120 a week), but be ready to put up with noise and highly visible – if harmless – drug dealers and prostitutes, not to mention some fairly seedy digs. Staying in the hostel along the bay in Fort Mason is a safer, more scenic option.

Wherever you lay your head, you'll be expected to pay in advance, which can be taken care of by allowing the concierge to take an imprint of your credit card. Some places also request a deposit of a night's room rate when you make your reservation and many will want a credit card number for security, which they will not hesitate to use for the cost of one night's stay should you fail to arrive. Reservations are held until 5pm or 6pm unless you've told the hotel you'll be arriving late.

Payment in cash or US dollar travelers' checks is usually acceptable, though most places prefer to take a swipe of your credit card and have you sign for the full amount when you check out – normally noon, though some hotels in high season attempt to push guests out by 10am, and others will extend your checkout to 2 or

3pm if you have a late departure in low season. At hotels, a continental breakfast, including coffee and tea, is often included in the room rate.

Downtown and Chinatown

Allison, 417 Stockton St at Sutter ☎1-800/628-6456 or 415/986-8737. Two blocks from Union Square and Chinatown, this clean hotel is one of the best all-around values in San Francisco. Ask about their "family suite" for five people, which can often be had for a steal when it's not already booked. ③–④

Baldwin, 321 Grant Ave ☎1-800/6-BALDWIN or 415/781-2220. One of the best-situated hotels in town, two blocks off Union Square, at the foot of Chinatown and cable cars and adjacent to a parking garage. Recently renovated rooms and bathrooms are clean but spartan. ⑤

Campton Place, 340 Stockton St at Sutter ☎415/781-5555. Smallish Union Square hotel that draws in a quiet, affluent crowd. Luxurious without being overly showy. ⑦–⑧

Cartwright, 524 Sutter St at Powell ☎1-800/227-3844 or 415/421-2865. Distinguishes itself from its rivals with little touches such as fresh flowers, afternoon tea and bend-over-backwards courtesy. Good location one block north of Union Square. ⑥

Clarion-Bedford Hotel, 761 Post St ☎415/673-6040. Charming old-world mid-sized boutique hotel in the traditionally pricey Theater District. Daily wine reception in the Victorian lobby. Rooms are a bit cramped but lushly decorated. ⑤

Clift, 495 Geary St ☎1-800/658-5492 or 415/775-4700. One of the city's oldest and most reliable hotels for business travelers, with a gym, restaurant, and all the best amenities, including huge rooms equipped with data ports and great views. ⑦

Commodore International, 825 Sutter St at Jones ☎415/923-6800. Classic Art Deco structure near Union Square with spacious, affordable rooms and a trendy, casual atmosphere. ⑤

Foley's Inn, 235 O'Farrell St at Fifth St ☎415/397-7800. Surprisingly affordable, clean rooms over an Irish pub of the same name, between Market St and Union Square in the heart of downtown. ③

Grant Plaza, 465 Grant Ave at Pine ☎415/434-3883. Clean, comfortable Chinatown hotel. One of the best values in San Francisco, given its location and quality. ③

Harbor Court, 165 Steuart St between Mission and Howard ☎1-800/346-0555 or 415/882-1300. Plush rooms, some of which offer the best bay views in the city; guests have free use of the excellent YMCA health club next door. ⑤–⑦

Mandarin Oriental, 222 Sansome St at California ☎1-800/622-0404 or 415/276-9888. You'll need silly amounts of money – rooms *start* at $395 – if you want to stay in what are reputedly San Francisco's most luxurious hotel rooms, but the views, which start on the 38th floor, are undoubtedly breathtaking. Amenities include valet, concierge, and 24hr room service. ⑧

Monaco, 501 Geary St at Taylor ☎1-800/214-4220 or 415/292-0100. Best of the new wave of San Francisco hotels, offering great style and decor. Next door to the sumptuous but reasonable *Grand Café*. ⑦

Prescott, 545 Post St between Taylor and Mason ☎1-800/283-7322 or 415/563-0303. The flagship of hotelier Bill Kimpton's San Francisco properties, this small Union Square hotel offers understated luxury, four-star comfort – and preferred seating at the popular restaurant, *Postrio*, with which it shares space (see p.242). ⑦

Ritz-Carlton, 600 Stockton St at California ☎1-800/241-3333 or 415/296-7465. Another luxurious San Francisco hotel, perched on the stylish slope of Nob Hill with gorgeously appointed rooms, a swimming pool, multimillion dollar art collection and one of the city's best spots for high tea (see p.241). ⑧

Accommodation

See p.54 for a map with downtown hotels.

Accommodation

Royal Pacific Motor Inn, 661 Broadway at Stockton ☎415/781-6661. Standard motel in the heart of Chinatown and near to North Beach and Russian Hill. ④

Sheehan Hotel, 605 Sutter St ☎415/775-6500 or 1-800/848-1529. Cozy, plush rooms in a centrally situated hotel with an Irish inn decor. ⑤

Sir Francis Drake, 450 Powell St ☎415/392-7755 or 1-800/227-5480. Don't be put off by the doormen – dressed as Beefeaters – this is a colonial California hotel whose greatest attraction is the 21st-floor *Harry Denton's Starlight Room* (see p.274). ⑥

Triton, 342 Grant Ave at Bush ☎415/394-0500 or 1-888/364-2622. Über-cool hotel with a wacky lobby that looks like an animated Istanbul of the distant future. Fitness center, air conditioning, bar, and lounge. ⑥

Westin St Francis, 335 Powell St ☎415/397-7000 or 1-800/WESTIN1. This completely renovated landmark hotel has a sumptuous lobby, four restaurants and lounges, a fitness center, and a spa. Yet aside from the views, the rooms are disappointingly plain. Worth entering the lobby to see the famous clock, ornate ceiling, painting of Queen Elizabeth amidst American celebs, and the steps where President Gerald Ford almost met his end from a would-be-assassin's bullet. ⑦

Women's Hotel, 642 Jones St ☎415/775-1711. Comfortable, secure, women-only building, unfortunately situated in the shabby Tenderloin district. Weekly rates only. ②

York, 940 Sutter St at Hyde ☎415/885-6800 or 1-800/808-YORK. Quiet, older hotel on the western edge of downtown, recently remodeled and thus also known as the "New York" hotel. An essential stop for Hitchcock fans, this is where the dramatic stairway scenes in *Vertigo* were filmed. ⑤

A map of hotels in the North Beach area appears on p.69.

North Beach and Nob Hill

Amsterdam, 749 Taylor St at Bush ☎1-800/637-3444 or 415/673-3277. On Nob Hill, but actually closer to the Tenderloin, with clean, good-value rooms decorated in wood and marble, with newly improved bathrooms. Parking next door (24 hours) for $13. ⑤

Boheme, 444 Columbus Ave ☎415/433-9111. Cozy 15-room hotel in the heart of North Beach featuring sumptuous decor and canopied, queen-size beds. ⑤

Fairmont, 950 Mason St ☎415/772-5000. Most famous of the top-notch hotels, this gaudy palace has four restaurants and lounges, as well as fantastic views from the rooms. Don't miss the terrace garden, overlooking Powell, and the splendor of the *Tonga Room*, in the basement (see p.276). ⑦

Huntington, 1075 California St ☎415/474-5400. The rooms of this landmark were designed as residential apartments, and so are quietly elegant compared to its Nob Hill counterparts. This is *the* hotel for the wealthy who don't feel the need to flash their cash. Fax machines in every room make it perfect if you're doing business. ⑦–⑧

Mark Hopkins Inter-continental, One Nob Hill, 999 California St at Mason ☎415/392-3434. Formerly glorious and elegant residential hotel for writers, movie stars, and the very glamorous, the *Mark* caters mostly to business travelers these days, though its *Top of the Mark* rooftop bar is popular with tourists (see p.274). ⑧

Mary Elizabeth Inn, 1040 Bush St ☎415/673-6768. Run by the United Methodist Church; a safe but unexciting place for women. Weekly rates available, breakfast and dinner included. ②

Queen Anne, 1590 Sutter St ☎415/441-2828. Over-the-top period decor in a Victorian with an illustrious past. Complimentary afternoon tea and sherry. ⑤

San Remo, 2237 Mason St ☎415/776-8688 or 1-800/352-7366. Pleasant, old-fashioned rooms (shared but spotless bath) in nice North Beach Victorian house a block off Columbus Ave. Particularly friendly staff. ③

The northern waterfront and Pacific Heights

Bel Aire Travelodge, 3201 Steiner St at Greenwich ☎1-800/280-3242 or 415/921-5162. Good-value motel, one block from Lombard St. ②

Del Sol, 3100 Webster St ☎415/921-5520. Bright, sunny refurbished 1950s motor lodge in the heart of the Marina, near Union and Fillmore St shopping. A delight to the eye. ⑤

Edward II, 3155 Scott St at Lombard ☎1-800/473-2846 or 415/922-3000. Large and comfortable inn-style accommodation in the Marina district with free breakfast and afternoon sherry. ③–④

El Drisco, 2901 Pacific Ave at Broderick ☎1-800/634-7277 or 415/346-2880. Small luxury hotel high atop Pacific Heights, nestled between mansions with spectacular views of the bay. Close to Sacramento St antique shops. Breakfast and wine reception included. ⑥–⑦

Holiday Lodge, 1901 Van Ness Ave ☎415/776-4469. Comfortable motel with free parking and outdoor pool, near Fisherman's Wharf. ③

Jackson Court, 2198 Jackson St ☎415/929-7670. Lovely converted Pacific Heights mansion, popular with locals for weekend romantic getaways. Ten rooms, including bath. Reservations essential. ⑥–⑦

Laurel Inn, 444 Presidio Ave ☎1-800/552-8735 or 415/567-8467. Just-renovated hotel in Laurel Heights, steps from Sacramento St's antique shops and near the bustling Fillmore strip of cafés and stores. All rooms come with a VCR. Pets allowed. ⑤

Sherman House, 2160 Green St between Webster and Fillmore ☎415/563-3600. This small Pacific Heights hotel is one of the city's lesser-known jewels, with plush, intimate rooms and impeccable service, but you'll pay the price. ⑧

Tuscan Inn, 425 North Point at Mason ☎1-800/648-4626 or 415/561-1100. The most upmarket hotel on the waterfront, with afternoon wine reception and free limo downtown in the mornings. ⑥

Van Ness Motel, 2850 Van Ness Ave at Chestnut ☎415/776-3220. Large rooms, within walking distance of Fort Mason. ③–④

Wharf Inn, 2601 Mason St at Jefferson ☎415/673-7411. Comfortable, family-style hotel close to the waterfront with free parking. ⑤

Accommodation

SoMa, the Tenderloin, and Civic Center

Atherton, 685 Ellis St ☎1-800/474-5720 or 415/474-5720. Cozy, clean, good-value hotel four blocks from Civic Center. ⑤

Bay Bridge Inn, 966 Harrison St at Sixth ☎415/397-0657. Basic and somewhat noisy but perfectly sited for late nights in SoMa's clubland. ②

Golden City Inn, 1554 Howard St at 12th ☎415/255-1110. Best of the inexpensive SoMa hotels, renting overnight rooms from May to Sept and on a weekly basis only from Oct to April. ①

Inn at the Opera, 333 Fulton St ☎415/863-8400. Very plush, intimate hotel across the street from the Opera House. ⑥

Palace Hotel, 2 New Montgomery St, at Market ☎415/512-1111. San Francisco's most elegant historic property couldn't be more conveniently situated. Now owned by Sheraton, it has all the amenities you'd expect at the price. ⑧

For a complete description of the Palace Hotel, see p.95.

Palomar, 12 Fourth St ☎1-877/294-9711 or 415/348-1111. Trendy new boutique hotel done up in plush, 1930s Art Deco with a French twist. ⑥

Pension San Francisco, 1668 Market St ☎415/864-1271. A good, clean and basic base near the Civic Center, walkably close to SoMa and the Castro. ④

The Phoenix, 601 Eddy St ☎415/776-1380. Converted Fifties-style motel in a slightly dodgy neighborhood on the edge of the Tenderloin, but the hip crowd lounging around the pool sipping cocktails doesn't seem to mind. ⑤

Accommodation

Airport hotels

Best Western Grosvenor, 380 South Airport Blvd ☎1-800/722-7141 or 650/873-3200. Large comfortable hotel with pool and free shuttle service to the airport. ④–⑤

Days Inn, 1113 Airport Blvd ☎1-800/329-7466 or 650/873-9300. Basic rooms and a free shuttle to the airport. ④

Goose & Turrets Bed and Breakfast, 835 George St, Montara ☎650/728-5451. In the seaside hamlet of Montara, a more intimate B&B alternative to other airport accommodation. Close to the beaches and hiking trails. ⑤

Hyatt Regency San Francisco Airport, 1333 Bayshore Hwy ☎1-800/223-1234 or 650/347-1234. Gigantic hotel south of the airport with all the amenities (pool, jacuzzi, bars) and a free shuttle to the airport. ⑤–⑥

La Quinta Inn, 20 Airport Blvd ☎650/583-2223. Overnight laundry service and a pool make this a comfortable stopover near the airport. Free shuttle service to the airport. ③

Motel 6, 1101 Shoreway Rd, Belmont ☎650/591-1471. A no-frills motel offering a clean environment to freshen up during a long and uncomfortable journey. ③

Park Plaza, 1177 Airport Blvd ☎1-800/411-7275 or 650/342-9200. Great facilities include restaurant, pool, jacuzzi, live music, and a free shuttle to the airport. ⑤

The Renoir, 45 McAllister St, at Seventh and Market ☎415/626-5200. Convenient location near Civic Center. Glitzy lobby and large, comfy rooms in an historic flatiron close to major sights and transportation. ⑤

Travelodge, 1707 Market at Valencia ☎415/621-6775. Very basic motel-style lodging, but couldn't be more conveniently located. ④

The Mission and the Castro

For B&Bs in the Mission and the Castro, see p.226.

Beck's Motor Lodge, 2222 Market St at Church ☎415/621-8212. Standard motel close to the Castro – the only accommodation in these parts that's not a B&B. ③

West of Civic Center and Haight-Ashbury

Best Western Miyako, 1800 Sutter St at Buchanan ☎1-800/528-1234 or 415/921-4000. Immaculate Japantown hotel, with quiet rooms. ⑤

The Carl, 198 Carl St ☎1-888/661-5679 or 415/661-5679. Hidden jewel in Cole Valley, near Golden Gate Park, Haight-Ashbury, and restaurants of the Inner Sunset. ④

Grove Inn, 890 Grove St at Fillmore ☎1-800/829-0780 or 415/929-0780. Nothing fancy (some shared baths), but good value and a fine location on Alamo Square in the Western Addition. ④

Stanyan Park, 750 Stanyan St ☎415/751-1000. Gorgeous small Victorian hotel in a great setting across from Golden Gate Park, with friendly staff and free continental breakfast. ⑤

The Richmond and the Sunset

Ocean Park Motel, 2690 46th Ave ☎415/566-7020. A fair way from downtown (25min by Muni), this is nonetheless a great Art Deco motel (San Francisco's first), opposite the zoo and the beach. Outdoor hot tub and jacuzzi, and a play area for children. ③

Oceanview Motel, 4340 Judah St ☎415/661-2300. No-frills lodging out in the Sunset District. ④

Sunset Motel, 821 Taraval St ☎415/681-3306. One of the finest little motels in San Francisco – clean, friendly, and safe. ③

East Bay

Bancroft Hotel, 2680 Bancroft Way, Berkeley ☎1-800/549-1002 or 510/549-

1000. Small hotel of 22 rooms with good location and service. Breakfast included. ⑤

The Beau Sky Hotel, 2520 Durant Ave, Berkeley ☎1-800/990-2328 or 510/540-7688. Centrally located boutique hotel in a 1911 Victorian with simple, fully renovated rooms. ④–⑤

The Claremont Resort & Spa, 41 Tunnel Rd, Berkeley ☎1-800/551-7266 or 510/843-3000. The lap of luxury among Berkeley hotels in a 1915 building on 22 acres nestled against the Berkeley hills. Two pools, ten tennis courts, and four saunas. Rooms have coffeemakers, data ports, hairdryers, cable TV and huge windows. ⑦

Durant, 2600 Durant Ave, Berkeley ☎1-800/238-7268 or 510/845-8981. 140 somewhat plain rooms in an upscale hotel in the heart of UC Berkeley. ⑤

French, 1538 Shattuck Ave, North Berkeley ☎510/548-9930. Small and comfortable hotel, with eighteen standard rooms in the heart of Berkeley's Gourmet Ghetto. ⑤–⑥

Golden Bear Motel, 1620 San Pablo Ave, West Berkeley ☎1-800/525-6770 or 510/525-6770. The most pleasant of the many motels in the "flatlands" of West Berkeley, though somewhat out of the way. Cottages here are about twice the price of the budget motel rooms. ③–⑤

Holiday Inn Bay Bridge, 1800 Powell St, Emeryville ☎510/658-9300. Not outrageously pricey considering the great views to be had from the upper floors. Free parking. ⑤

Jack London Inn, 444 Embarcadero West, Oakland ☎510/444-2032. Kitschy motorlodge located next to Jack London Square. ④

The Mac, 10 Cottage Ave, Point Richmond ☎510/235-0010. Built in 1907, the recently refurbished *Mac* boasts luxurious rooms with unbeatable prices. This was supposedly John Rockefeller's favorite place to stay when visiting his Standard Oil enterprise. ④

Marriott City Center, 1001 Broadway at Tenth St, Oakland ☎1-800/228-9290 or 510/451-4000. Huge chain hotel two blocks from a BART station with health center, pool, business center, in-room movies, and a restaurant. ⑤

The Shattuck, 2086 Allston Way, Berkeley ☎510/845-7300. Comfortable, central rooms in a well-restored older hotel. ⑤

Travelodge, 423 Seventh St, downtown Oakland ☎1-800/255-3050 or 510/451-6316. Spacious rooms, some of which have kitchens, make this a good option for families or groups. ③

Travelodge, 1820 University Ave, Berkeley ☎510/843-4262. Six blocks to UC. Clean, basic rooms. ③

Waterfront Plaza Hotel, 10 Washington St, Oakland ☎510/836-3800 or 1-800/729-3638. Plush, modern hotel moored on the best stretch of the Oakland waterfront. ⑥

The Peninsula

Best Western, 100 El Camino Real, Menlo Park (☎650/322-1234). Very pleasant first-class hotel near Stanford University. ④

Best Western Inn, 455 S Second St, San Jose (☎408/298-3500). Right in downtown San Jose, with pool and sauna. ④–⑤

The Cardinal, 235 Hamilton Ave, Palo Alto (☎650/323-5101). Affordable rates and comfortable rooms in the heart of downtown Palo Alto. Some rooms with shared bath. ④–⑤

The Craig, 164 Hamilton Ave, Palo Alto (☎650/853-1133). Somewhat threadbare, but right downtown and dirt cheap. ②

Days Inn, 4238 El Camino Real, Palo Alto ☎1-800/325-2525 or 650/493-4222. A mile from anywhere but the rooms are particularly clean and well kept. ③

The De Anza, 233 W Santa Clara St, San Jose (☎408/286-1000 or 1-800/843-3700). High standard rooms in this 1931 landmark downtown with complimentary deli buffet, snacks, and videos. ⑥–⑦

Accommodation

Accommodation

Wine Country restaurants are listed on p.271.

Executive Inn, 1215 S First St, San Jose ☎408/280-5300. Basic rooms downtown near the few cafés in the city. ④

The Fairmont, 170 S Market St, San Jose ☎408/998-1900 or 1-800/527-4727. San Jose's finest hotel in the heart of downtown on the Plaza. Features all the expected amenities, such as room service, heated pool, and lounge. ⑤–⑦

Pacifica Motor Inn, 200 Rockaway Beach Ave, Pacifica ☎650/359-7700. Large rooms just a block off the beach in hamlet alongside Hwy-1. ④–⑤

Sea Breeze Motel, 100 Rockaway Beach Ave, Pacifica ☎650/359-3903. Beachfront hotel with attached restaurant. ④

Valley Inn, 2155 The Alameda, San Jose ☎408/241-8500. Standard motel not far from the Rosicrucian Museum. ④

Marin County

The Acqua, 555 Redwood Hwy, Mill Valley ☎415/380-0400. Newly opened sumptuous hotel on Richardson Bay run by the owners of the *Mill Valley Inn*. ⑥

Casa Madrona, 801 Bridgeway, Sausalito ☎1-800/567-9524 or 415/332-0502. Deluxe hideaway tucked into the hills above the bay. ⑥

Colonial Motel, 1735 Lincoln Ave, San Rafael ☎415/453-9188. Quiet, cheap and friendly motel in a residential neighborhood. ③

The Grand, 15 Brighton Ave, Bolinas ☎415/868-1757. Budget rooms in a funky, run-down old hotel. ②

Mill Valley Inn, 165 Throckmorton Ave, Mill Valley ☎415/389-6608 or 1-800/595-2100. By far the best hotel in Marin County. Gorgeous European-style inn with elegant rooms and two private cottages. ⑥–⑦

Ocean Court Motel, 18 Arenal St, Stinson Beach ☎415/868-0212. Just a block from the beach, west of Hwy-1. Large simple rooms with kitchens. ④

Stinson Beach Motel, 3416 Shoreline Hwy, Stinson Beach ☎415/868-1712. Basic roadside motel right on Hwy-1, with tiny rooms. Five minutes' walk to the beach. ②

Wine Country

Astro Motel, 323 Santa Rosa Ave, Santa Rosa ☎707/545-8555. Cheapest, no-frills rooms in the Wine Country. ②–③

Best Western Hillside Inn, 2901 Fourth St, Santa Rosa ☎707/546-9353. Clean, attractive motel with swimming pool. ③

Calistoga Inn, 1250 Lincoln Ave, Calistoga ☎707/942-4101. Comfortable rooms with one bed, most with private bath, in a landmark building with its own restaurant and microbrewery. ③–④

The Chablis Inn, 3360 Solano Ave, Napa ☎707/257-1944. One of the cheaper places in the valley, with reasonable rooms, a pool, and hot tub. ⑤

Comfort Inn, 1865 Lincoln Ave, Calistoga ☎707/942-9400. Quiet, modern motel on the edge of town with heated mineral pool, steam room, and sauna. ④–⑤

Dr Wilkinson's Hot Springs, 1507 Lincoln Ave, Calistoga ☎707/942-4102. Legendary health spa and hotel downtown with spacious, well-lit, sparsely furnished rooms facing a peaceful courtyard or the pool patio. ④–⑤

El Bonita Motel, 195 Main St, St Helena ☎707/963-3216. Old roadside motel recently redone in Art Deco; surrounded by a 2.5-acre garden with a pool and jacuzzi. ⑤–⑦

El Pueblo Inn, 896 W Napa St, Sonoma ☎707/996-3651. Basic highway motel with a pool. ④

Fife's, 16467 River Rd, Guerneville ☎1-800/7-FIFES-1 or 707/869-0656. One of the original Guerneville gay resorts, built on 15 acres of land right on the river. Disco, gym, private beach, and restaurant. Lodging options run the gamut from private bungalow to campsite. ③–④

Golden Haven Hot Springs, 1713 Lake St, Calistoga ☎707/942-6793. Basic hotel just east of downtown with spa services. ③

Harvest Inn, 1 Main St, St Helena ☎1-800/950-8466 or 707/963-9463. English Tudor cottages at the edge of a vineyard with huge rooms loaded with perks like a down-feather bed, fireplace and private terrace overlooking the garden or a 14-acre vineyard. Two outdoor heated pools, whirlpool spas, and on-site trails. ⑥

Indian Springs Resort, 1712 Lincoln Ave, Calistoga ☎707/942-4913. Posh place to be packed with mineral-rich mud before soaking in the oldest Olympic swimming pool in Northern California – filled with natural mineral water. Comfortable, sunny rooms and attentive staff. ⑥

Jack London Lodge, 13740 Arnold Drive, Glen Ellen ☎707/938-8510. Modern motel near the Jack London State Park, with a good restaurant and pool. A nice place to try if Napa and Sonoma hotels are booked, or if you want a truly rural setting and fine star-gazing. ④

Motel 6, 2760 Cleveland Ave, Santa Rosa ☎707/546-1500. A little distant from the main wine areas, but good and cheap. ②

Hotel La Rose, 308 Wilson St, Santa Rosa ☎1-800/LAROSE-8. Restored lodging on Railroad Square. Clean new rooms with two phone jacks in each room for Internet use. ④–⑤

Motel 6, 3145 Cleveland Ave, Santa Rosa ☎707/525-9010. Second Santa Rosa location of clean, cheap motel. ②

Mount View Hotel and Spa, 1457 Lincoln Ave, Calistoga ☎1-800/816-6877 or 707/942-6877. Lively Art Deco-style hotel with nightly jazz and an excellent Cajun restaurant, *Catahoula*, on the ground floor. ⑤

Nance's Hot Springs 1614 Lincoln Ave, Calistoga ☎707/942-6211. Modest hotel with full spa, perfect for the budget traveler. Funky rooms with kitchenettes. ③–④

Russian River Resort 16390 Fourth St, Guerneville ☎707/869-0691. The "Triple R" is one of Guerneville's legendary gay resorts, with a bar, pool, jacuzzi, restaurant, and bungalow-style rooms. ④

The St Helena, 1309 Main St, St Helena ☎707/963-4388. Slightly claustrophobic (or cozy, depending on your mood) country-style hotel right downtown. 17 rooms (14 with private bath) and a decor rich in antiques, hand-carved wood, and marble. European breakfast included each morning. ⑤–⑥

The Sonoma, 110 W Spain St, Sonoma ☎707/996-7014. Newly renovated with French/American country decor. ⑤–⑥

The Swiss Hotel, 18 W Spain St, Sonoma ☎707/938-2884. A ninety-year-old landmark on the plaza with five cramped but quaint rooms in the rustic, pine interior. ⑤–⑥

Triple-S Ranch 4600 Mount Home Ranch Rd, Calistoga ☎707/942-6730. Up the hill from Calistoga, in the middle of the wilderness, these clean cabins offer few frills, but the cheap rates and secluded environment are hard to beat. ③

Vintage Inn, 6541 Washington St, Yountville ☎1-800/351-1133 or 707/944-1112. Huge luxury rooms in a modern hotel complex – all with fireplaces – with swimming pool and free bike rental. ⑦

White Sulphur Springs, 3100 White Sulphur Springs Rd, west of St Helena ☎707/963-8588. A relaxing retreat from the tourism of the Napa Valley – simple rooms in a newly remodeled 300-acre hillside resort, surrounded by hiking trails, with outdoor sulphur pool, jacuzzi, and swimming pool. ④–⑤

The Willows, 15905 River Rd, Guerneville ☎707/869-2824. Rustic, country-style modest lodge on 5 acres along the Russian River. Features a community kitchen, jacuzzi, and sauna and 13 rooms, nine with private bath. ④–⑤

Wine Country Inn, 1152 Lodi Lane, St Helena ☎707/963-7077; *www.winecountryinn.com*. Twenty-four rooms, most equipped with fireplaces, patterned after the inns of New England, with on-site strolling gardens and swimming pool. ⑤–⑥

Accommodation

Accommodation

Bed and Breakfast

Bed and breakfasts around the Bay Area offer good-value luxury, a more intimate alternative to the standard hotel or motel experience. Plus, most are housed in vintage buildings, such as Victorians in the city, Julia-Morgan-designed homes in the East Bay, or historic lumber-money buildings across the Golden Gate Bridge. Europeans, accustomed to shabby B&Bs in faded seaside resorts and greasy bacon-and-eggs, may be pleasantly surprised – though the rates, of course, are proportionately higher than in Europe.

Even the largest of establishments tend to have no more than ten rooms, with brass beds, plentiful flowers, stuffed cushions and a sometimes-contrived homey atmosphere. Other places may consist merely of a couple of furnished rooms in someone's home, or an entire apartment where you won't even see your host. The latter makes particularly good sense for families or those traveling with small children. Most B&Bs are bookable through the various specialist agencies listed in this chapter's introduction (see p.217).

While always including breakfast, the breakfasts themselves vary from coffee and tea with granola, fresh fruit, and scones, to a full-blown spread of pancakes, eggs, and bacon. If you need a big blowout to start the day, be sure to check. Prices vary greatly, anything from $60 to $200 a night, depending on location and season. Most B&Bs are booked weeks or months in advance, especially during peak times.

Downtown

Beresford Arms, 701 Post St ☎415/673-2600. Luxury B&B in the heart of town with a redbrick facade and an interior done up in crushed velvet and chandeliers. Roomy suites offer the best value, as they come with jacuzzi bathtubs, kitchen, and wet bar for slightly more than the nondescript double rooms. ④–⑤

Petite Auberge, 863 Bush St at Taylor ☎1-800/365-3004 or 415/928-6000. An opulent B&B with complimentary afternoon tea, wine, and hors d'oeuvres as well as full breakfast. Rooms are styled in oak and floral prints. ⑤–⑥

White Swan Inn, 845 Bush St between Taylor and Mason ☎415/775-1755. Dressed up in English manor theme: raging fires, oak-paneled rooms, and afternoon tea. ⑥

North Beach and Nob Hill

Art Center, 1902 Filbert St at Laguna ☎415/567-1526. Quirky little inn that's a real home away from home. ⑤

Bed and Breakfast Inn, 4 Charlton Court off Union St ☎415/921-9784. One of the first B&Bs to be established in the city, this lovely, sun-drenched Victorian house, tucked away down a quiet side street, offers some of San Francisco's most pleasant accommodation. ④–⑤

Washington Square Inn, 1660 Stockton St ☎415/981-4220. Cozy B&B right on North Beach's lovely main square. ⑤

The northern waterfront and Pacific Heights

Circa 1870, 2119 California St at Laguna ☎415/928-3224. Plush four-room B&B whose period rooms reflect the name. Each is brightly lit, has a fireplace and private bath, and is decorated in roses, oak, and vines. ⑤

The Slack Mansion, 2224 Sacramento St ☎415/447-7600. 1900-era B&B atop Pacific Heights. Five rooms, each with fireplace and private bath. ⑥–⑦

The Mission and the Castro

Andora Inn, 2438 Mission at 20th ☎1-800/967-9219 or 415/282-0337. Fully restored 12-room Victorian manor located in the heart of the Mission with an awesome staff. ④–⑤

Black Stallion Inn, 635 Castro St ☎415/863-0131. Clothing is optional at this gay B&B in a renovated Victorian. ④

Dolores Park Inn, 3641 17th St ☎415/621-0482. Kitchens and fireplaces are standard in this B&B; also has a hot tub. ④

Inn on Castro, 321 Castro St ☎415/861-0321. Luxury B&B; well worth the price for the large rooms and good breakfasts. Smack in the middle of the Castro. ④–⑤

24 Henry, 24 Henry St ☎415/864-5686. Quiet, intimate guesthouse near the heart of the Castro. ③–④ Another branch is nearby at 4080 18th St ☎415/864-0994. ⑤

Twin Peaks Hotel, 2160 Market St at Dolores ☎415/621-9467. Set in the hills above, this is a quieter and prettier location not far from the Castro, even if the rooms are small and short on luxury. ②

The Willows, 710 14th St ☎415/431-4770. Affordable, well furnished, and near the Castro. ④–⑤

West of Civic Center and the Haight-Ashbury

Albion House Inn, 135 Gough St at Oak ☎415/621-0896. Small and comfortable B&B above a fine restaurant. ④–⑤

Archbishop's Mansion, 1000 Fulton St ☎415/563-7872. Grandly camp Alamo Square mansion that was once a school for wayward Catholic boys and is now a gay-friendly B&B with attentive, personalized service, and a variety of "theme" rooms. The ballroom chandelier from *Gone With the Wind* is on display, and amenities include everything from fitness training to image consultancy. ⑥–⑦

Baby Bear's House, 1424 Page St ☎1-888/9BEAR4U or 415/255-9777. Lovely B&B in a restored Haight Victorian. ④–⑥

Château Tivoli, 1057 Steiner St ☎1-800/228-1647 or 415/776-5462. Victorian just off Alamo Square built by William H. Armitage for a lumber baron and decorated with furnishings from the estates of Charles de Gaulle and J. Paul Getty; Mark Twain loved it. ⑤–⑥

The Herb'N Inn, 525 Ashbury St ☎415/553-8542. Four-room B&B in the Haight run by the guides of the "Flower Power" walking tour. ④

The Red Victorian Bed, Breakfast and Art, 1665 Haight St ☎415/864-1978. Bang in the middle of Haight-Ashbury, a lively New Agey B&B, which also calls itself the Peace Center, with a hippie art gallery. A real Sixties relic. ④

East Bay

Berkeley City Club, 2315 Durant Ave, Berkeley ☎510/848-7800. Two blocks to UC, this property was designed by Julia Morgan (see p.150), and has an indoor swimming pool and exercise room. Each of the spacious rooms has a private bath. ④

Dean's Bed and Breakfast, 480 Pedestrian Way, Rockridge ☎510/652-5024; *hometown.aol.com/dimped*. A hidden gem with heated swimming pool and Japanese garden, near the Rockridge BART stop. Tidy but simple rooms with private bath, cable TV, and private phone line with answering machine. Highly recommended. ④

East Brother Light Station, 117 Park Place, San Pablo Bay ☎510/233-2385; *www.ebls.org*. A handful of rooms in a converted lighthouse, on an island in the middle of the bay. Not a handy base for seeing the sights, but an adventurous retreat for a foggy evening. Price includes gourmet dinner and breakfast. ⑧

Elmwood House, 2609 College Ave, Berkeley ☎510/540-5123 *www.elmwoodhouse.com*. Attractive, c.1900 home with B&B rooms, not far from UC

Accommodation

For more B&Bs in the East Bay, phone the Berkeley & Oakland Bed and Breakfast Network at ☎510/547-6380.

Gay accommodation

Not surprisingly, San Francisco has a few **bed and breakfasts** that cater specifically to **gay travelers**, almost all of them situated in the Castro (see above). Most accommodation in the Bay Area, though not gay specific, tends to be gay friendly. **Lesbian-specific accommodation** is virtually non-existant, though the *Mary Elizabeth Inn* and the *Women's Hotel* (see p.220) cater almost exclusively to **women**.

Accommodation

For more B&Bs, contact one of the reservation services listed on p.217.

For more B&Bs in Marin, phone the Bed and Breakfast Exchange at ☎415/485-1971.

For more on the Green Gulch Zen Center, see p.188.

Berkeley. Each of the four rooms is modeled in the style of a different famous architect. ④

Gramma's Rose Garden Inn, 2740 Telegraph Ave, Berkeley ☎510/549-2145. Pleasant if slightly dull rooms with fireplaces in a pretty mock-Tudor mansion half a mile south of UC Berkeley. ⑤

Union Hotel and Gardens, 401 First St, Benicia ☎707/746-0100. A longtime bordello, this fully converted B&B now has twelve comfortable rooms. ⑤

The Peninsula

Cowper Inn, 705 Cowper St, Palo Alto ☎650/327-4475. Restored Victorian with pleasant parlor and attractive rooms close to University Ave. ④

Old Thyme Inn, 779 Main St, Half Moon Bay (☎650/726-1616). Half a dozen rooms, each with private bath, in a lovely Victorian house surrounded by luxuriant herb and flower gardens. ⑤–⑥

San Benito House, 356 Main St, Half Moon Bay ☎650/726-3425. Twelve restful rooms in a hundred-year-old building, just a mile from the beach. Excellent restaurant downstairs. ⑤

Marin County

Blue Heron Inn, 11 Wharf Rd, Bolinas ☎415/868-1102. Lovely double rooms in an unbeatable locale. Breakfast is served at the owner's cozy restaurant, *The Shop Café* at 46 Wharf Rd, which also serves lunch and dinner. ④

Lindisfarne Guest House, Green Gulch Zen Center, Muir Beach ☎415/383-3134. Restful rooms in a meditation retreat set in a secluded valley above Muir Beach. Price includes excellent vegetarian meals. ④

Mountain Home Inn, 810 Panoramic Highway, Mill Valley ☎415/381-9000. Romantically located on Mount Tamalpais' crest, this bed and breakfast offers great views and endless hiking. Some rooms with hot tubs. ⑥

Olema Inn, 10000 Sir Francis Drake Blvd, Olema ☎1-800/532-9252 or 415/663-9559; *www.olemainn.com*. Comfy, quiet rooms near the entrance to Point Reyes National Seashore on a site that's been a hotel since 1876. ⑤

Pelican Inn, 10 Pacific Way, Muir Beach ☎415/383-6000. Very comfortable rooms in a romantic pseudo-English country inn, with good bar and restaurant downstairs, ten minutes' walk from beautiful Muir Beach. ⑥

Ten Inverness Way, 10 Inverness Way, Inverness ☎415/669-1648. Quiet and restful, with a hot tub, in small village of good restaurants and bakeries on the fringes of Point Reyes. ⑤

Wine Country

Ambrose Bierce House, 1515 Main St, St Helena ☎707/963-3003. Converted former home of the eminently quotable misanthropic ghost-story writer. ⑥

Applewood Inn & Restaurant, 13555 Hwy-116, Guerneville ☎1-800/555-8509 or 707/869-9093. Popular Wine Country retreat furnished with antiques and surrounded by gardens, patios, a pool and spa. ⑤–⑥

Calistoga Wine Way Inn, 1019 Foothill Blvd, Calistoga ☎1-800/572-0679 or 707/942-0680. Small and friendly B&B with lovely garden and antique-filled rooms, a short walk from the center of town. ⑤

Churchill Manor 485 Brown St, Napa ☎707/253-7733. Regal nineteenth-century mansion hidden on an unlikely suburban street. Antique furnishings, delicious breakfasts, and free use of tandem bikes. ⑤–⑥

Cinnamon Bear 1407 Kearney St, St Helena ☎1-888/963-4600 or 707/963-4653. Quirky, sumptuously furnished inn, for 22 years a favorite. ⑤

The Cottage, 302 First St E, Sonoma ☎707/996-0719. Owned by two interior designers, this calm downtown B&B has a hot tub and courtyard. ⑤

Creekside Inn and Resort, 16180 Neely Road, Guerneville ☎1-800/776-6586 or 707/869-3623. Homey B&B with a heated pool and restaurant; rooms are named for the type of wood they're decorated in and cottages nicknamed the "Ewok Village" for their resemblance to the treetop lodging of *Return of the Jedi*. ③–⑤

Gaige House Inn, 13540 Arnold Drive, Glen Ellen ☎1-800/935-0237 or 707/935-0237. Beautifully restored Queen Anne Victorian farmhouse in a quiet and contemporary country setting. No children under twelve permitted. ⑥–⑦

Kenwood Inn & Spa, 10400 Sonoma Hwy, Kenwood ☎1-800/353-6966 or 707/833-1293. Deluxe, beautiful, and secluded Italian villa-style bed and breakfast. ⑦

Ramekins Bed and Breakfast Inn, 450 W Spain St, Sonoma ☎707/933-4052. Italian-villa style lodging above a famous cooking school. ⑥

Sunny Acres Bed & Breakfast, 397 Main St, St Helena ☎707/963-2826. Restored Victorian home – located on a vineyard – of valley pioneer Dr George Belden Crane, who planted zinfandel grapes at this estate in 1862. Today the quaint inn is surrounded by 26 acres of grapes which supply the Robert Biale label. ⑥

Thistle Dew Inn, 171 W Spain St, Sonoma ☎1-800/382-7895 or 707/938-2909; *www.thistledew.com*. Near the central plaza, Sonoma's most elegant B&B has fully restored rooms, some with a private hot tub and patio, and one of the best breakfasts in town. ⑤–⑥

Hostels

At the bottom end of the price scale, there are a number of **hostels** in San Francisco and around the Bay Area, some in very beautiful settings. Dormitory rooms are sex-segregated, and beds go for around $15. Many hostels also offer cut-rate single and double rooms, and most have Internet service available, sometimes for free.

You can really expect little more from a hostel than a clean, safe bed and somewhere to lock your valuables. Some are livelier and more liberal than others, though those with more regulations (ie nightly curfews and bans on alcohol) also tend to be the safest – for women traveling alone they can often be good places to feel secure and meet other people. The hostels vary between **private** establishments, where things may in general be more relaxed, and the **official HI hostels**, which can often be cleaner and better equipped but normally have some kind of curfew and will charge you a few bucks more if you're not a HI member.

There are also a couple of well-located **YMCAs**, and a few rooms become available in **university dorms** during the summer vacation over in Berkeley – a great option for younger travelers, with single and double rooms ranging from $25 right up to $75, and good facilities including gyms and swimming pools.

If you're planning to stay in a hostel, it's always a good idea to **bring your passport**, even if you're American: many places will insist on seeing it before renting you a bed. This is intended to preserve the hostels for travelers. For similar reasons, many hostels also impose a nominal maximum stay of three to five days.

Accommodation

San Francisco

Green Tortoise, 494 Broadway ☎1-800/867-8647 or 415/834-1000. Funky North Beach hostel with dorm beds $16–19 per night and double rooms for $42–48; both options include complimentary breakfast, use of sauna, and Internet access. ②

For information on Green Tortoise's excursions, see p.15.

HI-San Francisco Union Square, 312 Mason St ☎415/788-5604. Large downtown hostel with dorm beds from $14–16 and twins $28–32. Members only, though acquiring a day membership is just $3. The cleanest and most central hostel, and, consequently, the most popular. ①

Interclub/Globe Hostel, 10 Hallam Place ☎415/431-0540. Lively South of Market

Accommodation

The Año Nuevo State reserve is described on p.179.

hostel with young clientele and no curfew. $15 per person; doubles $36. ①–②

Pacific Tradewinds Guesthouse, 680 Sacramento St ☎415/433-7970. Great location in Chinatown, and no curfew. Laundry and a host of other services. $14–16 per person. ①

San Francisco International Guest House, 2976 23rd St ☎415/641-1411. Popular with European travelers, this Mission District Victorian has dorms and a few private rooms. From $15 per person daily, with a 5-day minimum stay, less if you stay a month. Two kitchens; no curfew, and no reservations accepted. ①

San Francisco International Youth Hostel, Building 240, Fort Mason ☎415/771-7277. On the waterfront between the Golden Gate Bridge and Fisherman's Wharf. One of the most comfortable and convenient hostels around. From $16 per person, $32 for a twin room including breakfast. ①

YMCA Central Branch, 220 Golden Gate Ave ☎415/885-0460. Good central single and double rooms, two blocks from Civic Center. Rates include breakfast and use of gym, pool, and sauna. $30 single, $40 double. ①–②

East Bay

Berkeley YMCA, 2001 Allston Way at Milvia St, a block from Berkeley BART ☎510/848-6800. Berkeley's best bargain accommodation; rates include use of gym and pool. ②

Haste-Channing Summer Visitor Housing, 2424 Channing Ave, Berkeley ☎510/642-4444. Summer-only dorm rooms. ②

The Peninsula

HI-Hidden Villa, 26807 Moody Rd, Los Altos Hills ☎650/949-8648. Located on an 1800-acre ranch in the foothills above Silicon Valley; closed June–Sept. $15 a night. ①

HI-Pigeon Point Lighthouse, Hwy-1, just south of Pescadero ☎650/879-0633. Worth planning a trip around, this beautifully sited hostel, fifty miles south of San Francisco, is ideally placed for exploring the redwood forests in the hills above or for watching the wildlife in nearby Año Nuevo State Reserve. Outdoor hot tub perched on the rocky coast. Office hours 7.30–9.30am & 4.30–9.30pm; doors locked at 11pm. Members $13 per night, nonmembers $16; reservations essential in summer. Private rooms $30 a night, minimum two people. ①

HI-Point Montara Lighthouse, 16th St/Hwy-1, Montara ☎650/728-7177. Dorm rooms in a converted 1875 lighthouse, 25 miles south of San Francisco and accessible by bike or SamTrans bus #1L or #1C (Mon–Fri until 5.50pm, Sat until 6.15pm). Like Pigeon Point, its outdoor hot tub is dramatically situated over the ocean on the coastal rocks. Office hours 7.30–9.30am & 4.30–9.30pm; doors locked 11pm. Members $13 per night, nonmembers $16; reservations essential in summer. ①

Sanborn Park Hostel, 15808 Sanborn Rd, Saratoga ☎408/741-0166. Comfortable rooms in a beautiful wooded area fifteen minutes outside San Jose. $8.50 members; $10.50 nonmembers. ①

Marin County

HI-Marin Headlands, Building 941, Fort Barry, Marin Headlands (closed 9.30am–4.30pm) ☎415/331-2777. Hard to get to unless you're driving – it's near Rodeo Lagoon just off Bunker Road, five miles west of Sausalito – but worth the effort for its setting, in cozy old army barracks just across the Golden Gate Bridge. Dorm beds $12–14 a night, plus $1 linen rental. ①

HI-Point Reyes, in the Point Reyes National Seashore (closed 9.30am–4.30pm) ☎415/663-8811. Like the hostel above, hard to reach without your own transportation: six miles west of the visitor center and two miles from the beach, in an old ranch house surrounded by meadows and forests. Dorm beds $12–14 a night. ①

Campgrounds

Summertime's mild temperatures and the Bay Area's wealth of natural splendor make camping possible outside San Francisco. **Campsites** are usually groomed, meaning there's a flat area for your tent with a fire pit, and nearby drinking water and toilets are available. Campgrounds fill up fast; reservations are strongly recommended, though some backcountry sites operate on a first-come, first-served basis. Contact ParkNet (☎1-800/444-7275) for reservations at state parks, or call the park's information center for information on available places.

Closest to San Francisco, the parkland of **Angel Island** allows camping during summer months, but weather conditions mandate the availability.

Alternatively, the vast swaths of nature within the **Marin Headlands** are too large to be monitored by rangers and see many do-it-yourself camps, as do **beaches** throughout the Bay Area. Camping under the Bay Area's clear skies amidst the foggy, salty air, makes for a beautiful, though chilly, evening. Be sure your tent is beyond the high-tide mark, keep fires in a pit or hole, and leave the area cleaner than when you found it.

East Bay

Chabot Family Campground, off I-580 in East Oakland ☎510/562-2267. Walk-in, tent-only places, with hot showers and lots of good hiking nearby; reserve through ParkNet (☎1-800/444-7275) in summer; $20.

Mount Diablo State Park, 20 miles east of Oakland off I-680 in Contra Costa County ☎510/837-2525. RV and tent places; likewise, book through ParkNet (☎1-800/444-7275) in summer; $16.

The Peninsula

Butano State Park, Pescadero ☎650/879-2040. RV and tent spaces in a beautiful redwood forest; $16.

Costanoa Luxury Camping, 2001 Costanoa Rd, on the eastern side of Hwy-1, just south of Pescadero ☎1-800/738-7477. Offering a pampered night under the stars. Easy access to Whitehouse Ridge Trail and the ocean, which is just over the dune across Hwy-1. Accommodation ranges from austere tent cabins ($55–65) to deluxe tents with beds ($115–135) to cabins with fireplaces ($175–200).

Half Moon Bay State Beach, Half Moon Bay ☎650/726-8820. Sleep out (illegally but safely) along the beach for free, or in the campground for $16.

Marin County

China Camp State Park, off N San Pedro Rd, north of San Rafael ☎415/456-0766; reserve through ParkNet April–Oct ☎1-800/444-7275. Walk-in plots (just 600ft from the parking lot) overlooking a lovely meadow. First-come, first-served. $16.

Kirby Cove, just across the Golden Gate Bridge in the Marin Headlands; Apr–Oct ☎415/331-1540, reservations Tues–Thurs 10am–2pm; rest of year call ☎415/561-4304. The best of five campgrounds in the Headlands at the northern foot of the Golden Gate Bridge. $20.

Mount Tamalpais State Park, above Mill Valley ☎415/388-2070, reserve cabins via ParkNet ☎1-800/444-7275. Sixteen plots for backpackers on the slopes of the mountain ($16), and a few rustic cabins ($30 a night), along the coast at Steep Ravine.

Point Reyes National Seashore, forty miles northwest of San Francisco ☎415/663-1092, reserve sites up to two months in advance ☎415/663-8054, Mon–Fri 9am–2pm. A wide range of hike-in sites for backpackers, near the beach or in the forest. $10.

Samuel Taylor State Park, on Sir Francis Drake Blvd, fifteen miles west of San Rafael ☎415/488-9897; in summer, reserve through ParkNet at ☎1-800/444-7275. Deluxe, car-accessible plots with hot showers, spread along a river. Don't miss the swimming hole and bat caves. $16.

Accommodation

For complete details on Angel Island, see p.192.

Wine Country

Austin Creek State Recreation Area, Armstrong Woods Rd, Guerneville ☎707/865-2391. $14.

Bothe-Napa Valley State Park, four miles north of St Helena off Hwy-29 ☎1-800/444-7275 or 707/942-4575. Daily May–Sept. Lovely, tucked-away park with hiking and mountain bike trails and a public swimming pool. $16.

Johnson's Beach and Resort, 16241 First St, Guerneville ☎707/869-2022. $10.

Spring Lake Regional Park, Newanga Ave, outside Santa Rosa ☎707/539-8092. Daily May–Sept, weekends only Oct–April. $15.

Sugar Loaf Ridge State Park, 2605 Adobe Canyon Rd, Sonoma ☎707/833-5712. Fri–Sat $16, Sun–Thurs $15.

Chapter 15

Restaurants and cafés

San Franciscans consider their city the best in the world for **eating**, and the culinary standards here are undeniably high, leaving room for few complaints about choice or quality. Indeed, with some 3500 restaurants crammed onto the tiny tip of this peninsula – only Paris has more per capita – food is pretty much *the* culture, and the average resident spends nearly $3000 annually dining out. If you happen to be on an expense account, you could easily blow as much in a few weeks in some of the city's more expensive restaurants, though even if you're on a strict budget, you'll still be able to fare quite well.

Wherever you end up eating – and indeed, most neighborhoods are well stocked with restaurants and, for lighter meals, cafés, so you shouldn't really go hungry anywhere – you'll find that ingredients are fresh, well-prepared, and plentiful. California is, after all, one of the most agriculturally rich – and health-conscious – parts of the country. Locally grown fruits and vegetables, abundant fish and seafood, and top-quality meat and dairy products all find their way into the city's kitchens.

For smokers, lighting up after a fine meal will prove difficult. State law decrees that there is **no smoking** in any public space, restaurants included.

Breakfast and brunch

Breakfast tends to be the best-value meal of the day – for a hearty serving of eggs, bread or pancakes, bacon or sausage, home fried potatoes, and coffee for $5–10, head to a **diner** or **coffee shop**, all of which serve breakfast until at least 11am (though diners sometimes offer it all day).

Weekend **brunches** (generally 10am–2pm) offer you the chance to sample the cuisine of some of the city's

Brunch spots

The following restaurants, listed along with the neighborhoods in which they are located and cross-referenced to their reviews, are our choices for some of the best brunches in town – though new hot spots are popping up all the time, so keep your eyes open.

Bitterroot (Mission)	p.253	**Kate's Kitchen** (Lower Haight)	p.258
Boogaloo's (Mission)	p.253	**Miss Millie's** (Noe Valley)	p.255
Café Flore (Castro)	p.236	**Pork Store** (Haight)	p.258
Doidge's (Pacific Heights)	p.247	**Sears** (downtown)	p.241
Ella's (Pacific Heights)	p.248	**Ti Couz** (Mission)	p.256
Greens (northern waterfront)	p.248	**2223** (Castro)	p.255

Restaurants and cafés

more upscale restaurants without emptying your wallet in the process, though you can expect major queues at the most popular establishments (see box).

Lunch and fast food

Most workers take their **lunch break** between 11.30am and 2.30pm. During those hours many of the city's restaurants offer excellent low-cost **set menus**. Though not as large a meal as dinner, this can often be a welcome opportunity to sample sushi and other delights for half of what you'd pay later in the day.

Chinese **dim sum**, is another popular afternoon meal, while Mexican food is remarkably cheap at any time – a massive **burrito** generally costs less than $5 and makes a perfect lunch. A slice of **pizza** will set you back not more than a couple of bucks, while a **sandwich** costs only a little more. Help-yourself, pay-by-the-pound **salad bars**, full of fresh fixings, are scattered around the downtown.

Cafés, bakeries, and ice-cream parlors

Perhaps more than any other American city, San Francisco's **café** scene is an inescapable part of daily life and culture. Though most cafés offer tea, light snack food, and a variety of pastries, along with, of course, as many types of coffee as you could imagine, it's the lingering regulars that give these places life, and make them as much a part of the social scene as bars are in many places. In San Francisco, North Beach and the Haight are major spots for café life, and Berkeley's campus across the bay supports a big scene as well. **Bakeries** and **ice-cream parlors** are less prevalent in the Bay Area than in some parts of America, though there are a few notable addresses.

Downtown and Chinatown

Café Metropol, 168 Sutter St at Kearny ☎415/732-7777. Office workers thank their lucky stars for the flavorful ethnic salads and gourmet sandwiches served in this large space on an otherwise unpromising stretch of high-rises.

Specialty's, multiple locations including 101 New Montgomery at Mission ☎415/896-BAKE. Gooey, cheesy breads, towering sandwiches, hearty soups, and monster cookies make this chain of luncheon bakeries an almost mandatory part of the local workday routine. Get your lunch to go, and eat with locals on the front steps of offices along Market St.

Yakety Yak, 679 Sutter St at Taylor ☎415/885-6908. Catering to a large contingent of backpackers and fellow travelers with poetry readings and

Coffee talk

For those who've managed to miss out on the gourmet coffee craze that has taken over the United States over the last ten years or so, San Francisco's serious coffee culture will come as a rude awakening. This quick glossary of coffee lingo should bring tea drinkers up to full caffeinated speed.

Cafe au lait: coffee with frothy steamed milk.
Cafe mocha: hot chocolate with a shot of espresso.
Caffe latte: steamed milk with a shot of espresso.
Cappuccino: espresso topped with foamed milk.
Espresso: a shot of thick coffee, made by filtering steam through finely ground coffee.
Espresso con panna: espresso topped with whipped cream.
Espresso machiato: espresso "stained" with milk.
Latte macchiato: milk "stained" with espresso.

Internet access. Coffee, pastries, and basic snacks.

North Beach and Nob Hill

Caffe Trieste, 601 Vallejo St at Grant ☎415/392-6739. Even after a hearty Italian meal at one of the neighboring restaurants, it's hard to resist all the pastries in the window; thankfully, they sell coffee to revive you afterwards.

Imperial Tea Court, 1411 Powell St at Broadway ☎415/788-6080. Steep yourself in the ambience of an old-world tea house worthy of the last emperor. All the usual leaves are brewed here, but the soothing space might prompt you to let down your guard and sip into something a little more exotic.

Mario's Bohemian Cigar Store, 566 Columbus Ave at Union ☎415/362-0536. The "bohemian" in the name is dead on, as are the cheap sandwiches that draw locals with thin wallets. One of the few holdovers from the area's Beat heyday.

Stella Pastry, 446 Columbus Ave at Green ☎415/986-2914. Narrow little pastry shop selling a variety of delectable baked puffs to go with your coffee. Sadly, there's almost nowhere to sit.

Steps of Rome Café, 348 Columbus Ave at Vallejo ☎415/397-9435. By day just another moderately cool café, by night a noisy favorite of everyone from taxi drivers running on double espressos to young hipsters looking for a date.

Swenson's Ice Cream, Union and Hyde sts ☎415/775-6818. Luscious handmade ice cream and milkshakes from a neighborhood landmark. A perfect place to take a break after slogging up and down Russian Hill or after hopping off the Powell–Hyde cable car.

Tosca Café, 242 Columbus Ave at Broadway ☎415/391-1244. A beautiful old bar with tile on the floor, bow ties on the bartenders, and opera on the jukebox.

The northern waterfront and Pacific Heights

Bepple's Pies, 1934 Union St at Laguna ☎415/931-6225. A bakery-café offering both sweet and savory baked goods, including some semi-legendary pumpkin muffins. You can get everything to go from the counter or sit in the sunny dining room for a cheap break from the Union St shopping traffic.

SoMa, the Tenderloin, and Civic Center

Brainwash, 1122 Folsom St at Seventh ☎415/861-FOOD. A good gimmick and yummy food to go with it – munch on burgers, salads, or sandwiches while your laundry spins at the attached laundromat. There's even live music in the evening.

Caffé Museo, 151 Third St at Howard ☎415/357-4500. Though the prices are a little higher than they ought to be, this is still a decent spot to grab an Italian panini sandwich or biscotti cookie and listen in on some critical art debates.

Caffe Centro, 102 South Park at Jack London Way ☎415/882-1500. A terrific spot to grab an ahi-tuna salad sandwich with the nouveau-riche cyber set. Though sit-down service is available, the lunchtime take-out window is a better bargain.

Farley's, 1315 18th St at Texas ☎415/648-1545. Grab a cup of coffee or a basic sandwich to go and enjoy Potrero Hill's gorgeous views of the city, or just settle in with your snack and one of their innumerable magazines.

Mr Ralph's Café, 90 Natoma St, near Howard, at Second ☎415/243-9330. *Mr Ralph's* is a pleasant neighborhood café in search of a neighborhood. Hidden in a grubby little alley, it serves a good selection of home-style soups and sandwiches.

Primo Patio, 214 Townsend at Third ☎415/957-1129. Sandwiches and burgers, spiced with a subtle Brazilian twist. The backyard patio offers a pleasant escape from the industrial environs.

South Beach Café, 800 Embarcadero at Townsend ☎415/974-1115. A find where simple pastas and entrees of sur-

Restaurants and cafés

prisingly high quality rarely cost over $7. Perfect for picking up a pre-prepared sandwich or antipasto to eat by the water.

The Mission and the Castro

Café Flore, 2298 Noe St at Market ☎415/621-8579. From its plant-filled patio on Market St, you can while away a morning or afternoon watching the locals cruise, sipping espresso, or nibbling on one of the excellent pasta dishes or salads.

Café La Boheme, 3318 24th at Mission ☎415/643-0481. A diverse crowd and a staggering range of coffees keeps the Mission's caffeine addicts coming from sunup until late at night.

Café Macondo, 3159 16th at Guerrero ☎415/863-6517. Named after Garcia Marquez's fictional town, this scruffy café entertains a steady stream of notepad poets and coffee-cup philosophers. With pictures of Frida Kahlo and Louis Armstrong lining the walls, the atmosphere is self-consciously bohemian.

Lovejoy's, 1195 Church at 24th ☎415/648-5895. A rarity in a coffee-obsessed town, this cozy café in Noe Valley specializes in teas. Packed with overstuffed furniture and bric-a-brac, the ambience has a pleasantly musty Victorian quality.

Mitchell's, 688 San Jose Ave at 29th ☎415/648-2300. In a fairly desolate southern corner of the neighborhood is the perfect spot for an after-dinner treat. *Mitchell's* serves homemade ice cream in an array of exotic tropical flavors, including such oddities as macapuno and halo halo.

Red Dora's Bearded Lady, 485 14th St at Guerrero ☎415/626-2805. A small coffee shop catering primarily to the local lesbian community, with frequent spoken-word nights and performances by local artists.

St. Francis Fountain, 2801 24th St ☎415/826-4200. A classic 1950s-style ice cream and dessert counter, with glass jars filled with candy and shakes so deliciously thick you'll get a headache sucking them through the straw.

West of Civic Center and Haight-Ashbury

Bean There, 201 Steiner St at Waller ☎415/255-8855. Tucked away on a residential street, a great place to linger on sunny afternoons, sipping coffee with the local crowd.

Café International, 508 Haight St at Fillmore ☎415/552-7390. Host to a variety of open-mike poetry and singer songwriter nights, allowing the sufficiently daring to show off their talents, or lack thereof.

Horseshoe Café, 566 Haight St at Steiner ☎415/626-8852. Dangerously dark pints of coffee served in a dank atmosphere far more reminiscent of a biker bar than any *Starbucks*.

Jammin' Java, 701 Cole St at Waller ☎415/668-JAVA. Strictly for coffee, tea, or pastries but providing some calm respite on a corner midway between Haight St and the more upscale Cole Valley.

Momi Toby's Revolutionary Café, 528 Laguna ☎415/626-1508. No Red Scare flashbacks here, just a cozy neighborhood café. As a bonus, they've put out board games to help while away the time.

Pendragon, 400 Hayes St at Gough ☎415/552-7017. Not much to look at, until you see the freshly made food. Salad offerings are unusually flavorful and the baked items tend toward the oversized.

People's Café, 1419 Haight St at Masonic ☎415/553-8842. A big space, so you almost never have to wait. The salads and sandwiches are standard and cheap.

Squat and Gobble I and Too, 237 Fillmore St at Haight ☎415/487-0551 and 1428 Haight St at Ashbury ☎415/864-8484. Offering copious, cheap sandwiches, crepes, and caffeine to help you refuel before venturing into one of the neighboring clothing or record shops.

The Richmond and the Sunset

Cool Beans, 4342a California at Sixth Ave ☎415/750-1955. Neighborhood spot where the locals go to meet and greet over a game of backgammon or chess.

The Toy Boat, 401 Clement St at Fifth ☎415/751-7505. A perfect spot for the kids. Serving ice cream and other treats for the little ones and cups of coffee to help mom and dad keep up with them.

Berkeley

Anna's, 1801 University Ave at Grant ☎510/849-2662. A local institution, thanks to owner Anna de Leon's prominent involvement with city politics; relax in one of the space's plush sofas with a hot tea or coffee and you might catch one of her regular singing gigs.

Café Fanny, 1603 San Pablo, Berkeley ☎510/524-5447. Delicious and relatively cheap breakfasts or soup-and-salad lunches in a small and unlikely space with a sparse industrial decor. Owned by Alice Waters, of *Chez Panisse* fame, insuring that the food is a cut above the average lunch-counter fare.

Café Intermezzo, 2442 Telegraph Ave at Dwight ☎510/849-4592. A perennial favorite among budget-conscious Berkeley students. You get a hunk of homemade wholewheat bread and a gigantic salad with lots of toppings at a price no one can argue with.

Café Mediterraneum, 2475 Telegraph Ave, Berkeley ☎510/841-5634. Berkeley's oldest café, straight out of the Beat archives: beards and berets optional, battered paperbacks de rigueur.

Café Milano, 2522 Bancroft Way, Berkeley ☎510/644-3100. Airy, arty café across from UC Berkeley. Grad students fill the place, and their creative output hangs on the walls.

Café Strada, 2300 College Ave, Berkeley ☎510/843-5282. Upmarket, open-air café where art and architecture students cross paths with would-be lawyers and chess wizards.

Yogurt Park, 2433a Durant Ave, Berkeley ☎510/549-0570. Frozen yogurt is, obviously, the specialty; open until midnight for the student throngs.

Oakland

Coffee Mill, 3363 Grand Ave, Oakland ☎510/465-4224. Spacious room that doubles as an art gallery, and often hosts poetry readings.

Dreyers Grand Ice Cream Parlor, 5925 College Ave, Oakland ☎510/658-0502. Oakland's own rich ice cream – which is also distributed throughout California – is served at this small, slightly dull Rockridge café.

Fenton's Creamery, 4226 Piedmont Ave, North Oakland ☎510/658-7000. A brightly lit 1950s ice cream and sandwich shop, popular as much for its good basic lunch fare as its ice cream and decor.

Mama Bear's, 6536 Telegraph Ave, North Oakland ☎510/428-9684. Mainly a women's bookstore, it doubles as a café and meeting place and has regular readings, often for women only, by lesbian and feminist writers.

Royal Ground, 6255 College Ave, Oakland ☎510/653-5458. Bright, modern and relaxing spot in the Rockridge area, with outdoor seating.

Peninsula

Café de Matisse, 371 First St, San Jose ☎408/298-7788. Modern art hangs on the walls of this funky artist studio space, which serves fresh coffee and pastries.

Café at Printer's Inc, 320 California Ave, Palo Alto ☎650/323-3347. Good food and coffee, adjacent to Palo Alto's best bookstore.

Caffe Verona, 236 Hamilton Ave, Palo Alto ☎650/326-9942. Relaxing hangout for Palo Alto's intellectual crowd.

M Coffee, 522 Main St, Half Moon Bay ☎650/726-6241. Coffees, teas, sandwiches, and ice cream in a small, homey eatery.

Marin

Café Trieste, 1000 Bridgeway, Sausalito ☎415/332-7770. This distant relative of

Restaurants and cafés

Restaurant prices

The restaurants have been coded using the following key. **Price** represents the approximate cost for a three-course meal for one person, not including wine, tax, or tip.

Budget	under $10	Moderate	$20–40
Inexpensive	$10–20	Expensive	over $40

San Francisco's North Beach institution serves good coffee, a wide menu of pastas and salads, and great gelato.

Caledonia Kitchen, 400 Caledonia St, Sausalito ☎415/331-0220. Relaxing, cheery café serving simple sandwiches, fresh pastries, and a variety of salads across from a small park.

Depot Bookstore and Café, 87 Throckmorton Ave, Mill Valley ☎415/383-2665. Sharing space inside an old train station with a bookstore and newsstand, this lively café hosts weekly readings from local and nationally known authors.

Fairfix Café, 33 Broadway, Fairfax ☎415/459-6404. Excellent Mediterranean food with occasional evening poetry readings.

Java Rama, 546 San Anselmo Ave, San Anselmo ☎415/453-5282. Specialty coffees and pastries along with modern rock on the stereo attracts a young crowd.

New Morning Café, 1696 Tiburon Blvd, Tiburon ☎415/435-4315. Lots of healthy wholegrain sandwiches, plus salads and omelettes.

Sweden House, 35 Main St, Tiburon ☎415/435-9767. Great coffee and marvelous pastries on a jetty overlooking the yacht harbor, all at surprisingly reasonable prices.

Wine Country

Alexis Baking Company, 1517 Third St, Napa ☎707/258-1827. Fancy food shop and coffee bar.

The Model Bakery, 1357 Main St, St Helena ☎707/963-8162. A bakery serving good soups and lunches.

Restaurants

Even if it often seems swamped by more fashionable regional and ethnic cuisine, traditional **American cooking** can be found all over the Bay Area.

California Cuisine, based around "the cult of the ingredient," is raved about by foodies – and rightly so, especially in Berkeley, its acknowledged birthplace and home to a not-to-be-missed "Gourmet Ghetto." Basically a development of French *nouvelle cuisine*, utilizing the wide mix of fresh, locally available foods, California Cuisine is a healthy and aesthetically pleasing alternative, which doesn't fool around too much with the ingredients themselves. In San Francisco, many restaurants foster close relationships with individual growers and farmers, with produce basically coming straight from the fields, resulting in fresh portions and, quite often, very high prices – not unusually $50 and up a head for a full dinner with wine. At some bistro-style places, however, or even bars of high-end restaurants, you can do much better pricewise. To whet your appetite, typically California Cuisine might be dishes like cracker-crusted pizza with shrimp and arugula, seared ahi-tuna salad with wontons and wasabi lime aioli, grilled goat's cheese wrapped in grape leaves, or gratin of crab and sea urchin. San Franciscan chefs being the innovators that they are, it's standard procedure to **combine** culinary styles – Asian with French, for example – and it is often very difficult to categorize restaurants ethnically. Rather than stay rooted in one tradition, most chefs utilize the myriad variety of talent and produce available in the Bay Area, creating something peculiarly San Franciscan.

Restaurants and cafés

Late night diners

For a town that claims to like to party as much as San Francisco does, the city shuts pretty early, and it can be hard to find a snack at 3 or 4 am. The following exceptions will do in a pinch.

Bagdad Café, 2295 Market St at 16th, Castro ☎415/621-4434. Only open until midnight, but probably the best option on this end of town, for both charm and value.

International House of Pancakes, 2299 Lombard St at Pierce, Marina ☎415/921-4004. All-night chain specializing in pancakes, waffles, and breakfasts, but serving burgers, shrimp, and steaks as well.

Lori's Diner, 336 Mason St at Geary and O'Farrell, downtown ☎415/392-8646. Longstanding 24hr diner two blocks from Union Square, selling breakfast, omelettes, burgers, and sandwiches.

Mel's Diner, 2165 Lombard St at Fillmore, Marina ☎415/921-3039. Retro diner filled with pretty Marina people who get the munchies after the bars and clubs close. Open until 3am weekends and 1am weeknights.

Orphan Andy's, 3991 17th St at Market and Castro, Castro ☎415/864-9795. Popular neighborhood 24hr diner, though a bit pricey.

Pine Crest, 401 Geary Blvd at Mason, downtown ☎415/885-6407. Moderately downbeat greasy spoon 24hr diner filled with hardscrabble Tenderloin residents and tourists from the local hotels.

Sparky's, 242 Church St at 15th, Castro ☎415/621-6001. Service with attitude and a very standard menu at inflated prices, but in the wee hours, this 24hr diner is the only thing hopping on the block.

Mexican food is so common it often seems like (and historically is) an indigenous cuisine. Certainly, in the Mission district you can't go more than a couple of doorways without encountering a Mexican restaurant. What's more, day or night, it's the least expensive type of food to eat; even a full dinner with a few drinks rarely costs over $10 anywhere, except in the most upmarket establishment.

Other ethnic cuisines are plentiful, too. **Chinese**, **Thai**, and **Vietnamese** food are everywhere, and can often cost as little as Mexican; **Japanese** is more expensive and more trendy, sushi being worshipped by some Californians. **Italian** food is popular everywhere, above all in **North Beach**, but can be expensive once you leave the simple pastas and explore exotic pizza toppings or specialist regional cuisine. Ultra-thin-crust pizzas fired in a wood oven are the most recent rage, and are often reasonably priced even in the more expensive joints. **French** food, too, is widely available, though always pricey – the cuisine of social climbers and power-lunchers. **Indian** restaurants, on the other hand, are thin on the ground and often very expensive – though the situation is slowly changing for the better, with a sprinkling of moderately priced outlets, particularly in West Berkeley.

Not surprisingly, health-conscious San Francisco also has a wide range of **vegetarian** and **wholefood** restaurants, and in general, it's rare to find a menu anywhere that doesn't have at least several meat-free items (see box, p.248).

During the week, Bay Area restaurants outside San Francisco cater more to the locals and less to tourists, so exploring the many eateries there provides an authentic taste of neighborhood foods at what tend to be more reasonable prices. In particular, breakfast- and brunch-oriented cafés and diners are full of character, though they rarely take reservations and usually command a line of hungry customers awaiting seats.

Finally, remember that the vineyards of the Napa and Sonoma valleys are on the city's doorstep and produce prize-fighting

Restaurants and cafés

grapes that are good – and cheap – enough to make European wine growers nervous. Quality **wine** is a high-profile and standard feature of most San Franciscan restaurants.

In the listings that follow, the restaurants are arranged by neighborhood and thereafter by cuisine. Use the keys on the district maps for quick reference.

Downtown and Chinatown

AMERICAN

Aqua, 253 California St at Battery ☎415/956-9662. Gorgeously decorated, with mix-and match decor that varies with the season. Mainly seafood menu pulls in a discerning Financial District crowd who hobnob over seared ahi tuna and prawns. *Expensive.*

Bix, 56 Gold St at Montgomery ☎415/433-6300. The after-work crowd comes early for the bar, and music fans slip in later for the supper club where the old-fashioned dishes, such as filet mignon or roast chicken, are as rich as the jazzy setting. *Expensive.*

Clown Alley, 42 Columbus at Jackson ☎415/421-2540. Giant clown murals on

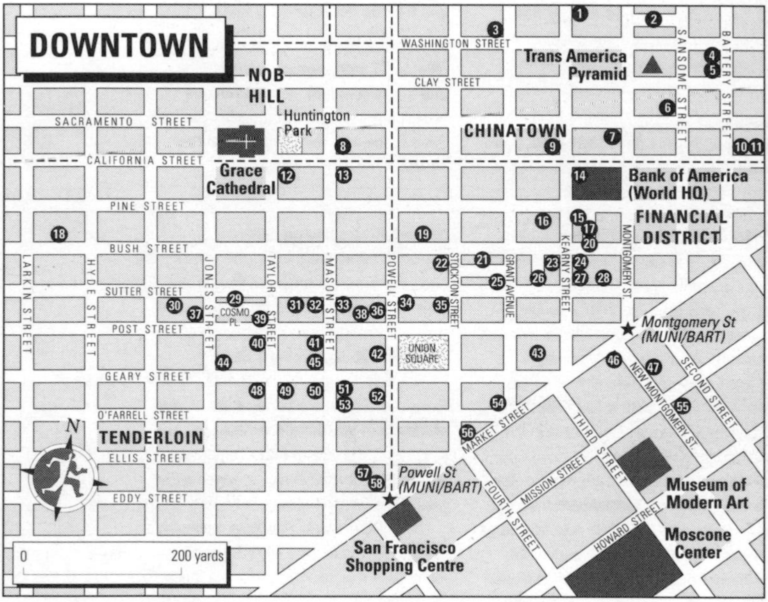

DOWNTOWN

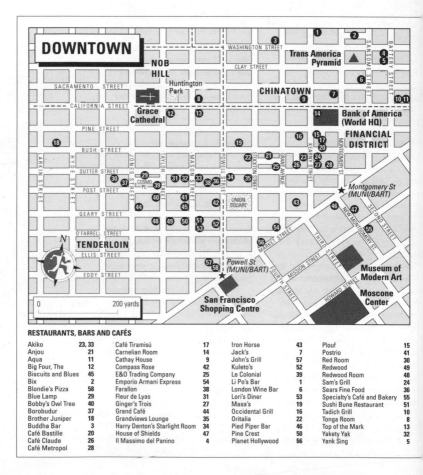

RESTAURANTS, BARS AND CAFÉS

Akiko	23, 33	Café Tiramisú	17	Iron Horse	43	Plouf	15
Anjou	21	Carnelian Room	14	Jack's	7	Postrio	41
Aqua	11	Cathay House	9	John's Grill	57	Red Room	30
Big Four, The	12	Compass Rose	42	Kuleto's	52	Redwood	49
Biscuits and Blues	45	E&O Trading Company	25	Le Colonial	39	Redwood Room	48
Bix	2	Emporio Armani Express	54	Li Po's Bar	1	Sam's Grill	24
Blondie's Pizza	58	Farallon	38	London Wine Bar	6	Sears Fine Food	36
Blue Lamp	29	Fleur de Lyas	31	Lori's Diner	53	Specialty's Café and Bakery	55
Bobby's Owl Tree	40	Ginger's Trois	27	Masa's	19	Sushi Bune Restaurant	51
Borobudur	37	Grand Café	44	Occidental Grill	16	Tadich Grill	10
Brother Juniper	18	Grandviews Lounge	35	Oritalia	22	Tonga Room	8
Buddha Bar	3	Harry Denton's Starlight Room	34	Pied Piper Bar	46	Top of the Mark	13
Café Bastille	20	House of Shields	47	Pine Crest	50	Yakety Yak	32
Café Claude	26	Il Massimo del Panino	4	Planet Hollywood	56	Yank Sing	5
Café Metropol	28						

the walls and a staff of tattooed toughs make this an appealingly odd spot for a burger and fries. *Budget.*

Harry Denton's Bar & Grill, 161 Steuart St at Howard ☎415/882-1333. Lively saloon atmosphere with a great cocktail bar and hearty brasserie-style cuisine. *Inexpensive.*

Iron Horse, 19 Maiden Lane at Kearny ☎415/362-8133. Wood-paneled men's-club atmosphere and hearty traditional American fare in a quaint alley off of Union Square. There's a takeout window at lunch hour. *Inexpensive.*

Jack's, 615 Sacramento St at Montgomery ☎415/421-7355. Open since 1864, and while the heart-stopping roast meats have kept them in business, it's the mimosas that made *Jack's* famous – legend has it that Alfred Hitchcock invented it here. *Expensive.*

John's Grill, 63 Ellis St at Powell ☎415/986-0669. Dashiell Hammett was such a regular at this meat-and-potatoes joint that he gave it a free plug in *The Maltese Falcon.* Noir fans have been flocking ever since. *Inexpensive.*

MacArthur Park, 607 Front St at Jackson ☎415/398-5700. Gathering place for young business types who seem to have stepped out of the frat house and into a corner office. The food is basic American at bull-market prices. *Inexpensive.*

Sears Fine Food, 439 Powell St at Post ☎415/986-1160. A classic breakfast joint with a hearty old-fashioned ambience. Try the big plate of tiny pancakes. *Budget.*

Tadich Grill, 240 California St at Battery ☎415/391-1849. One of the oldest restaurants in town, this traditional steak house oozes class from every inch of its wood-panel and brick walls. Expect power ties and old money, to go along with the grilled seafood and thick cuts of meat. *Expensive.*

Restaurants and cafés

Afternoon Tea

One of the nicest ways to finish an afternoon of intense consuming in the downtown stores is to partake of afternoon tea in one of the plush Union Square hotels. In true California style, the food is exquisite, and you'll be offered the gamut from cucumber and watercress sandwiches to fresh fruit sorbets and scones with cream.

Compass Rose, 335 Powell St ☎415/774-0167. Upscale nibbles, California Cuisine style, is what sets this tea service apart from the rest. Served daily from 3–5pm.

Garden Court, at the *Sheraton Palace*, 2 New Montgomery St at Market ☎415/392-8600. This landmark hotel recently restored its exquisite lobby, where you can sip fine teas while enjoying the soothing live harp music. Make reservations, it fills up. Wed–Sat 2–4.30pm & Sun 2–3.30pm.

Imperial Tea Court, 1411 Powell St at Broadway ☎415/788-6080. A traditional Chinese tea house, with decor evocative of old Shanghai. Open daily 11am–6.30pm.

King George Hotel, 334 Mason St between Geary and O'Farrell ☎415/781-5050. A Laura Ashley nightmare, where customers nibble at finger sandwiches in mock-British cottage surroundings. Only for Anglophiles and homesick Brits. Tues–Sun 3–6.30pm.

Mark Hopkins, 999 California St ☎415/392-3434. Standard high teas, served on lovely Wedgwood china by white-jacketed waiters. Mon–Fri 3–5pm.

Neiman Marcus, 150 Stockton St ☎415/362-3900. Tea is served in the glorious *Rotunda* restaurant at the top of the store. Watch the social butterflies nibble fearfully at the calorie-laden food. Daily 2.30–5pm.

Ritz-Carlton, 600 Stockton St ☎415/296-7465. The fanciest of them all, this is the place to slurp tea to the accompaniment of a tinkling harp. Mon–Fri 2.30–4.30pm, Sat & Sun 1–4.30pm.

Restaurants and cafés

CALIFORNIA

Cypress Club, 500 Jackson St at Montgomery ☎415/296-8555. Jackson Square hot spot known for its delicately presented, inventive California cooking, served up in an incredibly stylish dining room – a cross between the *Ritz-Carlton* and a Bedouin tent. With live jazz nightly. *Moderate*.

Farallon, 450 Post St at Powell ☎415/956-6969. Probably the most spectacular dining room in the city, done up in a visually dramatic underwater theme with elaborate draping glass lamps shaped like jellyfish and sea urchins. Even if you can't afford the pricey seafood entrees, it's worth a stop to have a drink at the bar. *Moderate*.

Oritalia, 590 Bush St ☎415/346-1333. A fusion trend-setter that's been rather eclipsed by its successors, serving light Italian with an inventive eastern-fusion flair, such as spicy beef carpaccio with gingered tomato confit and burdock salad. *Expensive*.

Postrio, 545 Post St at Mason ☎415/776-7825. Though Wolfgang Puck's name on the marquee adds celebrity value, the real draw here is the ambience, thanks to three floors offering entirely different dining experiences, from intimate elegance to casual cocktails. Prices for all three options are surprisingly moderate. *Moderate*.

Waterfront Café, at *Pier 7*, Embarcadero at Broadway ☎415/391-2696. Really two restaurants in one. Upstairs is ritzier, thanks to a recent high-profile makeover, while the more casual downstairs offers top-notch seafood. Bay views from either. *Moderate–expensive*.

CHINESE

Chef Jia's, 925 Kearny St at Columbus ☎415/398-1626. Just a couple of doors down from the *House of Nanking*, they serve quick, tasty, and cheap specialties that, if not quite equal to the offerings of its famous neighbor, is a decent substitute when the queue at *Nanking* gets too long. *Budget*.

Empress of China, 838 Grant Ave at Clay ☎415/434-1345. The grand-dame of Chinatown restaurants, serving better-than-average food in an antique-filled setting offering a lovely view over North Beach. Naturally, the prices match the setting. *Moderate*.

Gold Mountain, 644 Broadway at Jackson ☎415/296-7733. Not the best Chinese food in town, but there's always room to sit down for a quick meal or dim sum on weekends in the vast dining room. *Inexpensive*.

Great Eastern, 649 Jackson at Kearny ☎415/986-2500. Behind an impressive pagoda facade, this rather elegant, traditional Chinese restaurant serves some unusual dishes, like the excellent turtle soup. *Inexpensive*.

Harbor Village, 4 Embarcadero Center ☎415/781-8833. Downtown's best dim sum, served seven days a week, but especially popular on Sundays. Dinners are fresh classic Cantonese dishes, but don't expect much in the way of service besides a passing cart. *Inexpensive*.

House of Nanking, 919 Kearny at Jackson ☎415/421-1429. This tiny spot has become a legend: expect a long but rapidly moving queue, curt service, and a fabulous, underpriced meal. Those in the know let the waiters do the ordering for them. *Budget*.

Kowloon, 909 Grant Ave at Washington ☎415/362-9888. This tiny storefront dim sum house also serves sit-down meals and specializes in delicious vegetarian dishes made with seitan and wheat gluten. *Budget*.

Lotus Garden, 532 Grant at Bush. ☎415/982-3656. Run by a Taoist sect, this legendary vegetarian restaurant is situated one floor beneath a temple. Try the plate of mock vegetarian meats for a unusual and copious appetizer. *Budget*.

Lucky Creation, 854 Washington at Waverly ☎415/989-0818. Another Chinatown vegetarian option, with imaginative faux-meat dishes created from tofu and wheat gluten. Try the assorted glutens to see how far-fetched things can get. *Budget.*

Pot Sticker, 150 Waverly Place, off Clay St between Stockton and Grant ☎415/397-9985. Extensive menu offering your average Szechuan and Hunan dishes in this inexpensive, touristy Chinatown joint. Basic and plain but quick. *Budget.*

Sam Woh, 813 Washington St at Grant ☎415/982-0596. Popular late-night spot where Kerouac, Ginsberg, and others used to hold court. The food is mediocre, and the service famously brusque. Walk through the kitchen and up the cramped stairs to reach the dining room. *Budget.*

Yank Sing, 427 Battery St at Clay ☎415/781-1111. One of the better places for dim sum in the city. Despite being routinely packed during lunch hours, the waitstaff can almost always find a spot for you in the seemingly endless warren of dining rooms. *Inexpensive.*

Yuet Lee, 1300 Stockton St at Broadway ☎415/982-6020. Beckoning passersby with an exceedingly bright green exterior and rewarding those who venture inside with superior – albeit pricey – fish and seafood dishes. Open until 3am. *Inexpensive.*

FRENCH

Anjou, 44 Campton Place at Post ☎415/392-5373. Serving a bargain-priced prix-fixe lunch menu, it draws a steady downtown lunch crowd. Things become considerably more sedate during dinner hours. *Inexpensive.*

Café Bastille, 22 Belden Place at Bush ☎415/986-5673. Moderately priced French sandwiches, salads, and crepes in a French bistro setting, especially popular with the downtown lunch crowd. *Inexpensive.*

Café Claude, 7 Claude Lane at Sutter ☎415/392-3505. Down an alley from Union Square and with prices that are a cut below the competition for equal quality. On a warm evening, with a live band playing music outdoors, it can seem almost like you're in Paris. *Inexpensive.*

Fleur de Lys, 777 Sutter St at Taylor ☎415/673-7779. Romantic French restaurant with a pristine white tablecloth and candlelit setting where you'll have to book in advance – and be prepared to drop a wad of money. *Expensive.*

Grand Café, 580 Geary St at Jones ☎415/441-8080. This oversized continental dining room is a last refuge of elegance overlooking the seedy slopes of the Tenderloin, serving classic dishes such as braised beef cheeks. The service and food are a cut above, though the visually striking tile and stone-column decor can amplify the noise. *Expensive.*

Masa's, 648 Bush St at Stockton ☎415/989-7154. The fine cuisine gets it on most of the "best French restaurants in the country" lists – with four and five course prix-fixe meals hovering near $100 per person before wine, you would expect as much. *Expensive.*

Plouf, 40 Belden Lane at Bush ☎415/986-6491. The higher-priced bistro on Belden Lane, with a particular focus on Southern French seafood dishes and an airy café atmosphere. *Moderate.*

GREEK

Kokkari Estiatorio, 200 Jackson St at Front ☎415/981-0983. By far, the best Greek restaurant in town. Though the decor is purely Northern California, the cuisine is classic Greek, relying on staples such as lamb and eggplant, served both separately and cooked together as moussaka. *Moderate.*

ITALIAN

Blondie's, 63 Powell St at Ellis ☎415/982-6168. The doughy pizza at this hole in the wall is certainly nothing to write home about, but it wins points for convenience. *Budget.*

Café Tiramisu, 28 Belden Place at Bush ☎415/421-7044. The name makes it tempting to skip straight to dessert, but this hideaway also makes light

Restaurants and cafés

Restaurants and cafés

Mediterranean-style pasta dishes that are worth a detour. *Inexpensive.*

Il Massimo del Panino, 441 Washington St at Sansome ☎415/834-0290. Down the street from the Transamerica Building, but more importantly, next door to the Instituto Italiana di Cultura, which means they had better get their details right. The salads and grilled panini prove they do. *Budget.*

Kuleto's, 221 Powell St at O'Farrell ☎415/397-7720. Entertaining the pre-theater crowd with hearty pastas – try the gorgonzola tortellini with radicchio – and a dramatic centerpiece taken from the historic *Palace Hotel. Moderate.*

JAPANESE

Akiko, 431 Bush St at Kearny ☎415/397-3218 or 542 Mason St at Post ☎415/989-8218. Two tiny locations in remote corners of Union Square offer the lucky few who can squeeze in the chance to sample inexpensive, yet first rate and fresh sushi. *Inexpensive.*

Sushi Bune, 389 Geary St at Mason ☎415/781-5111. At the center of this sushi bar there's a small canal on which your food comes drifting by on little boats. Not the best sushi in town, but the gimmick keeps this little place bobbing along. *Inexpensive.*

SOUTHEAST ASIAN

Borobudur, 700 Post St at Jones ☎415/775-1512. A little pocket of authentic Indonesia, just a couple of blocks from Union Square. Thick curries, which mix Indian and Thai influences, are particularly good. Come early to avoid the karaoke. *Budget.*

Le Colonial, 20 Cosmo Place at Taylor ☎415/931-3600. Traditional Vietnamese curries and light, uncooked spring rolls, followed by French crème caramel. *Moderate.*

North Beach and Nob Hill

AMERICAN

Fog City Diner, 1300 Battery St at Embarcadero ☎415/982-2000. Near the hysterics of Fisherman's Wharf, this classic diner with its shiny facade serves the usual burgers and fries. *Inexpensive.*

Harris' Restaurant, 2100 Van Ness at Pacific ☎415/673-1888. Proudly proclaiming itself the city's best steak house – with the prices to match. Everything about the setting is simple and elegant, leaving nothing to distract you from a choice cut of meat. *Moderate.*

Yabbie's, 2237 Polk St at Green ☎415/474-4088. Shellfish of every variety served in every way imaginable, though oysters chilled on the half shell are the specialty. The grilled sea bass or tuna entrees are also good. *Moderate.*

CALIFORNIA

Bistro Zare, 1507 Polk at California ☎415/775-4304. Right on the border between Nob Hill and the Tenderloin, well-prepared, pan-Mediterranean specialties. *Moderate.*

Globe, 290 Pacific at Battery ☎415/391-4132. Open late, this industrial-chic spot is the place where chefs go after work to get *their* dinner. Meat and fish entrees, grilled or from the wood oven, are universally fresh and savory. *Moderate.*

mc2, 470 Pacific at Montgomery ☎415/956-0666. The masterminds behind this upscale spot supposedly spent upwards of $1 million on the decor alone, sprucing up an already striking Barbary Coast brick structure. Don't worry – they didn't decide to save any money on groceries either. Entrees tend toward the francophilic, with rabbit, duck, and sweatbreads all featured in simple yet precise presentations. *Expensive.*

FRENCH

Charles Nob Hill, 1250 Jones St at Clay ☎415/771-5400. Head chef Ron Siegel rocketed to international celebrity status after he appeared on the cult Japanese cooking/game show *Iron Chef*, a sort of cooking demolition derby. In his own

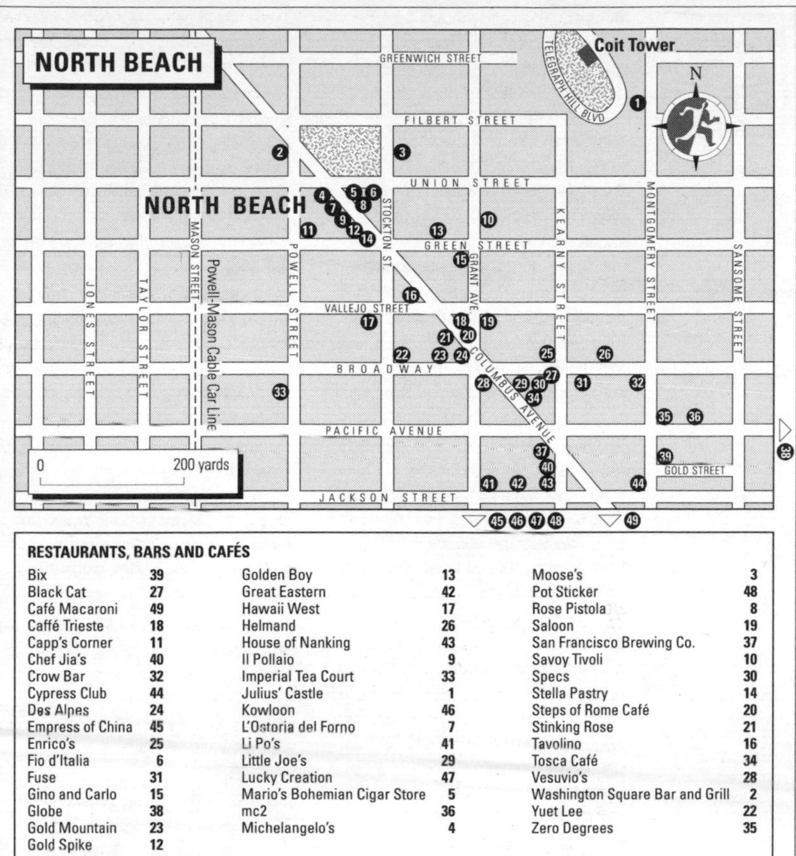

kitchen, Siegel prefers to keep things simple, mixing tired and true French preparations with fresh local ingredients. *Expensive.*

Des Alpes Basque Restaurant, 732 Broadway at Columbus ☎415/391-4249. Serves a seven-course menu of heartily sauced meat and potatoes and other continental comfort food. *Inexpensive.*

Julius' Castle, 1541 Montgomery at Telegraph Hill ☎415/392-2222. One of the most romantic restaurants in town, thanks to an enchanting cliffside view of the bay and a dose of Gallic charm. Not the top French spot in town, but the California-ized Provençal cooking is more than a match for the scenery. *Expensive.*

La Folie, 2316 Polk St at Green ☎415/776-5577. The classic Lyonnais cuisine is done to a perfection which you'll pay for, but the whimsical atmosphere has a sense of humor about the whole business, as does the non-pretentious staff. *Expensive.*

Matterhorn, 2323 Van Ness Ave at Vallejo ☎415/885-6116. An array of meat and cheese fondues served in a kitschy Swiss chalet setting. *Moderate.*

Restaurants and cafés

Moose's, 1652 Stockton at Filbert ☎415/989-7800. The latest word in power-lunching for the media-politico crowd. Rich chops and roast meats served in a men's-club environment. *Expensive.*

Pastis, 1015 Battery St at Green ☎415/391-2555. A stylish but relaxed atmosphere just off Levi's Plaza near Embarcadero, where the well-executed French Basque dishes – including quail and foie-gras – are every bit as good as those you'll find in more centrally located addresses but a tad less pricey. *Moderate.*

Washington Square Bar and Grill, 1707 Powell St at Union ☎415/982-8123. It may have lost a little of its caché over the years, but the luster remains: for the scotch and cigar set, the old-fashioned paneled main room is still the place to sip cocktails by the bar and sample braised meats cooked to rich and heavy perfection. *Moderate.*

ITALIAN

Albona Ristorante Istriano, 545 Francisco at Mason ☎415/441-1040. In a far-off corner of North Beach, near Fisherman's Wharf, and serving the Slavic-influenced food of Trieste combined with creamy Northern Italian dishes like lasagna and gnocchi. *Moderate.*

Black Cat, 501 Broadway at Kearny ☎415/981-2233. The latest creation of local restaurant mogul Reed Hearon (*Lulu's* and *Rose Pistola*) is a combination nightclub, lounge, and restaurant. The result is glitzy, if a bit all over the map – the menu runs from ravioli to dim sum. For snacks and live jazz, head downstairs to the *Blue Bar. Moderate.*

Café Macaroni, 59 Columbus Ave at Jackson ☎415/956-9737. Cramped space serving an extensive menu of well-made antipasti and main courses at close to budget prices. Even if they can't squeeze you in the door, the friendly staff is always welcoming. *Inexpensive.*

Capp's Corner, 1600 Powell St at Green ☎415/989-2589. While most of North Beach has gone noticeably upscale, *Capp's* can make you a heaping plate of old-fashioned pasta to fit a tight budget. *Inexpensive.*

Enrico's, 504 Broadway at Kearny ☎415/982-6223. Though its days as a comedy club are probably gone for good, this intrepid North Beach spot retains a spirited atmosphere and above-average cooking. *Inexpensive.*

Fior d'Italia, 601 Union St at Stockton ☎415/986-1886. Claiming (a bit dubiously) to be the oldest Italian restaurant in the US, *Fior* maintains a deliberately old-fashioned aura with bow-tied waiters practically bowing after taking your order. *Moderate.*

The Gold Spike, 527 Columbus Ave at Green ☎415/986-9747. A beloved institution: filled with memorabilia dating back to the begining of the twentieth century, this down-home spot serves hearty meats and pastas, without any fuss. *Inexpensive.*

Golden Boy, 542 Green St at Columbus ☎415/982-9738. As snack offerings in North Beach are fairly limited, this skinny little hole in the wall, serving simple square slices of pizza, is a haven for afternoon and late-night cravings. *Budget.*

Il Forniao, 1265 Battery at Greenwich ☎415/986-0100. Hidden from the crowds at Fisherman's Wharf by a bend in the Embarcadero, and serving better food at lower prices than the nearby tourist traps, this Italian bakery makes flavorful sandwiches with homemade bread. *Budget.*

Il Polliao, 555 Columbus Ave at Union ☎415/362-7727. You'd be hard-pressed to spend more than $15 for a blowout meal at this postage stamp-sized roast-chicken restaurant, where sheer value more than makes up for the lack of elbow room. *Inexpensive.*

Little Joe's, 523 Broadway at Columbus ☎415/433-4343. Food worth singing about – at least the cooks think so. In truth, the pastas are average, but the kitchen staff puts on quite a show:

shouting, banging, and flinging pots about with happy abandon. *Inexpensive.*

L'Osteria del Forno, 519 Columbus at Green ☎415/982-1124. They don't do much, but what they do, they do very well. This exceedingly simple kitchen specializes in pizzas and baked sandwiches, with only one or two pasta specials nightly. *Inexpensive.*

Maye's Oyster House, 1233 Polk at Bush ☎415/474-7674. The self-proclaimed second-oldest restaurant in town still serves classic seafood dishes like oysters Rockefeller, along with hearty Italian dishes. *Moderate.*

Michelangelo's, 579 Columbus at Union ☎415/986-4056. A cool triangular space, with bare walls and sharp angles, where the rich pastas and salads offer a comforting contrast. No reservations, so expect a wait. *Inexpensive.*

Rose Pistola, 532 Columbus at Green ☎415/399-0499. Local restaurateur Reed Haron's popular venture serves light, flavorful California-style Italian antipasti – snack-like servings that are meant to encourage sampling and experimentation. *Moderate.*

The Stinking Rose, 325 Columbus at Broadway ☎415/781-7673. If you're fond of their gimmick, you'll leave happy; otherwise, you might be in for indigestion: nearly every dish, including the desserts, features garlic as the prime ingredient. The romantic decor does a bit to override the restaurant's potent smell. *Moderate.*

Tavolino, 401 Columbus Ave at Vallejo ☎415/392-1472. A terrific spot for people-watching, not just because of the wonderful view of Columbus St, but because the first-rate finger food will have you more than happy to linger. *Inexpensive.*

SOUTHEAST ASIAN

The Golden Turtle, 2211 Van Ness Ave at Broadway ☎415/441-4419. Located in a stately Victorian mansion set back from the street and offering light Vietnamese cooking that balances the cool flavors of cucumbers and mint with spicy hot soups and curries. *Inexpensive.*

The northern waterfront and Pacific Heights

AMERICAN

Belle Roux, 2801 Leavenworth at Beach ☎415/771-5225. The fake swamp-hut look of this Cajun restaurant is pretty silly, but the quality is a cut above most of the Fisherman's Wharf tourist traps, with good gumbo and blackened catfish. *Inexpensive.*

Bistro Aix, 3340 Steiner at Chestnut ☎415/202-0100. On Sundays through Thursdays *Aix* offers a two-course prix-fixe menu, including a sizeable appetizer and a well-made entree such as roast chicken or fish, for less than the price of an entree at most comparable restaurants. *Inexpensive.*

Café Florio, 1915 Fillmore St at Pine ☎415/775-4300. Unusually posh bistro serving basic steak-frites dinners. If you're in need of a hefty French meal, dodge the power-tie types and step into the copper and wood interior. *Inexpensive.*

Doidge's, 2217 Union St at Fillmore ☎415/921-2149. One of the most popular weekend brunch spots in town. Locals will drive all the way across town for the fabulous biscuits and eggs Benedict. *Inexpensive.*

Elite Café, 2049 Fillmore at California ☎415/346-8668. Believe the first half of the name. This expensive Cajun restaurant and bar can get frighteningly packed, though it's often easier to sit down for dinners of buttery blackened catfish and thick gumbo than it is to cozy up to the bar for a drink. *Moderate.*

Izzy's Steaks and Chops, 3345 Steiner at Lombard ☎415/563-0487. While Van Ness might boast an impressive array of steak joints, this is *the* spot for top-notch red meat at a moderate price. It's not quite cheap, but with the best grilled meat in town, you're still getting more than you pay for. *Moderate.*

Restaurants and cafés

CALIFORNIA

Betelnut, 2030 Union St at Buchanan ☎415/929-8855. Perpetually packed, this high-volume dining room opens onto the Union St shopping district. While seeing and being seen certainly tops locals' lists, you'll still appreciate the well-presented California-style Asian cuisine, including an array of salads and dumplings, along with exotic main courses such as lychee tea-smoked quail. *Moderate.*

Café Kati, 1963 Sutter St at Fillmore ☎415/775-7313. Top restaurants don't tend to stay hidden for long in food-obsessed San Francisco, and though this tiny restaurant is no exception, its cozy little dining room still makes you feel as if you've stumbled upon a happy secret. They constantly reinvent the globe-trotting menu to surprise even repeat visitors. *Expensive.*

Ella's, 500 Presidio Ave at California ☎415/441-5669. Perhaps the most notorious breakfast wait in town, so put on some comfortable shoes before braving the queue that forms outside for scrumptious Californian interpretations of American classics like mandarin pancakes with mango syrup. *Moderate.*

Greens, Fort Mason Center, Building A ☎415/771-6222. The queen of San Francisco's vegetarian restaurants, thanks to a picturesque setting on a pier at Fort Mason Center that offers spectacular views of the bay. If dinner is too pricey to consider, the Sunday brunch is a terrific way to start out that day. *Moderate.*

Plumpjack Café, 3127 Fillmore at Greenwich ☎415/563-4755. Having helped initiate the craze for Mediterranean-themed dining, Gavin Newsome – a local celebrity and minor politician – also showcases an encyclopedic wine list, including many of his own vintage. *Expensive.*

CHINESE

Dragon Well, 2142 Chestnut St at Steiner ☎415/474-6888. A good lunch option that forgoes the oily standards in favor of light and healthy appetizers and noodle dishes. *Inexpensive.*

INDIAN

Gaylord, in Ghirardell Square, 900 North Point at Larkin ☎415/771-8822. Eating Indian at Fisherman's Wharf is a little like opting for fish and chips in Calcutta. Still, dining on passable tandooris and curries in a lovely setting, several floors above the tumult of tourists can seem oddly appropriate. *Moderate.*

ITALIAN

Columbus Ristorante, 3347 Fillmore at Chestnut ☎415/781-2939. Chef May Ditano has gone against the grain of her posh Marina neighborhood by cre-

Vegetarian restaurants

As you might expect, San Francisco has a number of options for **vegetarians**: most restaurants – however carnivore-friendly – have a number of vegetarian selections, and some of the city's best restaurants are entirely vegetarian, though innovative enough to attract even meat-loving foodies. The following restaurants have been cross-referenced here for their strictly vegetarian theme.

Ganges (Richmond and Sunset)	p.262	**Lucky Creation** (Chinatown)	p.242
Greens (northern waterfront)	above	**Millennium** (Civic Center)	p.252
Herbivore (Mission)	p.255	**Organica** (Sunset)	p.261
Kowloon (Chinatown)	p.242	**Red Crane** (Richmond)	p.261
Lotus Garden (Chinatown)	p.242	**Valentine's** (Noe Valley)	p.255

ating a family-style Italian eatery where you wouldn't feel ashamed tucking your napkin into your shirt before digging into hearty pastas and roasts. *Inexpensive.*

Jackson Fillmore, 2506 Fillmore at Jackson ☎415/346-5288. A casual trattoria serving fresh pasta dishes and salads, at a surprisingly reasonable price considering the upscale neighborhood and clientele. *Inexpensive.*

Mozzarella di Bufala, Fillmore at California ☎415/346-9928. A menu full of fairly standard pizza and pasta is embellished by the unusual addition of some hearty Brazilian entrees, such as chicken with black beans. *Inexpensive.*

Pizza Orgasmica, 3157 Fillmore St at Greenwich ☎415/931-5300. May not quite live up to its name, but this is one of the few spots in the Marina to get a lunch for under five bucks. Pizzas come in both thin- and thick-crust varieties, with a wide array of toppings. *Budget.*

Via Veneto, 2244 Fillmore St at Sacramento ☎415/346-9211. The classics, such as pasta al pesto, of Italian cooking, presented with deference and flair. Resist the temptation to steal the well-designed plates after the meal is over. *Inexpensive.*

Zinzino, 2355 Chestnut at Scott ☎415/346-6623. A rare blend of gourmet cooking and down-home setting, specializing in wood-oven fired thin-crust pizzas, with the exotic toppings, such as pears and gorgonzola, that Californians crave. *Inexpensive.*

JAPANESE

Ace Wasabi, 3339 Steiner at Lombard ☎415/567-4903. Formerly *Kamikaze Sushi*, this place is still fast, cheap, loud, and dishes up a touch of rock 'n' roll attitude with every order, thanks to the voluble crew of goateed hipsters working behind the counter. *Inexpensive.*

MEXICAN

Andale, 2150 Chestnut St at Steiner ☎415/749-0506. This San Francisco installment of a Santa Cruz-based taqueria chain offers standard burrito and tacos; high-quality, fresh ingredients make it a cut above the rest. *Budget.*

Café Marimba, 2317 Chestnut at Scott ☎415/776-1506. While California chefs have spruced up just about every cuisine under the sun, the food of the state's southern neighbor has been curiously underserved. This tasty, yuppified spot gives beans and corn an upscale makeover. *Inexpensive.*

MIDDLE EASTERN

La Méditerranee, 2210 Fillmore St at Sacramento ☎415/921-2956. The small dining room can feel a little like eating in a hallway, but the kitchen compensates with the best falafel, *babaghanouj* and tabouli in town. *Inexpensive.*

SOUTHEAST ASIAN

The Blue Monkey, 2414 Lombard St at Scott ☎415/776-8298. If you can forgive a fondness for cutesy names, the *Monkey* serves Americanizations of Thai dishes such as Pad Thai and *tom yum* soup, which incorporate such distinctly Western ingredients as salmon and cornish game hen. *Inexpensive.*

Irrawaddy, 1769 Lombard St at Octavia ☎415/931-2830. Sink into one of the overstuffed booths to sample some of the best Burmese cuisine in the city. Even if you're familiar with Burmese cooking, the original menu should present numerous discoveries, including a remarkably broad array of curries. *Inexpensive.*

Lhasa Moon, 2420 Lombard St at Scott ☎415/674-9898. Incongruously located on the motel-packed strip of Lombard St, a rare opportunity to sample the cooking of Tibet in a serene atmosphere that seems to invite meditation. Uncooked garlic bread makes for an unusual appetizer and sauteed greens are tart and succulent, though sadly, the traditional accompaniment of yak-butter tea is unavailable. *Inexpensive.*

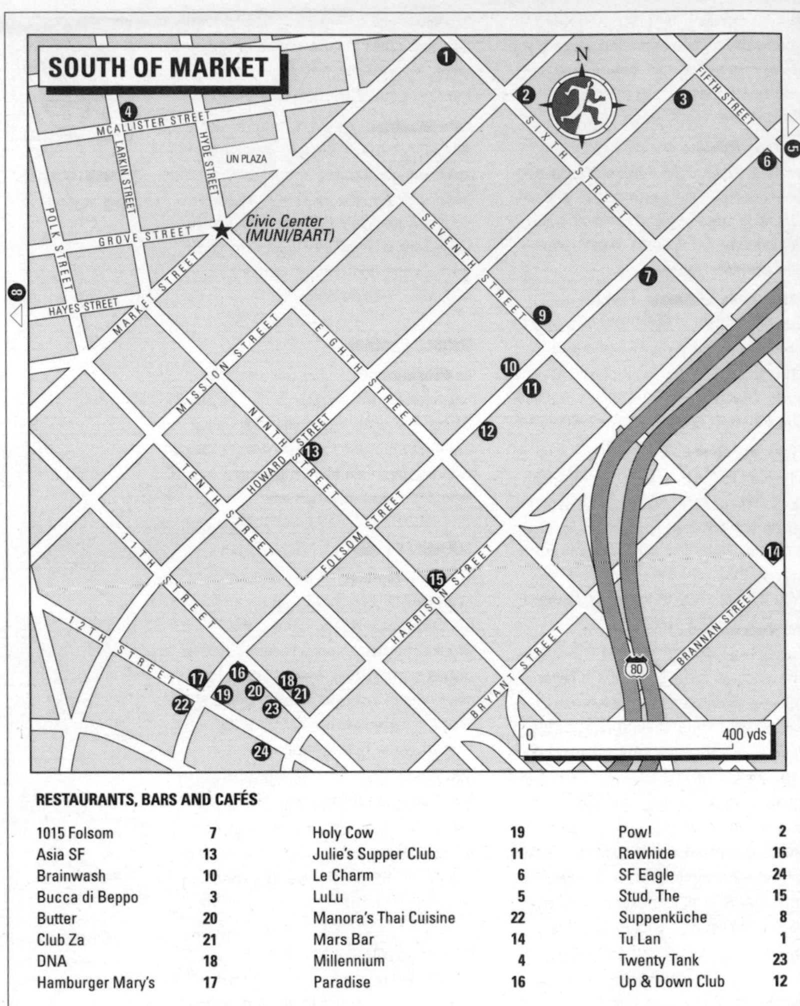

RESTAURANTS, BARS AND CAFÉS

1015 Folsom	7	Holy Cow	19	Pow!	2
Asia SF	13	Julie's Supper Club	11	Rawhide	16
Brainwash	10	Le Charm	6	SF Eagle	24
Bucca di Beppo	3	LuLu	5	Stud, The	15
Butter	20	Manora's Thai Cuisine	22	Suppenküche	8
Club Za	21	Mars Bar	14	Tu Lan	1
DNA	18	Millennium	4	Twenty Tank	23
Hamburger Mary's	17	Paradise	16	Up & Down Club	12

SoMa, the Tenderloin, and Civic Center

AMERICAN

Boulevard, 1 Mission St at Steuart ☎415/563-6084. Situated along the Embarcadero and boasting one of the few wood-exteriors in the downtown vicinity to survive the 1906 fires, this impressive space with its Art Nouveau interior is the setting for Nancy Oakes' classic American cooking, which relies on old-fashioned ingredients such as squash and fennel. *Expensive*.

Delancey Street Restaurant, 600 Embarcadero at Brannan ☎415/512-5179. Comfort food from around the world – from Chinese noodles to burgers – cooked up for a good cause: the restaurant's staff are ex-convicts attempting to get back into life on the right foot. In a classy touch, they serve high tea from 3 until 5 in the afternoon. *Inexpensive.*

Gordon Biersch, 2 Harrison at the Embarcadero ☎415/243-8246. Come for the beer, stay for the food. This brew-pub offshoot of the extremely successful local microbrewery features refined renditions of traditional bar food, such as burgers with blue cheese. *Inexpensive.*

The Grubstake, 1525 Pine St at Polk ☎415/673-8268. Rating four stars for ambience, this old-fashioned diner, housed in a decommissioned cable car, serves all the basics, though the brave go for the meat loaf. *Inexpensive.*

Hamburger Mary's, 1582 Folsom St at 12th ☎415/626-1985. Just the spot to get some starch and red meat in you before heading out for a night of serious drinking. Open late, this boisterous combination bar and restaurant caters to local clubgoers eager to keep the evening hopping. *Budget.*

Hawthorne Lane, 22 Hawthorne Lane at Folsom ☎415/777-9779. There's a certain machismo to the Gold Rush glitz here – though the big test of strength is proving you're tough enough to make it from the elegant Asian-influenced appetizers through the entrees to dessert without busting your gut. For those on a diet or thin in the wallet, the front room café is a lighter, better-value option. *Expensive.*

Infusion, 555 Second St at South Park ☎415/543-2282. A hopping front room bar specializing in fruit-infused vodka martinis hides a dining room where young computer professionals blow their newly minted cash on regional American cooking that has been spiced up with dashes of the fruity vodka. *Moderate.*

Red's Java House, Pier 28, the Embarcadero, no phone. A friendly throwback to the days when San Francisco was a rough and tumble seafaring town. The menu is short and heavy on the grease, but if you're in the mood for a chili dog, this is the place to go. *Budget.*

Swan Oyster Depot, 1517 Polk at California ☎415/673-1101. No frills – and officially, no full meals – at this cheap seafood counter. Grab a stool and hang onto it (it gets crowded and competitive in here) and suck down some cheap shellfish and seafood. *Inexpensive.*

Tommy's Joynt, 1101 Geary Blvd at Van Ness ☎415/775-4216. Serving massive platters of grilled and roasted meat without any California frills. Prepare to eat until the bursting point, since everything here is oversized, and sharing is scowled upon. *Inexpensive.*

BRAZILIAN

Café do Brasil, 1106 Market St at Seventh in the *Renoir Hotel* ☎415/626-6432. Pleasnt family operation dishes out traditional Brazilian meat – *churrasco rodizio* – and fish dishes. Weekends are given over to an all-you-can-eat buffet with grilled meats and salad. *Inexpensive.*

CALIFORNIA

Asia SF, 201 Ninth St at Howard ☎415/255-2742. More of an "experience" than a restaurant, featuring a staff of drag queens who put on a nightly revue during diner. Though it can't compete with the show, the food, if pricey, isn't too bad, either. Try the tuna burgers or duck quesadillas. *Moderate.*

California Culinary Academy, Polk St at Turk ☎415/771-3500. This legendary cooking school's *Careme Room* offers dinner service nightly and a discounted buffet on Fridays from 6 to 8pm. The menu and quality vary wildly, depending on the talent of the students who happen to be doing their homework in the kitchen. *Moderate.*

Fifth Floor, 12 Fourth St ☎415/348-1555. Plush modernist surroundings above the *Hotel Palomar*. One of the latest hot spots for its modern interpretations of French classics like gingersnap-crusted foie gras steak with brandied sour cherries. Reservations essential. *Expensive.*

Restaurants and cafés

Restaurants and cafés

42 Degrees, 235 16th St at Third ☎415/777-5558. Fashionable jazz supper club, in an appealingly remote location down on the old dockyards with a stark modern interior and a well-prepared French, Spanish, and Italian influenced menu. *Expensive*.

Julie's Supper Club, 1123 Folsom St at Seventh ☎415/861-0707. The cuisine, both at the bar and in the backroom restaurant, is a light, eclectic mix of influences, happily upgrading bar snacks such as tostadas and burgers with top-notch ingredients such as duck confit and blood oranges. The decor is straight out of the *Jetsons*. After 9pm there's a cover charge for live jazz, R&B, and retro bands. *Moderate*.

Lulu, 816 Folsom St at Fourth ☎415/495-5775. Thanks largely to its huge dining room and showy open kitchen, which turns out roast meats and Mediterranean sides at a frantic pace, *Lulu* has become a prime spot among multimedia moguls who work in the neighborhood. *Moderate*.

Millennium, 246 McAllister at Larkin ☎415/487-9800. A restaurant to settle many an argument: not only is *Millennium* one of the only vegan (no meat nor dairy) restaurants in town, it's also one of the city's best restaurants, period. Specialties like the savory Thai Napoleon and wild mushroom ragout are to die for, as is the wine list, which features an impressive selection of organic and sulfite-free varietals. *Moderate*.

xyz, 181 Third St at Howard ☎415/817-7836. This imposingly sleek new restaurant near the Yerba Buena Center vicinity serves crisply prepared and well-presented dishes that incorporate unusual ingredients like seaweed and wild greens. *Expensive*.

CHINESE

Long Life Noodle House and Jook Joint, 139 Steuart St at Howard ☎415/281-3818. A jook is a traditional Chinese porridge, made by boiling rice down to a thick broth and then adding meats and vegetables for flavor. They also do more familiar noodle dishes for tamer palates. *Inexpensive*.

FRENCH

Bizou, 598 Fourth St at Brannan ☎415/543-2222. Popular with SoMa trendies thanks to large windows where you can see and be seen. The inexpensive bistro fare, including French staples such as roast duck, lamb, and braised beef cheeks is simple and well-presented. *Moderate*.

Le Charm, 315 Fifth St at Folsom ☎415/546-6128. An unpretentious French bistro sprouting up through SoMa's post-industrial cracks. The light, airy space is easily matched by Southern French bean or fish soups and large, satisfying salads. *Inexpensive*.

South Park Café, 108 South Park at Third ☎415/495-7275. Don't let the name fool you – this is a high-end French bistro and even simple lunches will knock you back a good twenty bucks. But for dinner, the serene setting is appealing. *Moderate*.

INDIAN

Shalimar, 532 Jones St at Geary ☎415/928-0333. A happy find in the otherwise downtrodden Tenderloin. This hole-in-the-wall serves delicious, cheap Indian food, all of it made to order before your eyes, so you know it's fresh. *Budget*.

ITALIAN

Buca di Beppo, 855 Howard St at Fifth ☎415/543-7673. Crammed floor to ceiling with papal knickknacks and photographs, this family-style Italian-theme restaurant is a good spot for entertaining a crowd with a festive atmosphere and plentiful if standard food. *Inexpensive*.

Club Za, 371 11th at Harrison ☎415/552-5599. On the 11th St nightclub strip, this basic pizza joint is nearly vacant for most of the day. Come nightfall, there's often a line of drunken revelers looking for some quick carbohydrates to keep them going. *Budget*.

Ristorante Ecco, 101 South Park St at Jack London Alley ☎415/495-3291. Serving deliciously light and fresh pastas and salads to the newly wealthy South Park multimedia moguls in a cool café atmosphere. *Moderate.*

JAPANESE

Moshi Moshi, 2092 Third St at 17th St ☎415/861-8285. This calm spot is a bit away from everything but serves quality sushi, in addition to a wider-than-usual array of tempura, dumplings, and noodle soups. *Inexpensive.*

Shiki Japanese Restaurant, 251 Third St at Folsom ☎415/512-8138. Across the street from the Yerba Buena Center and specializing in cheap bento boxes of sushi and teriyaki that are perfect for taking to the park. *Budget.*

SOUTHEAST ASIAN

Manora, 1600 Folsom St at 12th ☎415/861-6224. There's no gimmick here beyond light, flavorful Thai cooking of the highest order, such as papaya salad and well prepared soft-shell crab. It's no surprise that the locals keep the place packed night after night. *Inexpensive.*

Tu Lan, 8 Sixth St at Market ☎415/626-0927. A legend ever since Julia Child first sampled the Vietnamese cooking in this cramped, dingy space on one of the seediest blocks in town. Should you sit at the sticky counter, you'll be nearly singed by the flames from the stove. Nevertheless, the food is consistently fresh, authentic, and flavorful. *Budget.*

SPANISH

Thirsty Bear Brewing Company, 661 Howard at New Montgomery ☎415/974-0905. A combination brew-pub and tapas bar. Packed in the evenings, when local workers go to drink and snack their cares away, it makes for an above-average lunch destination for garlicky shrimp and roast potatoes. *Inexpensive.*

The Mission, the Castro, and south

AFRICAN

Baobab, 3388 19th St at Mission ☎415/643-3558. Covering a lot of bases: all-American egg and French toast breakfasts in the morning, West African food, such as fried bananas and fish stew in the evening, and a popular bar later at night. *Inexpensive.*

AMERICAN

Bitterroot, 3122 16th St at Valencia ☎415/626-5523. With picket fences along the street and maps of the old west painted onto the walls, you know you're in for some old-fashioned American grub. This being San Francisco, the sausages are "chicken apple" and the burgers come with real blue cheese instead of processed cheese product. *Inexpensive.*

Blue, 2337 Market St at Noe ☎415/863-2583. Ugly 1980s-style decor offset by homey 1950s-style cooking. Mom's favorites, such as chicken pot pie or chili, get some mild dressing up. But you know a place with a root beer list as long as most's wine lists isn't aiming for snob appeal. *Moderate.*

Boogaloo's, Valencia at 22nd ☎415/824-3211. Every weekend the crowds line up for breakfast outside this fairly basic diner where the staple pancakes and eggs are decent, though often heavy on the grease. Try the vegetarian biscuits and gravy for an unusual twist on down-home comfort food. *Budget.*

Café Cuvée, 2073 Market and Church ☎415/621-7488. Well situated as a hub serving the Mission, Castro, Civic Center, and Lower Haight. The small, sun-filled dining room dishes up mostly Mediterranean soups and salads, though the menu can sometimes stray well beyond that. *Moderate.*

Firefly, 4288 24th St at Douglas ☎415/821-7652. Tucked away in the tree-lined folds of Noe Valley, *Firefly* is a bright spot in an otherwise sleepy neighborhood, offering down-home American

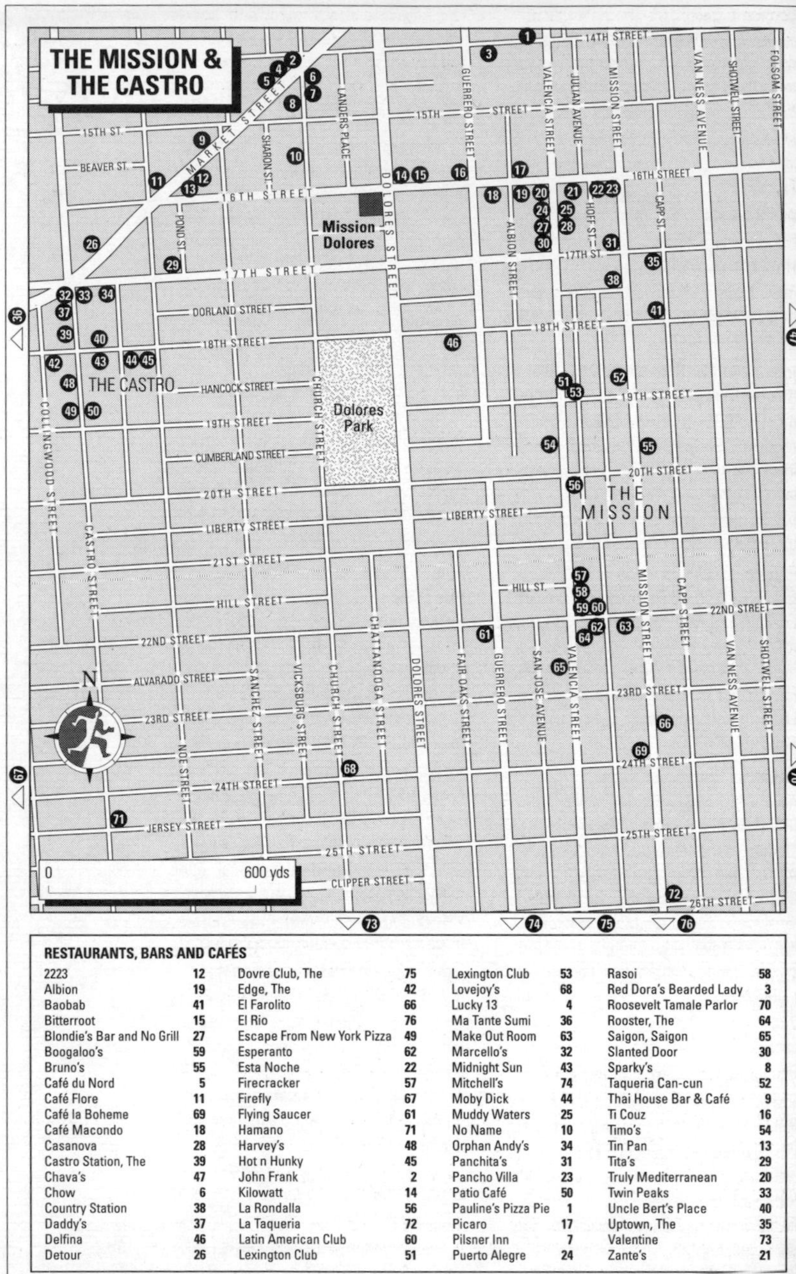

RESTAURANTS, BARS AND CAFÉS

2223	12	Dovre Club, The	75	Lexington Club	53	Rasoi	58
Albion	19	Edge, The	42	Lovejoy's	68	Red Dora's Bearded Lady	3
Baobab	41	El Farolito	66	Lucky 13	4	Roosevelt Tamale Parlor	70
Bitterroot	15	El Rio	76	Ma Tante Sumi	36	Rooster, The	64
Blondie's Bar and No Grill	27	Escape From New York Pizza	49	Make Out Room	63	Saigon, Saigon	65
Boogaloo's	59	Esperanto	62	Marcello's	32	Slanted Door	30
Bruno's	55	Esta Noche	22	Midnight Sun	43	Sparky's	8
Café du Nord	5	Firecracker	57	Mitchell's	74	Taqueria Can-cun	52
Café Flore	11	Firefly	67	Moby Dick	44	Thai House Bar & Café	9
Café la Boheme	69	Flying Saucer	61	Muddy Waters	25	Ti Couz	16
Café Macondo	18	Hamano	71	No Name	10	Timo's	54
Casanova	28	Harvey's	48	Orphan Andy's	34	Tin Pan	13
Castro Station, The	39	Hot n Hunky	45	Panchita's	31	Tita's	29
Chava's	47	John Frank	2	Pancho Villa	23	Truly Mediterranean	20
Chow	6	Kilowatt	14	Patio Café	50	Twin Peaks	33
Country Station	38	La Rondalla	56	Pauline's Pizza Pie	1	Uncle Bert's Place	40
Daddy's	37	La Taqueria	72	Picaro	17	Uptown, The	35
Delfina	46	Latin American Club	60	Pilsner Inn	7	Valentine	73
Detour	26	Lexington Club	51	Puerto Alegre	24	Zante's	21

cooking with ingredients from virtually every land and an unusually abundant array of vegetarian options; the pleasant result provides a touch of class with nary a hint of pretension. *Moderate.*

Herbivore, 983 Valencia at 21st ☎415/826-5657. Midway between a café and full-fledged restaurant, serving passable vegan food such as seitan sandwiches. *Budget.*

Hot n' Hunky, 4039 18th St at Castro ☎415/621-6365. The clientele is even hunkier than the massive burgers at this Castro diner. *Budget.*

Johnfrank, 2100 Market St at Church ☎415/503-0333. Sitting at one of the most trafficked corners in town, this medium-swank bistro has quickly jumped into the city's top ranks. Amazingly popular, though the dishes are rather unsurprising, pushing the inevitable sun-dried tomatoes and portabella mushrooms in predictable contexts. *Moderate.*

Just for You, 1453 18th St at Connecticut ☎415/847-3033. There isn't room for many more than just you in this homey breakfast spot atop Potrero Hill. The owners sling the hash while chatting with their loyal customers. *Budget.*

Tita's Hale Aina, 3870 17th St at Noe ☎415/626-2477. According to most American jokes, Hawaiian cuisine consists of ham, spam, and pineapple. To prove that this can be a *good* thing, this cozy Castro spot turns out roasts (heavy on the pork) and Spam stir fries. *Inexpensive.*

Tom's Peasant Pies, 4117 18th St at Castro ☎415/621-3632. Also at 4108 24th St and 1039 Irving St. Tiny little savory pies at prices fit for a king. Despite the offensiveness of the name, palm-sized treats such as leek and potato tails make for a decent between-meals snack. *Budget.*

CALIFORNIA

Flying Saucer, 1000 Guerrero St at 23rd ☎415/641-9955. *Flying Saucer* attracts fans from far and wide with inventive, exquisitely presented cuisine. The consistently daring menu changes weekly, but the prices remain a relative bargain when compared to the competition in this class. *Moderate.*

Mecca, 2029 Market at 14th St ☎415/621-7000. A frightfully imposing exterior hides a swank supper club. The aggressively moneyed atmosphere can be a major turn-off, but dishes offer an unusual mix of Asian seasonings (Japanese shiso) and Southern comforts (pecan nuts) to keep you focused on your plate. The thrifty can sidle up to the bar for cocktails, small plates of food, and live jazz in the background. *Expensive.*

Miss Millie's, 4123 24th St at Church ☎415/282-5598. A weekend brunch institution, thanks to fresh homemade baked goods. Expect a wait of close to an hour and be prepared to have your conversation interrupted by your co-diners' babies. *Inexpensive.*

Tin Pan, 2251 Market St at Sanchez ☎415/565-0733. Asian–Californian fusion cuisine in an elegantly understated interior. *Moderate.*

2223, 2223 Market at Sanchez ☎415/431-0692. Rather less daunting than *Mecca*, the Castro's other prime-dining destination. While the top-notch food should have you glowing, the room's warm tones cast even the drabbest date in a kind light. *Moderate.*

Valentine's, 1793 Church St at 30th ☎415/285-2257. This small, casual vegetarian restaurant is popular for wholesome American standards and Indian-inspired staples such as *saag paneer.*

CHINESE

Firecracker, 1007 Valencia St at 21st ☎415/642-3470. Upscale Chinese, with slightly fancified prices to match. If you're willing to take the extra hit to your wallet, you'll be rewarded with flavorful renditions of the old standbys, minus the grease and MSG. *Inexpensive.*

Garden of Tranquility, 2001 17th St at Kansas ☎415/861-8610. It's worth

Restaurants and cafés

Restaurants and cafés

making a trip to out-of-the-way Potrero Hill for its delicious, discounted lunch menu of *kung pao* chicken and Hunan beef. *Budget.*

FRENCH

Ma Tante Sumi, 4243 18th St at Douglass ☎415/552-6663. A popular Castro spot with an interesting angle – French food with a Japanese twist, such as goat-cheese salad with nigiri salmon rolls. *Moderate.*

Ti Couz, 3108 16th St at Valencia ☎415/252-7373. Specializing in the cuisine of France's Brittany, this Mission favorite dishes out delicious soups, salads and, most importantly, savory buckwheat crepes. Later, the sweeter flour dessert crepes come with American toppings like ice cream, fresh fruit, or caramel, for a decadent conclusion to your meal. *Inexpensive.*

INDIAN

Rasoi, 1037 Valencia at 21st ☎415/695-0599. Curries, tandooris and all your other Indian favorites, served in modern, track-lit surroundings. Portions can be small and the food isn't quite as spiffy as the decor, but it's still a stylish and popular dinner spot. *Inexpensive.*

Zante's, 3489 Mission between 30th St and Cortland ☎415/821-3949, and 3083 16th St at Valencia ☎415/621-4189. Getting points for uniqueness, if not for ambience and charm, this scruffy mini-chain specializes in Indian pizza, a uniquely flavorful invention. *Budget.*

ITALIAN

Chow, 215 Church St at Market ☎415/552-2469. An instant hit for its bargain first-rate pastas and wood-fired pizzas. No reservations accepted, and the wait can be long. *Inexpensive.*

Dago Mary's, in the Hunter's Point Shipyard ☎415/822-2633. The name isn't exactly PC and the out-of-the-way location is downright dangerous at night, but this is a true San Francisco original. Formerly a 1930s brothel – the ornate fireplace once belonged to Gold Rush millionaire James Flood – it is now a family-style eatery with hearty Italian basics at affordable prices. *Inexpensive.*

Delfina, 3621 18th St at Guerrero ☎415/552-4055. This tiny space has become one of the hottest restaurants in town, thanks mostly to top-notch dishes and service. The downside is that with tables packed tightly in a row, you'll often leave dinner feeling more intimate with the folks at the next table than with your date. *Moderate.*

Escape from New York, 508 Castro St at 18th ☎415/252-1515, with another location in the Haight at 1737 Haight St at Cole ☎415/668-5577. An impressively random array of celebrity photographs line the walls of this by-the-slice pizza joint, where the specialty – a sun-dried tomato, artichoke, and feta gourment slice – has little to do with New York or its pizza. *Budget.*

Marcello's, 420 Castro St at 17th ☎415/863-3900. Competing with *Escape from New York* for the title of best New York-style pizza in the city; the delicious slices come dripping with grease and cheese. *Budget.*

Pauline's, 260 Valencia St at 14th ☎415/552-2050. A sit-down pizza place right next door to the old Levi Strauss building, serving up a pie that's more than worth spending some time over. *Budget.*

JAPANESE

Blowfish, 2170 Bryant St at 20th ☎415/285-3848. Blowfish isn't on the menu, but the raw fish is better than average, and the red, black, and chrome design is glossy-chic, with Japanamation playing on TV sets above the bar. *Moderate.*

Country Station, 2140 Mission St at Sycamore ☎415/861-0972. An excellent sushi house buried in the center of one of the creepiest blocks in the Mission. The very friendly service ranges from leisurely to agonizingly slow. Though it's not always available, ask for the fish roe sushi soaked in burning-hot-wasabi. *Inexpensive.*

Hamano Sushi, 1332 Castro St at 24th ☎415/826-0825. Another excellent and popular sushi bar, this one in Noe Valley; dinner for two will set you back around $45 but it's worth it for the fresh goods. *Moderate.*

Yokoso Nippon, 314 Church St at 15th, no phone. Known by thrifty locals who frequent the place for its fresh food as "no name sushi" since there's no sign on the door. *Budget.*

MEXICAN

Chava's, 3245 18th St at Shotwell ☎415/552-9387. Traditional Mexican stews like *birria* or *menudo* (made with tripe), a reputed hangover cure, are stirred up daily in this basic spot. *Budget.*

La Taqueria, 2889 Mission St at 25th ☎415/285-7117. *La Taqueria* consistently packs them in by focusing on the basics – tacos and the like – and getting them right every time. *Budget.*

Panchita's, 3091 16th St at Valencia ☎415/431-4232; 3316 17th St at Mission ☎415/431-8852; and 3115 22nd St at Capp ☎415/821-6660. This neighborhood chain specializes in Central American cooking – not hugely different from Mexican food, except for the *papusa*, a sort of corn pancake filled with meat or cheese and served with a salad that most closely resembles coleslaw. *Budget.*

Pancho Villa, 3071 16th St at Valencia ☎415/864-8840. The food at this oversized taqueria, in contrast to that of some of the neighborhood's grungier establishments, is consistently fresh and flavorful. *Budget.*

Roosevelt Tamale Parlor, 2817 24th St ☎415/550-9213. Just one of their massive and delectable tamales – steamed corn and meat served inside corn husks – can easily serve two people. *Budget.*

Taquaria Cancun, 2288 Mission St at 19th ☎415/252-9560, and 3211 Mission at Valencia ☎415/550-1414. No messing around with fancy ingredients here, just simple, delicious burritos, devoured by a cross section from the neighborhood – from bike messengers to grandmas. *Budget.*

MIDDLE EASTERN

Truly Mediterranean, 3109 16th St at Valencia ☎415/252-7482, with another location at 1724 Haight St at Cole ☎415/751-7482 in the Haight. *Truly Mediterranean*'s version of the falafel is wrapped in thin, crispy lavash bread, though once you get it, you'll find barely anywhere to sit in the tiny windowfront restaurant. The busy staff's spontaneous singing and dancing comes free of charge. *Budget.*

SOUTHEAST ASIAN

Saigon, Saigon, 1132 Valencia St at 22nd ☎415/206-9635. Serving Vietnamese food with a vaguely French twist, this unpretentious neighborhood stalwart has lost some of its thunder to the flashier *Slanted Door* down the street, but it's a lot cheaper and you don't need a reservation. *Inexpensive.*

Slanted Door, 584 Valencia St at 16th ☎415/861-8032. While the menu isn't particularly unusual, running the gamut from spring rolls to curries, the unusually precise, light cooking makes every flavor stand out and is accentuated by the excellent wine list. The place is no secret, so be sure and reserve at least a week in advance. *Moderate.*

Thai House, 151 Noe at Henry ☎415/863-0374, and 2220 Market St at 15th ☎415/864-5006. Two locations just blocks apart make this perennial Castro favorite a study in contrasts. The Noe spot is warm and intimate, while the big windows on the Market St location make it a prime spot for people watching. In both cases, the staple dishes such as Pad Thai are reliably well-prepared. *Inexpensive.*

SPANISH

Esperpento, 3295 22nd St at Valencia St ☎415/642-8867. Catering to rowdy

Restaurants and cafés

young locals, with a wide variety of Spanish tapas cooked with enough garlic to clear out Keith Richards' bloodstream. There's often a wait, but if a wandering mariachi band stops by, you probably won't mind. *Inexpensive.*

Timo's, 842 Valencia at 19th St ☎415/647-0558. Don't expect a quiet sit-down meal here: this small, dark tapas restaurant packs them in every night for Spanish favorites such as fried squid and *papas bravas* (roast potatoes) accompanied by sangria. *Inexpensive.*

West of Civic Center and Haight-Ashbury

AFRICAN

Axum Café, 698 Haight St at Pierce ☎415/252-7912. It's not every neighborhood coffee shop where you can chow down on well-made Ethiopian specialties such as *fit-fit* and *gored*, all served up with the traditional flat bread known as *injera*. While the food may be mildly exotic, the relaxed atmosphere easily makes *Axum* feel like home. *Budget.*

Massawa, 1538 Haight St at Clayton ☎415/621-4129. Slightly more expensive than *Axum*; you're paying for screened ambience, not for a remarkable difference in the cuisine, which is equally tasty and filling here. *Inexpensive.*

AMERICAN

Big Sherm's, 250 Fillmore at Haight ☎415/864-1850. It's unclear who exactly Big Sherm is, but he certainly provides the inspiration for a mean sandwich. With a much longer menu than most sandwich shops, there's something for everyone. *Budget.*

Crescent City Café, 1418 Haight St at Masonic ☎415/863-1374. The New Orleans grub isn't fancy (things don't get "blackened," they get burnt) but the gumbo still sticks to your ribs. *Budget.*

Kate's Kitchen, 471 Haight at Fillmore ☎415/626-3984. When you first stare down at the monstrously large plates of breakfast fare served here, it's a little hard to think about saving room for extras. But do treat yourself to some hushpuppies – deep fried lumps of corn meal served with deliciously sweet honey-touched "pooh butter." *Budget.*

Mad Dog in the Fog, 530 Haight St at Fillmore ☎415/626-7279. This cozy pub is a great place to grab a cold pint of beer and a plate full of corned beef and cabbage. *Budget.*

Magnolia, 1398 Haight at Masonic ☎415/864-PINT. A brewpub with a mildly fancy selection of good grilled foods and salads. In keeping with the location, the Grateful Dead provide a seemingly permanent soundtrack. *Inexpensive.*

Martin Mack's, 1568 Haight St at Clayton ☎415/864-0124. Yet more British Isles nostalgia, which translates into lots of wood paneling and a menu full of hearty staples such as shepherd's pie. *Budget.*

Moishe's Pipic, 425 Hayes St at Gough ☎415/431-2440. Pipic, in case you were wondering, is Yiddish for belly button. *Moishe's* makes traditional Jewish deli food that should fill your belly to the bursting point. *Inexpensive.*

Pork Store, 1451 Haight St at Masonic ☎415/864-6981. The food is fairly standard coffee shop fixings (eggs, potatoes, and toast), but it's a popular neighborhood standby, nonetheless. *Budget.*

Powell's Soul Food, 511 Hayes St at Octavia ☎415/863-1404. The mayor's favorite restaurant specializes in Southern-fried chicken, along with all the traditional fixings – grits, greens and corn bread. *Budget.*

Rosamunde Sausage Grille, 545 Haight St at Fillmore ☎415/437-6851. Offerings at this no-frills grill range from the mundane (bratwurst) to the more exotic (a spicy Basque sausage). *Budget.*

Spaghetti Western, 576 Haight St at Fillmore ☎415/864-8461. Despite the name, the specialty here is breakfast food, cooked with plenty of grease. *Budget.*

Restaurants and cafés

Zare, 1640 Haight St at Clayton ☎415/861-8868. While the pleasantly plain front room of this understated restaurant doesn't look like much, the real draw is the idyllic back patio where Mediterranean-themed soups and salads are served. *Inexpensive.*

BRAZILIAN

Terra Brazilis, 602 Hayes at Laguna ☎415/241-1900. An original, somewhat hit-or-miss, menu that includes rarities such as sugar cane-skewered grilled meat; the striking decor feels like a Bauhaus interpretation of a rainforest. *Moderate.*

CALIFORNIA

Asqew Grill, 1607 Haight St at Clayton ☎415/701-9301. Cheap food with a good gimmick – everything, be it Thai lime chicken or American barbecue, gets stuck on a spit and grilled. *Budget.*

EOS, 901 Cole St at Carl ☎415/566-3063. A somewhat daunting wine list, thankfully available by the glass, gets paired with visually spectacular East–West fusion cooking, including ginger Caesar salad and lemon grass risotto. *Expensive.*

Hayes Street Grill, 320 Hayes at Gough ☎415/863-5545. Excellent grilled fish and standard American fare, perfectly prepared with fresh ingredients, draw a conservative crowd at lunch and opera – and theatergoers at dinner. *Moderate.*

Indigo, 687 McAllister St at Gough ☎415/673-9369. Stylish without being pretentious, this newcomer to the Cal-cuisine scene delivers generous portions of inventive, seasonal entrees at moderate prices, accompanied by top-notch service. *Moderate.*

Jardinière, 300 Grove St at Franklin ☎415/861-5555. Run by big-name chef Tracy Des Jardins, this boxy brick space caters to a pre-theater crowd with valet parking and plenty of pizzazz. A splurge, but you'll get what you pay for; there's an emphasis on indulgence from beginning (foie gras) to end (aged cheese platter). *Expensive.*

Zuni, 1658 Market St at Gough ☎415/552-2522. Once nouveau and now a staple, *Zuni* features the most famous Caesar salad in town – made with home-cured anchovies – and an equally legendary focaccia hamburger. Always perfect for people-watching from the picture windows. *Moderate.*

CHINESE

The Citrus Club, 1790 Haight St at Cole ☎415/387-6366. A rare escape from the oddly grease-heavy offerings of most Haight St establishment. Noodles are the theme here, whether sautéed in a wok or served in a variety of broths. *Budget.*

Eliza's, 205 Oak St at Gough ☎415/621-4819. One of the few restaurants in the city serving Chinese food in a true white linen and tablecloth setting. Above-average quality, reasonably priced. *Inexpensive.*

FRENCH

Absinthe, 398 Hayes St at Gough ☎415/551-1590. The forbidden elixir is nowhere to be found, but the inventive cocktails make a fine accompaniment to the pricey bistro fare. *Moderate.*

Crêpes on Cole, 100 Carl St at Cole ☎415/664-1800. Come for breakfast or lunch and you'll join the crowds of locals chowing down on thick servings of feta cheese, eggs, and spinach wrapped in crepes with heaping sides of potatoes. *Inexpensive.*

Piaf's, 1686 Market at Gough ☎415/864-3700. Appealing to a very particular niche market – nostalgics for *la chanson française*. Every meal begins with complimentary lobster bisque before proceeding to bistro favorites such as steak frites and truffles. But the atmosphere is the real draw, with nightly singers performing numbers from Edith's own songbook in the dark, purple interior – a Californian interpretation of gay old Paris. *Moderate.*

Restaurants and cafés

GERMAN

Suppenküche, 601 Hayes St at Laguna ☎415/252-9289. Traditional beer-garden fare, such a spaetzel, sausages, and sauerkraut, gets paired with an appropriately good selection of lagers and lemony wheat beers. Beerhall atmosphere, along with some ample hops, encourages you to get chatty with your neighbor. *Inexpensive.*

INDIAN

Indian Oven, 233 Fillmore St at Waller ☎415/626-1628. One of the best of the lot, in a city curiously lacking top-notch Indian cooking. Baked tandoori items are the specialty here, though the curries aren't half bad, either. *Moderate.*

ITALIAN

Caffé Delle Stelle, 395 Hayes St at Gough ☎415/252-1110. Good renditions of the hearty cooking of Northern Italy, with an emphasis on rich flavors and roasted meats. Particularly recommended are the cabbage leaves stuffed with smoked mozzarella. *Moderate.*

Papadoro, 1649 Haight St at Belvedere ☎415/621-7272. Decent baked pastas to enjoy in vinyl-cushioned booths, a nice break from the rowdy neighborhood. *Budget.*

Stelline, 429 Gough St at Hayes ☎415/626-4292. An even more casual outpost of the already casual *Caffé Delle Stelle* down the street. Instead of white linen and roasts you'll find red-checkered table-cloths and pastas. *Inexpensive.*

Vicolo, 20 Ivy St, off Franklin ☎415/863-2382. The place to go for prototypically Californian pizza, baked over a wood fire and with a thin, corn meal-sprinkled crust. Be warned: the restaurant is hidden in a tiny alley and can be hard to find. *Inexpensive.*

JAPANESE

Isobune, 1737 Post St at Webster inside the Japantown mall ☎415/563-1030. Sushi that floats around the table on little boats. Watch the crowd cringe a bit every time the sea cucumber roll comes around; best stick with the more familiar tuna and shrimp rolls. *Inexpensive.*

Kushi Tsuru, 1737 Post St at Webster inside the Japantown mall ☎415/922-9902. Basic noodle house offering a wide array of options. *Inexpensive.*

Mifune, 1737 Post St at Fillmore inside the Japantown mall ☎415/922-0337. More elegant than its neighbors, this noodle house has a large array of soup toppings and a small selection of sushi. *Inexpensive.*

On the Bridge, 1581 Webster St at Post inside the Japantown mall ☎415/922-7765. Strange Japanese versions of Western staples, such as spaghetti with *kim chi* (pickled cabbage). *Inexpensive.*

Sapporo-ya, 1581 Webster St at Post inside the Japantown mall ☎415/563-7400. Homemade buckwheat ramen – the old-fashioned noodle machine is right in the window – served up in thick and flavorful miso or pork broths. *Budget.*

Yoshida-Ya, 2909 Webster St ☎415/346-3431. Genuine sushi bar, where you kick off your shoes and eat at low tables on futon covered floors. *Inexpensive.*

MEXICAN

El Balazo, 1654 Haight St at Clayton ☎415/864-8608. Offering fairly run-of-the-mill California–Mexican fare, with the exception of an unusual focus on *nopales*, or edible cactus. *Budget.*

Zona Rosa, 1797 Haight St at Shrader ☎415/668-7717. By no means an "authentic" burrito – they use too many vegetables for that – but with a good and flavorful selection of *mole* and *verde* sauce-smothered fillings. *Budget.*

MIDDLE EASTERN

Kan Zaman, 1793 Haight St at Shrader ☎415/751-9656. While the food is good, the chance to recline on pillows and eat in a semi-horizontal position, puffing on a hookah while watching the belly dancers, is even better. *Inexpensive.*

SOUTHEAST ASIAN

Thep Phanom, 400 Waller St at Fillmore ☎415/431-2526. Widely considered the best Thai restaurant in the city, for its well-prepared dishes and pungent curries. *Inexpensive.*

SPANISH

Cha Cha Cha, 1801 Haight St at Clayton ☎415/386-5758. Abundantly flavorful tapas creations served in a subtle Caribbean decor. Be warned: the fried shrimp comes piled high enough to be a meal of its own, and the wait to get in can be interminable. *Inexpensive.*

The Richmond and the Sunset

AMERICAN

Avenue 9, 1243 Ninth Ave at Irving ☎415/664-6999. The anchor of the Inner Sunset dining scene offers some fierce competition to downtown's top eateries. Southern-style dishes such as baked chicken get significantly spruced up with swiss chard, arugula, and applewood bacon. *Moderate.*

Beach Chalet, 1000 Great Highway ☎415/386-8439. The food isn't exceptional, but the setting is, along the windy stretches of Ocean Beach and on the second floor of a pretty WPA-era building. Combination brewpub-restaurant, with live music on weekends. *Moderate.*

Cheer's, 127 Clement St at Third ☎415/387-6966. Serving brunch and fancy sandwiches in a cool, tiled setting. While dinner entrees can be overly ambitious and a bit pricey, the French toast and eggs breakfasts are a safer bet. *Inexpensive.*

Cliff House, 1900 Point Lobos Ave ☎415/386-3330. Much maligned as a tourist trap, but still an unbeatable spot to enjoy a meal and a drink while gazing out on the Pacific Ocean. The sumptuous all-you-can-eat champagne buffet brunch is to die for. *Moderate.*

Einstein's Cafe, 1336 Ninth Ave at Cabrillo ☎415/665-4840. Serving big, cheap sandwiches that clear your conscience while filling your gut – proceeds from all sales go to fund a not-for-profit organization that works with troubled youth. *Budget.*

Louis', 902 Point Lobos Ave ☎415/387-6330. By all rights this basic diner overlooking the ocean and the ruins of the Sutro Baths should be a blatant tourist trap, but things haven't changed much since the 1940s. *Budget.*

PJ's Oyster Bed, 737 Irving at Ninth ☎415/566-7775. Besides oysters, they also serve Southern-style cooking to a devoted and extremely festive crowd of regulars. *Inexpensive.*

Q, 225 Clement St at Third ☎415/752-2298. The over-the-top decor is so hip you could scream, but the Southern-style food is down-home and authentic. *Inexpensive.*

CALIFORNIA

House, 1269 Ninth Ave at Irving ☎415/682-3898. East–West fusion cuisine – like a Caesar salad with wok-fried scallops or garlic soy chicken wings – served in quirky, funhouse decor. *Moderate.*

Organica, 1224 Ninth Ave at Irving ☎415/665-6519. Formerly called *Raw*, this culinary oddity specializes in food that hasn't been cooked. It's more than salads – there's even a completely raw, and quite tasty, pizza. *Inexpensive.*

CHINESE

Coriya Hot Pot City, 852 Clement St at Tenth ☎415/387-7888. Eating at *Coriya* is a festive occasion: you prepare your own food at a tabletop grill, dipping it into one of the numerous sauces when it's done. Best experienced with a group. *Inexpensive.*

Formosa, 1125 Clement St at 12th ☎415/386-2198. A rare Taiwanese restaurant translates such unusual offerings as sea cucumber and quail's eggs into relatively mild-flavored preparations. *Budget.*

Red Crane, 1115 Clement St at 12th ☎415/751-7226. A strictly vegetarian

Restaurants and cafés

Restaurants and cafés

Chinese restaurant with interesting meatless interpretations of traditional dishes. *Inexpensive.*

Ton Kiang, 5821 Geary St at 22nd ☎415/387-8273. This massive Richmond restaurant is the prime place in the entire city for dim sum. Even with one of the biggest dining rooms around, a wait is almost inevitable. *Budget.*

FRENCH

Châpeau!, 1408 Clement St at 15th ☎415/750-9787. Downtown quality French food at foggy Richmond prices, packed with locals enjoying a relaxed provincial atmosphere. *Moderate.*

Clementine, 126 Clement St at Second ☎415/387-0408. Not quite the equal to its beloved predecessor *Alain Rondelli*. Still, a charming spot for French fare at a decent price. *Moderate.*

Luzern, 1429 Noriega at 22nd Ave ☎415/664-2353. Remote location has drawn fans of traditional Swiss food for decades. The cheese and meat fondues, the latter of which are augmented by a variety of dipping sauces, are particularly delicious. *Inexpensive.*

INDIAN

The Ganges, 775 Frederick at Lincoln ☎415/661-7290. The kitchen's always original and inventive vegetarian Indian creations range from the delicious to the plain weird. If you nab the back room, you can recline in splendor on cushions while dining. *Moderate.*

ITALIAN

Park Chow, 1240 Ninth Ave at Lincoln ☎415/665-9912. The sequel to popular *Chow* near the Castro. Solid, consistent renditions of pizzas, pastas, and the like, perfect for a post-park lunch. *Inexpensive.*

JAPANESE

Ebisu, 1283 Ninth Ave at Irving ☎415/566-1770. Generally considered the best sushi in town, based simply on the freshness and unobtrusive preparation of the fish. No reservations, so plan to stand out in the San Francisco fog while you wait to be seated. *Moderate.*

Hotei, 1290 Ninth Ave at Irving ☎415/753-6045. Down the street offshoot of popular *Ebisu* (see above), but focusing its attention more on soba and ramen dishes. *Inexpensive.*

KOREAN

Brother's, 4128 Geary Blvd at Sixth ☎415/387-3991. The oldest among a burgeoning row of Korean barbecue houses along Geary St, and one of the few with the name written in English outside (making it the easiest to find), *Brother's* specializes in family-sized feasts of grilled, marinated meats. *Inexpensive.*

MEXICAN

Tommy's, 5929 Geary Blvd at 23rd ☎415/387-4747. A perennially festive restaurant and bar with some of the best margaritas in town. The hearty food helps you keep your balance walking out the door. *Inexpensive.*

MIDDLE EASTERN

Yaya Cuisine, 1220 Ninth Ave at Lincoln ☎415/566-6966. Romantic, candlelit Middle Eastern restaurant near Golden Gate Park, with a Californian twist. Good vegetarian selection and overall excellent value. *Inexpensive.*

RUSSIAN

The Russian Bear, 939 Clement St at Eighth ☎415/752-8197. The traditional dishes such as borscht and veal served at this visually boggling restaurant (every surface seems to be gilt or mirrored) helps the recent Russian immigrants filling the neighborhood assuage any homesickness. *Moderate.*

Russian Renaissance, 5241 Geary Blvd at 17th ☎415/752-8558. Come on a weekend night, slide into a plush red booth, and order a bottle of vodka and a bowl of borscht or goulash for a completely decadent experience. *Inexpensive.*

SOUTHEAST ASIAN

Angkor Wat, 4217 Geary Blvd at Sixth ☎415/221-7887. The best Cambodian food in town, even if it doesn't have tons of competition – even the pope ate here when he visited. *Inexpensive.*

Khan Toke, 5937 Geary Blvd at 25th ☎415/668-6654. This Thai restaurant is popular with families who routinely pack the dining room, heaping curries and Pad Thai onto each others' plates. *Inexpensive.*

King of Thai Noodle House, 639 Clement St at Eighth ☎415/752-5198. Certainly not the fanciest Thai food in town, but when it comes to big bowls of soup, prepared before your eyes, you can't do much better. Try the pan-fried noodles as well. *Budget.*

La Vie, 5830 Geary Blvd at 23rd ☎415/668-8080. Slightly upscale Vietnamese cuisine, in an environment that's a cut above your run-of-the-mill noodle joint. The sautéed catfish is particularly excellent when available. *Inexpensive.*

Mandalay, 4348 California St at Fifth ☎415/386-3895. If you've never had the chance to sample traditional Burmese dishes such as Green Tea Salad, Poodhi or the enigmatically named "Ants Climb Tree," this is a terrific place to start. The food, particularly some remarkable homemade tofu, is deliciously refined. *Inexpensive.*

Marnee Thai, 2225 Irving St at 23rd ☎415/665-9500. Another excellent Thai restaurant; the mango and sticky rice is particularly divine. *Inexpensive.*

Singapore Malaysian Restaurant, 836 Clement St at Seventh ☎415/750-9518. Bare bones setting for cheap and tasty Malay cooking. *Inexpensive.*

Strait's Café, 3300 Geary Blvd at Parker ☎415/668-1783. Traditional Singaporean cuisine presented with all the precision of the sleek decor, attracting the neighborhood's largely Asian population as well as foodies from far away. *Inexpensive.*

East Bay

AFRICAN

Blue Nile, 2525 Telegraph Ave, Berkeley ☎510/540-6777. Offering tasty Ethiopian food at the end of the teeming Telegraph Ave strip; soothing atmosphere, though the service can be downright glacial. *Inexpensive.*

AMERICAN

Ann's, 3401 Fruitvale Ave, Oakland ☎510/531-9861. Massive portions of hearty fare that don't stop coming until you're ready to drop from your stool. A typical breakfast will include eggs, sausage, pancakes, scones, cereal if you want it, and all the coffee you can stomach. *Budget.*

Barney's, 4162 Piedmont Ave, Oakland ☎510/655-7180; 5819 College Ave, Rockridge ☎510/601-0444; and 1591 Solano Ave, Berkeley ☎510/526-8185. The East Bay's most popular burgers – including meatless ones – smothered in dozens of different toppings. *Budget.*

Bay Wolf, 3853 Piedmont Ave, Oakland ☎510/655-6004. Comfortable restaurant serving an ever-changing menu of grilled meat and fish dishes. *Moderate.*

Bette's Ocean View Diner, 1807 Fourth St, Berkeley ☎510/548-9494. Serving up some of the best casual diner fare in town. Very popular on weekends, when you may have to wait an hour for a table, so come for lunch during the week if possible. *Inexpensive.*

Café Rouge, 1782 Fourth St, Berkeley ☎510/525-1440. Specializing in delicately prepared organic meats – they have their own butcher shop – including an elevated version of the lowly hamburger. *Moderate.*

Fatapple's, 1346 Martin Luther King Jr Way, Berkeley ☎510/526-2260. Crowded but pleasant family-oriented restaurant with excellent cheap American breakfasts and an assortment of sandwiches and burgers for lunch or dinner. *Inexpensive.*

Restaurants and cafés

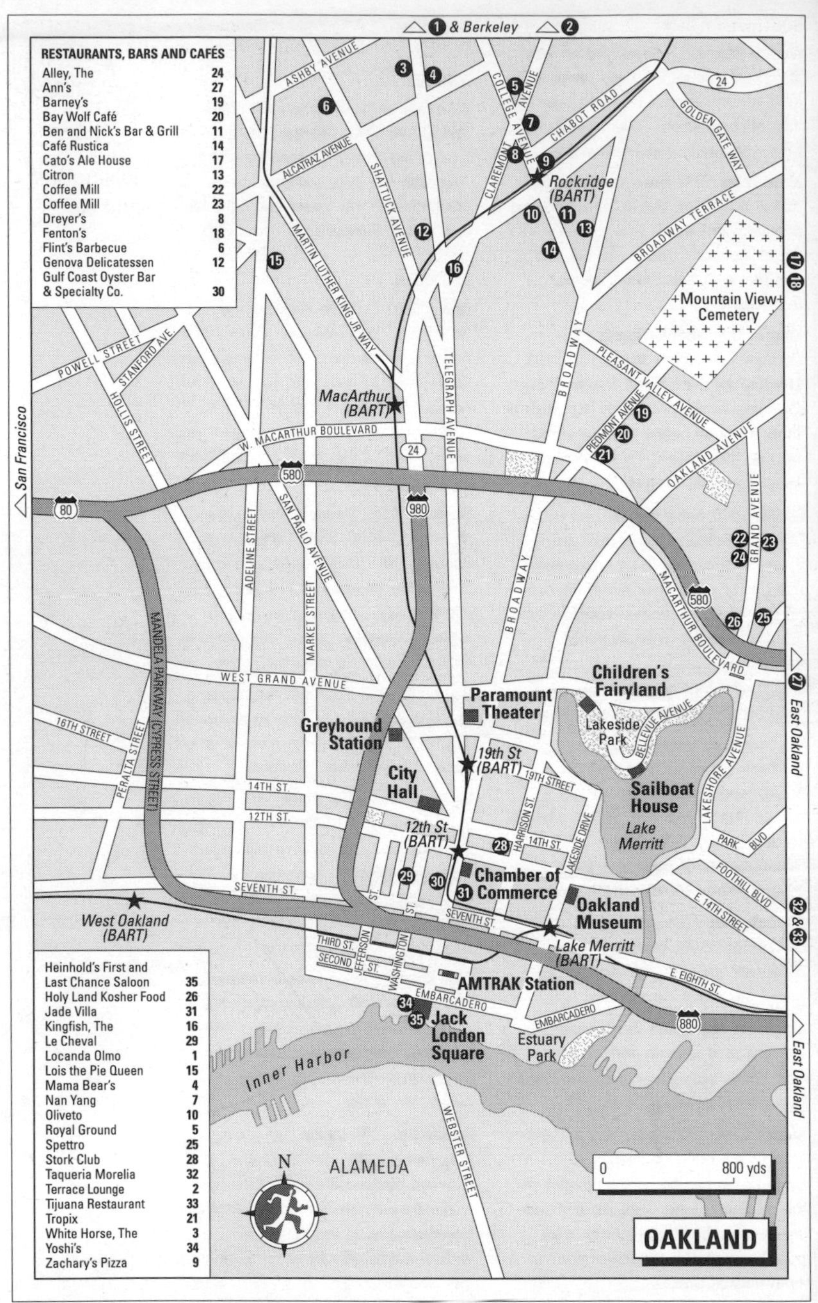

RESTAURANTS, BARS AND CAFÉS
Alley, The 24
Ann's 27
Barney's 19
Bay Wolf Café 20
Ben and Nick's Bar & Grill 11
Café Rustica 14
Cato's Ale House 17
Citron 13
Coffee Mill 22
Coffee Mill 23
Dreyer's 8
Fenton's 18
Flint's Barbecue 6
Genova Delicatessen 12
Gulf Coast Oyster Bar & Specialty Co. 30
Heinhold's First and Last Chance Saloon 35
Holy Land Kosher Food 26
Jade Villa 31
Kingfish, The 16
Le Cheval 29
Locanda Olmo 1
Lois the Pie Queen 15
Mama Bear's 4
Nan Yang 7
Oliveto 10
Royal Ground 5
Spettro 25
Stork Club 28
Taqueria Morelia 32
Terrace Lounge 2
Tijuana Restaurant 33
Tropix 21
White Horse, The 3
Yoshi's 34
Zachary's Pizza 9
& Berkeley
San Francisco
East Oakland
East Oakland
Rockridge (BART)
MacArthur (BART)
19th St (BART)
12th St (BART)
West Oakland (BART)
Lake Merritt (BART)
Mountain View Cemetery
Children's Fairyland
Paramount Theater
Greyhound Station
City Hall
Lakeside Park
Sailboat House
Lake Merritt
Chamber of Commerce
Oakland Museum
AMTRAK Station
Jack London Square
Estuary Park
Inner Harbor
ALAMEDA
N
0 800 yds
OAKLAND

Flint's Barbecue, 3314 San Pablo Ave, Oakland ☎510/653-0593. Open until the early hours of the morning for some of the best ribs and link sausages west of Chicago. *Inexpensive.*

Genova Delicatessen, 5095 Telegraph Ave, Oakland ☎510/652-7401. Friendly deli, complete with hanging sausages, serving up superb sandwiches. *Budget.*

Gulf Coast Oyster Bar & Specialty Co, 736 Washington St, Oakland ☎510/836-3663. Popular Cajun-flavored seafood. *Inexpensive.*

Homemade Café, 2454 Sacramento St, Berkeley ☎510/845-1940. Non-traditional California-style Mexican and Jewish food ranging from blintzes to burritos served for breakfast and lunch at tables you'll be sharing with others during the tight-squeezed breakfast rush. *Inexpensive.*

Lois the Pie Queen, 851 60th St at Adeline, Oakland ☎510/658-5616. Famous around the bay for its Southern-style sweet potato and fresh fruit pies, this cozy diner also serves massive, down-home breakfasts and Sunday dinners. *Budget.*

Rick & Ann's, 2922 Domingo Ave, Berkeley ☎510/649-8538. Every weekend the crowds line up outside this neighborhood diner for meatloaf and mashed potatoes. *Inexpensive.*

Saul's Deli, 1475 Shattuck Ave, Berkeley ☎510/848-DELI. For pastrami, corned beef, kreplach, or knishes, this is the place. Great sandwiches and picnic fixings to take away, plus a full range of sit-down evening meals. *Budget.*

Spenger's, 1919 Fourth St, West Berkeley ☎510/845-7771. About as far as you can get from the subtle charms of Berkeley's high-style restaurants, *Spenger's* is, nonetheless, a local institution, serving up tons of seafood to thousands of customers daily. Recently the menu was updated to include more fresh fish and fewer fried items. *Inexpensive.*

Top Dog, 2534 Durant Ave, Berkeley ☎510/843-7450. Lots of different types of delicious dogs at this tiny stand, which is plastered with all manner of anarchist literature. *Budget.*

BRAZILIAN

Café de La Paz, 1600 Shattuck Ave, Berkeley ☎510/843-0662. *La Paz* creates Cal-cuisined versions of food from throughout the continent, including fried pancakes from both Venezuela and Ecuador. *Inexpensive.*

CALIFORNIA

Chez Panisse, 1517 Shattuck Ave, North Berkekey ☎510/548-5525. The California restaurant to which all others are compared. Chef Alice Waters is widely given credit for first inventing California cuisine. She hasn't lost a step in the years since, and her menu still changes daily, always relying on the local organic produce that made the name legendary. *Expensive.*

Citron, 5484 College Ave, Rockridge ☎510/653-5484. Neighborhood gem quietly rivaling the top restaurants for years with warm, unpretentious service and exquisite food. *Moderate.*

Lalime's, 1329 Gilman St, North Berkeley ☎510/527-9838. A culinary dissertation on irony: leftist Berkeley professors chowing down on rich veal, pâté, and foie gras in an understated setting. *Moderate.*

Rivoli, 1539 Solano Ave, Berkeley ☎510/526-2542. Delivering all that is wonderful about Berkeley dining: first-rate fresh food that's closer to Italian than anything else, courteous service and a casual, friendly atmosphere. The hot fudge sundae is always on the menu and worth splurging on. *Expensive.*

Spettro, 3355 Lakeshore Ave, Oakland ☎510/465-8320. With light Italian, Caribbean, and Thai influenced cuisine and the friendliest staff in the area, the ususual decor (reminiscent of a modernist graveyard) seems a bit less spooky. *Moderate.*

Restaurants and cafés

CARIBBEAN

Tropix, 3814 Piedmont Ave, Oakland ☎510/653-2444. Reasonable prices, with authentic jerk sauce and thirst-quenching mango juice. *Inexpensive.*

CHINESE

Jade Villa, 800 Broadway, downtown Oakland ☎510/839-1688. For endless dim sum lunches or traditional Cantonese meals, this is one of the best places in Oakland's thriving Chinatown. *Inexpensive.*

Long Life Vegi House, 2129 University Ave, Berkeley ☎510/845-6072. Thanks to bargain prices and the liberal use of fake flesh, the vegetarian cooking is perpetually popular with Cal students, despite a plain setting. *Budget.*

FRENCH

Britt-Marie's Cafe and Wine Bar, 1369 Solano Ave, Albany ☎510/527-1314. Eclectic home cooking drawn from across Europe, nicely accompanied by a fine selection of mostly Californian wines by the glass, is followed by an outstanding chocolate cake. *Inexpensive.*

La Note, 2337 Shattuck, Berkeley ☎510/843-1535. The appropriately sunny, light cuisine of Provence set to the tune of jam sessions involving students and teachers dropping in from the jazz school next door. *Inexpensive.*

INDIAN

Ajanta, 1888 Solano Ave, Berkeley ☎510/526-4373. The chefs rotate dishes from different regions of India every month, to good effect. *Moderate.*

Breads of India, 2448 Sacramento, Berkeley ☎510/848-7648. Curry might have been originally invented to help preserve less-than-fresh food, but this gourmet curry house turns that notion on its head, preparing only a few specials daily, each of them deliciously fresh. *Budget.*

Vik's Chaat Corner, 726 Allston Way at Fourth ☎510/644-4412. A terrific lunchtime destination offering wide array of Indian snacks. The ambiance is minimal, leaving nothing to distract you from the large selection of delicious morsels. Begin with samosas and naan; from there the small portions only open more possibilities for experimentation. *Budget.*

ITALIAN

Café Rustica, 5422 College Ave, Oakland ☎510/654-1601. Intimate adobe-style eatery for designer pizza with pesto, sun-dried tomatoes and the like. Less expensive is the tapas bar upstairs, where you can sample many of the same items for less. *Inexpensive–expensive.*

Cheese Board Pizza, 1512 Shattuck Ave, Berkeley ☎510/549-3055. Tiny storefront selling some of the world's best "designer pizza" at very reasonable prices: $2 a slice, with a different topping every day. *Budget.*

Oliveto, 5655 College Ave, Rockridge ☎510/547-5356. Back-to-basics recipes and a dependence on homegrown ingredients has put chef Paul Bertolli's *Oliveto* on a level with the best Italian restaurants in the country. *Expensive.*

Zachary's, 5801 College Ave, Rockridge ☎510/655-6385, and 1853 Solano Ave, North Berkeley ☎510/525-5950. One of the few Bay Area restaurants offering deep-dish, Chicago-style pizza. *Inexpensive.*

JAPANESE

Kirala, 2100 Ward St, Berkeley ☎510/549-3486. Some of the best sushi in the East Bay with an emphasis on freshness. *Moderate.*

O Chame, 1830 Fourth St, West Berkeley ☎510/841-8783. One of the very best Japanese restaurants in the US, with beautifully prepared sashimi and sushi as well as a full range of authentic Japanese specialties. *Inexpensive.*

Yoshi's, 510 Embarcadero West, Oakland ☎510/238-9200. Classy sushi restaurant attached to the equally classy jazz club (see p.288), which is the cornerstone of the redeveloped Jack London Square district. *Moderate.*

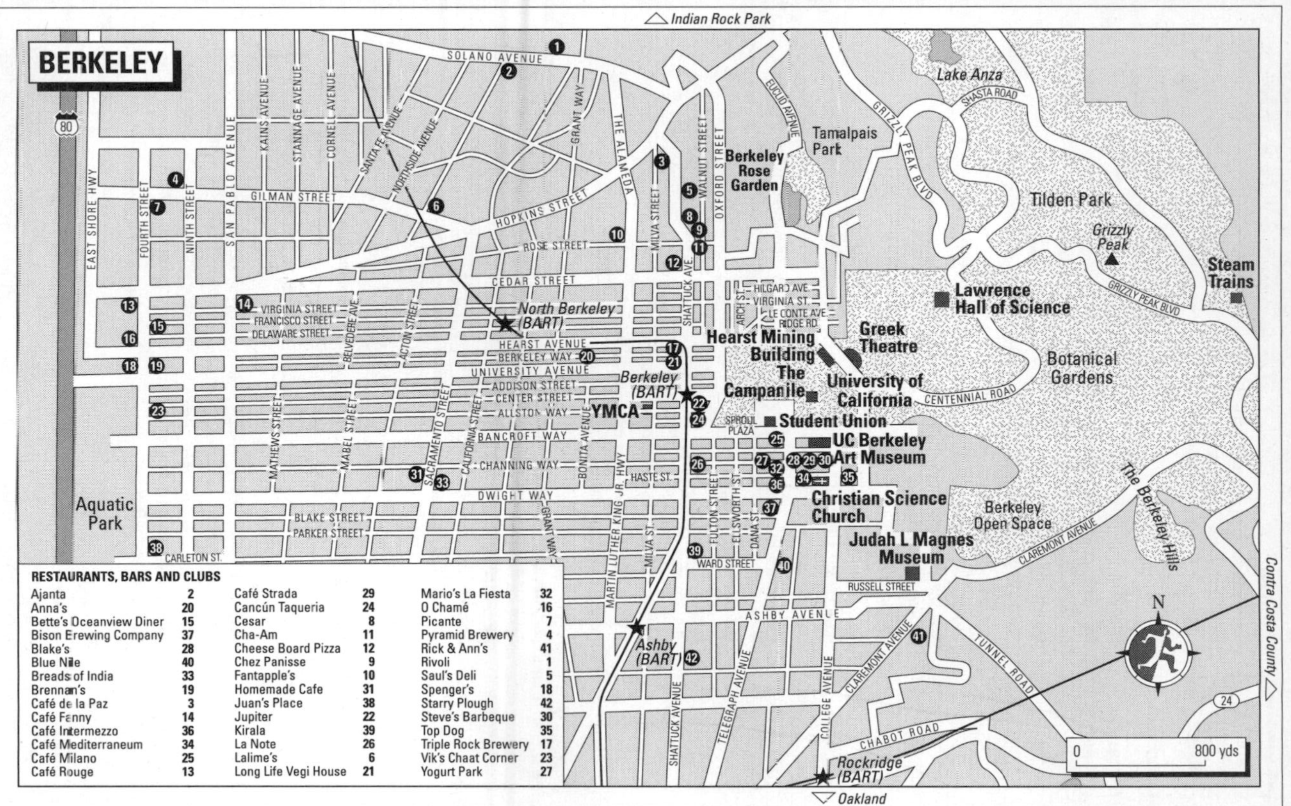
BERKELEY
Indian Rock Park
Oakland
Contra Costa County
Lake Anza
Tilden Park
Grizzly Peak
Steam Trains
Tamalpais Park
Berkeley Rose Garden
Lawrence Hall of Science
Greek Theatre
Botanical Gardens
Hearst Mining Building
The Campanile
University of California
Student Union
UC Berkeley Art Museum
Christian Science Church
Berkeley Open Space
Judah L Magnes Museum
The Berkeley Hills
YMCA
North Berkeley (BART)
Berkeley (BART)
Ashby (BART)
Rockridge (BART)
Aquatic Park
SPROUL PLAZA
SOLANO AVENUE
GRANT WAY
THE ALAMEDA
HOPKINS STREET
GILMAN STREET
ROSE STREET
CEDAR STREET
HEARST AVENUE
BERKELEY WAY
UNIVERSITY AVENUE
ADDISON STREET
CENTER STREET
ALLSTON WAY
BANCROFT WAY
CHANNING WAY
HASTE ST.
DWIGHT WAY
BLAKE STREET
PARKER STREET
CARLETON ST.
WARD STREET
RUSSELL STREET
ASHBY AVENUE
EAST SHORE HWY
FOURTH STREET
NINTH STREET
SAN PABLO AVENUE
KAINS AVENUE
STANNAGE AVENUE
CORNELL AVENUE
SANTA FE AVENUE
NORTHSIDE AVENUE
VIRGINIA STREET
FRANCISCO STREET
DELAWARE STREET
BELVEDERE AVE
ACTON STREET
MATHEWS STREET
MABEL STREET
SACRAMENTO STREET
CALIFORNIA STREET
BONITA AVENUE
MARTIN LUTHER KING JR. HWY
MILVA STREET
MILVA ST.
SHATTUCK AVE.
SHATTUCK AVENUE
WALNUT STREET
OXFORD STREET
ARCH ST.
HILGARD AVE.
VIRGINIA ST.
LE CONTE AVE.
RIDGE RD.
EUCLID AVENUE
GRIZZLY PEAK BLVD
SHASTA ROAD
CENTENNIAL ROAD
FULTON STREET
ELLSWORTH ST.
DANA ST.
TELEGRAPH AVENUE
COLLEGE AVENUE
CLAREMONT AVENUE
TUNNEL ROAD
CHABOT ROAD
24
80
N
0 800 yds
RESTAURANTS, BARS AND CLUBS
Ajanta 2
Anna's 20
Bette's Oceanview Diner 15
Bison Erewing Company 37
Blake's 28
Blue Nile 40
Breads of India 33
Brennan's 19
Café de la Paz 3
Café Fanny 14
Café Intermezzo 36
Café Mediterraneum 34
Café Milano 25
Café Rouge 13
Café Strada 29
Cancún Taqueria 24
Cesar 8
Cha-Am 11
Cheese Board Pizza 12
Chez Panisse 9
Fantapple's 10
Homemade Cafe 31
Juan's Place 38
Jupiter 22
Kirala 39
La Note 26
Lalime's 6
Long Life Vegi House 21
Mario's La Fiesta 32
O Chamé 16
Picante 7
Pyramid Brewery 4
Rick & Ann's 41
Rivoli 1
Saul's Deli 5
Spenger's 18
Starry Plough 42
Steve's Barbeque 30
Top Dog 35
Triple Rock Brewery 17
Vik's Chaat Corner 23
Yogurt Park 27

Restaurants and cafés

KOREAN

Steve's Barbeque, in the Durant Center, 2521 Durant Ave, Berkeley ☎510/848-6166. Excellent Korean food with *kim chi* to die for. *Inexpensive.*

MEXICAN

Cancun Taqueria, 2134 Allston Way, Berkeley ☎510/549-0964. Popular neighborhood burrito joint with live music some nights. *Budget.*

Juan's Place, 941 Carleton St, West Berkeley ☎510/845-6904. The original Berkeley Mexican restaurant, with great food (tons of it) and an interesting mix of people. *Budget.*

Mario's La Fiesta, 2444 Telegraph Ave, Berkeley ☎510/540-9123. Always crowded with students and other budget-minded souls who flock here for heaping portions of good, inexpensive Mexican food. *Budget.*

Picante, 1328 Sixth St, West Berkeley ☎510/525-3121. Good, cheap tacos with fresh salsa, plus live jazz on weekends. *Budget.*

Taqueria Morelia, 4481 E 14th St, East Oakland ☎510/535-6030. Excellent burritos and more unusual (and more authentically Mexican) *tortas. Budget.*

Tijuana Restaurant, 1308 E. 14th St, East Oakland ☎510/532-5575. This is the real thing – excellent authentic food served in a place that caters to a primarily Latin clientele. Famed for its *mariscada* – a plate piled high with garlicky seafood and fresh vegetables. *Budget.*

MIDDLE EASTERN

Holy Land Kosher Food, 2965 College Ave, Berkeley ☎510/665-1672. Casual diner-style restaurant serving Israeli food, including excellent falafels, to the student population. *Budget.*

SOUTHEAST ASIAN

Cha Am, 1543 Shattuck, Berkeley ☎510/848-9664. Climb the stairs to this always crowded little restaurant for deliciously spicy Thai food at bargain prices. *Inexpensive.*

Le Cheval, 1007 Clay St, Oakland ☎510/763-8495. Serving simple Vietnamese, the way it was meant to be. A pristine setting augments noodle and soup dishes, all served with your choice of chicken, beef, pork, or vegetables. *Inexpensive.*

Nan Yang, 6048 College Ave, Oakland ☎510/655-3298. Burmese food served in colorful, large portions. The chef – a political refugee – will happily discuss all his esoteric delicacies with inquisitive diners. *Inexpensive.*

SPANISH

Cesar, 1515 Shattuck Ave, Berkeley ☎510/883-0222. Eternally crowded tapas bar serving small, often fried dishes overflowing with taste, further enhanced by rich sauces such as aioli and romseco. *Inexpensive.*

The Peninsula

AMERICAN

Alpine Inn, 3915 Alpine Rd, Woodside ☎650/854-4004. Stagecoach stop in the hills turned greasy burger joint with outdoor picnic tables and an interesting mix of locals and computer guys. *Budget.*

Barbara's Fish Trap, 281 Capistrano Rd, off Hwy-1, Princeton-by-the-Sea ☎650/728-7049. Oceanfront seafood restaurant with good-value fish dinners and an unbeatable view. *Inexpensive.*

Blake's Steakhouse and Bar, 17 N San Pedro St, San Jose ☎408/298-9221. If you're craving a New York strip or a steamed lobster, washed down with a fine martini, this is the place. Entrees begin at $20. *Moderate.*

Duarte's, 202 Stage Rd, Pescadero ☎650/879-0464. Platefuls of traditional American food, (especially fish) are served in this somewhat overrated restaurant connected to a bar full of locals in cowboy hats, famous for it's outrageously priced artichoke soup. *Moderate.*

Joanie's Cafe, 447 California Ave, Palo Alto ☎650/326-6505. Homestyle breakfasts and lunches in a comfortable neighborhood restaurant. *Inexpensive.*

John's Market, Town and Country Village, Embarcadero at El Camino, Palo Alto ☎650/321-8438. Steer past the high-school kids on lunch break to get one of the best (and biggest) deli sandwiches around. Located across the street from Stanford Stadium. *Budget.*

Mongo's, 83 S Second St, San Jose ☎408/280-1738. San Jose's most unique eatery. You pile the veggies and meats onto your plate, and then watch as the cook stir fries it for you. *Inexpensive.*

Original Joe's, 301 S First St, San Jose ☎408/292-7030. Grab a stool at the counter or settle into one of the comfy vinyl booths and enjoy a burger and fries or a plate of pasta at this San Jose institution. *Budget.*

Peggy Sue's, 29 N San Pedro St, San Jose ☎408/298-6750. Inexpensive milkshakes, burgers, and fries served in a 1950s setting. Also has a vegetarian and kids' menu. *Inexpensive.*

Peninsula Creamery, 566 Emerson St, Palo Alto ☎650/323-3175. Nearly authentic 1950s American diner, serving the staples and shakes. *Inexpensive.*

St Michael's Alley, 806 Emerson St, Palo Alto ☎650/326-2530. Small, cozy café for students and locals, serving light breakfasts, lunches, and dinners. Art exhibits on the walls and live music at night. *Budget.*

71 Saint Peter, 71 N San Pedro St, San Jose ☎408/971-8523. Patio dining and oyster bar centered around a menu of filet mignon, pork loin, chicken, and salads. Extremely hot with the in-crowd. *Moderate.*

CALIFORNIA

AP Stump's, 163 W Santa Clara St., San Jose ☎408/292-9928. Best place to go if you have an unlimited expense account; one of *the* places to be seen in Silicon Valley. Great wine list. *Expensive.*

Cafe Marchella, 368 Village Lane, Menlo Park ☎408/354-8006. After nearly a decade, the cuisine here still surprises trend-conscious foodies. *Moderate.*

Eulipia, 374 S First St, San Jose ☎408/280-6161. Stylish spot featuring well-prepared versions of California-cuisine staples like grilled fish and fresh pastas. *Moderate.*

FRENCH

Bistro Vida, 641 Santa Cruz Ave, Menlo Park ☎408/462-1686. Giving Silicon Valley a much-needed style infusion by serving Left Bank Parisian bistro fare. *Inexpensive.*

Château des Fleurs, 523 Church St, Half Moon Bay ☎650/712-8837. The exquisite flower garden in front welcomes you to this small, reasonably priced French restaurant. *Moderate.*

L'Amie Donia, 530 Bryant St, Palo Alto ☎650/323-7614. A $30 three-course prix-fixe menu at this classy French bistro allows you to splurge while pretending to stay on a budget. *Moderate.*

GREEK

Evvia Estatiatorio, 420 Emerson St, Palo Alto ☎650/326-0983. California/Greek lamb and fish dishes served in a chic, yet cozy dining room. *Moderate.*

ITALIAN

Beppo, 643 Emerson St, Palo Alto ☎650/329-0065. Part of the same oddball chain as San Francisco's *Buca di Beppo*, everything about this place is fun, from the family-style Italian meals to the photos of the pope and Frank Sinatra on the walls. *Inexpensive.*

Fresco, 3398 El Camino Réal, Palo Alto ☎650/493-3470. Wide selection of pastas, pizzas, and salads with palpably fresh ingredients in unusual combinations. *Inexpensive.*

Mike's Cafe, Etc, 2680 Middlefield Rd, Palo Alto ☎650/473-6453.

Restaurants and cafés

Restaurants and cafés

Unpretentious neighborhood restaurant hidden behind a hardware store. Excellent fresh salads, pastas, and simple meat dishes are usually brought to your table by Mike himself. *Inexpensive.*

Palermo, 452 University Ave, Palo Alto ☎650/321-9908. Friendly staff and delicious Southern Italian pasta dishes served in a lively and cramped dining room. *Inexpensive.*

Spiedo, 151 W Santa Clara St, San Jose ☎408/971-6096. Handmade pasta, pizza, calamari, salmon, and more delight the tastebuds at lunch and dinner daily. *Inexpensive.*

JAPANESE

Miyake, 140 University Ave, Palo Alto ☎650/879-0464. Excessively popular restaurant serving decent and extremely cheap sushi to a boisterous crowd. The California rolls are the best (and biggest) around. *Inexpensive.*

MEXICAN

Casa Castillo, 206 S First St, San Jose ☎408/971-8132. Moderately priced Mexican food and a full bar serving monster margaritas made with Cuervo 1800. *Inexpensive.*

Los Gallos Taqueria, 3726 Florence St, Redwood City (just north of San Jose off Hwy-101) ☎650/369-1864. Simply put, the best burritos on the Peninsula. Take the Marsh Rd exit from Hwy-101 and look for the Marsh Manor shopping center. *Budget.*

SOUTHEAST ASIAN

E&O Trading Company, 96 S First St, San Jose ☎408/938-4100. Upscale outpost of the San Francisco Southeast Asian grill featuring curried fish and other Vietnamese/Indonesian fare. *Moderate.*

Krung Thai Cuisine, 1699 W San Carlos St, San Jose ☎408/295-5508. Excellent range of satays and delicious, unusual seafood dishes. Start off with a *po-tak* soup of clams and crab legs in citrus broth. *Inexpensive.*

Little Garden, 4127 El Camino Réal, Palo Alto ☎650/494-1230. Simple, spicy, well-prepared Vietnamese food – fried chicken on a bed of cabbage, shrimp and hot peppers in peanut sauce – in unpretentious surroundings. *Inexpensive.*

Marin County

AMERICAN

Bubba's Diner, 566 San Anselmo Ave, San Anselmo ☎415/381-0298. Old-fashioned diner with a friendly, hip atmosphere. Try a fresh biscuit with your meal. *Inexpensive.*

Dipsea Café, 200 Shoreline Hwy, Mill Valley ☎415/381-0298. Hearty pancakes, omelettes, sandwiches, and salads. Breakfast and lunch only. *Inexpensive.*

Hilda's, 639 San Anselmo Ave, San Anselmo ☎415/457-9266. Great breakfasts and lunches in this down-home, cozy café. *Inexpensive.*

The Lark Creek Inn, 234 Magnolia Ave, Larkspur ☎415/924-7766. The contemporary American food at this classy, restored Victorian is exquisite, and the service first rate. *Expensive.*

Mountain Home Inn, 810 Panoramic Hwy, above Mill Valley ☎415/381-9000. A place that's as good for the view as for the food, with broiled meat and fish dishes served up in a rustic lodge on the slopes of Mount Tamalpais. *Moderate.*

Pelican Inn, 10 Pacific Way, Muir Beach ☎415/383-6000. Traditional roast beef and fine ale in a candlelit coach-house atmosphere complete with stone fireplace. *Moderate.*

Sam's Anchor Café, 27 Main St, Tiburon ☎415/435-4527. This rough-hewn, amiable waterfront café and bar has been around for more than 75 years. Good burgers, sandwiches, and very popular Sunday brunches are best enjoyed on the outdoor deck. *Inexpensive.*

Station House Café, 11180 Hwy-1 (Main St), Point Reyes Station ☎415/663-1515. Serving three meals daily, this friendly local favorite entices diners from miles around to sample their grilled seafood and great steaks. *Inexpensive.*

Stinson Beach Grill, 3465 Shoreline Hwy, Stinson Beach ☎415/868-2002. Somewhat pricey, but relaxed, with outdoor dining and decent pub grub – look out for the bright-blue building right in the heart of town. *Inexpensive.*

CALIFORNIA

Mikayla, 801 Bridgeway, Sausalito ☎415/331-5888. Mediterranean staples meet California cuisine in this expensive, but highly rated restaurant in the *Casa Madrona* hotel (see p.224). Romantic views of the harbor and excellent seafood. Huge Sunday brunch buffet. *Moderate.*

ITALIAN

Gatsby's, 39 Caledonia St, Sausalito ☎415/332-4500. Slick pizza parlor a block from the waterfront on the north side of town. Bright new interior and an expansive menu. *Inexpensive.*

Piazza D'Angelo, 22 Miller Ave, Mill Valley ☎415/388-2000. Good salads, tasty pasta and affordable pizzas, served up in a lively but comfortable room right off the downtown plaza. *Inexpensive.*

MEXICAN

Cactus Café, 393 Miller Ave, Mill Valley ☎415/388-8226. Small and friendly restaurant serving fun Cal-Mex food flavored with homemade hot sauce. *Inexpensive.*

Guaymas, 5 Main St, Tiburon ☎415/435-6300. Situated on a dock by the bay – meaning you get some remarkable views of the city to accompany some terrific Cal-Mex cuisine. *Moderate.*

SOUTHEAST ASIAN

Rice Table, 1617 Fourth St, San Rafael ☎415/456-1808. From the shrimp chips through the crab pancakes and noodles on to the fried plantain desserts, these fragrant and spicy Indonesian dishes are worth planning a day around. *Inexpensive.*

Wine Country

AMERICAN

Bear Flag Cafe, 18625 Sonoma Hwy, Sonoma ☎707/938-1927. Exceptional European-influenced food at an airy bistro just outside of downtown Sonoma. *Inexpensive.*

Cafe Sarafornia, 1413 Lincoln Ave, Calistoga ☎707/942-0555. Long lines on weekends for enormous breakfasts and lunches. Let the gregarious owner talk your ear off. *Inexpensive.*

Calistoga Inn, 1250 Lincoln Ave, Calistoga ☎707/942-4101. Good seafood appetizers to help you hold down your wine. *Inexpensive.*

Catahoula Restaurant, 1457 Lincoln Ave, Calistoga ☎707/942-2275. Though perhaps slightly out-of-place in the Wine Country setting, the Cajun offerings – such as gumbo and blackened catfish – at this local eatery have quickly drawn crowds. *Moderate.*

The Diner, 6476 Washington St, Yountville ☎707/944-2626. Good diner food at a classic (if self-consciously retro) roadside joint. Evenings feature Mexican options. *Inexpensive.*

Ford's Diner, 22900 Broadway, Sonoma ☎707/938-9811. Hearty working-class American food served to locals in this out-of-the-way diner. The generous breakfast is worth the trip. *Inexpensive.*

Greystone Restaurant, at the Culinary Institute of America, 255 Main St, St Helena ☎707/967-1010. Book ahead if you want a table at this restaurant run by the country's premier cooking school. *Expensive.*

Hydro Bar and Grill, 1403 Lincoln Ave, Calistoga ☎707/942-9777. Pub grub and fancy beers. *Inexpensive.*

PJ's Cafe, 1001 Second St, Napa ☎707/224-0607. A Napa institution, popular for its pancakes, pizzas, and sandwiches. *Budget.*

Rutherford Grill, 1180 Rutherford Rd, Rutherford ☎707/963-1920. Large

Restaurants and cafés

portions of basic American food served in a handsome dining room. *Inexpensive.*

The Spot One, One mile south of St Helena on Hwy-29 ☎707/963-2844. Tacky roadside diner, convenient for a quick pit-stop. *Inexpensive.*

Third Street Aleworks, 610 Third St, Santa Rosa ☎707/523-3060. American fare like burgers and pizza coupled with microbrewed beer. *Budget.*

CALIFORNIA

Bistro Ralph, 109 Plaza St, Healdsburg ☎707/433-1380. Sparse modern decor and deliciously simple seasonal meat and fish dishes. *Moderate.*

Glen Ellen Inn, 13670 Arnold Drive, Glen Ellen ☎707/996-6409. Husband-and-wife team cook and manage this romantic dinner-only restaurant which holds only half a dozen tables, serving elegantly simple fare meant to be sampled with regional wine. *Moderate.*

Mustards, 7399 St Helena Hwy, Yountville ☎707/944-2424. Serving tapas-like tidbits rather than main meals, unusual choices inlcude blood orange salads and seared tuna on crackers. *Moderate.*

Napa Valley Grille, 6795 Washington St, Yountville ☎707/944-8506. Perfect for relaxing after a hard day tasting wine. The hearty comfort food such as roast chicken and mashed potatoes won't suprise you but will fortify you for the drive home. *Moderate.*

Pairs, 420 Main St, St Helena ☎707/963-7566. A menu of classy California options designed to go with local wines. If you're stumped they can help with a suggestion. *Moderate.*

Wappo Bar and Grill, 1226 Washington St, Calistoga ☎707/942-4712. Named after Jack London's ranch and affecting a certain rustic quality. Expect odd combinations such as chili rellenos with walnut pomegranate sauce. *Moderate.*

FRENCH

Bouchon, 6524 Washington St, Yountville ☎707/944-8097. French classics such as sweetbreads from the former chefs at the *French Laundry. Moderate.*

Domaine Chandon, 1 California Drive, Yountville ☎707/944-2892. Cal-French cooking such as squab – served grilled or rare – in the vineyard's own restaurant. Lovely views over the vines. *Expensive.*

French Laundry, 6640 Washington St, Yountville ☎707/944-2380. Worth a pilgrimage for impeccable service and a rotating menu of innovative French cuisine. *Expensive.*

La Boucane, 1778 Second St, Napa ☎707/253-1177. Hearty traditional dishes – so no calorie counting – with savory, buttery sauces, good meats, and shellfish. Open for dinner only and quite pricey. *Moderate.*

ITALIAN

Café Citti, 9049 Sonoma Hwy, Kentwood ☎707/833-2690. Casual trattoria in an area surprisingly thin in decent Italian options. *Inexpensive.*

Checkers Pizza, 1414 Lincoln Ave, Calistoga ☎707/942-9300. Pies with fancy toppings, plus soups and side dishes. *Inexpensive.*

MEXICAN

The Cantina, 500 Fourth St, Santa Rosa ☎707/523-3663. A lovely garden setting and good Mexican standards. *Budget.*

La Casa, 121 E Spain St, Sonoma ☎707/996-3406. Friendly, festive, and inexpensive Mexican restaurant just across from the Sonoma Mission. Excellent salsa – they'll sell you some to take home. *Budget.*

Chapter 16

Bars, clubs, and live music

Unlike in bigger cities, the distinction between **bars** and **nightclubs** in San Francisco can often be quite vague – with local promoters and DJs routinely transforming a grim dive into a packed hotspot in the blink of an eye. Many popular **live music** venues are little more than a neighborhood saloon with a stage in the back, and bands routinely have to battle barroom chatter for the audience's attention. There are a smattering of massive multilayer dance clubs for those who feel lonely in a crowd of less than a thousand, not to mention some remarkably stylish concert halls, including the landmark Fillmore, touchstone for the 1960s psychedelic rock movement. But even on weekends in the biggest venues, cover charges are almost universally quite low – often less than $10 per person.

While no one is going to force you to buy a drink, few venues admit patrons under 21, since that's the **legal age for purchasing alcohol** in the United States; even if you look twice as old, plan on carrying valid identification (generally a driver's license or passport) if you want to be sure to be admitted. Bars can legally open at 6am – though few do – and stay open until 2am. The same hours pertain to buying alcohol in a store, even those open 24 hours. All clubs serve alcohol, but many keep their doors open after 2am while switching to non-alcoholic beverages; on weekends, dance clubs tend to stay open till 4am. That said, San Francisco is not a 24-hour town, so partying until dawn requires a bit of determination and advance planning.

Visitors from Europe and other parts of the US are routinely shocked to discover that **smoking is now illegal** in virtually all bars and clubs in California, though a few bars bend the rules for their nicotine-dependent clientele. The penalty if you're caught smoking is a $95 ticket, though the law is only erratically enforced, and you're more likely to be reprimanded by health-conscious locals than written a citation.

Before heading out, make sure to grab one of the city's free weeklies – the *San Francisco Bay Guardian*, *SF Weekly*, and, in Berkeley, the *East Bay Express*, all have excellent listings sections – or stop by a record shop for invites to special club nights and flyers promoting one-time events. On the Web, both CitySearch (*www.bayarea.citysearch.com*) and SF Station (*www.sfstation.com*) offer comprehensive listings.

Bars, clubs, and live music

Rooftop bars

Carnelian Room, 555 California St at Kearny ☎415/431-7500. The best of the rooftop cocktail lounges, 52 floors up in the Bank of America Building. A truly elegant spot for some smart cocktails that attracts mostly businessmen on corporate accounts – so bring smart money, too.

Equinox, *Hyatt Regency*, Embarcadero ☎415/788-1234. Revolving cocktail lounge; you never have to leave your seat for a full 360° perspective of the city. The drinks aren't cheap, but prices are less lofty than those of meals in the adjoining dining room.

Grandviews Lounge, *Grand Hyatt*, 345 Stockton St at Sutter ☎415/403-4847. Good views over the bay at prices one would expect to pay for them.

Harry Denton's Starlight Room, *Sir Francis Drake Hotel*, 450 Powell St at Sutter ☎415/395-8595. Dress up and drink martinis. This is a sophisticated scene with a moneyed crowd who come for the live jazz.

Top of the Mark, *Mark Hopkins Hotel*, California St at Mason ☎415/616-6916. The most famous of the rooftop bars, though it tends to attract mostly tourists.

View Lounge, *Marriott Hotel*, 55 Fourth St at Market St ☎415/896-1600 ext 6374. Somewhat chintzy decor, but majestic views of the city. Drink prices are elevated, but then so is the bar.

Bars

San Francisco has an array of eclectic drinking establishments, each reflecting the character of the neighborhood in which it is situated. The **downtown** bars are generally packed just after work, when the inevitable happy-hour specials are in full swing, though they're dead at any other time of day. Nearby **North Beach** boasts several historic bars dating back to the city's wildest days, while the **Marina** has a big **yuppie singles** scene. **SoMa** boasts more clubs than bars, with the exception of the **gay bar circuit** situated along **Folsom Street**, notorious for its **leather crowd**. Among the **Tenderloin**'s bars are some of the seediest in the city, though there are a few pleasant exceptions scattered throughout the neighborhood. There are a few bars and pubs in the **Haight**, but anyone in search of a psychcedelic groove may be sadly disappointed by how pedestrian things have become. The **Castro** boasts a high concentration of gay bars, most of them surprisingly sedate except during the annual parade. The neighboring **Mission** district has the city's most diverse collection of bars, with everything from dank dives to swank hot spots. Out in the **Richmond** and the **Sunset**, there are a number of pubs and taverns catering to locals, but nothing worth a special trip.

There's not a whole lot in the way of Bay Area nightlife outside San Francisco, though **Berkeley**'s bar scene swarms with students from the local UC campus. Nearby **Oakland** features a few historic spots catering to a somewhat scruffy local contingent. Don't bother heading to either **Marin** or the **Peninsula** looking for a hot night on the town – most local venues tend to be rather low key. Those who travel to the **Wine Country** will doubtlessly spend their time at the vineyards, not in bars, though a few watering holes offer a non-pretentious escape from connoisseur culture.

Downtown and Chinatown

The Big Four, *Huntington Hotel*, 1075 California St at Taylor ☎415/771-1140. Classy hotel bar, aimed squarely at the sedate set who want a well-made drink in civilized surroundings.

The Bubble Lounge, 714 Montgomery St at Columbus ☎415/434-4204.

Champagne bar that attracts a young, label-touting crowd; the prices of the bubbly here are surprisingly reasonable.

Buddha Bar, 901 Grant Ave at Washington ☎415/362-1792. This Chinatown bar feels far removed from urban America, filled with older locals slapping down mahjong tiles.

Cathay House, 718 California St at Grant ☎415/982-3388. Don't be put off by the diners in the window – sitting smack in the middle of a run-of-the-mill restaurant is an inviting circular bar, centered on a large Buddha.

Compass Rose, at the *Westin St Francis Hotel*, 335 Powell St at Union Square ☎415/774-0167. Though you can get a perfectly passable fancy meal here, better to stop in at the bar for a couple of their more affordable cocktails.

E&O Trading Company, 314 Sutter St at Grant ☎415/693-0303. A brewpub restaurant and bar serving spring rolls and other Asian-style appetizers to go with some more exotic cocktails.

Ginger's Trois, 246 Kearny St at Bush ☎415/989-0282. A charmingly divey gay bar smack in the heart of downtown, welcoming a group of diehard regulars who like to sing along with the showtunes occasionally played by the bartenders.

Harrington's Bar and Grill, 245 Front St at California ☎415/392-7595. After work the long bar is packed with businessmen in need of some liquid comfort. Later in the evening the back room fills with diners searching for more hearty nourishment.

Li Po's Bar, 916 Grant Ave at Jackson ☎415/982-0072. Named after the Chinese poet, *Li Po's* is something of a literary hangout among the Chinatown regulars. Enter through the false cavern front and sit at the very dimly lit bar where Wayne Wang filmed *Chan is Missing*.

The London Wine Bar, 415 Sansome St at Sacramento ☎415/788-4811. Claiming to be America's first wine bar, this place is as pretentious and expensive as you might expect. Still the wine list is undeniably extensive.

Occidental Grill, 453 Pine St at Kearny St ☎415/834-0848. This Barbary Coast-style den is supposedly the birthplace of the martini – in any case, they certainly make a mean one.

Pied Piper Bar, in the *Palace Hotel*, 2 New Montgomery St at Market ☎415/392-8600. A mahogany-paneled watering hole inside the city's most elegant old hotel with lush landscape paintings lining the walls and powerful personages sipping expensive drinks.

Red Room, 827 Sutter St at Jones ☎415/346-7666. Like the name says, everything is red – walls, furniture, glasses, and many of the drinks – in this popular lounge that caters to a trendy set.

The Redwood Room, *Clift Hotel*, 495 Geary St at Taylor ☎415/775-4700. Old money in suitably sedate Art Deco surroundings. One of the most tastefully decorated drinking spots in town.

Royal Exchange, 301 Sacramento St at Front ☎415/956-1710. Where the young suits come after a long day getting rich to work the frenzied singles scene.

Zero Degrees, 490 Pacific St at Montgomery ☎415/788-9376. A sleek, minimalist café/bar where you can relax with wine and brandy or wind yourself up with caffeine and sugar.

North Beach and Nob Hill

The Crow Bar, 401 Broadway at Montgomery ☎415/788-2769. Down at the heels and nonthreatening; on a club-saturated strip of North Beach, this hole-in-the-wall is an appealing escape.

Fuse, 493 Broadway at Kearny ☎415/788-2706. The industrial decor is a welcome retreat from North Beach's omnipresent Italian kitsch. Quiet on weeknights, but packed with an under-thirty crowd on weekends.

Gino and Carlo, 548 Green St at Grant ☎415/421-0896. Transforming gracefully

Bars, clubs, and live music

Bars, clubs, and live music

SAN FRANCISCO BEERS

San Francisco **microbreweries** abound, so expect to be confronted by **lagers** (light, such as Becks or Heineken), **ales** (golden brown, such as Bass), and **stouts** (dark, such as Guinness), along with a few more esoteric varieties thrown in for good measure, all marketed under unfamiliar brand names. For the cream of the local product, stop by the Anchor Steam Brewery, 1705 Mariposa (☎415/863-8350) on Potrero Hill for a **tour**, though the product is universally available at bars and stores. Other popular regional alternatives are Sierra Nevada Pale Ale, Red Tail, Full Sail, and the rich Anderson Valley Boont Ales, from Sonoma County. Expect to pay between $3 and $5 for a 16oz pint or a 12oz bottle.

San Francisco

Beach Chalet	p.261	Potrero Brewing Company	p.279
Gordon Biersch	p.278	Thirsty Bear	p.253
San Francisco Brewing Company	below	Twenty Tank	p.278

East Bay

Bison Brewing Company	p.281	Pyramid Ale Brewery	p.281
Jupiter	p.281	Triple Rock	p.282

with age from a dive into a landmark, this is the classic drunken pressman's bar, with history oozing from every wooden nook and cranny.

Hawaii West, 729 Vallejo St at Stockton ☎415/362-3220. A cursing parrot, a drag-queen owner and a pool table you don't have to wait in line for. If you're lucky, the owner will serenade the crowd with some karaoke.

John Barleycorn, 1415 Larkin St at California ☎415/771-1620. Ye olde time bar, with plenty of bourbon behind the counter and pictures of men with handlebar mustaches above it.

San Francisco Brewing Company, 155 Columbus Ave at Pacific ☎415/434-3344. Probably the most touristy of the various microbrewpubs around town, with a bland crowd of non-locals and big shining tanks of beer.

Savoy Tivoli, 1434 Grant Ave at Green ☎415/362-0435. North Beach's most attractively decorated and populated bar, with a well-worn wooden interior. Also serving good, reasonably priced food – although the emphasis is on the standard array of beers and cocktails.

Spec's, 12 Saroyan Place at Columbus ☎415/421-4112. Calls itself a museum for its collection of knickknacks, but how many museums do you know where you can get cross-eyed on cocktails?

Tonga Room, *Fairmont Hotel*, Powell and Mason sts ☎415/772-5278. This basement tiki lounge has grass huts and a floating band at night, not to mention an indoor rainstorm every fifteen minutes. Come for happy hour to bring down the otherwise lofty prices.

Tosca Café, 242 Columbus Ave at Broadway ☎415/986-9651. A beautiful old bar with tile on the floor, bow ties on the bartenders, and opera as the soundtrack. Come early as the bass from the *Club Millenium* nightclub upstairs can get bothersome late night.

Vesuvio Cafe, 255 Columbus Ave at Broadway ☎415/362-3370. The famed beatnik haunt, just down the street from City Lights Bookstore. The aura of intellectual ferment is long gone, but what's left behind is still a warm neighborhood joint.

Bars, clubs, and live music

The northern waterfront and Pacific Heights

Balboa Café, 3199 Fillmore St at Greenwich ☎415/921-3944. Though its fortunes have waned somewhat in the past few years, this bar is still a magnet for the Pacific Heights singles scene.

Buena Vista Café, 2765 Hyde St at Beach, Fisherman's Wharf ☎415/474-5044. The best Irish coffee in town (after all, they claim to have introduced it to North America). Crowds aiming to sample the concoction often pack in to the bursting point.

City Tavern, 3200 Fillmore St at Greenwich ☎415/567-0918. A weekend favorite with the young and wealthy, with crowds routinely spilling out onto the street.

Eastside West, 3154 Fillmore St at Greenwich ☎415/885-4000. Along with *the Balboa Café* and the *City Tavern*, one of the three essential stops on the Pacfic Heights singles circuit. As with the others, you can get something from the kitchen, though the bar-side meat market is the standard main course.

Harry's on Fillmore, 2020 Fillmore St at Pine ☎415/921-1000. More posh than the *Boom Boom Room*, its better pedigreed neighbor down the hill, *Harry's* features bar-rocking blues on weekends.

Perry's, 1944 Union St at Buchanan ☎415/922-9022. Made legendary by Maupin's *Tales of the City*, this institution is a hugely popular pub with a friendly atmosphere.

Pier 23, Pier 23 ☎415/362-5125. Sit out on the deck and enjoy heatlamps and cocktails by the bay, plus a gorgeous view of the Bay Bridge.

Silver Cloud, 1994 Lombard St at Webster ☎415/922-1977. A pleasantly run-of-the-mill all-American burger joint and bar with a popular karaoke room in the back.

Trapdoor, 3251 Scott at Chestnut ☎415/776-1928. Tapas and drinks attract a wealthy Marina singles scene, who listen to occasional jazz acts amidst the sleek decor.

SoMa

Butter, 354 11th St at Folsom ☎415/431-6545. Stylized "white trash" bar and diner featuring imitation trailer park decor smack in the middle of club land. Your chance to listen to DJs while eating tater tots with the über-chic.

Gay bars and clubs

The bulk of San Francisco's gay **bars** are situated in three neighborhoods: the Castro (p.279), SoMa (above) – especially along Folsom Street near Ninth Street – and Polk Gulch near the Tenderloin district (p.278). The gay men's scene here tend to be less exclusive than in other cities, and gay-friendly straights are welcome wherever they are comfortable.

Virtually every **nightclub** in town has a "queer" night, though the following large venues are the surest bet for dancing cheek to cheek with a member of the same sex; also, be sure and check out flyers for roving hotspots such as *The Box*.

The Café	p.288	The EndUp	p.289
Cat Club	p.288	King Street Garage	p.289
Club Townsend	p.288	Liquid	p.289
Co-co Club	p.288	The Stud	p.289
El Rio	p.289	1015 Folsom	p.290

The city's **lesbian scene** isn't quite as distinct and visible as it once was, but sporadic women's nights at some of the venues listed above still attract decent crowds – albeit highly mixed ones.

Bars, clubs, and live music

The Caribbean Zone, 55 Natoma at Second ☎415/541-9565. Twilight Zone is more like it. Hidden under a Bay Bridge onramp, with indoor waterfalls and the fuselage of the Doobie Brothers' airplane converted into a seating area.

Gordon Biersch Brewery, 2 Harrison St at Embarcadero ☎415/243-8246. Bayfront outpost of the successful Peninsula microbrewery housed in a converted Hills Brothers coffee warehouse with a lovely view of the bridge, good bar food and some of the best beers in San Francisco.

Hole in the Wall Saloon, 289 Eighth at Folsom ☎415/431-HOWL. A hardcore gay biker bar where almost anything can happen and usually does. Not exactly the best place to show off your Armani.

House of Shields, 39 New Montgomery St at Mission ☎415/392-7732. A last bastion of the three-martini lunch. If you get drunk enough, saunter over to the piano and sing along.

The Lone Star, 1354 Harrison St ☎415/863-9999. A friendly, no-frills gay bar attracting bears and the cubs who love them.

Mars, 798 Brannan St at Seventh ☎415/621-MARS. So loud you can barely hear your cell phone ringing. The dressy young crowd of computer professionals packs in at 6pm and stays until late, looking for the right interface.

My Place, 1225 Folsom St ☎415/863-2329. Among the more notorious addresses on Folsom St for gay men. There's a dark and smoky back area where regulars disregard more than just the city's smoking policy.

111 Minna, 111 Minna St at Second ☎415/974-1719. A combination bar, art gallery, and performance venue showcasing the best in local arts, *111 Minna* is many things to many people, which is probably why it's usually packed.

POW!, 101 Sixth St at Mission ☎415/278-0940. A hipster bar in an unlikely part of SoMa; unique Japanamation theme and graffiti art on the walls.

Powerhouse, 1347 Folsom St ☎415/861-1790. Dark and cruisey gay men's bar in the dark depths of the Folsom scene.

The Ramp, 855 China Basin ☎415/621-2378. Way out on the old docks, this is well worth the half-mile trek from downtown to sit out on the patio and sip beers overlooking the abandoned piers and new boatyards.

The SF Eagle, 12th at Harrison St ☎415/626-0880. A good, old fashioned leather bar. Particularly popular on Sundays when they hold a late afternoon "beer bust."

Twenty Tank, 316 11th St at Folsom ☎415/255-9455. Vast vats of beer rise to the ceiling in this home-brewer's dream. Centrally located, this is a good place to grab a cheap drink before heading off clubbing.

The Tenderloin and Civic Center

Backflip, *Phoenix Hotel*, 601 Eddy St ☎415/771-FLIP. A little bit of LA in the north. Aspiring models and rockers lounge by the poolside bar, pretending it's 80 degrees outside.

Bobby's Owl Tree, 601 Post St at Taylor ☎415/776-9344. With more owls than you can count on every wall, from clocks to statues to paintings, the motif can get a bit creepy, but it's all in good fun.

Edinburgh Castle, 950 Geary St at Polk ☎415/885-4074. Just your average Scottish bar, except that it's run by Koreans. Be sure to order some fish and chips, which are delivered from the co-owned restaurant down the block. With occasional bands and plays (usually starring British expat cast members) upstairs.

Kimo's, 1351 Polk at Bush ☎415/885-4535. Polk Gulch drag bar that is home to the weekly rock night *Alcoholocaust*. Probably a little extreme for most tastes.

The Motherlode, 1081 Post St at Larkin ☎415/928-6006. The oldest and most famous transvestite bar in town – the ladies here don't usually take kindly to newcomers, especially gawkers.

Bars, clubs, and live music

The Castro

Bar, 456 Castro St at 18th ☎415/626-7220. Swank new bar in the heart of the strip where the drinks are cheaper and the crowd friendlier than the plush interior may lead you to expect.

Café Flore, 2298 Market St at Noe ☎415/621-8579. Very much the in-spot before dark. Attractive café, with matching clientele and leafy outdoor area, and no shortage of people eyeing each other up. Popular with gay men but a favorite of all.

Detour, 2348 Market St at Castro ☎415/861-6053. Brutally loud and dark techno bar curiously lacking a dance floor and catering to a young, fit gay crowd.

Harvey's, 500 Castro St at 18th ☎415/431-HARV. A lively corner hot spot drawing a friendly gay and lesbian crowd for socializing and the occasional drag show. Serves food, too.

Lucky 13, 2140 Market St at Church ☎415/487-1313. A primarily hetero rocker bar on the border between the Castro and the Lower Haight. Even if the crowd isn't always raging loudly, the music is.

Martuni's, 4 Valencia St at Market ☎415/241-0205. Sing along to Judy Garland with a well-heeled, middle-aged, and primarily gay crowd. There are regular open-mic nights for would-be torch stars.

Midnight Sun, 4067 18th St at Castro ☎415/861-4186. Flashy video bar filled with well-dressed white boys shopping for husbands. The weekly showings of popular television programs are a big draw.

The Mint, 1942 Market St at Guerrero ☎415/626-4726. A generally middle-aged crowd sips cocktails and croons ballads at this popular karaoke bar.

Orbit Room, 1900 Market St at Laguna ☎415/252-9525. Deco joint with tie-clad bartenders serving up specialty cocktails, plus the usual coffees and café food. Big bay windows let you observe the goings-on of Market St.

Pilsner Inn, 225 Church St at Market ☎415/621-7058. An old gay tavern that turned trendy one day, though no one can quite say why. The place packs them in every weekend; otherwise, not much more goes on here than the occasional pool game accompanied by an Eighties song on the jukebox.

Potrero Brewing Company, 535 Florida St at 17th ☎415/552-1967. Decent selection of snacks and homebrewed suds, plus a deck overlooking the Mission's more industrial stretches.

Twin Peaks, 401 Castro at 17th ☎415/864-9470. One of the Castro's first gay bars, with large picture windows looking out at the street. Draws a low-key older crowd who gather for quiet drinks and conversation.

The Mission

The Albion, 3139 16th St at Albion ☎415/552-8558. The sign above the bar says "service for the sick." If that sounds enticing, stay. There's pool in the back and occasional bands on the tiny stage by the door.

Casanova, 527 Valencia St at 16th ☎415/863-9328. Lots of cool lamps and an even niftier selection of music on the jukebox attract the young and stylish.

Dalva, 3121 16th St at Albion ☎415/252-7740. Though the wafer-thin space is easy to miss, that doesn't stop the crowds from packing in to lean against one of the narrow tables. They even manage to squeeze live bands and DJs into the slender front room.

Esta Noche, 3079 16th St at Valencia ☎415/861-5757. Nightly drag acts attract a largely Latino crowd.

La Rondalla, 901 Valencia St at 20th ☎415/647-7474. It's always Christmas at this festive Mexican dive. Sit at the bar if you don't need food with your margaritas, and prepare to duck beneath trombones and violins: they manage to

Bars, clubs, and live music

squeeze a full mariachi band into the narrow space.

Latin American Club, 3286 22nd St at Valencia ☎415/647-2732. Though the space is small, they've squeezed in a pool table for the crowd of hipsters who frequented the place until recently. Thankfully, newer hotspots have drawn the bulk of them away, making this a pleasant escape once again.

Lexington Club, 3464 19th St at Lexington ☎415/863-2052. A laid-back, no-frills lesbian bar packed with both the pretty as well as the butch. Great jukebox.

The Lone Palm, 3394 22nd St at Guerrero ☎415/648-0109. A dim, candlelit cocktail lounge with tablecloths, potted ferns, and classic American movies playing on monitors above the bar.

Tip Top, 3001 Mission St at 26th ☎415/824-6486. Catering to locals of the punk persuasion. Expect a cover on weekend evenings, when rock acts perform in the small back room.

Wild Side West, 424 Cortland Ave at Wool ☎415/647-3099. Quiet and off the beaten track, way out there in Bernal Heights. A neighborhood bar with a predominantly lesbian clientele.

Zeitgeist, 199 Valencia St at Division ☎415/255-7505. This "biker bar" (mostly bicycle messengers) has a large patio, making it a haven for smokers.

West of Civic Center and the Haight

An Bodhran, 688 Haight St at Pierce ☎415/431-4724. Not quite on par with the *Mad Dog* up the block, but occasional live Irish folk music and near-constant drunken revelry make this a popular spot for the young and inebriated.

Club Deluxe, 1511 Haight St at Ashbury ☎415/552-6949. Hangout for the wing-tipped, zoot-suit crowd, in a stretch of Upper Haight otherwise dominated by shaggy hippies.

Hayes and Vine, 377 Hayes St at Gough ☎415/626-5301. A fancy, dimly lit wine bar with a strong local selection. Depending on your mood it can either be intensely romantic or nap-inducing.

Mad Dog in the Fog, 530 Haight St at Fillmore ☎415/626-7279. Aptly named by the two lads from Birmingham, England who own the joint, this is one of the Lower Haight's most loyally patronized bars, with darts, English beer, copies of the *Sun* newspaper and a typical pub menu that includes bangers and mash, hearty ploughman's, and the like.

Marlena's, 488 Hayes St at Octavia ☎415/864-6672. An old drag bar that refuses to cave to gentrification, *Marlena's* attracts a friendly, aging crowd clinging to dreams of Seventies wildness.

Martin Macks, 1568 Haight St at Clayton ☎415/864-0124. Popular for its pub food, but you can still grab a pint of Guinness by the bar – if you can squeeze past the crowd, that is.

Molotov, 582 Haight St at Steiner ☎415/558-8019. Though ravers have largely displaced the rocker element in the neighborhood, leather jackets still predominate here.

Noc Noc, 557 Haight St at Steiner ☎415/861-5811. Decor straight out of an Orwellian sci-fi film, with static-filled televisions in every corner. The bar doesn't have a license to sell hard alcohol, so all cocktails are made from sake.

Persian Aub Zam Zam, 1663 Haight St at Clayton ☎415/861-2545. Open at totally arbitrary hours. Getting kicked out by Bruno, the owner/bartender, is a local tradition, as are his famous gin martinis.

Place Pigalle, 520 Hayes St at Gough ☎415/552-2671. Art on the walls and live music and readings many nights of the week have made this bar a hub for the local creative community.

Trax, 1437 Haight St ☎415/864-4213. The only gay bar in the Haight is a smoker's paradise, which also helps attract regulars of all orientations.

The Richmond and the Sunset

Bitter End, 441 Clement St at Fifth ☎415/221-9538. In fact, a pleasant Irish bar. Locals nip in throughout the day for a pint, pool, or a game of darts. Open front makes it perfect for afternoon people-watching.

Blarney Stone, 5701 Geary Blvd at 21st ☎415/386-9914. The Irish expat community crowds in on weekends to watch English League football matches with accompanying pints of bitter.

The Courtyard, 2436 Clement St at 25th ☎415/387-7616. A pretty standard bar and grill, but with a pleasant back patio. Come early – after dusk it can get brutally cold.

Pat O'Shea's Mad Hatter, 3848 Geary Blvd at Third ☎415/752-3148. Divey Irish pub with spare decor and regulars who seem bolted to their stools.

Pig & Whistle Pub, 2801 Geary Blvd at Wood ☎415/885-4779. Good range of English and California microbrews, a pool table and dartboards, plus very good pub food.

Trad'r Sam's, 6150 Geary Blvd at 26th ☎415/221-0773. Classic tiki bar, complete with flaming bowls of exotically named cocktails.

Yancy's Saloon, 734 Irving St at 8th ☎415/665-6551. Mellow, plant-festooned collegiate bar with free darts and cheap drinks.

East Bay

The Alley, 3325 Grand Ave, Oakland ☎510/444-8505. Sing along with the drunken locals at this cozy piano bar. Suggestions welcome from a songbook of favorites.

Ben-N-Nick's Bar and Grill, 5612 College Ave, Oakland ☎510/923-0327. A family-friendly beerhall with crayons for the kiddies and and twenty microbrews on tap for the parents.

Bench and Bar, 120 11th St, Oakland ☎510/444-2266. Primarily African-American and Latino club hot spot, with a loyal gay following. Particularly known for its weekend salsa nights, though the crowd and vibe can vary wildly depending on the evening's theme.

Bison Brewing Company, 2598 Telegraph Ave, Berkeley ☎510/841-7734. Eat and drink where some of the best and best-priced Bay Area beers are brewed – Honey Basil ale is highly recommended. Noisy bands on the weekends.

Brennan's, Fourth St and University, Berkeley ☎510/841-0960. Solidly blue-collar hangout that's a great place for drinking inexpensive beers and watching a game on TV.

Cato's Alehouse, 3891 Piedmont Ave, Oakland ☎510/655-3349. Casual local spot with a good beer selection to accompany their pizza and sandwich offerings.

Heinhold's First and Last Chance Saloon, 56 Jack London Square, Oakland ☎510/839-6761. Authentic waterfront bar that has hardly changed since the 1900s, when Jack London was a regular. They still haven't bothered to fix the slanted floor caused by the 1906 earthquake.

Jupiter, 2181 Shattuck Ave, Berkeley ☎510/843-8277. Many types of beer to select from at this local favorite. Live jazz on weekends, excellent atmosphere, and an outdoor beer garden.

The Kingfish, 5227 Claremont Ave, Oakland ☎510/655-7373. More like a tumbledown shed than a bar, selling low-priced pitchers of cold beer to UC Berkeley rugby players and other headbangers.

Pyramid Brewery, 901 Gilman St, Berkeley ☎510/528-9880. Huge post-industrial space actually makes for a surprisingly casual spot to sip the suds. Outdoor film screenings on weekend nights during summer.

Rickey's Sports Lounge, 15028 Hesperian Blvd, San Leandro, near Bayfair BART ☎510/352-0200. With seven giant-screen TVs and 35 others spread around the cavernous room, this bar-cum-restaurant is the place to go to watch sports.

Shattuck Avenue Spats, 1974 Shattuck Ave, Berkeley ☎510/841-7225. A

Bars, clubs, and live music

restaurant early evenings, though most come late for the exotic cocktails with names like "the Dankobar Screamer" and "Zelda's Zonker." Plush velvet couches create a soothing atmosphere.

Triple Rock Brewery, 1920 Shattuck Ave, Berkeley ☎510/843-2739. Buzzing, all-American beer bar with a good selection of beers brewed on the premises for the young, student crowd.

The White Horse, 6560 Telegraph Ave at 66th St, Oakland ☎510/652-3820. Oakland's only gay bar – a small, friendly place, with mixed nightly dancing for men and women.

Peninsula

Agenda, 399 S First St, San Jose ☎408/287-4087. A popular bar/restaurant/lounge in San Jose's "SICFA" district with live jazz and DJs spinning dance tunes nightly.

Backbeat, 777 Lawrence Expressway, Sunnyvale ☎408/241-0777. Uncharacteristically dressy Peninsula hot spot, resorting to the velvet rope treatment on weekends when the dance floor gets hopping.

Blue Chalk Café, 630 Ramona St, Palo Alto ☎650/326-1020. Yuppies and other young Siliconites congregate at this wildly successful bar/pool-hall/restaurant.

Douglass Beach House, Miramar Beach, two and a half miles north of Half Moon Bay just west of Hwy-1 on Medio Ave ☎650/726-4143. Two-story country beach house with fireplace and outside deck hosting West Coast jazz performers.

The Edge, 260 California Ave, Palo Alto ☎650/324-EDGE. Cheap drinks and low (or no) cover charge make this dance club a lively option. Good live touring bands some nights, when tickets cost $5–10.

Fanny & Alexander's, 412 Emerson Street, Palo Alto ☎650/326-7183. Thirtysomething crowd munches on decent bar snacks and gets down to pub rock nightly. On warm nights, make a beeline for the backyard garden.

Gordon Biersch Brewery, 640 Emerson St, Palo Alto ☎650/323-7723. Among the first and still the best of the Bay Area's microbrewery-cum-restaurants. Also in SF (see p.278) and in downtown San Jose at 33 E San Fernando St ☎408/294-6785.

Henfling's, 9450 Highway 9, Ben Lomond ☎831/336-8811. Cozy small-town pub and restaurant serving a mountainside community of aging hippies and bikers.

Moss Beach Distillery, Beach and Ocean, Moss Beach ☎650/728-0220. If you don't feel like paying out $20 per entree at the popular restaurant, snuggle up under a wool blanket, order a drink and an appetizer, and watch the sunset from the patio overlooking the ocean.

The Saddle Rack, 1310 Auzerais Ave, San Jose ☎408/286-3393. A massive barn housing the state's largest country-and-western bar – in fact, seven bars in one, plus a mechanical bull and line dancing.

Tied House Café and Brewery, 954 Villa St, Mountain View ☎650/965-2739. Spacious brewpub featuring an ample selection of hops. You can escape the frequent computer industry bashes out back, in the pleasant beer garden.

Marin

Café Amsterdam, 23 Broadway, Fairfax ☎415/256-8020. Live alternative folk rock nightly, to go with microbrews, espresso drinks, and an extensive menu.

Fourth Street Tavern, 711 Fourth St, San Rafael ☎415/454-4044. No-frills beer bar with free, bluesy music most nights.

Marin Brewing Company, 1809 Larkspur Landing, Larkspur ☎415/461-4677. Lively pub opposite the Larkspur ferry terminal, with half a dozen tasty ales – try the malty Albion Amber or the Marin Hefe Weiss – all brewed on the premises.

No Name Bar, 757 Bridgeway, Sausalito ☎415/332-1392. A smoky ex-haunt of the Beats which hosts live jazz several times per week.

Pelican Inn, Hwy-1, Muir Beach ☎415/383-6000. Fair selection of traditional English and modern Californian ales, plus fish and chips (and rooms to rent in case you overdo it).

Sam's Anchor Cafe, 27 Main St, Tiburon ☎415/435-4527. Popular waterfront spot with Marin day-trippers and locals alike. You can get a drink or two (or brunch) while waiting in the sun for the ferry back to San Francisco.

Smiley's Schooner Saloon, 41 Wharf Rd, Bolinas ☎415/868-1311. The bartender calls the customers by name at one of the oldest continually operating bars in the state. Basic hotel rooms are available in back for $59–69.

Sweetwater, 153 Throckmorton Ave, Mill Valley ☎415/388-2820. A comfortable saloon which doubles as Marin's prime live music venue, with gigs ranging from jazz and blues all-stars to Jefferson Airplane survivors.

Wine Country

Fab, 16135 Main St, Guerneville ☎707/869-5708. Rather out-of-place gay glam bar, catering to Russian River weekenders with drag shows and disco nights.

Mixx, 135 Fourth St, Santa Rosa ☎707/573-1344. Has a lovely old wooden bar for leaning on, and a decent, if somewhat standard, menu.

Murphy's Irish Pub, 464 First St E, Sonoma ☎707/935-0660. Small bar with an eclectic interior and a few outdoor tables serving basic pub grub and European beers.

Pancha's, 6764 Washington St, Yountville ☎707/944-2125. An actual dive bar – amid all the Napa Valley wine tasting – in the form of a western saloon.

Rainbow Cattle Company, 16220 Main St, Guerneville ☎707/869-0206. Dark, rustic bar catering to a primarily gay and lesbian crowd of weekenders vacationing along the nearby Russian River.

Santa Rosa Brewing Company, 458 B St, Santa Rosa ☎707/544-4677. Jumping brewpub with occasional live music and basic pub grub.

Third Street Aleworks, 610 Third St, Santa Rosa ☎707/523-3060. A microbrewery offering exotic seasonal concoctions, such as the Award-winning One Ton Blackberry Ale.

Live Music

San Francisco's music scene reflects the character of the city as a whole: laid-back, eclectic, and a little nostalgic. The options for catching **live music** are many, and the scene is progressive, if a bit provincial, characterized by the frequent emergence of decent young bands who like to play close to home.

The city has never recaptured the heyday it experienced in the 1960s when the Grateful Dead, Jefferson Airplane, and other psychedelic **rock** bands dominated the local scene, but nowadays the local musical community is at least a good deal more varied. You'll find good bands performing virtually every genre of music under the sun to an equally diverse and knowledgeable audience.

In addition to **Latin**, **Celtic**, and **country** music, **jazz** is very good and not just confined to the city proper: the East Bay in particular is very strong on jazz and **blues** bands. In recent years the Bay Area has helped launch **acid jazz** – a beat-heavy, electronic form of jazz that makes for pleasant background music – and a classic **swing** revival. Not quite as popular, but with a loyal following, is a community of **avant-garde jazz** musicians gathered around Oakland's Mills College.

Another scene that shows no immediate signs of disappearing is the **pop-punk** sound, which grew out of a deeply rooted Bay Area punk community, exploding into popularity in the early

Bars, clubs, and live music

Bars, clubs, and live music

1990s with bands such as Rancid and Green Day.

San Francisco's **club** scene, meanwhile, has experienced a particularly dramatic transformation, fed by a mind-boggling array of technologically innovative **electronic** musicians, DJs, and fledgling record labels. Local artists have been particularly prominent within the **ambient, house, and drum 'n' bass** scenes.

The best of local music can be heard at the smaller clubs and bars concentrated mostly in the Mission, Haight, and SoMa areas of San Francisco, as well as around Berkeley University in the East Bay. When a musical event isn't free, cover charges rarely go far over five dollars, unless the act has gained national or international attention.

The big venues

The best sources for **buying tickets** to the following venues are BASS (☎510/762-BASS), the Bay Area Seating Service, founded by local music mogul Bill Graham, and, for certain events, Ticketmaster (☎408/998-8497). Expect to pay a fee in addition to the ticket price, whether buying with a credit card over the phone or in person at RiteAid drugstores, Tower Records and Wherehouse record stores. Selling tickets to smaller venues, Ticketweb (*www.ticketweb.com*) generally charges a smaller fee than BASS. Bear in mind that some of the Bay Area's best large-scale venues, where the big names tend to play, are actually across the bay in Oakland and Berkeley.

For more on the Paramount Theater, see p.143.

Bimbo's 365 Club, 1025 Columbus at Chestnut ☎415/474-0365. Though Frank Sinatra would have felt right at home crooning the night away in Bimbo's plush setting, the current line-up features an eclectic array of first-class rock and world music acts.

For more on the Fillmore Auditorium, see p.115.

The Fillmore Auditorium, 1805 Geary St at Fillmore ☎415/346-6000. A local landmark, the Fillmore was at the heart of the 1960s counterculture; these days it plays host to the likes of Cowboy Mouth and Alanis Morissette.

The Great American Music Hall, 859 O'Farrell St at Polk ☎415/885-0750. Originally founded as a bordello in the 1900s, the Music Hall's fortunes went into decline over the ensuing decades. Revived in the 1970s, the gorgeous setting plays host to a wide variety of rock, country, and world music acts.

The Warfield, 982 Market St at Sixth ☎415/775-7722. In many ways the equal to the more historic Fillmore Auditorium, with both a beautiful music hall setting and top-name touring bands, the Warfield also has seating, which that other venue does not.

BAY AREA

Berkeley Community Theater, 1930 Allston Way at Martin Luther King Jr, Berkeley ☎510/644-8957. Emphasizing the "community" in its own name, this major East Bay venue hosts a variety of benefits, in addition to regular concerts by successful locals such as Bonnie Raitt and the surviving members of the Grateful Dead.

Greek Theater, UC Berkeley Campus, Berkeley ☎510/642-9988. Generally only active during summer. A large, open-air venue that entertains the students with a strong roster of successful college rock acts.

Oakland Coliseum, 7000 Coliseum Way, Oakland ☎510/569-2121. A massive venue for big-name acts.

The Paramount Theater, 2025 Broadway Ave, Oakland ☎510/465-6400. Formerly a movie house, this Art Deco treasure – designated a landmark by the federal government – regularly plays host to big-name performers drawn by the beautiful setting. In keeping with its past life, the Paramount also screens classic movies on Friday nights.

Shoreline Amphitheatre, 1 Amphitheatre Parkway, Mountain View ☎415/962-1000. The spot where huge touring acts stop in San Francisco, though ocean winds blowing into the open-air arena can make for a bitterly cold night.

Zellerbach Hall, UC Berkeley Campus, Berkeley ☎510/642-9988. In addition to being the regular home of the Berkeley Symphony, this UC Berkeley auditorium hosts world music, dance, and various avant-garde performances.

Rock, blues, folk, and country

Biscuits and Blues, 401 Mason St at Geary ☎415/292-BLUE. Both a tourist trap and one of the best spots in town to catch classic New Orleans jazz and delta blues. They also serve up some heart-stoppingly good soul food. $5–15.

Blue Light Café, 1979 Union St at Buchanan ☎415/922-5510. An attempt by local blues musician Boz Skaggs (who also owns the SoMa rock club *Slim's*) to bring some Southern-fried flavor to Union St; the result is a fairly bland blues bar, though rare visits by touring artists can spice up the mix.

Boom Boom Room, 1601 Fillmore St at Geary ☎415/673-8000. Don't expect legendary bluesman and owner John Lee Hooker to stop by too often, but the various touring acts performing here nightly do an adequate job of filling his shoes. $3–15.

Bottom of the Hill, 1233 17th St at Missouri ☎415/621-4455. The best place in town to catch up-and-coming or determinedly obscure rock acts. Frequently packed for shows, there's a small patio out back to catch a breath of fresh air or, on Sundays, have a bite of barbecue. $7–15.

Club Boomerang, 1840 Haight St at Shrader ☎415/387-2996. It's something of a local joke that every band in town gets its start at the Boomerang. The line-up features a variety of wet-behind-the-ears local acts. $5–10.

Cocodrie, 1024 Kearny at Broadway ☎415/986-6678. Despite a North Beach location, once the center of San Francisco's punk scene, this primarily metal and punk club is hit-or-miss. $5–10.

Covered Wagon Saloon, 917 Folsom St at Fifth ☎415/974-1585. A serious dive and determined to stay that way with a line-up of snarling gutter punk acts and raunchy drag shows. $3–8.

Hotel Utah, 500 Fourth St at Bryant ☎415/421-8308. Singer-songwriters take the stage at this small South of Market bar. $5–10.

Last Day Saloon, 406 Clement St at Fifth ☎387-6343. A center for live music in the otherwise sleepy Richmond district, booking an array of local funk, country, and rock acts, with a general emphasis on getting the crowd dancing. $5–15.

Lost and Found Saloon, 1353 Grant at Columbus ☎415/392-9126. This neighborhood watering hole hosts live music on weekends – whatever will get them going on the dance floor. $5–10.

Lou's Pier 47, 300 Jefferson St at Jones ☎415/771-0377. Blues joint by the bay packs them in nightly. On off nights and weekend afternoons, things settle down slightly with local jazz performers. $3–10.

The Make-Out Room, 3225 22nd at Mission ☎415/647-2888. Primarily a bar, this ultra-hip Mission spot hosts live acts early in the week for performances that tend to be jovial and homey. $5–10.

Mick's Lounge, 2513 Van Ness Ave at Union ☎415/928-0404. Who's on stage is generally secondary to whoever is lined up at the bar at this Marina singles spot. For the record, live bands tend toward jam rock and funk. $5–15.

Paradise Lounge, 308 11th St at Folsom ☎415/861-6906. Three stages vie for your attention at this cornerstone of the 11th St club district. If rock, punk and country aren't your thing, duck upstairs to play pool by the bar. $5–10.

Purple Onion, 140 Columbus St at Pacific ☎415/398-8415. Straight out of a

Bars, clubs, and live music

1950s B-movie, where the crowd is often as entertaining as the punk and garage rock bands on the minuscule stage. $3–10.

The Saloon, 1232 Grant Ave at Vallejo ☎415/989-7666. This bar has stood for more than a hundred years and has served as a whorehouse and Prohibition speakeasy. Today, the old structure creaks nightly as blues bands and crowds of young dancers shake it up to live funk and R&B.

Slim's, 333 11th St at Folsom ☎415/522-0333. Owned by local Boz Skaggs (who also owns *Blue Light Café*) what was once a blues bar is now a prime venue to catch an array of punk, alternative, world music, and country bands. $7–15.

BAY AREA

Blake's, 2367 Telegraph Ave, Berkeley ☎510/848-0886. A good place to relive your college glory days, with UC Berkeley students happily drinking their youth-away while listening to funk and rock bands. $3–5.

Cactus Club, 417 S First St, San Jose ☎408/491-9300. One of two very good clubs near each other in downtown San Jose, hosting some of the better up-and-coming bands with music ranging from roots reggae to hard-core thrash.

The Edge, 260 California St, Palo Alto ☎650/324-3343. A strong line-up of national punk, rock, and metal acts play to angry suburban youths. $5–15.

Freight and Salvage, 1111 Addison St, Berkeley ☎510/549-1761. Born out of the 1960s folk revival, this Berkeley institution has broadened its focus to include traditional music from around the world. $10–15.

FX: The Club, 400 S First St, San Jose ☎408/298-9796. The other good San Jose club, more jazz/hip-hop than the *Cactus Club*, great for drinking and dancing; 21 and over only. Closed Mon & Tues; free before 10pm, $6 after.

924 Gilman, 924 Gilman St, Berkeley ☎510/525-9926. Run entirely by volunteers with a semi-religious commitment, this rough and tumble all-ages punk club has been the launching pad for numerous nationally famous acts such as Green Day. $3–5.

Sweetwater, 153 Throckmorton Ave, Mill Valley ☎415/338-2820. Marin's main location for live music, hosting everything from hippy rock to bluegrass, not to mention a mixture of local and nationally famous bands. $5–10.

Jazz, Latin, and world music

Bahia Cabana, 1600 Market St at Franklin ☎415/626-3306. A prime spot for getting a groove on to Brazilian music and Caribbean salsa, with a mix of DJs and live performers nightly. $2–10.

Black Cat, 501 Broadway at Kearny ☎415/981-2233. A reincarnation of the famed 1960s nightspot, which was one of the first bars in town to regularly host a drag revue. Today it's an upscale supper club serenading a rather more straight-laced clientele with swing and acid jazz. $5.

Blue Lamp, 561 Geary St at Jones ☎415/885-1464. Rather unfriendly looking Tenderloin hole-in-the-wall offers live blues, funk, and jam rock just a short walk from the hotel district.

Bruno's, 2389 Mission St at 20th ☎415/550-7455. So self-consciously retro you might feel out of place without a fedora. But in the comfort and anonymity of an overstuffed booth you can enjoy the jazzy sounds in style. $3–6.

Café du Nord, 2170 Market St at Sanchez ☎415/861-5016. Primarily a jazz club, the varied booking provides constant surprises, and the warm, wood-paneled setting should put you in a receptive mood. $3–10.

Clarion Music Center, 816 Sacramento at Grant ☎415/391-1317. A cozy little theater located in the back of a music instrument store. The schedule of local and touring world music acts (usually on

Fridays at 8pm) is an equally pleasant surprise. $10.

Elbo Room, 647 Valencia St at 17th ☎415/552-7788. The birthplace of acid jazz, a popular local variant that emphasizes a danceable groove over complex improvisation. Also hosts world-music performers. $5–10.

Enrico's, 504 Broadway at Kearny ☎415/982-6223. Bustling supper club and jazz bar serves Italian food and soothing sounds nightly. No cover.

Gold Dust Lounge, 247 Powell St at Geary ☎415/397-1695. Dixieland jazz in the high-rent district. It's an enjoyably Disneyish rendition of the city's Barbary Coast days. No cover.

HiBall Lounge, 473 Broadway at Kearny ☎415/39-SWING. Swing and salsa, seven days a week (or at least until new trends come along). $5–10.

Paragon, 3251 Scott St at Francisco ☎415/922-2456. Slick Marina supper club that's more about the music and drinking than eating, though that too is tasty. Nightly jazz and a smooth crowd. Jam-packed on weekends.

Pearl's, 256 Columbus at Broadway ☎415/291-8255. Nightly sets by a rotating cast of regulars, many of whom have gigged with the biggest names around. No cover, two-drink minimum.

The Plough and Stars, 116 Clement St at Second ☎415/751-1122. The Irish expat community crams in here for hearty pints of Guinness.

The Plush Room, 940 Sutter at Leavenworth ☎415/885-6800. A throwback to days of yore, with cabaret singers and swanky crooners entertaining a contented older clientele. $20 and up.

Radio Valencia, 1199 Valencia St at 23rd ☎415/826-1199. Somewhere between a café and a bar, booking a wide array of bluegrass and performers most nights of the week. No cover.

The Ramp, 855 China Basin at Illinois ☎415/621-2378. A bayside restaurant serving up live salsa on summer Sunday afternoons. Be warned, the bar closes early.

Rasselas, 2801 California St at Divisadero ☎415/567-5010. Soon to be part of the new Fillmore Jazz District. For now, an unusual spot to see live jazz while munching Ethiopian food. $5 on Wednesdays.

Red Devil Lounge, 1695 Polk St at Clay ☎415/921-1695. Competing with the *Elbo Room* for fans of acid jazz, funk and pretty much any other variety of danceable music. Often the more appealing, less crowded option. $5–10.

Roccapulco, 3140 Mission St at Cesar Chavez ☎415/648-6611. Catering to the Mission's Latino population, this large club books salsa and Tejano music, including many performers rarely heard in the US. $8–15.

The Seventh Note, 915 Columbus at Lombard ☎415/921-2582. Jacket and tie is generally mandatory for this salsa and jazz club, except on the occasional nights when they open the doors to alternative rock acts or top-name DJs. $10–25.

The Up & Down Club, 1151 Folsom at Seventh ☎415/626-2388. A mix of live and DJ-spun acid jazz and the happy knowledge that you're dancing in a bar owned by supermodel Christy Turlington. $5.

BAY AREA

Ashkenaz, 1317 San Pablo Ave, Berkeley ☎510/525-5054. Offering dance lessons before many concerts, this prototypically Berkeley space books upbeat African and world-music acts. $5–8.

Eli's Mile High Club, 3629 Martin Luther King Jr Way, Oakland ☎510/655-6661. An informal atmosphere attracts happily raucous crowds and regular visits from some legendary blues musicians. $5 on weekends.

Kimball's East, 5800 Shellmound St, Emeryville ☎510/658-2555. Formerly one of the Bay Area's top jazz clubs, Kimball's has lately opened its stage to

Bars, clubs, and live music

Bars, clubs, and live music

The Mexican bus

Ironically named *El Volado* (loosely translated as "the Flier"), though it looks like it can barely make it to third gear, let alone take flight, this brightly painted school bus offers a way to get from party to party while keeping the mood festive en route. The circuit varies nightly, though salsa Thursdays are a particular highlight, and prices run around $35 per person. Email *dance@mexicanbus.com* or call ☎415/546-3747 for more info.

comedians and funk acts popular with Oakland's African-American community. $10–20.

Mr. E's, 2286 Shattuck Ave, Berkeley ☎510/848-2009. Owned by salsa performer Pete Escovedo (the father of Prince percussionist Sheila E) and with a salsa-centric schedule to match. Don't show up slobby: a dress code is enforced. $10–15.

Yoshi's, at Jack London Square, 510 Embarcadero W, Oakland ☎510/238-9200. The centerpiece of Oakland's newly revived Jack London Square, this combination jazz club and sushi bar routinely attracts the biggest names in jazz. $15–25.

Nightclubs

Thankfully, the velvet rope is all but non-existent in San Francisco **nightclubs** and while you might not want to wear gym shoes and shorts for your night out on the town, you can also skip packing your latest straight-from-the-catwalk fashions. If anything, those dressed to the nines will stick out more than those dressing for casual comfort. Nevertheless, the disco diva is not an entirely dead phenomenon, and attitude (generally good-humored) abounds, particularly in the city's thriving gay club circuit. In place of exclusivity, expect innovation, as appreciative audiences pack small venues searching for the latest DJ styles. At larger spaces, house still reigns supreme, and the young and aerobically fit dominate the dance floors.

Outside of the city, there's not a lot in the way of serious nightclubbing; consequently, most everyone looking for an all-night dance party in the greater Bay Area makes the sometimes lengthy commute into town, especially on Friday and Saturday nights when San Francisco's clubs are packed to bursting.

Big Heart City, 836 Mission at Fifth ☎415/777-0666. Snazzy space, with an impressive wall of video monitors and several theme rooms for hiding out, hosting multiple theme nights. $10.

The Café, 2367 Market St at Castro ☎415/861-3846. Catering to a gay and lesbian clientele with a postage stamp-sized dance floor and a line out the door. After working up a sweat on the dance floor, check out the action from the balcony which overlooks a major hub of pedestrian traffic. No cover.

Cat Club, 1190 Folsom St at Eighth ☎415/431-3332. Predominantly lesbian club often mixing live entertainment with dancing and successfully catering to a grown-up set that still likes to boogie. $5–10.

Club Townsend, 177 Townsend St at Third ☎415/974-6020. A massive barn, generally packed to the gills with sweaty dancers getting down to the latest in house and techno. Site of long-running gay and lesbian dance parties (*Club Q* for women, *Club Universe* and *Pleasuredome* for men) on Fri, Sat and Sun respectively. Call ahead for the latest events. $10–15.

Co-Co Club, 139 Eighth St at Mission ☎415/626-2337. A bar and café with a small floor for dancing. Intimate and frequently packed with young ladies who are definitely on the prowl yet still quite good humored about it. $4–7.

DNA Lounge, 375 11th St at Harrison ☎415/626-1409. Changes its music style nightly, but draws the same young hipsters. Large dance floor downstairs and when that gets to be too much you can lounge around on comfy sofas on the mezzanine. $10–15.

El Rio, 3158 Mission at Valencia ☎415/282-3325. A locals-only bar on weeknights that strings up the velvet rope on weekends when the popular funk and world-music nights take over. As a bonus, there is a large backyard patio and on Fridays they dole out free oysters on the half shell. $5–10.

The EndUp, 401 Sixth St at Harrison ☎415/357-0827. Open all night (though you can only drink until 2am), and attracting hardcore clubbers of all orientations and tastes by daybreak when the dance floor is at its fullest. Changes its bill weekly, but things start out mostly gay on Fri and lesbian on Sat. $5.

550 Barneveld, 550 Barneveld Ave at Oakdale ☎415/289-2001. A warehouse club in an iffy part of town. Be careful not to get lost along the way and you'll be rewarded with classic house and techno. $5–15.

Harry Denton's, 161 Steuart St at Howard ☎415/882-1333. An affluent older crowd comes for the expensive, hearty American cooking and the two dance floors to help them work it off. $5–15.

Holy Cow, 1531 Folsom at 11th ☎415/621-6080. Offering the chance to dance to disco and house with no cover and no attitude. Of course, there's usually a queue to get in.

Jelly's, 295 China Basin Way at Pier 50 ☎415/495-3099. A mix of locals and tourists come to dance by the bay to live funk and salsa. $7.

Kate O'Brien's, 579 Howard St at Second ☎415/882-7420. From the outside it looks like your run-of-the-mill businessman's bar, which it is until late on weekend evenings when a surprisingly good range of DJs stop in. $5.

King Street Garage, 174 King St ☎415/665-6715. Large space hosting a variety of theme nights catering to very distinct clienteles. On certain Saturday's, it becomes an extension of *Club Townsend* to which it is joined, forming one giant club. Check the listings to see what's up before heading out. $5–10.

Liquid, 2925 16th St at Capp ☎415/431-8889. You could walk right on by without noticing it, but this tiny club on a rather sketchy street is a rare place for serious dancing in the Mission's otherwise loungey bar district. $5–10.

Nickie's BBQ, 460 Haight St at Fillmore ☎415/621-6508. Hugely popular, year after year, this modest, bar-sized club lets you groove to New Orleans funk, Indian techno and world beat. $5–10.

The Palladium, 1031 Kearny St at Broadway ☎415/434-1308. Darker and sexier than the high-school cafeteria, the *Palladium* is one of the city's few 18-and-over clubs, attracting suburban youths not yet old enough to drink.

Six, 60 Sixth St at Market ☎415/863-1221. A test of your commitment to dance, since you'll have to walk through a thicket of panhandlers to get here. Hopping on weekends. $5.

Sound Factory, 525 Harrison at First ☎415/979-8686. An 18-and-over club where the dance floor serves as a testing ground for the serious adult clubbers of tomorrow. $12–15.

Storyville, 1751 Fulton at Masonic ☎415/441-1751. Named after the historic Red Light district in New Orleans, but catering to a clean-cut collegiate crowd, this large bar and club books a broad range of DJs and live acts, including the occasional big-name jazz combo. $5–15.

The Stud, Folsom St at Ninth ☎415/252-7883. This San Francisco legend attracts one of the most mixed

Bars, clubs, and live music

Bars, clubs, and live music

crowds in town – gay, lesbian, and straight – with theme nights most evenings. $3–5.

1015 Folsom, 1015 Folsom at Seventh ☎415/431-1200. The most across-the-board popular spot in town for late-night dancing, with folks of all persuasions moving to classic house grooves. $8–15.

330 Ritch Street, 330 Ritch at Townsend ☎415/541-9574. Well-chosen DJ music to stimulate your brain as well as your feet. On different nights you'll hear everything from classic groove jazz to Britpop. $5–15.

The Top, 424 Haight at Webster ☎415/864-7386. Tiny, but the best place in the city to catch terrific up-and-coming DJs. $5–10.

26 Mix, 2024 Mission at 26th ☎415/248-1319. Low-key Mission spot to catch top DJs. There's plenty of plush seating for you to relax in after having a go on the dance floor. $3–5.

The Velvet Lounge, 443 Broadway at Montgomery ☎415/788-0228. About the only spot for the under-thirty set to dance in North Beach; the stage is often open to live rock bands. $5.

Chapter 17

The performing arts and film

San Francisco – and the Bay Area in general – has an excellent reputation, accusations of provincialism notwithstanding, for the **performing** arts, boasting, for example, no fewer than five major symphonies based in the vicinity. It's also the only city on the West Coast to have its own professional **opera** and **ballet** companies to boot, and all of the above rank among the most highly regarded in the country.

Theater is even more accessible and less costly, with discount tickets readily available, though most of the mainstream downtown venues – barring a few exceptions – are mediocre, forever staging Broadway reruns. You'd do better to take some time to explore the infinitely more interesting **fringe circuit**.

As far as **comedy** goes, it has a decent reputation and tradition here, but these days there are only a few cabarets at which to have your funnybone tickled.

Film, on the other hand, is almost as big an obsession as eating in San Francisco. The range of movie choices is first-class, and you may well be surprised by the sheer number of cinemas – repertory and current-release – that flourish along with numerous film festivals.

Classical music, Opera, and Dance

Major companies

The Philharmonia Baroque ☎415/392-4400; *www.philharmonia.org*. The nation's biggest and most successful company playing traditional Medieval European instruments. Over years the orchestra's repertoire has expanded beyond its strict chronological boundaries, but its sound remains distinctive. The Philharmonia performs in various Bay Area venues throughout the fall and spring seasons.

San Francisco Ballet at the War Memorial Opera House, Van Ness Ave at Grove ☎415/864-3330; *www.sfballet.org*. Despite mourning the retirement of beloved prima ballerina Evelyn Cisneros, the third oldest ballet company in the US remains in top form. Founded in 1933, it was the first to stage full-length productions of *Swan Lake* and *The Nutcracker*. Following a period of decline and near-bankruptcy in the 1970s and early 1980s, the arrival as artistic director of Helgi Tomasson, "premier danseur" of the New York City Ballet, ushered in an era of revived prominence. Since the SF Ballet shares the War Memorial's stage with the Opera, the season is limited to Feb–May. Tickets begin at $30, with discounts for students and seniors.

San Francisco Opera at the War Memorial Opera House, 301 Van Ness Ave at Grove ☎415/864-3330; *www.sfopera.org*. Thanks to the leadership of Iranian émigré Lotfi Mansouri, the San Francisco Opera has long been held in high international regard. A typical

The performing arts and film

season offers a mixture of avant-garde stagings by composers such as John Adams or André Previn along with acclaimed productions of perennial favorites by Wagner or Puccini. The War Memorial Opera House provides a suitably opulent setting: opened in 1932 and recently restored, the building's design by Arthur Brown, Jr – also responsible for City Hall and Coit Tower – is a rich confection in gold with plush felt seats. The season runs from September through December, with a short summer season in June and July, and tickets cost upwards of $20. Standing-room tickets are a real bargain at only $15.

San Francisco Performances at Herbst Theater, 401 Van Ness Ave at Grove ☎415/392-2545. Schedules a diverse array of classical recitals, readings, and dance programs throughout the spring and fall. A relative upstart in the Bay Area classical community, performances can vary in both name recognition and quality. Tickets typically range from $25–40.

San Francisco Symphony at Louise M. Davies Symphony Hall, 201 Van Ness Ave at Hayes St ☎415/431-5400; *www.sfsymphony.org*. With the arrival of conductor Michael Tilson Thomas, this once musty institution has catapulted to the first rank of American orchestras. Though Thomas' relentless self-promotion can be off-putting, he has undoubtedly added vibrancy to the Symphony's programming, bringing a significant emphasis on twentieth-century composers to the program. The season runs from September through May, and depending on the performance tickets generally range between $25 and $80, with discounted $12 tickets for seats behind the stage available 2 hours before performances.

Smaller companies

The city is also host to several innovative smaller companies, who sometimes come close to equaling the ballet's national prominence. Berkeley choreographer **Mark Morris**' work is based in classical dance, but quickly departs from tradition into spectacular flights of fantasy. Between world tours, his extravagant (and stylishly costumed) productions regularly grace Berkeley's Zellerbach Hall. More traditional is San Francisco's **Smuin Ballet**, founded by former San Francisco Ballet director Michael Smuin, which spruces up traditional dance with snazzy bits of jazz and pop. Neither company has a stage to call home, so keep an eye out for performances in various large halls around town.

BAY AREA

Berkeley Symphony at Zellerbach Hall on the UC Berkeley campus ☎510/841-2800; *www.berkeleyopera.org*. Though largely overshadowed by the San Francisco Symphony, Berkeley can boast a first-rate symphony of its own, complete with internationally recognized conductor and artistic director Kent Nagano. The split fall and spring season is shorter than San Francisco's and features works by lesser-known composers. Tickets are $20–35, with lower student prices.

Cal Performances at Zellerbach Hall on the UC Berkeley campus ☎510/642-9988. Booking a roster of guests that has included notables such as modernist choreographer Merce Cunningham, Bertold Brecht's theater troupe, Ballet Folklorico de Cuba, and African musician Femi Kuti, Cal Performances offers a little something for every adventurous spirit. The schedule runs from fall through spring. Tickets usually $20–40.

Theater

The majority of San Francisco's larger **theaters** congregate downtown in the Theater District, with most of the alternative fringe venues in the Mission District. Tickets to even the largest productions can usually be had for under $50, with smaller productions starting at less than $10.

Most tickets can be purchased either through the individual theaters' box offices or by calling **BASS** (☎510/762-BASS). For last-minute bargains try the

Tix Bay Area booth on Stockton Street in Union Square (Tues–Thurs 11am–6pm, Fri & Sat 11am–7pm; ☎ 415/433-7827).

In early September, the **San Francisco Fringe Festival** (☎ 415/931-1094 or 673-3847) is a marathon of more than 250 experimental performances by some fifty companies at several local venues including Exit Theater and The Marsh.

Large theaters

Alcazar Theater, 650 Geary St at Leavenworth ☎ 415/441-4042. Mostly notable for its extravagant facade – a rare dose of color in the dingy Tenderloin – which was designed by a local Shriner's group to resemble an Islamic mosque. A former Masonic Temple, the theater now hosts hit-and-miss cabaret acts and musicals. Tickets start around $20.

American Conservatory Theater (ACT), Geary Theater, 415 Geary St at Taylor ☎ 415/742-2228. The Bay Area's leading resident theater group mixes new commissioned works and innovative renditions of the classics. Particularly noteworthy is the company's inventive set design and staging. Discount tickets cost as little as $10, though most cost upwards of $20.

Center for the Arts Theater at Yerba Buena Gardens, 701 Mission St at Third ☎ 415/978-ARTS. Hosting performances by prominent avant-garde dance, theater, and music companies, including regular visits by local classical music stars the Kronos Quartet, perhaps most famous for rendering Jimi Hendrix as chamber music. Tickets $10 and up.

Curran Theater, 445 Geary St at Taylor ☎ 415/551-2000. This former vaudeville theater presents both hit Broadway plays and musicals. Tickets cost $30–60.

Golden Gate Theater, 1 Taylor St at Golden Gate ☎ 415/551-2000. Constructed in the 1920s and recently restored to its original splendor, this splendid theater's elegant Rococo decor frequently outclasses its schedule of touring Broadway productions. Cheap seats cost around $20, while most tickets cost upwards of $30.

Orpheum Theater, 11192 Market St at Eighth ☎ 415/551-2000. Probably the most spectacular of the big houses, though the line-up of lesser Broadway shows is perhaps not as grand as the digs. The most expensive tickets in town, running upwards of $40.

Stage Door Theater, 420 Mason St at Geary ☎ 415/788-9453. Owned by ACT, this pleasant, 500-seat space is rented out to small but established local and touring productions. Prices vary with the production.

Theater on the Square, 450 Post St at Powell ☎ 415/433-9500. Converted Gothic theater with drama, musicals, and mainstream crowd pleasers. Tickets start around $20.

Smaller spaces

Beach Blanket Babylon, *Club Fugazi*, 678 Green St at Powell ☎ 421-4222. Founded by the late Steve Silver, a prominent local personality, *Babylon* is more or less a permanent theatrical institution in town, combining the silliness of a small-town pageant with the over-the-top tackiness of a Vegas revue. The story is based somewhat on the idea of Little Red Riding Hood being lost in the big bad city, but it's the massively oversized wigs and hats the performers wear – some as big as the performers themselves – that seems to keep locals and tourists alike pouring in. Alcohol is served and performances are 21 and over except Sunday matinees. Tickets start at $25.

Cable Car Theater, 430 Mason St at Geary ☎ 1-800/660-8462. Cheap, campy productions delivering an evening of easy fun directly downstairs from the Stage Door theater.

Exit Theater, 156 Eddy St at Taylor ☎ 415/673-3847. The house is tiny – only fifty seats – and the Tenderloin address is dodgy, but this is one of the best spots in town for cutting-edge experimental theater. Tickets start around $10.

The performing arts and film

Fort Mason Center, Laguna St at Marina Blvd ☎415/474-8935. A complex of smaller theaters, including the Cowell, Magic, and Bayfront (in descending order of size), hosting live music, dance, and theatrical performances. Ticket prices vary.

Intersection for the Arts, 446 Valencia St at 16th ☎415/626-2787. Frequently political, community-oriented productions in a tiny space.

The Lab, 2948 16th St at Capp ☎415/864-8855. Next door to Theater Rhinoceros, this scruffy community space presents a program focusing on radical works by and for women, with tickets generally under $10.

The Marsh, 1062 Valencia at 21st ☎415/641-0235. Longstanding alternative space hosting solo shows, many with a political bent. Monday nights are test nights for works in progress. Tickets go from under $10 to close to $20.

San Francisco Mime Troupe ☎415/285-1717. A leading light of 1960s radical theater, the troupe's punchy, not-so-subtle political comedies, performed for free at parks throughout the city, have become a summertime tradition.

San Francisco Shakespeare Festival, Golden Gate Park ☎415/422-2222. Free Shakespeare productions in the park (weekends Sept & Oct, 1.30pm). Arrive by noon to be sure to get a seat.

Theater Artaud, 450 Florida St at Mariposa ☎415/621-7797. Successful art space in a converted warehouse, hosting the cream-of-the-crop among local dance and theater performers. Closer to the mainstream than the name might imply. Tickets $10–20.

Theater Rhinoceros, 2926 16th St at S Van Ness ☎415/861-5079. The city's prime gay-oriented theater space actually has two theaters hosting productions ranging from heartfelt political drama to raunchy cabaret acts. Tickets start at $10.

Venue 9, 252 Ninth St at Howard ☎415/978-2345. Small, respected stage offering theater productions and experimental music. Tickets are often less than $10; can be as much as $15.

BAY AREA

Alice Arts Center, 1428 Alice St at 14th St, Oakland ☎510/652-0752. Home to the Oakland Ensemble Theater and host to weekly concerts and performances by East Bay artists.

Berkeley Repertory Theater, 2025 Addison St, Berkeley ☎510/845-4700. One of the West Coast's most highly respected theater companies, presenting updated classics and contemporary plays in an intimate modern theater. Tickets $30–50, with a small number of discounted tickets sold the day of the show.

Black Repertory Group, 3201 Adeline St, Berkeley, near Ashby BART ☎510/652-2120. After years of struggling, this politically conscious African-American company, that encourages new talent, moved into its own specially built home in 1987. Typically under $10.

California Shakespeare Festival, Siesta Valley, Orinda ☎510/548-3422. After fifteen seasons in a North Berkeley park, this summer-long outdoor festival moved to a larger home in the East Bay hills. Tickets $8–30.

Forest Meadows Amphitheater at Dominican College in San Rafael ☎415/457-4400. An outdoor amphitheater hosting summertime productions.

Julia Morgan Theater, 2963 College Ave, Berkeley ☎510/845-8542. Small theater on a treelined street, hosting some of the Bay Area's most successful performances, everything from intimate operas to radical political works. Tickets $8–20.

Comedy

From Lenny Bruce to Whoopie Goldberg, **comedians** have traditionally found a welcoming audience in San Francisco, a city in which comedians can end up taking center stage in City Hall, as the city saw when stand-up performer Tom

Amiano gave Mayor Willie Brown the run for his money during the 1999 election. Nonetheless, following a boom period in the late 1980s and early 1990s, most local venues have shut their doors.

Cobb's Comedy Club, The Cannery, 2801 Leavenworth St at Beach ☎415/928-4320. Pricey and usually full of tourists, but the standard of the acts is fairly consistent. Worth a look if everything else is booked up. Tickets start around $10, plus two-drink minimum.

The Punch Line, 444 Battery St at Washington ☎415/397-7573. Frontrunner of the city's "polished" cabaret venues, this place has an intimate, smoky feel that's ideal for downing expensive cocktails and laughing your head off. The club usually hosts the bigger names in the world of stand-up and is always packed. Tickets start around $10, plus two-drink minimum.

Films

Maybe it has something to do with the foggy weather, but San Franciscans attend more **movies** than residents of any other city in America. There are plenty of repertory houses, several of them beautiful Spanish-revival and Art Deco buildings that are, in themselves, a delight to behold, screening a wide range of non-mainstream flicks – though if you're looking for Hollywood releases you'll find those too.

AMC 1000, 1000 Van Ness at O'Farrell ☎415/922-4AMC. After opening in 1998 to much fanfare, this escalator-riddled multiplex proved something of a disappointment, beset by a variety of technical woes. Still, the steeply inclined "arena style" seating is a major bonus.

Artists' Television Access (ATA), 992 Valencia St at 21st ☎415/824-3890; *www.atasite.org*. A scrappy not-for-profit storefront space showing weekend programs of short underground films, often with a political or social theme.

The Bridge, 3010 Geary St at Blake ☎415/352-0810. A large screen in this old, vaguely Art Deco cinema, shows wide-release art films to appreciative masses.

The Castro Theater, 429 Castro St at Market ☎415/621-6120. This gorgeous old movie palace offers foreign films, classic revivals, festivals, and the most enthusiastic audience in town. Come early for evening screenings to listen to the Wurlitzer organ and stare at the spectacular chandelier.

Center for the Arts Screening Room at Yerba Buena Center ☎415/978-ARTS; *www.yerbabuenaarts.org*. This museum offshoot seems to revel in out-of-date lowbrow oddities, regularly screening 1960s soft-core porn and 1970s blaxploitation films.

The Coronet, 3575 Geary St at Arguello ☎415/752-4400. The massive expanse of this single-screen theater in the Richmond is the perfect place to catch the latest oversized Hollywood spectacle.

Embarcadero Cinema, 1 Embarcadero Center on Sansome ☎415/352-0810. This downtown art-house multiplex is a good spot to catch up on next year's Oscar contenders.

The Foreign Cinema, 2534 Mission St at 21st ☎415/648-7600. Not really a movie theater, but this expensive supper club and bar shows classic foreign films on its back patio.

Four Star, 2200 Clement St at 23rd ☎415/666-3488. Funky Richmond theater screening a mix of art films and Hong Kong action flicks for the local Asian community.

Kabuki 8 Cinemas, 1881 Post St at Fillmore ☎415/922-4AMC. Part of the Japan Center complex, this multiplex screens a mixture of indie and big-budget titles. Validated parking at the underground parking lot.

Lumiere, 1572 California St at Polk ☎415/352-0810. Offering a mix of short-run rarities and new-release foreign films.

The performing arts and film

The Metreon, 101 Fourth St at Mission ☎415/537-3400. 15 screens arrayed along one very long hallway on the second floor of Sony's brand new urban mall. Good sound and steeply sloped "arena style" seating.

The Metro, 2055 Union St at Webster ☎415/931-1685. Spacious, recently restored old movie house with a large curved screen.

Opera Plaza, 60 Van Ness at Golden Gate ☎415/352-0810. Generally the last place to catch a movie before it shows up at the video store – though some of the sub-compact screens aren't much bigger than a large-screen TV set.

The Red Vic, 1727 Haight St at Cole ☎415/668-3994. Grab a wooden bowl filled with popcorn and kick your feet up on the benches at this friendly collective. Cult faves predominate.

The Roxie, 3117 16th St at Valencia ☎415/863-1087. An adventurous rep house and film distributor, the Roxie is one of the few theaters in the country willing to take a risk on documentaries and little-known foreign directors.

San Francisco Cinematheque at the San Francisco Art Institute, 800 Chestnut and the Yerba Buena Center, 701 Mission ☎415/558-8129; *www.sfcinematheque.com*. Don't expect to find anything resembling mainstream Hollywood fare at this home of the high-art film community.

BAY AREA

Camera Three, 288 S Second St, San Jose ☎408/998-3300. Offbeat films to accompany the beers and snacks from the cinema's café.

Fine Arts, 2541 Shattuck at Haste, Berkeley ☎510/848-1143. Run by a

Area film festivals

San Francisco International Asian-American Film Festival (March) ☎415/255-4299; *www.naatanet.org/festival*. The nation's premier festival of both films from Asia and films by Asian Americans, with a varied roster ranging from campy kung-fu flicks to intense political dramas.

San Francisco International Film Festival (April) ☎415/931-FILM; *www.sfiff.org*. The first film festival in America and still of one of the best. Large program of foreign and independent American films, with a consistently high standard of quality. Screenings are repeated in Berkeley and Marin.

San Francisco International Lesbian and Gay Film Festival (June) ☎415/703-8650; *www.frameline.org*. Short films and features, with quality ranging from amateurish to MTV slick, all of it cheered on by an exuberantly supportive audience at the world's oldest and largest festival of its kind.

San Francisco Jewish Film Festival (July) ☎415/621-0556; *www.sfjff.org*. Films from throughout the Jewish Diaspora, from thought-provoking documentaries to racy Israeli soap operas.

Cine Accion Festival de Cine Latino (Sept) ☎415/553-8135; *www.cineaccion.com*. A rare window into the heavily political film culture of South America, dominated by documentary exposés and dramas.

Mill Valley Film Festival (Oct) ☎415/383-5256; *www.finc.org/mvff*. Providing an early peak at next year's art-house fare, this Marin festival can sometimes seem like a Miramax promotional catalogue, but also schedules some rare premieres.

Film Arts Festival (Nov) ☎415/ 552-8760; *www.filmarts.org*. A longstanding festival of Northern California filmmakers – particularly strong programs of documentaries and short films, many of which go on to the Sundance festival.

couple of film buffs and perhaps not long for this world. While it lasts, the program of rare premieres and classic revivals is worth a look.

Grand Lake, 3200 Grand Ave, Oakland ☎510/452-3356. A grand dame of East Bay picture palaces, right on Lake Merritt, showing current major releases.

Pacific Film Archive, 2575 Bancroft Way at Bowditch, Berkeley ☎510/642-1124. Inventive programming with a subtle educational bent offers up an array of unusual gems. Double features nightly.

Parkway, 1834 Park Blvd at 18th, Oakland ☎510/814-2400. Offering the chance to eat pizza and drink beer while watching a movie. Beyond that, the first-run films offered are pretty standard.

Rafael Film Center, 1118 Fourth St at A, San Rafael ☎415/454-1222. Recently revived art-house that's a prime spot to catch quality flicks.

Stanford Theater, 221 University Ave ☎650/342-3700. Built in 1925 and recently fully restored, showing major releases.

UC Theater, 2036 University Ave at Shattuck, Berkeley ☎510/843-3456. Revival house popular with UC Berkeley students. Thursdays are given over to Hong Kong action films.

Chapter 18

Shops and galleries

For a city of its size, San Francisco has a good concentration of **shopping** options – all the international names are displayed in downtown storefronts,

Shopping streets

Outside of the dense shopping clustered around Union Square downtown, San Francisco is really a coalition of a dozen or so independent enclaves, each self-sufficient, small-townish, and centered around a main commercial street – an anomaly in mall-manic America. Below we've given San Francisco's prime **shopping strips**, alphabetized according to the neighborhood in which each is situated, though wandering down less-traveled roads will sometimes lead to surprise discoveries as well.

The Castro – Castro Street, between 17th and 19th sts and Market Street, between Castro and Church sts. Gay-oriented boutiques, clubwear, unusual designer clothes, and shoes.

Cow Hollow – Union Street, between Octavia and Fillmore. Expensive boutiques and shoe stores – most for women.

The Haight-Ashbury – Haight Street, between Stanyan and Masonic. Tons of head and record shops, as well as used clothing, retro fashion, and bookstores.

Hayes Valley – Hayes Street, between Franklin and Laguna and along Market near Gough. An array of upscale galleries and gift stores aimed at the pre-opera crowd.

Jackson Square – Jackson Street, between Montgomery and Sansome. A cluster of antique rug, furnishings, and clock shops.

Laurel Heights – Sacramento Street, between Arguello and Divisadero. Antique magnet of San Francisco, with vintage used clothes for women.

The Marina – Chestnut Street, between Broderick and Fillmore. Health foods, wine shops, and women's clothing boutiques.

The Mission – Valencia Street, between 14th and 21st sts. A dense collection of used furniture, clothing, and bookshops.

Noe Valley – 24th Street, between Castro and Church. Women's clothing, music, and bookstores.

Pacific Heights – Fillmore Street, between Jackson and Geary. Home furnishings, antiques, and designer clothes.

Polk Gulch – Polk Street, between Clay and Geary. Used bookstores, shoe stores, and porn outlets.

The Richmond – Clement Street, between Second and Tenth aves. Bustling Chinese groceries near some of the best used bookstores in the city.

The Sunset – Irving Street, between Seventh and 23rd aves. Book, music, and houseware shops.

Shops and galleries

Shopping categories

and there's an abundance of smaller-scale outlets, great for picking up odd and unusual things you wouldn't find at home. Most are clustered in neighborhood blocks alongside cafés, restaurants and movie theaters, making for a relaxed day of browsing.

If you want to run the gauntlet of designer labels, or just watch the style brigades in all their consumer fury, **Union Square** is the city's most chic, big-name shopping center. Be sure and watch out for the steel washbasins at Levi's on Post Street where teens line up to take the plunge to shrink-fit their new jeans. Across the square on Geary, Macy's recently renovated palace raised the bar for neighboring competition. The area of Market Street near Fourth Street has become another booming area for commerce, with massive new chain stores, such as Old Navy and Virgin Megastore, that lure young shoppers with their raucous interiors, resembling multileveled nightclubs more than stores.

Nearby, at **Fourth and Mission streets**, the brand new Sony Metreon is a futuristic center where it's easy to play with the high-tech merchandise but difficult to find a cash register at which to buy it, so high is the consumer demand for the technological gadgets on display.

Less chaotic are the **outer neighborhoods**, each of which has a central shopping street along which can be found more intimate book, record, houseware, clothing, and antique stores than any downtown chain could ever offer (see box, opposite).

You can fill whole afternoons browsing San Francisco's thoroughly-stocked **independent booksellers** and **music stores**, some focusing solely on rarities like first editions or specific genres, others providing a taste of everything.

Across the bay, Berkeley's college crowd is a ripe market for more book and record stores as well as **secondhand apparel** and other used items; Berkeley's resale shops often stock high-quality contemporary trendwear as well as much-sought-after vintage clothing.

One major difference between San Francisco and other American cities is the early closing times for most shops. Typically, stores are open from Monday to Saturday, 9am until 6pm, and on Sunday, 10am to 5pm, though many **supermarkets**, such as Safeway, are open 24 hours a day, vending essentials like toiletries, magazines, flowers, film, and alcohol.

Credit cards are accepted in most stores for purchases above a minimum

Shops and galleries

of $10; **travelers' checks** are as good as cash, provided they're in US dollar denominations and that you have your passport or other photo ID.

Department stores and shopping malls

San Francisco has remained more immune to the establishment of large **shopping malls** than most American cities, though to be sure there are still a few where all your needs will be catered to. The downtown plays host to several **department stores** around Union Square, though these are branches of upscale national chains that can be found in most major American cities.

Department stores

Macy's Union Square, Stockton and O'Farrell ☎415/397-3333. A dangerous place to go with a full wallet, this is probably the city's best-stocked store, with beautifully presented merchandise beckoning from every side. Underwent a massive facelift in 1999, with its men's department being moved across Stockton St to a new space.

Nieman Marcus, 150 Stockton St at O'Farrell ☎415/362-3900. The sheer cheek of the pricing department has earned this store the nickname "Needless Mark-up." Undoubtedly Union Square's most beautiful department store, nevertheless, with a glass-domed rotunda capping a top-floor restaurant and bar from which you can watch shoppers struggling with packages in Union Square down below.

Nordstrom, 865 Market St at Powell ☎415/243-8500. Shoppers flock here for the high-quality (and expensive) fashions, as well as a chance to ride on the spiral escalators that climb the four-story atrium from the San Francisco Shopping Center below.

Sak's Fifth Avenue, 384 Post St at Powell ☎415/986-4300. A scaled-down version of its New York sister store, geared largely to the middle-aged shopaholic, Saks is *the* high-end specialty shopping store.

Shopping malls

Crocker Galleria, 50 Post St at Kearny ☎415/393-1505. A modern, Italianate atrium, this Financial District mall features some very pricey showcase boutiques; a nice place for a wander.

Embarcadero Center, at Embarcadero BART/Muni station at the foot of California St ☎415/772-0500. Ugly, eight-square-block shopping complex with 125 stores and a few unremarkable restaurants, distinguished from other anodyne shopping malls only by its location on the ground floors of a complex of four sleek, white office buildings joined at the base.

Ghirardelli Square, 900 North Point at Larkin ☎415/775-5500. This attractive c.1900 building used to be a chocolate factory, but is now home to 43 stores and five restaurants – one of the nicer places to drop dollars at the wharf if you must.

Japan Center, Post St at Buchanan ☎415/922-6776. Surprisingly characterless five-acre complex of stores, movie theaters, and restaurants with a Japanese theme. A few redeemable antique, paper, and art shops.

San Francisco Shopping Center, Fifth and Market sts ☎415/495-5656. A good-looking mall; glass, Italian marble, polished green granite, and spiral escalators up and down its eight stories all add to the seductive appeal of spending money with California-style panache. Sumptuous Parisian cakes at *La Nouvelle Patisserie* vie for your attention with Bugs Bunny paraphernalia at the Warner Bros store.

Sony Metreon, Fourth St and Mission ☎415/369-6000. Anchored on the ground floor by a Discovery Channel shop and on top by a state-of-the-art movie theater, this latest San Francisco mall is pure "shoppertainment." The Microsoft Store is a fun place to play free video games or check your email,

24-hour pharmacies

The following branches of **Walgreen's** are **open 24 hours**:

498 Castro St ☎415/861-6276

3201 Divisadero at Lombard ☎415/931-6415

25 Point Lobos between 42nd and 43rd aves near Geary, near Ocean Beach and the Coast Trailhead ☎415/386-0706

Rite Aid has one 24-hour branch at 5280 Geary Blvd in the Richmond ☎415/668-2041

Shops and galleries

and the views of the Modern Art Museum and Yerba Buena Gardens make the patio a great place to have a drink.

Stonestown Galleria Shopping Center, 19th Ave and Winston Drive ☎415/759-2623. Way out in the Sunset, one block from SF State University, this 120-store complex has a Macy's, a Border's Books, a Nordstrom, and upscale clothing and shoe stores along with the usual mall choices.

Drugstores, beauty products, and toiletries

Standard **drugstores** can be found in every San Francisco neighborhood. A few are open 24 hours a day, selling essentials like film, batteries for your Walkman, aspirin, tampons, condoms, etc, and all have a pharmacy that can dispense medications and fill prescriptions.

Though **Rite Aid** has opened a slew of new stores throughout the city, **Walgreen's** remains, for the moment, the largest chain pharmacy with numerous branches throughout the city, selling prescription drugs and general medical supplies, as well as cosmetics and toiletries. Most are open long hours (Mon–Sat 8am–10pm, Sun 9am–8pm), and the most central location, at 135 Powell St ☎415/391-4433, is open till midnight most days.

Outlets for such indulgences as body oils and bubble bath tend to congregate in the pricier neighborhoods.

Drugstores

Embarcadero Center Pharmacy, 1 Embarcadero Center ☎415/788-4511. Prescription drugs and general medical and toiletry supplies. Not open late.

Fairmont Pharmacy, 801 Powell St ☎415/362-3000. Huge pharmacy, perfumery, and toiletry supply store that also has a good selection of maps and books on San Francisco.

Mandarin Pharmacy, 895 Washington St ☎415/989-9292. This amiable, well-stocked drugstore is a sanctuary in the bustle of Chinatown.

Rite Aid Pharmacy, 760 Market St ☎415/397-0837. Also 1946 Market St ☎415/626-9972; 1300 Bush ☎415/771-3303; 100 Church ☎415/626-0470; and several other locations around town. Fill a prescription, pick up toiletries, and develop a roll of film, all in one stop.

Toiletries and beauty supplies

The Beauty Store Upper Market, 3600 16th St at Market ☎415/861-2019. Also at 1560 Haight St. Makeup, hair color, and massage oils.

BeneFit, 2117 Fillmore ☎415/567-0242, and 2219 Chestnut ☎415/567-1173. Hip beauty-products store stocked with Gen X essentials like pearl-white lip pencils and rose and bronze tints for the cheeks and eyes. Full salon in back.

Body Time, 2072 Union St ☎415/922-4076, with outlets at 1932 Fillmore St and 1465 Haight St. Though this Bay Area-born company sold the original name to the UK-based Body Shop, they still put out a full range of aromatic natural bath oils, shampoos, and skin creams, and will custom scent anything.

Shops and galleries

Body Treats, 634 Irving Ave ☎415/661-2284. Soaps, gels, scrubs, and bath oils amidst cozy Irving ave's fun shops.

Common Scents, 3920 24th St ☎415/826-1019. Essential oils and bath salts, as well as hair and skincare products, stocked in bulk and sold by the ounce. They'll refill your empties.

Isa's Hair Studio, 3836 24th St at Church ☎415/641-8948. Great hairdressing salon upstairs and a wide selection of hair and skin-care products in the shop below. Good place for stocking up on quality essentials.

Merle Norman Cosmetics Studio, 150 Powell St near O'Farrell ☎415/362-2387. Make-up lessons available as well as an exhaustive range of cosmetics. Girlie heaven.

Sephora, 1 Stockton St ☎415/392-1545. Swank three-story beauty warehouse off Union Square selling hundreds of its own signature lipsticks, nail polishes and lip and eye pencils. Browsing and sampling strongly encouraged; stations are stocked with brushes and makeup remover.

Skin Zone, 575 Castro St ☎415/626-7933. Every unguent imaginable at very reasonable prices. Look for Skin Zone's own brand for real bargains.

BAY AREA

Body Time, 2911 College Ave, Berkeley ☎510/845-2101, with outlets on Shattuck Ave and in SF. Natural scents, lotions, soaps, and hair-product collection.

Whole Foods Market, 3000 Telegraph Ave, Berkeley ☎510/649-1333. For the alternative-remedy addict, an excellent selection of homeopathic herbs and medicinal products in an upscale natural-foods supermarket.

Clothes and accessories

Perhaps more than anywhere else in the US, San Francisco's power-dressing **designer clothes** stores are distinct from the bulk of the city's clothing outfitters. Most locally based designers' shops are located around Union Street in Cow Hollow, though a fair amount can be found in the Mission and Inner Sunset. Otherwise, most designers of international importance have shops around Union Square, where only they can afford the rent.

Though Ralph Lauren chic definitely rules the Financial District, style elsewhere in the city is a much more open concept. The dot-com generation has chased suits from the halls of power, replacing them with casual khakis and shirts. Formal business attire was so out of vogue by 2000 that stalwarts Bullock & Jones and Sulka closed their San Francisco stores.

Dozens of stores like the Gap, Banana Republic, and Old Navy sell very Californian **casual wear**, mainly jeans or cargo pants and earth-toned shirts. If you're feeling adventurous, check out the countless **secondhand clothes** stores specializing in period costume, from 1920s gear to leftover hippie garb. Better still, explore the myriad charitable **thrift stores**, where you can pick up high-quality castoffs for virtually next to nothing (although in the more upscale shopping areas, even these prices have climbed). For a thorough listing of these, Rummaging Through Northern California publishes a free guide to over 1800 local resale shops and outlets; call ☎707/939-9124 or check out their Web site at *www.secondhand.com*.

Designer clothes

Agnes b, 33 Grant Ave ☎415/772-9995. French pop designs near Union Square.

Backseat Betty, 1684 Haight St at Clayton ☎415/431-8393. Small range of exquisite, affordable dresses and very feminine separates by lesser-known designers. Recommended.

Betsey Johnson, 2031 Fillmore St at California ☎415/567-2726. One of the few American designers who doesn't see women in business suits. Her clothes are stylish and have flair without being silly, and, by designer standards, they are also affordable.

Shops and galleries

Bryan Lee, 1840 Union St ☎415/923-9918. Small Cow Hollow boutique carrying local designers, with a line of men's and women's urban weekend styles – mainly clubwear, and not cotton.

Catherine Jane, 1234 Ninth Ave ☎415/664-1855. Inner Sunset shop featuring luxurious "fog coats" (shawls made from cashmere and angora) and fashions in silk dupioni, crepe de chine, and other cozy fabrics.

Dema, 1038 Valencia Ave ☎415/206-0500. This shop in the Mission, sells jewelry and original designs in linen and cotton voile.

Diesel, 101 Post St ☎415/982-7077. Home of those puffy jackets and baggy pants that everyone under age 30 seems to be wearing. This flagship store has five-stories-worth of the stuff, including an entire floor of jeans.

Duchess, 1429 Haight St ☎415/255-1214. The theme here is "fitted, not tarty," as designer Keri White described in *San Francisco* magazine. Ruffled dresses, jackets, and pants that you could wear for work or play.

Emporio Armani, 1 Grant Ave at O'Farrell and Market ☎415/677-9400. European chic. This large store with its own café is the perfect place to deck yourself out in simple style if you have the bucks.

Loehmann's, 222 Sutter ☎415/982-3215. Designer thrift store featuring cast-off Donna Karan, Versace, BCBG, and other major labels.

Luba Designs, 751 Irving Ave ☎415/665-6112. Platform shoes, capri pants, midriff-baring tops, and printed nylon tees.

MAC (Modern Appealing Clothing), 1543 Grant Ave at Union in North Beach ☎415/837-1604. Showcase for exclusive designers and locals such as Vivienne Westwood, Think Tank, etc. Quality stuff, fine tailoring, and affordable. They also have a men's store at 5 Claude Lane off Sutter between Grant and Kearny ☎415/837-0615.

Manifesto, 514 Octavia St ☎415/431-4778. Flagship shop of local designers Sarah Franko and Suzanne Castillo for their line of 1950s-ish, roomy clothing.

Metier, 355 Sutter ☎415/989-5395. A gallery of up-and-coming designers, with everything from sweaters and scarves to jewelry and handbags.

Rolo, 2351 Market St at Church ☎415/-431-4545) and 450 Castro ☎415/626-7171. Moderately priced and well-made menswear in simple, easy-to-wear styles.

Under Cover, 535 Castro St at 19th ☎415/864-0505. Tiny store, crammed with unusual and body-hugging club wear by lesser-known designers. Activewear, swimwear, and lots of underwear. Mostly gay clientele.

Utopia Planitia, 624 Bush St ☎415/362-1277. Original designs in leather, wool, and cotton by Minnie Yeh, who is often behind the counter.

Wilkes Bashford, 375 Sutter St at Stockton ☎415/986-4380. Four floors of fabulous designer finery for men; and now one floor for women. Reportedly mayor Willie Brown's favorite clothier.

Designer accessories: bags, shoes, hats, jewelry

China Gem Co., 500 Grant Ave at Pine ☎415/397-5070. Good place for jade, pearls, opal, and precious gems.

The Coach Store, 190 Post St at Grant ☎415/392-1772. Well-made, simple and expensive handbags and luggage. Definitely worth the investment if you've got the money, as they come with a lifetime guarantee.

Ghurka, 170 Post St ☎415/392-7267. *The place* in San Francisco to buy leather goods like wallets, handbags, and luggage. The products have quite a following due to their durability; scratches wipe off instantly.

Gimme Shoes, 50 Grant Ave ☎415/434-9242. Whatever your footwear need – from sandals to evening wear to trainers – the outgoing staff will try to satisfy your every whim.

Gucci, 200 Stockton St at Geary, Union Square ☎415/392-2808. Classic Italian

Shops and galleries

shoes, bags, and apparel that you need a trust fund to indulge in. Snoop around the store and be fascinated by the rich ladies who come in and say "I'll have one of those, two of those, one of those," etc.

Hats on Post, 210 Post St at Grant, 2nd floor ☎415/392-3737. Interesting, odd designs, very contemporary, but only worth shelling out for if you're *really* into hats.

Hermes, 212 Stockton St at Geary ☎415/391-7200. Classy French luggage and accessories for the super-rich. Again, good only for spying on those who can afford it.

Kenneth Cole, 2078 Union St at Webster ☎415/346-2161, also at 865 Market at Powell ☎415/227-4536. State-of-the-art boutique selling the well-designed shoes of this New York designer. His men's shoes are imaginative and funky, but the women's stuff is more wearable.

Laku, 1069 Valencia St ☎415/695-1462. Hand-made exquisite silk slippers by local designer Yakeo Yamashita. Also sells velvet hair accessories.

Mapuche, 500 Laguna St ☎415/551-0725. Very unique handbags hand-crafted at their Hayes Valley shop.

Pearl of the Orient, 900 North Point, Ghirardelli Square ☎415/441-2288. Reputedly the largest stock of pearls in the Bay Area; quality ones, too.

Shapur, 245 Post St at Union Square ☎415/392-1200. Unusual fittings for uniquely cut diamonds and various other gems; each piece is created individually.

Shreve & Co, 200 Post St at Grant ☎415/421-2600. The oldest jeweler in town and quite possibly the best. Known for their fine silverware and flawless diamonds. You can get a replica of the pearl necklace given by the Japanese emperor to Marilyn Monroe on her honeymoon with local hero Joe DiMaggio.

Tiffany, 350 Post St at Powell ☎415/781-7000. Luxurious two-storied site, where the extraordinarily courteous staff is happy to let you try the stuff on even if it's obvious that you can't afford it.

BAY AREA

Jil Cappuccio, 3026 Ashby Ave ☎510/549-9316. One-of-a-kind designs, including popular men's shirts patched together from mismatched cloth found at garage sales.

Molly B, 2112A Vine St ☎510/843-1586, and 1811 Fourth St, Berkeley ☎510/548-3103. Eclectic designer frocks for gals with dough.

Nordstrom Rack, 1285 Marina Blvd, San Leandro ☎510/614-1742. After merchandise has been in the San Francisco store for three months, it's sold at a fifty percent discount here.

The Walk Shop, 2120 Vine St, Berkeley ☎510/849-3628. Down-to-earth, stylish shoes that feel good to walk in.

Casual wear

Banana Republic, 256 Grant Ave at Sutter ☎415/788-3087. Also at Embarcadero Center. Stylish, if overpriced clothes for the traveling yuppie, in this main branch of the San Francisco-based nationwide chain owned by Gap, Inc.

Daljeets, 541 Valencia St at 16th ☎415/626-9000; 1744 Haight St at Cole ☎415/752-5610. Amazing selection of shoes from the sensible to the bizarre and a nice little sideline in sex toys and fetish wear.

Esprit, 499 Illinois Ave at 16th ☎415/957-2550. Warehouse-sized store in SoMa that is the flagship of the wildly successful international chain selling sporty "California-style" casual wear in California colors. For basics, T-shirts, and the like, it's pretty good.

The Gap, 890 Market St at Powell ☎415/788-5909. Also at 1975 Market St at Dolores ☎415/861-8442, and all over the city and Bay Area and the country and the world. Large branch of the hugely successful chain store selling rather plain jeans, T-shirts, and casual wear.

Groger's Western Wear, 1445 Valencia St at 25th ☎415/647-0700. Mission store selling cowboy boots, Stetson hats, boot tips, and traditional brand-name Western clothes. Fun shopping. Closed Mon and Tues.

Levi's, 300 Post St at Stockton ☎415/501-0100. Four levels of jeans, tops, and jackets set against a thumping backdrop of club music. You can have your denims custom tailored (a computer scans your exact dimensions), and even shrink-fit a pair in the store by sitting in the warm-water tub and then passing through the stand-up dryer.

North Beach Leather, 190 Geary St at Stockton ☎415/362-8300. Leather everything, and in some pretty sickly colors, but for basic black jackets and simple pieces there are some well-made styles. The owner began by clothing the Hells Angels in 1967 and later outfitted the San Francisco police department before dressing Elvis Presley in 1969.

Patagonia, 770 North Point, near Fisherman's Wharf ☎415/771-2050. Functional, outdoor clothing that has a cult, semi-yuppie following.

Ragwood, 1764 Haight St at Cole ☎415/221-9760. Smart and distinctive designs that won't break the bank in this unusual store that also sells old furniture.

Villains, 1672 and 1682 Haight St at Belvedere ☎415/626-5939. Youthful, fun clothing and wild shoes. For when you want to dress up in club gear, but don't want to splash out.

Secondhand clothes

Aaardvark's Odd Ark, 1501 Haight St ☎415/621-3141. Large secondhand clothing store in Haight-Ashbury. Vintage and contemporary wear and an infinite supply of perfectly faded Levi's.

American Rag Co, 1305 Van Ness Ave at Bush ☎415/474-5214. As secondhand clothing stores go, this one is expensive, but has a superior collection of stylish clothing.

Buffalo Exchange, 1800 Polk St at Washington ☎415/346-5726, also at 1555 Haight St ☎415/431-7733. Cheap and occasionally tatty, but if you've got the patience to search through the piles of clothing, you may turn up some gems.

Clothes Contact, 473 Valencia St ☎415/621-3212. Where the punkers come for bomber jackets. Pay by the pound ($8), as weighed at checkout on a vintage scale.

Departures from the Past, 2028 Fillmore St ☎415/885-3377. A hybrid costume/vintage clothing shop. Tuxedo jackets and shirts, lots of scarves and vests, none exactly priced to move.

Jeremy's, 426 Brannan St ☎415/849-0701. Specializing in casual and designer clothes for men and women, seconds, and fashion show outtakes.

Retro Fit Vintage, 910 Valencia St ☎415/550-1530. Bowling shirts, smoking jackets, and a selection of mid-twentieth-century furniture, which often gets rented out for photo shoots and movie sets.

Schauplatz, 791 Valencia St ☎415/864-5665. The name is German for "happening scene" – the sort to which the colorful, upscale, used clothing sold in this boutique might be worn.

Third Hand Store, 1839 Divisadero St at Bush ☎415/567-7332. While other stores cash in on the craze for vintage clothing, this Western Addition store keeps its prices reasonable and has some interesting pieces.

Wasteland, 1660 Haight ☎415/863-3150. The granddaddy of Haight-Ashbury vintage-clothing stores. It's a day's work just getting through it all.

Worn Out West, 1850 Castro St at 19th ☎415/431-6020. Gay secondhand cowboy gear – a trip for browsing, and if you're serious about getting some Wild West kit, this is the least expensive place in town to pick out a good pair of boots, stylish Western shirts and chaps.

BAY AREA

Buffalo Exchange, 3333 Lakeshore Ave, Oakland ☎510/452-4464, also at 2512 Telegraph Ave, Berkeley ☎510/644-9202. Part of the secondhand clothing chain, this branch is the dumping ground

Shops and galleries

for residents of the upscale Piedmont community. High-class treasures aplenty. The Telegraph Ave store has last year's castoffs from the college crowd, current fashions and the classic Levi's 501s.

Carousel Consignment, 1955 Shattuck Ave, Berkeley ☎510/845-9044. Classy women's contemporary clothing and accessories.

Crossroads Trading Company, 5636 College Ave, Oakland ☎510/420-1952. Secondhand clothing of high quality, but more casual wear than vintage apparel. Styles for men and women.

Jeremy's, 2967 College Ave, Berkeley ☎510/849-0701. Casual wear, designer samples, and end-of-the-year castoffs.

Sharks, 2505 Telegraph Ave, Berkeley ☎510/841-8736. Great prices on retro-Americana. Dress up as the young Frank Sinatra or as his date.

Slash Clothing, 2840 College Ave, Berkeley ☎510/841-7803. Barely room to walk in this tiny, nontrendy basement with secondhand Levi's piled from floor to ceiling.

Thrift stores

Bargain Mart, 1823 Divisadero St at Bush ☎415/921-7380. Downscale secondhand clothes that look as though they're about to fall apart, but are ideal if you need to get decked out on the cheap.

Community Thrift, 625 Valencia St at 18th ☎415/861-4910. Thrift store in the Mission with clothing, furniture, and general junk. All proceeds are divided up among local charities.

Goodwill, 241 10th St at Howard ☎415/252-1677; also 822 Geary St at Hyde ☎415/922-0405; 2279 Mission St at 19th ☎415/826-5759; and 1700 Haight at Cole. There are Goodwill outlets all over the city, stocking everything from lampshades to handbags to three-piece suits. Exhaustive selection of junk and gems.

Repeat Performance San Francisco Symphony Thrift Store, 2223 Fillmore St ☎415/563-3123. Casual as well as formal wear and a few vintage items, all selling at top dollar, as the Pacific Heights location would suggest. Also jewelry, kitchenware, and shoes. All proceeds go to the Symphony.

Ross Dress for Less, 5200 Geary Blvd ☎415/386-7677, and 799 Market St ☎415/957-9222. Specializing in clothing and housewares remaindered from major department stores. A wide selection of men's, women's, kids', and lingerie, as well as picture frames, pillows, and cooking utensils, all for at least half off original retail prices.

St Vincent de Paul, 6298 Mission St in Daly City ☎650/992-9271. Queen of the junk stores, St Vinnies will keep you amused for hours. You could spend money all day and still have change from $50.

Seconds-To-Go Resale Shop, 2252 Fillmore St ☎415/563-7806. Nice clothes and housewares sold to benefit the Sacred Heart school. As with other used-clothing stores along Fillmore St, you'll find the prices higher than elsewhere.

Thrift Town, 2101 Mission St at 17th ☎415/861-1132. Huge and well-displayed selection, with some of San Francisco's better-quality trash as well as pretty stylish secondhand clothing bargains.

BAY AREA

Berkeley Flea Market, Ashby BART Station, cnr of Ashby Ave and Martin Luther King Jr. Way, Berkeley. ☎510/644-0744. Parking lot is open on weekends for independent vendors to sell secondhand clothes, furniture, and myriad bits. Perfect for booty-hunting.

Salvation Army Thrift Store, 1382 Solano Ave, Albany ☎510/524-5100. Low-priced clothes, shoes, and furnishings from gunk to great.

Food and drink

Food faddists will have a field day in San Francisco's many **gourmet stores**, which are on a par with the city's

24-hour stores

If you're caught short by hunger in the middle of the night, the following are just a few of the many stores open **24 hours**: Safeway at 15 Marina Blvd in the Marina, 2020 Market St and 2300 16th St in the Mission; and Cala Foods at 4201 18th St in the Castro, on California St near Hyde, at 6333 Geary Blvd and another at the end of Haight St opposite Golden Gate Park.

restaurants for culinary quality and diversity. The simplest neighborhood deli will get your taste buds jumping, while the most sophisticated places are enough to make you swoon.

Be sure to try such **local specialties** as Boudin's sourdough bread, Gallo salami and Anchor steam beer. Bear in mind, too, that however overwhelming the food on offer in San Francisco itself may seem, some of the very best places are to be found across the bay in Berkeley. For more basic stocking up there are, of course, **supermarkets** all over the city (Safeway is probably the most widespread name), some of them open 24 hours per day.

Most stores carrying food sell alcohol – including a range of Californian wines – provided you show an ID proving you're at least 21 years of age, though for the best variety, you should head to a specialist retailer.

Delis and groceries

Andronico's Market, 1200 Irving St between Funston and 14th Ave ☎415/753-0403; also four locations in Berkeley. The California gourmet's answer to Safeway. Pricey but gorgeous produce: microbrews, good wine, craft breads, fancy cheeses, an olive bar, and a pretty good deli. Not the cheapest, but way better quality than your average supermarket.

Casa Lucas, 2934 24th St at Guerrero ☎415/826-4334. Mission store with an astonishing array of exotic fruits and vegetables.

The Cheesery, 427 Castro St at 18th ☎415/552-6676. Reasonably priced coffees (from $4/lb) and cheeses from around the world.

David's, 474–480 Geary St at Taylor ☎415/771-1600. The consummate Jewish deli, open until midnight. A downtown haven for the after-theater crowd and night owls.

Harvest Ranch Market, 2285 Market St at Church ☎415/626-0805. Make an organic feast from the by-the-pound gourmet salad bar and eat with other locals on one of the benches out front.

Lo-Cost Market, 498 Haight St at Fillmore ☎415/621-4338. Inexpensive Asian market selling a wonderful selection of meats and seafood for cash only.

Lucca Ravioli, 1100 Valencia St at 22nd ☎415/647-5581. Fresh pasta factory that you can spy on through the big picture windows before you go into the store.

Molinari's, 373 Columbus Ave ☎415/421-2337. Bustling North Beach Italian deli, jammed to the rafters with goodies.

Pasta Gina, 741 Diamond at 24th in Noe Valley ☎415/921-7576. Fresh pasta and sauces to heat and eat. Everything you need, including wine, for an Italian dinner when you don't want to dine out or cook.

Rainbow Grocery, 1745 Folsom St ☎415/863-0620. Progressive politics and organic food in this huge SoMa wholefood store.

San Francisco Health Foods, 333 Sutter St at Grant ☎415/392-8477. Dried fruits, juices, and wholefood.

San Francisco Herb Company, 250 14th St between Mission and S Van Ness ☎415/861-3018. SoMa-based store with large quantities of fresh herbs at wholesale prices.

Shops and galleries

Sunrise Deli and Café, 2115 Irving St at 22nd ☎415/664-8210. Specialty Middle Eastern foodstuffs – stuffed vine leaves, *baba ghanoush* and hummus.

Swan Oyster Depot, 1517 Polk St ☎415/673-1101. Fantastic clam chowder, half-shell oysters, lobster, crabs, and seafood salad. Take your fish home to cook, or let one of the seven brothers who run the place serve you on their stainless-steel lunch counter.

Farmers' markets

Ferry Plaza Farmer's Market, on the Embarcadero in front of the Ferry Building at Market St; Sat 8.30am–2pm. Higher prices accompany the mostly organic produce in this very popular downtown market. Beautiful produce and fine foodstuffs.

Heart of the City Farmer's Market, United Nations Plaza at Market St near Civic Center; Wed & Sun 7am–5pm; ☎415/558-9455. Huge, friendly, certified farmer's market (which means everything is sold by the growers themselves), distinguished from others by catering to the multiethnic inner-city clientele at low prices. Mouthwateringly fresh local produce.

San Francisco Farmer's Market, 100 Alemany Blvd at Crescent Ave; Sat dawn–dusk; ☎415/647-9423. Covered market, established since the 1940s, offering customers the chance to purchase food fresh from the farms at fresh-from-the-farm prices. Invaluable if you're cooking for crowds or just love a bargain. Check out the flea market on Sunday.

BAY AREA

Berkeley Bowl, 2777 Shattuck Ave, Berkeley ☎510/841-6346. Converted bowling alley is now an enormous produce, bulk, and health-food market. Least expensive grocery in town with the largest selection of fresh produce. But be warned: the Bowl is so popular that it takes longer to get through the checkout line than it does to do your shopping.

Cheese Board, 1504 Shattuck Ave, Berkeley ☎510/549-3183. Collectively owned and operated since 1967, this was one of the first outposts in Berkeley's "Gourmet Ghetto" and is still going strong, offering more than 200 varieties of cheese and their own freshly baked bread.

Genova Delicatessen and Ravioli Factory, 5095 Telegraph Ave, Oakland ☎510/652-7401. Traditional Italian deli complete with an array of hanging sausages. Enormous and cheap sandwich creations.

Market Hall, 5655 College Ave, Oakland ☎510/601-8208. Conveniently located next to Rockridge BART. Offers all possible gourmet eats to local yuppies and students. Comprises a variety of small, fine-food shops serving to eat there or take out.

Monterey Market, 1550 Hopkins St, Berkeley ☎510/526-6042. An incredible variety of produce at stupendous prices, lots of it organic. Next door to a great deli, fish market, and cheese shop.

Ratto's, 821 Washington St, Oakland ☎510/832-6503. One hundred years old and looks the part. Dry-goods store and deli has remained in refurbished "Old Oakland," providing an excellent selection of gourmet fine foods.

Trader Joe's, 5700 Christie Ave in Powell St Plaza, Emeryville ☎510/658-8091. Also in San Francisco at 3 Masonic Ave, ☎415/346-9964. A grocer with a cult following, Joe's eclectic selections are available at bargain-basement prices. Unusual frozen foods and gourmet versions of ordinary supermarket items, beers, and wine. Highly recommended.

Yasai's Produce Market, 6301 College Ave, Oakland ☎510/655-4880. Beautiful selection of fruits, vegetables, and Asian spices.

Bread, pastries, and sweets

Bakers of Paris, 3989 24th St near Noe ☎415/863-8725. Noe Valley bakery that serves up mountains of baguettes and croissants.

Boudin, 156 Jefferson St, Fisherman's Wharf ☎415/928-1849. The sourdough bread at this chain is the best around, made using a 150-year-old recipe.

Godiva Chocolates, 865 Market St at Fifth ☎415/543-8910. Rich Belgian chocolates at around a $1.50 a nibble. Heaven for the chocaholic.

Italian French Baking Co., 1501 Grant Ave at Union ☎415/421-3796. In the heart of North Beach, selling mouthwatering breads, rolls, muffins, and homemade biscotti.

Just Desserts, 248 Church St at Market St ☎415/626-5774, and 836 Irving St near Ninth Ave ☎415/681-1277. Hugely popular chain of café-style bakeries specializing in a line of fresh if somewhat over-frosted cakes.

Liguria Bakery, 1700 Stockton St at Filbert, North Beach ☎415/421-3786. Marvelous old-world Italian bakery, with deliciously fresh focaccia.

Specialty's Cafe & Bakery, 101 New Montgomery St at Mission, plus many other downtown locations ☎415/896-BAKE. Convenient to the SoMa museums and arts centers, they offer big sandwiches on freshly baked bread, plus a staggering array of cakes, cookies, pastries, and flavored breads baked daily on the premises.

Sweet Inspirations, 2239 Market St at Sanchez St ☎415/621-8664, and 2123 Fillmore ☎415/931-2815. Monstrous portions of decadent desserts, like the excellent white-chocolate and blueberry tart; some can be a bit too rich, though.

Teuscher, 255 Grant Ave ☎415/398-2700. To-die-for confectioner off Union Square.

BAY AREA

Grace Baking, 5655 College Ave ☎510/428-2662. In Market Hall (see p.308), Grace Baking is a wonderful place for breakfast. Take home a fresh loaf of one of more than thirty different breads.

La Farine, 6323 College Ave, Oakland ☎510/654-0338. Home of the popular morning bun, a sticky cinnamon and sugar roll best eaten warm.

Your Black Muslim Bakery, 5836 San Pablo Ave, Oakland ☎510/658-7080, also 365 17th St ☎510/839-1313. Awesome sweet rolls best nibbled while thumbing through an ever-changing array of political pamphlets.

Tea, coffee, and spices

Bombay Bazar, 548 Valencia St at 17th ☎415/621-1717. Exotic spices and tons of legumes, grains, and other staples.

Freed, Teller & Freed, 1326 Polk St at Bush ☎415/673-0922. Polk Gulch coffee and tea emporium. Every conceivable legal addiction and all the paraphernalia to go with it.

Graffeo Coffee, 733 Columbus Ave at Filbert ☎415/986-2420. Huge sacks of coffee are piled up all around this North Beach store – you can smell the place from half a block away.

Haig's Delicacies, 642 Clement St ☎415/752-6283. Curries, teas, pickles, and spices from around the world.

Peet's Coffee and Tea, 2156 Chestnut St at Steiner ☎415/931-8302; 2257 Market (Upper Castro); and 2139 Polk at Vallejo. Marina-based San Francisco flagship of this venerable Berkeley coffee-roaster, offering some thirty different varieties.

Tea and Company, 2207 Fillmore ☎415/929-TEAS. Teapots and 89 varieties of tea.

Wines and spirits

California Wine Merchant, 3237 Pierce St at Chestnut ☎415/567-0646. Before you set off for the Wine Country, pick up a sample selection at this Marina wine emporium so you know what to look out for.

Cannery Wine Cellars, 2801 Leavenworth St, The Cannery, Fisherman's Wharf ☎415/673-0400. An astounding selection of wines and imported beers, as well as Armagnac and Scotch, line the walls.

Shops and galleries

Coit Liquor, 585 Columbus Ave at Union ☎415/986-4036. North Beach specialty wine store, with the accent on rare Italian vintages. Good stock of regular booze.

D & M Wine & Liquor Co., 2200 Fillmore St at Sacramento ☎415/346-1325. Great selection of Californian wines, but located as they are in Pacific Heights, their specialty is champagne; bargains abound.

The Jug Shop, 1567 Pacific Ave at Polk ☎415/885-2922. The Jug Shop is famous for its cheap Californian wines, but it also has more than 200 varieties of beer that are similarly well priced. One of the city's best places for booze.

Urban Cellars, 3821 24th St at Church ☎415/824-2300. The dipsomaniac's dream – hundreds of wines and exotic spirits taking booze shopping to its zenith.

The Wine Club, 953 Harrison St at Sixth ☎415/512-9086. Huge warehouse lacking in comfort, but filled with wine on which the mark-up is sometimes as low as five percent. Makes you realize how much you're being ripped off in other places.

BAY AREA

Beverages & More, 836 San Pablo Ave, Albany ☎510/525-9582, and at Jack London Square, Oakland ☎510/208-5126. Huge selection of wines, craft brews, and spirits; also cigars and party nibbles.

Paul Marcus Wines, 5655 College Ave, Oakland ☎510/420-1005. In trendy Market Hall, where employees are used to matching patron's gourmet groceries with appropriately sophisticated selections.

Takara Sake USA, 708 Addison St, Berkeley ☎510/540-8250. The producers of ShoChiku Bai sake give free tastings in an intimate bar, from noon to 6pm.

Trader Joe's, 5700 Christie Ave in Powell St Plaza, Emeryville ☎510/658-8091, also in San Francisco at 3 Masonic Ave, ☎415/346-9964. This popular grocery store has the widest range of affordable wines, many of them imports, in the Bay Area.

Vino!, 6319 College Ave, Oakland ☎510/652-6317. Small Bay Area chain works at stocking rare but affordable (under $10) selections. Very knowledgeable, friendly staff.

Bookstores

San Francisco boasts some truly excellent **bookstores**, not surprising for a city with such a literary reputation. The established focus for literature has long been in North Beach, in the area around the legendary City Lights Bookstore, but increasingly the best spots, particularly for contemporary creative writing, are to be found in the lower-rent Mission district, which is home to some of the city's more energized – and politicized – bookstores. There are a few **secondhand booksellers** in the city too, but these can't compare with the diverse bunch across the bay in Oakland and Berkeley. Most bookstores tend to open every day, roughly 10am–8pm, though City Lights is open daily until midnight.

General

The Booksmith, 1644 Haight St near Cole ☎415/863-8688. Good general bookstore stocking mainstream and countercultural titles.

Borders Books and Music, 400 Post St at Powell ☎415/399-1633. Massive, emporium-style bookstore with some 160,000 books to chose from as well as CDs, videos, and software on four floors. There's also a café, popular with cruising singles.

City Lights Bookstore, 261 Columbus Ave at Broadway ☎415/362-8193. America's first bookstore to carry paperbacks exclusively. Now, one of the city's best overall bookstores, with a range of titles including City Lights' own publications. Check out the basement's "Evidence" section, an X-Files fans'

Eden of conspiracy theories and ET sightings.

A Clean, Well Lighted Place for Books, Opera Plaza, 601 Van Ness Ave at Golden Gate ☎415/441-6670. Good selection of rather high-minded titles and a truly interesting calendar of readings from authors.

Green Apple, 506 Clement St ☎415/387-2272. A funky, cluttered shop sprawling over three storefronts in the Richmond, with a good kid's section and a large used book and music annex next door.

Tillman Place Bookstore, 8 Tillman Place, off Grant Ave, near Union Square ☎415/392-4668. Downtown's premier general bookstore and certainly one of the oldest, with a beautifully elegant feel.

BAY AREA

Barnes & Noble, 2532 Shattuck Ave at Durant, Berkeley ☎510/644-0861. Full-service bookstore with a Zen-like fountain in the central courtyard surrounded by park benches. Huge selection of books of every stripe.

Serendipity Books, 1201 University Ave, Berkeley ☎510/841-7455. This vast garage-like bookstore is off the loop of Berkeley bookstores but an absolute must for collectors of first editions, obscure fiction and poetry, and African-American writing. Its stock in each of these categories is unrivaled in the world, the prices are fair, and the owner – incredibly, given the towers of unshelved books – knows exactly where everything is to be found.

Walden Pond Books, 3316 Grand Ave, Oakland ☎510/832-4438. Large used and new bookstore carries the best selection of international fiction around at reasonable prices.

Secondhand

Aardvark Books, 227 Church St ☎415/552-6733. Carries all sorts of titles, but is particularly strong on mysteries and lesbian fiction. Buys used books everyday, so the stock is always changing.

Acorn Books, 1436 Polk St ☎415/563-1736. Specializes in first and rare editions. Smells and looks the way an old bookstore should.

Around the World, 1346 Polk St at Pine ☎415/474-5568. Musty, dusty, and a bit of a mess, this is a great place to spend hours poring over first editions, rare books, and vinyl records.

Chelsea Bookshop, 637 Irving Ave ☎415/566-0507. Next to Green Apple, one of the better used bookstores in town.

Columbus Books, 540 Broadway at Union ☎415/986-3872. North Beach store with a good selection of new and used books, and a large travel section.

Phoenix Books and Records, 3850 24th St at Sanchez ☎415/821-3477. Wide selection of new and used books at knockdown prices. Come out with armloads for $20.

Russian Hill Bookstore, 2234 Polk St at Vallejo ☎415/929-0997. Used books in very good condition.

BAY AREA

Pegasus Fine Books & CDs, 1855 Solano Ave ☎510/525-6888, and 2349 Shattuck Ave, Berkeley ☎510/649-1320. Picky selection of used books (ie not the ones you're trying to unload), plus used CDs (mostly jazz) and a smaller selection of quality new books and magazines.

Specialty

Bound Together Anarchist Collective Bookstore, 1369 Haight St ☎415/431-8355. Haight-Ashbury store specializing in radical and progressive publications.

China Books, 2929 24th St ☎415/282-2994. Mission bookstore with books and periodicals from China, and a good number of publications on the history and politics of the Third World.

A Different Light, 489 Castro St at 18th ☎415/431 0891. Well-stocked gay/lesbian bookshop, diverse and popular and a good place to meet people, especially

Shops and galleries

during the popular readings held here periodically.

Fields Bookstore, 1419 Polk St at Pine ☎415/673-2027. Metaphysical and New Age books.

Get Lost, 1825 Market St ☎415/437-0529. Despite the name, the friendliest and best travel bookshop in town; also has a decent assortment of maps and gear.

Good Vibrations, 1210 Valencia St at 23rd ☎415/974-8980, and 2504 San Pablo, Berkeley ☎510/841-8987. A comfortable, decidedly un-sleazy place to buy how-to sex books and erotica. So keen is this outfit to promote women's sexuality they even publish their own titles under the Down There Press imprint. Also sells a bewildering diversity of sex toys, condoms, and intimate apparel.

Great Expectations, 1512 Haight St at Ashbury ☎415/863-5515. Radical liberal bookstore with hundreds of T-shirts bearing political slogans, some funnier than others.

Kinokuniya, 2nd floor, Japan Center, 1581 Webster St ☎415/567-7625. Large stock of Japanese and English-language books, but they really excel in art books.

See p.153 for a more complete look at Berkeley bookstores.

The Maritime Store, San Francisco Maritime National Historic Park, Hyde Street Pier ☎415/775-2665. All seafaring enthusiasts stop here for maritime history, navigation, boat-building, and sailing books.

Modern Times, 888 Valencia St at 20th ☎415/282-9246. Good selection of gay and lesbian literature, many radical feminist publications, and a hefty stock of Latin American literature and progressive political publications. Stages regular readings of authors' works.

Rand McNally Map & Travel Store, 595 Market St at Second ☎415/777-3131. Large store selling travel guides, maps and paraphernalia for the person on the move.

Sierra Club Bookstore, 85 Second St at Mission ☎415/977-5600. Indispensable for the camper or hiker; check in here before you wander off to explore the great wide.

Stacey's Professional Bookstore, 581 Market St between First and Second ☎415/421-4687. A wide general selection but best in business and medical tomes.

William Stout Architectural Books, 804 Montgomery St at Jackson ☎415/391-6757. One of San Francisco's world-class booksellers, with an excellent range of books on architecture, building, and urban studies.

BAY AREA

Comic Relief, 2138 University, Berkeley ☎510/843-5002. All the mainstream stuff, plus self-published mini-comics by locals.

Dark Carnival, 3086 Claremont Ave, Berkeley ☎510/654-7323. Dedicated to science fiction, fantasy, and mysteries.

Gaia Books, 1400 Shattuck Ave, Berkeley ☎510/548-4172. Voted best specialty bookstore by readers of the local paper *The Express*, this New Age and spirituality depot is a hoot. They also host readings by your favorite out-there authors.

Mama Bear's Women's Bookstore, 6536 Telegraph Ave, Oakland ☎510/428-9684. Cozy women-owned bookstore and café with an enormous selection of lesbian and feminist literature.

Music

San Francisco's **record stores** are of two types: massive, anodyne warehouses pushing all the latest releases, and impossibly small specialist stores crammed to the rafters with obscure discs. The big places like Virgin Megastore are more or less identical to those throughout the world, though foreign visitors tend to find the prices marginally cheaper than back home. More exciting is the large number of **independent** retailers and **secondhand and collectors' stores**, where you can track down anything you've ever wanted, especially in West Coast jazz or psychedelic rock.

General Interest

Aquarius Records, 3961 24th St at Noe ☎415/647-2272. Small neighborhood store with friendly, knowledgeable staff. Emphasis on indie rock, jazz, and blues.

CD & Record Rack, 3987 18th St at Castro ☎415/552-4990. Castro emporium with a brilliant selection of dance music including a few Seventies twelve-inch singles. The accent is definitely on stuff you can dance to.

Discolandia, 2964 24th St at Mission ☎415/826-9446. Join the snake-hipped groovers looking for the latest in salsa and Central American sounds in this Mission outlet.

Hear Music, 1314 Howard ☎415/487-1822. Amazing selection of world music and indies, with dozens of listening stations. Another location in Berkeley; see overleaf.

Musica Latina/American Music Store, 2653 Mission St between 22nd and 23rd sts ☎415/664-5554. Mission store selling music from all over the Latino world, especially South America.

Record Finder, 258 Noe St at Market ☎415/431-4443. One of the best independents, with a range as broad as it's absorbing. Take a wad and keep spending.

Tower Records, Columbus Ave and Bay St, near Fisherman's Wharf ☎415/885-0500. Main San Francisco location of the multinational empire.

Virgin Megastore, 2 Stockton at the corner of Market St ☎415/397-4525. Three floors packed with music in a wide variety of styles. The third floor has a good stock of current, popular books, videos, and a café with windows overlooking Market St.

Secondhand and specialty music

Amoeba Records, 1855 Haight St ☎415/831-1200, and 2455 Telegraph, Berkeley ☎510/549-1125. This big sister to Berkeley's renowned emporium is one of the largest used-music retailers in America. Both locations are stocked to the gills with hard-to-find releases, both new and used, on vinyl and CD, including rarities of every stripe.

Flat Plastic Sound, 24 Clement St ☎415/386-5095. Actually specializes in classical music, but DJs come here for the wide array of obscure retro vinyl – an out-of-print album by Mr. T, say.

Green Apple, 506 Clement St ☎415/387-2272. Used and new cassette and CD shop beside the annex to the bookstore of the same name (see p.311).

Groove Merchant Records, 687 Haight St ☎415/252-5766. Very groovy Lower Haight soul and jazz shop.

Jack's Record Cellar, 254 Scott St at Page ☎415/431-3047. The city's best source for American secondhand records – R&B, jazz, country, and rock'n'roll. They'll track down rare discs and offer you the chance to listen before you buy.

The Jazz Quarter, 1267 20th Ave near Irving ☎415/661-2331. A bit of a trek from downtown, but if you're a jazz fiend on the lookout for rarities, it's worth the effort.

Let It Be Records, 2434 Judah St at 29th Ave ☎415/681-2113. Beatles memorabilia and other rock rarities.

Medium Rare, 2310 Market St ☎415/255-7273. Shoebox-sized Castro store carrying an offbeat selection of Fifties cocktail-lounge albums.

Reckless Records, 1401 Haight St at Masonic ☎415/431-3434. With other locations in Chicago and London, all specializing in buying and selling both new and used independent music.

Recycled Records, 1377 Haight St at Masonic ☎415/626-4075. Good all-round store, with a decent selection of music publications, American and imported.

Rocket Records, 1377 Ninth St ☎415/664-2324. Quality stash of old

and used LPs, and CDs, too. In the Inner Sunset.

Rooky Ricardo's, 448 Haight St at Fillmore ☎415/864-7526. Albums and singles specializing in Fifties to Seventies soul, funk, and jazz. Vinyl only.

Streetlight Records, 3979 24th St ☎415/282-3550, also at 2350 Market St ☎415/282-8000. A great selection of used records, tapes, and CDs. The perfect opportunity to beef up your collection on the cheap.

BAY AREA

Down Home Music, 10341 San Pablo Ave, El Cerrito ☎510/525-2129. As you might guess from the name, Down Home stocks an excellent selection of folk, blues, and bluegrass music, making it well worth the trek across to the East Bay. One of the best record stores of its kind in the US.

Hear Music, 1809 Fourth St., Berkeley ☎510/204-9595. Like the San Francisco location (see overleaf), boasts an extensive selection of jazz, Celtic, and international artists.

Mod Lang, 2136 University Ave at Shattuck, Berkeley ☎510/486-1850. Mail order ☎510/486-1880. Knowledgeable staff will inform and sell you a whole range of indie and progressive CDs and vinyl.

Rasputin's, 2350 Telegraph Ave, Berkeley ☎510/848-9004. Open until 11pm, and good for jazz, rock, and ethnic recordings.

Art Galleries

At first glance the low-profile San Francisco **art scene** seems provincial compared to the glamorous internationalism of New York and Los Angeles. And in many respects it is. But with a large concentration of artists living in the Bay Area, there is a scene of sorts, one that drifts freely from the stylistic vagaries of the world art market.

Out-of-towners tend to find it difficult to get a sense of what's going on, as most younger artists shun **commercial galleries**, especially the mainstream ones around Union Square, and prefer to show their work in their favorite cafés and bars. That said, there is a core of relatively innovative galleries around the South of Market area, though even there the asking prices can be pretty steep. For a complete listing of art galleries in the city, just pick up a copy of *SF Weekly*, available free from street-corner boxes and most cafés; or contact the SF Bay Area Gallery Guide, 1369 Fulton St ☎415/921-1600; or the SF Art Dealer's Association, 1717 17th St ☎415/626-7498. Most galleries are open Tues–Sat 11am–5pm, and until 7.30pm on the first Thursday of each month in a special promotion designed for the after-work crowd.

If you're around in October, take advantage of the annual Open Studios event ☎415/861-9838, in which around 800 local artists open their creative spaces to the public for free.

Union Square and around

American Indian Contemporary Arts, 23 Grant Ave, 6th floor ☎415/989-7003. Nonprofit gallery run by and for contemporary Native American artists.

Atelier Dore, Inc., 771 Bush St at Mason ☎415/391-2423. Salon-style gallery hung floor-to-ceiling with top-quality paintings. Historical genre paintings from California, including WPA works, and about the only place that carries the work of nineteenth- and twentieth-century black American painters.

Bond St. Gallery, 478 Post St at Mason ☎415/362-1480. Specializes in Latin American painting, sculpture, and graphics, with an emphasis on contemporary Mexican artists.

Caldwell Snyder Gallery, 228 Grant Ave, between Post and Sutter ☎415/392-2299, and 357 Geary St at Mason ☎415/296-7896. Well-known contemporary artists at prices to match their notoriety.

Fraenkel Gallery, 49 Geary St at Kearney and Market ☎415/981-2661. Sharing space with seven other galleries, including Rena Bransten (see opposite),

Fraenkel focuses on photography and fine art from the nineteenth and twentieth centuries. Exhibitions change about every two months.

Hackett-Freedman Gallery, 250 Sutter St at Grant ☎415/362-7152. One of the more interesting ones, the first in California to be dedicated to promoting contemporary realist painting, drawing, and sculpture.

James Willis Gallery, 77 Geary St at Grant ☎415/398-7545. Tribal artifacts from India, Africa, and Indonesia. Unusual carvings and fabrics.

Japonesque, 824 Montgomery St at Jackson ☎415/391-8860. Museum-quality Japanese art, including pottery, sculpture and prints.

John Berggruen Gallery, 228 Grant Ave at Post ☎415/781-4629. Ultra-trendy gallery on three floors, showing big-name American and international artists in painting and sculpture.

John Pence Gallery, 750 Post St at Jones ☎415/441-1138. American academic realist painting and sculpture. Some beautiful pieces.

Modernism, 685 Market St at Third, suite 290 ☎415/541-0461. Futurism, expressionism, Pop Art, minimalism and American modern art.

Rena Bransten Gallery, 77 Geary St at Kearney and Market ☎415/982-1807. In the same space as Fraenkel (see opposite), Bransten exhibits photography, video, sculpture, and painting by established and up-and-coming modern artists such as the East Bay's Henry Wessel.

Shapiro Gallery, 250 Sutter St between Grant and Kearny, 3rd floor ☎415/398-6655. Twentieth-century black-and-white photographs from the f/64 group, whose stars include Ansel Adams, Imogen Cunningham, and Edward Weston.

Smile, A Gallery with Tongue in Chic, 500 Sutter St at Powell ☎415/362-3436. From the whimsical to the very serious, this gallery is one of very few into it just for the fun of it. They'll exhibit anything.

Vorpal Gallery, 393 Grove St at Franklin ☎415/397-9200. Contemporary Californian and international artists from more than thirty countries.

SoMa and elsewhere

Art Collective Gallery, 3654 Sacramento St at Spruce ☎415/474-9999. An art gallery collective showing work from different galleries all over the Bay Area.

The Audium, 1616 Bush at Franklin ☎415/771-1616. The brainchild of sound engineer Stan Shaff, who has been running it by himself for the past 25 years, the space-age room is filled with over 150 speakers, which Shaff uses to put on shows illustrating the three-dimensional possibilities of sound (Fri & Sat, 8.30pm; $10).

Clarion Alley, next to the Community Thrift Store at 625 Valencia ☎415/861-4910. Hosts an ever-evolving exhibition of public art – a series of murals that brighten an otherwise rather glum block.

Creativity Explored, at 3245 16th St ☎415/863-2108. Runs a full-time art center for developmentally disabled adults. Work produced at the school has been shown at galleries around the world, including the SF MoMA, and some is usually available for purchase.

Crown Point Press, 20 Hawthorne St, around the corner from the SF MoMA. ☎415/974-6273. Two showrooms; limited editions of etchings changing every six weeks.

Encantada Galley of Fine Art, 904 Valencia ☎415/642-3939. Varied and typically lovely Mexican and Latin American art gallery in the Mission.

Erickson & Elins Gallery, 345 Sutter at Grant ☎415/981-1080. Nineteenth- and twentieth-century fine art.

Folk Art International-Boretti Amber, 900 North Point, Ghirardelli Square ☎415/928-3340. Latin American art and Baltic amber jewelry.

Galeria de la Raza, 24th and Bryant sts (Tues–Sat noon–6pm); ☎415/826-8009.

Shops and galleries

Shops and galleries

See p.162 for more on the art world in Benicia.

Hosts community activities and exhibitions by artists from the Mission district.

Joseph Chowning Gallery, 1717 17th St at Carolina ☎415/626-7496. Massive forum for modern and contemporary painting and sculpture.

Mission Cultural Center, 2868 Mission St at 25th ☎821-1155. Home to the Galeria Museo, one of the largest galleries in town, devoted exclusively to Hispanic art. The center offers classes as well as a wide variety of community events, from street fairs to political actions.

New Langton Arts, 1246 Folsom St at Ninth ☎415/626-5416. Noncommercial theater and gallery organization showing experimental works in all media, and hosting new music and jazz concerts, readings, and performances.

Ruby Artists Cooperative Gallery, 3602 20th St ☎415/550-8052. Twenty-five local artists take turns producing work for the shop – everything from lampshades to cuff links to decorative boxes and soaps.

San Francisco Art Institute, 800 Chestnut St at Jones ☎415/771-7020. Local avant-garde contemporary art and student work.

SF MoMA Rental Gallery, Building A, Fort Mason ☎415/441-4777. Large space where more than 1300 artists try to break into the commercial art world. Sales as well as rentals.

Terrain, 165 Jessie St between Third and New Montgomery, 2nd floor ☎415/543-0656. South of Market gallery exhibiting contemporary painting, sculpture, constructions, and mixed media by diverse local and international artists.

Xanadu, 900 North Point, Ghirardelli Square ☎415/441-5211. Tribal and ethnic art from West Africa, textiles and jewelry from Indonesia, India, and Asia.

East Bay

Arts Benicia Gallery, 991 Tyler St, Benicia ☎707/747-0131. A resource for the Benicia arts scene, the gallery presents workshops, poetry readings, slide lectures, and a changing series of exhibitions, Fri–Sun noon–4pm. The first weekend in May, Arts Benicia hosts open studios all over town.

Pro Arts, 461 Ninth St, Oakland ☎510/763-4361. Changing exhibitions, concentrating on local artists and community issues, six times a year in this bright, modern space. Worth a look, and a good resource for the East Bay art scene.

Specialty stores

In among the designer clothes stores and art galleries of the Union Square area, a handful of stores sell **antiques and other treasurable objects**; though prohibitively expensive, many repay a look-in at least. We've also pulled together in this section some of the city's odd shops specializing in things you often need desperately but never know where to find – stationery, birthday cards, nuts and bolts, flowers, camping gear, children's toys, and so on.

Antiques and collectibles

Antonio's Antiques, 701 Bryant St ☎415/781-1737. Three floors of antiques from around the world. Good porcelain and sculpture.

Asakichi Japanese Antiques and Art, Japan Center, 1730 Geary Blvd at Webster ☎415/921-2147. Lovely pieces, but definitely geared toward the tourist dollar.

Biordi, 412 Columbus Ave at Vallejo ☎415/392-8096. North Beach store selling lovely hand-painted Italian dinnerware and ornaments. It's unlikely that you'd ever buy this kind of stuff while traveling, but it makes for very enjoyable browsing.

Genji Antiques, 22 Peace Plaza, Japantown ☎415/931-1616. Expensive oddments and beautiful wooden chests.

Gump's, 135 Post St at Kearny ☎415/982-1616. Famous for its jade, oriental rugs and objects cast in crystal, silver, and china. Fuel for fantasies rather than genuine consumption.

Miscellaneous

Body Manipulations, 3234 16th St at Guerrero ☎415/621-0408. Piercing, branding and other fun-filled leisuretime activities.

Brooks Cameras, 125 Kearny St at Post ☎415/362-4708. High-quality camera store with full repair department.

Cliff's Variety, 479 Castro St at 18th ☎415/431-5365. Hardware store selling everything useful from toilet paper to gimlets to kettles and more. A brilliant browsing store if you're into home improvements.

Cottage Industry, 4068 24th St ☎415/821-2465 and 2326 Fillmore ☎415/885-0326. Friendly housewares shop packed with candlesticks, incense, Buddhas and fountains from Japan, China, and India.

The Dreaming Room, 245 Columbus Ave ☎415/788-7882. Incredibly unique selection of exotic folk art, Buddhist, Hindu, and tribal icons, statues, and instruments.

FAO Schwarz, 48 Stockton St at O'Farrell ☎415/394-8700. Mega-toystore on three floors designed to turn children into monsters.

Fillamento, 2185 Fillmore ☎415/931-2224. Fabulous knickknack shop for bath, kitchen, and living room.

Fredericksen Hardware, 3029 Fillmore ☎415/292-2950. Since 1896, this store has been selling everything from old clocks to kitchen, gadgets to Cow Hollow residents.

Good Vibrations, 1210 Valencia St at 23rd ☎415/974-8980 and 2504 San Pablo, Berkeley ☎510/841-8987. Adult book and sex-toy emporium, owned and operated by women who have created a safe and friendly atmosphere for women, men, and giddy couples to probe the depths of their sexuality.

Le Video, 1231 Ninth Ave ☎415/566-3606. Two adjacent stores containing the most comprehensive collection of videos in the country. Where else can you find a copy of the Japanese edition of Italian director Dario Argento's third *giallo* film, digitally remastered in a letter-boxed edition with yellow subtitles?

Lost Weekend Video, 1034 Valencia St ☎415/643-3373. Video shop perfect for homesick Brits or Anglophiles, with a huge BBC section.

Mom's Bodyshop, 1408 Haight ☎415/864-MOMS. Tattoos for those who want to go home with a permanent souvenir. Large selection of Chinese, Celtic, and Tibetan scripts.

Psychic Eye, 301 Fell ☎415/863-9997. Pick up the roots and herbs you need to cast spells, or browse the books on ancient sexual positions. The staff will do a psychic reading on you, or you can sign up for the Tarot for Dummies class, at $10 a session.

Star Magic, 4026 24th St at Castro ☎415/641-8626. Situated down in Noe Valley, this is the ultimate New Age store, full of crystals to cleanse your chakras and the like.

Under One Roof, 549 Castro St ☎415/503-2300. A unique San Francisco store selling decorative gift items, with 100 percent of the profits going to 51 AIDS-services organizations. Nine years of operation has raised $5.4 million.

Union Street Papery, 2162 Union St at Fillmore ☎415/563-0200. Excellent, pricey stationers selling fine writing paper and a range of cards and pens.

BAY AREA

The Bone Room, 1569 Solano Ave, Berkeley ☎510/526-5252. Animal and human bones, skulls, preserved insects and whatnot, for the natural historian or just the curiosity-seeker.

East Bay Vivarium, 1827-C Fifth St, Berkeley ☎510/841-1400. The largest collection of living reptiles for sale under one roof. Even if you're not in the market, there's no harm in looking.

Narain's, 1320 San Pablo Ave, Berkeley ☎510/527-2509. Custom sewing and outdoor-gear repair shop, also with a good line in travel pouches.

Chapter 19

Sports and outdoor activities

Given its mild climate, large swaths of protected parkland, and rugged natural beauty, it comes as no surprise that the Bay Area is full of people who love **outdoor activities**. Aside from rollerblading, hiking, mountain biking, and running, locals have a wealth of **spectator sports** to choose from and several professional and collegiate teams to which they pledge their undying loyalty. The fitness exuded by many locals isn't quite the cosmetic "body-beautiful" kind that Southern California is renowned for; still, a healthy percentage of San Franciscans consider a gym membership a basic necessity of life in the modern age. Keep in mind that even when the skies are gray, as they often are, the sun's ultraviolet rays pierce through the clouds, giving many unprepared tourists an surprise **sunburn** as a souvenir.

Spectator sports

San Franciscans have been spoiled with successful professional sports teams – mainly in American football – since the early 1980s. Though American football is generally noteworthy for its physical brutality and ethos of toughness, the 49ers dominated the sport for much of the 1980s and 1990s with an unusually elegant style of play, epitomized by the legendary duo of Joe Montana and Jerry Rice. The beloved team ran off sixteen consecutive winning seasons, a streak that ended in 1999 when the local celeb quarterback Steve Young suffered one concussion too many and was forced to the bench – eventually retiring the next year. Nevertheless, 49er games continue to sell out, a testament to local fans' loyalty.

A fierce rivalry exists between Oakland and San Francisco's baseball and football teams, and their different playing styles reflect the cities they represent: Oakland's baseball and football players are seen as blue-collar types, with the franchises making do with limited budgets and few stars, while San Francisco's teams enjoy higher spending sprees and have egos to match.

The competition peaked over a decade ago, when the two baseball sides, the Oakland A's and San Francisco Giants, faced off in the **1989 World Series**, a "Battle of the Bay" that was temporarily postponed when the Loma Prieta earthquake struck before the beginning of Game Three. After halting play for over a week while the Bay Area picked up the pieces, the A's swept the Giants for the championship.

Tickets to big events like 49ers games are sold out years in advance, and the opening of the gorgeous new Pac Bell Ballpark on downtown San Francisco's waterfront means Giants games are a hot commodity for curious fans. For other events, it's generally possible to show up on the day of a game for tickets. A seat in the sun-drenched "bleachers" in Oakland's outfield grandstand, for example, can go for as little as $1 and as high as $4, with seats closer in topping the scale at around $30. Advance tickets for all Bay Area sports events are available through the **BASS** charge-by-phone ticket service (☎415/478-BASS or 510/762-BASS; *www.basstickets.net*), as well as from the teams themselves.

Baseball

Baseball's once-dominant (early 1970s and late 1980s) and recently resurgent **Oakland Athletics (A's)** play at the usually sunny **Coliseum**, 7900 Coliseum Way (☎510/638-0500). Despite their low payroll and slim ticket sales, the organization was voted baseball's Organization of the Year in 1998 and 1999 for its smart use of its young talent. Ticket prices range from $4 for bleacher seats to $125 for a field-side box, but promotions, like Wednesday Dollar Days (where most seats, hot dogs, and soft drinks are $1), make seeing a baseball game here the cheapest major sports event in town. BART stops outside the stadium.

In April 2000, the National League's **San Francisco Giants** began play in new **Pac Bell Ballpark** in SoMa along the waterfront at King Street (☎1-800/544-2687). The Giants are anchored by perennial All-Star outfielder Barry Bonds, one of the best – and long-considered one of the most self-serving – players in baseball.

In their new stadium, home runs over the right-field fence splash into the bay inlet, renamed McCovey Cove after a former Giants great. If you can't get a ticket to the game – most seats for the entire first season were sold before the sod was even in place – head down to the new stadium anyhow by walking along the Embarcadero or taking Muni's N Line from downtown. A see-through fence along the the right-field wall allows you to spy on a game for free, or chase home runs that have left the park.

If you must get inside the park, the Giants hold 500 bleacher-seat tickets for sale on every game day. Check *www.sfgiants.com* or stop by the stadium concourse, Willie Mays Plaza, at Seventh and Brannan for schedules and ticket availability.

The **San Francisco Seals** is the city's minor league team, playing ball in San Rafael's Albert Park at 618 B St (June–Sept ☎415/431-2899). The team is comprised of top college players on break, and the spirit in the stands is as lively as a Main Street parade. Expect cheap beers, the smell of hot dogs on barbecues, a live blues band, and stunning views of the hills. Here's baseball the way it was meant to be played.

Football

Football's once-fabulous **San Francisco 49ers**, many-time Super Bowl champions, play at 3Com Park (☎415/468-2249) at windswept Candlestick Point to the south; however, there are controversial plans for a new stadium/mall, an idea strongly backed by Mayor Brown to keep the team in the city. After owner Eddie DeBartolo Jr threatened to move, voters narrowly passed two measures in 1997 that will provide $100 million in city-issued bonds to help finance a gigantic $525 million stadium/shopping mall at Candlestick Point, an idea that's now on hold as the struggle for 49ers ownership carries on between Eddie – recently convicted of bribery and banned from the league for a year – and his sister Denise, who sued him for possession of the franchise. It's almost impossible to get hold of a ticket to a 49ers game, despite a few sub-par seasons. Your best bet is to show up in the parking lot of game day and look for scalpers; you may have to fork out as much as $100 for a good seat.

There are always tickets available to see the Silver and Black do battle in the Coliseum (☎510/639-7700), where the **Raiders** are working-class heroes to Oaklanders but cheap-shot thugs to the rest of the nation. Tickets are at least $60 since the team moved back to Oakland in 1995 after having abandoned the city

Sports and outdoor activities

In brief, the baseball season runs from April to October, with 81 home games; basketball from November to June, with 41 home games; and football from September to January, with 8 home games.

Sports and outdoor activities

for Los Angeles thirteen years before, only to return to Oakland when the fan base didn't prove as profitable as hoped. Raiders' fans are the most boisterous in professional sports, often donning serious face paint and costumes at gametime.

Basketball, hockey, soccer, and college games

For **professional basketball**, the Bay Area is limited to the woeful **Golden State Warriors**, who dribble at Oakland Arena (☎510/762-BASS), next to the Coliseum. For the past decade, the team has been one of the losingest in the league, capturing headlines for poor moves and outbursts such as player Latrell Sprewell choking his coach during practice. Sprewell went on to fame and fortune for the New York Knicks, while the coach remained for a few more years of purgatory with the Warriors before being fired in 1999.

The **National Hockey League's San Jose Sharks** (☎408/999-5721 or 288-8666) play at their own brand-new arena in the South Bay. After many years of inane play, the Sharks, lead by Owen Nolan, became very good in 1999–2000, when they knocked the NHL's top team out of the playoffs.

The Bay Area's newest sports team is the **San Jose Earthquakes** (☎408/985-GOAL or 241-9922), a **Major League Soccer** club that plays at San Jose State's Spartan Stadium.

University of California's Bears play in the Pac-10 conference, one of America's toughest intercollegiate leagues. Tickets (☎1-800/GO-BEARS) for men's and women's basketball and soccer, as well as men's football and basketball are usually less than $15. All events usually have some seats for sale before game time, save for football's annual "Big Game" between Cal and arch-rival Stanford during which whooping college fans are a show in themselves.

Cycling and mountain biking

For detailed information and maps on mountain biking trails, visit one of the following Web sites: www.mtbr.com; www.marin-trails.com/bike; *or* xenon.stanford.edu/~rsf/mtn-bike.html.

San Francisco is a city full of unspoiled parks and rugged natural landscapes, perhaps best experienced by **cycling** through them. Golden Gate Park and Ocean Beach (chapter 8) as well as the Marina and the Presidio (chapter 4) have great, paved trails and some good off-road routes. For a tranquil trek through less developed nature, head north over the Golden Gate Bridge (the western side is reserved solely for bikes) and into the Marin Headlands for a series of improved, off-road trails along ocean-hugging cliffs and into valleys (see p.185). For the more ambitious, day-trips to Angel Island (see p.192) offer less-worn trails. Overnight bike tours of the Wine Country (see p.200) are hard to beat for flat, sunny roads and a liquid reward at every tasting stop.

The Bay Area's contribution to cycling was the invention in the early 1970s of the **mountain bike**, when Tamalpais High School students began cruising down the fire roads of Marin County's Mount Tamalpais on one-speed, coaster brake Schwinn cruisers, heavy beach bikes with thick balloon tires that could handle the road's rough terrain. Over time, riders like Otis Guy, Joe Breeze, and Gary Fisher began adding gears and drum brakes, and by 1976 the bikes had become so popular that a race, the Repack, was begun. The event generated major press coverage, leading to a national craze.

For **serious mountain bikers**, consider a trip outward to El Corte de Madera Open Space Preserve, San Mateo County (Fir Trail); East Bay Regional Park, Oakland Hills (Westridge Trail); Mount Diablo State Park, Contra Costa County (Blood Trail/Devil's Elbow); and Fairfax, Marin County (Pine Mountain Loop).

For **rentals**, Park Cyclery, 1749 Waller St, in the Haight, near Golden Gate Park (☎415/751-7368), has mountain bikes for $5 per hour, $25 per day. Downtown, for Golden Gate Bridge rides, try American Bicycle Rental, 2715 Hyde St, near Fisherman's Wharf (☎415/931-0234), and Blazing Saddles, 1095 Columbus in North Beach (☎415/202-8888). Both rent bikes for $5 per hour, $25 per day as does Adventure Bicycle

Company, 968 Columbus Ave (☎415/771-TREK), which also rents tandem bikes ($45) and jogging strollers ($15). Within Golden Gate Park, Surrey Bikes and Skates Rental (☎415/668-6699) is housed in the boathouse at Stow Lake. They rent mountain bikes ($21/day), rollerblades ($10–15/day), tandem bikes ($25/day), strollers ($15/day), and even fringed surreys ($15–25/day).

For **motorcyclists** the 87-mile ride from Livermore Valley's vineyards (southeast of Oakland) to San Jose begins on I-580, heading east toward Stockton, exiting to the right at South Livermore Road. Gas up in town, as the next fuel is in San Jose. Follow the road to its end, turn left on Tesla Road, then right on Mines Road, where sticking to the left flank of the road leads you through 31 twisty, gorgeous miles of backcountry. To continue to San Jose, take a right on San Antonio Valley Road and head 31 miles up the back of Mount Hamilton, past the Lick Observatory, and then down Mount Hamilton Road for a 25-mile downhill ride into Silicon Valley. Superb.

Skating

San Francisco's steep roads and pathways aren't exactly skater-friendly, but there's enough flat, paved ground around the Marina and, to a lesser extent, in Golden Gate Park to make **inline skating** a popular weekend activity. On Sunday, most of Golden Gate Park's roads are closed to autos, bringing out hordes of bladers and bikers. On other days of the week, skaters use the flat sidewalk along Ocean Beach, and the good trails around Lake Merced, although both are away from the action of downtown. San Francisco's many plazas are more welcoming to **skateboarding**, even if local law conspires to ban thrashers from city limits. The flat expanse of the Embarcadero is a popular place to shred. Skates on Haight, 1818 Haight St (☎415/752 8375), sells and rents both for $6/hr.

For those preferring to put their blades to ice, the Bay Area has a couple of excellent **ice-skating** rinks. Each winter, from early November to mid February, **Kristi Yamaguchi's Holiday Skating Rink** is set up in Justin Herman Plaza at the Embarcadero (Sun–Thurs 10am–10pm, Fri & Sat 10am–11.30pm; $6 entrance; skate rental $3 for figure skates, $4 for hockey skates; ☎415/956-2688).

Also in San Francisco, but operating year-round, the **Rooftop at Yerba Buena Gardens** atop Moscone Center, 750 Folsom at Fourth Street (Mon–Fri 1–5pm, Fri & Sat 7.30–10.30pm; $6, including skate rental; ☎415/777-3727), has both a regulation-size hockey rink and Olympic-size figure-skating surface.

The Bay Area's preeminent ice rink is located in the East Bay, where the Olympic-sized **Oakland Ice Center**, 519 189th St (☎510/268-9000), has indoor skating year round, at least whenever Olympic medalists aren't training; Kristi Yamaguchi and Brian Boitano often practice here (daily noon–5pm, also Fri & Sat 7–10pm; $8 skate rental and all-day use). Occasional NHL exhibition hockey games also take place here.

Jogging

To some extent, cycling and rollerblading have supplanted the Bay Area's former obsession, **jogging**, though you'll still see people running in Golden Gate Park, and late May's **Bay-to-Breakers Race** continues to thrive. During this distinctly San Franciscan event, throngs of costumed joggers – waiters carrying wine glasses, giant centipedes and the like – follow a few world-class runners from the Embarcadero, seven and a half miles across the city to Ocean Beach. If you're tempted to join in, call ☎415/777-2424 for details. In Marin County's much more serious **Dipsea Race**, which takes place on the second Sunday in June, several hundred runners race across the mountains from Mill Valley to Stinson Beach. If you want to participate, contact Dipsea Race, PO Box 30, Mill Valley, CA 94942, for an application, or email *edda@concentric.net*.

Sports and outdoor activities

For updated news on bicycle races, marathons, and intramural running and swimming associations, pick up a copy of City Sports *(*www.citysportsmag.com*), a monthly publication available for free at area health clubs.*

Sports and outdoor activities

Surfing, windsurfing, and kayaking

The water off the San Francisco coast tends to be pretty chilly, so **surfing** remains more of a Southern California phenomenon. However, wet- and dry-suited enthusiasts do get radical off most Bay Area beaches, particularly Ocean Beach, Stinson Beach in northern Marin County and along the Peninsula at Linda Mar Beach in Pacifica. If you're feeling up to it, Aquaholics, 2830 Sloat at Ocean Beach in San Francisco (☎415/242-9283) rents and sells gear. Outside town, Sonlight Surfshop at 575 Crespi Drive in Pacifica (☎650/359-0353) and Marin Surf Sports in Mill Valley (☎415/381-9283) both rent surfboards and wet or drysuits. Mavericks Beach, just off Pillar Point west of Princeton, with the largest waves in North America, attracts some of the world's best (and craziest) surfers when conditions are right – just watching them can be an exhilarating way to spend an hour or so.

See chapter 8 for more information on San Francisco's many beaches.

Windsurfing is especially visible around Crissy Field and the Presidio, from where sailors race out and around the Golden Gate. Call Cityfront Sailboards (☎415/929-7873) for info on lessons and rentals. At the Berkeley Marina, another center for windsurfers, you can also rent sailboats from the Cal Sailing Club (☎510/287-5905) and cruise around the bay.

For those who don't care about the temperature of the water, **kayaking** can be done in the East Bay and Marin for about $25–50 per day. For exploring the bay, kayaks are best rented near the calmer waters that surround Sausalito. Sea Trek (☎415/332-4465) rents single or double sea kayaks beginning at $20 for two hours' worth of paddling the bay. They offer sit-on-top kayaks, lessons, and safe routes for first-timers or closed kayaks and directions around Angel Island for more experienced paddlers. Cal Adventures in the Berkeley Marina (☎510/642-4000) is good if you're in the East Bay, and Stinson Beach Health Club (☎415/868-2739) on Hwy-1 is best if you prefer to paddle the waters along the coast. Without experience, you may be required to take a two-to-four-hour lesson.

Sunbathing and swimming

For simple **suntanning** or sandcastle-building, there are two good beaches within the city itself: Baker Beach, just west of the Golden Gate Bridge, and the more protected but smaller China Beach near Lincoln Park. Baker has a **nude sunbathing** area at its north end, making it America's most frequented urban nude beach. Ocean Beach along the western edge of the city is also popular, but can be too windy to be enjoyable.

If you'd prefer not to brave the frigid waters of the Pacific, Mission Pool, on 19th Street between Valencia and Guerrero (☎415/695-5002; $3), has outdoor recreational and lap **swimming**. If you'd prefer to stay indoors, head over to the Richmond and the University of San Francisco's **Koret Center** on Parker Avenue at Turk (☎415/422-6820), where there's usually a free lane in an Olympic-sized pool (Mon–Thurs 6am–9.30pm, Fri 6am–9pm, Sat 8am–7pm, Sun 8am–6pm; $4).

For dry sunbathing, the blanket of green that covers Mission Dolores Park (see p.105) is almost always sun-drenched, at which times it becomes packed with sunbathers only too aware that the long trip out to the beaches may turn up nothing but wind and fog.

Hiking and climbing

For the best **hiking** in town, head up to Bernal Heights or Twin Peaks for stunning vistas over the bay, or go under the canopy of the cypresses which line the **Pacific Coast trail**, beginning from Sutro Heights at Ocean Beach or Land's End. The trail hugs San Francisco's northern edge, following the bed of an old train track, giving awesome views of the Golden Gate Bridge to which the trail leads. Cross the bridge and continue the trail till it reaches the abandoned clifftop gun encampments of the Marin Headlands (see p.185).

South of San Francisco, the least-used beach-and-bluff hiking area is around **Thornton State Beach**, south of Fort Funston at the end of Olympic Way where a trail leads down to a very isolated beach and green ridges populated only by wind-swept cypress trees and horse stables.

Further south, the **Whitehouse Ridge Trail**, a spectacular 1.5-mile uphill loop through the redwoods of the Santa Cruz Mountains, starts on Hwy-1 near Año Nuevo State Park (see p.179). Approaching from San Francisco, you can pick it up between Gazos Creek and Año Nuevo, where a sign marks the Skylark Ranch. Turn left on the dirt road next to the ranch's sign and look for the clearing 2.5 miles ahead where the trailhead begins.

Those who wish to put the connection between mind and body through a rigorous test may go **rock-climbing**. There are many climbing walls for beginners as well as advanced climbers with ropes. Some outdoor walls include Mickey's Beach off of Tiburon and Berkeley's famous Indian Rock, off Indian Rock Road. Climbing enthusiasm has led to indoor climbing walls, too – Mission Cliffs in San Francisco at 2295 Harrison St (☎415/550-0515) and Ironworks in Emeryville at 800 Potter St (☎510/654-2510), run by the same company, are both housed in industrial buildings and have everything from top-roping to lead-climbing. The daily entrance fee includes use of the full adjoining gyms (Mon, Wed & Fri 6.30am–10pm, Tues & Thurs 11am–10pm, Sat 10am–6pm; $16).

For rock climbing **lessons**, try hitting UC Berkeley's Cal Adventure's Wall, in the Strawberry Canyon Recreation Center on Centennial Street (☎510/642-4000).

Miscellaneous activities

Besides the above, there's a whole range of considerably less athletic things to do in the great outdoors. If you're into gambling or just a great day out and a few drinks, you might fancy a trip to Golden Gate Fields in Albany in the East Bay (☎510/559-7300), the Bay Area's only **horse-racing** track. If you prefer to **ride horses** yourself, Miwok Livery (☎415/383-8048) in Marin County charges $50 for two hours' trail-riding in fine locations. The only equestrian facility in the city proper is at Golden Gate Stables, John F. Kennedy Drive and 36th Avenue in Golden Gate Park (☎415/668-7360); it offers guided rides on horses or ponies through the park and along Ocean Beach for $26 an hour. Reservations must be made in advance.

The truly daring may be interested in **hang gliding** at Fort Funston on the southernmost portion of Ocean Beach. For a pretty penny – upward of $150 – the instructors at the San Francisco Hang Gliding Center (☎510/528-2300) will take you up on a tandem flight.

With some 120 public courts, a place to play **tennis** in San Francisco is not hard to come by. For directions to the nearest courts, the most scenic of which are in Alta Vista and Dolores Parks, call the San Francisco Park and Recreation Department (☎415/753-7001). You can rent a racket for around $5 a day at the Tennis Shack, 3375 Sacramento St (☎415/928-2255).

San Francisco is home to some beautiful and surprisingly reasonable **golf courses**, such as the Lincoln Park Golf Course, at 34th Avenue and Clement Street ($23 greens fee, $27 on weekends; $25 club rental; ☎415/221-9911), which features stunning views of the ocean and Golden Gate Bridge. The Golden Gate Park Course ($10, $13 on weekends; $6 club rental; ☎415/751-8987) is a cheaper alternative featuring nine tricky par-3 holes.

Perhaps the most exceptional outdoor adventure available in the Bay Area is **whale-watching**, following pods of mighty California gray whales on their annual migration – generally between December and April (see box, p.196). You can usually spot them from

Sports and outdoor activities

Sports and outdoor activities

headlands like Point Reyes (see p.195), but to get a real sense of their size and might, you have to join them on the seas. The best local operator of boat trips is the nonprofit Oceanic Society, Building E, Fort Mason Center (☎415/441-1106), which offers seven-hour whale-watching trips along the Point Reyes National Seashore (Oct–June; $50). During summer months, the society operates tours (July–Sept; $50) out to the Farrallon Islands, where, even if it's not the right time of year for gray whales, you'll see thousands of seabirds – pelicans, cormorants and rarer creatures – and possibly the world's largest mammal, the glorious blue whale. Reservations for the Point Reyes trips are recommended two weeks in advance, while rides to the Farrallon fill-up months in advance. You can begin booking the Farrallon trip in May.

When the whales are not migrating, you might try deep-sea salmon **fishing** as a way of seeing the ocean. Trips by Huck Finn Sportfishing out of Half Moon Bay (☎650/726-7133) last from 5.30am to 3pm and cost around $50.

Another possibility for wildlife-watchers (especially good for those prone to seasickness) happens around the same time as the whale migration – the mating season of the massive and grotesquely beautiful Northern **elephant seals**. These two-ton creatures spend most of January and February at Año Nuevo State Reserve, down the coast thirty miles south of San Francisco. If you fancy watching the trunk-nosed males as they battle it out for the right to make babies, see p.179 for details.

As for tame but fun indoor pursuits, there's **bowling** at Japantown Bowl, 1790 Post St in the Richmond district (Sun–Thurs 9am–1am, Fri & Sat open 24 hours $3/game weekday, $3.60 weekends; shoe rental $2; ☎415/921-6200); or if you feel like shooting some **pool**, Amusement Center downtown at 447 Broadway (☎415/398-8858), has hourly table rental (Sun–Thurs noon–midnight, Fri & Sat noon–2am; $6). You'll also find pool tables in numerous bars around the city; see chapter 15 for the possibilities.

Fitness centers

If you need a workout during your stay in the Bay Area and your hotel doesn't have all the equipment you need, there are a number of **fitness centers** with daily rates for out-of-towners. San Francisco gyms are the setting of a major social scene, which can be enjoyed regardless of how much exercise you end up doing.

Among the most well known is Gold's Gym, which has locations at 1001 Brannan St at Ninth Ave (Mon–Thurs 5am–midnight, Fri 5am–11pm, Sat 7am–9pm, Sun 8am–8pm; ☎415/552-4653); 2072 Addison St, Berkeley (daily 24 hrs; ☎510/548-4653); and 600 Meridian Ave, San Jose (weekdays 5am–midnight, weekends 6am–9pm; ☎408/279-6441). Day passes to all are $15.

Cheaper options can be found at Cathedral Hill Plaza Athletic Club, 1333 Gough at Geary St (weekdays 6am–9.30pm, weekends 8am–6pm; $10 day pass; ☎415/346-3868), which also has tennis (additional $10 for 2hr) and swimming, and Pacific Heights Health Club, 2356 Pine at Fillmore St (Mon–Sat 6am–10pm, Sun 8am–8pm; day pass $10; ☎415/563-6694).

Meanwhile, the Muscle System, 2275 Market at 17th St (Mon–Fri 6am–10pm, Sat 8am–8pm, Sun 8am–6pm; $8 day pass; ☎415/863-4700), and 364 Hayes Ave at Franklin St (same hours and price; ☎415/863-4701), is a **men-only club** with an almost exclusively gay clientele and some rather creaky old equipment.

Chapter 20

Directory

ADDRESSES When pinpointing an **address** verbally to a cab driver or when giving directions, San Franciscans always give the crossroad rather than the number (eg Valencia and 18th), and you'd do well to follow their example. You may, however, see numbered addresses written down (in this *Guide*, for example), in which case there is a formula for working out where it is on the city's very long thoroughfares. All streets work on blocks of 100 from their downtown source, which on north–south streets is Market Street; on east–west streets it is the Embarcadero or Market Street in the case of those streets that don't extend all the way east to the bay. For example, 950 Powell St is on the tenth block of Powell north of Market; 1450 Post St is on the fifteenth block of Post west of Market; 220 Castro St is on the third block of Castro south of Market. Unlike many American cities, most streets have names rather than numbers, the only grid of numbered streets being that radiating into the docks area south of Market. Further out from downtown, in the Richmond and Sunset, the avenues all have their origin at the foot of the Presidio and travel south in increasing blocks of 100. Block numbers are usually also posted above the street sign, with an arrow indicating whether the numbers are increasing or decreasing.

AIDS/HIV INFORMATION: AIDS Hotline (☎415/863-2437). 24hr information and counseling. **California AIDS Ride**, (☎1-800/825-1000; *www.aidsride.org*). Annual six-day SF–LA bike ride in June to raise money for AIDS research. 2500 riders participate yearly, and they're always looking for more. You just need to bring your bike, as camping gear, food, and a bus ride back to SF is provided for fundraisers. **Names Project Bay Area Chapter and Visitor Center**, 2362 Market St (☎415/863-1966). The history of the quilt which first brought national awareness to AIDS in the 1980s. Information on the AIDS crisis in the Bay Area, as well as resources for volunteer work and activism. **Project Inform**, 205 13th St, Suite 2001 (☎1-800/822-7422). The best source for detailed HIV treatment information, puts out free factsheets on a variety of AIDS-related medical issues written in accessible laymen's terms. **SF AIDS Foundation**, 25 Van Ness Ave (☎415/864-4376). Referral service providing advice, testing, support groups.

AMERICAN EXPRESS 560 California St between Kearny and Montgomery (Mon–Fri 9am–5pm; ☎415/536-2600). Park at the garage at 635 Sacramento, as they validate. Travel Service Office, 455 Market St at First St (Mon–Fri 8.30am–5.30pm, Sat 9am–2pm). Also at 333 Jefferson at Jones in Fisherman's Wharf (Mon–Thurs 10am–6pm, Fri & Sat 10am–9pm, Sun 11am–6pm).

APARTMENT HUNTING If you decide that you love San Francisco so much that you can't leave, you may want to think again; a booming economy combined with a serious shortage of housing have brought the city's vacancy rate down to less than 0.5 percent, the worst rental market in

Directory

history. Prices are sky-high, and an apartment showing usually attracts more than 25 applicants within hours or even minutes. If you do want to apply for a flat, bring along a copy of your credit report, identification, proof of employment, and the names and addresses of former landlords for reference. In general, expect to pay $800–1000 a month for a studio apartment in the cheaper parts of town, $1200 and up for somewhere a bit more central. One-bedroom apartments start anywhere from $950 to $1500 depending, again, on the neighborhood. Shared housing is a more affordable solution, and roommate ads abound in the local press. Most landlords expect one month's rent as a deposit, plus one month in advance. Utilities, such as gas and electricity, are all charged monthly. To find a place, consider walking the neighborhood where you want to live; with the high demand, most landlords don't bother to pay for advertising. If you're very lucky, you might catch a building manager at home at the moment a vacancy in his or her building occurs. Otherwise, check *www.craigslist.org*, or *www.ucsf.edu* for free access to the latest postings. Alternatively, you might scour the *San Francisco Chronicle*, *Examiner* or, more usefully, the many free papers such as the *Bay Guardian* or the *East Bay Express;* and, for women, *Bay Area Women's News*. Several housing agencies operate in town. Among the most reputable are RentTech, 4054 18th St at Hartford (☎415/863-7368; *www.renttech.com*) in the Castro, and Spring Street, 3059 Fillmore (☎415/441-2309) and 2285 Jackson (☎415/771-0447; *www.springstreet.com*). Both charge around $80 for access to their listings, and both rent pagers and cell phones; they can issue your credit report for an additional $25. See p.44 for more details on long-term stays in the city.

BABYSITTING Bay Area Child Care (☎650/991-7474).

CHURCHES Grace Cathedral on Nob Hill at 1051 Taylor St has an Episcopalian (Anglican) congregation, and Catholics can worship at St Mary's Cathedral, 600 California St. The grandest synagogue is Congregation Emanu-El, 2 Lake St, at the eastern edge of the Richmond district by the Presidio.

CIGARETTES AND SMOKING Despite being banned in all public indoor spaces and frowned upon elsewhere, cigarettes are sold in virtually any food store, drugstore, or bar, and are also available from vending machines on the outside walls of these establishments. You may be asked to show ID that you are at least 18 years of age. Heavy taxes mean a packet of twenty costs upward of $4, about $35 for a carton. For discount smokes, hit a Cigarettes Cheaper outlet, where a pack goes for under $3 (dozens of locations around town). While many local pubs turn a blind eye to patrons' lighting up, be aware that if you're spotted by a beat cop patrolling the neighborhood, you and the bartender can each be given a $75 fine.

CITY CLINIC 356 Seventh St (☎415/487-5500). STD testing $10 a visit.

CONSULATES Australia (for New Zealand as well), 1 Bush St (☎415/362-6160); China, 1450 Laguna St (☎415/674-2900); France, 540 Bush St (☎415/397-4330); Germany, 1960 Jackson St (☎415/775-1061); India, 540 Arguello Blvd (☎415/668-0683); Ireland, 44 Montgomery St (☎415/392-4214); Japan, 50 Fremont St (☎415/777-3533); Korea, 3500 Clay St (☎415/921-2251); Netherlands, 1 Maritime Plaza (☎415/981-6454); UK, 1 Sansome St (☎415/981-3030).

DENTAL TREATMENT For a free referral to the nearest dentist, call the national Dental Referral Service (☎1-800/511-8663). The San Francisco Dental Office, 131 Steuart (☎415/777-5115) offers 24hr emergency service and comprehensive dental care.

DRUG CRISIS LINE ☎1-800/711-6375. Answering 24 hours, 365 days a year.

DRUGS Possession of under an ounce of the widely consumed marijuana is a non-criminal offense in California, and the worst you'll get is a $200 fine. Being caught with more than an ounce, however, means facing a criminal charge for dealing, and a possible prison sentence. Other drugs are, of course, completely illegal and it's a much more serious offense if you're caught with any, though judging from the sheer number of the strung-out youths hanging out around parts of the city begging for change, you might not believe it. Of the major drugs, heroin has come back in vogue somewhat, and ordinary cocaine, while still largely a drug of the rich, has seen its street price drop and is more prevalent these days. The fad for designer drugs such as ecstasy has waned, though the popularity of particulary nasty synthetic concoctions like crystal methadone is at an all-time high.

ELECTRICITY 110V AC. All plugs are two-pronged and rather insubstantial. If you're a foreign visitor, note that some travel plug adapters don't fit American sockets.

EMERGENCIES Dial ☎911 for police, fire, or ambulance services.

FLOORS British travelers should note that the *first* floor in the US is what would be the ground floor in Britain; the *second* floor would be the first floor, and so on.

INTERNET You'll find free access via iMacs downtown at CompUSA, 760 Market, and in the Microsoft store on the second floor of the Sony Metreon mall at Yerba Buena Gardens in SoMa. Many hostels (see p.229) offer Internet access as well, though there's often a wait. Alternatively, if you don't mind paying or just want to enjoy a good cup of joe while surfing, head to *Coffee Net*, at 744 Harrison in SoMa (☎415/495-7447; $2.50/hour before 10am, $5/hour after 10am). The nearby *CyberWorld Café* at 528 Folsom (☎415/278-9669) charges $10/hour, $8 if you're a member (membership costs $2). Finally, if you have your own laptop, you can plug into a phone line at *Circadia*, a plush café in the Mission at 2727 Mariposa St (☎415/552-2649). Access here is $2.95/hour ($3.95 for a T1 line).

LAUNDRY All but the most basic hotels do laundry; a wash and dry in a laundromat costs a lot less (about $1.25 for wash and 25¢ for 10 minutes of dryer time). There's a laundromat on nearly every other residential block in town. *Brainwash*, 1122 Folsom St in SoMa, is a combo bar-and-laundromat. The Little Hollywood Launderette, 1906 Market at Guerrero (*www.launderette.com*), next to the *Orbit Room Café*, is open until midnight.

LEFT LUGGAGE Greyhound Bus, 155 Fremont between Howard and Mission, on the ground level of the Transbay Terminal (☎415/495-1555); open daily 6am–8pm.

LEGAL ADVICE Lawyer Referral Service, 465 California (☎415/989-1616).

LIBRARY Main public branch, Civic Center, at 100 Larkin St at Grove (☎415/557-4400). Mon 10am–6pm, Tues–Thurs 9am–8pm, Fri 11am–5pm, Sat 9am–5pm, Sun noon–5pm. The new facility's multi-million-dollar design confounds most of its users, and doesn't include enough shelfspace for all the library's books; the free Internet access is available only to members who must show proof of local residency.

MEASUREMENTS AND SIZES No metric system here, if that's what you're accustomed to: measurements are in inches, feet, yards, and miles; weight in ounces, pounds, and tons. American pints and gallons are about four-fifths of imperial ones. Clothing sizes are always two figures less than what they would be in Britain – a British women's size 12 is a US size 10 – while British shoe sizes are one and a half below American ones.

PASSPORT AND VISA OFFICE US Dept of Immigration, 630 Sansome St (☎1-800/375-5283).

PHARMACIES Walgreen's, 498 Castro St (☎415/861-6276), is open 24 hours every day; see box p.301.

PUBLIC TOILETS There are no public toilets as such, although there are some new pay French-style public toilets along Market St. Bars, and to a lesser extent restaurants and fast-food outlets, are your best bets, although technically you should be a customer. If you're desperate,

Directory

Directory

department stores and upscale hotels all have rather smart lavatories.

SUICIDE PREVENTION ☎415/781-0500. 24 hours.

TAX Sales tax is added to virtually everything you buy in a store, save for food, but isn't part of the marked price. In San Francisco and the East Bay the sales tax is 8.5 percent, 8.25 percent in the South Bay, and 7.25 percent in Marin County. Hotel tax will add fourteen percent onto your bill.

TELEGRAMS Western Union has numerous locations around the Bay area; call ☎1-800/325-6000 to find the nearest.

TEMPERATURES Always given in Fahrenheit.

TIME The West Coast runs on Pacific Standard Time (PST), always three hours behind the East Coast, and, with the exception of two weeks out of the year, eight hours behind GMT.

TIPPING You really shouldn't depart a bar or restaurant without leaving a tip of *at least* 15 percent (unless the service is absolutely terrible). The whole system of service is predicated on tipping; not to do so causes a great deal of resentment, and will result in a short pay packet for the waiter or waitress at the end of the week. About the same amount should be added to taxi fares – and round them up to the nearest 50¢ or dollar. A hotel porter who has lugged your suitcases up several flights of stairs should get $1 per bag; though many people tip much more. When paying by credit or charge card, you're expected to add the tip to the total bill before filling in the amount and signing.

TRAVEL AGENTS Council Travel, 530 Bush St (☎415/421-3473); STA Travel, 51 Grant Ave (☎415/391-8407); Ticket Planet, 59 Grant (☎1-800/799-8888). For good service and prices to the UK and Ireland, try Quinn Travel (☎415/665-7330; *www.flyirish.com*), 319 West Portal Ave, in the West Portal neighborhood (off Muni train M or K lines). Gay and lesbian travelers can call the Travel Alternatives Group (☎1-800/464-2987) to be routed to the nearest gay-friendly agent.

VOLUNTEER WORK Bay Area Volunteer Information Center (*www.meer.net/users/taylor*); San Francisco Volunteer Center, 425 Jackson (☎415/982-8999, *www.vcsf.org*); Volunteer Centers of the Bay Area (☎1-800/227-3123; *www.volunteerbayarea.com*).

Part 5

Contexts

A history of San Francisco

Though its recorded history may not stretch back very far by European standards, in its 150 years of existence San Francisco has more than made up for time. The city first came to life during the California Gold Rush of 1849, an adventure that set a tone for the place that it sustains to this day, both in its valuing of individual effort above corporate enterprise and in the often nonconformist policies that have given it perhaps the most liberal image of any US city. The following account is intended to give an overall view of the city's development; for a rundown of the figures – both past and present – who have helped to shape the city, see the "San Francisco people" glossary on p.358.

Native peoples

For thousands of years prior to the arrival of Europeans, the **aboriginal peoples** of the Bay Area lived healthily and apparently fairly peacefully on the naturally abundant land. Numbering around 15,000, and grouped in small, tribal villages of a few hundred people, they supported themselves mainly by hunting and fishing rather than agriculture. Most belonged to the coastal **Miwok** tribe, who inhabited most of what is now Marin County, as well as the Sonoma and Napa valleys; the rest were **Ohlone**, who lived in smaller villages sprinkled around the bay and down the south coast of the peninsula.

Very few artifacts from the period survive, and most of what anthropologists have deduced is based on the observations of the early explorers, who were by and large impressed by the Indian way of life – if not their "heathen" religion. One of the first colonists characterized them as "constant in their good friendship, and gentle in their manners." Indian boats, fashioned from lengths of tule reed, were remarkably agile and seaworthy. Of the buildings, few of which were ever intended to last beyond the change of seasons, the most distinctive was the *temescal* or sweat lodge. Kule Loklo, a replica Miwok village in the Point Reyes National Seashore, provides a good sense of what their settlements might have looked like.

Since there was no political or social organization beyond the immediate tribal level, it did not take long for the colonizing Spaniards effectively to wipe them out, if more through epidemics than through outright genocide. Nowadays no Bay Area Native Americans survive on their aboriginal homelands.

Exploration and conquest

Looking at the Golden Gate from almost any vantage point, it's hard to imagine that anyone might fail to notice such a remarkable opening to the Pacific. Nevertheless, dozens of **European explorers**, including some of the most legendary names of the New World conquest – Juan Cabrillo, Sir Francis Drake, Sebastian Vizcaino – managed to sail past for centuries, oblivious of the great harbor it protected. Admittedly, the passage is often obscured by fogs, and even on a clear day the Bay's islands, and the East Bay hills that rise up behind, do disguise the entrance to the point of invisibility.

The Englishman **Sir Francis Drake** came close to finding the Bay when he arrived in the *Golden Hind* in **1579**, taking a break from plundering Spanish vessels in order to make repairs. The "white bancks and cliffes" of his supposed landing spot – now called Drake's Bay, off Point Reyes north of San Francisco – reminded him of Dover. Upon going ashore, he was met by a band of Miwok, who greeted him with food and drink and placed a feathered crown upon his head; in return, he claimed all of their lands, which he called Nova Albion (New England), for Queen Elizabeth. Supposedly, he left behind a brass plaque; although this has been proved to be a fake, a copy remains on display in the Bancroft Library at the University of California in Berkeley.

Fifteen years later the Spanish galleon **San Augustín** – loaded to the gunwales with treasure from the Philippines – moored in the same spot, but met with tragically different results. After renaming Drake's Bay to honor their patron saint, San Francisco de Asis (Francis of Assisi), disaster struck: the ship was dashed against the rocks of Point Reyes and wrecked. The crew was able to salvage some of the cargo and enough of the ship to build a small lifeboat, on which they traveled south all the way to Acapulco, the Spanish base of operations in the Pacific, hugging the coast for the entire voyage and still sailing right past the Golden Gate. Indeed it was not until the end of 1769 that Western eyes set sight on the great body of water now called San Francisco Bay.

Colonization: the mission era

The **Spanish occupation** of the West Coast, which they called "Alta California," began in earnest in the late 1760s, following the Seven Years' War, partly due to military expediency (to prevent another power from gaining a foothold), and partly to Catholic missionary zeal to convert the heathen Indians. Early in **1769**, a company of three hundred soldiers and clergy, led by Father **Junipero Serra**, set off from Mexico to establish an outpost at Monterey, half of them by ship, the other half overland. A number stopped to set up the first California mission at San Diego, while an advance party – made up of some sixty soldiers, mule skinners, priests and Indians, under the leadership of **Gaspàr de Portola** – continued up the coast, blazing an overland route. It was hard going, especially with their inadequate maps, and not surprisingly they overshot their mark, ending up somewhere around Half Moon Bay.

Trying to regain their bearings, Portola sent out two scouting parties, one north along the coast and one east into the mountains. Both groups returned with extraordinary descriptions of the Golden Gate and the great bay, which they thought must be the same "Bahia de San Francisco" where the *San Augustín* had come to grief almost two centuries earlier. On November 4, 1769, the entire party gathered together on the ridgetop, overwhelmed by the incredible sight: Father Crespi, their priest, wrote that the bay "could hold not only all the armadas of our Catholic Monarch, but also all those of Europe." Portola's band barely stayed long enough to gather up supplies before turning around and heading back to Monterey; that mission was to become the capital and commercial center of Spanish California.

It took the Spanish another six years to send an expedition 85 miles north to the bay Portola had discovered. In May **1775**, when he piloted the *San Carlos* through the Golden Gate, Juan Manuel de Ayala became the first European to sail into San Francisco Bay. The next year Captain **Juan Bautista de Anza** returned with some 200 soldiers and settlers to establish the **Presidio of San Francisco** overlooking the Golden Gate, as well as a mission three miles to the southeast, along a creek he named *Nuestra Señora de Dolores* – "Our Lady of Sorrows." From this came the mission's popular – and still current – name, **Mission Dolores**.

Over the coming years four other Bay Area **missions** were established along the *El Camino Reàl*, the "Royal Road" built between 1769 and 1823 to link the 21 missions in the chain which ran along the California Coast from San Diego, eventually reaching up to Sonoma at its conclusion. Santa Clara de Asis, forty miles south of Mission Dolores, was founded in 1777; San José de Guadalupe, set up in 1797 near today's Fremont, grew into the most successful of the lot. In 1817, the *asistencia*, or auxiliary mission, San Rafael Arcangel was built in sunny Marin County as a convalescent hospital for priests and Indians who had been taken ill at Mission Dolores. The last, San Francisco Solano, built at Sonoma in 1823, was the only mission established under Mexican rule.

Each of the mission complexes was broadly similar, with a church and cloistered residence structure surrounded by irrigated fields, vineyards and more distant ranchlands, the whole protected by a small contingent of soldiers. Indian catechumens were put to work making soap and candles, but were treated as retarded children, often beaten and never educated. Objective facts about the missionaries' treatment of the Indians are hard to come by, though mission registries record twice as many deaths as they do births, and their cemeteries are packed with Indian dead. Many of the missions suffered from Indian raids; the now ubiquitous red-tiled roofs replaced the earlier thatch to resist fire.

To grow food for the missions and the forts or presidios, **towns** – called *pueblos* – were established, part of the ongoing effort to attract settlers to this distant and as yet undesirable territory. The first was laid out in 1777 at San Jose in a broad fertile valley south of the Mission Santa Clara. Though it was quite successful at growing crops, it had no more than a hundred inhabitants until well into the 1800s. Meanwhile, a small village – not sanctioned by the Spanish authorities – was beginning to emerge between Mission Dolores and the Presidio, around the one deep-water landing spot, southeast of today's Telegraph Hill. Called **Yerba Buena**, "good grass," after the sweet-smelling minty herb that grew wild over the windswept hills, it was little more than a collection of shacks and ramshackle jetties. Although the name "San Francisco" was not applied to it until the late 1840s, this tiny outpost formed the basis of today's metropolis.

The Mexican revolutions and the coming of the Americans

The emergence of an independent **Mexican state** in 1821 spelled the end of the mission era. Within a few years the new republic had secularized the missions and handed over their lands to the few powerful families of the "Californios" – mostly ex-soldiers who had settled here after completing their military service. The Mexican government exerted hardly any control over distant Yerba Buena, and was generally much more willing than the Spanish had been to allow foreigners to remain as they were, so long as they behaved themselves. A few trappers and adventurers had passed by in the early 1800s and, beginning in the early 1820s, a number of British and Americans started arriving in the Bay Area, most of them sailors who jumped ship, but also including a few men of property. The most notable of these immigrants was **William Richardson**, an Englishman who arrived on a whaling ship in 1822 and stayed for the rest of his life, marrying the daughter of the Presidio commander and eventually coming to own most of southern Marin County, from where he started a profitable shipping company and ran the sole ferry service across the tricky bay waters. In Richardson's wake, dozens followed – almost without exception males who, like him, tended to fit in with the existing Mexican culture, often marrying into established families and converting to the Catholic faith.

As late as the mid-1840s, Monterey was still the only town of any size on the entire West Coast, and tiny Yerba Buena (population 200 or so) made its livelihood from supplying passing ships, mainly Boston-based whaling vessels and the fur-traders of the English-owned **Hudson's Bay Company**. Though locals lived well, the Bay Area was not obviously rich in resources, and so was not by any means a major issue in international relations. However, from the 1830s onwards, the **US government** decided that it wanted to buy all of Mexico's lands north of the Rio Grande, California included, in order to fulfil the "Manifest Destiny" of the United States to cover the continent from coast to coast. Any negotiations were rendered unnecessary when, in June 1846, the Mexican–American War broke out in Texas, and US naval forces quickly took over the entire West Coast, capturing San Francisco's Presidio on **July 9, 1846**.

A revealing – although historically insignificant – episode, which set the tone for the anarchic growth of the Bay Area over the next fifty years, took place around this time. An ambitious US Army captain, John C. Fremont, had been working to encourage unhappy settlers to declare independence from Mexico, and to set himself up as their leader. By assembling an unofficial force of some sixty sharpshooting ex-soldiers, and by spreading rumors that war with Mexico was imminent and unstoppable, he managed to persuade settlers to take action: the **Bear Flag Revolt**. On June 14, some thirty farmers and trappers descended upon the abandoned Presidio in Sonoma and took the retired commandant, Colonel Guadupe Vallejo, captive, raising a makeshift flag over the plaza and declaring California independent. The flag – which featured a roughly drawn grizzly bear above the words "California Republic" – was eventually adopted as the California state flag, but this "Republic" was short-lived. Three weeks after the disgruntled settlers hoisted their flag in Sonoma, it was replaced by the Stars and Stripes, and California was thereafter **US territory**.

Ironically, just nine days before the Americans took formal control, **gold** was discovered on January 24, 1848, in the Sierra Nevada foothills a hundred miles east of the city – something that was to change the face of San Francisco forever.

The Gold Rush

At the time gold was discovered, the Bay Area had a total (non-native) population of around two thousand, about a quarter of whom lived in tiny **San Francisco**, which had only changed its name from Yerba Buena the year before. By the summer of 1848, rumors of the find attracted a trickle of gold seekers, and when news of their subsequent success filtered back to the coast, soldiers deserted and sailors jumped ship.

The first prospectors on the scene made fantastic fortunes – those working the richest "diggings" could extract more than an ounce every hour – but the real money was being made by merchants charging equally outrageous prices for essentials. Even the most basic supplies were hard to come by, and what little was available cost exorbitant amounts: a dozen eggs for $50, a shovel or pickaxe twice that. Exuberant miners willingly traded glasses of gold dust for an equal amount of whiskey – something like $1000 a shot. Though it took some time for news of the riches to travel, soon men were flooding into California from all over the globe to share the wealth, in the most madcap migration in world history. Within a year some 100,000 men – known collectively as the **Forty-Niners** – had arrived in California. About half of them came overland, after a three-month slog across the continent, and headed straight for the mines. The rest arrived by ship and landed at San Francisco, expecting to find a city where they could recuperate before continuing on the arduous journey. They must have been disappointed with what they found: hulks of abandoned ships formed the only solidly constructed buildings, rats overran the filthy streets, and drinking water was scarce and often contaminated.

Sam Brannan, who had originally come west to found a Mormon paradise, was just one of many ruthless businessmen who cashed in on the gold hysteria: using his Portsmouth Square shop to relay tales of fabulous wealth to recent arrivals, he milked them for as much as he could get, an endeavor that proved far more lucrative than any missionary work.

Few of the new arrivals stayed very long in ruthless San Francisco, but, if anything, life in the mining camps proved even less hospitable. As thousands of moderately successful but worn-out miners returned to San Francisco, especially during the torrential rains of the **winter of 1849–50**, the shanty-town settlement began to grow into a proper city. Ex-miners set up foundries and sawmills to provide those starting out with the tools of their trade, and traders arrived to profit from the miners' success, selling them clothing, food, drink, and entertainment. The city where the successful miners came to blow their hard-earned cash was a place of luxury hotels and burlesque theaters, which featured the likes of Lola Montez, whose semi-clad "spider dance" enthralled legions of fans. Throughout the early 1850s immigrants continued to pour through the Golden Gate, and although the great majority hurried on to the mines, enough stayed around to bring the city's population up to around 35,000 by the end of 1853. Of these, more than half were from foreign parts – a wide-ranging mix of Mexicans, Germans, Chinese, Italians, and others.

Within five years of the discovery of gold the easy pickings were all but gone, and as the free-wheeling mining camps evolved into increasingly large-scale, corporate operations, San Francisco swelled from frontier outpost into a substantial city, with a growing industrial base, a few newspapers, and even its own branch of the US Mint. When revenues from the gold fields ceased to expand in the late 1850s, the speculative base that had made so many fortunes quickly vanished. Lots that had been selling at a premium couldn't be given away, banks went bust, and San Francisco had to declare itself **bankrupt** as a result of years of corrupt dealings. The already volatile city descended into near-anarchy, with vigilante mobs roaming the streets enforcing their particular brand of justice. By the summer of 1856 the "Committee of Vigilance," led by William Coleman and the ever-present Sam Brannan, and composed of the city's most successful businessmen, was the **de facto government** of the city, having taken over the state militia and installed themselves inside their "Fort Gunnybags" headquarters, outside which they regularly hanged petty criminals (admittedly after giving them a trial), to the amusement of gathered throngs.

Events reached a boiling point when the future California Supreme Court Justice **David Terry** shot a committee member (Terry would go on to shoot the state's first senator a few years later), bringing the vigilantes into direct confrontation with the official government. A few of the most radically minded proposed secession from the

US, but calmer heads prevailed, and the city was soon restored to more legitimate governance. Ironically, the task of defending the rabidly pro-slavery Terry fell to a failed banker and young local military commander named **William Sherman**, who would later go into the history books for razing much of the state of Georgia during the Civil War.

The boom years (1860–1900)

In the 1860s San Francisco enjoyed a bigger boom than that of the Gold Rush, following the discovery of an even more lucrative band of precious **silver ore** in the Great Basin mountains of western Nevada. Discovered just east of Reno in late 1859 and soon known as the **Comstock Lode**, it was one of the most fantastic deposits ever encountered: a single, solid vein of silver, mixed with gold, that ranged from ten to over a hundred feet wide and stretched a little over two miles long, most of it buried hundreds of feet underground. Mining here was in complete contrast to the freelance prospecting of the California gold fields, and required a scale of operations unimagined in the California mines. Many of San Francisco's great engineers, including George Hearst, Andrew Hallidie, and Adolph Sutro, put their minds to the task.

As the mines had to go increasingly deeper to get at the valuable ore, the mining companies needed larger and larger amounts of capital, which they attracted by issuing shares dealt on the burgeoning San Francisco **Stock Exchange**. Speculation was rampant, and the value of shares could rise or fall by a factor of ten, depending on the day's rumors and forecasts; Mark Twain got his literary start publicizing, for a fee, various new "discoveries" in his employers' mines. Hundreds of thousands of dollars were made and lost in a day's trading, and the cagier players, like James Flood and James Fair, made millions.

While the Comstock silver enabled many San Franciscans to enjoy an unsurpassed prosperity throughout the 1860s, few people gave much thought to the decade's other major development, the building of the **transcontinental railroad**, completed in 1869 using imported Chinese laborers. Originally set up in Sacramento to build the western link, the **Central Pacific** and later **Southern Pacific** railroad soon expanded to cover most of the West, ensnaring San Francisco in its web. Wholly owned by the so-called **Big Four** – Charles Crocker, Collis P. Huntington, Mark Hopkins, and Leland Stanford – the Southern Pacific "octopus," as it was caricatured in the popular press, exercised an essential monopoly over transportation in the Bay Area. Besides controlling the long-distance railroads, they also owned San Francisco's streetcar system, the network of ferry boats that crisscrossed the bay, and even the cable-car line that lifted them up California Street to their Nob Hill palaces (see p.76).

Not everyone, however, reaped the good fortune of the Nob Hill elite. The coming of the railroad usurped San Francisco's primacy as the West Coast's supply point, and products from the East began flooding in at prices well under anything local industry could manage. At the same time the Comstock mines ceased to produce such enormous fortunes, and depression began to set in. The lowering of economic confidence was compounded by a series of droughts which wiped out agricultural harvests, and by the arrival in San Francisco of thousands of now unwanted **Chinese workers**. As unemployment rose throughout the late 1870s frustrated workers took out their aggression in racist assaults on the city's substantial Chinese population. Railroad baron **Leland Stanford** campaigned for governor on an anti-immigrant platform, though his company's employment of masses of Chinese laborers on construction gangs seriously undercut his candidacy, and at mass demonstrations all over the city, thousands rallied behind the slogan "The Chinese Must Go!"

Though San Francisco was popularly seen as being powered by ignoble motives and full of self-serving money-grabbers, there were a few exceptions, even among its wealthiest elite. **Adolph Sutro**, for example, was a German-born engineer who made one fortune in the Comstock mines and another buying up land in the city – in 1890 he was said to own ten percent of San Francisco, even more than the Big Four. But Sutro was an unlikely millionaire, as compassionate and public-spirited as the Big Four were ruthlessly single-minded; in fact, when the Southern Pacific tripled fares to a quarter on the trolley line out to Golden Gate Park, Sutro built a parallel line that charged a nickel. He also built the Sutro Baths and the Cliff House and in 1894 was elected mayor of San Francisco on the Populist Party ticket, campaigning on an anti-Southern Pacific manifesto which promised to rid San Francisco of "this horrible monster which is devouring our substance and debauching our people, and by its devilish instincts and criminal methods is every day more firmly grasping us in its tentacles." Sutro died in 1898, with the city still firmly in the grasp of the "octopus."

The Great Earthquake and after

San Francisco experienced another period of economic expansion in the **early years of the 1900s**, due in equal part to the Spanish–American War and the Klondike Gold Rush in Alaska. Both of these events increased ship traffic through the port, where dockworkers were beginning to organize themselves into **unions** on an unprecedented scale. The mighty longshoremen's association they formed was to become a political force to be reckoned with. The fight to win recognition and better wages was long and hard; unrest was virtually constant, and police were brought in to scare off strikers and prevent picket lines from shutting down the waterfront. But this economic instability was nothing compared to the one truly earth-shattering event of the time: the **Great Earthquake of 1906.**

The quake that hit San Francisco on the morning of April 18, 1906 was, at 8.1 on the Richter Scale, the most powerful ever to hit anywhere in the US, before or since (over ten times the force of the 1989 earthquake). It destroyed hundreds of buildings, but by far the worst destruction was wrought by the **post-earthquake conflagration**, as ruptured gas mains exploded and chimneys toppled, starting fires that spread rapidly across the city. It all but leveled the entire area from the waterfront, north and south of Market Street, west to Van Ness Avenue, whose grand mansions were dynamited to form a firebreak. Comparatively few people, around 500 in total, were killed, but about half of the population – some 100,000 people – were left homeless and fled the city. Many of those who stayed set up camp in the barren reaches of what's now Golden Gate Park, where soldiers from the Presidio undertook the mammoth task of establishing and maintaining a tent city for about 20,000 displaced San Franciscans.

During the ensuing ten years, San Francisco was rebuilt with a vengeance, reconstructing the city as it was and largely ignoring the grand plan drawn up by designer Daniel Burnham just a year before the disaster. The city council had given its approval to this plan, which would have replaced the rigid grid of streets with an eminently more sensible system of axial main boulevards filled in with curving avenues skirting the hills and smaller, residential streets climbing their heights. However, such was the power and influence of the city's vested interests that the status quo was quickly reinstated, despite the clear opportunity afforded by the earthquake.

To celebrate its recovery, and the opening of the Panama Canal – a project that had definite implications for San Francisco's trade-based economy – the city fathers set out to create the magnificent **1915 Panama Pacific International Exhibition**. Land was reclaimed from the bay for the exhibition and on it an elaborate complex of exotic buildings was constructed, including Bernard Maybeck's exquisite Palace of Fine Arts and centering on the 100yd-high, gem-encrusted Tower of Jewels. Hundreds of thousands visited the fair, which lasted throughout the year, but when it ended all the buildings, save the Palace of Fine Arts, were torn down, and the land was sold off for the houses that now make up the Marina district.

The great success of the exhibition proved to the world that San Francisco had recovered from the earthquake. But the newly recovered civic pride was tested the next year when, on the eve of America's involvement in **World War I**, a pro-war parade organized by San Francisco's business community was devastated by a **bomb attack** that killed ten marchers and severely wounded another forty. In their haste to find the culprit, the San Francisco police arrested half a dozen radical union agitators. With no evidence other than perjured testimony, activist **Tom Mooney** was convicted and sentenced to death, along with his alleged co-conspirator Warren Billings. Neither, fortunately, was executed, but both spent most of the rest of their lives in prison; Billings wasn't pardoned until 1961, 45 years after his fraudulent conviction.

The Roaring Twenties

The war years had little effect on San Francisco, but the period thereafter, the **Roaring Twenties**, was in many ways the city's finest era. Despite Prohibition, the jazz clubs and speakeasies of the Barbary Coast district were in full swing. San

Francisco was still the premier artistic and cultural center of the West Coast, a role it would relinquish to Los Angeles by the next decade, and its status as an international financial hub (both major international credit-card companies – today's Visa and Access – had their start here) was as yet unchallenged by the upstart southern megalopolis. The strength of San Francisco as a banking power was highlighted by the rise of the Bank of America – founded as the Bank of Italy in 1904 by A.P. Giannini in North Beach – into the largest bank in the world.

The buoyant 1920s gave way to the Depression of the 1930s, but, despite the sharp increases in unemployment, there was only one major battle on the industrial relations front. On "**Bloody Thursday**" – July 5, 1934 – police protecting strike-breakers from angry picketers fired into the crowd, wounding thirty and killing two longshoremen. The Army was sent in to restore order, and in retaliation the unions called a **General Strike** that saw some 125,000 workers down tools, bringing the Bay Area economy to a halt for four days. It was one of the largest strikes in the nation's history. Otherwise there was remarkably little unrest, and, thanks in part to **WPA sponsorship**, some of the city's finest monuments – Coit Tower for example and, most importantly, the two great bridges – were built during this time. Before the **Bay and Golden Gate bridges** went up, in 1936 and 1937 respectively, links between the city and the surrounding towns of the Bay Area were provided by an impressive network of **ferry boats**, some of which were among the world's largest. In 1935, the ferries' peak year, some 100,000 commuters per day crossed the bay by boat; just five years later the last of the boats was withdrawn from service, unable to compete with the increasingly popular automobile.

World War II

The Japanese attack on Pearl Harbor and US involvement in **World War II** transformed the Bay Area into a massive war machine, its industry mobilizing quickly to provide weaponry and ships for the war effort. **Shipyards** opened all around the bay – the largest, the Kaiser Shipyards in Richmond, was employing more than 100,000 workers on round-the-clock shifts just six months after its inception – and men and women flooded into the region from all over the country to work in the lucrative concerns. Entire cities were constructed to house them, many of which survive – not least Hunter's Point, on the southern edge of the San Francisco waterfront, which was never intended to last beyond the end of hostilities but still houses some 15,000 of the city's poorest people. A more successful example is Marin City, a workers' housing community just north of Sausalito, which – surprisingly, considering its present-day air of leisured affluence – was one of the most successful wartime shipyards, able to crank out a ship a day.

The war effort inadvertently helped establish San Francisco as a **gay center**, as young gay men pressed into service in the Bay Area found kindred spirits far from home, only to be dishonorably discharged by the thousands immediately after the war. Many of those so dismissed chose to settle in the city, helping found the roots of the current community.

The Fifties

After the war, thousands of GIs returning from the South Pacific came home through San Francisco, and many decided to stay. The city spilled out into new districts, and, especially in suburbs like the Sunset, massive tracts of identical dwellings, subsidized by federal loans and grants, were thrown up to house the returning heroes – many of whom still live here. The accompanying economic prosperity continued unabated well into the 1950s, and in order to accommodate increasing numbers of cars on the roads, huge **freeways** were constructed, cutting through the city. The Embarcadero Freeway in particular formed an imposing barrier, perhaps appropriately dividing the increasingly office-oriented Financial District from the declining docks and warehouses of the waterfront, which for so long had been the heart of San Francisco's economy.

As the increasingly mobile and prosperous middle classes moved out from the inner city, new bands of literate but disenchanted middle-class youth began to move into the areas left behind, starting, in the middle part of the decade, in the bars and cafés of North Beach, which swiftly changed from a staunch Italian neighborhood into the Greenwich Village of the West Coast. The **Beat generation**, as they became known, reacted against what they saw as the empty materialism of 1950s America by losing themselves in a bohemian orgy of jazz, drugs, and Buddhism, expressing their disillusionment with the status quo through a new, highly personal and expressive brand of fiction and poetry. The writer **Jack Kerouac**, whose *On the Road* became widely accepted as the handbook of the Beats, both for the style of writing (fast, passionate, unpunctuated) and the lifestyle it described, was in some ways the movement's main spokesman, and is credited with coining the term "Beat" – meaning "beatific" – to describe the group. Later, columnist Herb Caen somewhat derisively turned "beat" into "beatnik," after Sputnik. San Francisco, and particularly the **City Lights Bookstore**, at the center of North Beach, became the main meeting point and focus of this diffuse group, though whatever impetus the movement had was gone by the early 1960s.

The Sixties

Though the long-term value of their writing is still debatable, there's no doubt that the Beats opened people's minds. However, it was an offshoot of the group, the **hippies**, that really took this task to heart. The term was originally a Beat put-down of the inexperienced but enthusiastic young people who followed in their hedonistic footsteps. The first hippies appeared in the early 1960s, in cafés and folk-music clubs around the fringes of Bay Area university campuses. They, too, eschewed the materialism and the nine-to-five consumer world, but preferred an escapist fantasy of music and marijuana that became adapted as a half-baked political indictment of society and where it was going wrong.

The main difference between the Beats and the early hippies, besides the five years that elapsed, was that the hippies had discovered – and regularly experimented with – a new hallucinogenic drug called LSD, better known as **acid**. Since its synthesis, LSD had been legally and readily available, mainly through psychologists who were interested in studying its possible therapeutic benefits. Other, less scientific research was also being done by a variety of people, many of whom, from around 1965 onward, began to settle in the **Haight-Ashbury district** west of the city center living communally in huge low-rent Victorian houses, in which they could take acid and "trip" in safe, controlled circumstances. **Music** was an integral part of the acid experience, and a number of bands – the **Charlatans**, **Jefferson Airplane**, and the **Grateful Dead** – came together in San Francisco during the summer of 1966, playing open-ended dance music at such places as the Fillmore Auditorium and the Avalon Ballroom.

Things remained on a fairly small scale until the spring of **1967**, when a free concert in Golden Gate Park drew a crowd of 20,000 and, for the first time, media attention. Articles describing the hippies, most of which focused on their prolific appetites for sex and drugs, attracted a stream of newcomers to the Haight from all over the country, and within a few months the **"Summer of Love"** was well under way, with some 100,000 young people descending upon the district.

In contrast to the hippie indulgence of the Haight-Ashbury scene, across the bay in Berkeley and Oakland **revolutionary politics**, rather than drugs, were at the top of the agenda. While many of the hippies opted out of politics, the student radicals threw themselves into political activism, beginning with the Free Speech Movement at the University of California in 1964. The FSM, originally a reaction against the university's banning of on-campus political activity, laid the groundwork for the more passionate, **anti-Vietnam War** protests that rocked the entire country for the rest of the decade. The first of what turned out to be dozens of **riots** occurred in June 1968, when students marching down Telegraph Avenue in support of the Paris student uprising were met by a wall of police, leading to rioting that continued for the next few days. Probably the most famous event in Berkeley's radical history took place in **People's Park**, a plot of university-owned land that was taken over as a community open space by local people. Four days later an army of police, under the command of Edwin Meese – who later headed the US Department of Justice in the Reagan years – teargassed and stormed the park, accidentally killing a bystander and seriously injuring more than 100 others.

Probably the most extreme element of late 1960s San Francisco emerged out of the impoverished flatlands of Oakland – the **Black Panthers**, established by Bobby Seale, Huey Newton, and Eldridge Cleaver in 1966. The Panthers were a heavily armed but numerically small band of militant black activists with an announced goal of securing self-determination for America's blacks. From their Oakland base they set up a nationwide organization, but the threat they posed, and the chances they were willing to take in pursuit of their cause, were too great. Thirty of their members died in gun battles with the police, and the surviving Panthers lost track of their aims: Eldridge Cleaver later became a right-wing Republican, while Huey Newton was killed over a drugs deal in West Oakland in 1989.

The Seventies

The unrest of the 1960s continued into the **early 1970s**, if not at such a fever pitch. One last headline-grabber was the kidnapping in 1974 of heiress Patty Hearst from her Berkeley apartment by the Symbionese Liberation Army, or **SLA**, a hard-core bunch of revolutionaries who used their wealthy hostage to demand free food for Oakland's poor. Hearst later helped the gang to rob a San Francisco bank, wielding a submachine gun. Otherwise, certainly compared to the previous decade, the 1970s were quiet times, which saw the opening of the long-delayed **BART** high-speed transportation system, as well as the establishment of the **Golden Gate National Recreation Area** to protect and preserve 75,000 acres of open space on both sides of the Golden Gate Bridge.

Throughout the 1970s, it wasn't so much that San Francisco's rebellious thread had been broken, but rather that the battle-lines were being drawn elsewhere. The most distinctive political voices were those of the city's large **gay and lesbian communities**. Inspired by the so-called Stonewall Riots in New York City in 1969, San Francisco's homosexuals began to organize themselves politically, demanding equal status with heterosexuals. Most importantly, gays and lesbians stepped out into the open and refused to hide their sexuality behind closed doors, giving rise to the gay liberation movement that has prospered worldwide. One of the leaders of the gay community in San Francisco, **Harvey Milk**, won a seat on the Board of Supervisors, becoming the first openly gay man to take public office. When Milk was **assassinated** in City Hall, along with Mayor George Moscone, by former Supervisor Dan White in 1978 – see p.109 – the whole city was shaken. The fact that White was found guilty of manslaughter, not murder, caused the gay community to erupt in riotous frustration, burning police cars and laying siege to City Hall.

The Eighties

The **1980s** saw the city's gay community in retreat to some extent, with the advent of **AIDS** in the early part of the decade devastating the confidence of activists and decimating its population. An enormous education and prevention effort grew out of a largely grassroots effort, leading to the eventual stabilization of new infection rates by the 1990s. Treatment and caretaking efforts for those infected by HIV, meanwhile, remained largely driven by volunteers' fundraising efforts, nearly exhausting the energies of the community, which became almost exclusively focused on the crisis. City Hall, led by Mayor **Dianne Feinstein**, who took over after the death of Moscone, responded to the crisis more quickly and efficiently than other cities hard-hit by the virus, supporting the community's herculean efforts with well-funded urban relief and education programs.

At the same time, the mayor oversaw the construction of millions of square feet of office towers in downtown's Financial District, despite angry protests against the **Manhattanization** of the city. Although Feinstein's attempts to spend the city out of its financial slump dumped a tangled mess of financial worries into the lap of her successors, she went on to become senator in 1992 and remains one of the most prominent female politicians in America today.

But before the already tough 1980s came to an end, the city was shaken by a major **earthquake** in October 1989, 7.1 on the Richter Scale – an event watched by 100 million people on nationwide TV, since it hit during a World Series game between Bay Area rivals, the San Francisco Giants and the Oakland A's.

Contemporary San Francisco

Following this rather grim decade, the **1990s** seemed sunnier, at least for some of the city's residents. A national boom in high-tech industries, initiated by companies such as Apple, Oracle, Netscape, and Yahoo based south of the city in **Silicon Valley**, proved particularly lucrative for the Bay Area. The rush for new-technology jobs – at one peak moment, the Valley was supposedly cranking out 63 new millionaires per day – has created a region-wide population boom. In San Francisco, the influx of wealthy young computer professionals into an incredibly tight housing market has led to the rapid **gentrification** of large sections of town, with rents skyrocketing by as much as 100 percent per year. Long-impoverished neighborhoods such as the Mission have been rapidly transformed into playlands for the newly wealthy, while an entirely new upscale community has sprung up along the South Beach waterfront.

Merrily riding the wave of prosperity has been **Willie Brown**, self-dubbed "da Mayor," who began his remarkable climb to power from child of African-American sharecroppers in Texas by driving a cab to fund his law degree, eventually becoming the most influential man in California's state senate and one of the most powerful black politicians in the nation. As mayor, Brown has initiated ambitious programs to fix the city's overburdened mass transit system and aging public housing. His detractors, however, say he's all style and no substance, and the failure of the city's newfound wealth to solve such longstanding problems as homelessness seem to argue in their favor. Evidence that gentrificiation hasn't completely killed the city's liberal spirit came during Brown's campaign for reelection in 1999, when write-in candidate Tom Ammiano, a popular gay stand-up comedian and head of the city's board of supervisors, nearly staged an upset with his progressive agenda. Still, the victory was Brown's, and it remains to be seen how he'll deliver on his second round of promises to help the disenfranchised even while protecting corporate interests. For both the poor and the wealthy, the major question of the moment is the same: just how far can the local economy be inflated?

Writers on San Francisco

Writers seem to pull out all the stops trying to capture San Francisco's great beauty and unique energy. Some of the city's best writing has been in the form of journalism or firsthand observations; the first two pieces below are essentially dispatches from various key points in its history, while the third is an excerpt from a semi-autobiographical novel.

Mark Twain

The author of the literary hallmark Adventures of Huckleberry Finn, **Mark Twain** *was based in San Francisco for many years; his famous line about the city's weather – "The coldest winter I ever spent was the summer I spent in San Francisco" – is inevitably cited whenever the fog rolls in. Indeed, Twain never held back his criticism of the town, subtly dismissing its provincial pretension with his sharp wit, as evidenced in the following account of an earthquake published in 1872.*

Roughing It

San Francisco, a truly fascinating city to live in, is stately and handsome at a fair distance, but close at hand one notes that the architecture is mostly old-fashioned, many streets are made up of decaying, smoke-grimed wooden houses, and the barren sand-hills toward the outskirts obtrude themselves too prominently. Even the kindly climate is sometimes pleasanter when read about than personally experienced, for a lovely, cloudless sky wears out its welcome by and by, and then when the longed for rain does come it *stays.* Even the playful earthquake is better contemplated at a dis–

However there are varying opinions about that.

The climate of San Francisco is mild and singularly equable. The thermometer stands at about seventy degrees the year round. It hardly changes at all. You sleep under one or two light blankets Summer and Winter, and never use a mosquito bar. Nobody ever wears Summer clothing. You wear black broadcloth – if you have it – in August and January, just the same. It is no colder, and no warmer, in the one month than the other. You do not use overcoats and you do not use fans. It is as pleasant a climate as could well be contrived, take it all around, and is doubtless the most unvarying in the whole world. The wind blows there a good deal in the Summer months, but then you can go over to Oakland, if you choose – three or four miles away – it does not blow there. It has only snowed twice in San Francisco in nineteen years, and then it only remained on the ground long enough to astonish the children, and set them to wondering what the feathery stuff was.

During eight months of the year, straight along, the skies are bright and cloudless, and never a drop of rain falls. But when the other four months come along, you will need to go and steal an umbrella. Because you will require it. Not just one day, but one hundred and twenty days in hardly varying succession. When you want to go visiting, or attend church, or the theatre, you never look up at the clouds to see whether it is likely to rain or not – you look at the almanac. If it is Winter, it will *rain* – and if it is Summer, it *won't* rain, and you cannot help it. You never need a lightning-rod because it never thunders and it never lightens. And after you have listened for six or eight weeks, every night, to the dismal monotony of those quiet rains, you will wish in your heart the thunder *would* leap and crash and roar along those drowsy skies once, and make everything alive – you will wish the prisoned lightnights *would* cleave the dull firmament asunder and light it with a blinding glare for *one* little instant. You would give *anything* to hear the old familiar thunder again and see the lightning strike somebody. And along in the Summer, when you have suffered about four months of lustrous, pitiless sunshine, you are ready to go down on your knees and plead for rain – hail – snow – thunder and lightning – anything to break the monotony – you will take an earthquake, if you cannot do any better. And the chances are that you'll get it, too.

[I remember enjoying] ...my first earthquake. It was one which was long called the "great" earthquake, and is doubtless so distinguished till this day. It was just after noon, on a bright October day. I was coming down Third street. The only objects in motion anywhere in sight in that thickly built and populous quarter, were a man in a buggy behind me, and a street car wending slowly up the cross street. Otherwise, all was solitude and a Sabbath stillness. As I turned the corner, around a frame house, there was a great rattle and jar, and it occurred to me that here was an item! – no doubt a fight in that house. Before I could turn and seek the door, there came a really terrific shock; the ground seemed to roll under me in waves, interrupted by a violent joggling up and down, and there was a heavy grinding noise as of brick houses rubbing together. I fell up against the frame house and hurt my elbow. I knew what it was, now, and from mere reportorial instinct, nothing else, took out my watch and noted the time of day; at that moment a third and still severer shock came, and as I reeled about on the pavement trying to keep my footing, I saw a sight! The entire front of a tall four-story brick building in Third street sprung outward like a door and fell sprawling across the street, raising a dust like a great volume of smoke! And here came the buggy – overboard went the man, and in less time than I can tell it the vehicle was distributed in small fragments along three hundred yards of street. One could have fancied that somebody had fired a charge of chair-rounds and rags down the thoroughfare. The street car had stopped, the horses were rearing and plunging, the passengers were pouring out at both ends, and one fat man had crashed half way through a glass window on one side of the car, got wedged fast and was squirming and screaming like an impaled madman. Every door, of every house, as far as the eye could reach, was vomiting a stream of human beings; and almost before one could execute a wink and begin another, there was a massed multitude of people stretching in endless procession down every street my position commanded. Never was solemn solitude turned into teeming life quicker.

Of the wonders wrought by "the great earthquake," these were all that came under my eye; but the tricks it did, elsewhere, and far and wide over the town, made toothsome gossip for nine days. The destruction of property was trifling – the injury to it was wide-spread and somewhat serious.

The "curiosities" of the earthquake were simply endless. Gentlemen and ladies who were sick, or were taking a siesta, or had dissipated till a late hour and were making up lost sleep, thronged into the public streets in all sorts of queer apparel, and some without any at all. One woman who had been washing a naked child, ran down the street holding it by the ankles as if it were a dressed turkey. Prominent citizens who were supposed to keep the Sabbath strictly, rushed out of saloons in their shirt-sleeves, with billiard cues in their hands. Dozens of men with necks swathed in napkins, rushed from barber-shops, lathered to the eyes or with one cheek clean shaved and the other still bearing a hairy stubble. Horses broke from stables, and a frightened dog rushed up a short attic ladder and out on to a roof, and when his scare was over had not the nerve to go down again the same way he had gone up. A prominent editor flew down stairs, in the principal hotel, with nothing on but one brief undergarment – met a chambermaid, and exclaimed:

"Oh, what *shall* I do! Where shall I go!"

She responded with naive serenity:

"If you have no choice, you might try a clothing-store!"

A certain foreign consul's lady was the acknowledged leader of fashion, and every time she appeared in anything new or extraordinary, the ladies in the vicinity made a raid on their husbands' purses and arrayed themselves similarly. One man who had suffered considerably and growled accordingly, was standing at the window when the shocks came, and the next instant the consul's wife, just out of the bath, fled by with no other apology for clothing than – a bath-towel! The sufferer rose superior to the terrors of the earthquake, and said to his wife:

"Now *that* is something *like*! Get out your towel my dear!"

The plastering that fell from ceilings in San Francisco that day, would have covered several acres of ground. For some days afterward, groups of eyeing and pointing men stood about many a building, looking at long zig-zag cracks that extended from the eaves to the ground. Four feet of the tops of three chimneys on one house were broken square off and turned around in such a way as to completely stop the draft. A crack a hundred feet long gaped open six inches wide in the middle of one street and then shut together again with such force, as to ridge up the meeting earth like a slender grave. A lady sitting in her rocking and quaking parlor, saw the wall part at the ceiling, open and shut twice, like a mouth, and then drop the end of a brick on the floor like a tooth. She was a woman easily disgusted with foolishness, and she arose and went out of there. One lady who was coming down stairs was astonished to see a bronze Hercules lean forward on its pedestal as if to strike her with its club. They both reached the bottom of the flight at the same time, – the woman insensible from the fright. Her child, born some little time afterward, was club-footed. However – on second thought, – if the reader sees any coincidence in this, he must do it as his own risk.

The first shock brought down two or three huge organ-pipes in one of the churches. The minister, with uplifted hands, was just closing the services. He glanced up, hesitated, and said:

"However, we will omit the benediction!" – and the next instant there was a vacancy in the atmosphere where he had stood.

After the first shock, an Oakland minister said:

"Keep your seats! There is no better place to die than this" –

And added, after the third:

"But outside is good enough!" He then skipped out at the back door.

Such another destruction of mantel ornaments and toilet bottles as the earthquake created, San Francisco never saw before. There was hardly a girl or a matron in the city but suffered losses of this kind. Suspended pictures were thrown down, but oftener still, by a curious freak of the earthquake's humor, they were whirled completely around with their faces to the wall! There was great difference of opinion, at first, as to the course of direction the earthquake traveled, but water that splashed out of various tanks and buckets settled that. Thousands of people were made so sea-sick by the rolling and pitching of floors and streets that they were weak and bed-ridden for hours, and some few for even days afterward. – Hardly an individual escaped nausea entirely.

The queer earthquake – episodes that formed the staple of San Francisco gossip for the next week would fill a much larger book than this, and so I will diverge from the subject.

Hunter S. Thompson

One of America's most exciting and controversial essayists, **Hunter S. Thompson** *is a troublemaker and muckraker of the first order. Equally wild away from his typewriter, his experiences have included a spell with the Hell's Angels in San Francisco, about whom he wrote his first book. His later fascination with Richard Nixon reached its culmination in his long and consistently unforgiving book* The Great Shark Hunt, *from which the extract below is taken. After lying relatively low for a while at his Colorado ranch, he resurfaced in the 1980s to write a column for the* San Francisco Examiner, *pieces of which have been brought together in* Generation of Swine; *and he has continued into the 1990s, writing* Better than Sex, *dispatches from the 1992 campaign trail.*

The "Hashbury" Is the Capital of the Hippies

In 1965 Berkeley was the axis of what was just beginning to be called the "new left." Its leaders were radical, but they were also deeply committed to the society they wanted to change. A prestigious faculty committee said the Berkeley activists were the vanguard of "a moral revolution among the young," and many professors approved.

Now in 1967 there is not much doubt that Berkeley has gone through a revolution of some kind, but the end result is not exactly what the original leaders had in mind. Many one-time activists have forsaken politics entirely and turned to drugs. Others have even forsaken Berkeley. During 1966, the hot center of revolutionary action on the coast began moving across the bay to San Francisco's Haight-Ashbury district, a run-down Victorian neighborhood of about forty square blocks between the Negro/Fillmore district and Golden Gate Park.

The "Hashbury" is the new capital of what is rapidly becoming a drug culture. Its denizens are not called radicals or beatniks, but "hippies" and perhaps as many as half are refugees from Berkeley and the old North Beach scene, the cradle and the casket of the so-called Beat Generation.

The other half of the hippy population is too young to identify with Jack Kerouac, or even with Mario Savio. Their average age is about twenty, and most are native Californians. The North Beach types of the late nineteen-fifties were not nearly as provincial as the Haight-Ashbury types are today. The majority of beatniks who flocked into San Francisco ten years ago were transients of the East and Midwest. The literary artistic nucleus – Kerouac, Ginsberg, et al – was a package deal from New York. San Francisco was only a stop on the big circuit: Tangier, Paris, Greenwich

Village, Tokyo and India. The senior Beats had a pretty good idea what was going on in the world; they read newspapers, traveled constantly and had friends all over the globe.

The word "hip" translates roughly as "wise" or "tuned-in." A hippy is somebody who "knows" what's really happening, and who adjusts or grooves with it. Hippies despise phoniness; they want to be open, honest, loving, free. They reject the plastic pretense of twentieth-century America, preferring to go back to the "natural life," like Adam and Eve. They reject any kinship with the Beat Generation on the ground that "those cats were negative but our thing is positive." They also reject politics, which is "just another game." They don't like money, either, or any kind of aggressiveness.

A serious problem in writing about the Haight-Ashbury is that most of the people you have to talk to are involved, one way or another, in the drug traffic. They have good reason to be leery of strangers who ask questions. A twenty-two-year-old student was recently sentenced to two years in prison for telling an undercover narcotics agent where to buy some marijuana. "Love" is the password in the Haight-Ashbury, but paranoia is the style. Nobody wants to go to jail.

At the same time, marijuana is everywhere. People smoke it on the sidewalks, in doughnut shops, sitting in parked cars or lounging on the grass in Golden Gate Park. Nearly everyone on the streets between twenty and thirty is a "head," a user of either marijuana, LSD, or both. To refuse the proferred joint is to risk being labeled a "nark" – a narcotics agent – a threat and a menace to almost everybody.

With a few loud exceptions, it is only the younger hippies who see themselves as a new breed. "A completely new thing in this world, man." The ex-beatniks among them, many of whom are now making money off the new scene, incline to the view that hippies are, in fact, second-generation beatniks and that everything genuine in the Haight-Ashbury is about to be swallowed – like North Beach and the Village – in a wave of publicity and commercialism.

Haight Street, the great white way of what the local papers call "hippieland," is already dotted with stores catering mainly to the tourist trade. Few hippies can afford a pair of $20 sandals or a "Mod outfit" for $67.50. Nor can they afford the $3.50 door charge at the Fillmore Auditorium and the Avalon Ballroom, the twin wombs of the "psychedelic, San Francisco, acid-rock sound." Both the Fillmore and the Avalon are jammed every weekend with borderline hippies who don't mind paying for the music and the light shows. There is always a sprinkling of genuine, barefoot, freaked-out types on the dance floor, but few of them pay to get in. They arrive with the musicians or have other good connections.

Neither of the dance palaces is within walking distance of the Hashbury, especially if you're stoned, and since only a few of the hippies have contacts in the psychedelic power structure, most of them spend their weekend nights either drifting around on Haight Street or loading up on acid – LSD – in somebody's pad. Some of the rock bands play free concerts in Golden Gate Park for the benefit of those brethren who can't afford the dances. But beyond an occasional Happening in the park, the Haight-Ashbury scene is almost devoid of anything "to do" – at least by conventional standards. An at-home entertainment is nude parties at which celebrants paint designs on each other.

There are no hippy bars, for instance, and only one restaurant above the level of a diner or a lunch counter. This is a reflection of the drug culture which has no use for booze and regards food as a necessity to be acquired at the least possible expense. A "family" of hippies will work for hours over an exotic stew or curry in a communal kitchen, but the idea of paying $3 for a meal in a restaurant is out of the question.

Some hippies work, others live on money from home and many are full-time beggars. The post office is a major source of hippy income. Jobs like sorting mail don't require much thought or effort. A hippy named Admiral Love of the Psychedelic Rangers delivers special-delivery letters at night. The Admiral is in his mid-twenties and makes enough money to support an apartmentful of younger hippies who depend on him for their daily bread.

There is also a hippy-run employment agency on Haight Street and anyone needing part-time labor or some kind of specialized work can call and order as many freaks as he needs; they might look a bit weird, but many are far more capable than most "temporary help," and vastly more interesting to have around.

Those hippies who don't work can easily pick up a few dollars a day panhandling along Haight Street. The fresh influx of curiosity-seekers has proved a great boon to the legion of psychedelic beggars. During several days of roaming around the area, I was touched so often that I began to keep a supply of quarters in my pocket so I wouldn't have to haggle over change. The panhandlers are usually barefoot, always young and never apologetic. They'll share what they collect anyway, so it seems entirely reasonable that strangers should share with them.

The best show on Haight Street is usually on the sidewalk in front of the Drog Store, a new coffee bar at the corner of Masonic Street. The Drog Store features an all-hippy revue that runs day and night. The acts change sporadically, but nobody cares. There will always be at least one man with long hair and sunglasses playing a wooden pipe of some kind. He will be wearing either a Dracula cape, a long Buddhist robe, or a Sioux Indian costume. There will also be a hairy blond fellow wearing a Black Bart cowboy hat and a spangled jacket that originally belonged to a drum major in the 1949 Rose Bowl parade. He will be playing the bongo drums. Next to the drummer will be a dazed-looking girl wearing a blouse (but no bra) and a plastic mini-skirt, slapping her thighs to the rhythm of it all.

These three will be the nucleus of the show. Backing them up will be an all-star cast of freaks, every one of them stoned. They will be stretched out on the sidewalk, twitching and babbling in time to the music. Now and then somebody will fall out of the audience and join the revue; perhaps a Hell's Angel or some grubby, chain-draped impostor who never owned a motorcycle in his life. Or maybe a girl wrapped in gauze or a thin man with wild eyes who took an overdose of acid nine days ago and changed himself into a raven. For those on a quick tour of the Hashbury, the Drog Store revue is a must.

Most of the local action is beyond the reach of anyone without access to drugs. There are four or five bars a nervous square might relax in, but one is a Lesbian place, another is a hangout for brutal-looking leather fetishists and the others are old neighborhood taverns full of brooding middle-aged drunks. Prior to the hippy era there were three good Negro-run jazz bars on Haight Street, but they soon went out of style. Who needs jazz, or even beer, when you can sit down on a public curbstone, drop a pill in your mouth and hear fantastic music for hours at a time in your own head? A cap of good acid costs $5, and for that you can hear the Universal Symphony, with God singing solo and the Holy Ghost on drums.

Drugs have made formal entertainment obsolete in the Hashbury, but only until somebody comes up with something appropriate to the new style of the neighborhood. This summer will see the opening of the new Straight Theater, formerly the Haight Theater, featuring homosexual movies for the trade, meetings, concerts, dances. "It's going to be a kind of hippy community center," said Brent Dangerfield, a young radio engineer from Salt Lake City who stopped off in San Francisco on his way to a job in Hawaii and is now a partner in the Straight. When I asked him how old he was he had to think for a minute. "I'm twenty-two," he said finally, "but I used to be much older."

Another new divertissement, maybe, will be a hippy bus line running up and down Haight Street, housed in a 1930 Fagol bus – a huge, lumbering vehicle that might have been the world's first house trailer. I rode in it one afternoon with the driver, a young hippy named Tim Thibeau who proudly displayed a bathtub under one of the rear seats. The bus was a spectacle even on Haight Street: people stopped, stared and cheered as we rumbled by, going nowhere at all. Thibeau honked the horn and waved. He was from Chicago, he said, but when he got out of the Army he stopped in San Francisco and decided to stay. He was living, for the moment, on unemployment insurance, and his plans for the future were hazy. "I'm in no hurry," he said. "Right now I'm just taking it easy, just floating along." He smiled and reached for a beer can in the Fagol's icebox.

Dangerfield and Thibeau reflect the blind optimism of the younger hippy element. They see themselves as the vanguard of a new way of life in America – the psychedelic way – where love abounds and work is fun and people help each other. The young hippies are confident that things are going their way.

The older hippies are not so sure. They've been waiting a long time for the world to go their way, and those most involved in the hip scene are hedging their bets this time. "That back to nature scene is okay when you're twenty," said one. "But when you're looking at thirty-five you want to know something's happening to you."

Ed Denson, at twenty-seven, is an ex-beatnik, ex-Goldwaterite, ex-Berkeley radical and currently the manager of a successful rock band called Country Joe and the Fish. His home and headquarters is a complex of rooms above a liquor store in Berkeley. One room is an art studio, another is an office: there is also a kitchen, a bedroom and several sparsely furnished areas without definition.

Denson is deeply involved in the hippy music scene, but insists he's not a hippy. "I'm very pessimistic about where this thing is going," he said. "Right now it's good for a lot of people. It's still very open. But I have to look back at the Berkeley scene. There was a tremendous optimism there, too, but look where all that went. The beat generation? Where are they now? What about hula-hoops? Maybe this hippy thing is more than a fad; maybe the whole world is turning on but I'm not optimistic. Most of the hippies I know don't really understand what kind of a world they're living in. I get tired of hearing about what beautiful people we all are. If the hippies were more realistic they'd stand a better chance of surviving."

Amy Tan

Born in Oakland in 1952, **Amy Tan** *first visited China in 1987. Her father, who was educated in Beijing and worked for the United States Information Service after the war, came to America in 1947. Her mother came to the United States in 1949, shortly before the Communists seized control of Shanghai. Amy Tan now lives in San Francisco and New York. Her first work of fiction,* The Joy Luck Club, *explores the nuances of Chinese-American identity through the relationships between four Chinese mothers and their American daughters, each of whom narrate their own stories, rich in detail and atmosphere. Here junior chess champion Waverly Jong takes a plunge into San Francisco's Chinatown.*

The Joy Luck Club

My mother imparted her daily truths so she could help my older brothers and me rise above our circumstances. We lived in San Francisco's Chinatown. Like most of the other Chinese children who played in the back alleys of restaurants and curio shops, I didn't think we were poor. My bowl was always full, three five-course meals every day, beginning with a soup full of mysterious things I didn't want to know the names of.

We lived on Waverly Place, in a warm, clean, two-bedroom flat that sat above a small Chinese bakery specializing in steamed pastries and dim sum. In the early morning, when the alley was still quiet, I could smell fragrant red beans as they were cooked down to a pasty sweetness. By daybreak, our flat was heavy with the odor of fried sesame balls and sweet curried chicken crescents. From my bed, I would listen as my father got ready for work, then locked the door behind him, one-two-three clicks.

At the end of our two-block alley was a small sandlot playground with swings and slides well-shined down the middle with use. The play area was bordered by wood-slat benches where old-country people sat cracking roasted watermelon seeds with their golden teeth and scattering the husks to an impatient gathering of gurgling pigeons. The best playground, however, was the dark alley itself. It was crammed with daily mysteries and adventures. My brothers and I would peer into the medicinal herb shop, watching old Li dole out onto a stiff sheet of white paper the right amount of insect shells, saffron-colored seeds, and pungent leaves for his ailing customers. It was said that he once cured a woman dying of an ancestral curse that had eluded the best of American doctors. Next to the pharmacy was a printer who specialized in gold-embossed wedding invitations and festive red banners.

Farther down the street was Ping Yuen Fish Market. The front window displayed a tank crowded with doomed fish and turtles struggling to gain footing on the slimy green-tiled sides. A hand-written sign informed tourists, "Within this store, is all for food, not for pet." Inside, the butchers with their bloodstained white smocks deftly gutted the fish while customers cried out their orders and shouted, "Give me your freshest," to which the butchers always protested, "All are freshest." On less crowded market days, we would inspect the crates of live frogs and crabs which we were warned not to poke, boxes of dried cuttlefish, and row upon row of iced prawns, squid, and slippery fish. The sanddabs made me shiver each time; their eyes lay on one flattened side and reminded me of my mother's story of a careless girl who ran into a crowded street and was crushed by a cab. "Was smash flat," reported my mother.

At the corner of the alley was Hong Sing's, a four-table café with a recessed stairwell in front that led to a door marked "Tradesmen." My brothers and I believed the bad people emerged from this door at night. Tourists never went to Hong Sing's, since the menu was printed only in

Chinese. A Caucasian man with a big camera once posed me and my playmates in front of the restaurant. He had us move to the side of the picture window so the photo would capture the roasted duck with its head dangling from a juice-covered rope. After he took the picture, I told him he should go into Hong Sing's and eat dinner. When he smiled and asked me what they served, I shouted, "Guts and duck's feet and octopus gizzards!" Then I ran off with my friends, shrieking with laughter as we scampered across the alley and hid in the entryway grotto of the China Gem Company, my heart pounding with hope that he would chase us.

My mother named me after the street that we lived on: Waverly Place Jong, my official name for important American documents. But my family called me Meimei, "Little Sister." I was the youngest, the only daughter. Each morning before school, my mother would twist and yank on my thick black hair until she had formed two tightly wound pigtails. One day, as she struggled to weave a hard-toothed comb through my disobedient hair, I had a sly thought.

I asked her, "Ma, what is Chinese torture?" My mother shook her head. A bobby pin was wedged between her lips. She wetted her palm and smoothed the hair above my ear, then pushed the pin in so that it nicked sharply against my scalp.

"Who say this word?" she asked without a trace of knowing how wicked I was being. I shrugged my shoulders and said, "Some boy in my class said Chinese people do Chinese torture."

"Chinese people do many things," she said simply. "Chinese people do business, do medicine, do painting. Not lazy like American people. We do torture. Best torture."

Books

Where the books we recommend below are in print, the publisher's name is given in parentheses after the title: the US publishers first, separated, where applicable, from the UK publisher by an oblique slash. Where books are published in only one of these countries, we have specified which one; when the same company publishes the book in both, it appears just once. The titles listed as being out of print (o/p) in both countries should be easy enough to find in secondhand bookstores.

Travel/impressions

Martin Amis *The Moronic Inferno and Other Visits to America* (Penguin). An assortment of essays that pull no punches in their dealings with American life and culture, including the moral majority, militarism and high-energy consumerism.

John Miller (ed) *San Francisco Stories* (US Chronicle Books). Patchy collection of writings on the city with contributions from Lewis Lapham, Tom Wolfe, Dylan Thomas, and Hunter S. Thompson to name a few.

Czeslaw Milosz *Visions from San Francisco Bay* (US Farrar, Straus & Giroux). Written in Berkeley during the unrest of 1968, these dense and somewhat ponderous essays show a European mind trying to come to grips with California's nascent Aquarian Age.

Mark Twain *Roughing It* (Penguin). Vivid, semi-fantastical tales of frontier California, particularly evocative of life in the silver mines of the 1860s Comstock Lode, where Twain got his start as a journalist and storyteller. His descriptions of San Francisco include a moment-by-moment description of an earthquake. An excerpt from this work appears on p.341.

Edmund White *States of Desire* (Picador/Plume). Part of a cross-country sojourn that includes a rather superficial account of the gay scene in 1970s San Francisco.

Tom Wolfe *The Electric Kool-Aid Acid Test* (Bantam/Black Swan). Wolfe at his most expansive, floridly riding with the Grateful Dead and Hell's Angels on the magic bus of Ken Kesey and the Merry Pranksters as they travel through the early 1960s, turning California on to LSD.

History, politics, and society

Walton Bean *California: An Interpretive History* (UK McGraw-Hill). Blow-by-blow account of the history of California, including all the shady deals and back-room politicking, presented in accessible, anecdotal form.

Gray Brechin *Imperial San Francisco* (US University of California Press). Crisply written, tough-minded account of the shady dealings that helped drive the city's rapid growth around the end of the nineteenth century.

James Brook, editor *Reclaiming San Francisco* (City Lights Books). A collection of essays evaluating the city's history and current state from an avowedly leftist point of view. Tackles a wide variety of specific contemporary and historical subjects, with varying degrees of success.

Herb Caen *Baghdad by the Bay* (US Comstock Editions); *The Best of Herb Caen* (Chronicle Books). Two collections by the city's most indefatigable promoter. Though rather light, Caen's bemused writing always portrays the city as a charming cosmopolitan stomping ground.

Barnaby Conrad *Name Dropping: Tales from My Barbary Coast Saloon* (US Harper San Francisco). Author, bullfighter, and once-proud owner of the happening 1950s Bay Area bar *El Matador* spills the beans on his celebrity clientele, which included the likes of Kerouac, Sinatra, and Marilyn Monroe. Conrad also recently edited a new book about one of his longtime pals, *The World of Herb Caen* (Chronicle Books).

Peter Coyote *Sleeping Where I Fall* (Counterpoint). The author, an actor of minor rate, chronicles his hippie days, giving out food as a member of the Diggers and directing radical theater with the SF Mime Troupe.

Joan Didion *Slouching Toward Bethlehem* (Farrar, Straus & Giroux/Flamingo). Selected essays from one of California's most renowned journalists, taking a critical look at the West Coast of the Sixties, including San Francisco's acid culture and a profile of American hero John Wayne. In a similar style, *The White Album* (Penguin/Flamingo) traces the West Coast characters and events that shaped the Sixties and Seventies, including The Doors, Charles Manson, and the Black Panthers.

Edmund Fawcett and Tony Thomas *America and the Americans* (o/p). A wide-ranging and engagingly written rundown on the US in all its aspects from politics to sport and religion. An essential beginner's guide to the nation.

Frances Fitzgerald *Cities on a Hill* (US Simon & Schuster). Intelligent, thorough and sympathetic exploration of four of the odder corners of American culture, including San Francisco's Castro district, the Rajneeshi community of Oregon, and TV evangelism.

Milton Gould *A Cast of Hawks* (US Copley Books). Rather floridly written account of San Francisco's early days, when the distinction between crook and statesman was vague to say the least; does provide a few interesting details on the city's vigilante government.

Joyce Jansen *San Francisco's Cable Cars* (Woodford Publishing). An informal history of the city's most prominent moving landmarks with some good historic photos of them.

David A. Kaplan *The Silicon Boys* (US Perennial). A witty, entertaining, and thorough account of the history and culture of the Silicon Valley.

Charles Perry *The Haight-Ashbury* (US Random House). Curiously distant but detailed account of the Haight during the Flower Power years, written by an editor of *Rolling Stone*, a magazine that got its start there.

Rand Richards *Historic San Francisco* (US Heritage House). Part history and part guide book, this is a good introduction to the city's odd narrative, with some handy sight descriptions.

Mel Scott *The San Francisco Bay Area: A Metropolis in Perspective* (o/p). Though somewhat dry and academic, this enormous tome will tell you all you ever wanted to know about the evolution of San Francisco and the Bay Area.

Randy Shilts *The Mayor of Castro Street: The Life and Times of Harvey Milk* (St. Martin's Press). Exhaustively researched epic biography of Milk; explores the assasinated supervisor's place in the struggle for gay rights. Shilts also wrote the most thorough account of the early days of the AIDS epidemic, *And the Band Played On* (St. Martin's Press).

Jay Stevens *Storming Heaven: LSD and the American Dream* (HarperCollins/Grafton). An engaging account of psychedelic drugs and their effect on American society through the Sixties, with an epilogue covering "designer drugs" – Venus, Ecstasy, Vitamin K, and others – and the inner space they help some modern Californians to find.

Susan Stryker and Jim Van Buskirk *Gay By the Bay* (US Chronicle). Pithy illustrated history of the city's gay and lesbian community. Though they touch on the city's history, the authors focus their attention on the post-World War II boom in the gay scene and the subsequent movement for artistic expression and political liberation.

Sunset Editors *California Missions: a Pictorail History* (Sunset Books). The best of the many books on the missions, packed with photos and drawings, along with "accounts" of early mission life and descriptions of more recent restoration efforts.

Hunter S. Thompson *Hell's Angels* (Ballantine). The book that put Thompson's "gonzo" journalism on the map, as he chronicles violent parties with the notorious biker gang. *The Great Shark Hunt* (Ballantine/Picador) (see excerpt p.343). Collection of often barbed and cynical essays on 1960s American life and politics – thought-provoking and hilarious. *Generation of Swine* (Random/Picador) is a more recent collection of caustic musings on the state of America and those who control it, assembled from his regular column in the *San Francisco Examiner*.

Tom Wolfe *Radical Chic & Mau Mauing the Flak Catchers* (US Farrar, Straus & Giroux). Wolfe's waspish account of Leonard Bernstein's fundraising party for the Black Panthers – a protracted exercise in character assassination – is coupled with an equally sharp analysis of white guilt and radical politics in City Hall, San Francisco. Often ideologically unsound, always very funny.

Specific guides

Daniel Bacon *Walking San Francisco on the Barbary Coast Trail* (Quicksilver). A highly detailed guide focusing on every detail of a small cluster of locations along what was once the Barbary Coast – sites of some of the pivotal events in the city's history.

Adab Bakalinsky *Stairway Walks in San Francisco* (US Wilderness Press). Small, nicely illustrated guide detailing pretty back streets and stairways through San Francisco's hills. Excellent for turning up lesser-known spots on a walking tour.

Bicycle Rider Directory (US Cycle America). Low-cost guide to do-it-yourself bicycle touring around the Bay Area and Napa and Sonoma valleys, with good fold-out route maps.

California Coastal Commission *California Coastal Access Guide* (US UC Press). The most useful and comprehensive plant and wildlife guide to the California coast, packed with maps and background information.

Don Herron *The Literary World of San Francisco* (US City Lights). A walk through the San Francisco neighborhoods associated with authors who have lived in and written about the city. Detailed and well presented, it's an essential handbook for anyone interested in San Francisco's literary heritage. For a more specific approach, try *The Dashiell Hammett Tour* by the same author.

Judith Kahn *Indulge Yourself* (o/p). The ideal companion for the café animal, this book covers San Francisco's most famous and beautiful coffee spots, giving hints on when to go, what sort of people you'll see and what's on offer.

Karen Liberatore *The Complete Guide to the Golden Gate National Recreation Area* (o/p). Easy-to-read book covering San Francisco's extensive waterfront areas and large green spaces, with historical perspective. Lots of photos.

Grant Peterson *Roads to Ride* (US Heyday Books). As its subtitle says, this is a bicyclist's topographic guide to the whole Bay Area, and is particularly good on the back roads of Marin County.

Don Pitcher *Berkeley Inside/Out* (o/p). This is an extremely well-written, fully illustrated and encyclopedic guidebook to the most dynamic small town in the Bay Area.

Walking the West Series: *Walking the California Coast; Walking California's State Parks* and others (HarperReference). Well-written and produced paperbacks, each covering over a hundred excellent day-walks from two to twenty miles. They're strong on practical details (maps, route descriptions, and so on), and boast inspiring prose and historical background. Recommended.

Peggy Wayburn *Adventuring in the San Francisco Bay Area* (US Sierra Club). If you are planning to spend any time hiking in the Bay Area's many fine wilderness regions, pick up this fact-filled guide, which also details a number of historic walks through the city's urban areas.

Fiction and poetry

Ambrose Bierce *The Enlarged Devil's Dictionary* (Dover/Penguin). Spiteful but hilarious compilation of definitions (i.e. "Bore: a person who talks when you wish him to listen") by this journalist working at the end of the nineteenth century. Bierce also wrote some great horror stories, including the stream-of-consciousness "An Occurrence at Owl Creek Bridge," collected in *Can Such Things Be* (US Citadel) and his *Collected Works* (Citadel/Picador).

James P. Blaylock *Land of Dreams* (Grafton o/p/Ace Books). A fantastic tale of the arrival of the twelve-year Solstice in a Northern Californian coastal town.

Richard Brautigan *The Hawkline Monster* (US Houghton-Mifflin). Whimsical, surreal tales by noted Bay Area hippie writer.

Philip K. Dick *The Man in the High Castle* (Vintage/Penguin). Long-time Berkeley- and Marin County-based science-fiction author imagines an alternative San Francisco, following a Japanese victory in World War II. Of his dozens of other brilliant novels and short stories, *Bladerunner* (Balantine/Panther) and *The Trans-migration of Timothy Archer* (Random House/Gollancz o/p) make good use of Bay Area locales.

John Dos Passos *USA* (NAL-Dutton/Penguin). Massive, groundbreaking trilogy, combining fiction, poetry and reportage to tap the various strands of the American Experience. Much of the first part, *The 42nd Parallel*, takes place around Sutro Baths and Golden Gate Park.

William Gibson *Virtual Light* (Bantam Books). Cyberpunk sci-fi author's futuristic vision of the city, complete with squatters on the Golden Gate Bridge and heroic bike messengers.

Allen Ginsberg *Howl and Other Poems* (US Friendship Press). The attempted banning of the title poem assured its fame; *Howl* itself is an angry rant that often descends into wince-inducing Beatnik jive, but a Whitmanesque voice often shines through.

Oakley Hall, *Ambrose Bierce and the Queen of Spades* (Penguin). Rich mystery of old-time San Francisco, in which colorful characters of the city's late nineteenth-century cultural scene collide against a backdrop of murder, corruption, big business and investigative journalism.

Dashiell Hammett *The Four Great Novels* (Random House/Picador). Seminal detective stories including *The Maltese Falcon* and starring Sam Spade, the private investigator working out of San Francisco. See also Diane Johnson's absorbing *The Life of Dashiell Hammett* (Fawcett/Picador).

Maxine Hong Kingston *Chinamen* (Vintage International). Hugely popular and affecting magical-realist depiction of one family's immigration from China to the gold coast. Kingston manages to combine both telling period details and the larger mythic quality of the passage of generations.

Jack Kerouac *On the Road* (Penguin). The book that launched a generation with its "spontaneous bop prosody," it chronicles Beat life in a series of road adventures, featuring some of San Francisco and a lot of the rest of the US. His other books, many set in the Bay Area, include *Lonesome Traveler* (Grove-Atlantic/Paladin), *The Dharma Bums* (Penguin/Paladin), and *Desolation Angels* (Riverhead Books/Paladin).

David Lodge *Changing Places* (Penguin). Thinly disguised autobiographical tale of an English academic who spends a year teaching at UC Berkeley (renamed in the book) and finds himself bang in the middle of the late-1960s student upheaval.

Jack London *Martin Eden* (Penguin). Jack Kerouac's favorite book, a semi-autobiographical account tracking the early years of this San Francisco-born, Oakland-bred adventure writer. The lengthy opus tells of his rise from waterfront hoodlum to high-brow intellectual and of his subsequent disenchantment with the trappings of success.

Armistead Maupin *Tales of the City* (HarperCollins/Black Swan); *Further Tales of the City* (HarperCollins/Corgi); *More Tales of the City* (HarperCollins/Corgi); *Babycakes* (HarperCollins/Corgi); *Significant Others* (HarperCollins/Black Swan); *Sure of You* (HarperCollins/Black Swan). Six lively consecutive soap operas, wittily detailing the sexual and emotional antics of a select group of archetypal San Francisco characters, taking them from the late 1970s to the end of the 1980s.

Ken McGoogan *Kerouac's Ghost* (US Robert Davies). Beatnik homage in which author raises Kerouac from the dead and sticks him in the 1970s to write about Haight-Ashbury and play mentor to a struggling French-Canadian writer.

Seth Morgan *Homeboy* (Random House/Vintage). Novel charting the sleazy San Francisco experiences of the former junkie boyfriend of Janis Joplin.

John Mulligan *Shopping Cart Soldiers* (Scribner). Fictionalized memoir of a homeless vet who hangs out in Washington Square, where he meets the ghost of Robert Louis Stevenson. Offbeat and well written.

Fae Myenne Ng *Bone* (US HarperPerennial). Well-crafted first novel that gives a good taste of hardscrabble life in San Francisco's Chinatown.

Frank Norris *McTeague: A Story of San Francisco* (Norton/Penguin). Dramatic, extremely violent but engrossing saga of love and revenge in San Francisco at the end of the nineteenth century; later filmed by Erich von Stroheim as *Greed*. Norris's *Octopus* (Penguin) tells the bitter tale of the Southern Pacific Railroad's stranglehold over the California economy.

Thomas Pynchon *The Crying of Lot 49* (HarperCollins/Vintage). Follows the labyrinthine adventures of conspiracy freaks and potheads in 1960s California, revealing the exotic side of stamp collecting.

Kenneth Rexroth *An Autobiographical Novel* (New Directions). Rather stiffly written account of the influential poet and translator's freewheeling life and times. A leading figure in San Francisco's postwar artistic community, Rexroth's experimental nature was an inspiration to a younger generation of Beat writers.

Douglas Rushkoff *The Ecstasy Club* (HarperCollins West/Hodder & Stoughton). Cyberculture pundit concocts a fun if transparent piece of future schlock rife with conspiracy theories and occult esoterica. Ravers, Deadheads, and other Bay Area riffraff wander in and out of the plot.

Vikram Seth *The Golden Gate* (Random House/Faber). Slick novel in verse, tracing the complex social lives of a group of San Francisco yuppies, by the subsequent author of the spellbinding blockbuster *A Suitable Boy* Harperperennial Phoenix.

Gary Snyder *Left Out in the Rain* (US Farrar, Straus & Giroux). One of the original Beat writers, and the only one whose work ever matured, Snyder's poetry is direct and spare, yet manages to conjure up a deep animistic spirituality underlying everyday life.

Amy Tan *The Joy Luck Club* (Putnam/Minerva). Four Chinese-American women and their daughters gather together to look back over their lives. Moving story of immigrant struggle in the sweatshops of Chinatown. An excerpt of this work can be found on p.346.

William T. Vollman *The Rainbow Stories* (Penguin/Deutsch). Brutal, gut-level portraits of street life: Tenderloin whores, Haight Street skinheads, beggars, junkies, and homeless Vietnam vets. Involving stuff for those who can handle it.

San Francisco on Film

San Francisco is a favorite with Californian film-makers, the city's staggering range of settings and chameleon-like geography making an often economical choice for the director who needs sunny beaches, swirling fogs, urban decay, and pastoral elegance all at once. Thrillers, in particular, seem to get good mileage out of the city; Hitchcock loved it, while the ridiculous gradients are almost ideally suited to the car chases that Hollywood loves so much. Below is a list of the obvious and not-so-obvious films made about or in California's most beautiful city.

Ten classic San Francisco films

Barbary Coast (Howard Hawks 1935). Set in misty, fog-bound, c.1900 San Francisco, where Edward G. Robinson finds he has competition when he tries to seduce the exotic dancer played by Miriam Hopkins. A brawling adventure film that captures the spirit of a lawless San Francisco.

Bullitt (Peter Yates 1968). Though Steve McQueen is the star of the this cops vs crooks crash up, San Francisco steals the show in the definitive high-speed, hillside car chase the film revolves around.

The Conversation (Francis Ford Coppola 1974). Local boy Coppola directed this brilliant Watergate-era thriller, starring Gene Hackman as a surveillance expert slowly descending into paranoia. A foggy Union Square provides the perfect backdrop.

Days of Wine and Roses (Martin Manulis 1962). Jack Lemmon plays a likeable drunk who drags his wife into alcoholism, too, only to leave her there once he's on the road to recovery. Smart satirical comedy that occasionally slips into melodrama.

Dirty Harry (Don Siegel 1971). Sleek and exciting sequel-spawning thriller casts Clint Eastwood in definitive role as neofascist San Francisco cop. Morally debatable, technically dynamic.

Greed (Erich von Stroheim 1924). Legendary, lengthy silent masterpiece based on Frank Norris's *McTeague* – see p.351 – detailing the squalid, ultimately tragic marriage between a blunt ex-miner with a dental practice on San Francisco's Polk Street and a simple girl from nearby Oakland. Dated but nonetheless unforgettable, including the classic finale in Death Valley.

The Maltese Falcon (John Huston 1941). Possibly the greatest detective movie of all time, starring a hard-bitten Humphrey Bogart as private dick Sam Spade and Peter Lorre stroking a remarkably suggestive cane.

Out of the Past (Jacques Torneur 1947). Genuine tough guy Robert Mitchum stars in this iconic film noir about one man's date with destiny. Moody and mysterious.

The Times of Harvey Milk (Robert Epstein 1984). Academy Award-winning documentary chronicling Milk's career in San Francisco politics and the aftermath of his 1978 assassination.

Vertigo (Alfred Hitchcock 1958). Known during production as the "San Francisco movie," Hitchcock's remarkable film looks at fear, obsession, and voyeurism. Jimmy Stewart gives an uncharacteristically dark performance as an ex-cop slowly coming unhinged because of a romantic obsession. Excellent use of locations, including Nob Hill, Fort Point, Muir Woods, and Mission Dolores.

Documentaries

Berkeley in the Sixties (Mark Kitchell 1990). Well-made documentary about the heyday of political protest in Berkeley. Combination of modern-day interviews with startling clips showcasing nearly every movement that occurred back in the day.

Common Threads: Stories from the Quilt (Robert Epstein 1989). The maker of *The Times of Harvey Milk* documents the history of the Names Project Memorial Quilt, talking to six bereaved partners of people who died from AIDS complications.

Crumb (Terry Zwigoff 1994). Disturbing portrait of Robert Crumb, the wildly eccentric comic artist whose Mr. Natural became a 1960s icon, and his even wilder relatives.

Fillmore (Richard T. Heffron 1972). Bad rock movie about San Francisco's famous music venue in the last week of its existence. Good footage of the Grateful Dead, Jefferson Airplane, and Boz Scaggs, but Bill Graham's egomaniacal ranting between the acts soon becomes wearying.

Gimme Shelter (David & Albert Maysles/Charlotte Zwerin 1970). Legendary film about the Rolling Stones' Altamont concert (see p.119). Lots of shots of Mick Jagger looking bemused during and after the notorious murder.

Jimi Plays Berkeley (Peter Pilafian 1971). The historic Memorial Day Jimi Hendrix concert in Berkeley, interspersed with lots of shots of rampaging students waving their peace signs. Hendrix ignores the peripheral action and just plays.

Last Call at Maude's (Paris Poirier 1993). Sweet ode to a bygone lesbian bar – a window into over twenty years of Bay Area lesbian history.

Neighborhoods: the Hidden Cities of San Francisco (Peter L. Stein 1997). A popular four-part mini-series on the history of San Francisco, focusing on Chinatown, the Castro, the Fillmore, and the Mission.

Thrillers

Basic Instinct (Paul Verhoeven 1992). Sharon Stone is vampish as a bisexual writer pursued by bug-eyed Michael Douglas around the dramatic city landscape in this conventional murder mystery that drew protests from San Francisco's gay and lesbian community over alleged homophobia.

Chan is Missing (Wayne Wang 1982). A friend's disappearance provides an excuse for a good-humored tour through Chinatown's back alleys in local director Wang's breakthrough indie hit.

Copycat (Jon Amiel 1995). An exceedingly run-of-the-mill serial-killer story, featuring Holly Hunter and Sigourney Weaver, but has some nice hilltop photography.

Dark Passage (Delmer Davies 1947). Classic couple Humphrey Bogart and Lauren Bacall steam up foggy San Francisco as they try to clear the wrongfully accused Bogey's good name. Good locations and some exotic camerawork.

D.O.A. (Rudolph Mate 1949). A thriller with a terrific gimmick: a poisoned man with only a few hours to live searches to uncover his murderer. Excellent use of LA and San Francisco locales.

The Enforcer (James Fargo 1976). *Dirty Harry* Part Three finds Clint Eastwood in a typically aggressive mood, at odds with the liberal supervisors who want him to stop killing every teenage delinquent in sight. Slight relief is provided by Tyne Daly, as a female cop facing ridiculous odds.

Escape from Alcatraz (Don Siegel 1979). Clint Eastwood reteams with *Dirty Harry* director Don Seigel for this well-made retelling of a true-life escape attempt from the infamous prison.

Experiment in Terror (Blake Edwards 1962). The inspiration for David Lynch's *Twin Peaks*, this entertaining Cold War period piece has dozens of FBI agents trying to track down an obscene phone caller in San Francisco's Twin Peaks neighborhood.

Eye of the Cat (David Lowell Rich 1969). *Psycho*-esque thriller in which a man with a cat phobia goes to stay with an aunt who has an army of them.

Family Plot (Alfred Hitchcock 1976). The master's light-hearted final film is a lark about stolen jewels, kidnapping, and psychic sleuthing in and around San Francisco.

Fog over Frisco (William Dieterle 1934). A very young Bette Davis plays a wayward heiress who is kidnapped in this terse thriller.

48 Hours (Walter Hill 1982). Eddie Murphy puts in a slick comic performance as the criminal sidekick to Nick Nolte's tough-talking cop, who has 48 hours to wrap up a homicide case. Fantastic shots of San Francisco and quick-witted dialogue make this fast-paced comedy-thriller immensely entertaining.

Foul Play (Colin Higgins 1978). Goldie Hawn and Chevy Chase team up to thwart an albino and a midget from assassinating the pope in this enjoyably silly action-comedy, which highlights North Beach and the Opera House.

The Game (David Fincher 1996). Stylish but strangely pointless thriller from the director of *Seven* follows a wealthy executive who becomes involved in an all-too-real role-playing game, which results in his nearly drowning in the Bay.

Interview with a Vampire (Neil Jordan 1994). Jordan's stylish adaptation of Anne Rice's hugely popular novel is well-filmed, even if the leading actors, Tom Cruise and Brad Pitt, are miscast. Pivotal scenes were shot on the Golden Gate Bridge and along Market Street.

Invasion of the Body Snatchers (Philip Kaufman 1978). Instead of indulging in Cold War paranoia, this remake of the 1960s horror classic parodies New Age culture. With a distinctly alien-looking Donald Sutherland as earth's last best hope: an uptight restaurant inspector.

It Came From Beneath the Sea (Charles Schneer 1955). A giant octopus attacks the city and tries to destroy Golden Gate Bridge in this B-grade monster flick.

The Killer Elite (Sam Peckinpah 1975). Typically violent outing from tough-guy auteur Peckinpah, with James Caan as an agent bent on revenge against his double-crossing bosses.

The Lady From Shanghai (Orson Welles 1948). Orson Welles' brief marriage to Rita Hayworth resulted in this twisted mystery about a double-crossing couple. The finale, shot in a hall of mirrors, is one of the most famous scenes in film history.

The Laughing Policeman (Stuart Rosenberg 1973). Walter Matthau and Bruce Dern team up in yet another brutal San Francisco cop thriller, centered around the gunning down of a busload of people in the Mission district. Queasy use of gay characters.

The Lineup (Frank Cooper 1958). Film adaptation of the TV series *San Francisco Beat*, about the SFPD capturing a junkie gunman. An unconvincing plot, but polished acting and fantastic shots of San Francisco.

Magnum Force (Ted Post 1973). The sequel to *Dirty Harry*, with more shots of Clint Eastwood looking tough and the city skyline looking beautiful.

The Organization (James Webb 1971). Sidney Poitier returns again as uptight cop Virgil Tibbs, from *In the Heat of the Night*, and ends up breaking the law to help a radical group trying to stop the flow of heroin into the inner city.

Pacific Heights (John Schlesinger 1990). Michael Keaton is the tenant from hell trying to evict his landlords from their lovingly restored Victorian. Shaky plot mechanics, though the picture delivers a few rusty thrills and a tour through the city's contentious rental laws.

Point Blank (John Boorman 1967). Lee Marvin plays a double-crossed gangster out for revenge on his cheating bosses. Remarkable, stylish camerawork and set design embellish a borderline abstract plot that moves from LA to Alcatraz. Angie Dickinson plays a convincingly faithless wife.

The Presidio (Peter Hyams 1988). TV star Mark Harmon tries the big screen in this bland mystery about murder on the military base. Costar Sean Connery seems to be wishing he was elsewhere.

The Rock (Michael Bay 1996). Embarrassingly enjoyable actioner stars Nicholas Cage as an FBI scientist trying to save the city from biological warheads hidden on Alcatraz. Sean Connery, as the only man to ever escape from the island prison, looks on with droll amusement during the absurd proceedings. Features a geographically impossible car chase.

They Call Me Mister Tibbs! (Gordon Douglas 1970). Another benign follow-up thriller to *In the Heat of the Night*, with Sidney Poitier as Virgil Tibbs, the black San Francisco cop who sleuths his way to unraveling a murder mystery.

THX-1138 (George Lucas 1970). Shot in the then brand-new BART's tunnels, the *Star Wars* mogul's debut is a bleak look at an Orwellian future.

Time After Time (Nicholas Meyer 1979). Courtesy of the Time Machine, Malcolm McDowell chases Jack the Ripper into twentieth-century San Francisco accompanied by a lot of cheap jokes and violence.

The Towering Inferno (John Guillermin/Irwin Allen 1974). An all-star cast – including Steve McQueen, Faye Dunaway, Fred Astaire, and Paul

Newman – gets alternately burned, blown-up, smashed or dropped from great heights in this borderline camp disaster epic about a fire in the world's tallest building.

Drama

Birdman of Alcatraz (John Frankenheimer 1962). Earnest but overlong study of real-life convicted killer Robert Stroud (Burt Lancaster) who becomes an authority on birds while kept in America's highest security prison.

The Counsellor (Alberto De Martino 1973). Italian Mafia movie, dubbed into English and shot in San Francisco. Little more than a takeoff of *Bullitt* and *The Godfather.*

Crackers (Louis Malle 1983). Donald Sutherland rescues what is otherwise a limp art film about struggling on the back streets of San Francisco. One of a million films to romanticize being poor.

Dragon – The Bruce Lee Story (Rob Cohen 1993). Odd mixture of biography and cartoonish chop-socky action, detailing the early years of the international film star, including his early hipster days working as a cook in Chinatown.

Freebie and the Bean (Richard Rush 1974). Former psychedelic auteur Rush descends into formula with this tough-but-funny dramedy about mismatched police partners.

The Frisco Kid (Samuel Bischoff 1935). James Cagney stars in this rough-and-tumble tale of a shanghaied sailor who rises to power amid the riffraff of the 1860s Barbary Coast.

Gentleman Jim (Raoul Walsh 1942). Rich evocation of 1880s San Francisco with Errol Flynn playing the charming, social-climbing boxer, Gentleman Jim Corbett.

Hammett (Wim Wenders 1982). German director Wenders, never known for keeping things short and sweet, financially ruined Coppola's Zoetrope production company with this tribute to Dashiell Hammett's quest for material in the back alleys of Chinatown.

I Remember Mama (George Stevens 1948). Sentimental, nostalgic tribute to family life circa 1910 for a group of Norwegian immigrants in San Francisco. Told through the memories of a now successful author, who dwells on her tough past and credits it with making her the woman she is.

Joy Luck Club (Wayne Wang 1993). Epic weepy based on the best-selling novel about first generation Chinese women's struggle to make it in America.

Murder in the First (Marc Rocco 1995). Draining courtroom drama based on the true story of an incarcerated petty thief driven to a jailhouse murder by years of solitary confinement and torture. Period trappings, including antique streetcars, plus decent turns by Gary Oldman, Christian Slater, and Kevin Bacon.

Pirates of Silicon Valley (Martyn Burke 1999). Made-for-TV docudrama about the rivalry and rise of Microsoft's Bill Gates and Apple's Steve Jobs during the early days of Silicon Valley. Surprisingly, Gates comes off the better of the two.

Shoot the Moon (Alan Parker 1981). Albert Finney and Diane Keaton star in this strained tale of self-obsessed Marin County trauma and heartbreak. About as affecting as an episode of *Dallas.*

Star Trek IV – The Voyage Home (Leonard Nimoy 1986). In a surprising twist this warm-hearted comic installment of the sci-fi series sends Kirk and company back in time to contemporary San Francisco in order to save some whales.

Comedy and romance

After the Thin Man (W.S. Van Dyke 1936). Dashiel Hammett's drunken detectives Nick and Nora Charles retire to a fabulous mansion, which seems from the views to be situated on top of Coit Tower, only to have their relaxation interrupted by a high-society murder.

The Bachelor (Gary Sinyor 1999). This remake of the Buster Keaton classic stars Chris O'Donnell as a non-committal multimillionaire desperately pursued by every woman in town. The foolishness culminates with a thousand would-be brides chasing O'Donnell through the Stockton tunnel.

Dim Sum (Wayne Wang 1985). Appealing little film about a more-or-less Westernized Chinese family in San Francisco. A treat.

Flower Drum Song (Ross Hunter 1961). Patronizing, remorselessly cute Rodgers and Hammerstein musical about love dilemmas in San Francisco's Chinatown.

The Frisco Kid (Howard Koch Jr 1979). Implausible but amusing comedy about a rabbi who befriends an outlaw on his way to San Francisco. Silly and sentimental, it nonetheless has good comic performances from Gene Wilder and Harrison Ford.

Guess Who's Coming to Dinner (Stanley Kramer 1967). Well-meaning but slightly flat interracial comedy in which Spencer Tracy and Katharine Hepburn play the supposedly liberal but bewildered parents of a woman who brings home the black man (Sidney Poitier) she intends to marry.

Harold and Maude (Hal Ashby 1971). Black comedy about a romance between a death-obsessed teenager and the eighty-year-old woman he befriends at various funerals. Intolerable for some, a cult classic for others.

High Anxiety (Mel Brooks 1977). Mel Brooks' spoof on *Vertigo*, and psychiatry in general, is one of the director's best – if you have a high tolerance for rampant silliness.

I Love You, Alice B. Toklas (Hy Averback 1968). Long before Austin Powers hit the screen, Peter Sellers' performance in this groovy film with a script by Larry Tucker and Paul Mazursky set the standard for Swinging Sixties farces. By today's standards, though, the film's portrayal of women seems almost as dated as the wardrobe.

Mother (Albert Brooks 1996). Albert Brooks, the West Coast's answer to Woody Allen gives Debbie Reynolds a memorable role as an overly attentive mother in the Sausalito area.

Mrs. Doubtfire (Chris Columbus 1993). Dippy claptrap about a caddish man (Robin Williams) who pretends to be a British nanny in order to be close to his kids.

Nina Takes a Lover (Alan Jacobs 1996). Small independently produced romantic comedy about love and loneliness, well shot against the backdrop of San Francisco's street scenes.

Pal Joey (Fred Kohlmar 1957). Frank Sinatra, Rita Hayworth, and Kim Novak star in this slick musical about a rising nightclub entertainer. Begins well, but slides alarmingly into cheap sentiment.

Petulia (Richard Lester 1968). San Francisco surgeon George C. Scott takes up with unhappily married kook Julie Christie in richly detailed, deliberately fragmentary comedy drama set in druggy, decadent society.

Play It Again, Sam (Herbert Ross 1972). Woody Allen leaves his beloved New York and enters film history as a nerdy young cinophile obsessed with Humphrey Bogart in this sweet, mildly amusing comedy.

Psych-Out (Richard Rush 1968). Pumped out quickly to capitalize on the "Summer of Love." Good performances from Jack Nicholson and Bruce Dern can't save what is basically a compendium of every hippie cliché in the book. That didn't stop it from quickly becoming a cult movie, though.

San Francisco (W.S. Van Dyke 1936). Elaborate, entertaining hokum about a Barbary Coast love triangle circa 1906. The script is upstaged by the climactic earthquake sequence.

Serial (Bill Persky 1980). Sharply observed comedy about social neurosis and hypocrisy among wealthy ex-hippies in Marin.

Skidoo (Otto Preminger 1968). Carol Channing, Jackie Gleason, and friends drop acid on Alcatraz, under the observant eye of a stoned God, played by Groucho Marx. With a soundtrack by Harry Nilsson.

Take the Money and Run (Woody Allen 1969). Allen's hilarious hippie spoof on the Paul Newman prison flick *Cool Hand Luke* features a crime spree through Northern California. One of Allen's most purely slapstick efforts.

Tales of the City (Alastair Reid 1993). Widely loved mini-series based on Maupin's popular books. When it was first shown on public television, it generated a great deal of controversy for its gay content, and went on to become the most popular progam ever aired on PBS. Still, only cable would touch the sequels – *More Tales of the City* (Pierre Gang 1998) and *Further Tales of the City* due to be released in 2001.

What's Up, Doc? (Peter Bogdanovich 1972). Wildly likeable screwball comedy pastiche starring Barbra Streisand and Ryan O'Neal as a cook and a naive professor, with a famous moment shot in Alta Plaza park (see p.86).

The Woman In Red (Gene Wilder 1984). Initially sophomoric comedy about one man's obsessive lust for a beautiful stranger. Takes a pleasant twist when Wilder's character (very belatedly) realizes there's more to love than physical attraction, and more to parking on San Francisco's hills than shifting to P.

Glossaries

Every city has a jargon all its own, and San Francisco is no exception. We've compiled a few of the terms you'll find sprinkled throughout the guide – to get a real sense of the slang you're going to have spend a few hours hanging out in one of the neighborhoods with a local. We've also included a rundown to some prominent figures, both past and present, who have helped give the city by the bay its unique personality.

San Francisco people

ADAMS Ansel The world's most famous landscape photographer and the man responsible for turning Yosemite's Half Dome into a national monument.

BIAFRA Jello Lead singer of the Dead Kennedys and a seminal figure in the San Francisco punk music scene who has taken the local spotlight as an anarchist activist and mayoral candidate.

BIERCE Ambrose Author of *The Devil's Dictionary*. Came to San Francisco on an army assignment, where he began his literary career as a journalist and went on to become the *San Francisco Examiner*'s most satirical and witty staff writer.

BRANNAN Samuel Founded a Mormon colony in the early years of the city and founded San Francisco's first newspaper, the *California Star*. Most famous, however, as the man who brought the news of the discovery of gold in the Sierras. Made a fortune in real estate before drinking his way into poverty and spending his last years alone and forgotten in Escondido, San Diego.

BRIDGES Harry Inspired by Jack London's fiction to leave his native Australia and come to San Francisco to work on sailing vessels, Bridges went on to become the militant leader of the International Longshoremen's Association, a career which brought him disciples and enemies in equal numbers as he led the union through often violent battles with the Pacific Coast shipowners in 1934, and again in 1971 when he came out of retirement on behalf of his longshoremen. A genuine working-class hero.

BRODERICK David US Senator in the 1850s and San Francisco's leading politician of the time, shot and mortally wounded in a duel at Lake Merced with the former California State Supreme Court Justice David Terry.

BROWER David California-born conservationist, Brower was longtime director of the Sierra Club (1952–69) and went on to help found Friends of the Earth.

BROWN Arthur Oakland-born architect who built San Francisco's City Hall and Coit Tower.

BROWN Jerry California's former "Governor Moonbeam," a turtleneck-wearing iconoclast who succeeded his long-ruling father in the statehouse. After dropping out of political life to work with Mother Theresa, Brown staged a low-rent comeback as the mayor of Oakland.

BROWN Willie A former Texas sharecropper who financed his college education by driving a city cab, Brown was elected to the California State Assembly. Forced out by term limits, Brown's working retirement as San Francisco mayor has given him a very public platform from which to flaunt his smooth political style.

BRUBECK Dave Oakland-born jazz pianist and composer, notably of *Take Five*, Brubeck brought attention to the cooler sounds of West Coast Jazz.

BRUNDAGE Avery Michigan-born engineer, Brundage went on to become the president of the International Olympic Committee. But he is best known for his enormous collection of Oriental art, donated to San Francisco's de Young Museum and now known as the Asian Art Museum.

BURNHAM Daniel Chicago architect who was invited by San Francisco's mayor, James D. Phelan, to plan the city's development in the early twentieth century, creating the Beaux Arts complex of Civic Center – though this was in fact only a small part of his ambitious scheme.

CAEN Herb San Francisco's most prominent columnist, urban booster, and mythologist, Caen wrote for the *San Francisco Examiner* for eons, until his death in 1997. Though rather overrated, he could definitely dig up good dirt about the Nob Hill upper crust.

CLARK, Jim and ANDREESSEN, Marc Cofounders, in 1994, of Netscape, the first computer program to allow casual users to surf the Internet – previously the domain of academics and government officials.

COIT Lillie Renowned for her unusual behavior, Coit came to San Francisco as a child and was reared in the best social circles. Married briefly to Howard Coit, on her death she left $100,000 to the city in order to build Coit Tower, Telegraph Hill's principle landmark, as a memorial to San Francisco's volunteer firefighters.

COLEMAN William Leader of the "Vigilance Committees," extra-legal police squads who controlled (and often terrorized) San Francisco in the mid-1800s.

COOLBRITH Ina San Francisco poet who introduced Jack London to literature when working for the Oakland Public Library. Her poems are collected in the books *Singer of the Sea, A Perfect Day* and *Songs of the Golden Gate*. In recognition of her organization of the World Congress of Authors, for the Panama Pacific Exhibition in 1915, the legislature made her the state's first Poet Laureate.

COPPOLA Francis Ford The director of the *Godfather* trilogy and *Apocalypse Now*, Coppola founded the American Zoetrope film production company in the hopes of making Northern California a new center of film production. He still lives in the area and owns a winery, plus the Columbus Tower in North Beach.

DE AYALA Juan Manuel The first European to enter the San Francisco bay, soon followed by Juan Batista de Anza, who founded the original bayside colony.

DIEBENKORN Richard Bay Area artist who gained renown in the 1960s with his Ocean Park series of paintings. Along with other artists, Diebenkorn's combination of mundane subjects and an expressionist-influenced painting style came to be known as the Bay Area Figurative School.

FEINSTEIN Dianne Ex-San Francisco mayor who stepped in when George Moscone and Harvey Milk were assassinated and is now a US Senator. She is very much a career politician; rumors abound about her dealings with big corporations in the late 1970s that led to massive development in San Francisco's Financial District.

FERLINGHETTI Lawrence Founder and still owner of City Lights Bookshop, America's first paperback bookshop, who fought a legal battle for the right to sell Allen Ginsberg's *Howl* and became a prominent figure in the Beat movement in the 1950s.

FREMONT John Leader of the tiny "Bear Flag Revolt" which declared Californian independence from Mexico.

GARCIA Jerry The late lead guitarist and vocalist for psychedelic rock gods the Grateful Dead.

GINSBERG Allen Though he was born and died in New York, Ginsberg is associated with San Francisco because he wrote the controversial book-length poem *Howl*, which depicted homosexuality and social discontent, while living in North Beach.

GRAHAM Bill Rock promoter and owner of the Fillmore who helped organize numerous psychedelic rock concerts in the 1960s, before making his fortune through bloated arena rock excess. Noted for his charitable work, Graham died in a plane crash in 1992.

GROVE Andy A Hungarian refugee hired by fledgling microprocessor Intel; his management style made the company so successful that, now, 80 percent of the world's computers depend on Intel hardware.

HALLIDIE Andrew English-born engineer who emigrated to San Francisco in the nineteenth century to work in the Comstock mines. In 1873 he invented the universally loved cable car and thereby made travel over San Francisco's ridiculous gradients possible.

HAMMETT Dashiell Hammett, who traveled to San Francisco as a young man and worked for the Pinkerton Detective Agency, drew on his experiences to write the hard-boiled detective novels *The Maltese Falcon* and *The Thin Man*. In his later years, Hammett was involved with the Hollywood Ten McCarthy witch-hunts concerning alleged "un-American" activities and was sent to jail for refusing to testify.

HEARST Patty Kidnapped by the Symbionese Liberation Army, an obscure 1970s radical group, this wealthy debutante reappeared in the surveillance video of a Sunset district bank she helped the group rob at gunpoint. Upon her arrest Hearst claimed she had been brainwashed and was spared jail time.

HEARST William Randolph Publishing magnate and the practitioner of inflammatory "yellow journalism" who as a young man worked on the *San Francisco Examiner* and went on to acquire a string of successful daily newspapers, motion picture companies, and radio stations. He later ran for senator of New York before settling into a lavish lifestyle in the incredible Hearst Castle at San Simeon, south of the city, which was parodied in Orson Welles' *Citizen Kane*.

HOBART Lewis P. Missouri-born architect who came to study at the University of California and went on to design the Bohemian Club, Grace Cathedral, and the Steinhart Aquarium.

JOBS, Steve A college drop-out from a blue-collar background, Jobs cofounded Apple computers and became one of the two most powerful men in the computer industry. After leaving to found the Pixar animation studio, Jobs recently returned to Apple and introduced the popular iMac.

JONES Jim Western Addition minister for a multiracial congregation, Jones grew into a major cult figure during the 1970s. Paranoid about nuclear war, he moved his congregation to Guyana, where he led them to a horrific mass murder and suicide.

JOPLIN Janis Texas-born Joplin came to San Francisco at the age of eighteen and began her singing career with Big Brother and the Holding Company. She was a central figure in the psychedelic scene; her problem was not LSD, but booze and heroin, an overdose of which finally killed her in 1970.

KEROUAC Jack A leading figure of the Beat movement in New York, Kerouac came out in the 1950s to San Francisco, where he drew on his experiences to write the Beats' bible *On the Road*. He spent much of his life with his mother in Massachusetts and eventually drank himself into an early grave at the age of 46.

KESEY Ken Oregon-reared Kesey enrolled in a creative writing program at Stanford University, during which time he became involved with psychiatric experiments with LSD – experiences that inspired him to write *One Flew over the Cuckoo's Nest*. Important, too, for his involvement in San Francisco's psychedelic scene, Kesey toured the country with his busload of Merry Pranksters in the Sixties, a time richly chronicled in Tom Wolfe's *The Electric Kool-Aid Acid Test*.

KINGSTON Maxine Hong The first Asian-American author to reach mainstream audiences. Rather than trucking in Orientalist exoticism, Kingston's magical-realist style revels in the details of Americanization and generational clashes.

LONDON Jack London was an illegitimate child who grew up in rough and tumble Oakland with little formal education but read books compulsively, a habit that was later to serve him well when he began his prolific writing career that produced *The Call of the Wild*.

LUCAS George *Star Wars* producer, and one of the film industry's most powerful men – who has set up shop in the foothills of Marin. A recent contract with the city will allow Lucas to build a mini-studio in converted military buildings in the Presidio.

MAUPIN Armistead Author of the ongoing serial of stories, collected as *Tales of the City*, which celebrated San Francisco's youthful swinger culture of the 1970s.

MAYBECK Bernard Early modern architect responsible for some of the most beautiful buildings in the Bay Area, including the magnificent Palace of Fine Arts for the Panama Pacific Exhibition in 1915.

MAYS Willie Remarkably graceful center fielder for the San Francisco Giants during the 1960s, the "Say Hey Kid" eased the team's transition when it moved from New York.

MIEGGS Henry Mieggs came to San Francisco at the beginning of the Gold Rush and made a small fortune carrying lumber from upstate New York. He went on to become a civic leader and built Mieggs Wharf – today's Fisherman's Wharf. Later in life he was involved in a scandal concerning forged city treasury warrants and fled to South America.

MILK Harvey San Francisco's (and arguably America's) first openly gay politician, Milk played a key role in the gay emancipation of the 1970s, only to be assassinated at the height of his career and popularity by political rival, Dan White (see p.109).

MITCHELL, Jim and Artie Popular counterculture figures, the Mitchell brothers skyrocketed to ame when they premiered their pornographic film *Behind the Green Door* at France's Cannes film festival. The duo also owned and managed the successful O'Farrell theater, described by (their friend) Hunter S. Thompson as "The Carnegie Hall of public sex in America." It all came crashing down in 1991 when Jim shot and killed his brother.

MONTANA Joe All-American quarterback for the San Francisco 49ers football team who led the team to four Super Bowl titles.

MONTGOMERY John B. Nineteenth-century naval captain in command of the *Portsmouth* during the Mexican War. His troops occupied San Francisco in 1846 and raised the American flag on the plaza that was the one-time waterfront.

MOONEY Tom Radical socialist labor leader, charged with planting the bomb that killed ten people during a Preparedness Day Parade on San Francisco's Market Street in 1916. He was sentenced to hang for the killings, but his unjust conviction became a cause célèbre for years and in 1939 he was pardoned.

MORGAN Julia Berkeley architect who designed William Randolph Hearst's impressive San Simeon estate and the Chapel of the Chimes in Oakland.

MOSCONE George San Francisco's well-liked liberal mayor who was assassinated along with Harvey Milk in 1978.

MUIR John Father of the American environmental movement, Muir campaigned for the establishment of national parks, notably Yosemite, and was honored in the naming of Marin's lush Muir Woods.

NEWTON Huey Black Panthers leader who advocated militancy as a means of achieving equal rights. Newton was murdered in what was presumed to be a botched drug deal in 1989.

NORRIS Frank Highly respected writer, who studied at the University of California and went on to produce acclaimed works such as *McTeague*, *The Octopus* and *The Pit*, strong accomplishments for one who died when barely past 30.

NORTON Joshua Abraham "Emperor" London-born character who came to be known as Emperor Norton after declaring himself "Emperor of the United States"; see box p.55.

POLK Willis An architect, he came to San Francisco as a young man and became involved with a bohemian group known as Les Jeunes. He also headed Daniel Burnham's San Francisco office (see p.336) and worked on his city plan. Known for his elegant brown-shingle designs.

REXROTH Kenneth Poet and translator whose apartment in the Lower Haight served as a crash pad for the younger generation of Beat writers.

RIVERA Diego Mexican painter known for his murals of working-class scenes, and whose influence can still be seen in the public art on view all around San Francisco, notably the Mission district.

ROSSETTO Louis Founder/publisher of *WIRED*, the design-centered new technology magazine that has made it cool to like computers.

SANTANA Carlos San Francisco-based guitar virtuoso renowned for his blending of Latin rhythms into pop music and having enjoyed a recent resurgence in popularity.

SAVIO Mario Leading figure of the Berkeley Free Speech movement of the early 1960s. When students opposed to the war in Vietnam were prohibited from passing out literature on campus, the protests shut down the campus and led staunchly right-wing Governor Ronald Reagan to call in armed contingents of the National Guard.

STANFORD Leland One of the Big Four local oligarchs of the nineteenth century who constructed the Central Pacific Railroad. During a two-year term as governor he was a staunch union supporter, although he is perhaps best known now for the creation of the university in Palo Alto that bears his name.

STEEL Danielle The immensely successful romance novelist owns the historic Spreckels Mansion at the summit of Pacific Heights.

SUTRO Adolph Prussian-born philanthropist who came to San Francisco and made his fortune in the Comstock silver bonanza. Heavy investment in San Francisco real estate led to his ownership of almost a twelfth of the entire city, to which he donated many developments, including the Cliff House, Sutro Baths, and the Sutro Library.

TWAIN Mark (Samuel Langhorne Clemens) Spent his early years in Missouri before embarking on a journalistic career that brought him to San Francisco in 1864. A regular contributor to such publications as *The Golden Era*, *Californian* and *Territorial Enterprise*, he gained his biggest popularity after writing *Roughing It*, telling exaggerated tales of adventures in the Comstock mining era.

WHITE Dan The murderer of Harvey Milk and George Moscone, White was a disgruntled ex-policeman and city supervisor whose trial came to be known for the "Twinkie Defense" after his lawyer claimed that White was suffering from temporary insanity caused by harmful additives in fast food. White's controversially brief five-year sentence caused a wave of rioting after the verdict was announced.

WOZNIAK, Steve Along with Steve Jobs, co-founder of Apple computers. It was in Wozniak's garage that the company's famous computers first took shape.

Terms and acronyms

Art Deco Style of decoration popular in the 1930s, characterized by elegant geometrical shapes and patterns.

Art Nouveau Art, architecture, and design of the 1890s typified by stylized organic forms.

Atrium Enclosed, covered pedestrian space often forming the lobby of a corporate building.

The Avenues Catch-all term for the Richmond and Sunset neighborhoods.

BART (Bay Area Rapid Transit) Slightly musty underground train system linking San Francisco to Oakland, Berkeley, and other parts of the East Bay.

The Beats Free-spirited and hard-drinking literary types who descended on North Beach in the 1950s, led by Jack Kerouac and Allen Ginsberg.

Beaux Arts Style of Neoclassical architecture taught at the Ecole de Beaux Arts in Paris at the end of the nineteenth century, the best example of which in the Bay Area is Civic Center.

The Big Four Collis P. Huntington, Mark Hopkins, Charles Crocker, and Leland Stanford – the four railroad barons who made their fortune building the Central Pacific Railroad in the late 1800s.

Black Panthers African-American political party born in 1960s Oakland, which adopted a martial stance toward the state and federal governments.

Cal Nickname for the University of California's Berkeley campus.

City Hall Not just the building, but also used to describe the local government as a whole.

Clapboard House covered with overlapping timber boards, in evidence throughout the city.

Critical Mass Loosely-organized bike ride that takes over the city's streets on the last Friday of every month.

Dot-com Any business affiliated with the Internet; employees of which may be known as dot-commers.

Food Not Bombs Homeless activist organization handing out free meals at United Nations Plaza.

Hippies The 1960s offspring of the Beats, generally associated with long hair, peace symbols, and hallucinogenic drugs.

IPO Initial Public Offering – the method by which many Internet companies in the 1990s cashed in and made their employees paper millionaires.

La Raza Refers to *mestizo*, or mixed-race indigenous and Latin, people from throughout Central and South America.

Multimedia Gulch SoMa district along Townsend and Third streets that hosts an unusual number of Internet and new-media companies.

Muni (San Francisco Municipal Railway) Not just a railway, but a system of buses, trolley buses, cable cars, and streetcars that serves the city.

Plaza Wide open space that acts as a pedestrian forecourt to a skyscraper or set of buildings.

Project Blocks of public housing.

Project Open Hand Support organization providing free meals to homebound AIDS victims.

Silicon Valley Communities south of Palo Alto that are home to many of the biggest computer companies in the world.

Sisters of Perpetual Indulgence Troupe of Catholic-themed drag queens who campaign publicly for various social causes.

Skyscraper The word comes from the highest sail on a sailing ship, and hence refers to any high building.

The South Bay Common term for the communities on the peninsula south of San Francisco.

Techie An employee of the computer industry.

WPA (Works Project Administration) Work-relief agency begun by Roosevelt in 1935. The WPA's Public Works of Art Project produced many murals in public buildings and a renowned set of guidebooks to the entire country.

INDEX

D

E

F

T

U

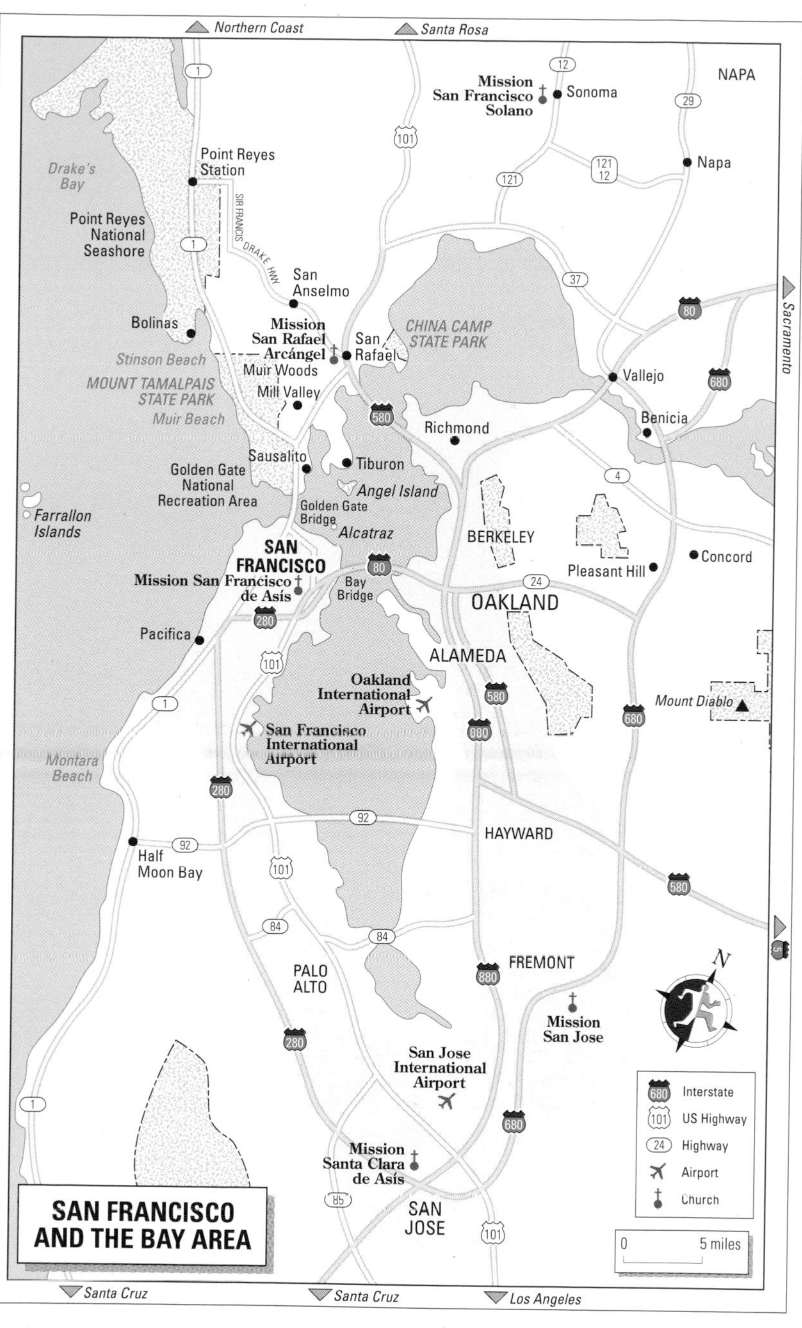

Northern Coast
Santa Rosa
Sacramento
Santa Cruz
Santa Cruz
Los Angeles
Mission San Francisco Solano
Sonoma
NAPA
Napa
Point Reyes Station
Drake's Bay
Point Reyes National Seashore
SIR FRANCIS DRAKE HWY
San Anselmo
Bolinas
Mission San Rafael Arcángel
San Rafael
CHINA CAMP STATE PARK
Stinson Beach
Muir Woods
MOUNT TAMALPAIS STATE PARK
Mill Valley
Muir Beach
Vallejo
Benicia
Richmond
Sausalito
Tiburon
Golden Gate National Recreation Area
Angel Island
Farrallon Islands
Golden Gate Bridge
Alcatraz
BERKELEY
SAN FRANCISCO
Concord
Pleasant Hill
Mission San Francisco de Asís
Bay Bridge
OAKLAND
Pacifica
ALAMEDA
Oakland International Airport
Mount Diablo
San Francisco International Airport
Montara Beach
HAYWARD
Half Moon Bay
PALO ALTO
FREMONT
Mission San Jose
San Jose International Airport
Mission Santa Clara de Asís
SAN JOSE
N
Interstate
US Highway
Highway
Airport
Church
0
5 miles
SAN FRANCISCO AND THE BAY AREA

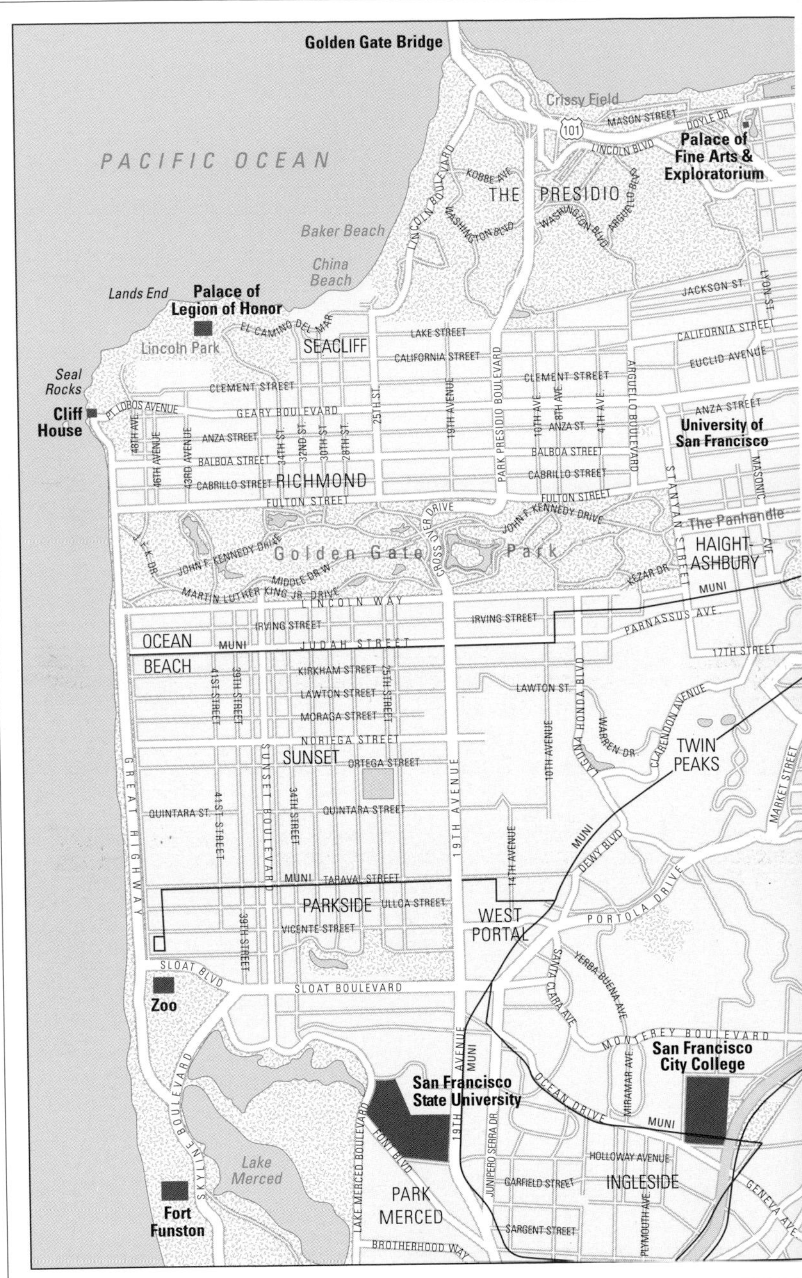

Golden Gate Bridge
PACIFIC OCEAN
Crissy Field
MASON STREET
DOYLE DR.
101
LINCOLN BLVD
Palace of Fine Arts & Exploratorium
KOBBE AVE
THE PRESIDIO
LINCOLN BOULEVARD
WASHINGTON BLVD
ARGUELLO BLVD
Baker Beach
China Beach
Lands End
Palace of Legion of Honor
EL CAMINO DEL MAR
Lincoln Park
SEACLIFF
LAKE STREET
CALIFORNIA STREET
JACKSON ST.
LYON ST.
CALIFORNIA STREET
EUCLID AVENUE
Seal Rocks
Cliff House
PT. LOBOS AVENUE
CLEMENT STREET
GEARY BOULEVARD
25TH ST.
19TH AVENUE
PARK PRESIDIO BOULEVARD
10TH AVE.
8TH AVE.
4TH AVE.
ARGUELLO BOULEVARD
ANZA STREET
University of San Francisco
48TH AVE.
46TH AVENUE
43RD AVENUE
ANZA STREET
34TH ST.
32ND ST.
30TH ST.
28TH ST.
ANZA ST.
BALBOA STREET
BALBOA STREET
CABRILLO STREET
RICHMOND
CABRILLO STREET
STANYAN STREET
MASONIC AVE.
FULTON STREET
FULTON STREET
CROSS OVER DRIVE
JOHN F. KENNEDY DRIVE
The Panhandle
J. F. K. DR.
JOHN F. KENNEDY DRIVE
Golden Gate Park
HAIGHT-ASHBURY
MIDDLE DR W
MARTIN LUTHER KING JR. DRIVE
KEZAR DR
MUNI
LINCOLN WAY
IRVING STREET
IRVING STREET
PARNASSUS AVE.
OCEAN BEACH
MUNI
JUDAH STREET
17TH STREET
KIRKHAM STREET
41ST STREET
39TH STREET
25TH STREET
LAWTON STREET
LAWTON ST.
LAGUNA HONDA BLVD
MORAGA STREET
CLARENDON AVENUE
WARREN DR.
NORIEGA STREET
10TH AVENUE
TWIN PEAKS
SUNSET
ORTEGA STREET
GREAT HIGHWAY
SUNSET BOULEVARD
19TH AVENUE
MARKET STREET
QUINTARA ST.
41ST STREET
34TH STREET
QUINTARA STREET
14TH AVENUE
MUNI
DEWEY BLVD
MUNI
TARAVAL STREET
PORTOLA DRIVE
PARKSIDE
ULLOA STREET
WEST PORTAL
39TH STREET
VICENTE STREET
SANTA CLARA AVE
YERBA BUENA AVE
SLOAT BLVD
SLOAT BOULEVARD
Zoo
MONTEREY BOULEVARD
San Francisco City College
MUNI
San Francisco State University
SKYLINE BOULEVARD
19TH AVENUE
OCEAN DRIVE
MIRAMAR AVE.
MUNI
LAKE MERCED BOULEVARD
FONT BLVD
JUNIPERO SERRA DR.
HOLLOWAY AVENUE
Lake Merced
PARK MERCED
GARFIELD STREET
INGLESIDE
GENEVA AVE.
Fort Funston
SARGENT STREET
PLYMOUTH AVE.
BROTHERHOOD WAY

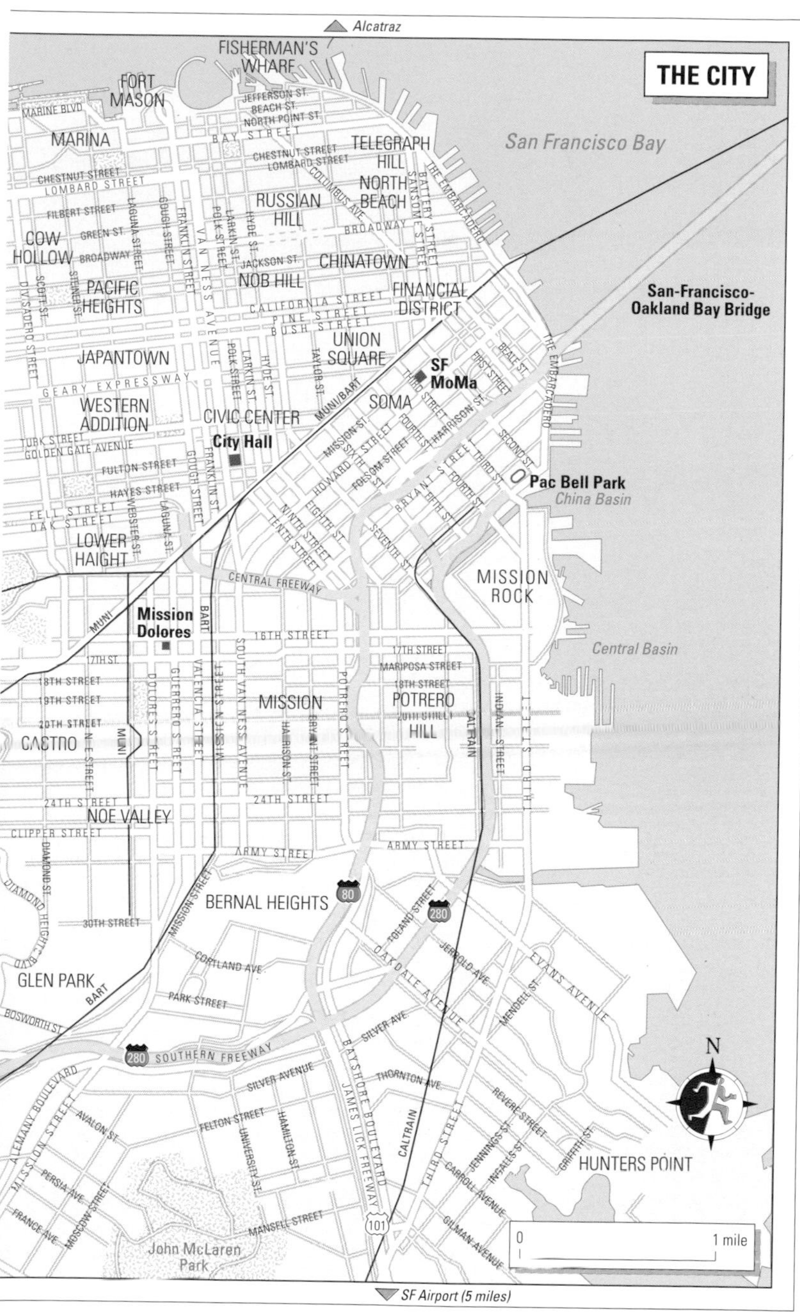

Alcatraz
THE CITY
San Francisco Bay
FISHERMAN'S WHARF
FORT MASON
MARINA
TELEGRAPH HILL
NORTH BEACH
RUSSIAN HILL
COW HOLLOW
PACIFIC HEIGHTS
CHINATOWN
NOB HILL
FINANCIAL DISTRICT
San-Francisco-Oakland Bay Bridge
UNION SQUARE
JAPANTOWN
SF MoMa
SOMA
WESTERN ADDITION
CIVIC CENTER
City Hall
Pac Bell Park
China Basin
LOWER HAIGHT
MISSION ROCK
Mission Dolores
Central Basin
MISSION
POTRERO HILL
CASTRO
NOE VALLEY
BERNAL HEIGHTS
GLEN PARK
HUNTERS POINT
John McLaren Park
MARINE BLVD
JEFFERSON ST.
BEACH ST.
NORTH POINT ST.
BAY STREET
CHESTNUT STREET
LOMBARD STREET
COLUMBUS AVE.
THE EMBARCADERO
BATTERY STREET
SANSOME STREET
BROADWAY
FILBERT STREET
GREEN ST.
LAGUNA STREET
GOUGH STREET
FRANKLIN STREET
VAN NESS AVENUE
POLK STREET
LARKIN ST.
HYDE ST.
JACKSON ST.
SCOTT ST.
STEINER ST.
DIVISADERO STREET
CALIFORNIA STREET
PINE STREET
BUSH STREET
TAYLOR ST.
BEALE ST.
FIRST STREET
GEARY EXPRESSWAY
MUNI/BART
THIRD STREET
HARRISON ST.
MISSION ST.
FOURTH ST.
SECOND ST.
TURK STREET
GOLDEN GATE AVENUE
FULTON STREET
SIXTH STREET
HOWARD ST.
FOLSOM STREET
HAYES STREET
FELL STREET
OAK STREET
WEBSTER ST.
BRYANT STREET
FIFTH ST.
EIGHTH ST.
NINTH STREET
TENTH STREET
SEVENTH ST.
CENTRAL FREEWAY
MUNI
BART
16TH STREET
17TH ST.
17TH STREET
MARIPOSA STREET
18TH STREET
19TH STREET
20TH STREET
DOLORES STREET
GUERRERO STREET
VALENCIA STREET
MISSION STREET
SOUTH VAN NESS AVENUE
HARRISON ST.
POTRERO STREET
CALTRAIN
INDIANA STREET
THIRD STREET
24TH STREET
CLIPPER STREET
DIAMOND ST.
ARMY STREET
80
280
TOLAND STREET
DIAMOND HEIGHTS BLVD
30TH STREET
CORTLAND AVE
OAKDALE AVENUE
JERROLD AVE.
EVANS AVENUE
MENDELL ST.
PARK STREET
BOSWORTH ST.
SILVER AVE.
SOUTHERN FREEWAY
BAYSHORE BOULEVARD
JAMES LICK FREEWAY
THORNTON AVE.
REVERE STREET
SILVER AVENUE
ALEMANY BOULEVARD
AVALON ST.
FELTON STREET
HAMILTON ST.
UNIVERSITY ST.
JENNINGS ST.
INGALLS ST.
GRIFFITH ST.
CARROLL AVENUE
PERSIA AVE.
MOSCOW STREET
FRANCE AVE.
MANSELL STREET
101
GILMAN AVENUE
N
0
1 mile
SF Airport (5 miles)

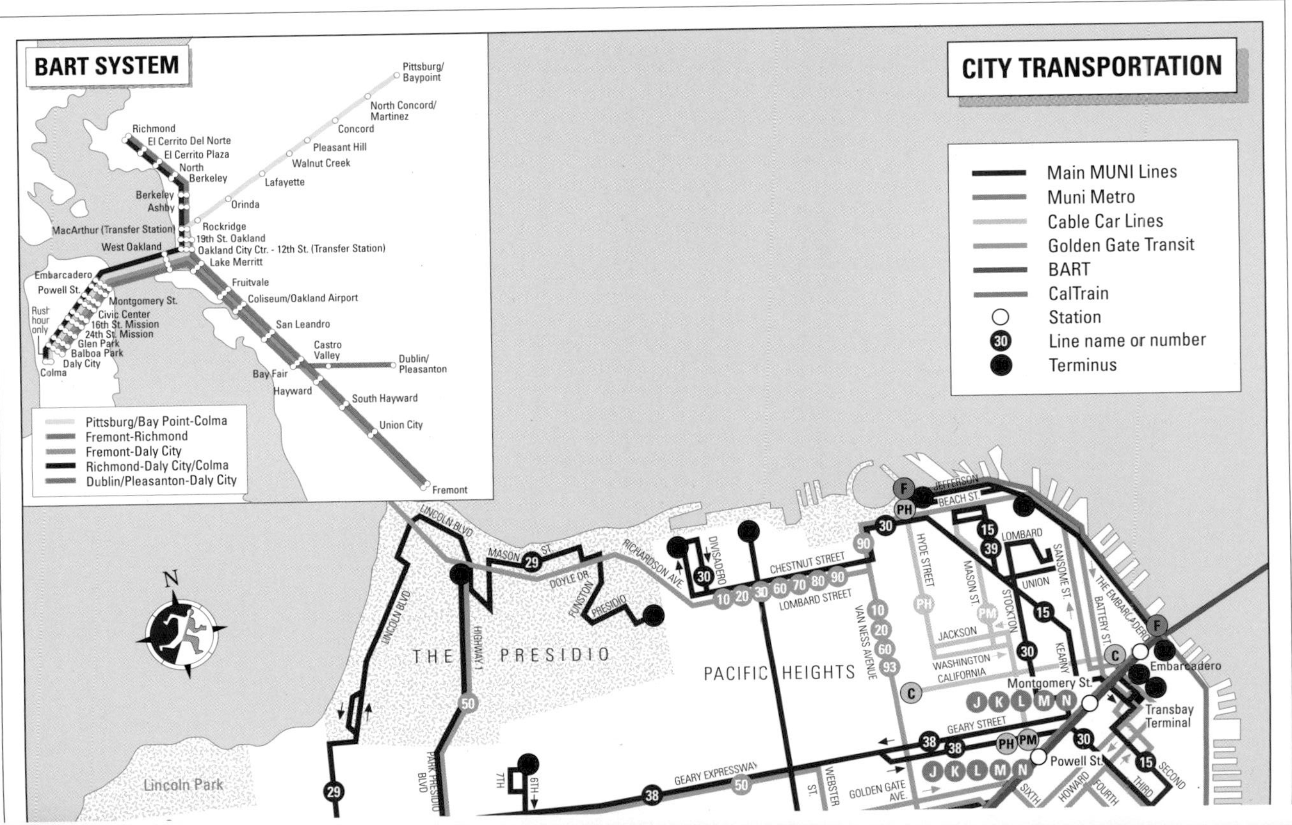

BART SYSTEM
Pittsburg/Baypoint
North Concord/Martinez
Concord
Pleasant Hill
Walnut Creek
Lafayette
Orinda
Rockridge
Richmond
El Cerrito Del Norte
El Cerrito Plaza
North Berkeley
Berkeley
Ashby
MacArthur (Transfer Station)
19th St. Oakland
Oakland City Ctr. - 12th St. (Transfer Station)
Lake Merritt
West Oakland
Embarcadero
Powell St.
Montgomery St.
Civic Center
16th St. Mission
24th St. Mission
Glen Park
Balboa Park
Daly City
Colma
Rush hour only
Fruitvale
Coliseum/Oakland Airport
San Leandro
Castro Valley
Dublin/Pleasanton
Bay Fair
Hayward
South Hayward
Union City
Fremont
Pittsburg/Bay Point-Colma
Fremont-Richmond
Fremont-Daly City
Richmond-Daly City/Colma
Dublin/Pleasanton-Daly City
CITY TRANSPORTATION
Main MUNI Lines
Muni Metro
Cable Car Lines
Golden Gate Transit
BART
CalTrain
Station
Line name or number
Terminus
N
Lincoln Park
LINCOLN BLVD
HIGHWAY 1
PARK PRESIDIO BLVD
MASON ST.
DOYLE DR.
FUNSTON
PRESIDIO
RICHARDSON AVE
DIVISADERO
THE PRESIDIO
7TH
6TH
GEARY EXPRESSWAY
CHESTNUT STREET
LOMBARD STREET
PACIFIC HEIGHTS
WEBSTER ST.
GOLDEN GATE AVE.
VAN NESS AVENUE
JEFFERSON
BEACH ST.
HYDE STREET
MASON ST.
LOMBARD
STOCKTON
UNION
JACKSON
WASHINGTON
CALIFORNIA
KEARNY
SANSOME ST.
BATTERY ST.
THE EMBARCADERO
GEARY STREET
Montgomery St.
Embarcadero
Transbay Terminal
Powell St.
SIXTH
HOWARD
FOURTH
THIRD
SECOND

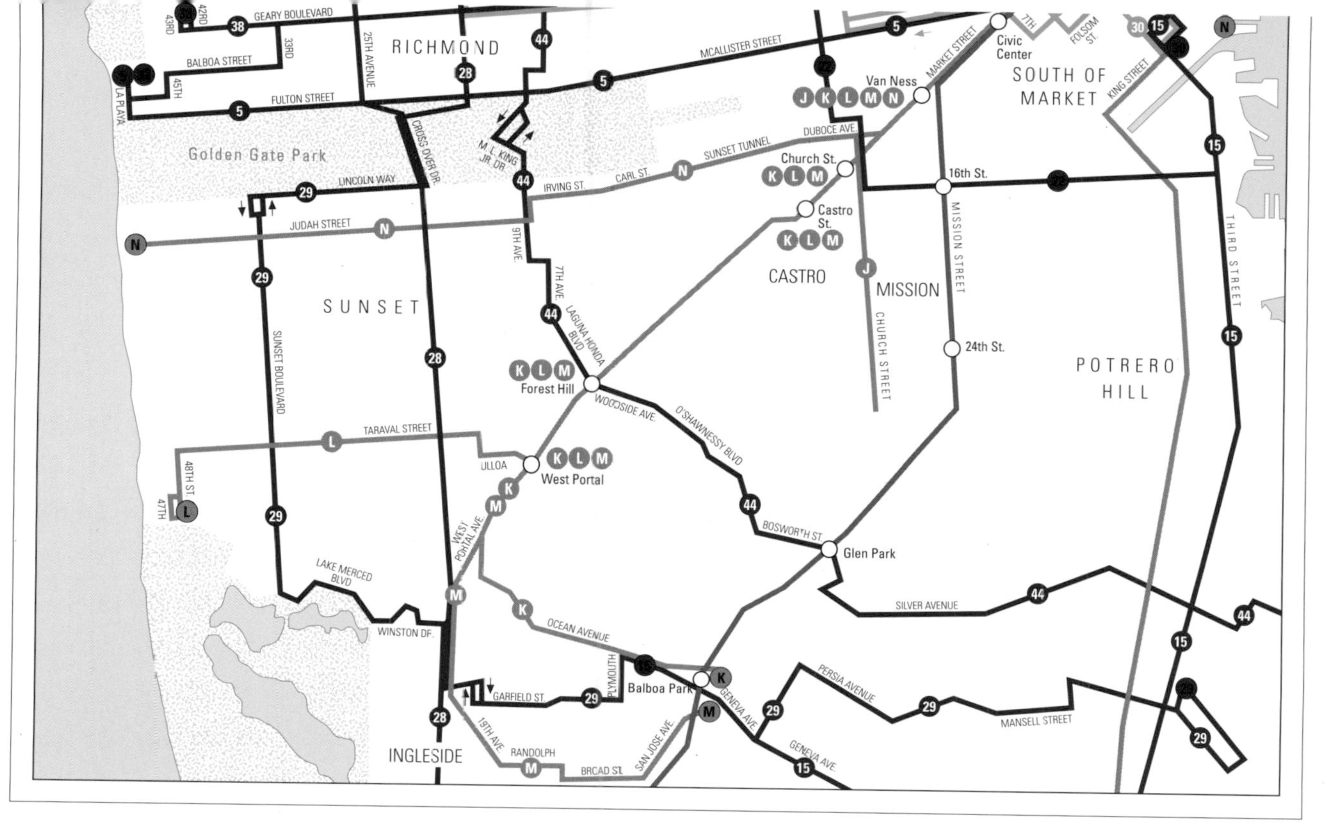

RICHMOND
GEARY BOULEVARD
42RD
43RD
33RD
BALBOA STREET
45TH
LA PLAYA
FULTON STREET
25TH AVENUE
MCALLISTER STREET
Golden Gate Park
CROSS OVER DR.
M. L. KING JR. DR.
LINCOLN WAY
JUDAH STREET
IRVING ST.
CARL ST.
SUNSET TUNNEL
DUBOCE AVE.
9TH AVE.
7TH AVE.
LAGUNA HONDA BLVD
SUNSET
SUNSET BOULEVARD
TARAVAL STREET
48TH ST.
47TH
LAKE MERCED BLVD
WINSTON DR.
INGLESIDE
GARFIELD ST.
19TH AVE.
RANDOLPH
BROAD ST.
SAN JOSE AVE.
PLYMOUTH
Balboa Park
GENEVA AVE.
OCEAN AVENUE
WEST PORTAL AVE.
ULLOA
West Portal
Forest Hill
WOODSIDE AVE.
O'SHAWNESSY BLVD
BOSWORTH ST.
Glen Park
SILVER AVENUE
PERSIA AVENUE
MANSELL STREET
Civic Center
7TH
FOLSOM ST.
SOUTH OF MARKET
KING STREET
MARKET STREET
Van Ness
Church St.
Castro St.
CASTRO
MISSION
CHURCH STREET
16th St.
MISSION STREET
24th St.
THIRD STREET
POTRERO HILL

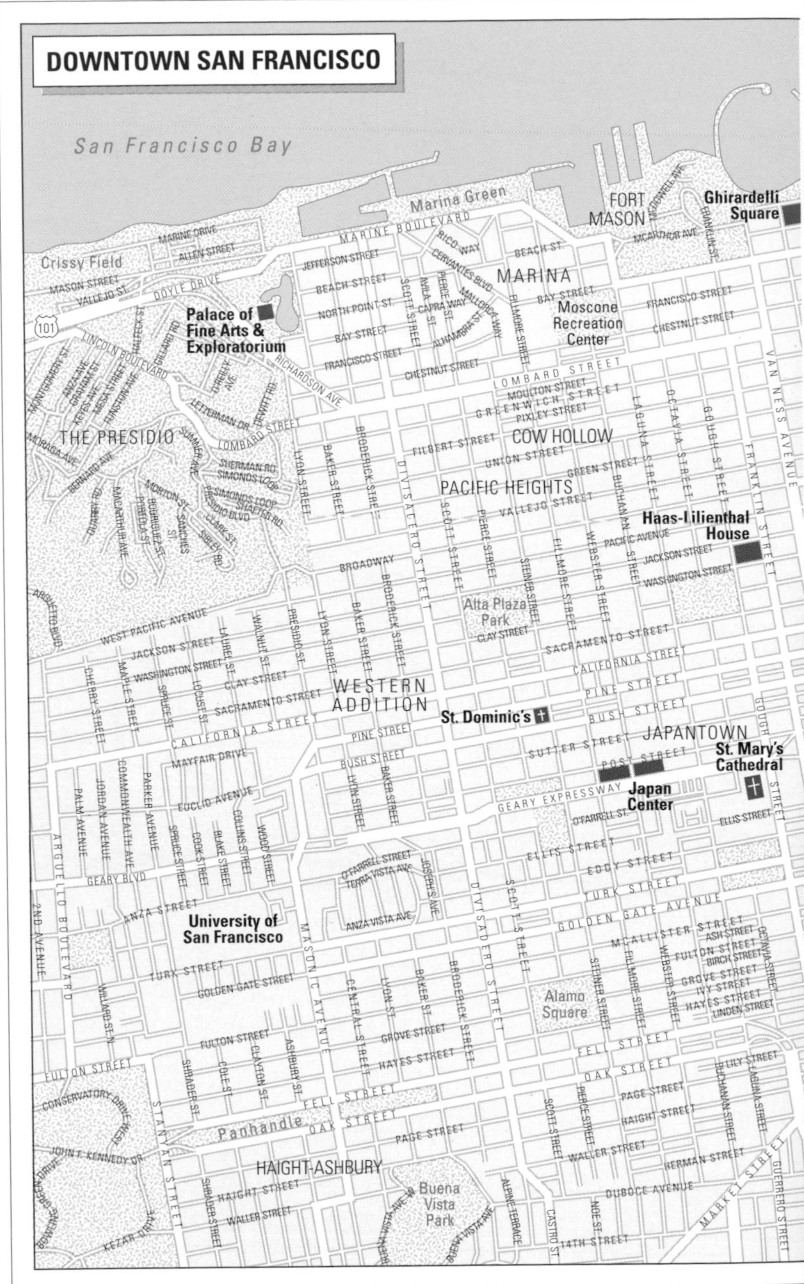
DOWNTOWN SAN FRANCISCO
San Francisco Bay
Marina Green
FORT MASON
Ghirardelli Square
Crissy Field
MARINE DRIVE
ALLEN STREET
MASON STREET
VALLEJO ST.
DOYLE DRIVE
101
MARINE BOULEVARD
JEFFERSON STREET
BEACH STREET
NORTH POINT ST.
BAY STREET
FRANCISCO STREET
CHESTNUT STREET
LOMBARD STREET
MOULTON STREET
GREENWICH STREET
PIXLEY STREET
FILBERT STREET
UNION STREET
GREEN STREET
VALLEJO STREET
PACIFIC AVENUE
JACKSON STREET
WASHINGTON STREET
CLAY STREET
SACRAMENTO STREET
CALIFORNIA STREET
PINE STREET
BUSH STREET
SUTTER STREET
POST STREET
GEARY EXPRESSWAY
O'FARRELL ST.
ELLIS STREET
EDDY STREET
TURK STREET
GOLDEN GATE AVENUE
MCALLISTER STREET
FULTON STREET
GROVE STREET
HAYES STREET
FELL STREET
OAK STREET
PAGE STREET
HAIGHT STREET
WALLER STREET
DUBOCE AVENUE
HERMAN STREET
14TH STREET
MARKET STREET
MARINA
Moscone Recreation Center
COW HOLLOW
PACIFIC HEIGHTS
Haas-Lilienthal House
Alta Plaza Park
WESTERN ADDITION
St. Dominic's
JAPANTOWN
St. Mary's Cathedral
Japan Center
Alamo Square
University of San Francisco
Palace of Fine Arts & Exploratorium
THE PRESIDIO
LINCOLN BOULEVARD
RICHARDSON AVE.
LETTERMAN DR.
LOMBARD STREET
WEST PACIFIC AVENUE
MAYFAIR DRIVE
EUCLID AVENUE
GEARY BLVD
ANZA STREET
ANZA VISTA AVE
TERRA VISTA AVE
O'FARRELL STREET
Panhandle
HAIGHT-ASHBURY
Buena Vista Park
CONSERVATORY DRIVE WEST
JOHN F. KENNEDY DR.
KEZAR DRIVE
BOWLING GREEN DRIVE
STANYAN STREET
ARGUELLO BOULEVARD
2ND AVENUE
MASONIC AVENUE
DIVISADERO STREET
SCOTT STREET
PIERCE STREET
STEINER STREET
FILLMORE STREET
WEBSTER STREET
BUCHANAN STREET
LAGUNA STREET
OCTAVIA STREET
GOUGH STREET
FRANKLIN STREET
VAN NESS AVENUE
LYON STREET
BAKER STREET
BRODERICK STREET
PRESIDIO ST.
WALNUT ST.
LAUREL ST.
LOCUST ST.
SPRUCE ST.
MAPLE STREET
CHERRY STREET
PALM AVENUE
JORDAN AVENUE
COMMONWEALTH AVE.
PARKER AVENUE
COOK STREET
BLAKE STREET
COLLINS STREET
WOOD STREET
CENTRAL STREET
SHRADER ST.
COLE ST.
CLAYTON ST.
ASHBURY ST.
CASTRO ST.
NOE ST.
ALPINE TERRACE
BUENA VISTA AVE.
GUERRERO STREET
LILY STREET
ASH STREET
BIRCH STREET
IVY STREET
LINDEN STREET
WILLARD ST. N.
ARGUELLO BLVD
MCARTHUR AVE
FRANKLIN ST.
MCDOWELL AVE.

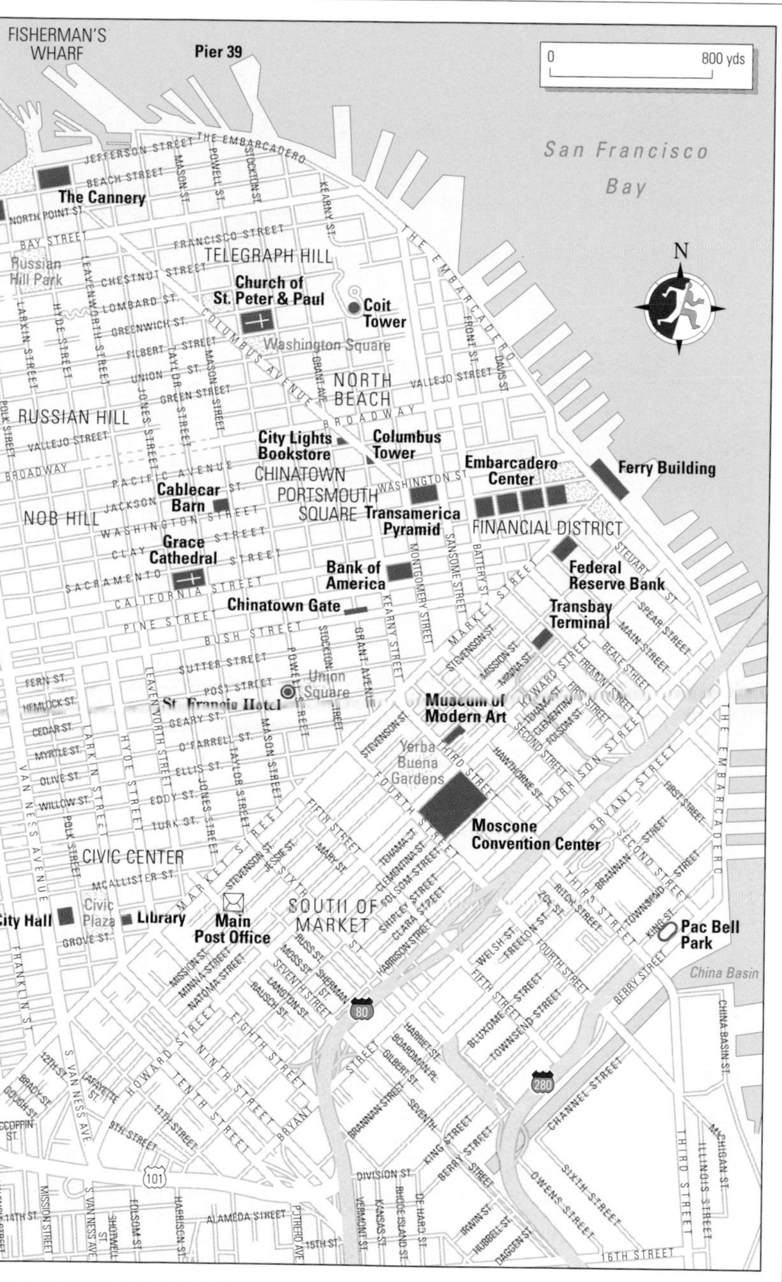
FISHERMAN'S WHARF
Pier 39
0
800 yds
San Francisco Bay
N
The Cannery
JEFFERSON STREET
THE EMBARCADERO
BEACH STREET
NORTH POINT ST.
BAY STREET
FRANCISCO STREET
TELEGRAPH HILL
Russian Hill Park
CHESTNUT STREET
LOMBARD ST.
GREENWICH ST.
FILBERT STREET
UNION ST.
GREEN STREET
VALLEJO STREET
BROADWAY
Church of St. Peter & Paul
Coit Tower
Washington Square
COLUMBUS AVENUE
NORTH BEACH
RUSSIAN HILL
City Lights Bookstore
Columbus Tower
CHINATOWN
PORTSMOUTH SQUARE
Embarcadero Center
Ferry Building
Cablecar Barn
NOB HILL
Transamerica Pyramid
FINANCIAL DISTRICT
Grace Cathedral
Bank of America
Federal Reserve Bank
Chinatown Gate
Transbay Terminal
Union Square
St. Francis Hotel
Museum of Modern Art
Yerba Buena Gardens
Moscone Convention Center
CIVIC CENTER
City Hall
Civic Plaza
Library
Main Post Office
SOUTH OF MARKET
Pac Bell Park
China Basin
80
280
101
16TH STREET

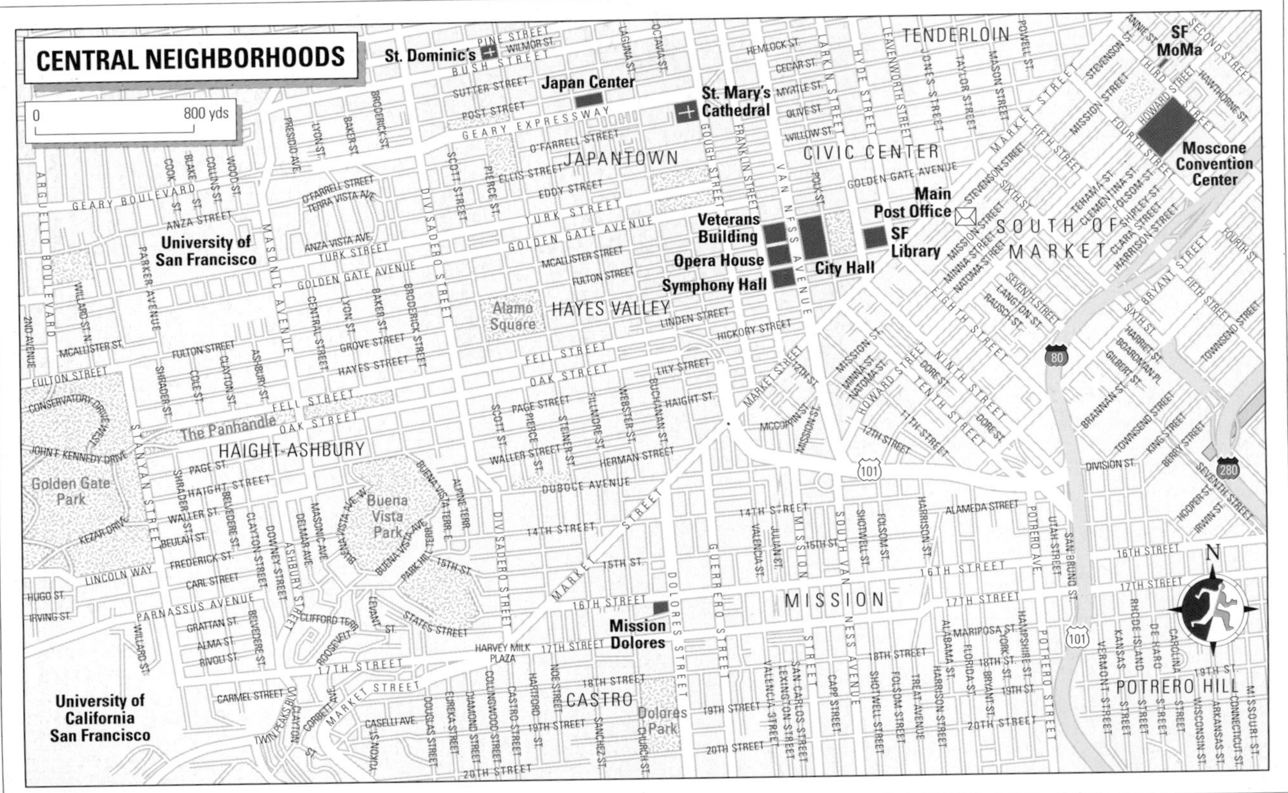
CENTRAL NEIGHBORHOODS
0
800 yds
TENDERLOIN
CIVIC CENTER
JAPANTOWN
SOUTH OF MARKET
HAYES VALLEY
HAIGHT-ASHBURY
MISSION
CASTRO
POTRERO HILL
St. Dominic's
Japan Center
St. Mary's Cathedral
SF MoMa
Moscone Convention Center
Main Post Office
SF Library
Veterans Building
Opera House
City Hall
Symphony Hall
University of San Francisco
Alamo Square
The Panhandle
Golden Gate Park
Buena Vista Park
Mission Dolores
Dolores Park
University of California San Francisco
HARVEY MILK PLAZA
N
GEARY EXPRESSWAY
GEARY BOULEVARD
ARGUELLO BOULEVARD
MASONIC AVENUE
DIVISADERO STREET
GOLDEN GATE AVENUE
VAN NESS AVENUE
SOUTH VAN NESS AVENUE
MARKET STREET
STANYAN STREET
LINCOLN WAY
PARNASSUS AVENUE
DUBOCE AVENUE
GUERRERO STREET
DOLORES STREET
POTRERO STREET
PINE STREET
BUSH STREET
SUTTER STREET
POST STREET
O'FARRELL STREET
ELLIS STREET
EDDY STREET
TURK STREET
MCALLISTER STREET
FULTON STREET
FELL STREET
OAK STREET
PAGE STREET
HAIGHT STREET
WALLER STREET
HERMAN STREET
14TH STREET
15TH ST.
16TH STREET
17TH STREET
18TH STREET
19TH STREET
20TH STREET
LARKIN STREET
HYDE STREET
LEAVENWORTH STREET
JONES STREET
TAYLOR STREET
MASON STREET
POWELL ST.
GOUGH STREET
FRANKLIN STREET
POLK ST.
OCTAVIA ST.
LAGUNA ST.
SCOTT STREET
PIERCE ST.
BRODERICK ST.
BAKER ST.
LYON ST.
PRESIDIO AVE.
MISSION STREET
HOWARD STREET
FOLSOM ST.
HARRISON STREET
BRYANT STREET
BRANNAN ST.
TOWNSEND STREET
KING STREET
BERRY STREET
FOURTH STREET
FIFTH STREET
SIXTH ST.
SEVENTH STREET
EIGHTH STREET
NINTH STREET
TENTH STREET
11TH STREET
12TH STREET
DIVISION ST.
SAN BRUNO ST.
UTAH STREET
POTRERO AVE.
VERMONT STREET
KANSAS STREET
RHODE ISLAND STREET
DE HARO STREET
CAROLINA STREET
WISCONSIN ST.
ARKANSAS ST.
CONNECTICUT ST.
MISSOURI ST.
CASTRO STREET
NOE STREET
SANCHEZ ST.
CHURCH ST.
80
101
280